The British Empire

The British Empire

Themes and Perspectives

Edited by Sarah Stockwell

Blackwell
Publishing

© 2008 by Blackwell Publishing Ltd
BLACKWELL PUBLISHING

350 Main Street, Malden, MA 02148–5020, USA
9600 Garsington Road, Oxford OX4 2DQ, UK
550 Swanston Street, Carlton, Victoria 3053, Australia

The right of Sarah Stockwell to be identified as the author of the editorial material in this work has been asserted in accordance with the UK Copyright, Designs, and Patents Act 1988.

The publisher and the author make no representations or warranties with respect to the accuracy or completeness of the contents of this work and specifically disclaim all warranties, including without limitation warranties of fitness for a particular purpose. No warranty may be created or extended by sales or promotional materials. The advice and strategies contained herein may not be suitable for every situation. This work is sold with the understanding that the publisher is not engaged in rendering legal, accounting, or other professional services. If professional assistance is required, the services of a competent professional person should be sought. Neither the publisher nor the author shall be liable for damages arising herefrom. The fact that an organization or website is referred to in this work as a citation and/or a potential source of further information does not mean that the author or the publisher endorses the information the organization or website may provide or recommendations it may make. Further, readers should be aware that Internet websites listed in this work may have changed or disappeared between when this work was written and when it is read.

First published 2008 by Blackwell Publishing Ltd

1   2008

Library of Congress Cataloging-in-Publication Data
The British Empire: themes and perspectives/ edited by S.E Stockwell.
p. cm
Includes bibliographical references and index
ISBN-13: 978-1-4051-2534-5 (hardcover: alk. paper)
ISBN-13: 978-1-4051-2535-2 (pbk.: alk. paper)
1. Great Britain—Colonies—History. 2. Commonwealth countries—History.
3. Imperialism—History.
I. Stockwell, S.E
DA16. B6956 2008
909'.0971241--dc22
2007018994

A catalogue record for this title is available from the British Library.
Set in 10/12.5 pt Classical Garamond
by Prepress Projects Ltd, Perth, UK

The publisher's policy is to use permanent paper from mills that operate a sustainable forestry policy, and which has been manufactured from pulp processed using acid-free and elementary chlorine-free practices. Furthermore, the publisher ensures that the text paper and cover board used have met acceptable environmental accreditation standards.

For further information on
Blackwell Publishing, visit our website at
www.blackwellpublishing.com

Contents

Notes on Contributors   vii
Preface   xi
Abbreviations Used in Notes   xvii
Maps   xviii

1 Britain's Empires   1
   John Darwin

2 Foundations of Empire, 1763–83   21
   Eliga H. Gould

3 Empire and the British State   39
   Andrew Thompson

4 The British Empire on the Move, 1760–1914   63
   Kent Fedorowich

5 The Economics of Empire   101
   A. R. Dilley

6 Religion in the British Empire   131
   Elisabeth Elbourne

7 Empire and Ideology   157
   Stephen Howe

8 Colonial Knowledge   177
   Tony Ballantyne

9 Culture and Identity in Imperial Britain   199
   Catherine Hall

10 Imperial Identities Abroad   219
    Stuart Ward

11 Agency, Narrative, and Resistance   245
    Jon E. Wilson

12 Ends of Empire   269
    Sarah Stockwell

    Consolidated Bibliography   295
    Index   343

Notes on Contributors

Tony Ballantyne is an associate professor of history and international and Area studies at Washington University in St Louis. He works on South Asian cultural and intellectual history as well as the history of colonial knowledge within the British Empire. His publications include *Orientalism and Race* (2002) and *Between Colonialism and Diapora: Sikh Cultural Formations in an Imperial World* (2006).

John Darwin teaches imperial and global history at Oxford University, where he is a Fellow of Nuffield College. He is the author of *Britain and Decolonization: The Retreat from Empire in the Post-War World* and *The End of the British Empire: The Historical Debate*. His *After Tamerlane: The Global History of Empire* has recently been published by Allen Lane/Penguin Press.

Andrew Dilley is a lecturer in imperial and commonwealth history at King's College London. He recently completed a doctorate on "Gentlemanly Capitalism and the Dominions: London Finance, Australia and Canada, 1900–1914" at Oxford University and is now preparing a book on the subject.

Elizabeth Elbourne is associate professor in the department of history, McGill University, where she teaches British and South African history and the history of British colonialism. Her publications include *Blood Ground: Colonialism, Missions and the Contest for Christianity in Britain and the Eastern Cape, 1799–1853* (2002). Her current research explores struggles over the status of indigenous peoples in the white settler colonies of the late eighteenth and early nineteenth century British empire, with attention to networks between different imperial locations, including Christian humanitarian networks and the movement of indigenous people themselves.

Kent Fedorowich is reader in British imperial and commonwealth history at the University of the West of England, Bristol. He is the author of *Unfit for Heroes: Reconstruction and Soldier Settlement between the Wars* (1995) and co-editor, with Martin Thomas, of *International Diplomacy and Colonial Retreat* (2001), and, with Carl Bridge, *The British World: Diaspora, Culture and Identity* (2003). He has also co-authored with Bob Moore, *The British Empire and its Italian Prisoners of War, 1940–1947* (2002).

Eliga Gould is associate professor of history at the University of New Hampshire, where he teaches early American and British Atlantic history. His publications include *The Persistence of Empire: British Political Culture in the Age of the American Revolution* (2000), which won the Omohundro Institute of Early American History and Culture's Jamestown Prize, and *Empire and Nation: The American Revolution in the Atlantic World* (2004), co-edited with Peter Onuf. He is currently writing a book on the American Revolution and the legal geography of the Atlantic world.

Catherine Hall is professor of modern British social and cultural history at University College London. Her recent work has centered on questions of "race," ethnicity, and difference in the history of the nineteenth century nation and empire. Recent publications include *Defining the Victorian Nation: Race, Class, Gender and the Reform Act of 1867* (2000), jointly authored with Keith McClelland and Jane Rendall; *Civilising Subjects. Metropole and Colony in the English Imagination 1830–1867* (2002); and *At Home with the Empire. Metropolitan Culture and the Imperial World*, edited with Sonya O. Rose (2006). She is an editor of *History Workshop Journal*.

Stephen Howe is professor in the history and cultures of colonialism at the University of Bristol. His books include *Anticolonialism in British Politics* (1993), *Afrocentrism* (1998), *Ireland and Empire* (2000), and *Empire. A Very Short Introduction* (2002). *The Intellectual Consequences of Decolonization* is forthcoming from Oxford, and his edited collection *New Imperial Histories* from Routledge.

Sarah Stockwell is senior lecturer in imperial and commonwealth history at King's College London. Her publications include *The Business of Decolonization: British Business Strategies in the Gold Coast* (2000) and, co-edited with S. R. Ashton, *Imperial Policy and Colonial Practice 1925–1945* (1996). Her current research interests include social and cultural consequences of end of empire for Britain.

Andrew Thompson is professor of commonwealth and imperial history, and co-director of the Institute of Colonial and Postcolonial Studies at the University of Leeds. He is author of *Imperial Britain. The Empire in British Politics, c.1880–1932* (2000) and *The Empire Strikes Back. The Impact of Imperialism on Britain from the Mid-Nineteenth Century* (2005). He is currently completing a study of the "cultural economy" of the British world from c.1840 to 1914, with Professor Gary Magee, as well as editing a companion volume to the *Oxford History of the British Empire* entitled *Britain's Experience of Empire During the Twentieth Century*.

Stuart Ward teaches imperial history at the University of Copenhagen, specializing in comparative settler-colonial societies. His major publications include *Australia and the British Embrace* (2001), the edited collections *British Culture and the End of Empire* (2001), and *Australia's Empire* (with Deryck M. Schreuder, forthcoming), and a special edition of the *Australian Journal of Politics and History: Post-Imperial Australia* (2005, with Graeme Davison). He is working on a comparative history of the break-up of the "British World."

Jon E. Wilson teaches the history of South Asia and the British empire at King's College London. He has written widely on the history of colonialism and resistance in early colonial Bengal. His first book, *The Domination of Strangers. Modern Politics in Colonial India, c.1780–1830* will be published in 2008, and will be followed by research on the history of politics in East Pakistan/Bangladesh in the second half of the twentieth century.

Preface[1]

Such has been the sea change in scholarly fashions, that it now seems barely necessary to state that in recent years there has been resurgent interest in the history of imperialism and colonialism. The current liveliness of historiography engaging with the history of British imperialism contrasts strikingly with the situation in the early 1980s. Then, such was the challenge posed to "imperial history" by the growth (and anti-imperial ideology) of regional studies that one historian was moved to ask "Can Humpty-Dumpty be put together again?"[2] Now more scholars than ever are drawn to a field that has been the site of some exciting conceptual debates, and which has also given historians of Britain a platform from which to reach a larger audience by relating the history of a small island state to wider processes.

Here is not the place for extended explanations of the dynamics of this renaissance, but we should acknowledge how the study of colonial discourse has allowed new insights first developed in literary studies to be brought to bear in analyzing colonial encounters and anatomizing power in colonial contexts, as well as redirecting attention to the ways in which imperialism shaped the discursive and cultural history of the colonizer as well as the colonized. Along with other factors, some derived from developments within the historiography of the British Isles, this has served to nourish historiographical projects reintegrating the history of Britain overseas with its domestic history. The impact of these new approaches in collapsing boundaries between imperial metropoles and peripheries has been accompanied, and in some cases reinforced, by other, quite distinct, historiographical trends. One such is a growing interest in the processes of globalization,[3] which has encouraged scholars to return to the history of British imperialism in a search for the historical roots of globalization, or to write "imperial history" as a form of global history.

Together, these various dynamics have contributed towards a trend for historians to eschew national frameworks in favor of the study of transnational networks and global interactions. Some of these approaches are manifest in the conceptualization of an early modern "Atlantic World," which involved the movement of peoples, goods and ideas across four continents, and in which Britain played a key part; in a later modern period, it is mirrored in an interest in the cultural and other networks which bound together a global diaspora of "neo-Britons" in a "British World."[4]

Perhaps inevitably, the very fecundity and methodological diversity of recent interventions in the history of the British empire has not always favored the creation of an integrated or coherent historiography. In the early twenty-first century, historians of Africa and Asia increasingly engage across the newly-delineated turf of "colonial encounters," while those of colonial North America and of Australia, Canada, New Zealand, and South Africa focus on the supranational currents and networks which bound their localities into wider regional or global histories: the literature concerning imperialism and colonialism has increasingly spun off into distinct (if interconnected) historiographies no longer arranged around an imperial center, but instead characterized through reference to more inclusive and decentralised "worlds," or as "colonial" or "post-colonial" studies.

In particular, significant differences of approach and interest are often now claimed to separate what has been termed a "new" imperial history from the "old."[5] Some would characterize the former by its interdisciplinarity and its concern with issues of culture, gender, and race—with what Catherine Hall has described as "new ways of theorizing difference."[6] Critics allege that it has involved an unhealthy neglect of the material and legal arm of British imperialism, while in practice still privileging the "metropolitan gaze."[7] In contrast, the "old" imperial history has been criticised by some for being unduly preoccupied with the constitutional, political, and economic, and construed within categories constituted by institutions of empire and the archives they generated.[8] This tradition arguably suffers from its early association with the imperial project itself. The "founder" of imperial history is often identified as Sir John Seeley, whose 1883 *The Expansion of England* anticipated the coming together of different areas of empire into a "Greater Britain"; and, beginning in the early twentieth century, it was the endowment of chairs in imperial history at British universities with money generated by imperialistic endeavors in southern Africa that helped develop a scholarly field.[9]

If portions of the literature seem at times to be constructed in opposition to each other this is no reason to confine one's attention exclusively to one tradition rather than another. This volume takes as its starting point that students of imperialism and colonialism should be familiar with imperialism in all its manifestations, including cultural, economic, and constitutional, and with historiographical developments across *all* relevant fields. It brings together a series of thematic essays on these different areas, designed to serve as a "companion" to the historiography and its contours for students at all levels. In so doing it also unites in one project historians sometimes associated with quite distinct methodologies and traditions. Collectively it is hoped that the essays illustrate not only the current liveliness of scholarship across all areas of the history of the British empire, arguably obscured by blanket characterizations of "old" and "new,"[10] but also continuities between established areas of historiography and some more recent contributions.

By taking as its subject British imperialism in all its different guises—such as the territories of white settlement, the tropical colonies and the "informal" empire—this book foregrounds the British empire at a time when others are abandoning such an approach. The editor makes no apology for this: whatever the undesirability of reading local, regional, or world history primarily through a lens of "imperial" history, the British empire—at its apogee one of the largest territorial empires the world has ever seen—profoundly shaped the lives of people both in Britain and overseas, and remains worthy of focused scholarly analysis in its own right alongside considerations approaching it in the context of more broadly conceived and comparative histories of colonialism and imperialism. At the same time it is hoped that the thematic approach successfully navigates the dangers of privileging an imperial institutional framework or of obscuring the complexities involved in dealing with so many disparate regions and historiographies.

The thematic organization underpins this book's claim to make a distinct contribution to the literature. Older thematic collections in imperial history now look dated; newer compendiums—such as recent collections focusing on culture, race and gender, or the *Companion* volumes in the *Oxford History of the British Empire (OHBE)*—usually concentrate on one theme alone. As far as general histories of empire go, most are organized chronologically, or, for example in the case of the five original *Oxford History* volumes, are multi-volume enterprises.

An editor following the approach adopted here unavoidably confronts the task of selecting themes for inclusion from a wide range of possibilities. A different editor would very likely have chosen differently. For example, some readers—encouraged by a recent outpouring of excellent writing—may look in particular for a chapter on gender and empire. The decision not to include a dedicated essay on this theme reflects a sense not of its marginality but of its ubiquity; all historians of empire must be sensitive to the gendered dimensions of their subject. Similarly, although the theme of race and categories of difference receive extended treatment in several essays in this book (especially that by Tony Ballantyne), there is no chapter devoted to race alone. True to the intention to contribute towards an integrated history of empire that does not maintain artificial boundaries between "new" and "old" imperial histories and is organized around themes rather than historiographical approaches, "post-colonialism" is also not here given separate treatment, although its insights will be encountered throughout.

Of those themes which *have* been selected for dedicated treatment, some are perhaps more obvious than others. The first chapter by John Darwin undertakes the essential task of surveying what he analyzes as Britain's very different empires, not least in terms of their distinct constitutional arrangements, which remain of fundamental importance to an understanding of the dynamics of British imperialism. The theme of economics and empire has a long historiographical tradition, and, as Andrew Dilley shows, is an aspect of the history of imperialism which, though attracting less sustained scholarly attention in recent years than in the past, remains crucial to a proper appreciation of the material forces shaping the lives and interactions of colonized and colonizer, not least in the waxing and waning of imperial power.[11] Much more attention has recently been paid to the role of imperialism in forging metropolitan culture and identity, here the subject of a chapter by one of its foremost analysts, Catherine Hall. Kent Fedorowich's chapter, "Empire on the move," addresses another important subject, the enormously significant migrations that were constitutive of, and occurred within, the British empire. These last two chapters are complemented by Stuart Ward's essay on identities in the colonies of white settlement, the subject of extensive and fascinating current scholarship. A chapter by Elizabeth Elbourne expands on a recent preoccupation for many scholars, missions and imperialism, to examine the broader relationship between religion and empire.

Two other essays address themes that have recently secured prominence. This is the case, for example, with Jon Wilson's chapter on "agency," a key concept in literature on non-European interactions with Europeans. Another important interface of colonizer and colonized is considered in Tony Ballantyne's discussion of the production of "colonial knowledge" and the debates surrounding the relationship between knowledge and power in colonial contexts.

Other chapters take as their subject less established themes. Stephen Howe's essay brings together different historiographical developments that, while generally identified under other headings, address a common concern with the relationship between ideology and British imperialism. A chapter on "Empire and the British State" similarly unites established areas of historiographical enquiry about the acquisition and management of empire in different regions and periods in a fresh way by focusing on the British state, too often neglected in writing about empire.[12] By considering ways in which British nationals sought to use the state for their own "imperial" ends, Andrew Thompson's chapter encompasses, and it is hoped invigorates, established debates on "free trade imperialism," associated with an older generation of imperial history, as well as more recent contributions, such as that concerned with "gentlemanly capitalism."

Finally, two chapters diverge from the otherwise thematic organization to address literatures on particular phases in the history of British imperialism. The first, by Eliga Gould, considers the "Foundations of Empire" from 1763 to 1783. This transitional period, following the crisis culminating in the independence of the thirteen American colonies, saw the loss of much of what is sometimes and controversially termed the "first" British empire and the emergence of a "second," with the acquisition of Quebec from France and the beginnings of empire in India. Thus far this chapter establishes a context for those that follow, but it also introduces readers to some of the concerns of an expanding literature on an "Atlantic World," much of which lies beyond the chronological scope of the volume. My own chapter discusses the rapidly developing literature on "Ends of Empire" after 1945, frequently now taught as a subject in its own right.

With the exception of those on foundations and ends of empire, each chapter addresses the broad chronological and geographical sweep of British imperialism, although inevitably some periods and regions are more apposite to some themes than to others. Restrictions of space have also forced contributors to make hard decisions as to what to include. As with any volume of this kind, though perhaps to an unusual degree, there are differences of style and approach between contributors, reflecting the varied interests of each, as well as the challenge of attempting to map the main contours of the subject while simultaneously surveying and critiquing the historiography of each. In particular, some chapters deal with historiographies generated around historical developments, whereas others address literatures which are more conceptually driven. It is hoped that far from rendering the book less useful, these variations will instead add to its appeal, enabling students and established scholars alike to see how a diverse set of historians have approached their themes, and how each theme works out over a long historical period.

In putting together this volume I have incurred a number of debts. Thanks are due to Christopher Wheeler, formerly of Blackwell, who commissioned the book and saw it through its very early stages, and subsequently to Tessa Harvey, Gillian Kane, Hannah Rolls, and Leanda Shrimpton at Blackwell, and also to Helen MacDonald and Catriona Vernal for their commitment and hard work in guiding it through to publication. I would also like to thank the anonymous referees who commented on the first proposal. As editor, I have benefited in various ways from the advice and assistance of Peter Marshall and Andrew Thompson, and I am especially grateful to two contributors who stepped in late in the day and who delivered with such style when those originally commissioned had to withdraw from the project. More generally, I have been fortunate in having a set of contributors willing and able to grapple with the complexities of their subjects across such a broad period and, in the case of those chapters dealing with comparatively novel arrangements, to breathe life into the themes they were handed. Above all, thanks are due to Arthur Burns, who has given characteristically generous support and wise advice, and, although less wittingly complicit in the production of this book, for their forbearance with my working life, to our three boys, James, Alasdair, and Douglas.

Sarah Stockwell

Notes

1 I wish to thank Arthur Burns, Andrew Thompson, and Jon Wilson for their comments on this preface.
2 Fieldhouse, "Humpty-Dumpty".
3 See on globalization, Hopkins (ed.), *Globalization in World History*.
4 See, for example, Armitage and Braddick (eds), *The British Atlantic World*; Bridge and Fedorowich (eds), *The British World*.
5 On the former, see, for example, K. Wilson (ed.), *A New Imperial History*, although Wilson herself (p. 3) notes that she aims not to "substitute a new orthodoxy for an established one . . . [nor evacuate] established political, social, or intellectual histories." On the differences between "traditional" imperial history and more recent writing, see D. Kennedy, "Imperial history".
6 C. Hall, "Introduction" in *id.* (ed.), *Cultures of Empire*, p. 16.
7 R. Price, "One big thing".
8 Cooper and Stoler, "Between metropole and colony," pp. 33–4.
9 Seeley, *Expansion of England*.
10 As Howe recently observed: S. Howe, "When—if ever—did empire end?", p. 586.
11 On the importance of which see, for example, Hopkins, *The Future of the Imperial Past*, p. 27; see also Cooper and Stoler, "Between metropole and colony," pp. 18–19.
12 As others are also noticing: see Price, "One big thing," p. 614.

Abbreviations Used in Notes

AIC	African Initiated Church movement
ANC	African National Congress
BBC	British Broadcasting Corporation
BDEEP	*British Documents on the End of Empire* project
BLFES	British Ladies Female Emigrants' Society
BWEA	British Women's Emigration Association
CAB	Cabinet Office
CLEC	Colonial Land and Emigration Commission
CMS	Church Missionary Society
CO	Colonial Office
EIC	East India Company
FO	Foreign Office
FMCES	Female Middle Class Emigration Society
HO	Home Office
H of C debs.	*House of Commons Debates*, Britain
ICS	Indian Civil Service
JAH	*Journal of African History*
JICH	*Journal of Imperial and Commonwealth History*
Jl	Journal
LMS	London Missionary Society
NA	National Archives, Kew, London
OHBE	*Oxford History of the British Empire*
Rev.	Review
SPCK	Society for Promoting Christian Knowledge
SPG	Society for the Propagation of the Gospel in Foreign Parts

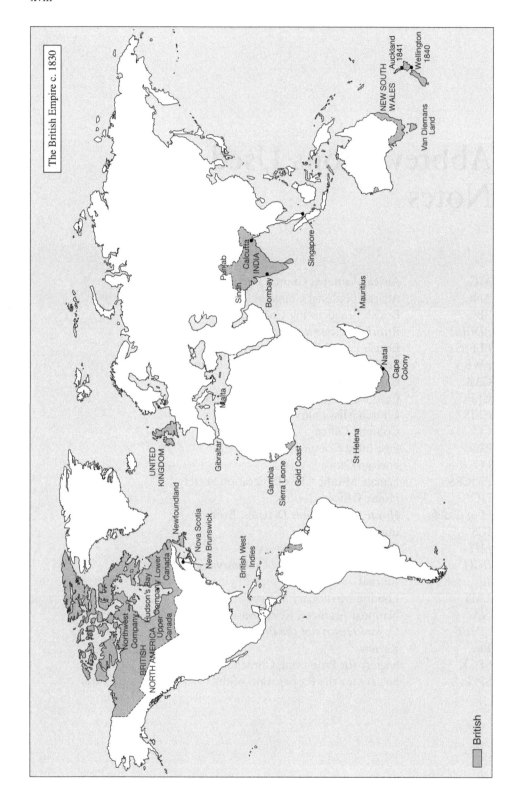

The British Empire c. 1830

Auckland 1841
Wellington 1840
NEW SOUTH WALES
Van Diemens Land

Punjab
Sindh
Calcutta
INDIA
Bombay
Singapore
Mauritius

Natal
Cape Colony

Malta

UNITED KINGDOM

Gibraltar

St Helena

Gambia
Sierra Leone
Gold Coast

Newfoundland

Nova Scotia
New Brunswick

Northwest Company
Hudson's Bay Company
Upper Canada
Lower Canada

BRITISH NORTH AMERICA

British West Indies

British

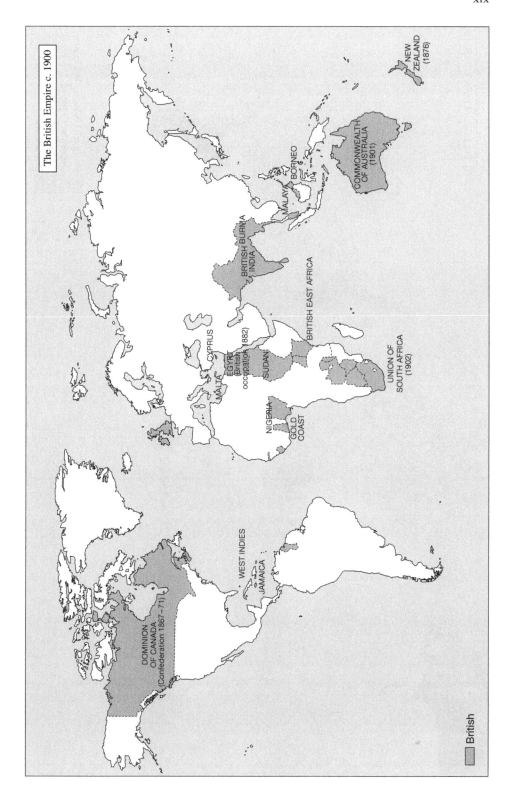

The British Empire c. 1900

NEW ZEALAND (1876)

COMMONWEALTH OF AUSTRALIA (1901)

BORNEO

MALAYA

BRITISH BURMA
INDIA

BRITISH EAST AFRICA

CYPRUS

EGYPT
(British occupation 1882)

SUDAN

UNION OF SOUTH AFRICA (1902)

MALTA

NIGERIA

GOLD COAST

WEST INDIES

JAMAICA

DOMINION OF CANADA
(Confederation 1867–71)

British

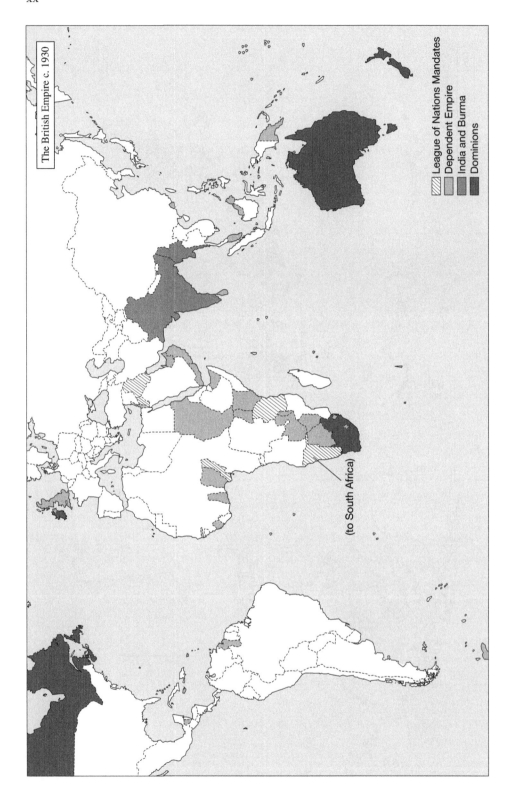

The British Empire c. 1930

League of Nations Mandates
Dependent Empire
India and Burma
Dominions

(to South Africa)

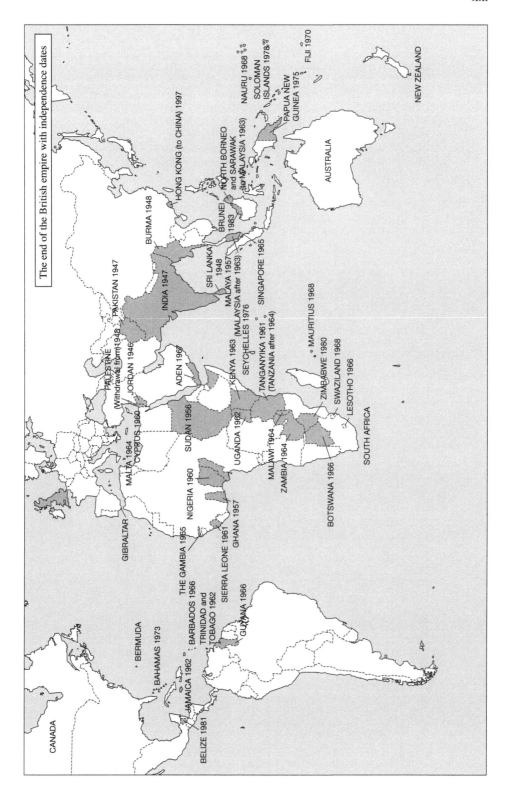

The end of the British empire with independence dates

1

Britain's Empires

John Darwin

I

In 1914 more than eighty separate territorial units acknowledged the sovereignty or accepted the protection of the British Crown. Indeed, since some of those units themselves comprised quite distinct parts, or, like the Indian states "agencies," grouped together many small territories for administrative ease, a realistic figure would be a good deal higher: certainly well over one hundred. Scattered over the globe, this fragmented colossus covered more than 11 million square miles and counted over 400 million subjects.

The size and scale of this globe-spanning juggernaut were its most obvious features. But perhaps just as striking was the variety of forms that British expansion had taken during three centuries of empire building beyond the home islands. Historians have long accepted the adage that British power worked in two modes, choosing between them according to circumstances. Where commercial or strategic objectives could be achieved without the trouble of annexation or rule, and the local elite was compliant or obliging, governments in London were more than happy with "informal empire." There was no British governor and no British flag, but the fact of Britain's predominance—whether commercial or military—was stamped indelibly on local affairs, constraining the freedom of nominally sovereign governments. Where this co-operative spirit was deficient or absent, and the ruling power on the ground resisted British interests, London had recourse to the "formal" alternative and British rule was imposed. In the classic formulation devised by Gallagher and Robinson, British expansion advanced "by informal control where possible; [by] . . . rule when necessary."[1] Thus, Britain's "empire" comprised two parallel sub-systems: divergent in style but common in purpose.

This is a start. But it is obvious enough that it cannot do justice to the extraordinary range of constitutional, political, economic, and cultural relationships contained within Britain's multiple imperial connections. There was, after all, a whole spectrum of differences just within the category of "formal empire." Unquestionably, part of that empire, painted red on the map, and acknowledging the British Crown as sovereign, were the five large colonies of settlement usually called (after the Colonial Conference in 1907) "dominions": Canada, Australia, New Zealand, South Africa, and Newfoundland.[2] The distinctive feature of the five dominions (the number rose to six in 1921 when Southern Ireland became a dominion as the Irish Free State, and fell back to five in 1933 when Newfoundland's bankruptcy led to its constitution being suspended) was their complete internal autonomy. They were self-governing states into whose domestic affairs (including the right to set tariffs) London had renounced interference. The key limitation on their complete independence until the interwar years lay in foreign affairs and defense. Since the British Crown was their sovereign, it could take them to war although acting solely on the advice of British ministers in London. But it was also acknowledged that the precise contribution that they might make to a war was a matter for the dominion governments themselves. Since the dominions differed significantly in their ethnic, racial, and geopolitical characteristics, this convention was vital. For what came to be called "dominion status" concealed the reality that each dominion had a different "British Connection."

The self-governing colonies were a world away from the "dependencies" that made up the bulk of British territory. But these too were far from uniform. Foremost among them was India, whose special position was signalled by its designation as the "Indian Empire," ruled by its "King-Emperor" (the British king) through a "viceroy." With a population of some 250 million, India was a giant among the colonial lilliputs. What made it unique was its huge colonial army (around 140,000 men), paid for by Indian taxpayers, the military instrument (alongside the large British garrison, for which India also had to pay) of British power in Asia. Partly as a result, it was left to the Viceroy (who had his own Foreign Office) to manage Britain's relations with a vast periphery extending from Aden, through the Persian Gulf, to Afghanistan, Nepal and Burma, the last of which was incorporated as an Indian province. The Indian government, which combined the administration of "British India" with paramount supervision of the Indian princely states, dealt with London on quite different terms, and with far more independence, than the British officials in the crown colonies and protectorates. But only a dreamer would have imagined that the mass of ill-assorted administrative zones into which those were divided (often with skeletal governments and still more skeletal revenues) could be driven and drilled by a fiat in London.

Finally, the "informal empire" of influence rather than rule was predictably diverse. Three different categories can be distinguished. Firstly, there were those states whose political sovereignty was beyond dispute, but whose economic development and external economic relations had been shaped by British-owned enterprise: banks, railway companies, and utilities. The classic case was Argentina. Secondly, there were states where the British had asserted effective control over their external relations, or (while denying the fact) sought a degree of authority over their internal government as great as was found in parts of the formal empire. Egypt was the supreme example of this, where the British engaged in a double pretense: that Egypt was still part of the Ottoman Empire, and that their role was simply to "advise" its government. Thirdly, there was China, where the British disclaimed any desire to annex or partition, but where British interests exploited the bundle of extra-territorial privileges, including rights of residence and municipal self-rule, extracted from China since the 1840s and enforced when practical by gunboat diplomacy. The extent to which London was able to impose its will on any particular issue, at any particular time, in any of these regions of "informal sway" was subject to wide variation.

Even at first glance, then, the British empire bore little resemblance to a centralised despotism whose "command and control" was directed in London. Far from being a "designer empire" whose links and connections could be neatly traced out from imperial center to colonial periphery, it looked like a half-finished "project of an empire" (in Adam Smith's phrase) bound loosely together by a maze of wiring of uncertain age and untested strength. The questions that matter are why this was so, and how it was possible for this chaotic conglomerate to survive for so long into the age of global war after 1914.

II

Of course, the untidiness of empire had been there from the beginning—in the earliest phase of *English* empire building in the British Isles before 1300. England was much the wealthiest and most powerful unit in a fragmented archipelago. Yet after more than three centuries of restless expansion, and periodically forceful assertions of English supremacy, little progress had been made towards absorbing the British "periphery" or creating a common British identity. Indeed, perhaps the opposite had happened: producing four identities not one, and a keener sense of cultural difference than had existed before. The reason for this, it has been persuasively argued, lay in the nature of English society. It was, paradoxically, its internal cohesion and institutional strength—the real sources of English power—that simultaneously restricted its cultural influence. The "closely-woven institutional structure of lowland England"[3] could not be easily replicated in other parts of Britain or the British Isles. The English had also acquired very early an acute ethnic self-consciousness. They had closed themselves off from the ready absorption of cultural influence from outside. The compromises needed to forge a pan-British identity were not easy to make.[4]

English colonization, if we follow this argument, was marked from the first by insistence upon the distinct and peculiar requirements of an English identity. If the means were lacking to attract or coerce non-English peoples into English ways, they might have to be left in their "barbarous" state. If the transition was too hard, realism dictated acceptance of a plural society, with two forms of governance and two kinds of law, one for the English colonists, another for the rest. This was the pattern of English rule in Ireland. Yet it was not without costs. The price to be paid, raged Sir John Davies, Elizabeth I's attorney general in Ireland, was perpetual instability. The failure to force upon Gaelic society English notions of individual property had allowed the survival of fractious tribal communities, whose internal disputes and predatory habits made them a constant source of disruption, severe enough at times to threaten English rule altogether.[5] In this respect, as in many others, the dilemmas of empire were already apparent in the medieval colonization of Ireland.

Yet, in the first great phase of empire building overseas, variety of this kind seemed a less serious problem. What eventually became the key cause of tension between mother country and colonies (and of the violent separation of the rebel Thirteen) was a different sort of variation: the extent to which colonial political institutions and culture had diverged more and more from those of the motherland. This divergence was rooted, and it could later be seen in the actual origins of English colonization in the Atlantic world. Colonization was not undertaken by governments, but by private interests. What they sought from the Crown was usually a license or charter, offering some claim to protection in the event of attack by rival Europeans, delegating the power to govern, and granting a monopoly over the trade of a designated tract. The Crown granted charters to companies (like the Virginia or Massachusetts companies), or "letters patent" to "proprietors" (like Lords Baltimore or Carlisle) that conferred on them seigneurial rights modelled on those enjoyed by the "Bishops Palatine" of Durham[6]—a reminder of how far English thinking about colonial governance was built on medieval precedents. But apart from devising the forms of authority, governments in London took almost no active part in directing English colonization. From almost the very beginning, the colonial societies created by emigration from the British Isles enjoyed considerable freedom to frame the customs and rules that best suited their interests. The successive attempts under Cromwell, Charles II, and James II to impose a more centralized system and assert more direct authority in the affairs of the colonies were half-hearted at best: the Revolution Settlement of 1689 effectively killed them. What followed was the age of "salutary neglect"[7] that lasted into the 1760s. London appointed the colonial governors but was content to leave them to their own devices in the face of elected local assemblies, whose grip on finance and executive power grew steadily stronger.

The result was a political culture markedly different from that in Britain where the influence of the court, the growth of the "fiscal-military state," and the social grip of the landed aristocracy were a far more powerful check on radical or populist tendencies in politics than anything that existed in the mainland colonies of English America. Symptomatic of this, from London's point of view, was the grudging and truculent response of the colonies to its requests for money and manpower in the American campaigns of the Seven Years War (1756–63). After the war, when British governments at home looked for ways of sharing the huge burden of debt that victory had brought with those whom they saw as its colonial beneficiaries, American resentment at imperial interference, the threat of imperial taxation, and the closer regulation of trade produced the explosion that wrecked the "First British Empire."[8]

Yet until the 1770s, the imperial "system" that had grown up higgledy-piggledy since the 1620s could still be imagined as the more or less straightforward expansion of English society. The colonies were populated by "free-born" Englishmen (or their Scottish equivalents) whose values, institutions, sympathies and allegiance bound them to Britain. Of course, in the southern colonies of the American mainland and in the British West Indies, this agreeable fiction was challenged by the presence of many thousands of blacks. But since almost all were slaves, and slavery was a form of "social death" extinguishing social and political rights, this awkward complication could be easily glossed over. The same was true as regards the potential divergence in economic interests. The control of colonial trade through the Navigation Laws required colonial producers to ship their products to Britain and to use British shipping. But for all their inequities, the mercantile rules seemed the price of security in a dangerous world in which the colonists faced the risk of foreign predation, the loss of their market to foreign competitors, and the shortage of coin.[9] And the overseas empire was still the English (or perhaps British) Atlantic,[10] an extension of Britain. Where British expansion had strayed outside the Western Atlantic, before 1760 it was confined to trading posts and "factories," perched on the flank of indigenous empires, not aspiring to rule over them, or create settlements in them.

The loss of the American colonies in 1783 was the most obvious sign that the "first" British Empire had reached the end of its tether. But by the mid-1780s, a whole series of changes had begun to signal the arrival of a much more diversified empire and of new kinds of British expansion. In what remained of the old Atlantic Empire, the conquered population of French Canadians (captured with Quebec in 1759) became much more important, since the city and province of Quebec became the key to British power on the American continent. In a crucial decision, the imperial government carefully separated the predominantly French districts of Quebec into a new province of "Lower Canada," and granted it representative government on the old American model.[11] This marked the extension of what had originally been thought of as a privilege reserved to those of British stock to a community whose allegiance to Britain could not be taken for granted. Before very long, its political wisdom began to look questionable. Meanwhile, Britain's relations with the West Indian colonies (who had rejected the path of rebellion on grounds of self-interest as well as of sentiment) were increasingly strained by the rapid growth of anti-slavery feeling in opinion at home.[12] Opposition to the slave trade and to the institution of slavery sharpened the sense that the whites in the islands were a class of brutal degenerates and that the West Indian proprietors who drew their profits from sugar were the bloated accessories of a great moral evil. More to the point, emancipating the slave population (delayed in practice until 1838) meant envisaging a colonial society composed of free blacks as well as free whites. Here, too, the question was raised of what kind of rule could be applied to colonies, the majority of whose citizens would have no obvious reason to feel loyal to Britain, and who might be tempted to regard their technical freedom not as the end of their struggle but just its beginning.

But the most dramatic example of the new imperial diversity lay in the East not the West. The East India Company was a trading corporation whose commercial activity had needed the permit of the Mughal emperors in Delhi. But by the 1750s, Mughal power had declined and the Company's agents had grown used to dealing with the local powers on the coast as well as relying on armed force and diplomacy to fend off their European rivals, especially the French. The Anglo-French conflict of the Seven Years War coincided with a crisis in the politics of Bengal, the most dynamic of the coastal states where the writ of the Mughals had become a dead letter. When the Bengali ruler, Sirajaud-Daula, turned on the Company, seized its fort at Calcutta, and drove out or imprisoned the Company's agents, internal divisions within the local elite allowed the Company's army, under Robert Clive, to sail back to Bengal and score an easy victory at Plassey in 1757. Within a very short time, Clive became the kingmaker in Bengali affairs, and in 1765 the Company took control of the province's revenues and hence of its government. There and in the south round Madras, it quickly became the governing power, using its army to extract treaties and tribute. But the threat of bankruptcy brought on by its huge military spending, the scandals surrounding its agents in India, and the stream of private wealth remitted home to Britain by the Company's "servants" provoked a furious outcry at home against a regime that eluded any public control.

At the center of the controversy over Indian affairs in the 1770s and 1780s were three closely linked issues. The first was how to bring the Company's officials in India under effective control from London, and restrain their appetite for privately profitable wars. The second was how to govern the Company's new empire. The third was how far this "Asiatic" dominion should be deliberately anglicised, in law and religion as well as in trade. All three raised very difficult questions. The government in London had an obvious interest in supervising the policies of the Company in India, especially since it could not stand aloof if the Company was threatened with military defeat or financial collapse. Troops had to be sent, money had to be lent. But there were also strong arguments against giving politicians in London too loud a voice in the Company's Indian government. They lacked specialized knowledge of the Indian "world" and it was widely feared that the Company's patronage (a much sought-after commodity) would be abused by ministers for party purposes. When it came to governing Indians, the most urgent tasks that faced the Company were collecting revenue and raising troops. Far from invoking an alien tradition of representative government, it preferred to step into the shoes of pre-existing regimes, redirecting the yield of the land revenue system to fill its tax-coffers. Nor were the Company men eager to anglicise India, fearing to offend the educated class on whose support they depended, and arouse religious antagonism. The result in the decades after 1780 was a pattern of compromise. The London government gained ministerial oversight through the "Board of Control," but the Company government remained in place in London and controlled all appointments. The civil administration of the Company's districts was placed in the hands of a dedicated administrative corps, the "Indian Civil Service," and the Company's commercial activity separated from it. But on the ground in India, the Company was left free to follow local practice, and though it was forced in 1813 to allow in Christian missionaries, it carefully avoided being seen as the aggressive proponent of an anglicised culture.[13]

Britain's eastern empire thus looked radically different from its western empire, where a settler population enjoying representative government remained the dominant mode. But in the 1780s a third sort of empire began to be glimpsed, a commercial empire. The American revolt had almost coincided with the publication of Adam Smith's *Wealth of Nations* in 1776. Part of Smith's book was taken up with an attack on the mercantile system, the battery of controls that was meant to secure the British merchants' monopoly in colonial trade and minimize imports from outside the empire. Smith derided "mercantilism", insisting instead that commercial freedom would encourage productivity and maximize wealth. The costly apparatus of an administrative empire, it was clearly implied, was a waste of money: what was needed instead was a web of merchant connections to expand the scope of commercial exchange as widely as possible. Here was the germ of an "empire of free trade," where the prize was not territory or rule over peoples but access to markets, suppliers, and customers. How far such an empire would need the application of military power to reinforce its commercial inducements was not apparent at first.

As it turned out, the interval between the fall of the first British Empire and the emergence of a new imperial system was filled by the global war waged almost continuously between 1793 and 1815. In the course of the conflict, the British greatly expanded their stake in the Indian sub-continent. They seized other colonial prizes from the French, the Dutch, and the Spanish, including Cape Colony, Ceylon (Sri Lanka), Mauritius, and Trinidad. They enlarged the "empire of rule" as against the "empire of settlement," and acquired a new population of alien Europeans (the Boers of the Cape), as well as non-Europeans with different political traditions. The variety of empire became even more marked. But perhaps the key outcome of the war was the effective destruction of the old mercantilist empires and their closed trading blocs. By 1815, British naval power was supreme and the world's seas lay open to British mercantile enterprise. The mid-Victorians' empire was about to be born.

III

In the 1830s and 1840s the horizons of British expansion were widened enormously. Parts of the world that had seemed inaccessible or had been closed to outsiders by reclusive regimes now offered the promise of trade, conversion, or settlement. Inland West Africa (where Richard Lander had revealed the course of the Nile), the Southern African highveld, Australia's transmontane, interior and even New Zealand (which drew a minor invasion of travellers and publicists in the 1830s) could now be imagined as zones of British enterprise, influence, or missionary endeavor. Trade treaties with the Ottoman and Iranian governments dangled the prospect of an extensive new commerce. The smashing open of China's back door in the "Opium War" of 1839–42, and the freedom to trade through Chinese merchants in a half dozen "treaty ports," suggested that even the largest and grandest of non-European empires could no longer resist the commercial demands of the West.

These changes coincided with the growing capacity of Britain itself to exert its power in the world. This was to be seen in the rising number of migrants whose annual exodus exceeded 100,000 for the first time in 1830. Of course, many of these were destined for the United States, but enough were left over to fuel Britain's demographic imperialism in British North America, Australia, and New Zealand (where settlement began in 1840). It was in the 1830s that steam power was applied successfully to production of cotton cloth (as opposed to yarn) and to locomotion. Both applications sharpened and deepened the penetrative power of British trade: together they promised to turn almost any part of the world into a profitable market. Thirdly, the 1830s also saw great attention being paid to the systematic collection and dissemination of geographical knowledge of the non-European world. The Royal Geographical Society (founded 1830) and John Arrowsmith's great atlas (Arrowsmith was a founder member and his maps drew upon the travellers' reports that the Society collected) were instrumental in alerting an ever-widening circle of British opinion to the religious, commercial, or agrarian prospects of hitherto little-known regions.

Yet this aggressive self-confidence had as its doppelgänger a strong undertow of anxiety and self-doubt. The abolition of slavery in 1833 was shadowed by the insistence that liberated slaves should remain as "apprentices" for a further five years. The humanitarian feeling that had sustained anti-slavery was consumed by the fear that the European impact upon "aboriginal" peoples in North America, Africa, and the South Pacific would be morally and culturally fatal, once the British predilection for trading in gew-gaws, selling cheap liquor, and buying sexual favours had taken its toll. Pristine communities awaiting the Christian faith would be drenched with the sins that had degraded the West. The brittle fragility of non-white societies (freed slave or "aboriginal") and their need for protection against the exploitative whites became the dominant theme in humanitarian thought. The 1830s were also a period in which Britain's dependence on industry and the export of manufactures seemed a dangerous risk, and when the saturation of markets abroad might throw thousands out of work, wrecking social order at home. Fears of this kind lay behind the insistence of ministers that (in Palmerston's words in 1839) "it was the duty of the Government to open new channels for the commerce of the country," and their claim that "the great object of the Government in every quarter of the world was to extend the commerce of the country."[14]

This formed the context from which the mid-Victorian empire emerged. The 1840s to the 1870s were the critical period in which the four different models of empire that characterized the British system down to the 1940s assumed something like their fully-fledged form. These were the settlement colonies enjoying almost complete self-rule under the tag of "responsible government"; India, whose curious "double government" was entrenched and civilianized when the Crown replaced the Company in 1858; the numerous "dependencies", from the Caribbean to Hong Kong ruled by "Crown Colony" government—a category largely invented by Victorian officials; and the various cases of "informal empire," those "spheres of interference" (in Sellars and Yeatman's phrase)[15] where British business or diplomats exerted a preponderant influence, but without risking recourse to, or needing the help of, colonial rule.

Self-governing settlement colonies that remained loyal to their "British connection" (refusing to take the American road) were perhaps the most strikingly individual feature of the Victorians' empire. Settler self-government—"responsible government"—derived from the old tradition of local colonial autonomy that went back, as we saw, to the earliest colonization of English North America. But the "representative government" of the first British Empire did not evolve smoothly into "responsible government." The transition was marked by colonial insurrection, prolonged instability, and a sense of nervous experiment. The scene of the crisis was British North America, where revolts broke out in 1837 in Upper Canada (the Anglophone district of the old Quebec province) and, far more seriously, in Lower Canada, which was predominantly French. While various social and economic grievances played a role in aggravating discontent, the flashpoint of conflict was resentment against the supposedly autocratic tendencies of the governors and the illicit influence of the camerillas around them (the "Family Compact" in Upper Canada, the "Chateau clique" in Lower). In reality, as has been powerfully argued,[16] the governors found themselves fighting a rearguard action against the progressive enlargement of the assemblies' power in much the same way as had happened in the Thirteen Colonies some fifty years earlier. What made the Lower Canadian rebellion especially worrying was that it threatened to mobilize religious (Catholic) and ethnic (French-Canadian) feeling behind the elite politicians (Louis Papineau was a wealthy lawyer) in much the same way as had happened in Ireland. This example was not lost on British officialdom.

London's response, once the uprisings were crushed, was to despatch an inquiry under Lord Durham. Durham's report crisply identified the disabling weakness of representative government. The assembly, he said, had every incentive to behave irresponsibly. It could hobble the executive by non-co-operation, but the governor and his officials were not answerable to it and it could not change them. The elected politicians could indulge in demagogy, and make the wildest proposals. Since they could never hold office, they lacked any motive to be moderate or practical and the unelected executive could always be blamed for whatever went wrong. The result, argued Durham, was not a strong government but a desperately weak one. The right answer, he claimed, was to ensure that the executive enjoyed the Assembly's support. The colonial governor should be instructed "to secure the co-operation of the Assembly in his policy, by entrusting its administration to such men as could command a majority."[17] Imperial interference in the colony's affairs should be reduced to the minimum. "I know not in what respect it can be desirable that we should interfere with their internal legislation in matters which do not affect their relations with the mother-country."[18] Indeed, it was safer to rely on the self-interest and loyalty of the settler communities to preserve the imperial connection than the clumsy apparatus of imperial control.

Durham's analysis was extremely influential. His key political insight can be glimpsed again and again in the working documents of the imperial government down to the time of the Simon Commission in India in 1928–30.[19] But for the moment at least, it seemed a step too far. British governors were urged to cultivate the assembly politicians and avoid confrontation. One governor, Lord Sydenham, formed what amounted to a political party and fought a successful election. By 1846, however, solutions like this had largely broken down in "Canada" (Upper and Lower Canada had been united in 1840 in the hope of "swamping" the French Canadians with new British settlers) and Nova Scotia. This time the British chose to bite the bullet. "It cannot be too distinctly acknowledged," the Colonial Secretary told the governor of Nova Scotia in November 1846, "that it is neither possible nor desirable to carry on the government of any of the British provinces in North America in opposition to the opinion of the inhabitants."[20] The corollary, as he explained soon after, was that the executive council should be composed only of those officers who enjoyed the Assembly's support and could be removed if they lost it.[21] This was ministerial or cabinet government, with ministers "responsible" to the elected assembly, and the governor in the role of a constitutional monarch, not the chief executive officer. Its credibility was soon to be tested. In the province of Canada it was threatened with breakdown almost immediately, when a new set of ministers offered compensation to those who had rebelled in 1837. The Rebellion Losses bill aroused violent opposition in Montreal which had a large British population fiercely hostile to the French-Canadian rebels. Rioting, arson, and a brutal campaign in the press were intended to force Lord Elgin, the governor-general, to veto the bill and dismiss the ministers. But Elgin stood firm. To side with the opposition would be to abandon the governor's "dignified neutrality." It would throw the imperial connection back into the maelstrom of local party politics from which "responsible government" had been intended to rescue it. The new constitution would have failed its first test. With London's backing, Elgin supported the ministers and the bill was passed.

Elgin had grasped that as a constitutional system, "responsible government" was based less on rules than discretion. The governor had to be willing to work with his ministers; if he became unpopular, then rather than risk the imperial connection, the government at home should disavow and replace him.[22] Indeed, "responsible government" remained an idea, a set of conventions and practices: it was not laid down in a statute. The imperial parliament retained the power to legislate for the self-governing colonies. The governors had the technical power to disavow legislation or reserve it for scrutiny in London. In practice these powers lay almost unused for fear of the conflict that Elgin had foreseen. In Canada and Australia (where the colonial parliaments had mostly adopted responsible government by the late 1850s) London carefully avoided confronting local opinion. It relied instead on the quiet diplomacy of the governors to protect the two key restrictions on local self-rule: foreign relations and constitutional change. No colony was permitted to make its own foreign policy or amend its own constitution—not at least without London's approval. Friction could also arise when British troops were deployed in a colony (as in New Zealand against the Maori and in Canada to counter the threat of American invasion). But on almost everything else, including the creation of colonial tariffs that affronted Victorian Britain's free-trading ideals, the Colonial Office preferred to let sleeping dogs lie.

Responsible government became the Magna Carta of the settlement colonies: it embodied the rights to which all settlers aspired. But its award was delayed where the settlement seemed too weak or too poor to carry the burden of self-rule. It was denied at the Cape until 1872 when the revenue from diamonds transformed the colony's prospects. It was withheld from Natal until the mid-1890s. But by 1870, if not earlier, it was well understood that settler societies could expect political freedom from London's commands. What remained to be worked out was how far they would share in the empire's wider concerns.

Mid-Victorian governments dealt with the settlement colonies on the somewhat grudging presumption that as British communities they could not be denied the political freedoms Britons enjoyed at home. They dealt with India on exactly the opposite basis. India was a conquest state: indeed, until mid-century, it still seemed in process of being conquered. The Company maintained a huge army, twice the size of the British army, and its style of government was notably militarized. Through the Board of Control in London (whose "President" functioned as the minister for India), the British government exercised fitful supervision of the Company's rule. It was not enough to restrain several impetuous viceroys from waging annexationist wars. In India itself, the Company's civilian officials had fashioned a hybrid regime.

Its externals looked British and all the key posts in the government hierarchy were filled with British expatriates. But the forms of taxation, the treatment of property, the apparatus of law, and the lower levels of government reflected the practices of pre-conquest rulers in different parts of the sub-continent. Indeed, the Company eagerly codified what it imagined to be the time-honoured customs of local society. It has been persuasively argued that, in the formative period when the *raj* was constructed between the 1790s and the 1840s, what really took shape was a "neo-traditional" regime. By allying with Indians who invoked (or invented) an historicized version of Indian political traditions, the Company hoped to bed down its often fragile authority and represent itself as a legitimate "Indian" power.[23]

This trend did not pass without challenge. A strenuous lobby of utilitarian reformers was determined to ensure the "modernization" of India through a market economy and an administrative system that would cut down the remnants of obsolete custom. Free traders in Britain, particularly Lancashire interests, were fiercely critical of the slothful attitude of the Company government toward building railways and roads. They accused it of being more concerned with protecting the interests of the Company servants than with opening up India to British manufactures. When the 1857 Indian Rebellion revealed the disorganization and weakness of the Company's government, its charter was abruptly wound up. But although India now became the direct responsibility of the British government, this had a limited impact on the shape of British rule in the sub-continent.

Part of the reason was the careful insulation of Indian affairs from the over-zealous attention of the British Parliament. Those who had once argued for keeping the Company cited the dangers of making the government of India directly accountable to British MPs. Parliamentarians, they said, were often ignorant and prejudiced. They had no understanding of India, let alone of the differences between its various peoples, religions and cultures. They would promote private interests with little regard for their political consequence. They would act on a whim of political fashion or to score an electoral point. Their pious enthusiasms would threaten the careful avoidance of religious controversy by the Indian government. To fend off this danger, the 1858 Act created a "Council of India," mainly recruited from retired British officials, to act as a firewall against parliamentary interference. As it turned out, a far better protection was parliamentary boredom, artfully maintained by the avalanche of reports—a printed mass of impenetrable detail—supplied by the Indian government. Few British MPs took more than an occasional interest in Indian affairs and a debate about India was sure to empty the Commons.

In fact, the main beneficiaries of the Company's fall were the administrative cadre of the "covenanted" civil service,[24] the so-called "Civilians." The mutiny put an end to the Company policy of annexing princely states. Alongside "British India," where the British governed directly, was "Native State India," where Indian princes ruled under the watchful eye of a British "resident." The Indian princes were now to be treated as the Queen's loyal henchmen, bound to her by a semi-feudal allegiance. The mutiny also brought a drastic reduction in the size of the Company's army, by almost two thirds. The conquest-state era had passed. The result was the heyday of "Civilian" influence. Indeed, the Civilians were not so much a "civil service" in the

Western sense of the word as a political oligarchy. Almost every senior non-military post was reserved for men with the magic initials "I. C. S." after their name. They invented an ideology of imperial service and amassed a scholarly literature in which India's history, society, economy, and culture were interpreted as a story of chaos from which only the "steel frame" of Civilian rule had been able to save them.[25]

The Civilians understood very well that freedom from London's interfering hand really depended upon their continuing to pay the "Imperial Dividend." The counterpart to reducing the Indian army had been the stationing of a large British garrison of around 70,000 men (or one British soldier to every two Indian) to guard against a second mutiny and to be a strategic reserve for the British empire in the Eastern world. The reformed Indian army was also expected to be on standby for imperial service as far afield as China, East Africa, or Egypt. The ordinary costs of all this fell on the Indian taxpayer, who thus paid for almost two thirds of the British Empire's standing military force.[26] The costs of the "Army in India" (the British garrison and the Indian army) were the first charge on the Indian budget. The Civilians had to cut their administrative coat according to this military cloth. They also had to bend to the pressure from home to spend more money on railways, opening up India's interior markets and swelling its exports of raw cotton and wheat. The "rent" that they paid for the "hire" of the British garrison, and the interest payments on the money they borrowed to build India's railways, made up the bulk of the "Home Charges," the annual "tribute" (as its Indian critics called it) remitted to London. While that was paid on time, order was kept, and another mutiny averted, the Civilians could expect their "masters" in Whitehall to prolong their license to rule.

But Civilian rule was not entirely unchallenged. From the mid-1880s the Indian National Congress (founded 1885) campaigned against the Civilians' refusal to extend representative government to India: what Indian politicians labeled in a brilliant phrase, "the unBritishness of British rule." The Civilians were periodically fearful that the Congress leadership would attract liberal sympathy in Britain and force them into concession. They were also uneasy at facing public criticism in India and knew that London would frown on the heavy-handed censorship of India's English-language newspapers. To keep the Congress at bay, the Civilians devised a skillful defense. They rejected outright the Congress demand that the Civil Service should be progressively Indianised (the Congress, like them, knew where the real power lay). They offered instead a limited concession to the Congress request for elective representation on the hand-picked legislative councils—India's lawmaking bodies. In 1892 and 1909, the legislative councils of the British Indian provinces were made somewhat more representative of Indian opinion and the principle of limited election admitted. The Congress had called for a steady advance towards the same political freedom as the settler colonies enjoyed under responsible government. What they actually got was something quite different. Representation in India was carefully crafted to echo the divisions between religions, castes, and communities which made up the Indian "reality" as the Civilians understood it. Closely constrained by procedural rules, denied budgetary power and fissured by communal differences, India's legislatures remained largely an adjunct of executive power, not a real check upon it. While India paid so much of Britain's military bill, disdain for Indians' political capacities harmonized neatly with British self-interest. There was no time in the future, the great Victorian radical John Morley told the House of Lords in 1911, when India would be fitted for parliamentary self-government.

The colonial dependencies were the great residual category of the Victorian empire. What they had in common was "Crown Colony" government. Its essential principle was the concentration of both executive and legislative power in the hands of a governor accountable to London. This did not exclude the creation of "legislative councils" in the colonies: indeed it was usually found wise to consult local opinion— or at least its most powerful exponents—when drafting new laws. But the legislative councils had to have an "official" majority of members appointed by the governor as his representatives and obliged to vote under his direction. This type of empire had first been tried out in Quebec between 1774 and 1791. But its wider adoption came with the conquests made during the wars of 1793–1815. The test case was Trinidad, captured from the Spanish in 1796. Some voices were raised to argue that as a West Indian island it should be granted the same constitution as other British West Indian colonies. Its early governors objected. The island had a large population of "free people of colour." If they gained the vote they would control any assembly; if they were denied it, they would be dangerously antagonised. Few of the white population were British, or Protestants.[27] A despatch from Lord Liverpool in 1810 eventually settled the question. He laid down as a general principle that no elected assembly should be established where the British were too few and the population was largely composed of "free people of colour."[28]

Crown colony rule was thus explicitly justified along racial lines. But by the middle years of the century, this racial argument had acquired a new twist. The arrival of British merchants, planters, and other expatriates led in a number of places to renewed demands for representative government and an elected assembly—for the British residents only. These were badly received in the Colonial Office, imbued by now with a deep-seated mistrust of the European treatment of indigenous peoples. When a petition arrived from the white planters in Ceylon (Sri Lanka) in 1847, James Stephen's reaction was crushing. "To myself," he wrote,

> It seems that Englishmen who resort to the number of a few hundred to a great Asiatic state . . . must, while residing there, be content to forego the franchises of their Native land. Such a legislature as is proposed would in fact be an absolute oligarchy, responsible to no one for their actions, but armed with a power, crushing and intolerable, to the great mass of the people among whom they live . . .[29]

The governor's power was the key to protecting the subject population from exploitation and ill-treatment. In the West Indian colonies, the abolition of slavery, creating a large population of "free people of colour," also shifted the argument. In the new social conditions, the survival of assemblies elected by small white minorities blocked the road to reform. "Lifting the negroes out of barbarous indolence and ignorance," remarked a Colonial Office official, neatly combining racial, social and intellectual condescension, "would only be possible if the assemblies' power was swept away."[30] But London shied away from constitutional surgery and waited for the assemblies to abolish themselves. In Jamaica, the chance came with the 1865 rebellion. Amid the turmoil that followed its violent suppression, the assembly agreed to wind itself up and "revert" to the status of Crown Colony rule.

Crown Colony government was thus well established in time for the great expansion of Britain's tropical empire in Asia and Africa after 1880. It provided a highly flexible formula that allowed colonial administrators to make local agreements with indigenous rulers, and tape together a wide variety of subordinate polities as "colonies" or "protectorates." Far from imposing a uniform model, Crown Colony rule gave colonial governors wide discretion on who to consult and how to select their law-making councils. And far from announcing a brusque centralizing regime, its real significance was the pragmatic acceptance of local custom and precedent in what were often divided and disparate colonial communities.

However, it is "informal empire" that is often held up as the most characteristic mode of Victorian empire. "Informal empire" is a slippery term: no contemporary used it. It was more than mere influence. It is best applied to cases where a country was adapted systemically to the political, economic or cultural requirements of a stronger power, but without the formal loss of its sovereignty. Just as much as other forms of empire, it depended on the co-operation of local elites to whom it might offer the rewards of status as well as something more tangible. Its sphere is harder to define with precision than that of other forms of empire: opinions differ as to whether informal imperialism was deployed successfully in any particular place or time. Yet it remains the indispensable category within which to include those extra-European states whose substantive (as opposed to technical) independence was compromised by their "special relationship" with a foreign power.

"Informal empire" expressed the Victorians' confidence that unblocking the channels of trade with even the most reclusive of states outside Europe would help them reform along liberal lines. "Not a bale of merchandise leaves our shores," declared Richard Cobden, "but it bears the seeds of intelligence and fruitful thought to the members of some less enlightened community . . . our steamboats and our miraculous railways are the advertisements and vouchers for our enlightened institutions."[31] But like the formal varieties of empire, informal empire differed considerably from place to place. In Latin America, where conditions generally disfavoured an armed intervention (although it was tried), or the creation of extra-territorial enclaves, informal empire was visible mainly in commerce. What began as diplomatic agreements for the freeing of trade and security for the lives and property of foreign merchants, grew by the late nineteenth century into something much larger. In Argentina, it meant large-scale British ownership of banks, utilities and transport infrastructure: British-owned railways, spreading fan-like into the pampas, helped to make Argentina one of the world's greatest producers of maize and meat by 1914. It created an influential expatriate community, from which British-owned firms recruited their staff. It meant the sometimes grudging compliance of the Buenos Aires government with the financial disciplines required by the City of London as the condition for credit and further investment. In China, however, where the interests of trade were also pre-eminent, informal empire took on a different guise.

Unrestricted commerce with the West had been forced on China at the point of the bayonet in 1842. Even then, British merchants were not free to wander in the interior of China. What they gained in the first of the "unequal treaties" was the right to trade in a number of "treaty ports," and freedom in those from Chinese administrative control. Extra-territorial privilege placed them instead under the jurisdiction of their own consuls, who would adjudicate any disputes with the Chinese. In several places this privilege included the right to a separate municipal area, like the International Settlement at Shanghai, which had its own town council and police force. With a garrison at Hong Kong, gunboats patrolling the coast and the Yangtse, and a swarm of "China consuls" to uphold the rights promised in the treaties, informal empire in China was much more visible than in Latin America (where British investment was six times as large), and much more dependent on the exertion of force.[32] A third case of informal empire was different again. In Egypt, where the British had both financial interests and a strategic investment in the Suez Canal, they had intervened militarily in 1882, ostensibly to prevent a xenophobic regime (under Arabi Pasha) from taking power in Cairo. But to avoid provoking a hostile coalition of European powers, and partly because they initially hoped to stage an early withdrawal, they carefully refrained from annexing the country or declaring a protectorate. Instead, London insisted that that the occupation was "temporary" (it actually lasted for seventy-four years), and that its representative in Cairo, the formidable Evelyn Baring (later Lord Cromer), was merely "consul-general," not (as he really was) a de facto proconsul whose "advice" the government of Egypt was bound to accept.[33]

IV

In the late Victorian era after 1880, the headlong expansion of the previous half-century was shored up strategically. Annexations, occupations, and diplomatic partitions extended the sphere of British control in Africa, Asia and the Pacific. The frontiers of empire, especially the sea route to India, acquired a new set of outworks. This was partly made possible by economic success. As the world's leading shipper, insurer, banker, and trader, Britain profited heavily from the rapid growth of world trade after the mid-1890s, and built up huge overseas assets. The last decade before 1914 was certainly not free from imperial anxieties, rumours of wars, or conflict over Ireland—that colony-at-home. But it also saw the re-affirming of free trade as the basis of British prosperity—a tacit acknowledgment that the empire of investment and services was of vital importance. Although "imperial federation" between Britain and the self-governing "dominions" (as the self-governing colonies were now usually styled) made no political headway, there was closer co-operation between them in defense and foreign policy than before 1900. Over India, where (as we saw) there had been a limited extension of political rights, London now exerted a tighter financial control through the adoption of the "gold exchange standard" as the basis of India's monetary policy. Against this settled pattern of empire—self-governing, Indian, dependent, and informal—World War I was to break with earth-shattering force.

It did not seem so at first. The dominions, like India and the rest of the formal empire, found themselves at war because the king—their king too—had declared it. The dominions could decide how much—or how little—to contribute. In practice, public opinion, except among Afrikaners and French-Canadians, was fiercely loyal to empire—their empire. In India, the Congress was also unimpeachably loyal; and the Indian army was despatched on imperial service to fight the Germans and Turks. But by 1916, after two years of war, the political scenery began to shift. For the dominion governments it became increasingly urgent to be seen to have influence over the conduct of the war that was inflicting such losses. In India, the need to "reward" loyalty was made all the more pressing by the signs of a grand coalition of Indian politicians, Hindu and Muslim, calling for advance toward responsible government. In 1917–18, with its growing dependence upon dominion and Indian resources to carry on the war, London had no choice but to make some concessions.

The result was a dramatic reshaping of imperial relations. At the Imperial War Conference held in March/April 1917, the dominions' claim to formal equality with Britain was all but acknowledged. Jan Smuts' complaint that "what ever we may say, whatever we may think, we are subject Provinces of Great Britain. That is the actual theory of the Constitution,"[34] was met by the Conference's Resolution IX. This laid down, as the basis for a future adjustment of the dominions' status, that they were henceforth to be regarded as "autonomous nations of an Imperial Commonwealth."[35] With the end of the war, the urgency of winning an adequate voice in Britain's foreign policy quickly receded. But Canadian and Irish dissatisfaction (Southern Ireland became a dominion in 1921 as the "Irish Free State") with the ambiguities of their constitutional position prompted a new attempt to define what had come to be called "dominion status" at the Imperial Conference in 1926. The legendary verbal finesse of Arthur Balfour, a former prime minister, was mobilised for the task. The result was a formula to which all could assent. Both Great Britain and the dominions, it said,

> Are autonomous Communities within the British Empire, equal in status, in no way subordinate one to another in any aspect of their domestic or external affairs, though united by common allegiance to the Crown, and freely associated as members of the British Commonwealth of Nations.[36]

Five years later the Statute of Westminster enshrined this statement in law. The British Parliament surrendered its right to legislate for the dominions and would only do so at their express request.

Was dominionhood still a variety of empire? Status equality allowed Irish or Afrikaner nationalists to say no. But majority opinion in Canada, Australia, and New Zealand, and among the South African "English" (around 40 percent of the white population) was equally sure that membership of the empire—defined as the collective enterprise of the British *peoples*—was entirely compatible with their national identity, and perhaps even essential to it. This opinion also took it for granted that the survival and safety of the British empire as a whole (insofar as it secured Britain's place as a world power) was a common interest they shared, since no other principle of world order could promise so much. Meanwhile, the Indian version of empire was also in flux. In 1917, to appease discontent and "rally the moderates" (a phrase never far from official lips in the twentieth-century empire), London had broken with pre-war tradition and announced that India too could advance to responsible government and implicitly therefore to dominion status. In 1919, partial self-government was granted in the Indian provinces. In 1935, full responsible government was prescribed for the provinces, and partial self-government for the Indian center—subject, however, to a mass of "safeguards" that included control over the Indian army and the military budget. Sandwiched between these announcements was a further promise made in 1929 that India would become a dominion sooner or later. But the 1935 act made progress towards dominionhood dependent on the achievement of an "All-India Federation" of "British India" and the Princely States. On the eve of World War II, there was little sign of this happening.

Nevertheless, the interwar years showed that the Victorian empire had had to adjust to the demands of nationalism. In Ceylon, a Crown Colony, the "Donoughmore constitution" conferred wide powers of self-government on an elected assembly. In Egypt the British renounced (at least formally) the pre-war practice of interfering in domestic affairs and declared Egypt to be an independent state—subject to British oversight of its foreign relations and British protection of foreign interests. In the case of Iraq, conquered from the Turks in 1918 and then ruled as mandate under the League of Nations, the British readily agreed to independent statehood in 1932, in exchange for the right to keep military bases. In both Iran and China, they accepted the need to give up the extra-territorial privileges that had underpinned their informal imperialism before 1914, although the final repudiation of the unequal treaties with China was delayed until 1943. The rhetoric of empire was softened: the idea of a "Commonwealth" of voluntary members, held together by shared interests and values, was heard more frequently. Its less sentimental corollary was the private belief of British politicians and officials that so long as Britain remained a world power, the flowery language would make little difference.

Indeed, in other parts of their empire the British seemed to be rowing in the opposite direction. In their African colonies, they showed little enthusiasm for electoral politics or the creating of nations. The reigning orthodoxy in colonial policy was "indirect rule." Indirect rule meant the conscious adoption (and codification) of tradition and custom. If they could not be found, then, with local help, they could be invented. The aim was to rule through "native authorities" (who were expected to be tribal chiefs) and "customary law," purged when necessary of disagreeable elements. Implicit in this version of empire was not only a doctrine of minimal cost but also the denial of the possibility of nationhood except in a future too remote to be planned for. Instead the active ingredients in the colonial polity were thought of as "tribes," or the subnational units of traditional rulers—Nigerian emirs or Malayan sultans. Empire of this kind was almost a stationary state: far from exerting the imperial will, it came close to a pact of non-interference in exchange for tranquility and a skeletal budget.

The most obvious casualty of the interwar years was the worldwide commercial empire of the City of London. Amid the financial crash of 1931, Britain abandoned free trade and the gold standard, the twin pillars of London's pre-war supremacy as the entrepôt of world trade. A new and more limited kind of commercial empire emerged, defended by tariffs and informal controls on the export of capital. This was the "sterling bloc," one of the trading and currency groups into which the world was divided by the mid-1930s. Yet its scale should not be disparaged. It included all of the formal empire—dominions, India, and dependencies, with the partial exception of Canada (a dollar country but inside the tariff barrier)—as well as Egypt, Iraq, and much of the Middle East. Its managers hoped that with Japan's co-operation it would also gather in China where monetary reform had become very urgent by the 1930s. Battered by depression and the "deglobalization" of the world economy, Britain was still the world's leading trader on the eve of World War II.

V

In retrospect, it seems obvious that the real substance of empire had been lost soon after the end of World War II. By 1947 India was independent. The partitioned sub-continent contributed nothing to the defense of Britain's empire east of Suez. Britain no longer had sole claim to the loyalty of the "white dominions." Canada, Australia, and New Zealand now looked to the United States, not Britain, as the best guarantor of their safety. (This was less true of South Africa, but there the triumph of the "purified nationalists" and their doctrine of apartheid made co-operation increasingly difficult after 1948.) The informal imperium in the Middle East, acquired in 1918, had all but collapsed by the late 1940s. Without the advantage of hindsight, the British tried to build a new empire to meet post-war conditions. In the tropical colonies, the "night-watchman" state of the interwar years became the "developmental state" to turn their sluggish economies into imperial assets, earning dollars for Britain and easing the grip of post-war austerity on its battered economy. The British held on in Malaya, the source of key raw materials, and at Singapore. They hoped to turn the white-ruled Central African Federation (today's Zambia, Zimbabwe and Malawi) into a proto-dominion whose huge copper reserves were a vital strategic material. They promoted a special relationship with Australia, the main destiny of post-war migration from Britain, and London's key partner in its nuclear programme—the strategic foundation of imperial survival into the atomic age. They expected an enlarged "British Commonwealth," into which the Afro-Asian dependencies would be admitted as members once they had advanced to self-rule, to remain a vast sphere where British influence was pre-eminent. While this version of empire remained credible, and the delusion persisted that the British economy would recover the strength to sustain a pattern of global commitments, a "European" future as the partner of France (a bogus world power of doubtful stability) and West Germany, had little appeal. In the 1950s it was still possible to imagine a new kind of empire built along these lines. But after 1960 a new round of crisis in the domestic economy brought a salutary realism. Before the end of the decade, Britain's last empire became too heavy a burden, and the pains of post-imperial adjustment began to be felt in earnest.

Notes

1 Gallagher and Robinson, "Imperialism of free trade," pp. 1–15.
2 Madden and Darwin (eds), *Dominions and India*, p. 12.
3 Davies, *First English Empire*, p. 195.
4 *Ibid.*, p. 198.
5 For Sir John Davies' views, see Pawlisch, *Sir John Davies*.
6 Letters Patent from Charles I to Lord Baltimore, 2 June 1632. See Madden and Fieldhouse (eds), *"Empire of the Bretaignes,"* p. 223.
7 Henretta, *"Salutary Neglect."*
8 Whether the Empire before the American Revolution can be usefully described as the "First British Empire," and (if so) when it gave way to a "Second" British Empire have been much debated. See Hyam, "British imperial expansion"; Mackay, "Direction and purpose"; Marshall, "First British Empire," pp. 43–53. The most forceful exponent of the change and its late eighteenth century timing was V. T. Harlow in his *Founding of the Second British Empire*.
9 Fear among merchants of a shortage of coin is stressed in Bailyn, *New England Merchants*.
10 See Steele, *English Atlantic*.
11 For the terms of the Canada Act 1791, see Madden with Fieldhouse (eds), *Imperial Reconstruction*, pp. 455–9.
12 See Drescher, *Capitalism and Antislavery*.
13 For a recent account see Marshall, *Making and Unmaking*, ch. 7.
14 *Parliamentary Debates*, 3rd series, 49, col. 1391 (Aug. 6, 1839).
15 Sellar and Yeatman, *1066 and all That*, p. 137.
16 Buckner, *Transition to Responsible Government*.
17 Madden with Fieldhouse (eds), *Imperial Reconstruction*, p. 565.
18 *Ibid.*, p. 566.
19 See Darwin, "Durham in the East," pp. 144–61.
20 Madden (ed.), *Settler Self-Government*, p. 154.
21 *Ibid.*, p. 158.
22 Elgin to Grey, January 14, 1850. Doughty (ed.), *Elgin-Grey Papers II*, p. 580.
23 Washbrook, "India 1818–1860," pp. 395–421.
24 So called because they signed a legal covenant on appointment.
25 See Metcalf, *Ideologies of the Raj*.
26 In the late nineteenth century the British army amounted to around 180,000 men, and the Indian army to 140,000, a total of 320,000 regular soldiers. Of these, 210,000 were on the "Indian budget."
27 Manning, *British Colonial Government*, pp. 350–1.
28 *Ibid.*, p. 361.
29 Minute by Stephen, January 14, 1847. Madden (ed.), *Dependent Empire*, p. 276.
30 *Ibid.*, p. 158: Minute by H. Taylor, May 30, 1865.
31 Cobden, *England, Ireland and America*, p. 11.
32 The classic accounts are Greenberg, *British Trade*; Fairbank, *Trade and Diplomacy*. For a recent account, Hevia, *English Lessons*, a much more interesting book than the subtitle suggests.
33 The best recent account of the Cromerian regime is R. Owen, *Lord Cromer*.
34 Madden and Darwin (eds), *Dominions and India*, p. 38.
35 *Ibid.*, p. 42.
36 *Ibid.*, p. 105.

Further Reading

The best introduction to the sheer variety of Britain's imperial expansion can be found in the five volumes of the *OHBE*, general editor W. R. Louis, and in the forthcoming companion volumes on Canada and Australia. In recent years, many historians of empire have shown a surprising indifference to constitutional matters, as if the rules of the political game did not matter intensely to contemporaries. This is a bizarre misjudgment. The best corrective can be found in the eight-volume collection of *Select Documents*, edited by F. Madden, beginning with his *Empire of the Bretaignes*. The constant interplay of constitutional, social, economic and ideological issues is revealed. The medieval origins of British expansion have now been elegantly analyzed in R. R. Davies, *The First English Empire*; the importance of medieval precedents for colonial governance was made clear earlier in A. F. M. Madden, "1066, 1776 and all that." The most stimulating introduction to the "first" British empire can be found in Steele, *The English Atlantic*. The relationship between the end of empire in the thirteen American colonies and the rise of empire in India, once described by V. T. Harlow as the "swing to the East" in his *Founding of the Second British Empire*, can now be followed in P. Marshall, *The Making and Unmaking of Empire*. The starting point for any serious analysis of the Victorians' imperial "system" remains J. Gallagher and R. Robinson, "The imperialism of Free Trade." Commentary and criticism can be found in W. R. Louis (ed.), *Imperialism: The Robinson and Gallagher Controversy*. A brilliant demonstration of how the idea of informal empire can be applied is P. Winn, "Britain's informal empire." British rule in India has been extensively studied. The most bracing interpretation of its symbiotic relationship with Indian nationalism is still A. Seal, "Imperialism and nationalism in India," the first chapter in Gallagher, Johnson and Seal (eds), *Locality, Province and Nation*. India's place in the British imperial system is the subject of the marvellous opening chapter of A. Seal, *The Emergence of Indian Nationalism*. For the interwar years, the best guides are Tomlinson, *The Indian National Congress* and Page, *Prelude to Partition*. The development of responsible government in the settler colonies is described in J. M. Ward, *Colonial Self-Government* and in Buckner, *The Transition to Responsible Government*. Britain's relations with the "white dominions" are assessed in J. Darwin "A third British Empire? The dominion idea in imperial politics," in Louis and Brown (eds), *OHBE: The Twentieth Century*. The authoritative study of anglo-dominion relations between the wars is R. F. Holland, *Britain and the Commonwealth Alliance*. Dominion attitudes to Empire are one focus of the developing historiography of the "British World." For the Canadian and South African cases, see the relevant chapters in Buckner and Francis (eds), *Rediscovering the British World*. The special case of Ireland is dealt with in D. McMahon, *Republicans and Imperialists*. "Crown colony government" has not received much by way of thematic, as opposed to particularized, attention. H. T. Manning, *British Colonial Government* provides the best introduction but M. Wight, *The Development of the Legislative Council* and the same writer's *British Colonial Constitutions* are indispensable.

2

Foundations of Empire, 1763–83

Eliga H. Gould

The closing months of 1775 easily rank among the most fraught and confused moments in Britain's imperial history. The previous spring, Parliament's long-running dispute with the American colonists had finally erupted in armed conflict, plunging North America's eastern seaboard into open rebellion and forcing the British people to brace for their third colonial war in as many decades. To the metropolitan public, much about the conflict was unclear. By general agreement, the government was engaged in an "unnatural civil war" involving people who, by the indissoluble ties of law, kinship, and religion, were as British as any of the king's subjects in Britain. "It is no longer our task to describe devastation in Poland, or slaughter on the Danube," lamented the *Annual Register*. "The evil is at home."[1] Yet there was also something different—even exotic—about what was taking place in the colonies. In the reports that inundated the British press, readers were assured that Americans had committed the most horrific atrocities, mistreating loyal women and children, refusing to care for wounded prisoners, and scalping enemy corpses.[2] Others noted the brutal underside of American society, especially the chicanery with which colonists swindled Indians and the widespread use of African slaves. As an English correspondent warned a friend in America, the colonists did not lack defenders on the near shores of the Atlantic, but it was by no means certain that they would ever appear "respectable in the eyes of Europe."[3]

Not so long ago, an essay on the early modern foundations of the British Empire could have opened by depicting the boundaries between Britain and its overseas colonies as fixed and unambiguous. For most of the post-World War II era—an era characterized, among other things, by decolonization in Britain and the rejection of formal empire across much of Western Europe—the scholarly tendency was to treat British and imperial history as distinct subjects, with "British history" invariably denoting the history of metropolitan Britain, and "Britain" usually serving as a synonym for the union's English core.[4] Today, the situation is far less clear-cut. Imperial themes pervade metropolitan scholarship on the nineteenth and twentieth centuries; India, Ireland, and America figure prominently in early modern narratives; and the British nation of England, Scotland, and Wales has regained its proper character as a "multiple monarchy" or empire. Students pursuing degrees in British history are likely to know as much about soil depletion in Virginia as crop rotation in Suffolk, as much about interracial sexuality in Bengal as worker radicalism in the Midlands, and a great deal more than earlier generations would have thought possible about marronage in Jamaica, Protestant missions in Africa, and educational reform in the Highlands.[5]

Taken as a whole, this renewed interest in the imperial dimensions of British history has produced a much clearer understanding of the history of Britain and the British Empire as two parts of the same whole, and of the fundamentally British character of events like the American Revolution—a "singular" conflict, as a writer described the looming war in 1775, that pitted "English subjects against English subjects."[6] Without doubt, the benefits of this broader perspective have been considerable, as the "Little Englandism" that long dominated metropolitan and imperial history has yielded to a more inclusive interpretation. Nonetheless, the prevailing trend raises a number of difficult questions. Among the more important is how, exactly, to deal with the spatial boundaries and sense of difference that featured so prominently in the British press reports from late 1775, especially the all-important distinction between Britain's history as one of the dominant "civilized states" of Europe and its expanding presence in the extra-European world. Georgian Britain may have been a "nation defined by empire," as Peter Marshall has written. It was, however, also a nation keenly aware of its empire's global, extra-European character, one where even colonists of British extraction were often viewed with deep ambivalence, if not outright hostility.[7]

Although there are numerous reasons for this paradox—including differences based on the colonies' racial diversity, religious heterodoxy, and variations in social structure—by far the most important for the British themselves was the legal geography that they used when thinking about matters of empire. For people throughout the British Empire, the law functioned as a kind of lingua franca for categorizing distinctions of all sorts, and it was law that gave constructs like race, nation, and class their dynamic, instrumental force. To most Britons at the time of the American Revolution, British colonists were their own "flesh and blood," natural-born Britons with the same rights and responsibilities as Britons who lived in Britain proper. At the same time, though, both English common law and the law of nations reinforced a perception of the world beyond Europe as a place so chaotic that even British nationals were free to act in ways that the British would have viewed as unacceptable closer to home.[8] The result was a set of conflicting, sometimes contradictory images. Despite regarding their overseas settlements as so many fragments of English society, Britons everywhere insisted that their overseas colonies were situated in lawless, perpetually warring zones, where the rules of European civil society often did not apply. In a sense, the same geography that gave the empire its British character placed limits on how far British subjects in the colonies could be expected to conform to metropolitan norms of behavior, even when the subjects in question were as British as the New Englanders who defied the king's troops on Lexington Common.

The lawlessness that the British attributed to the world beyond Britain's shores did not apply to all nations, especially the nations of Western Europe. Despite the xenophobia with which they regarded competitors like France and Spain, the British viewed Europe as a "kind of republic," what the Swiss jurist Emer de Vattel described as a law-bound system of states whose "members—each independent, but all linked together by the ties of common interest—unite for the maintenance of order and liberty."[9] Having helped thwart every European aspirant to "universal monarchy" since the Spanish Armada, Britons were immensely proud of their role in maintaining the "liberties of Europe" or, as it was sometimes called, the European balance of power. As an Irish pamphleteer observed during the American Revolution, Europe's modern history would have been an unrelenting story of slavery and impoverishment, "but for the intervention of Great Britain."[10] Because a Europe of independent states was allegedly a more peaceful, law-abiding regime than one dominated by a single power, the British attributed other, equally beneficial consequences to their efforts, including the triumph of a moral code that encouraged Europeans to temper the pursuit of their own interests by acknowledging the rights of others. "Even foreign wars abate of their cruelty," remarked David Hume of what he took to be the dominant trend during the 1750s, "and after the field of battle, where honour and interest steel men against compassion as well as fear, the combatants divest themselves of the brute, and resume the man."[11] "Europe hath for above a century past been greatly enriched by commerce and polished by arts," concurred East Apthorp, the New England-born vicar of Croydon, in 1776. "Whoever compares the present age with the last, will discern an almost total change to have taken place in the manners, customs, and government of Christendom."[12]

The question, which the American Revolution raised with particular urgency, was just how far this European "republic" extended. Did it include the British colonies in North America and the West Indies or, for that matter, the British forts and factories on the coasts of Africa, let alone the East India Company's possessions in Asia? If so, were Britons in such remote outposts obligated to follow the same rules of international behavior as Britons in Europe? In the main, British jurists took an expansive approach to such questions, holding the European treaties and diplomatic customs, known collectively as the law of nations, to be universal, with norms that were as binding in the "wilds" of America as at the center of Europe. This was partly because of the need to regulate relations between Europe's imperial powers and to prevent them from subjecting each other's colonists to what Bristol's Society of Merchant Venturers termed "uncivilized sistem[s] of war."[13] In Britain's case, the notion of a global jurisprudence derived added force from the doctrine that settlers who emigrated overseas retained all the rights of natural-born subjects, including the protection of both the common law and the law of nations. As William Blackstone noted in the *Commentaries*, the latter formed such a fundamental part of the British constitution that it was "adopted in it's full extent" wherever English law was in force. Were the situation otherwise, wrote Blackstone, contracts between merchants would be worthless, foreign treaties would lose their force, and Britain could expect neither friendship nor mercy from other governments; in a word, its people "must cease to be a part of the civilized world."[14]

As Blackstone's words suggested, the British Empire's place in Europe's "civilized world" was partly a function of the English basis of the colonies' law and government.

"The common law of England is the common law of the plantations," wrote the Admiralty's legal counsel, Richard West, in 1720. "Let an Englishman go where he will, he carries as much of law and liberty with him, as the nature of things will allow."[15] During the colonial taxation debates of the 1760s and 1770s, Anglo-Americans eagerly embraced such notions, insisting, in the words of the Virginia patriot Richard Bland, that Britons in America had the same "right to the liberties and privileges of *Englishmen*, as if they were actually resident within the kingdom."[16] Even colonists who remained loyal to the Crown in 1776 tended to conceive of their rights in liberal terms. In 1787, the governor of Barbados claimed that this sense of entitlement was so extensive that he was at the mercy of a "democracy," with the island's lower house claiming privileges that exceeded even those of "the House of Commons in England."[17] "The form of government here," wrote Edward Long in his *History of Jamaica* (1774), "resembles that of England almost as nearly as the condition of a dependent colony *can* be brought to resemble that of its mother country."[18] As the Virginia attorney general and future Loyalist John Randolph wrote in 1774,

> A more pleasing and natural Connection never subsisted between any different Bodies of Men than . . . between *Great Britain* and her Colonies. The *Americans* are descended from the Loins of *Britons*, and therefore may, with Propriety, be called the Children, and *England* the Mother of them. We are not only allied by Blood, but are still further united, by the extensive Trade and Commerce carried on between us. Our Manners are similar; our Religion, and Language, the same. There is no Diversity between the Laws of each Country, but such as local Circumstances have occasioned.[19]

Although the American Revolution eventually severed the "natural" bonds to which Randolph referred, such observations reinforced perceptions of Britain's Atlantic empire as a vast diasporic nation, a greater British polity whose North American and West Indian components figured as so many "cultural provinces" of the empire's English core.[20] During the transatlantic debates over colonial taxation, almost no one in Britain questioned the premise that the king's Anglo-American subjects were "fellow subjects" with the same rights and responsibilities as the king's subjects in Britain. As Lord Mansfield noted in defense of Parliament's right to levy revenue taxes in the colonies, there were "twelve millions of people in England and Ireland who are not represented" in Parliament, yet every one of them was subject to parliamentary taxation. Solicitor General Fletcher Norton made the same point, insisting that, by taxing the colonists without their consent, "we use North America as we use ourselves."[21] Although not all Britons accepted this way of thinking, even those who opposed taxing the colonists did so on the assumption that, as the English radical John Wilkes argued in 1771, there ought to be "no difference between an inhabitant of Boston in Lincolnshire, and of Boston in New England."[22] In the words of a British pamphleteer, whose dialog with "a candid merchant of America" appeared as war was about to erupt in 1775, "You are my fellow-subject, or we have been playing the fool for more than a century."[23]

If British settlers in America shared a common law and nationality with fellow subjects in Britain, their membership in the "civilized world" to which Blackstone referred also depended on the safeguards that the British government afforded all Britons under the law of nations, no matter where they lived. This was especially important in regions that lay outside the main areas of Anglo-American settlement, including the shipping lanes of the Atlantic, the hinterlands of North America's Indian country, and Africa and India (where sovereignty over Britain's outposts remained, ostensibly, in the hands of local rulers). Without the compensatory bulwark of English settlement, the law of nations was often the only security for Britons in such areas, backed, as far as possible, by the British government's watchful eye and military power. Whatever they thought of Britain's ill-fated attempts at colonial taxation, even Americans recognized the benefits of this protection, noting, among its many advantages, the safeguards conferred by Britain's agreements with other nations, the commercial prosperity that Britons everywhere gained from the navy's dominance of the high seas, and the security that came from the government's vigilance against hostile powers. For colonists in North America and the West Indies, Britain's maritime enforcement of the law of nations was particularly important, and many accepted that Parliament had a corresponding right to defray some of the costs by regulating the colonies' trade.[24] As Benjamin Franklin told the House of Commons in 1766, "the sea is yours":

> You maintain by your fleets, the safety of navigation in it, and keep it clear of pirates; you may have therefore a natural and equitable right to some toll or duty on merchandizes carried through that part of your dominions.[25]

As the move to repudiate the imperial sovereignty of the British Crown and Parliament gathered strength in North America, the question that gave many colonists the greatest difficulty was the likely effects on the maritime regime that Franklin described. In particular, because the law of nations only protected the subjects of internationally recognized governments, Americans worried that, by unilaterally declaring independence, they were about to embark on what Pennsylvania's John Dickinson called a dangerous attempt to "brave the Storm in a Skiff made of Paper."[26] Although writers like Tom Paine sought to allay such fears, assuring American readers that their new states would find compensatory markets and allies as long as "eating is the custom of Europe," more than a few Britons agreed.[27] According to Samuel Johnson, the only alternative to enjoying the benefits of civil society under the authority of the colonists' lawful sovereign was primitive savagery. "By turning fishermen or hunters, woodmen or shepherds," Johnson insisted, "[Americans] may become wild, but it is not so easy to conceive them free."[28] "Your Destruction is inevitable," concurred the Scottish advocate Sir John Dalrymple in his *Address to the Inhabitants of America* (1775),

> [I]f you are permitted to throw off [the] badges of supremacy, as madmen may call them, you are that instant independent states: you will form yourselves into independent principalities, republics, and we fear anarchies. A new political system will arise, not in Europe alone, but in the World.[29]

Statements like these attest to the misgivings with which people throughout the British Atlantic greeted the project of American independence, yet they also strengthened the countervailing belief that only settlers who accepted their obligations as British subjects were likely to enjoy the "felicity [that] is the envy of all nations."[30] Although American Loyalists frequently took the lead in advancing such claims, warning against the Republican tendency to "speak contemptuously of all government," metropolitan Britons were well aware of the safeguards that their government afforded them under the common law and the law of nations.[31] In the words of a loyal address adopted by the city of Exeter in September 1775, Americans would soon discover "that peace, and happiness, and liberty, are only to be secured . . . by the protecting power of this country."[32] "How shall I describe what I felt, when I first set my foot on British ground?" wrote Louisa Wells of South Carolina, upon landing at Deal in 1779.[33] As Beilby Porteus, the American-born bishop of Chester, told the House of Lords:

> Wherever our discoveries, our commerce, or our arms have penetrated, they have in general carried the laws, the freedom, and the religion of this country along with them. Whatever faults and errors we may be chargeable with in other respects, for these gifts at least, the most invaluable that one country can bestow upon another, it is not improbable that both the eastern and the western world may one day acknowledge that they were *originally* indebted to this nation.[34]

If Britons embraced an expansive notion of British nationality and international rights for themselves, there was less agreement about the rights and responsibilities of imperial subjects who were neither British nor European. Even when they lacked access to English courts, natural-born Britons in remote locations like North America's Indian country, the British forts of West Africa, and the dominions of the East India Company were all entitled to the same "law and liberty" as fellow subjects in Britain and the colonies; however, Britain's authority over the indigenous inhabitants of such territories more closely resembled a kind of protective union or alliance—what Edmund Burke, in his speech on Fox's East India Bill (1783), called an "external federal trust."[35] As the extensive use that the government made of Native American auxiliaries during the American Revolution showed, non-Europeans could be as reliably loyal as British subjects who claimed the rights of Englishmen. On the other hand, the laws that governed their actions invariably differed from those of either the British or their European neighbors, a fact that the American Congress duly noted on July 4, 1776, by denouncing George III for employing "merciless Indian Savages, whose known rule of warfare, is an undistinguished destruction of all ages, sexes and conditions."[36] Because the treaties and customs that governed relations within Europe's diplomatic republic owed their efficacy to a voluntary, culturally specific code of reciprocity, it was unclear how far, or in what ways, such norms applied to people "who observe no law," in the ominous words of Vattel.[37]

During the 1760s and early 1770s, the question of how to manage the British Empire's legal diversity emerged with particular urgency in the debates over what, if any, regulations Parliament ought to adopt for the Mughal provinces governed by the East India Company.[38] As Warren Hastings' protracted, seven year trial showed, the British public increasingly expected the government to "extend the protection of English justice over even the tribes of India."[39] At the same time, most proponents of reform admitted the near impossibility of transplanting "the laws of one country, to another differing entirely in its customs, habits, manners, and . . . regulations."[40] In the words of Harry Verelst, former governor of Bengal, one might as well expect the "gallantry of a Frenchman in the wilds of America, as hope that minds depressed by despotism can embrace the idea of a common interest, or conceive the dominion of laws."[41] "It is . . . the height of absurdity," wrote the Earl of Stair, "to think the Indians are unhappy because they do not live under the same constitution as the inhabitants of this island."[42] As the East India Company officer Alexander Dalrymple insisted in 1772:

> I am perfectly convinced [that] an attempt to introduce a Code of Laws [would] be ruinous: The Indians are so devoted to their own Customs, which they injoyed many ages before we had even painted Ancestors, that the English Laws are not suited to them . . . Every Conqueror of India must follow the example of former Conquerors and leave the Indians to themselves.[43]

Although these objections reflected a variety of concerns—some stemming from an awareness of the antiquity of India's history and culture, others having more to do with the Company's own interests—the most compelling objection of all was Britain's inability to impose its will unilaterally on Indian society. Speaking of the norms that governed marriage in India, Harry Verelst claimed that "women in the East are transferred with little ceremony," with suitors "rarely await[ing] their consent." "Were our laws of rape and rules of evidence enforced," insisted Verelst, "one half of the vales would incur the penalty of death."[44] Other writers highlighted differences in the rights of Indian landlords, in the relationship of law to religion, even in Indian conceptions of what the law was.[45] "A moment's consideration," wrote one observer, "will be sufficient to convince any man, that an act done in *England*, and attended with the forfeiture of life itself, may not be attended with any punishment at *Constantinople*," and the same was true of the administration of justice in India.[46] As Burke cautioned in his speech attacking Fox's East India Bill, India was a "vast mass, composed of so many orders and classes of men, . . . infinitely diversified by manners, by religion, by hereditary employment, through all their possible combinations." Let no one suppose that its affairs could be managed in the same way that Parliament might "regulate the tenants of a manor, or the shopkeepers of the next county town."[47]

Although the Asiatic territories of the East India Company differed in important respects from Britain's empire in America, admonitions of this sort resonated in part because of Britain's long experience with similar problems in the extra-European Atlantic. The Atlantic Ocean supplied ample evidence of the limits of Britain's imperial jurisdiction, and of the corresponding need to accommodate groups whose conceptions of the law often differed from those of both metropolitan and colonial Britons. Although the "golden age of piracy"—as one historian has called it—was over by the time of the American Revolution, the British public continued to regard the Atlantic as a "state of nature," a sort of maritime common where illicit trade was the norm, where even the king's regular navy sometimes bent the law, and where the privateers licensed by every European government continued to operate according to their own "piratical" customs.[48] In part, these apprehensions came from the British people's exposure to the autonomous, violent aspects of maritime culture in England, whether in the form of smuggling, naval impressment, or seamen's strikes. During the Liverpool strike of August 1775, when some two thousand sailors, idled by the fighting in America, seized cannons from a whaler and bombarded the Exchange, one observer "could not help thinking we had Boston here."[49] But the lawlessness that people attributed to the high seas also reflected the fact that the authority of what Blackstone called the British "maritime state" was, at best, a negotiated authority.[50] As Anna Maria Falconbridge recalled after being awakened by a deranged passenger on her Africa-bound vessel in 1791, her first thought was that "a gang of pirates had attacked the ship, and would soon put us all to death." Although Falconbridge's ship had yet to leave Gravesend, such stories conveyed an obvious lesson.[51] Men and women who ventured beyond Britain's shores entered a zone where the law differed in important respects from the law in England, sometimes terrifyingly so.

If the waters of the Atlantic exemplified the legal diversity of Britain's periphery, writers attributed the same lawless conditions to the "unoccupied" lands of America. Despite a tendency to describe North America's indigenous inhabitants as "noble savages," British and Anglo-American writers also viewed Indians as stateless people whose "barbarous" customs included torture, infanticide, and cannibalism. Following the notorious massacre at Fort William Henry in 1757, one Massachusetts soldier wrote that France's Indian allies killed indiscriminately: "men, women, and children were despatched in the most wanton cruel manner, and immediately scalped." Another New Englander claimed that the Indians tore "the Children from their Mothers Bosoms and their mothers from their Husbands."[52] According to the Scottish-born Boston antiquarian William Douglass, Native Americans were primitives, who lived in "small and distinct" tribes, only one stage removed from government by "distinct families," each "Isolé" from the others. Douglass also insisted that Indians possessed "no civil government, no religion, no letters; the French call them *les hommes des bois*, or men-brutes of the forest."[53] In the years before the American Revolution, ethnographic observations of this sort became so common that Tobias Smollett parodied the entire genre in the character of Lieutenant Obadiah Lismahago, a penniless Scot recently returned from the colonies, who regaled the cast of *Humphrey Clinker* (1772) with stories of being captured and tortured by the "Badger tribe" near Fort Ticonderoga, after which he was elected their *sachem* and married to a princess about whose neck hung "the fresh scalp of a Mohawk warrior."[54]

As we might expect, not all manifestations of the Atlantic world's reputed lawlessness were negative. On some occasions, the same conditions that gave rise to stories like that of Lieutenant Lismahago could yield profound insights, unimpeded by the trappings of excessive civility and refinement. As the English radical John Cartwright noted of a Labrador woman who accompanied his naval vessel to England in 1769, immense structures like the hospital at Portsmouth and St Paul's Cathedral made a "wonderful impression," but her greatest surprise—which Cartwright, in turn, found deeply revealing—came when she learned that an Englishman could be hanged for attempting to "go into the woods and kill venison."[55] Yet even when non-Europeans were cast in the role of noble savage, their unfamiliarity with British and European legal systems rendered them objects of suspicion, if not outright distrust. In the words that could just as easily have been used to describe British views of American Indians, Thomas Poplett, who spent the American Revolution in the British garrison at Goree, assured the Privy Council in 1789 that Africans were "lively, jealous, and vindictive."[56] Not surprisingly, Olaudah Equiano, whose *Interesting Narrative* became an international bestseller following its publication in 1789, was willing to go only so far in adopting the persona of primitive savant. Although the account of his early years in Africa established his natural humanity, the narrative's main purpose was to show that a man of color could master a range of European skills, including writing, sea-faring, theology, and the law.[57]

Despite the British Empire's increasingly global reach, these limits on the extra-European jurisdiction of both English common law and the European law of nations had the effect of sanctioning behavior on the part of Britons in the colonies that the British were unwilling to sanction at home. In the years before the American Revolution, the clearest indication of such attitudes was the growing British debate over the African slave trade and the colonial slavery that it helped sustain. In the aftermath of Lord Mansfield's momentous decision in Somerset versus Stewart (1772), a case widely perceived as abolishing slavery in England,[58] the British frequently reiterated Blackstone's dictum that a slave became free "the instant he lands in England."[59] Even abolitionists, however, admitted that merchants on the coasts of Africa were engaged in a legitimate commerce involving peoples whose enslavement was legal, according to the customs of their native country. According to most accounts, captives shipped to the colonies were either prisoners of war or convicted adulterers, witches, thieves, and murderers, all of whom would have faced the most horrendous death at the hands of their own rulers had they not been sold into slavery. As the *London Magazine* assured its readers during the 1740s, West Africa's petty despots wielded powers so arbitrary and "contrary to nature and reason" that it was an act of mercy to transplant their unfortunate dependents to colonies where they could live "under the benign influence of the law and Gospel."[60] "I cannot think the Slave Trade inconsistent with any moral, or religious law," wrote Anna Maria Falconbridge of what she observed during her travels in Sierra Leone:

> [I]n place of invading the happiness of Africa, [it] tends to promote it, by pacifying the murdering, despotic chieftains of that country, who only spare the lives of their vassals from a desire of acquiring the manufactures of this and other nations, and by saving millions from perdition, whose future existence is rendered comfortable, by the cherishing hands of Christian masters.[61]

Although the Indians' plight occasioned less comment, Britons and Anglo-Americans freely invoked many of the same prerogatives when justifying the confiscation of indigenous land in North America. According to writers on both sides of the Atlantic, the "primitive" character of Indian society—evident, most notably, in the absence of settled agriculture and a recognizable system of private property—gave British settlers the right to dispose of "vacant" native lands, by conquest and unilateral appropriation if the gentler means of diplomatic purchase did not suffice.[62] "The earth . . . produces little without cultivation," wrote the archdeacon of Carlisle, William Paley, of the moral underpinnings of this right in 1785:

> A nation of North American savages, consisting of two or three hundred, will take up, and be half starved upon, a tract of land, which in Europe, and with European management, would be sufficient for the maintenance of as many thousands.[63]

To be sure, not everyone accepted this way of thinking. As Samuel Johnson observed at the start of the Seven Years War, the struggle between Britain and France for control of the Ohio Valley resembled nothing so much as "the quarrel of two robbers for the spoils of a passenger."[64] For those who shared Johnson's qualms, however, an impressive battery of thinkers, including Locke, Pufendorf, and Vattel, confirmed that it was entirely legal for European settlers to seize "land of which the savages stood in no particular need, and of which they made no actual and constant use."[65]

Taken together, such assumptions made the extra-European world—including, significantly, much of North America—seem like a zone of endless possibility, what the literary critic Stephen Greenblatt has described as a place of "wonders", where the constraints that governed affairs in Europe simply did not apply.[66] At times, descriptions of this wondrous state could take on a spiritual, almost rhapsodic quality. As the English hymnist John Newton wrote of his years as a slave ship captain, life at sea "necessarily" lacked the benefits of "public ordinances and christian communion," but it also gave the "religious sailor" a rare opportunity "to observe the wonders of God in the great deep, with the two noblest objects of sight, the expanded ocean, and the expanded heaven."[67] On other occasions, the miraculous served more sinister purposes, as in the preamble to a Bermuda statute of 1730, which attributed the lenient treatment of whites who murdered "Negroes Indians Mulattoes and other Slaves" to the way "things are wonderfully altered" in Britain's American colonies.[68] In the years immediately preceding the American Revolution, yet another example of this imperial license was the tendency of Britons everywhere to remember 1759—the highpoint of Britain's victories during the Seven Years War—as a sort of *annus mirabilis*, a year of wonders when the king's forces conquered distant lands on a scale that seemed to belie Britain's commitment to the liberties of Europe.[69] In each instance, the "unsettled" regions of the British Atlantic appeared lawless, autonomous, and remote, even as British settlers continued to affirm their allegiance to metropolitan norms and laws.

As they braced for war with their American "brethren" in 1775, the British thus had two models of the empire with which to contend, one that emphasized the colonies' English character and membership in Europe's republic, the other the remoteness of the zone in which they were situated. In many ways, of course, the two models were compatible, even complementary. Although they lived on intimate terms with Indians and Africans, the reputed lawlessness of such groups freed British settlers to establish social and political systems based entirely on metropolitan forms. "The British dominions consist of Great Britain and Ireland, divers colonies and settlements," wrote the English agronomist Arthur Young in 1772. "The clearest method is to consider all as forming one nation, united under one sovereign, speaking the same language and enjoying the same liberty, but living in different parts of the world."[70] The Earl of Chatham invoked the same unified history in his final, desperate plea for British-American reconciliation in 1777. There was no reason, Chatham insisted, why Britain's colonists in America "should not enjoy every fundamental right in their property, and every original substantial liberty, which Devonshire or Surrey, or the county I live in, or any other county in England, can claim."[71] Although the British Empire contained millions of people who did not fit this anglicised model, the blindness of both English common law and the law of nations to Vattel's people without law made it all too easy for Britons everywhere to accept a vision of the empire as an extended consortium of English fragments.

As the reality of Britain's collapsing authority in North America began to sink in, the British were forced to acknowledge another, more troubling, imperial prospect, one tinged with fears that Britons who spent too much time in places without law might—in the words of John Newton—adopt "the tempers, customs, and ceremonies of the natives, so far as to prefer [their new] country to England."[72] When he wrote these words, Newton was thinking of Africa, but his words were no less applicable to British views of America, especially as those views began to harden during the crisis of 1775. In the allegations that followed the commencement of hostilities, ministerial writers accused patriot militias of engaging in Indian-style atrocities like scalping, firing from hidden emplacements, and mistreating prisoners of war.[73] The colonists' British critics also claimed to see connections between the unchecked liberty that American planters wielded over their African slaves and the equally extravagant rights that they were asserting against Parliament.[74] As William Innes observed in the House of Commons in 1775, people on both sides of the Atlantic maintained that "the colonists are the offspring of Englishmen, and as such, entitled to the privileges of Britons"; however, it was "well-known that they not only consist of English, Scots, and Irish, but also of French, Dutch, Germans innumerable, Indians, Africans, and a multitude of felons from this country."[75] In short, wrote Allan Ramsay, the king's American subjects seemed to be neither foreign nor English, but instead constituted a "new class of men."[76]

Although the British were spared from having to spell out the implications of Ramsay's words for the colonies that became the United States, the anti-settler feelings and sense of difference that underlay them had a number of far-reaching consequences within the remaining portions of the British Empire. The first was to clarify, if not positively to accelerate, the empire's changing legal foundations, from a polity based solely on the exportation of English law and customs by British settlers, to one that included a growing number of what Burke called "external trusts" over peoples who were neither British nor European. By the mid-1780s, the East India Company controlled territories, armed forces, and revenues in Asia that exceeded those of many governments in Europe; one of the defining features of these territories, however, was a conspicuous absence of British settlers and colonies of settlement. With this change came others, especially the determination to reform the administration of external trusts like India, curtailing, wherever possible, the autonomy of local magistrates and officials, and attempting (or so British reformers claimed) to make British rule more benevolent, accountable and—usually—authoritarian.[77] As F. W. Maitland would remark almost exactly a century after the American Revolution, the British ministers charged with governing Britain's global empire were required to "administer Mohammedan law and Hindoo law, French law, Dutch law, English law." "[T]he world has never seen a tribunal," claimed Maitland, "with such worldwide powers."[78]

As jurists like Maitland recognized, the British Empire's post-1783 foundations displayed more continuity in the Atlantic and the Antipodes, with British settlers claiming the same British nationality and common law rights as the North American colonists who rebelled in 1775, yet even in Canada, Australasia, South Africa, and the West Indies, the metropolitan public's sometimes pronounced hostility to settlers and its newfound sense of trusteeship made for some important differences. Although British and colonial racism ensured the continued dominance of natural-born Britons, those charged with governing the colonies of settlement assumed that, on some level, they had an obligation to safeguard the rights of the Crown's other subjects, including indigenous peoples and slaves. As the Treaty of Waitangi (1840) would show, the extra-European right of settlement, which to writers like William Paley had seemed so straightforward, was potentially in conflict under the new regime with the rights of indigenous people like New Zealand's Maori.[79] It was also difficult for British settlers to continue justifying either slavery or the slave trade. As Jamaica's Edward Long admitted in 1774, there was something grotesque in the spectacle of liberty-minded West Indians "clamouring with so much vehemence for what they den[ied] to so many thousand Negroes, whom they hold in bondage." Increasingly, the British public agreed, insisting that people like Long "[g]ive freedom . . . to others," as the absentee planter imagined a critic saying, "before you claim it for yourself."[80]

This, of course, was an empire to which most of Britain's North American subjects no longer wished to belong. Having insisted in 1776 on the "self-evident" truth that "all men are created equal," citizens of the newly independent United States showed little inclination to extend such rights to any but white settlers. According to the Constitution of 1787, Indians were "not taxed" (and therefore not citizens), and the federal census weighted each slave as three fifths of a freeman.[81] Although the individual states were free to abolish slavery, the only ones to do so immediately were in New England, where plantation slavery had never taken root. During the mid-1830s, at roughly the same moment as Parliament was compelling Britain's West Indian planters to emancipate their slaves, the government of the United States was engaged in the brutal process of expelling the so-called five "civilized" Indian nations from millions of acres in Georgia, Alabama, and Mississippi, all so that planters from the depleted farms of the eastern seaboard could convert the nutrient-rich soil to slave-based cotton agriculture.[82] Had Jamaica elected to join the American union in 1776, its history would almost certainly have followed a similar path. "Nineteenth-century Jamaican planters," as Trevor Burnard has written, "could only look at [states like] South Carolina with envy."[83]

If British settlers found things to admire in the United States, however, the Revolution did nothing to alter the maritime supremacy that enabled white Britons, in particular, to enjoy the most elusive right of all, the security under the law of nations that only a power with Britain's resources could provide. Although the Revolutionary War threatened this position, it did not destroy it. In 1783, Britain was still the dominant power in the extra-European Atlantic, with the largest navy, the most extensive trade, and the deepest pockets. The British were also well placed to claim a kind of moral imperium, whether through their leading role in the international movement to abolish slavery, their growing involvement in Protestant missions in Africa, America and Asia, or their gradual (and, at times, partial) embrace of free trade.[84] As Martin Daunton and Rick Halpern have written of the "ambivalent" place of humanitarian causes in the post-1783 empire, Britain's "imperial state" often appeared to be both the source of "the problem and the agent for its resolution."[85] As the next century would show, the "informal" dimensions of this empire extended well beyond the British Empire's formal boundaries, ensuring that even the erstwhile colonies in North America remained, to a surprising degree, within Britain's economic, diplomatic, cultural, and legal orbit.[86] "Great Britain is the nation which can do us the most harm of any one, or all on earth," wrote Thomas Jefferson in 1823, but the aging patriot was sure that any people "with her on [their] side . . . need not fear the whole world."[87] As a one-time subject of the British Crown, and as one of the British Empire's most trenchant critics and effective opponents, the sage of Monticello knew whereof he spoke.

Notes

1 *The Annual Register, or a View of the History, Politics, and Literature, for the Year 1775*, vol. 18 (London, 1776), p. iv.

2 See, for example, discussions of English press reports of American barbarism in anon. to Robert Carter Nicholas, Sept. 22, 1775: NA, CO 5/40/1/22; William Trent to Edward Bancroft, Oct. 15, 1775: CO 5/40/1/52; for the continuing resonance of such allegations, see Lind, J., *An Answer to the Declaration of the American Congress* (London 1776), p. 100.

3 Anon. letter, Sept. 22, 1775: NA, CO 5/40/1/17.

4 See esp. Pocock, "Limits and divisions."

5 Daunton and Halpern (eds), *Empire and Others*; K. Wilson (ed.), *New Imperial History*. On Britain as a composite empire, see esp. Pocock, "Empire, state, and confederation."

6 *Considerations upon the Different Modes of Finding Recruits for the Army* (London 1775), p. 14. See also Gould, *Persistence of Empire*; Conway, *British Isles*; Wilson, *Sense of the People*; Colley, *Britons*.

7 Marshall, "Nation defined by empire," pp. 208–22.

8 The argument here builds on Gould, "Zones of law." See also Pocock, "Limits and divisions."

9 E. de Vattel, *The Law of Nations, or, Principles of the Law of Nature, Applied to the Conduct and Affairs of Nations and Sovereigns. From the French of Monsieur de Vattel* (London, 1797), § 48 (p. 312). For contemporary views of the Europe and the law of nations in Britain and America, see Gould, "Zones of law," pp. 471–510; Onuf and Onuf, *Federal Union*; Armitage, "Declaration of Independence," pp. 39–64.

10 *Thoughts on the Present Alarming Crisis of Affairs: Humbly Submitted to the Serious Consideration of the People of Ireland* (Dublin, 1779), p. 14. See also Gould, "American independence," pp. 112–21.

11 "Of refinement in the arts and sciences," in Hume, *Essays*, p. 274.

12 E. Apthorp, *A Sermon on the General Fast, Friday, December 13, 1776, for the Pardon of Sins, Averting Judgments, Imploring Victory, and Perpetuating Peace to the British Empire* (London, 1776), p. 8. See also Gould, "American independence," pp. 107–41.

13 Memorial to the king (April 7, 1781), in Minchinton (ed.), *Politics and the Port*, p. 151. The subject of the petition was the king's order authorizing the confiscation of all enemy property on the West Indian islands of St Eustatius and St Martin, which Britain had seized from Denmark. By way of contrast, the petitions noted the "justice" that France demonstrated upon capturing Grenada from the British, whereby "the moveable property of every individual without distinction was preserved to him and the severe edicts which the French commander in Chief at first issued were reprobated and annulled by his Court" (p. 150).

14 Blackstone, *Commentaries*, vol. 4, p. 67. Blackstone's somewhat unusual claim that the common law had "no allowance or authority" in Britain's North American colonists would seem to weaken the universality of the law of nations in this particular instance; however, he readily conceded that English subjects who "planted" colonies in "an uninhabited country," which is how most Americans and many English envisioned North America at the time of first contact, did "carry their laws with them" wherever they went. Blackstone's reason for disallowing the common law's authority in North America was that the colonies had been founded by conquest or treaties with natives, meaning that the Indians' "ancient laws" remained in force, unless specifically modified by either the colonists themselves or the Crown. Blackstone did not specify any English colonies that were fully subject to common law (vol. 1, pp. 104–5). In the second edition, Blackstone's revisions suggest a greater awareness of the extent to which colonial law was based on English common law (see "Supplement to the first edition," vol. 4, pp. ii-iii).

15 West, "English common and statute law in settled colonies," June 20, 1720, in Madden with Fieldhouse (eds), *Select Documents*, vol. 2, p. 192.

16 Richard Bland, *An Enquiry into the Rights of the British Colonies* (London, 1769; orig. pub. 1766) in Greene (ed.), *Colonies to Nation*, p. 92.

17 Governor David Parry to Viscount Sydney, December 18, 1787, in Madden with Fieldhouse (eds), *Select Documents*, vol. 3, p. 331.

18 Long, *History of Jamaica*, vol. 1, pp. 9–11.

19 J. Randolph, *Considerations on the Present State of Virginia* (1774) in Scribner (ed.), *Revolutionary Virginia*, vol. 1, p. 210.

20 Clive and Bailyn, "England's cultural provinces," pp. 200–13; Gould, "Virtual nation," pp. 476–89.

21 Simmons and Thomas (eds), *Proceedings*, vol. 2, pp. 169 (Norton), 568 (Mansfield).

22 Wilkes to Junius, 6 Nov. 6, 1771: British Library, Add. MSS 30,881, 27.

23 *Common Sense: In Nine Conferences between a British Merchant and a Candid Merchant of America* (New York, 1970), p. 11.

24 Baugh, "Maritime strength."

25 "Examination of Benjamin Franklin (February 13, 1766)", in Almon (ed.), *Papers Relative to the Dispute*, p. 73.

26 John Dickinson, "Arguments against the independence of the Colonies" (remarks delivered in Congress, July 1, 1776), in Greene (ed.), *Colonies to Nation*, p. 293. See also Gould and Onuf, "Introduction," in id., *Empire and Nation*, pp. 1–15.

27 Thomas Paine, *Common Sense* (1776), in Greene (ed.), *Colonies to Nation*, p. 276.

28 [Samuel Johnson,] *Taxation No Tyranny* (1775), in Greene (ed.), *Political Writings*, p. 416.

29 Dalrymple, Sir J., *The Address of the People of Great-Britain to the Inhabitants of America* (London, 1775), p. 15.

30 *Ibid.*, p. 7.

31 Hung Finlay, surveyor of the posts in North America, to his brother, onboard *King Fisher*, May 29, 1775, in Roberts (ed.), *Calendar of Home Office Papers*, p. 366.

32 "The humble address of the Mayor, Aldermen, and Common Council of the City of Exeter" (September 25, 1775): NA, HO 55/11/7.

33 Aikman, *Jl of a Voyage*, pp. 61–2.

34 Porteus, B., *A Sermon Preached before the Lords Spiritual and Temporal, in the Abbey-Church, Westminster, on Friday, January 30, 1778* (London, 1778), p. 19.

35 E. Burke, *Mr. Burke's Speech, on the 1st December 1783 . . . on Mr. Fox's East India Bill*, (London 1784), p. 16. For the legal rights of British subjects in India—especially the right to a jury trial under English common law—see, for example, *Appendix to the Comment on the Petition of the British Inhabitants of Bengal, Bahar, and Orissa, to Parliament* (London, 1780). See also Marshall, "The whites of British India," pp. 26–44.

36 "The Declaration of Independence" (July 4, 1776), in Greene (ed.), *Colonies to Nation*, p. 300.

37 Vattel, *Law of Nations*, bk. iii, ch. viii, sect. 141 (p. 348).

38 Bowen, *Revenue and Reform*; Marshall, *Making and Unmaking*.

39 *Gazetteer*, February 16, 1788, quoted Marshall, "Britain without America," p. 584.

40 *Considerations on the Administration of Justice in Bengal* ([London], [1780]), p. 2.

41 H. Verelst, *A View of the Rise, Progress, and Present State of the English Government in Bengal* (London, 1772), p. 139. See also Ghosh, "Household crimes," pp. 599–623.

42 Stair, J. Dalrymple Earl of, *The Proper Limits of the Government's Interference with the Affairs of the East-India Company* (London, 1784), p. 15.

43 A. Dalrymple, *Considerations on a Pamphlet, Entitled 'Thoughts on Our Acquisitions in the East-Indies'* (London, 1772), p. 58.

44 Verelst, *A View of the Rise*, p. 141.

45 A. Dalrymple, *A Plan for Extending the Commerce of This Kingdom, and of the East-India-Company* (London, 1769), p. 101; Bolts, W., *Considerations on India Affairs; Particularly Respecting the Present State of Bengal and Its Dependencies*, 3 vols (London, 1772–5), vol. 1, p. viii; Dalrymple, A., *Considerations on a Pamphlet, Entitled 'Thoughts on Our Acquisitions in the East-Indies'* (London, 1772), p. 58.

46 *Considerations on the Administration of Justice in Bengal* ([London], [1780]), p. 3.

47 Burke, *Speech*, pp. 14–15.

48 Anonymous observation, quoted Rankin, *Golden Age*, p. 22.

49 Gilmour, *Riot, Risings, and Revolution*, p. 255.

50 Blackstone, *Commentaries*, vol. 1, pp. 405–9. For the "negotiated" character of Britain's imperial authority generally, see Greene, *Negotiated Authorities*, pp. 1–24.

51 Falconbridge, *Two Voyages*, p. 49.

52 Quoted Steele, *Betrayals*, pp. 117–18.

53 W. Douglass, *A Summary, Historical and Political, of the First Planting, Progressive Improvements, and Present State of the British Settlements in North-America* (London, 1755), vol. 1, pp. 152n, 153.

54 Smollett, *Expedition of Humphry Clinker*, p. 230.

55   Cartwright (ed.), *Life and Correspondence*, vol. 1, pp. 40–1. On hearing about the draconian nature of England's game laws, the woman reportedly burst into laughter and "exclaimed in a tone of the greatest contempt, 'Hanged for killing venison, oh you fool!'" (p. 41).

56   Lambert, ed., *Sessional Papers*, vol. 69, p. 10.

57   Allison, "Introduction: Equiano's worlds" in Equiano, *Interesting Narrative*, pp. 18–21.

58   James Somerset was an African slave who attempted to leave the service of his master, Charles Stewart, after accompanying him from Virginia to London. Although British abolitionists interpreted the decision much more broadly, Mansfield was careful to avoid ruling on the underlying legality of slavery in England, holding only that Stewart could not send Somerset out of England against his will.

59   Blackstone, *Commentaries*, vol. 1, p. 412. For the limited nature of the Somerset decision, as well as the misperception that it abolished slavery, see Paley, "After *Somerset*."

60   Quoted H. Thomas, *Slave Trade*, pp. 468–9.

61   Falconbridge, *Two Voyages*, p. 135.

62   R. A. Williams, *American Indian*, pp. 245–55.

63   W. Paley, *The Principles of Moral and Political Philosophy* (1785), in *The Works of William Paley* (Philadelphia, 1857), p. 45.

64   "Observations on the Present State of Affairs, 1756," in Greene, D. J. (ed.), *Political Writings*, vol. 10, *The Yale Edition of the Works of Samuel Johnson* (New Haven, 1977), p. 188.

65   Vattel, *Law of Nations*, bk. i, ch. xix, sect. 209 (p. 100). Pagden, "Struggle for legitimacy," pp. 34–54.

66   Greenblatt, *Marvelous Possessions*. See also Hall, *Worlds of Wonder*.

67   "Authentic Narrative, &c.," in Cecil (ed.), *Rev. John Newton*, vol. 1, p. 105.

68   Quoted Craton, *Sinews of Empire*, p. 171.

69   The actual use of the phrase with reference to 1759 seems to be the retrospective work of British historians, as in Holland Rose's description of William Pitt's "exultation" over the "triumph[s] of that *annus mirabilis*": Rose, "Frederick the Great," p. 260.

70   A. Young, *Political Essays*, p. 1.

71   Speech of December 20, 1777, in Taylor and Pringle (eds), *Correspondence*, p. 474n.

72   Newton, "Authentic Narrative," in Cecil (ed.), *Rev. John Newton*, vol. 1, p. 93.

73   Gould, "American independence," pp. 107–41.

74   C. L. Brown, *Moral Capital*.

75   Simmons and Thomas (eds), *Proceedings*, vol. 6, p. 203.

76   A. Ramsay, *Letters on the Present Disturbances in Great Britain and Her American Provinces* (London, 1777), p. 20. For changing views of Americans in Britain, see Gould, *Persistence of Empire*, chap. 6; Conway, "fellow-nationals," pp. 65–100.

77   Marshall, "Empire and authority," pp. 105–22.

78   Maitland, *Constitutional History*, p. 340. The history was based on a series of lectures that Maitland delivered at Cambridge in 1887 and 1888; the tribunal to which Maitland referred was the Judicial Committee of the Privy Council.

79   Pocock, "Law, sovereignty, history," pp. 226–55.

80   Long, *History of Jamaica*, vol. 1, p. 5.

81   "The Constitution of the United States" (September 17, 1787), article i, § 2, in Greene (ed.), *Colonies to Nation*, p. 548.

82   Wallace, *Long, Bitter Trail*.

83   Burnard, "Freedom, migration, and the American Revolution," in Gould and Onuf (eds), *Empire and Nation*, p. 300.

84 Brown, *Moral Capital*; Porter, "Church history," pp. 555–84; Gould, "American independence," pp. 134–41.

85 Daunton and Halpern, "Introduction: British identities, indigenous peoples and the empire," in *id. Empire and Others*, p. 13.

86 Gallagher and Robinson, "Imperialism of free trade," pp. 1–15. For the American response to Britain's economic and cultural dominance, see Yakota, "Post-Colonial America"; Schoen, "Fragile fabric of Union."

87 Jefferson to the President of the United States (James Monroe), October 24, 1823, in Peterson (ed.), *Thomas Jefferson*, p. 1482.

Further Reading

With good reason, historians no longer write "grand narratives" of Britain's eighteenth-century empire. For two different perspectives on the current state of the field, see P. J. Marshall (ed.), *The Eighteenth Century*; vol. 2 of *OHBE*; and Kathleen Wilson (ed.), *A New Imperial History*. For the metropolitan dimensions of Britain's eighteenth-century expansion, see Linda Colley, *Britons: Forging the Nation*; David Armitage, *Ideological Origins of the British Empire*; Kathleen Wilson, *The Island Race*. The early modern British Atlantic world is the subject of David Armitage and Michael J. Braddick (eds), *The British Atlantic World*; see also Eliga H. Gould, "Zones of law."

The multinational and multicultural character of Britain's Atlantic empire is discussed in Bernard Bailyn and Philip D. Morgan (eds), *Strangers within the Realm*. For non-European peoples, see Richard White, *The Middle Ground*; Robin Blackburn, *The Making of New World Slavery*; Martin Daunton and Rick Halpern (eds), *Empire and Others*. H. V. Bowen, *Revenue and Reform* traces the origins of the British movement to reform the East India Company. Richard Drayton, *Nature's Government*, explores the role of science in Britain's late-eighteenth-century expansion.

Historians have generally treated Britain's American and East Indian empires as distinct entities with separate histories; for the many connections between the crises that beset the two during the later eighteenth century, see P. J. Marshall, *The Making and Unmaking of Empires*. On politics in Britain and Ireland, see Eliga H. Gould, *The Persistence of Empire*; Stephen Conway, *The British Isles and the War of American Independence*. Christopher Leslie Brown, *Moral Capital*, examines the Revolution's consequences for British anti-slavery. The Revolution's impact on North America's indigenous peoples is discussed in Colin G. Calloway, *The American Revolution in Indian Country*; for the impact on the British Caribbean, see Andrew Jackson O'Shaughnessy, *An Empire Divided*. The imperial response to the French Revolution is the subject of C. A. Bayly, *Imperial Meridian*.

3

Empire and the British State

Andrew Thompson

Introduction

The "state" can be likened to the proverbial elephant in the room of Commonwealth-Imperial historiography: its presence is obvious, and yet curiously little remarked or reflected upon. Part of the aim of this chapter, therefore, is to take a closer and more critical look at how assumptions about the state have implicitly been built into existing theories of empire.

The first section ("The Empire Overseas") examines how two seminal theories of British imperialism—the "imperialism of free trade" and "gentlemanly capitalism"—conceptualize the state. Having considered the strengths and limitations of their approaches, it then moves on to ask how far what we know about the (changing) character of the state can help to explain when, why and how the British peoples expanded overseas. The focus here will be on five key attributes of the emerging "modern" state—fiscal-military; laissez-faire; professionalization; Whig-Imperial; and the legislative union—each of which influenced, constrained and modified the way in which Britain projected its power into the wider world. Some of these attributes were specific to parts of the period covered by this volume; for example, the term "fiscal-military" applies to the later-eighteenth and early-nineteenth centuries, while the Whig-Imperial conception of the state dates from the later nineteenth century—the point at which the neo-Britains, or colonies of settlement, assumed a significantly larger place in political discourse and the public imagination. Other attributes spanned much or all of the period under consideration, most notably, the growth of a professional ethic (which can be traced back to the early nineteenth century, even if professionalization gathered pace thereafter) and the legislative union (cemented by Ireland's incorporation into a new state, the United Kingdom, in 1800).

The second section of the chapter ("The Empire at Home") explores the interplay between "grand" narratives of British state formation and the "new" imperial history's concern with the manifestations of empire in metropolitan life. Specifically, we will consider how particular constructions of the twentieth-century British state, revolving around the notions of "difference," "decline" and "disintegration," have drawn upon readings of the imperial past to substantiate themselves. We will also examine the so-called "cost benefit" debate about empire, and the issue of how far the state was "used" by private citizens for their own "imperial" ends. Here reference will be made to the idea of "imperial circuits"—the dense webs and networks that connected Britain to its empire and gave settlers, lobbies, and other expatriate groups the opportunity to shape metropolitan views of the colonial "mission."

The final section ("The Empire Today") turns to the issue of citizenship after World War II. As the sun was setting on the empire, people from the West Indies and Indian subcontinent began migrating to the United Kingdom in increasing numbers and came to form a notable proportion of its citizenry. This migration prompted a major rethinking of concepts of British nationality in both official and wider public spheres. Its consequences remain with us today as the adequacy of the "multicultural" concept of the British state, hitherto so deeply entrenched in thinking about race relations, is increasingly called into question.

Throughout the chapter the "state" will be conceived as a set of institutions— encompassing the monarchy, executive, legislature, bureaucracy, and armed forces—which collectively make and enforce public policy, and structure relations between government and society.[1] This definition is, of course, a minimum working description. The forms and functions of these institutions were not fixed, and so the relationship between the empire and the state needs to be viewed from several historical vantage points. Moreover, the state can be understood as an ideological project as well as a set of institutions. For this reason it will also be important to take account of what political scientists term "instrumentalist" and "structuralist" views of the state, namely of whether the bureaucratic and military apparatus of colonial rule tended to serve particular interests in society, or whether the state functioned more independently in the making of imperial policy according to the preconceptions and precepts of ministers and officials. Beyond that, we will need to reflect on the adequacy of territorial and nation-state centric concepts of the state (policed by passport controls, immigration laws, and other means) when studying the transnational relations between British society at home and overseas British societies of the empire.

If the agency of the state, and concepts of state formation, have tended to suffer from neglect in Commonwealth-Imperial historiography,[2] this chapter seeks to provide a corrective by showing how, across the period from the later eighteenth to the later twentieth centuries, the British state has been inseparable from the idea of empire.[3]

The Empire Overseas

The idea of the state as an autonomous or semi-autonomous entity, capable of formulating and acting in pursuit of its own economic or geopolitical goals, is central to what has arguably been the most influential thesis in Commonwealth-Imperial historiography, namely the "imperialism of free trade."[4] The authors of this thesis, Ronald Robinson and Jack Gallagher, portrayed the nineteenth century as a period of relentless expansion, taking many different forms, whereby Victorian governments worked to establish British "paramountcy" by whatever means seemed locally most appropriate. The preferred mode of expansion was *informal*, resulting from economic and cultural forces; the actual annexation of overseas territory (*formal empire*) was always a last resort—a departure from the normal pattern of securing British interests in the wider world, undertaken not in response to organized opinion or electoral pressures, but in response to the perceptions of a policy-making elite (an *official* or *collective* mind). Imperialism's "official mind" was guided by its own traditions, memories and values, and set apart from the rest of society by birth, education and lifestyle. It developed a strong concept of the "national interest" centered on the maintenance of British supremacy in India, the unique political, economic, and strategic value of which meant that Victorian statesmen were prepared not only to intervene much more directly in its affairs than in those of other colonies, but to contemplate the acquisition of territory in other parts of the world to ensure its future safety and stability.

It should be acknowledged that Robinson and Gallagher never used the phrase "state autonomy."[5] Nor, in trying to uncover the motives that lay behind British territorial expansion, did they deny a place to public opinion: the thirst for "peace, economy and prestige," anti-slavery sensibilities and the tenets of trusteeship had all from time-to-time to be respected.[6] They did insist, however, that organized opinion, in whatever shape or form, rarely determined imperial policy. Rather, it was the perceptions of officials in the key departments of state—the India, Colonial and Foreign Offices—that were judged to be of overriding importance.

While it would be difficult to overestimate the impact of Robinson's and Gallagher's ideas in the development of Commonwealth-Imperial historiography, few scholars have been willing to ascribe the same degree of cohesion and consistency to the bureaucratic arm of the state.[7] In fact, a wide range of writing casts doubt on the idea that the British state was largely impervious to external pressures. Business history draws attention to the influence of commercial and financial lobbies (including the chartered companies); religious history to the influence of humanitarian and missionary movements; and political history to the influence of party machinery and electoral pressures. In each of these spheres, the state is considered by some to have been much more mindful of organized opinion than the notion of an "official mind" of imperialism allows.

The theory of "gentlemanly capitalism," as expounded by Peter Cain and Anthony Hopkins, presents a different view of the state as emanating from forces within society and the economy. According to this theory, the state's apparatus served to further the interests of financial capital,[8] and "gentlemanly capitalists" were less a lobby or pressure group, having to bang loudly on the doors of government to make themselves heard, than a part of its very fabric pursuing their goals from inside rather than outside Westminster and Whitehall. By taking such a starkly "instrumentalist" view of the British state, Cain and Hopkins likewise laid themselves open to criticism, in their case for exaggerating the unity of the financial-service sector, for failing to evidence its specific links to government, and for positing nonexisting barriers between industrial, commercial, and financial capital.[9]

Part of the challenge for any theory of imperialism, therefore, is to do justice to the intense pluralism and regional diversity of British society as it developed during the "long" nineteenth century, and the often "fuzzy" boundaries that existed between that society and the state. As we will see below, the empire appealed to a variety of people in British society, furthered a range of socioeconomic interests, and propagated many different values and beliefs. Trying to set the state apart from society ("the imperialism of free trade"), or to equate it to one particular segment of it ("gentlemanly capitalism"), is asking for trouble conceptually.

If the big theories of Commonwealth-Imperial historiography have struggled to conceptualize the role of the state satisfactorily, an alternate approach may be to begin more modestly with one of the key insights to recently emerge from the "new imperial history," namely that the history of the British empire began at home. What was it about the character of the "domestic" state that propelled, even compelled, it to project its power abroad? Rather than attempt a systematic survey of the modern state, as it emerged after c.1780, the rest of this section highlights five key attributes of British state building. Each of these attributes helped to generate the necessary momentum for British expansion overseas; each of them, in turn, were sustained and even strengthened by Britain's ongoing imperial commitment.

Fiscal-Military State

The British state emerged from the Revolutionary (1793–1802) and Napoleonic (1803–15) Wars having made substantial territorial gains and with considerably expanded aims and powers. In 1792, Britain possessed twenty-six colonies; by 1816 she could boast forty-three. Moreover, this period saw the British state establish itself as one of the largest and most efficient in Europe. Two formidable capacities were developed during its protracted struggle with France: the capacity to wage war on an unprecedented scale, and the capacity to levy taxes and to borrow money cheaply when required.[10]

Some scholars talk of the growth of a "Second" British empire at this time, the hallmark of which was a more authoritarian form of nationalism.[11] This new nationalistic spirit is partly attributed to the resurgence of the patriotic role and reputation of the Crown (witness, for example, the development of royal ritual and pageantry at home and among the expatriate British in the colonies),[12] and partly to the spread of racist hierarchies and stereotypes—based on the "governing race" principle and Britons' fitness to rule—through state-sponsored institutions such as the Anglican Church, military colleges and, of course, the East India Company.[13] Meanwhile, the role of the economic instruments of state power during the later Hanoverian era was the cause of considerable debate. Ultra-Tory ideologues developed an alternative imperial political economy that looked to the navigation laws and preferential tariffs to consolidate the political cohesion of Britain's new far-flung empire, to develop secure and permanent overseas markets for British trade, and to rectify the oversupply of domestic labour and capital via colonial (rather than foreign) emigration.[14] But others resisted such prescriptions, tending to see economic gains as the welcome "by-products of military advance" rather than the rationale for territorial expansion.[15] In this context, it is, of course, worth remembering that the areas of most intense commercial interest during the early 1800s—North and South America—were not ones over which there was any sustained attempt to exert formal control.[16]

Nowhere was the "fiscal military" state of the late eighteenth century more manifest than in India, where more money had to be raised and new territory taken to pay for the Company's burgeoning army and administration,[17] and over which a series of military victories were enthusiastically celebrated by the public at home.[18] Above all, it was under Lord Cornwallis (Governor-General from 1786–93) that new regulatory and coercive powers were developed. Cornwallis initiated an ambitious program of reforms aimed at making the Company's administration more efficient and less corrupt.[19] In addition to a "permanent settlement" of the taxation of land revenues that fixed landowners' obligations in perpetuity (1793), he instituted a new system of civil law courts, promulgated a new set of criminal regulations, brought the Indian police more closely under British supervision, and tried, but failed, to overhaul the entire military forces of India by amalgamating them under Crown control.[20] Equally important, Cornwallis and the Earl of Wellesley (Governor-General, 1798–1805) presided over a massive increase in the strength of the Company's armed forces from 90,000 in 1790 to nearly 200,000 in 1815—forces used not only for defense but for revenue collection and police duties too.[21]

Yet the ideological foundations of this "Second" British empire were soon to give way to a "Third." In India itself the Company's commercial privileges had been considerably circumscribed by 1802. Subsequently, in 1813, a long-running debate over the legal possession of its territories came to an end with the Charter Act that formally vested them in the Crown. Effectively what was once a "free-standing and independent trading company" was being refashioned as an "agency of imperial government," a process that continued with the loss of the China monopoly in 1833, and culminated in the full transfer of power to the Crown in 1857–8.[22] More generally, the French wars had led to an enormous increase in the national debt—from £133m in 1763, to £245m in 1783 and £700m in 1815—and, consequently, in excise and customs duties, the burden of which fell on consumers. These duties severely tested the patience of public opinion. Increasingly, people resented having to pay for such an elaborate and expensive machinery of state at home and abroad, regarding it not only as militaristic and monopolistic but as wasteful and inefficient to boot.

Laissez-Faire State

The transformation of the fiscal-military state of the French Wars into the laissez-faire state of the mid-Victorian era is too complex, indeed too contentious, a process to chart satisfactorily here, though it is worth noting that the transition was facilitated by passing some of the costs of government on to the colonies.[23] Suffice to say that by the 1820s and 1830s a preference for minimal government, retrenchment, and lower taxation were firmly on the political agenda in Britain; by the 1840s they had found legislative expression in the repeal of the Corn Laws (1846) and Navigation Acts (1849). And yet, notwithstanding the rapid advance of free trade and liberal ideas after 1815, Britain's appetite for territory did not diminish. In the next thirty years she gobbled up the Gambia (1816), Singapore (1819), the Gold Coast (1821), Malacca and part of western Burma (1824), Western Australia (1829), the Falklands (1833), South Australia (1836), Aden (1839), New Zealand (1840), Hong Kong (1842), Natal and Sind (1843), and North Borneo (1846). How is this continued impulse to imperial expansion to be explained? Historians tend to regard economic policy as the cornerstone of the "Third" British empire of the Victoria era. Whether in the guise of a drive for overseas markets by the first industrialized nation, or the search for further investment opportunities by portfolio capitalism, they present free trade as the defining feature of British expansion (see, especially, Robinson and Gallagher previously). Britain was the strongest industrial player, and, under the discipline of the unregulated market, became the "workshop of the world." At the same time, the City of London established itself as the center of international trade in foodstuffs and raw materials. Free trade was, in short, a form of imperialism that did not, perhaps dare not, speak its name.

For some contemporaries there was, of course, a more optimistic vision of free trade. It was based on the hope that the mutual exchange of commodities would bring about international peace and goodwill. A considerable body of mid-Victorian opinion—radicals, peace activists and positivists—espoused this vision and was consequently suspicious of formal empire, if not actively hostile toward it. For example, when Peel abandoned the Canadian corn and timber preferences in 1846, Cobden was not slow to rub the salt of unilateral free trade into the protectionist wounds of imperially-minded Tory backbenchers. As he declared to a Belgian official:

> I am not aware of any differential duty in favour of the Mother Country being kept in any of our Colonies whether in favour of shipping or manufactures. In fact our Colonies have ceased to be Colonies in the old sense of the word, because we have ceased to have exclusive dealings with them. They are your Colonies as much as ours.[24]

But had Peel really jettisoned the fiscal tools of imperial statecraft in favour of cosmopolitan political economy?[25] It seems unlikely. The consistency of Peel's imperial vision, based on a passionate belief in the moral as well as commercial advantages of empire, has been forcefully asserted.[26] Thus while the dismantling of the formal economic bonds of empire may have dealt a blow to the old colonial interests cushioned by the state,[27] it did little to stem the pressures for overseas expansion. Rather, in a world increasingly influenced by a rapidly-industrializing Britain, the consequence of free trade was to create a series of satellite economies overseas. Equality of access to markets sounded fine in theory; in practice, however, Britain was the country in by far the best position to take advantage of it.[28]

It is also worth noting that most Radicals were pragmatic. Even the famous "Manchester School" of northern free traders, led by Cobden and Bright, was happy for government to initiate and finance economic reform in India—railway building, the construction of roads and irrigation systems, increasing the supply of raw cotton—when it perceived Indian conditions to be hampering the free operation of commerce.[29] Several Radicals went a step further, supporting the deployment of armed forces to extend Britain's markets during the Opium Wars (1839–42, 1856–60). In the words of one scholar: "the Radical cry of anti-colonialism was designed to bring down that vast network of patronage and privilege which was the 'old colonial system,' and to replace it by a middle-class empire."[30]

But if free trade ultimately had more to do with "bellicose Britannia" than "pax Britannica," the formal acquisition of territory was not seen as a necessary or desirable part of this process. What *was* vital to the growth and security of the Victorian empire was supremacy at sea. The Royal Navy—the key institution of state when it came to collective imperial security—helped to protect the far-flung parts of the empire, to keep the shipping lanes open during wartime, to clamp down on privateering during peacetime, and to suppress the slave trade.[31] To be sure, not all of Britain's most significant international trade routes were imperial—Britain could not live without trade with Europe or the Americas. Nonetheless, the importance of the maritime concept of empire defense was as apparent to Victorian and Edwardian politicians as it has been to historians since. In particular, a "Blue Water" theory of naval power, widely propagated during the later-nineteenth and early-twentieth centuries, spoke of the empire as the "possession of the sea" and the "gift of sea power," and justified increasing levels of naval expenditure to a widening electorate in terms of the fleet's vital role in maintaining Britain's imperial communications and commitments.[32]

By the end of the nineteenth century, rapidly rising naval expenditure, fuelled by the pace of technological change, was putting the Gladstonian fiscal constitution of minimal government and low taxation under almost intolerable strain.[33] The quid pro quo for the grant of responsible self-government to the colonies of settlement during the 1840s and 1850s was that they should shoulder more of their own military and administrative costs, and thereby further the cause of retrenchment at home. There were, however, understandable limits to the colonies' willingness to foot part of the bill for the Royal Navy when they, as junior partners in the empire, rightly calculated that its ships were not equally available to them. Alongside the mounting costs of urban government, therefore, Britain's naval building programme exposed the inadequacy of the existing narrow base of taxation.[34] Then came the South African War (1899–1902), the bill for which put huge pressure on the national finances and forced a reassessment of the entire structure of government revenue.

One solution to this developing financial crisis was to raise more money through customs duties. This was the preferred method of the constructive imperialists, who, more than any other group of British politicians at this time, were intent on expanding the fiscal forms of state power. They looked specifically to preferential tariffs to consolidate Britain's colonial relationships and to forge stable and permanent markets for metropolitan and dominion producers. Under free trade, they argued, the United Kingdom had been turned into a cosmopolitan clearing-house for money and goods, while the resources of the empire had been shamefully neglected. What was required was creative and dynamic government and the active implementation of policies aimed at enhancing imperial unity. Constructive imperialists were especially critical of the free traders' search for immediate profits. They insisted that the state had a duty to act on behalf of wider communal rather than narrowly individual interests.[35] Government was to be guided not by a philosophy of *laissez-faire* but by *vouloir-faire* (the will to act) and *savoir-faire* (the knowledge to act).[36] Contemporary international developments were an influence on their thinking: state building in Europe and the expansion of frontiers in Russia and the USA seemed to show the necessity of organizing on a larger scale. Social Darwinist theory and evolutionary thought were important too, at least insofar as they suggested that smaller states were insignificant, unsafe, and essentially obsolete, or at least destined to become so.

It took three decades for constructive imperialist ideas to be translated into public policy. The Edwardian tariff reform movement was bedevilled by the spectre of "food taxes" during the elections of 1906 and 1910, which, to the chagrin of Stanley Baldwin (Conservative Prime Minister, 1923–4), reared their ugly head again in 1923. So it was not until the world economic depression of the early 1930s, when prices and production collapsed and unemployment soared, that a system of imperial preferential tariffs was finally introduced. Admittedly, the bilateral agreements introduced in Ottawa in July-August 1932 only partially fulfilled their proponents' aim of shifting trade from non-empire to empire channels.[37] Yet the Ottawa negotiations, and the London Economic Conference of 1933, during which Britain resolutely resisted American proposals for the extension of preferences to countries with whom she had "most-favoured-nation" arrangements, clearly spelt the "end of the road for British economic internationalism."[38]

Professionalization

The nineteenth century witnessed the rapid professionalization of both state and society in Britain.[39] Industrialization and urbanization loosened the bonds between the professions and the landed aristocracy, replacing the patron-profession relationship with the client-profession relationship. As a result, service no longer entailed dependency and professional ideals were able to diverge from the ideals of those to whom services were rendered. The proportion of professional men with landed origins declined, while that of recruits with professional fathers increased. Specialized training was also given greater emphasis. By the end of the nineteenth century, therefore, the professions had grown considerably in importance. Not only did professionals become more numerous, more prosperous, and more varied, they successfully strove for improved self-organization and were able to entrench their ethos of self-sacrificing service to the community ever more deeply in the public sphere. The empire contributed to each of these achievements, and, in so doing, to the emergence of a state in which aristocratic principles of governance increasingly gave way to professional ones.[40]

The contest between the aristocracy and the professions, as it manifested itself in the imperial sphere, was about where social authority ultimately lay. British rule could legitimate itself either by conservative appeals to "traditional" authority, or by placing emphasis on good governance and administration delivered by an impartial and trained civil service. The aristocratic view of governance was based on hereditary authority—some men were born to rule. The professional view saw authority as being acquired—some or all men could be trained to rule. An early shot across the bows from the professional middle classes came with the introduction of competitive entry into the Indian Civil Service (ICS) in 1853, a full year before the publication of the Northcote-Trevelyan report on the organization of the home civil service. Previously, the East India Company's directors had nominated young men to "writerships" and prepared them for their Indian careers at a special college—Haileybury. Now all appointments were to be made by examination alone.[41] As success in this examination guaranteed a career for life, the ICS began to enter increasingly into the calculations of professional men seeking employment for their sons.[42] The separation from home and family, and the difficult working conditions associated with service in India, meant that these opportunities particularly appealed to able young men of more modest middle class backgrounds, prepared to accept such disadvantages in return for the considerable financial rewards.

What was true of the ICS was also true of the officer corps of the Indian army, access to which was noticeably more meritocratic than the British army.[43] Although the purchase of commissions in Britain was abolished in 1871, soldiering remained an expensive occupation: in 1869 the pay of officers remained almost exactly what it had been during the reign of William II. The "best" regiments, in particular, tended to be guarded by considerations of wealth, social standing, and family connections. India was the exception. Under the East India Company, military appointments were disposed of gratis, and poverty was, if anything, a recommendation to the directors' benevolence. After the transfer of authority to the Crown, Indian army pay continued to be higher than that of the British army; and the cost of living was, of course, much lower in India. Hence it was possible for a relatively "poor" but able man to live on his salary, and officer recruits to the Indian army were generally from more modest backgrounds. There were just over 2,000 officers in the Indian army by the turn of the century. The biggest single source was sons of existing Indian army officers, and certain specialized units almost constituted themselves as a caste on this basis. The Indian army also thought of itself as attracting (and retaining) more able men than the home army. It was not until the 1880s that the rapid growth of the professions in Britain began to be properly reflected in the home army. By the 1920s, the distinction between the two forces had begun to diminish as British army pay became more competitive and officers received a living wage.

In Africa, too, the bulk of colonial administrators were drawn from a professional rather than landed elite. Admittedly, these men were not many in number—their salaries were paid out of the budgets of the colonies themselves, which severely restricted recruitment. But they did develop a distinctive ethos of public service based around the multifaceted concept of "character."[44] Repudiating the politics of aristocratic patronage, and suspicious of leisured independence and independent wealth, the professional elite that espoused the virtues of honesty, self-help, manliness, and devotion to duty saw the empire as their testing ground. These virtues were particularly prized in the colonies because they were felt to build up trust in government among subject populations by lifting British rule above the material imperatives of commerce and trade, and by injecting into it the moral imperatives of the "civilizing mission." The concept of character also spoke to another defining characteristic of Britain's late nineteenth-century imperial experience, namely the uncertainty and isolation that confronted the officer on the remote hill station or the soldier on the battlefield; in such situations the measure of a man was felt to be his ability not to "crack under pressure" or "let the side down."

The colonial state was not, however, the preserve of the upper-middle class administrators who ran the empire, or the soldiers who fought for it. The colonies provided a wealth of new career opportunities for professional people— opportunities so many and varied that it is impossible to do justice to them here. By way of illustration, one might briefly point to the generation of irrigation engineers who worked on government projects in India and Egypt—projects that developed new technological knowledge in hydraulic engineering; to the geographers who secured state funding for their overseas expeditions by helping colonial officials to demarcate spheres of territorial influence and to exploit colonial natural resources; to the doctors employed by the Indian and Colonial Offices who formed overseas branches of the British Medical Association to lobby for better representation in the higher echelons of the colonial bureaucracy; to the entomologists who searched for solutions to tropical diseases in the colonies; and to the nurses who, on the back of patriotic service in colonial wars, sought to raise funds, improve training, and secure state recognition and registration.[45] This burgeoning bureaucratic and professional middle class saw the British imperial world as their oyster; and their increasingly prominent and powerful position in the state is to be explained as much by their achievements abroad as at home.

Whig-Imperial State

The British state in the period from the 1880s to the 1950s, it has been suggested, was the child as well as the parent of the empire: "the grandeurs and servitudes of empire were of its very essence; and the same grandeurs and servitudes inevitably shaped the identity it claimed to embody."[46] This "Whig Imperialist" conception of the state stemmed from Britain's decision to seek an oceanic and imperial destiny, rather than a merely continental European one, and from the belief that the British were a uniquely global and freedom-loving people. According to the academic and ex-Labour party MP, David Marquand, it shaped the mentality of the entire political class, left as well as right, for the greater part of the twentieth century. Implicit in Marquand's reasoning is the idea that the state was imagined not just as a piece of territory, or a framework of administration, but as a genuine community of people, tied together by common sentiments and traditions, a shared sense of purpose, and a collective memory. This was very much the approach to the state taken by Sir John Seeley, whose highly influential *The Expansion of England* (1883), put the growth of an imperial state at the center of British history and identity: "men should conceive themselves as belonging, and belonging in such an intimate and momentous union, to a corporation which is not simply the family."[47] Seeley's "corporation" comprised not only the British Isles but a wider Britannic "federation":

> Our Empire is not an Empire at all in the ordinary sense of the word. It does not consist of a congeries of nations held together by force, but in the main one nation, as much as if it were no Empire but an ordinary state.[48]

The Whig-Imperial conception of the state was inspired by the vision of a "racial community of Britons"; its dynamic, therefore, was that of demographic expansion.[49] Here it should be remembered that at least 52 million people left Europe for overseas destinations between 1815 and 1930, a figure equivalent to approximately a quarter of Europe's natural population increase. The United Kingdom led the way, supplying a staggering 10 million migrants, or 23 percent of the total. Of course, not all these people went to the empire: the United States was the largest single recipient of migrants. That said, of the ten million migrants mentioned above, 2.3 million went to Canada, 1.7 million to Australia and New Zealand, and 671,500 to South Africa. Emigration, therefore, played an enormous social and imaginative role in the life of the British people. On arrival in the colonies, these migrants did not suddenly separate themselves from friends and family back home. On the contrary, through correspondence, return journeys and remittances, British migrants forged tightly personalized networks, stretching from their place of settlement all the way back to their place of origin.

For some leading British politicians the reality of emigration was very much a personal one. For example, the Tory leader and Prime Minister (1922–3), Andrew Bonar Law, widely regarded as an intensely practical businessman, was actually far from immune to the appeal of imperial sentiment. Having returned to Scotland from New Brunswick at the age of twelve (his father was a Presbyterian minister of the Free Church of Scotland in the parishes of Kingston and Richibucto), he left school at the age of sixteen and subsequently made his money in the Glasgow iron trade. Yet, according to his latest biographer, R. J. Q. Adams, Canada "was always close to Bonar Law's heart"; "he wished with all sincerity that [it] should remain joined by spiritual as well as economic and imperial links to Britain."[50] Similarly, when Harold Wilson, the future Labour Prime Minister (1964–70, 1974–6), went to see his family in Western Australia in 1926, the journey made a lasting impression. He was only ten years old, but returned to school in Milnsbridge, near Huddersfield, to regale teachers and classmates with stories of his Australian adventures. In the view of Ben Pimlott, "it is possible to believe Wilson's later claim that his sympathy for the Commonwealth idea began with his early experience in Australia."[51]

In view of this dense web of kith and kin ties that joined British society at home to the overseas British societies of the empire, it should not surprise us that new ideas about the state were occasionally beamed back from the colonies of settlement to the "mother country." This was especially true of Australia and New Zealand. Reformers in Britain kept a watchful eye on innovations in the spheres of social welfare and the constitution in both colonies. Liberalism flourished in New Zealand from 1891 to 1912 as the machinery of government was expanded to tackle the socioeconomic problems of the day. The colony prided itself on the progress it had made, and legislation on old age pensions and compulsory arbitration was particularly significant in terms of its influence upon labour movements and welfare policy in Britain. Labour legislation was also an aspect of Australian public policy in which there was an ongoing interest. For example, in the case of the British Trade Boards Act (1909)—which established boards of employers, employees, and government nominees in order to fix wages in certain "sweated" industries—there was a very clear Australian legislative precedent.

Advocates of state action in Britain borrowed the idea of wages boards from the colony of Victoria, and pored over the Victorian evidence in an effort to master their subject. According to one scholar, the Trade Boards Act "represented the most explicit attempt to imitate a colonial example."[52]

What the notion of the "Whig-Imperial" state seeks to capture, then, is the sentimental as well as strategic appeal of the imperial system in which British politicians, well into the twentieth century, found their identity.[53] At the same time, the ideologues of this global imperial identity were constantly confronted with the awkward reality that "territory," especially the contiguity of territory, was a defining characteristic of the modern state.[54] This may help to explain why there was always a tension in political constructions of the British people.[55] On the one hand they were a "worldwide people" who, although separated by vast oceanic distances from the "expatriate" British populations of Australia, New Zealand, Canada, and South Africa, were intimately connected to these colonies by family relationships and historic ties. On the other hand, they were apt to retreat into their island fortress, to eschew the potentially corrupting influences of the outside world, and to construct their political sovereignty along national-territorial lines. The influential historian and New Zealander, J. G. A. Pocock, perceived this tension only too clearly. In his view, one of the major (and most regrettable) effects of Britain's entry into the European Community in 1972 was to tip the scales decisively away from the Whig-Imperial toward a more insular view of the British state. Pocock's response was to call for a pluralized British history—a history that properly situated the United Kingdom "British" in the context of their settler empire.[56]

Multiple Kingdoms

Across the period covered by this chapter, Britain was a legislative union of the English, Scots, Welsh, and (later) Irish, joined together by the central institutions of Crown and Parliament, but among whom there were marked legal, educational, and economic differences.[57] Yet participation in the empire is also said to have helped them to look beyond their subnational identities and transcend their internal divisions.[58] By acquiring colonies in Africa and Asia, it is argued, the English, Welsh, Scots, and, somewhat more ambiguously, the Irish, came into protracted contact with an array of colonial "others" against which the British national character could be more sharply defined. Unity in a common imperial cause did not, however, mean uniformity. While a range of domestic forces—railways, education, migration, and sport—were working to "blend" different cultures within the United Kingdom,[59] regional distinctiveness was as likely to be underlined as undermined by the empire. In this vein, John MacKenzie points to the empire's tendency to perpetuate and enhance regional identities in Scotland.[60] He shows how the process of fashioning a British imperial identity was more about building on regional forms of association than liquidating them. In MacKenzie's view, therefore, "imperial Britishness" was not something superimposed over an array of disparate cultures and identities that made up the United Kingdom. Rather, to varying degrees, the Scottish, the Welsh, and the Irish (and, for that matter, some of the English regions) were to find in the empire a form of self-affirmation that helped them better contend with the political and cultural challenges they faced.

Of all the peoples of the United Kingdom, it is the Scots' contribution to the empire that stands out as disproportionate. They were the first peoples of the British Isles to take on an imperial mentality, and possibly the longest to sustain one. In the spheres of education, engineering, exploration, medicine, commerce, and shipping, the Scots earned a particularly strong reputation for empire building.[61] In fact, as a leading historian of Scotland has recently written, "virtually every sphere of Scottish life . . . was fashioned in a large part by engagement with the empire."[62] By contrast, the Welsh were more reticent: part of the purpose of the 1911 investiture of the Prince of Wales was to encourage them to take their full place in the British imperial enterprise. They were nonetheless deeply involved in establishing the gold-fields of Australia, where the eisteddfod became a well-known institution. There is also a sense in which the very character of the industrial economy of South Wales and its working population (dependent as they were on the global export trade) can be considered to have been "imperial."[63]

Ireland's imperial involvement is more complex; it can be seen both as a colonizing power and a country that was colonized. The Irish middle class—educated Catholic as well as Protestant—was well represented in the Indian civil and medical services. And the Irish working class were prolific migrants.[64] Nevertheless, the empire served a dual function for the Irish. This was the result of Ireland being an internally fractured society, and the subject of systematic English and Scottish colonization. Thus while many Irish nationalists were quick to identify themselves rhetorically with anti-imperialist movements, and to understand their sufferings in terms of an oppressive colonial state, Ulster "loyalists" saw themselves as a settler people, and, like other embattled groups in Natal and Rhodesia, constantly sought reassurance that their loyalty to Britain and the empire would not go unrecognized.[65] They also took considerable pride in Britain's achievements overseas.[66] As early as the 1880s, during the Home Rule debates, Ulster began to take on an imperial consciousness, but the South African War was something of a defining moment in Irish attitudes to the empire. For Irish Catholics it provided a classic example of colonial oppression— some actually fought alongside the Boers in the Transvaal.[67] For Unionists, the struggle in South Africa was a source of inspiration and unity: volunteer companies, memorials, press reporting, and commercial advertising all helped to "propagate a mass audience for the imperial message" among Irish Protestants.[68]

The Empire at Home

Three grand narratives of British state formation—namely, those of "difference," "decline," and "disintegration"—have looked to the imperial past to substantiate themselves. In the case of "difference," scholars who postulate a British *Sonderweg*—a separate path of development, making Britain "different" from other European powers—point to Britain's uniquely prominent imperial position to corroborate their claim. Others who see national "decline" as the main theme of post-war history either lament the loss of a worldwide empire and its effects on Britain's international standing, or, alternatively, turn to that empire for an explanation of Britain's economic backwardness and for inflated ideas of Britain's international role. And "disintegrationists," who present the (potential) break-up of the Union as a concomitant of decolonization, argue that without colonies the United Kingdom has been deprived of its *raison d'être*. What seems to be the case, therefore, is that the character of the post-war British state has been viewed through the prism of its prior imperial involvement.

Yet a major flaw of each of these narratives of state formation is their apparent assumption that the state was uniformly affected by Britain's expanding presence overseas. It is not at all clear that the key institutions of state responded to the empire in the same way, or to the same degree. While an imperial dimension was readily grafted on to the roles of the monarchy and the armed forces, other parts of the state's fabric—namely, the bureaucracy and parliament—proved much more resistant to change. Indeed, the gathering pace of territorial expansion had a surprisingly modest impact on the machinery of government at home.[69] There were several reasons why this was so. For most of the nineteenth century communication with the colonies was difficult and slow. Much of the business of governing the empire had therefore to be devolved to the "men-on-the-spot"—diplomats, proconsuls, army officers, and the like. Added to this, and in an effort to cut the cost of administration, the nineteenth century saw a big shift toward the devolution of power in the colonies of white settlement. Many decisions that had previously been taken in Whitehall were now to be taken locally by a new generation of colonial politicians. And, until the end of the century, there was little need for government to think about intervening in colonial economies: as the first power to industrialize, Britain's lead over its rivals was sufficient for trade to be left to look after itself.

Hence the Colonial Office during the nineteenth century was among the smallest departments of state; in the eyes of many contemporaries it was no more than a "political backwater." As the volume of its business grew, there was no corresponding increase in the size of its staff. No surprise, then, that when the ambitious and energetic Joseph Chamberlain became Colonial Secretary (1895–1903) he immediately set out to transform the administrative capabilities of his department. Yet Chamberlain was thwarted by an obstructive and parsimonious Treasury, and by a lack of support from cabinet colleagues.[70] He found that the Colonial Office's machinery was simply not up to the task of revitalizing the West Indian sugar economies or fostering interimperial trade.[71] Admittedly, after 1918 the functions of the department did expand, partly in the hope that colonial development would aid post-war British economic recovery. But the division of responsibilities into geographical departments continued to inhibit the promotion of initiatives across territories, while the introduction of new technical and scientific expertise tended to take the form of professional advisory committees rather than appointments of staff within the department itself.[72] Even after the passage of the Colonial Development Act (1929), the funds provided by the Treasury for such activity were very limited, and the Colonial Office's approach piecemeal. By the late 1930s, the department remained under-funded and wanting in vision, amateur in the way it selected development projects and incapable of initiating new ones of its own.[73]

   Much the same might be said of Parliament. Although there were powerful East and West Indian lobbies in the House of Commons during the later eighteenth and early nineteenth centuries, they did not find their equivalent during the Victorian era—the post-1832 reformed House of Commons was much less accessible to Indian nabobs or West Indian planters.[74] Indeed, there was a persistent underlying resistance to fundamental change on the part of Parliament, especially where this involved any suggestion of "federation" or power sharing with the colonies.[75] Why was this so? It has been shrewdly observed that the flexibility of the British Parliament was already stretched to the limits by the role it had to play in accommodating religious, legal, and educational differences *within* the United Kingdom.[76] No surprise, then, that there were limits to how far politicians in Britain were willing to draw on *colonial* knowledge and experience. To be sure, one can point to the way mid-Victorian parliamentarians formulated their views on citizenship in the light of what they already knew about the operation of colonial constitutions,[77] and the way later-Victorian feminists staked their claims to political rights and the franchise within Britain on the role they could play as imperial women.[78] But of equal, if not greater, significance here is the way constitutional schemes of the federal variety, implemented extensively and successfully across the empire, were invariably rejected as an option for the United Kingdom.[79] The first Home Rule bill is a case in point. When drafting this measure, the Liberal Prime Minister, W. E. Gladstone (1868–74, 1880–5, 1886), had assembled copies of the constitutions of the self-governing colonies, paying particular attention to the Canada Acts of 1840 and 1867.[80] Canada's constitution was, of course, federal, but legislative devolution in Scotland, England, or Wales was not seriously contemplated in 1886. In fact, the provincial legislatures of the Canadian system enjoyed far more wide-ranging powers than the proposed Irish legislature,[81] where significant "reserved powers" were specified, including defense, foreign, and fiscal policy.

   So much for the institutions of state. The empire expanded as much through the initiative and enterprise of its individual citizens as it did through official activity. Indeed, one of the most remarkable things about Britain's imperial experience is how it markedly extended the boundaries of domestic society. Doctors, engineers, explorers, journalists, settlers, missionaries, and traders—all these people (and others) gained experiences from the empire that they would never have had if their lives had been more centered on the British Isles. This raises the thorny question of how private citizens in Britain were able to "use" the state to advance their own "imperial" ends. Ever since the Radical-Liberal journalist, J. A. Hobson, published *Imperialism: A Study* (1902) there has been a tendency in the literature to assume that it was the already dominant classes in society who gained the most from overseas expansion.[82] Hobson identified international financiers as the biggest beneficiaries, though he also recognized other groups—including armament manufacturers, branches of the export trade and shipping interests—to have had a substantial stake in maintaining and defending British rule. In many ways, it is striking how little this cast of characters has changed in the intervening hundred years. According to one recent study of mid-century Victorian Britain:

For certain individuals and certain groups the empire undoubtedly proved splendidly rewarding, with the result that in imperial terms the prosperous classes, especially financiers, merchants, shippers, and the like, did well, while the majority of people continued to cheerfully and even proudly to shoulder the tax costs of an empire from which they obtained little in the form of material gains.[83]

Recent explorations of the costs and benefits of overseas expansion by economic historians provide quantitative evidence in support of this view that the empire, while a burden on the nation as a whole, nonetheless benefited an array of selfish class interests within it. Focusing on the most easily measured of imperial gains—financial returns on overseas investments—these studies conclude that the politically influential professional and rentier classes of the south-east of England creamed off far more from the colonies (in the form of dividends) than they ever sunk into them (in the form of taxes).[84] Such an approach seems unduly narrow. One does not even need to take account of the psychological and emotional satisfactions of empire (though we should certainly not discount them)[85] to appreciate that some items on imperial balance sheets are more easily accounted for than others—the material benefits of emigration, for example, are almost impossible to quantify, though new work on remittances suggests they may have been much more substantial than hitherto acknowledged.[86]

Rather than privilege any particular source of support for empire, the latest studies of the impact of imperialism on Britain highlight the intense pluralism and regional dynamism that fuelled overseas expansion.[87] The empire, it is argued, may have owed a great deal to the upper-middle classes who ran it, yet its reach went far beyond these people. A vast array of groups in British society became caught up in the processes of overseas expansion, albeit in vastly different and unequal ways. Moreover, there is now growing recognition of the often very "fuzzy" boundaries that existed between society and the state. Complex webs or networks of association—"imperial circuits"—connected private, provincial, and local interests in Britain with their overseas contacts, communities, and projects. The precise nature of state involvement in these circuits can prove very difficult to pin down.[88] Yet perhaps the most fruitful way of conceptualizing society's interaction with the state, in an imperial context, may be to think in terms of expatriate British communities on the periphery. Such communities had to establish a local infrastructure—or "bridgehead"—into which imperial power could be inserted. They also had to mobilize sufficient domestic support to be able to bend the policy-making process to their collective will.[89] Some were extra-parliamentary societies, dining clubs, or pressure groups, enjoying varying degrees of official patronage and involvement. Others brought together powerful business interests or differing types of administrative expertise, only to be absorbed by the state—chartered companies and emigration agencies are cases in point. There were also groups of colonial officials—most notably, the Royal Colonial Institute, the British Committee of the Indian National Congress, and the South African "kindergarten"—which were effectively lobbies for the shaping of public policy. Whatever form they took it was their ability to align local colonial with wider British interests and perspectives that was crucial to success.

The Empire Today

Among the state's most far-reaching powers is that of defining who its citizens are. The British Nationality Act of 1948 reaffirmed the right of people from the colonies to settle permanently in the United Kingdom.[90] As Henry Hopkinson (Minister of State at the Colonial Office, 1952–5), subsequently boasted to the House of Commons:

> As the law stands, any British subject from the Colonies is free to enter this country at any time as long as he can produce evidence of his British status. That is not something we want to tamper with lightly. In a world in which restrictions on personal movement and immigration have increased we can still take pride in the fact that a man can say *Civis Britannicus sum* whatever his color may be, and we can take pride in the fact that he wants and can come to the Mother country.[91]

This "open door" policy was felt to have the virtues of remedying shortages of labour, of presenting a liberal, progressive image of Britain to the rest of the world (especially America), and of helping to stabilize the Commonwealth system. During the 1950s and 1960s, the West Indies and Indian subcontinent were the two main sources of immigration. Approximately one and a half million "new" Commonwealth migrants were resident in Britain by the mid-1970s. Though they formed only 3 percent of Britain's total population, they were concentrated in the major conurbations of Greater London, the West Midlands, Manchester, Merseyside, and Yorkshire, and hence were more visible to the "indigenous" population.

From 1962 to 1981 successive British governments retreated from this "open door" policy and introduced a sequence of legislative controls that made it ever more difficult for former colonial subjects to gain right of abode or work permits in the United Kingdom.[92] The motives that lay behind these acts, and their precise effects, are the subject of dispute. What is not in doubt is that, by the 1960s, immigration from the "new" Commonwealth was widely being talked about as if it were a social "problem."[93] Colored people from the colonies may have had the legal right to migrate, yet they were not a welcome presence in the "mother country."[94] They tended to be perceived as outsiders or "aliens" who had little in common with UK residents, notwithstanding the fact that many of them and their families had fought alongside Britain during World War II.

How far, then, was there was a structural relationship between Britain's colonial past and the domestic racism of the post-war era? Certainly, some people of African-Caribbean and Asian backgrounds feel this to be so. According to the Indian-born novelist, Salman Rushdie, for example, it is impossible to grasp the essence of British racism without accepting its historical and colonial roots:

> Four hundred years of conquest and looting, four centuries of being told that you are superior to the Fuzzy-Wuzzies and the wogs, leave their stain. This stain has seeped into every part of the culture, the language and daily life; and nothing much has been done to wash it out.[95]

One does, of course, need to tread carefully here. There are plenty of other minorities in Britain—the Jews, Italians, and Germans—who were not former colonial subjects but who experienced discrimination. (The Irish could potentially be placed in this category too, depending on whether one sees them as having been "colonized" by the English). Moreover, the variety of experiences of African-Caribbean and Asian migrants, and the variety of levels of economic success they have achieved, caution against explaining exclusion and hardship simply in terms of racial prejudice.

Nonetheless, "new" Commonwealth immigration reversed the colonial encounter in ways that many people in Britain found profoundly uncomfortable. In particular, it called into question beliefs that were deeply rooted in decades of British rule, not least the enforcement of sexual boundaries and taboos against intermarriage between blacks and whites. In that sense it is clear that Britain's imperial past had done little to prepare it for the transition to a multiracial society during the 1960s and 1970s. Arguably, it is only in relatively recent times that African-Caribbean and South Asian people have begun to be embraced as an integral part of British social order. In that sense Catherine Hall is surely correct to claim that decolonization is as much a cultural as a political process, and one in which, in the early twenty-first century, we are all very much still engaged. With a younger generation expressing decidedly more liberal attitudes toward immigration, while, to differing degrees, the rest of the population struggles to live with racial difference at home, it seems that we have yet to close the "critical gap" between notions of "metropolitan superiority" and "colonial inferiority" upon which British power was for so long predicated.[96]

The suspicion and fear recently generated by militant forms of Islam, and the West's response to it at home and in Afghanistan and Iraq, has only served to heighten the sense of ethnic division and tension within Britain. At the time of writing we are facing what is widely acknowledged to be a crisis of our "multicultural" state. There is a growing feeling among those involved with race relations that the doctrine of multiculturalism—of cultural and religious pluralism—is failing to provide a sufficiently strong buffer against the social fragmentation that manifested itself, for example, during the 2001 riots in Bradford, Burnley, and Oldham. Hence the repeated calls that have come from Trevor Phillips and the Commission for Racial Equality for the state to be more actively involved in promoting a common citizenship and greater civic participation. Yet the vision of a more united society in which people of all backgrounds feel that they truly belong raises the tricky issue of what it means to be "British" when many of the supports that formerly propped up a sense of nationality— the empire, Protestantism, the monarchy, the BBC, or the public memory of World War II—have either collapsed or are much weaker now than they previously were. As the English, Scots, and Welsh retreat into their own identities, it may be the case that the only people left calling themselves "British" in twenty or thirty years time will be the Ulster Unionists, still in their mind "colonists" or a "frontier" people, and Britain's ethnic minorities, another product of the empire.

The real question for Britain's multicultural state, therefore, appears to be whether it can promote a more inclusive and flexible definition of national identity, transcending older colonialist ways of seeing and thinking about "other" non- European cultures and peoples, while at the same time fostering a sense of "core British values" which all people hold in common. Preaching racial and religious tolerance is unlikely in itself to be the answer here. Rather, the preconditions for the development of a stable and secure British identity among migrant communities need to be addressed. More has to be done to promote the integration of newcomers to Britain by providing them with better access to education and employment, spheres in which significant ethnic "penalties" persist, and by arresting the fracturing of social relations along ethnic lines (the levels of segregation in housing and schooling are of real concern).[97] More may also have to be done to define the fundamental political rights and freedoms that British citizens can expect to enjoy and are in turn obliged to respect. Whatever the way forward, dealing with the diversity of religion and culture in our post-colonial society is among the greatest challenges facing the British state this century. In that sense, the empire really has come home to roost.

Notes

1 The definition is drawn from Yudelman, *Emergence of Modern South Africa*, p. 17. Other institutions—not considered in this chapter—but often appended to this list would include the judiciary, police, schools, and churches. For the impact of colonial models of policing on British practices, see G. Sinclair, *End of the Line*. The subject of missionary activity is considered separately in the chapter by Elizabeth Elbourne; the churches (Anglican and Nonconformist) in Britain had a complex relationship with the colonial state, sometimes working in co-operation with it, sometimes cutting across its priorities and purposes: on this point see, especially, Porter, *Religion versus Empire*.

2 For a recent exception, see Armitage, *Ideological Origins*.

3 For the claim that the "imperial qualities" of the English (rather than British) state were "a fundamental aspect of both its materiality and its imagery," see Corrigan and Sayer, *Great Arch*, p. 11. Regrettably, although Corrigan and Sayer reiterate their claim (pp. 15–16) they do not develop it; their analysis focuses exclusively on English state formation in England. They do, however, entertain the possibility that the "external" (i.e., imperial) form of the state permeated its social power and enhanced its political legitimacy "at home" (p. 122).

4 Gallagher and Robinson, "Imperialism of free trade"; *id., Africa and the Victorians*. For an overview of their work and its historiographical significance, see Thompson, "Gallagher" and "Robinson."

5 As elaborated, for example, by Skocpol, "Bringing the state."

6 Gallagher (ed.), *Decline*.

7 See, for example, the appraisals in Louis (ed.), *Imperialism: Robinson and Gallagher*.

8 Cain and Hopkins, *British Imperialism*.

9 Cannadine, "Empire strikes back"; Daunton, "Gentlemanly capitalism"; Porter, "Gentlemanly capitalism."

10 See Brewer, *Sinews of Power*; Stone (ed.), *Imperial State at War*.

11 The term is most closely associated with Harlow, *Founding of the Second British Empire*. For the historical debates surrounding it, see Bayly, "Second British empire."

12 Colley, *Britons*, esp. ch. 5.

13 Bayly, *Imperial Meridian*, pp. 136–55.

14 Gambles, *Protection and Politics*, esp. chs 6–7.

15 Bayly, *Imperial Meridian*, pp. 105, 248.

16 For the case of South America, see Gallo, *Great Britain and Argentina*.

17 Peers, *Between Mars and Mammon.*

18 Marshall, "Cornwallis triumphant," pp. 57–74.

19 Reports of Company corruption and misrule had begun to circulate widely in British society from the mid-eighteenth century; it remains a moot point as to how far Cornwallis' reforms improved standards and behavior in the Company. See Bowen, *Business of Empire*, pp. 7, 15–18.

20 Bayly and Prior, "Cornwallis,"; Callahan, *East India Company*, pp. 60–70, 118–26; Wickwire and Wickwire, *Cornwallis*, chs 3–6.

21 Bayly, *Imperial Meridian*, p. 128.

22 Bowen, *Business of Empire*, p. 83.

23 For a perceptive analysis of the process, see Harling and Mandler, "Fiscal-military." See also Daunton, *Trusting Leviathan*, pp. 124–35.

24 Quoted A. Howe, "Pax Britannica," p. 4.

25 Gambles, *Protection and Politics*, pp. 197–9.

26 Eastwood, "Peel, the nation," pp. 37–8.

27 A. Howe, *Free Trade*, pp. 18, 63.

28 Hoppen, *Mid-Victorian Generation*, p. 156.

29 Brown, *Modern India*, pp. 70–1; Searle, *Entrepreneurial Politics*, pp. 127–8, 316–17; Silver, *Manchester Men*.

30 Semmel, *Rise of Free Trade*, p. 205.

31 P. Kennedy, *Rise and Fall*; Rodger, *Command of the Ocean*.

32 Thompson, *Imperial Britain*, ch. 5.

33 Friedberg, *Weary Titan*.

34 Daunton, *Trusting Leviathan*, pp. 302–5.

35 Cain, "Economic philosophy," pp. 47–8, 54–5; E. H. H. Green, *Crisis of Conservatism*, pp. 165–6, 171.

36 Leo Amery quoted in Thompson, *Imperial Britain*, p. 87.

37 For the view that the deals struck at Ottawa benefited the dominions more than Britain, see J. Davis, *History of Britain*, pp. 208–12; Tsokhas, *Markets, Money and Empire*, pp. 89–104.

38 Clavin, "World Economic Conference."

39 For brief but insightful remarks on the early period, see Brockliss, "Professions and national identity," esp. pp. 9–10; for an excellent extended treatment of the later period, see Perkin, *Rise of Professional Society*.

40 Of course, in parts of the empire—the Indian Princely States and Malaya, for example, the hereditary right to rule remained the basis of British administration up to the 1940s. For the importance of class and status in British perceptions of empire, see Cannadine, *Ornamentalism*. Ornamentalism is perhaps a less useful concept in Southern Africa where the British respect for hierarchy and status was not nearly so marked: see Price, "One big thing," p. 621.

41 Compton, "Open competition," pp. 265–84.

42 Dewey, "Education of a ruling caste," pp. 283–5.

43 Heathcote, *Indian Army*, ch. 7.

44 Cain, "Character and imperialism," pp. 177–200; Collini, *Public Moralists*, pp. 91–118.

45 Thompson, *Empire Strikes Back*, pp. 22–9.

46 Marquand, "How united?" pp. 286–8. For a fuller explication of Marquand's views, see "Twilight of the British state?" pp. 57–69.

47 Seeley, *Expansion*. For the argument that "the state provides perhaps the best example of the mutually constitutive relationship of empire and British history," see Price, "One big thing," pp. 613–14.

48 Seeley, *Expansion*, p. 44.

49 See, for example, Robert Colls' observation that "The crown colonies were administered by the imperial state but not considered a part of that state, except ceremonially. The "white" dominions were self-governing and considered close, close enough to be admitted to the counsels of state': Colls, *Identity of England*, p. 93.

50 Adams, *Bonar Law*, p. 26.

51 Pimlott, *Harold Wilson*, pp. 18–20.

52 Rickard, "Anti-sweating movement," [quote from p. 594].

53 Bridge and Fedorowich (eds), *British World*.

54 Armitage, *Ideological Origins*, p. 14.

55 Lawrence, "Politics of place," p. 93.

56 Pocock, "British history," pp. 601–28; *id.*, "History and sovereignty," pp. 358–89.

57 For the multinational character and cultural diversity of the British state, as it developed during the mid-eighteenth century, see Brockliss and Eastwood (eds), *Union of Multiple Identities*, especially the editor's Introduction.

58 Colley, "Britishness and otherness," pp. 309–29; Walton, "Britishness," pp. 518, 522.

59 K. Robbins, *Nineteenth Century Britain*, pp. 18–28, 183–5.

60 J. M. MacKenzie, "Empire and national identities," p. 231.

61 Devine, *Scotland's Empire*; J. M. MacKenzie, "Essay and reflection."

62 Devine, *Scotland's Empire*, p. 360.

63 Ellis, "Reconciling the Celt," pp. 391–418; Cardell, Cumming *et al.*, "Welsh identity," pp. 25–60; G. A. Williams, *Welsh in Their History*, pp. 175–85.

64 Jeffery (ed.), *Irish Empire*.

65 Falls, *Birth of Ulster*, pp. 230–54; Ignatieff, *Blood and Belonging*, ch. 6.

66 Loughlin, "Imagining 'Ulster'," p. 112.

67 McCracken, *Irish Pro-Boers*; *id.*, *MacBride's Brigade*.

68 Jackson, "Irish unionists," pp. 131–7; Loughlin, *Ulster Unionism*, p. 32.

69 Harrison, *Transformation of British Politics*, p. 56.

70 Kubicek, *Administration of Imperialism*, pp. 14–6, 23, 26–9, 42, 174–6.

71 Havinden and Meredith, *Colonialism and Development*, p. 90.

72 Constantine, *British Colonial Development Policy*, pp. 278–86.

73 H. L. Hall, *Colonial Office*, pp. 269–70.

74 For the respective influence of West Indian merchants and planters, the lobby of "Indian" MPs, and North American interests in the British Parliament, see Marshall, "British state overseas," pp. 179–80.

75 Marshall, "Imperial Britain" (1995), p. 382; Thompson, *Imperial Britain*, pp. 26–8.

76 For the importance of Parliament in cementing the "Unionist" British State, see Eastwood, Brockliss, and John, "From dynastic union," p. 193.

77 Hall, "Nation within and without"; Taylor, "1848 revolutions."

78 Burton, *Burdens of History*.

79 Kendle. *Federal Britain*, pp. ix-xiii.

80 Mansergh, *Commonwealth Experience*, p. 24; Matthew, *Gladstone*, pp. 216, 225, 227.

81 Morley, *Gladstone*, 3, p. 317.

82 For Hobson's political thought, see Cain, *Hobson and Imperialism*.

83 Hoppen, *Mid-Victorian Generation*, p. 226.

84 See esp. Davis and Huttenback, *Mammon*; Edelstein, *Overseas Investment*.

85 Offer, "British Empire."

86 Magee and Thompson , "Lines of Credit."

87 Marshall, "Imperial Britain" (1996); Thompson, *Empire Strikes Back?*, esp. pp. 1–9, 239–44.

88 Darwin, "Descent of empire." For a case study of such imperial networks and their relation to the state, see A. S. Thompson, "Imperial propaganda."

89 Darwin, "Imperialism and the Victorians," pp. 641–2.

90 The Act divided British citizenship into two categories: "UK and Colonies," and "independent Commonwealth countries"—this allowed Indian nationals to retain their status as British subjects even after India became a republic. Following Sonya Rose, I am defining "citizenship" as a "membership category," determining who does and does not belong to a particular national community: see S. Rose, *Which People's War*, pp. 15–16.

91 *H of C debs*, vol. 532, col. 827, 5 Nov. 5, 1954.

92 Prior to 1962, practical rather than legislative obstacles had been placed in the path of "new" Commonwealth immigrants—the Colonial Office limited the distribution of passports, increased application fees, and emphasized the likelihood of unemployment for new arrivals.

93 Kathleen Paul contends that the view of African-Caribbean and Asian immigrants creating a "color problem" stemmed chiefly from government, which fostered an unfavorable public atmosphere toward them: see Paul, *Whitewashing Britain*. Others argue that the public needed little encouragement to take this stance: see, for example, Wendy Webster on the British media's negative portrayals of Commonwealth immigrants, who, unlike those from Europe, were not deemed "suitable": Webster, *Englishness and Empire*, ch. 6.

94 For the various forms of discrimination (or color bars) experienced in Britain before and during the war, see S. Rose, *Which People's War?*, pp. 264–6.

95 Rushdie, "New empire within Britain," p. 130.

96 Hall, *Civilising Subjects*, pp. 1–22; *id.*, "Roundtable," pp. 534–5.

97 For a fuller discussion, see Thompson with Begum, "Asian 'Britishness'."

Further Reading

For the challenges involved in conceptualizing the modern state, and in charting its historical evolution, see Theda Skocpol, "Bringing the state back in," in Evans, Rueschemeyer, and Skocpol (eds), *Bringing the State Back In*. For the exploration of some of the issues raised by Skocpol in a specifically colonial context, see C. J. Fuller and V. Béné, *The Everyday State and Society in Modern India*. That said, the "state" and "state formation" remain under-theorized in Commonwealth-imperial historiography. For a brief reflection on imperial influences on British state formation, and the possibilities for further study, see especially Richard Price, "One big thing: Britain, its empire and their imperial culture." One field in which new research has taken place is that of official mentalities: see, for example, on the Raj, Clive Dewey's *Anglo-Indian Attitudes*, and, on South Africa, Saul Dubow's two seminal essays: "Colonial nationalism, the Milner kindergarten and the rise of 'South Africanism,' 1902–10," and "Imagining the new South Africa in the era of reconstruction," in David Omissi and Andrew Thompson (eds), *The Impact of the South African War*.

"Domestic" British historiography offers richer pickings for the study of the state. For the Hanoverian period, see especially John Brewer, *The Sinews of Power*, and Lawrence Stone (ed.), *An Imperial State at War*. Meanwhile, the idea of the

British state in the early and mid-Victorian era is skilfully explored in a collection of essays edited by Laurence Brockliss and David Eastwood, *A Union of Multiple Identities*, and by Philip Harling and Peter Mandler in "From 'fiscal-military' state to laissez-faire state, 1760–1850." For an important investigation of the limits of the state during the twentieth century, see S. J. D. Green and R. C. Whiting (eds), *The Boundaries of the State in Modern Britain*. The most chronologically sweeping study of the (English) state remains that by Philip Corrigan and Derek Sayer, *The Great Arch*—a provocative if, in places, difficult read.

4

The British Empire on the Move, 1760–1914

Kent Fedorowich

> For every "exile," there was an adventurer; for every alien, a settler.
>
> David Fitzpatrick, *Oceans of Consolation*[1]

The accession of George III to the throne in 1760 coincided with the beginning of a phenomenal upsurge in British migration to the New World. Between 1760 and 1820 there occurred several fundamental shifts in the categories, patterns, and destinations of British migrants, which, in turn, provided the all-important foundation for the movement of 22.6 million individuals from the British Isles between 1815 and 1914.[2] In terms of empire migration, the largest beneficiaries of this British 'dispersal' were the colonies of white settlement,[3] which later became the four self-governing or "white" dominions of Australia, Canada, New Zealand, and South Africa. Unsurprisingly, this flow of migrants to the former dominions has secured the closest attention from scholars, and is the focus of this chapter. Nonetheless, as Robert Bickers has reminded us, British communities in Argentina, Egypt, India, and Hong Kong—these "mini-Britains"—also deserve careful attention by historians.[4] Migration was not confined to the white races of Great Britain. Equally significant was the abolition of slavery and the slave trade initiated in 1807, its termination throughout the British Empire by 1837–8 and the emancipation and repatriation of some of these unfortunate souls.[5] Nor must we forget the initiation of a "new system of slavery" after 1834—indentured labour—which took many guises in many tropical regions of the British Empire involving 2.5 million South Asians, Africans, Chinese, and Pacific Islanders until it too was finally stopped in 1922.[6]

It is only within the last twenty years or so that British migration and the peopling of its immense empire of both free and un-free individuals have been (re)incorporated into the mainstream of British imperial historiography.[7] For too long, those interested in population studies and migration flows have concentrated on a specific ethnic, racial, gender, or socioeconomic group in a particular timeframe or region.[8] More recently, several scholars using a comparative framework have attempted a Braudellian-like sweep, to examine the competing forces and developing trends that have arisen over huge spans of time,[9] while others have provided an indispensable analysis of the migration of one specific ethnic group to many overseas destinations.[10] Today, the clarion call is for migration historians to embark upon bolder comparative studies that situate the experiences of specific migrant groups within the "wider histories they shared with others."[11] This includes the integration of European and African migrations, both free and coerced; an approach long advocated by David Eltis and recently reiterated by two early modern scholars.[12] While significant advances have been made in the field of British migration studies over the past two decades, in particular the growing awareness that migrants and their kinship networks were invaluable conduits in the transmission of political ideas, investment capital, cultural transfer, and identity (re)formation,[13] more remains to be done.

Bernard Bailyn, one of the pioneering historians of migration to colonial America, asked:

> What were the propelling or attracting forces . . . [that] drew or forced these thousands of people from their homes, led them to undertake transatlantic voyages that were both deeply disorientating and dangerous, and deposited them on the far margins of the British world?[14]

Such simple but taxing questions have confronted migration scholars for decades, and form the basis of the analytical framework of this essay. The objectives are threefold. First, it is necessary to map the changing contours of British outward migration since 1760 and provide the aggregate figures to identify major trends. Second, is the discussion surrounding the stimuli, both positive and negative, which influenced and impinged upon the decision to migrate; or, in the case of forced migration, which influenced various agencies to make such decisions for those who were denied the right to choose. Finally, this essay will point readers in the direction of neglected fields of study. For instance, Oonagh Walsh has argued for scholars to include "career" migrants such as missionaries, the professional classes, businessmen, soldiers, and policemen in the migrant pool.[15] Colonial administrators and civil servants must not be forgotten, the "hard wire" of the imperial system. With their families, they helped to construct a wider British identity and culture overseas and were influenced by their experiences, while serving abroad, that created a broader Britishness, some of which was exported back "home."[16] Similarly, the issue of return migration contributes to a more sophisticated understanding of the history of migration.

British Migration to the New World, 1700–76

The overwhelming consensus among migration historians is that prior to the American Revolution (1776–83) the composition of white migrant flows to British North America and the West Indies was dominated by indentured servitude. In fact, indenture—which was designed to increase labour mobility from (predominantly) England to the New World—became the spine of the entire migratory process in the colonial period. Between 1630 and 1780, for example, 50–60 percent of the labour streaming into Britain's New World possessions in the Americas and West Indies were servants.[17] Even more staggering is that nearly 75 percent of all immigrants arriving in the thirteen American colonies did so in some form of bondage: slaves, convicts, and servants.[18] Servitude, which became a pivotal institution throughout many regions of colonial America, was accepted as a "normal" practice in everyday society prior to 1776; "a complex world of the free and the unfree, occupying different conditions of liberty and bondage." [19]

British convicts became a vital source of involuntary labour during the eighteenth century such that "they did much to replace indentured servants as a source of bound labor [sic] from England."[20] Between 1718, with the inauguration of the Transportation Act, and 1775 when the practice was stopped, approximately 50,000 felons were transported to colonial America and sold as servants. This represented 25 percent of all British migrants arriving in colonial America at this time, the bulk of offenders—a staggering 80 percent—being transported to Maryland and Virginia.[21]

Unfortunately, due to the paucity and fragmentation of eighteenth-century migration records, especially for the first six decades, accurate statistics are wanting.[22] Yet, what is apparent is that while emigration from Great Britain during the seventeenth century was predominately English—and the scale was indeed astounding (as was the wastage due to high mortality rates[23])—the eighteenth century witnessed smaller numbers and a changing ethnicity amongst migrants. According to Nicholas Canny, the contribution made by English migrants was more significant in terms of quality than quantity; as these migrants on average were better educated and more skilled than their Scottish and Irish counterparts.[24] English migrants were aware that their skills were more highly valued in the colonies than in England,[25] and this migrant optimism was heightened as the cost of passage to America halved from £5-£6 in the early eighteenth century to £3 5s. by the mid-1770s.[26] Hence, for some at least, the New World was regarded not as a place of exile, but as a land of opportunity.

As English migration declined in proportional terms (50,000 migrants out of a grand total of 262,000 to the mainland colonies of America between 1700 and 1775), there was a notable increase—especially after 1760—both in the numbers of indentured and voluntary migrants from Scotland and Ireland, which imprinted a more "British" character on the flow of migrants arriving to the New World. One estimate for the period 1700 to 1780 states that as many as 70 percent of the 270,000 British migrants were Scots or Irish. As Alison Games has observed, migration may have had a "greater impact creating a *British* identity because of the ways in which migration patterns in this period eroded regional cultures and brought people from remote parts of Britain into contact with each other in both the British Isles and America."[27]

Games's point is equally and controversially applicable to the Irish. L. M. Cullen has argued that the 1760s and 1770s constituted the "greatest single watershed in the history of [Irish] migration overall." He contends that the 1760s and 1770s were an era of positive economic change and that increasing numbers of Irish migrants—both Protestant and Catholic—were deliberately making more informed decisions to emigrate.[28] This analysis reinforces the work of Akenson and others who have asserted that the Irish were not "victims" but willing "collaborators" in the subjugation of indigenous peoples overseas who eagerly participated in expanding Britain's colonial empire. Between 1630 and 1775 the net migration from Ireland to British North America and the West Indies was an estimated 165,000 souls; 40,000 of whom comprised the largest flow of white migration to the West Indies between the mid-seventeenth and early eighteenth centuries.[29] Irish migrants were highly visible among the lower-class white population in the West Indies and were modestly represented among the colonial gentry on a number of islands. Montserrat is a case in point where by 1730 most Irish households owned slaves. By 1800 a number of Irish Catholic and Protestant families had established lucrative slave plantations in the Caribbean, offering work to their fellow countrymen engaged as artisans, overseers, merchants, and indentured servants.[30]

When broken down along religious affiliations and demographic constituencies, the statistics for Irish migration for this period make interesting reading. Three-quarters of all transatlantic departures from Ireland between 1700 and 1775 were Protestants; a community which constituted between one quarter to one third of the Irish population. What's more, approximately 70 percent of the Protestant emigrants were Presbyterians—which in times of peace averaged between 1,000 and 2,000 emigrants per year after 1750—a highly mobile community whose experience in Ireland made them ideal settlers in the back blocks of colonial America.[31]

Scottish migration was also significant. Between 1700 and 1760 approximately 30,000 Scots migrated to America, with 90 percent coming from the Lowlands.[32] Indeed, it was the Act of Union of 1707 which opened the English empire to Scottish enterprise.[33] As a result, their involvement in the commercial development of the Caribbean—St Kitts, Tobago, and especially Jamaica—was striking. They were able to out do their English rivals, especially in the lucrative tobacco trade where Virginia was turned into a Scottish plantation. Spurred on by the Scottish Enlightenment, their endeavors continued to flourish throughout the latter part of the eighteenth century; an accomplishment helped, in part, by the reinvention of a system of clanship that allowed a restructuring of their social and commercial relations on a global scale within an imperial framework.[34]

It is interesting to examine why so many more Scots were leaving the British Isles. Bumsted argues that the two chief stimuli of Scottish emigration between 1763 and 1775 were lack of work and high rents. Periodic famine was also a contributing factor. With the conclusion of the Seven Years War in 1763, emigration from the Highlands and Islands increased, sparking intense public debate, led by the Highland lairds who wanted emigration banned. The irony here was that Scotland, like Ireland, was finally modernizing and over the course of the eighteenth century was slowly raising its standard of living. Lowland Scotland had experienced these forces in the earlier part of the eighteenth century and was beginning to reap the benefits. Modernization, especially in the Highlands and Islands, was achieved much later and at a higher social cost, generating pressures that encouraged Scots to abandon their country. Tom Devine has argued that there was a well-established 'culture of mobility' in Scottish society stretching back to the early modern period. However, the economic forces which were unleashed at this time and which led to the first Highland or People's Clearance, are crucial in explaining why emigration from Scotland became so extensive. Herein lay the paradox. As material conditions improved and living standards grew emigration accelerated rather than waned after 1750.[35]

With the exception of London, between 1773 and 1776 more people left the sparsely populated Highlands than from any other region in the British Isles: an incredible 18 percent of all British migrants.[36] Only a small proportion of Highland emigrants travelled as indentured servants; a further illustration of the changing dynamics of Scottish migration patterns. Customs returns for 1774–5 indicate that of 3,000 Scots emigrants, only 150 were indentured servants and the majority of these were from the Lowlands. Highlanders were employing their own resources and paying their own passage, which indicates that most came from the middling ranks of Highland society: people who had the skills, assets and access to capital to finance their passage and that of their families and kinsmen.[37]

Another distinctive feature of Highland emigration, especially in the west, was the role of military service in America in establishing migration networks. Fierce resistance to the Union and English rule, as epitomized in the Jacobite rebellions of 1715 and 1745, did not deter military recruiters or "crimpers" from tapping manpower in this region. Valued for their martial qualities and fighting spirit, men from the Highlands and Islands were highly prized by recruiters, who raised ten line regiments for overseas service during the Seven Years War.[38] When peace returned in 1763, three of these regiments which had fought in North America, including the 42nd (Black Watch), were disbanded and settled in Quebec and Nova Scotia. Fearing a possible rebellion by the newly-conquered French Canadians, detachments of these troops were disbanded in these colonies with the express hope that they would increase productivity and provide a first-rate militia for colonial defense. They were enticed by land grants, which ranged from 2,000 to 3,000 acres for subalterns and officers and 50–200 acres for ordinary soldiers and their non-commissioned officers, and which were usually located in areas where military considerations overrode agricultural viability. Nonetheless, soldier settlement plans were employed along the south bank of the upper St Lawrence River in Quebec and the St John River in New Brunswick after the American Revolution, and again after the Napoleonic Wars.[39]

The surge of humanity which arrived in North America from the British Isles between 1760 and 1775 totalled 125,000: 55,000 Protestant Irish, 40,000 Scots (10,000 of whom came from the Highlands), and 30,000 English. On average this meant that 15,000 people arrived annually, triple the yearly average prior to 1760. For the same period at least 12,000 Germans (mostly redemptioners) and 84,500 African slaves were imported into North America making for an aggregate total of 221,500.[40] This clearly demonstrates that the demand for labour and settlers had become so acute that, according to Aaron Fogleman, record numbers of African slaves, British convicts, indentured servants, and free passengers signalled a flourishing market in all four categories before the disruption caused by the American Revolution.[41]

Despite the fact that indentured servitude continued to dominate colonial labour markets the situation was changing and by the 1770s there was a growing chorus of opinion that suggested that "indentured servitude was an obstacle, not a stepping-stone, toward prosperity in America."[42] The erosion in the acceptance of indentured servitude as best practice in pre-revolutionary America also signalled the death knell of the hierarchical immigration system that had dominated the social and economic landscape for so long. When war broke out between Britain and the Thirteen Colonies in 1775 all forms of migration stopped. After 1783, when the transatlantic migration of Europeans recommenced to the fledgling United States of America it was characterized not by degrees of bondage and servitude but by free and voluntary migration. White migration patterns and practices to America had been irrevocably transformed.[43]

British Migration During the Revolutionary Era, 1783–1820

The loss of the thirteen American colonies introduced a number of fundamental changes to British migration patterns. An immediate problem was where to send Britain's convicts. Shortly after the outbreak of hostilities, American ports refused entry to British ships transporting criminals to its shores. It was not until August 1786 that the decision—more by default than design—was made to establish a convict colony at Botany Bay on the east coast of Australia.[44]

Another urgent problem was what to do with the United Empire Loyalists who stayed true to the British cause but were forced (or chose) to leave the United States during and after hostilities ceased in 1783. Between 1763 and 1775 substantial numbers of British migrants had been arriving on North American shores; but no more than 5,000 had settled in Quebec and Nova Scotia. However, the American Revolution persuaded approximately 60,000 settlers to stream north to the scattered imperial enclaves of what remained of British North America. Nova Scotia's population doubled, while a substantial non-French minority was established in Quebec in the Eastern Townships and along the St Lawrence River. The creation of New Brunswick in 1784 was made possible, in part, by a large influx of Loyalists to that region. Prince Edward Island also benefited enormously from this incursion of refugees as did several districts along the Ontario peninsula.

Former soldiers from disbanded British regiments, many recruited in the Scottish Highlands and Ireland, were also part of this exodus providing essential manpower in the future defense of these vulnerable colonies. However, the largest contingent within the Loyalist element was not first-generation British migrants but native-born Americans largely from New York and Pennsylvania. In fact, between 1790 and 1812 tens of thousands of the so-called late Loyalists arrived in the Canadas. These settlers were mostly Americans with apparently little or no Loyalist connection, attracted by the prospects of cheap land rather than by any desire to dwell under the British Crown. As a result, by 1815 a significant majority of the non-francophone community was of American origin. This, in turn, posed immediate problems concerning the future defense and security of this exposed and sparsely populated imperial periphery.[45]

The strategic port of Halifax, populated by disbanded soldiers in 1749, was the first major British example of a conscious soldier settlement plan. Gratuitous land grants were made between 1763 and 1775 and again between 1783 and 1812 where it seemed Scottish officers in particular had succeeded in carving out huge claims, mainly for speculative gain. The rhetoric rarely matched the reality as many ex-soldiers found it difficult to adjust to the pressures of pioneering life, abandoned their farms and moved into town. Nonetheless, despite these drawbacks, the military grant system remained an essential factor in imperial defense thinking throughout the nineteenth century.

The dilemmas faced by British administrators in North America concerning security and demography after 1783 were compounded by an anti-emigration lobby which had gathered pace, largely amongst the Scottish nobility, since the mid-1770s.[46] There were additional issues such as the drain on military manpower. Scotland and the Highlands especially were seen as important recruiting grounds for the British Army. Emigration drained military manpower and left the nation vulnerable in time of war. It also meant that if these Scottish nobles could not raise enough troops their privileged position within the British body politic would be undermined. The ability to grant or influence the distribution of military commissions to family and kinsmen was also essential in reinforcing patronage and prestige within the political circles of both Scotland and London.[47] Hence the tenacity with which many Scottish lairds supported the anti-emigration lobby.

The most successful advocate of anti-emigration was the masterful manipulator Henry Dundas. As Lord Advocate, it was Dundas who, for military reasons, succeeded in temporarily banning emigration from Scotland in 1775; and it was he who successfully introduced one of the most draconian pieces of mercantilist legislation— the Passenger Act of 1803—to stem the tide of Highland emigration. He failed, however, in persuading his government colleagues in 1786 to legislate a total ban on emigration throughout the British Isles.[48] Moreover, energetic administrators like Lieutenant-Governor John G. Simcoe of the newly-created province of Upper Canada (1792) would either ignore or work around such metropolitan diktats because the first priority was the need to extend and develop the colony. Emigrants were central to this strategy. Ironically, many of the proponents of Scottish emigration schemes were half-pay officers or disgruntled tacksmen who saw their position within an industrializing and modernizing Scotland hopelessly under threat. Thus, migrating overseas was seen by some as a way of securing a better, more stable future. Yet, there were others who deployed the threat of leaving Scotland to negotiate better tenancy agreements from their already jittery landlords.[49]

The problems of depopulation were raised in the province of Ulster where the politics of migration possessed an undeniable political edge. During the three decades after 1783, a further 100,000 were enticed overseas—increasingly self-sufficient from the respectable classes of Ulster society capable of paying their own way— the majority landing in the mid-Atlantic states of America. This continuous drain of loyal Protestants from Ulster was deeply worrying to the political leadership in the province, because of its implications in the power struggle between Protestants and Catholics. If emigration was left unchecked, the balance of power could shift decisively in favour of the Catholic population. It was the emigration scandal in Scotland which inspired the anti-emigration lobby in Whitehall, but there is no doubt that policy makers were acutely aware of the effects this legislation would have on curbing emigration from Ulster.[50]

Fearful that the life-blood of the nation was draining away, the indefatigable Dundas orchestrated the 'devious' Passenger Act of 1803 which was passed with hardly a comment. This triumph of mercantilism, which "equated population with wealth and saw emigration simply as a drain upon national strength" proved to be a pyrrhic victory as the beneficial effects of emigration were being promoted by a growing number of influential philanthropists and intellectuals.[51] By the end of the Napoleonic Wars in 1815 it was agreed that emigration would help resolve the menacing spectre of overpopulation and act as a safety valve for popular discontent that was beginning to sweep the country in the aftermath of a severe economic depression and chronic post-war unemployment. The economist, Patrick Colquhoun, advocated that emigration was a positive social force that would both increase the colonial demand for British manufactured goods, and provide a partial solution to the economic distress that was ravaging large parts of Great Britain.[52] Thomas Douglas, 5th Earl of Selkirk (1771–1820), was another inveterate supporter of these ideas, whose influence on the debate, until very recently has not been appreciated.[53] An avid promoter of overseas colonization, Selkirk established several settlements in Prince Edward Island, Upper Canada and, in 1812, the Red River colony in Canada's North West.

The more positive outlook given to emigration coincided with one of the worst periods of economic distress and political discontent ever experienced in the United Kingdom. As wartime industries shed workers and adjusted to the demands of a peacetime economy, wages declined, wheat prices fell, and poverty soared. The demobilization of 200,000 men from Britain's armed services fuelled an already distressing unemployment situation. Yet the price for bread and fuel remained high putting additional pressures on the already precarious household budgets of agricultural labourers and factory workers. One contemporary observer estimated that 15 percent of England's population was indigent. However, perhaps the most telling indicator of the rising social deprivation after 1815 was that in 1817–18 a staggering £8 million or 84 percent of the total sum available to parishes and local authorities was spent on poor relief.[54] For some, emigration was an attractive remedy to the overwhelming economic, political and social woes facing the country.

The Dawn of a New Age, 1820–60

Broadly speaking, the overall trends in British migration during the nineteenth century ebbed and flowed along the following lines. Figures for the 1820s were small, rose steadily in the 1830s, and swelled with the Irish Famine between 1845 and 1852 when, in just eight years, 2.5 million Britons emigrated overseas. By the late 1850s numbers began to decline but revived again in the 1860s, reaching a new peak in the years either side of 1870. Nonetheless, it was in the 1880s that numbers surged to their highest levels before another decline interceded until the end of the century.[55] What of their origins? Ulster Protestants predominated throughout the 1820s and 1830s, while in the middle decades it was the underprivileged from Catholic Ireland. After 1870 English and Scottish migrants prevailed and would do so far into the twentieth century.

Final destinations make for interesting comparison as well. Estimated at between 62 and 73 percent, the United States remained the foremost recipient of this flow of settlers from all parts of the British Isles throughout the nineteenth century.[56] Even so, there are some interesting trends that demonstrate how important British migration was in reinforcing the sense of Britishness in the colonies of white settlement. Half a million Irish (mostly Protestant) moved to British North America between 1815 and 1845, to be followed by a third of a million more after the Great Famine. The heaviest concentrations were in the province of Upper Canada where two-thirds of the Irish intake was Protestant, a feature that remained constant throughout the nineteenth century. In fact, between 1815 and 1865 Irish emigrants outnumbered the combined total of English, Scottish, and Welsh arrivals.[57] Of the colonies of white settlement, Canada remained the favored destination for British migrants until about 1870. In the 1830s, for instance, British North America was "especially prominent" and for the period 1815–40 as a whole held the advantage over the United States by the slimmest of margins. The dramatic shift to the United States as the preferred destination for British migrants occurred during the Irish Famine where, for the remainder of the century, the proportion between America and Canada ranged from five, to as high as nine, to one.

Even the Australian colonies made significant inroads into the (free) migrant traffic during specific years of the middle decades of the century. In the early 1840s and the 1850s after the Victorian gold rush Australian totals in several instances came close to matching American figures and streaked ahead of Canadian tabulations. In 1855, for example, 50,000 migrants left Liverpool for the United States, followed by 40,000 to Australia and only 15,000 to British North America.[58] The early 1860s were another boom period for migration to Australia before economic depression after the 1880s allowed Canada to reassert and maintain its popularity as the overriding imperial destination for British migrants until war once again interrupted migration in 1914. Within these general trends, the breakdown of aggregate figures into ethnic, gender and age categories for both state-assisted and voluntary migration provide further insights into British migrant flows over the course of the nineteenth century.

One scholar has argued that Lord Liverpool's administration (1815–26) was "unique" in the annals of migration policy. There were no less than six discrete experiments in state-assisted emigration, involving at most 11,000 people, which represented a "hesitant response" to the mounting socioeconomic pressures British society was facing in the decade after Waterloo. Although the number of participants was small compared to those who left Britain voluntarily or with philanthropic backing, from a colonial aspect these experiments were significant in boosting overall numbers on the frontier. In Upper Canada, for example, between one-sixth and one-fifth of the total number of emigrants arriving in the colony were state-aided. In one project alone involving the Bathurst district in the Ottawa valley, approximately 4,000 people received government assistance between 1815 and 1821. Between 1819 and 1821, the newly-acquired colony at the Cape of Good Hope was another test location where 3,500 British migrants were channelled by Colonial Office intervention to settle and consolidate British influence in the Zuurveld in the Eastern Cape.[59] Moreover, while the numbers were small comparative to those of unassisted migrants,[60] the debate on government-assisted migration continued.

In Scotland, the opposition to overseas migration had wilted. By 1820 an astonishing conversion in favour of fostering emigration was championed by Lowland politicians, such as the liberal-minded Lord Archibald Hamilton, whose constituencies in Glasgow, Lanarkshire, and Renfrewshire had experienced exceptionally severe economic dislocation and political radicalization.[61] Undoubtedly, there was an element of political opportunism at work amongst the political elite in Scotland. The fear of further radical insurrection as witnessed at Peterloo (1819), the Cato Street conspiracy (1820), and the Radical War between 1819 and 1820 galvanized Lowland politicians, landlords, and the press to support state-assisted schemes for the unemployed artisan as a way of reducing future disorder. Emigration became a political weapon in the fight to combat popular radicalism; a "safety valve," which would thin the ranks of the agitators while simultaneously diffusing radical political pressures.[62]

As with Dundas's attempts to ban emigration from Scotland in the last quarter of the eighteenth century, the public debate after 1815 over the pros and cons of pauper emigration from Scotland were much more politicized and engaged with by a broader spectrum of society than in the rest of the United Kingdom. Politics aside, there were compelling economic reasons for the advocacy of state assistance which were promoted by unemployed artisans themselves. Since the spring of 1819, artisan-led emigration societies had been organized in Glasgow and Lanarkshire to raise awareness of the plight of redundant workers, mainly in the textile industry. This, in turn, prompted leading officials like Lord Hamilton to coordinate these various agencies under the umbrella of the Glasgow Committee on Emigration so that maximum pressure could be put on the central authorities when petitioning for more government-assisted emigration schemes.[63]

In 1826–7 the imperial visionary R. J. Wilmot Horton, parliamentary under-secretary of state in the Colonial Office, presided over a select committee on emigration which certified his proposals for state-funded emigration to the colonies. The spectres of over-population and economic ruin once again confronted policy makers. This time, it was London's profound apprehension to stem the flood of impecunious Irish peasants into England and Scotland that lay behind parliamentary support for a new passenger act. Unless this deluge of economic refugees was redirected, an inundation which had been greatly facilitated by the growing cheapness of cross-channel fares, Irish paupers would swamp Great Britain.[64]

There was a "revolution" in government thinking and administration with regard to emigration policy. The deliberations over the series of passenger acts enacted between 1803 and 1872 were confirmation of this modernization when, for example, a corps of emigration officers was established in the 1830s.[65] Nevertheless, this was not the only "revolution" which was unfolding in the pre-Famine period. There was also the growth in philanthropy, with emigration being one of many tools used by middle-class Britons in their war against poverty, social decay, and declining public morals.

Combined with this evangelical zeal with which many philanthropists (and later trade unionists[66]) campaigned for greater state supervision in safeguarding and promoting overseas migration was a corresponding transformation in ship design, fare structures, and journey times. It was not until the 1860s that steam superseded sail on the Atlantic routes and that specialized passenger ships first made their appearance. But as Devine has argued, the steamship "did not so much as lower the costs of transatlantic travel as radically increase its speed, comfort and safety." On average it took two months to cross the Atlantic in the eighteenth and early nineteenth centuries. By the 1850s the crossing had been slashed to six weeks and had fallen to a week or less by 1914. In 1862, over 80 percent of transatlantic emigrants travelled by sail. While in 1863, this figure had plunged to 45 percent. By 1867 nine-tenths of the emigrant traffic to North America embarked on steamships. Despite the fact that fares on the steamships were between 30 and 50 percent higher, the journey was safer, faster, and moderately more comfortable, and as Devine noted, the shortened crossing times "removed one of the major costs of emigration, . . . during which there was no possibility of earning."[67]

One of the principal stimulants which helped channel greater numbers of migrants to British North America prior to 1850 was the increase in Atlantic trade. The ravenous demand for Canadian timber after 1815 combined with the continuous expansion of the cotton trade with the United States dramatically opened up facilities to British migrants which had not been accessible before. It was, as Maldwyn Jones observed, not just the case that there were more ships trading with North America between 1815 and 1850; or that the capacity of the sailing ships had doubled in the same period from 400 tons in 1820 to 800 tons by 1840, reaching 1,250 tons by the mid-1850s. It was the simple matter of spare capacity on the westward voyage. Cargo space could be converted to the use of passengers bound for North America. Shipping interests were quick to exploit this opportunity.[68]

During the 1820s, the emigrant trade became an organized branch of commerce, as shipping companies vied with each other for this increasingly lucrative traffic. This decade also saw the establishment of passenger brokers, an insalubrious collection of scoundrels, who established networks of agents throughout the major British ports to inveigle and convey emigrants overseas. Despite their dubious collective reputation, competition for clients kept fare prices down and buoyed up emigrant numbers.[69] This was matched by developments across the Atlantic where emigrants were attracted by land companies offering good terms and transportation to prospective settlers. Chartered in 1826, the Canada Company established a network of agents in the British Isles, the United States, and British North America which provided information about settlement opportunities in Upper Canada near Lake Huron. Two other companies, the British American Land Company, which promoted prospects in the Eastern Townships of Lower Canada, and the New Brunswick and Nova Scotia Land Company in New Brunswick, also enticed emigrants with promises of cheap, productive land. These commercial ventures, in association with increasingly confident and prosperous mercantile elites in British North America, were an integral part of an expanding network which was becoming indispensable in the field of imperial migration.[70]

For Maldwyn Jones the "private letter was beyond question the most trusted source of information about emigration and may well have been for that reason the most effective stimuli."[71] As well as emigrant letters, another catalyst was the printed word, which stimulated the growth of popular knowledge about specific destinations and the information flows which stemmed from them. Superior access to other forms of information was also vital and came in a wide variety of formats: travelogues, emigrant handbooks, colonization journals, illustrated magazines, periodicals, etchings, paintings, and of course, newspapers. Enhanced transport facilities in the Canadian colonies, including an improved postal system and an extension of banking services provided by the Bank of Montreal, facilitated a safe and sound way of transferring emigrant deposits and remittances, making "emigration less of an exile."[72]

Despite the problems historians face when trying to interpret the subtle nuances and hidden meanings within emigrant letters,[73] a common theme in many was the warning sent home to those thinking of emigrating that it was essential to possess realistic expectations about life on the frontier. In September 1832, Simeon Titmouse, a British farm labourer who had recently migrated to Dundas, Upper Canada with his wife and family, wrote to an acquaintance in Bassingbourn, Cambridgeshire:

> The country is discouraging at first, but the longer one is in it, the better one begins to like it. Any stout, hard labouring man, with a family, may do better in this country for them, than he can do at home. But remember, he will have to work pretty hard and long days.[74]

Another key factor which oiled the wheels of British migration was remittances or prepaid passages. MacDonagh has posited that the majority of nineteenth century Irish migration was financed this way. Increasing amounts of money travelled back across the Atlantic helping families to join their friends and relatives in North America. During 1849, British emigration officials reported that 75 percent of the Irish emigrants had received their fares in one form or another from across the Atlantic.[75]

Funds transferred this way were prodigious. In 1855 the Colonial Land and Emigration Commissioners recorded in their annual report that nearly £1.75 million had been remitted home from North America, although it was acknowledged that the actual sum was significantly greater.[76] In fact, the calculations of remittances sent to friends and relatives in the British Isles from family members in the United States and British North America between 1848 and 1880 was a staggering £23,510,669. Figures for Australia are more humble and less comprehensive, but between 1875 and 1880 a total of £265,183 was remitted.[77] These funds were not the monopoly of the Irish. The Cornish were exceptional practitioners too. For instance, in 1905 there were 7,000 Cornish miners on the gold fields in South Africa; and in that year alone an estimated £1 million was sent home.[78] Pioneering work on migrant remittances using money order systems operated by national and colonial postal networks indicates that between £200 and £270 million was despatched home over the period 1875 to 1913.[79] Even so, the transfer of such large sums of money and the increasing amount of information available to potential migrants would not have been possible without a revolution in communications itself. After 1865, with the development of the telegraph, transoceanic cables and wireless – the new "software of empire"[80] –

these pioneering delivery systems not only improved the speed, safety, and efficiency in transferring these monies; they also expanded old networks and information flows while simultaneously creating new ones which bound the British World closer.

In the 1830s the state renewed its efforts to deal effectively with the increasing problem of pauperism by passing the Poor Law Amendment Act in 1834. Famous for its insistence that the Poor Law should become more of a deterrent, the Act also recommended emigration as part of the new policy.[81] Section 62 of the New Poor Law allowed English parishes to elicit funds to pay for the emigration of destitute people to British colonies. This practice was adopted over wide areas of southern and eastern England, especially in East Anglia, Wiltshire, Sussex, and Kent. Between 1834 and 1860 approximately 27,000 people were given assistance to emigrate by their parish; on average just over 1,000 per year.[82] The numbers are infinitesimal when compared with the millions of unassisted migrants who left Britain in the nineteenth century. However, new research by British and Australian scholars has overturned the long-held contention that assisted migration was a cynical mechanism of "shovelling out paupers." For example, Gary Howells, whose pioneering work on parish-assisted migration from Norfolk, Northamptonshire, and Bedfordshire overturns the preconception that assisted emigration was nothing more than "a forced callous expulsion."[83] He argues that the "policy was neither haphazard nor accidental . . . nor was it a panicked response . . . The poor emigrants who were targeted were assisted because they were good labourers, not useless indigents incapable of providing for themselves."[84]

The charge that pauper emigrants who received poor law assistance were simply crafty manipulators of the new system and possessed a canny appreciation that their impoverishment could be exploited to put pressure on the authorities also needs serious re-evaluation.[85] Assisted emigrants were likely to be more "self-selecting" as well as more "adventurous and enterprising." Hence government policy was likely to assist the embarkation of the better class of emigrant. The process could be a positive one for both parties with constructive and progressive forces at work "facilitating the fulfilment of the poor's aspirations."[86]

Free and Un-Free Migration to the Southern British World

Political discontent in the Canadas during the mid-1830s, combined with a groundswell of negativity directed at pauper migration—which had peaked in 1836 and was predominantly Irish—made Canada less attractive to would-be British migrants. Open rebellion in 1837, compounded by a fragile Canadian economy, encouraged many more migrants to look elsewhere. Many looked to Australia where in the 1820s and 1830s a fundamental shift in migration policy and practices were unfolding. For thirty to forty years Botany Bay (1788), Port Philip Bay (1802), and Van Diemen's Land (1804), were nothing more than penal colonies perched on the far away margins of empire. The criminals, who came from all parts of the British Isles, were mainly convicted of larceny and were mostly first-time offenders: 70 percent of the Irish and 59 percent of the British.[87] Young single adults comprised the vast majority of convicts, with 75 percent of the males and 70 percent of the females aged between fifteen and twenty-nine years of age. Less than 1 percent were children aged between ten and fourteen; while only 3 percent of the convicts were fifty years of age or older. Between 1788 and 1853, when convict transportation was finally terminated to eastern Australia, 123,000 male and 25,000 female convicts had been landed. The Swan River colony (Western Australia), established in 1820, controversially initiated transportation only in 1850 when the practice was coming to an end on the eastern seaboard. Against stiff criticism, 9,668 hardened male convicts were shipped to penal facilities in Western Australia, until 1868, when the practice was ended once and for all.[88]

The final total of convicts varies from between 157,000 and 163,000. Over half were sentenced to seven years, one quarter were sentenced for life, while the remainder (until 1840) were sentenced to fourteen years. After 1840, the customary sentence was ten years, though the ticket of leave system might reduce the number of years served. (Even more startling is that between 5 and 10 percent actually managed to return to the United Kingdom.)[89] However, the character of transportation over these eighty years was as diverse as it was distinctive. During its initial stages prior to the French Revolutionary wars, the entire process was "simply a rather unorganized and slipshod method of relieving the overcrowded gaols." This carelessness is also reflected in the mortality rates, which were markedly high prior to 1814, averaging 11.3 per thousand. After Waterloo, the post-war increase in crime and the paranoia it generated amongst Britain's ruling elites, combined with the change in punishment which saw the move away from the death sentence initiated by the Home Secretary Sir Robert Peel in the late 1820s, saw annual averages of convicts climb dramatically as the system became more proficient. By 1815, 1,000 criminals were being sent annually to Australia. From 1816 to 1825, the yearly average reached 2,600, almost doubling to 4,900 by 1835 and peaking by 1840 at 5,000. After this, numbers declined to 4,000 per year between 1841 and 1845. Further reforms to the criminal justice system introduced by the Home Secretary, Sir George Grey, in the mid-1840s saw annual figures for transportees fall to 3,000 between 1846 and 1852.[90]

The geographic, occupational and ethnic profiles of the convicts make for interesting reading as well. Of the 4,077 men and 769 women conveyed to Australia between May 1787 and March 1792 a third of the English convicts and half of the 155 Irish felons were from London, Middlesex, and Dublin. In fact, most of the English convicts sent to Australia—who made up 60 percent of the global convict numbers—came from the cities, principally from London and its immediate environs. In 1819 one third of those transported came from London, which by 1840 had dropped to 20 percent. With industrialization and the growing political protest it generated, more convicts came from the mill towns and industrial conurbations of Lancashire, which apart from the capital, provided the largest number of transported English criminals to Australia. A disproportionate number were juveniles; and female convicts, although highly prized for their sexual currency, were an eagerly sought after commodity in an expanding colonial labour market that was crying out for experienced workers. This has prompted several scholars to argue that the economic value of female convicts has been woefully underestimated by historians.[91]

Between 1787 and 1868, nearly 30,000 men and 9,000 women were transported directly to Australia from Ireland. Another 6,000 Irishmen who had crossed over to find work in Great Britain fell into criminality and were transported as well. In all, about 34 percent of all convicts sent to Australia were Irish. Although Dublin accounted for about one fifth of all transported felons, it was the Irish peasant who made up almost two thirds of Irish convicts, especially after 1830. There were fewer juveniles and on average the Irish component was several years older than their British counterparts. Many more were married as well. Women made up one-quarter of all Irish transportees, which was double the proportion of Britain's female convicts.[92] There were regional variations too. Of those convicts despatched to New South Wales between 1788 and 1815, 21 percent were Irish.[93] By the 1840s, Belfast—which had long surpassed Cork as a centre for larceny—was beginning to rival Dublin; thus increasing the number of Irish offenders being transported from here. During the last phase of transportation to eastern Australia (1846–53), one which overlapped with the Great Famine and the repeal of the Corn Laws, proportionally more Irish than English convicts were sent. Yet doubts remain as to their criminality; Irish magistrates were using transportation as a social instrument to ease the impact of the famine on the growing number of deserving poor, keen to escape their plight.

This cannot be said of their counterparts from Scotland, who made up 5 percent of the final total. Marjory Harper argues that Scottish judges were more reluctant to impose transportation for sentences they deemed menial. Their restraint is indicated in the figures: more than 8,000 Scottish convicts were sent to Australia, a third of these after 1840. This last influx of convicts from Scotland was endowed with the same basic educational and work skills as assisted migrants were taking to the Antipodes. In fact, they seem to have been better educated than their allegedly more delinquent English and Irish cousins; yet, by the late 1840s, free labour outnumbered convicts and ex-convicts in the labour market.

The arrival of the first shipload of free settlers occurred in February 1793, but numbers remained small for decades. For instance, in 1828 there were only 4,600 free immigrants in New South Wales out of a total white population of 36,600.[94] By 1830, the non-aboriginal population in Australia was 70,000: 90 percent had either been transported or were the progeny of convicts. Ten years later, even after the first great waves of free migrants both assisted and unassisted had arrived, convicts and ex-convicts still comprised 71 percent of the white labour force. In contrast, by the end of the nineteenth century free immigrants—approximately 1.6 million— outnumbered convicts by ten to one. Of the 1.6 million free immigrants, 750,000 received state assistance.[95]

If convict transportation was the first wave of (un-free) British migration to Australia, in 1831 the convergence of a number of political, economic and social forces occurred which unleashed the second wave of (free) migration.[96] Convict labour was far from adequate to keep pace with the expansion of the pastoral economy with its emphasis on wool production and export. Unlike Canada and South Africa, the tyranny of distance dictated that Australia was deemed unsuitable for expensive trials involving British paupers. Yet some commentators believed that Australia could benefit from government-sponsored experiments in assisted migration that targeted other social groupings.

The failure of Wilmot Horton during the 1820s to persuade his political masters that large-scale government-assisted migration would cure Britain's social maladies was rescued by another enthusiast, Edward Gibbon Wakefield. His objective, writes Eric Richards, was the

> replication of English conditions in new systematic colonies that would meet the aspirations of respectable capitalists and working migrants alike. In practical terms it created a new mechanism that employed colonial land revenues to finance emigration to the antipodes . . . It combined the interests of the colony, the paupers, and the British taxpayer.[97]

Renewed disorder in the English countryside, predominantly in the south-east, prompted the imperial authorities to act. By 1831, as London began to mobilize its resources, several colonial governments in Australia began drafting their own state-aided migration schemes. Ironically, the first batches of free migrants who arrived between 1831 and 1836 included high percentages of poor English and Irish emigrants who had either received parish assistance or were funded through Australian land revenues.[98]

One of the most sought after groups of free immigrants were single women. The sexual imbalance between men and women had been a salient feature of convict society. This disparity needed urgent attention, for women were perceived to play a central feminizing role in civilizing the frontier, and instilling dignity and respectability into colonial life. Therefore, between 1832 and 1836 more than 3,000 single British women from diverse working and lower-middle class backgrounds were given free grants-in-aid of £8 to settle in Australia.[99] This unique but short-lived experiment floundered on objections levelled that female emigration was an exploitative practice tantamount to white slavery; a similar charge which had been directed at philanthropic agencies working with child migrants in South Africa.[100] The emphasis in mid-1830s Australia, as elsewhere, now shifted to assisting family groups.

Imperial patronage was indeed crucial in the early stages of free migration to Australia, and later New Zealand. So too was the role played by the colonial governments which brokered and subsidized these deals between London and the multifarious colonization companies established to sponsor migration and settlement between 1831 and 1850. These promotional strategies took several forms. Cheap land grants were authorized by colonial governments to colonization consortiums for resale to private investors. The capital raised by the companies was then used to subsidize emigrant passage and outfitting. For example, in the mid-1820s passage fares to Australia averaged more than £30 per head, with some of the cheaper fares eventually falling to between £18 and £20 by the mid-1830s. This stood in stark contrast to North Atlantic fares which averaged at £5 per head and which facilitated migration that was largely self-financed. British North America's advantageous geographical proximity, combined with its rapidly expanding economic integration with the British Isles, meant that without colonial government intervention fares to the Antipodes would remain prohibitive.[101] Another direct form of state inducement was a strict system of bounty regulations whereby specific age and gender groups, family units, and occupational categories were prioritized. The bounty system (1835–41), in conjunction with the government system (1837–40), allowed bounty agents, who worked on behalf of private shippers, to receive payments according to a rigid set of selection criteria, which targeted those occupations of which Australia was in desperate need: agricultural labourers, shepherds, farm servants, carpenters, wheelwrights, bricklayers, blacksmiths, and female domestics.[102]

This government-engineered bias in immigration flows aided by the generous greasing of the migration machinery with public funds was essential to offset the oppression of distance and expense prospective migrants would otherwise encounter when embarking for Australasia. This was doubly important, for in 1840 convict transportation to New South Wales was terminated. The scale of state subsidy was huge. In mid-1841 the Colonial Office learned that 74,315 bounty permits were still outstanding for New South Wales alone. Valued at £980,000, which was more than the total land revenue for the period 1837–40, London had to rein in the spendthrift New South Wales government by stopping all bounty payments after November 1841. Despite the financial retrenchment, the achievements of the New South Wales government that year had been astounding: more than 20,000 assisted migrants had landed on its shores compared with only 2,380 unassisted migrants.[103]

Private enterprise played a central role in peopling Australasia, perhaps more so than any other British territory, including Canada. Businessmen—spurred on by opportunities offered by state intervention—established colonization companies, mobilized and selected emigrants, transported them and their chattels to the colonies in their ships, and "decisively determined the conditions, pace, and quantity of their exodus to Australasia."[104] Here was a complex field of interchange where government and private business intermingled; where entrepreneurs could both implement and influence government policy at a variety of levels. Between 1836 and 1840, the South Australian Company introduced 12,206 migrants to the only colony not to be tainted by convictism. In newly acquired New Zealand, 12,017 British migrants were landed by the New Zealand and Plymouth Company between 1841 and 1850. In New South Wales between 1838 and 1842 private companies landed 37,999 bounty migrants or 65.6 percent of all arrivals to the colony.[105]

Demands for greater state control in the mid-1830s led to several significant developments which further facilitated migration to the Australian colonies. The first of these, in 1836, was the creation of an Agent-General for Emigration, with the appointment of the energetic and highly efficient T. F. Elliot. As "emigration was becoming an important part of the ordinary business of Government," it had to accept responsibility for assisted migration and thus develop the infrastructure whereby it could exercise that control.[106] In September 1840 the Colonial Land and Emigration Commission (CLEC) superseded the office of Agent-General. It acted as the main clearing house for migration activities, mainly to Australia, where it supervised shipping arrangements for emigrants and guided colonial funds to where they were most needed. Between 1840 and 1872 when the CLEC was terminated, over 340,000 people received assistance to relocate, mostly to Australia (but some to South Africa after 1844, as well as a handful to New Zealand and the Falkland Islands) at a cost of £4,860,000.[107] By 1878, once the total number of those who had finally accepted or had received their free or assisted passage had been factored in, the final figures reached 352,215 individuals or 27 percent of empire-bound migrants for the period 1840–1878.[108]

The 1840s signalled the beginning of several interesting shifts in British migration patterns to Australia. After sustained growth in the 1830s, which peaked in 1840–1, throughout the remainder of the decade the number of British migrants landing in New South Wales, for instance, was haphazard. This, in part, can be explained by the onset of a deep recession which plagued the colonial economy between 1842 and 1848 and had an immediate impact on labour requirements. The geographical origins of the immigrants were also changing. Whereas in the late 1830s the number of assisted Scots made up between 25 and 40 percent of New South Wales immigrant intake, the average between 1842 and 1850 oscillated wildly between 0 and 19 percent. The number of unassisted Scots who landed between 1832 and 1850 was approximately 7,000, nearly a quarter of the entire figure.[109]

The English and Welsh response to bounty passage was equally lacklustre. The 1841 emigration returns for New South Wales clearly demonstrate that only 22 percent responded to these financial enticements. In contrast, two thirds of the assisted immigrants in the 1841 returns for New South Wales were born in Ireland. Once almost entirely dominated by Protestants from Ulster, the influx of Irish from the late 1830s to the 1860s was now dominated by Catholic peasants from the south and west.[110] Pre-Famine statistics reveal another set of trends, showing a highly mobile population well before the cataclysmic events of 1845–52. With a bit of indulgent tinkering, one set of data indicates that 1.5 million Irish had left the Emerald Isle between 1815 and 1845; this included 30,000 migrants who obtained state assistance to make the long journey to Australia. Significantly, Irish emigration to the Antipodes was unique in that it was largely subsidized by metropolitan, colonial, and private agencies where during and immediately after the famine more than 80 percent of the Irish migrants received state assistance in a number of forms until the 1890s.[111]

While between 1 and 1.5 million people died of poverty- and hunger-related diseases during the Great Famine, emigration was, according to David Fitzpatrick, an even more significant "agent of depopulation than famine-related mortality." The havoc unleashed by want and sickness forced many to flee between 1846 and 1851, the year which saw famine-driven emigration peak in Ireland. Even during the 1850s and 1860s when prosperity returned, Irish migration remained intensive. Depending upon how the figures are calculated, it has been estimated that between 2.1 and 2.6 million departed Ireland; most never to return. A third of these were young people, most of whom travelled in family units or were sponsored by family members already established overseas. The topmost destinations for settlement were habitually the United States, followed by Britain, Canada, and Australia (where 300,000 arrived there between 1840 and 1914),[112] with a smattering in South Africa and New Zealand. In all, 5 million people left Ireland during the first seven decades of the nineteenth century; but it must be emphasized that the United States did not become the majority destination until the 1860s.[113]

The importance of the famine as an engine driving outbound migration from Ireland must not be overstated. For many families the famine was perhaps the last in a series of calamities which reduced them to acute poverty; or was the stimulus for them to escape grinding impoverishment.[114] For many others who had left before the famine, the fear of becoming destitute was a driving factor. As we have seen, pre-famine emigration, especially after 1825, was considerable; particularly the propensity of the rural Irish Catholic peasant to venture abroad, which by the late 1830s was growing at a phenomenal rate. This suggests that when news that colonies like New South Wales offered generous financial support, the scope and connectedness of information flows amongst Irish migrants became increasingly sophisticated. This same heightened receptivity applies to Poor Law relief, as many Irish migrants increasingly sought opportunities through local parishes when they invoked the various forms of migration assistance in the 1840s and 1850s.[115] It also indicates that shipping agents and their recruiters were tapping into a migrant flow that was not only in transition but, as with Catholic Ireland, it now reflected a greater propensity within that section of the community to emigrate overseas.[116] Ireland, therefore, had a number of crucial preconditions already in place before the catastrophe of 1845–52, which were *accelerated not stimulated* by the famine.

Colonial finances dictated the pace of assisted migration to Australia, which in the 1840s was suspended from time to time. The 1840s also witnessed the involvement of a number of philanthropic societies which targeted specific categories of migrants. Two schemes advanced by Mrs Caroline Chisholm were perhaps the most important of the period. The first programme was to reunite children of married couples left behind in the United Kingdom with their parents who had emigrated. Assistance and support for this project was provided by the Family Colonisation Loan Society, established by Chisholm in 1849. The second was the protection and support of young single women emigrants both in transit and when they arrived in Australia. Her lasting contribution, which became the model for future emigration societies, was the establishment of a system of matrons on board government emigrant ships. Their key function was to train, chaperon, and "protect" these young women especially from predatory members of the crew and other male passengers during the voyage to the Antipodes. Another practice adopted by Chisholm was to segregate her female charges from the rest of the ship's company and passengers. These practices were embraced by the British Ladies Female Emigrants' Society (BLFES), also known as the Matrons' Society, established in 1849, which over the next forty years assisted hundreds of single female immigrants to Britain's colonies.[117]

The issue of single female migration to colonial Australia intersects a number of key issues. In the 1850s, many schemes which introduced single women to Australia were initiated by British philanthropists and British government authorities for the express purpose of relieving poverty in Britain. Solving Britain's social woes was uppermost; colonial concerns were of secondary importance. Other schemes were initiated and financed by the colonial governments themselves, sometimes with the help of British or colonial-based emigration societies. The desire to redress the imbalance between the sexes was a primary factor. There was a perception in Britain that there were several hundreds of thousands of "surplus" but impoverished women, who with a little help could flee their destitution and become productive members of society in Australia where men outnumbered women. It was not just their reproductive capacity that was being exported; their domesticity would tame Australia's bachelorhood (and frontier) while their work skills would contribute not only to the development of a stable and harmonious family life but the women would also add to the local economy. Emigration offered a simple solution to the hard up "redundant" female.[118]

Poverty was the dictating prerequisite for entry into those schemes initiated in Britain in the 1850s. Indeed, British philanthropists like Sidney Herbert "increasingly looked to emigration as a means of relieving poverty *before* women were forced into the workhouse or onto the streets."[119] However, a more controversial project was the Irish orphan scheme where 4,000 girls between the ages of 14 and 18 were despatched to Australia from Irish workhouses in 1848 and 1849. In 1850 Herbert sought to assist the most destitute of all British workers, the needlewomen. Over the next three years 1,300 mostly working class women had some or all of their fares and seaboard outfit subsidized through Herbert's charitable funds. In Scotland, the Highland and Island Emigration Society, although not specifically a female emigration agency, had secured support and funds from the CLEC because of its ability to attract young single women to its schemes. Nearly one quarter of the 5,000 emigrants who sailed under the Society's auspices between 1852 and 1857 were young single working women.[120]

Morality and character were fundamental to the selection process whether it be through a philanthropic agency like the BLFES or Australian colonial authorities. Many working class women saw domestic service overseas as a vehicle for social improvement. There was a price to pay once this charity had been accepted: they were expected to be obedient, deferential, and grateful. Shaped by the middle class values and social expectations of their donors, the selection process imposed strict controls over the behavior of these female immigrants. Many candidates rejected the stereotype of assisted female immigrants as needy, intractable, and degenerate.[121]

By the end of the 1850s a backlash against pauper migration, particularly from Ireland, was building throughout Australia with demands from settlers that the colonial governments take a more direct role in organizing these schemes, especially for single women whose domestic skills were found wanting. The CLEC had been severely criticized for importing too many disadvantaged and untrained workers, especially single Irish women. New South Wales, Victoria, and South Australia took control of their own immigration funds and the selection process. If anything, the proprietary desire to control the women throughout all stages of the emigration process became even stronger than it had been with British philanthropic societies. Perhaps as a result it was through state-assisted schemes, like the one operated by the Tasmanian government between 1856 and 1863,[122] that the majority of these women, mainly Irish, were introduced to Australia; an estimated 90,000 by 1900.[123]

The discovery of gold in Victoria in 1851 and Otago on the South Island of New Zealand in 1861 attracted a third wave of immigration which lasted until 1870. These Antipodean gold rushes coincided with surging economic growth and accelerated processes which were already well under way.[124] As a result, between

1852 and 1866 the number of British migrants travelling to Australasia continually outstripped those landing in British North America. Between 1853 and 1860, for instance, 28.1 percent of British emigrants went to Australasia as opposed to only 9.1 percent to British North America. For the decade 1861–70 the differential had narrowed but the Antipodes still supplanted Canada as the premier destination. The continued allure of gold, combined with the reintroduction of selected and assisted emigration schemes in Australia and New Zealand meant that 17.2 percent of all British migrants were making for the Antipodes while only 8.3 percent made their way to Canada. The American Civil War (1861–65) undoubtedly had a negative impact on emigration to British North America.

Although the gap between the two closed in succeeding years, Australasia with its continued emphasis on state assistance maintained its dominance over British North America well into the next two census periods of 1871–80 and 1881–90: 17.8 and 14.5 percent as opposed to 10.7 and 11.7 percent respectively.[125] Canada's geographical advantage had been temporarily nullified, and was further reduced by the opening of the Suez Canal in 1869 and the comprehensive replacement of sail by steam in the passenger trade to the southern oceans by the 1880s; reducing dramatically the sailing time between Britain, India, and her Pacific possessions. This combination of mineral discoveries, assertive state aid, and technological advances allowed Britain and her Australasian colonies to draw closer together. Even more impressive statistically, during the 1850s and early 1860s the total number of British emigrants departing for Australasia achieved almost half the number who arrived in the United States, which continued to be the preferred destination for two thirds of British migrants until the end of the nineteenth century.[126]

The Victorian gold rush attracted 290,000 immigrants from the British Isles between 1852 and 1860, which was over half the total number of people who landed in Australia and New Zealand during those years. Just over one third, approximately 101,000, were Irish. Clearly, the gold rushes of 1851–60 made Irish Australia; by the end of the century the Irish comprised one quarter of the continent's European population.[127] Although assisted migration played an important role in attracting British migrants during the 1850s, only one fifth of all British migrants received state aid: almost four fifths paid their own passage possessing independent means that allowed them to move freely between gold strikes in the various Australian colonies and across the Tasman Sea to New Zealand.[128] This highly mobile population was not simply made up of working class people, such as miners from Derbyshire, Cornwall, Wales, and Somerset. The 1850s saw a larger, better educated, more prosperous middle class element taking passage overseas. Initially attracted by striking it big on the gold fields, many of these middle class migrants were drawn from a range of professional occupations which provided essential skills and services in support of the gold mining economy and the expanding communities it maintained.[129]

By the 1850s more British workers regarded emigration as a positive choice and many were in a position to finance their own passage. As William Van Vugt argues, rather than fleeing the spectres of poverty and unemployment, an increasing number of ambitious and increasingly urban-based British migrants saw emigration as a way of elevating their personal circumstances and prosperity. If unsuccessful in these ventures, they could easily return home; and many did, reflecting a greater itinerancy amongst British migrants, a phenomenon that would increase as the nineteenth century progressed.[130] The same could be said of their rural counterparts.[131]

With a few twists, the story of New Zealand shadows closely that of migration to and settlement in Australia. Between 1840 and 1880 the foundation of the Britain of the South was laid. Like Australia, Wakefieldian theories of colonization were instrumental during the 1830s and 1840s, where the New Zealand Company and several rival associates attempted to introduce a "better stock" of settler. New Zealand did not want to be tainted, as was colonial Australia, as a nation founded by convicts. This cultural construct was based on a falsehood. Many of the European pioneers who arrived in New Zealand prior to the 1840s were in fact convicts; and many more would arrive as emancipists or recycled convicts in the 1850s and 1860s when the trans-Tasman economy began to flourish and become more fully integrated. Australia remained second only to the United Kingdom as a source of migrants between 1850 and 1914. What's more, most British migrants arrived in New Zealand via Australia, with an unspecified number spending a brief sojourn in Australia before finally embarking for "New Eden." In fact, prior to 1850 approximately half of the European or Pakeha population arrived from Australia which gave many of the new settlements like Auckland a distinctly Australian flavour for decades to come. Another dimension of the foundation myth was the overinflated importance played by the land companies in establishing the first settlements. True, they played a key role, especially in propagandizing the benefits of life in this Pacific Eden by marketing new colonizing opportunities, creating new information flows, and establishing the first settlement communities which anchored future chain migration; but the remarkable fact is that only 15,600 or 4 percent of the founding population was enticed and shepherded by these companies.[132]

Credit must go to the provincial governments of the 1850s and 1860s, who were quite enterprising in attracting settlers to their domains. Also significant was the role played by the British Army, which between 1840 and 1870 encouraged hundreds of imperial regulars to take their discharges in New Zealand. The 58th regiment alone supplied 1,100 men before returning home in 1858. Military colonization also involved the settlement of retired military officers, primarily on the North Island, who were pensioned off in the 1850s and 1860s and given land grants or scrip for services rendered. In reality, loyalty to "Queen and Country" had very little to do with these awards: frontier security remained an urgent issue in the 1850s and 1860s as the Maori were a constant source of trouble to the settlers at the time.[133]

The real visionary, however, was the colonial politician Sir Julius Vogel, a London-born Jew who in the 1870s established a very successful and far-reaching state-sponsored immigration programme.[134] The 120,000 assisted passages approved by the New Zealand authorities between 1863 and 1880 testify to the pivotal role played by government; a crucial element of which was the appointment of an agent-general in London to represent New Zealand interests—the cornerstone of which was to promote and oversee this ambitious strategy. In August 1871, Sir Isaac Featherston, the veteran politician from Wellington, took up the post, in the initial stages of which he had access to a war chest containing £1 million.[135] In addition, the establishment of the nominee system, which allowed new arrivals to recommend family members for an outward bound passage from Britain, was equally critical in maintaining the supply of British stock in a highly competitive emigration field. Between a fifth and a quarter of the assisted immigrants arriving in New Zealand benefited from this system.[136]

As in 1850s Victoria, the gold strikes on the west coast of New Zealand in the 1860s lured more Europeans. In 1861 alone, Otago received 13,000 immigrants—mostly miners from the Victorian gold fields. By the end of the decade, 195,000 fortune hunters had travelled to New Zealand in the wake of the gold rushes, two thirds from Australia and the remainder from the United Kingdom.[137] The contribution of migration to population growth in the 1860s was exceptional: it accounted for approximately 70 percent of the total growth and over 50 percent the following decade.[138] Many moved on after the gold played out but a net gain of 114,000 was added to New Zealand's European population simply through these mineral discoveries. Between 1861 and 1890 nearly 300,000 new Britons made New Zealand their home.[139] A salient feature concerning the settlement and development in both the Australian colonies and New Zealand provinces was the trans-Tasman dimension, where the migration flows that emerged established their own rhythm creating distinctive linkages, networks and patterns of growth unique to the region.[140]

So who were these Britons eager to make a new paradise for themselves and their families in one of the furthest corners of the British Empire? Like Australia, the preference in New Zealand was for English, Scots, Welsh, and Ulster Protestants. Influenced by what was occurring in Australia, colonial authorities throughout New Zealand were fervently opposed to Irish Catholic migration. As a result, New Zealand attracted more Scots than Irish, with most of the latter arriving in the post-famine period.[141] In the 1850s the share of the English and Welsh population peaked at 62 percent of the overall European total, but it was never more than half for the rest of the century, despite the fact that the English would constitute the largest ethnic minority after overtaking the Maori in the 1860s. The Scots were over-represented in New Zealand's white population, where they comprised 24 percent of the total (as opposed to 10 percent in the United Kingdom), in which Lowlanders made up four-fifths of all Scots making for New Zealand.[142] This is hardly surprising for in the 1870s the New Zealand government inaugurated an extensive and highly successful system of immigration agents throughout Scotland. The 73 agents advertising in 288 Scottish newspapers blanketed the country with promises of paradise and offers of state assistance to settle there.[143] Not surprisingly, as James Belich has remarked, the "Scots were to New Zealand what the Irish were to Australia—the chief lieutenants of settlement." The largest concentrations were located around Otago and its hinterland on the South Island; and in some years as many as one third of all Scots emigrants came to New Zealand.[144]

As for the Irish, Ulster Protestants were the preferred stock but they never dominated the total Irish aggregate. Roughly speaking, 18 percent of New Zealand's European population was Irish, with one quarter of these being Protestant. This has prompted one historian, when comparing the patterns of nineteenth-century Irish migration flows to Australia, Canada, and New Zealand, to comment that the flow to

New Zealand, with its bias towards north-east Ulster, was a hybrid of the Australian and Canadian movements. From the early 1850s the northern Irish province reliably bestowed over 40 percent of the annual Irish intake to New Zealand, averaging over 50 percent after 1890, and numbering 50,000 individuals between 1840 and 1939.[145] However, it is abundantly clear that Irish Catholics dominated the overall figures whatever the bias towards Ulster Protestants and the bluster of colonial officials that Irish Catholics were not welcome. The fact remained that Irish Catholics, especially from Ulster, were exploiting emigration schemes and government-aid programmes that were intended for their Protestant neighbours. This not only demonstrates a striking similarity with trends that were unfolding in Australia: that Irish Catholics were more willing to emigrate than other ethnic groups from the British Isles. It also reveals that when it came to specific categories, such as single Irish women, the bureaucracy would cast aside its rhetoric and religious prejudices if it meant closing the sex ratio in the colony, which at mid-century stood at six women for every ten men.[146] In this instance, the practicalities of ensuring a viable colonial society invariably triumphed over the public posturing of a few bigoted politicians.

Women, Children, and Philanthropy, 1860–1914

As we have seen, single female emigration became a vigorous field for social reformers, evangelicals and philanthropists, particularly from the late 1840s. However, it was in the 1860s, with the establishment of the Female Middle Class Emigration Society (FMCES) under the auspices of the energetic but controversial Maria Rye (1829–1903), that the promotion of single female women took an interesting turn. Founded in 1862, the FMCES grew out of the early feminist movement of the 1850s, which campaigned strenuously for reform of married women's property rights. Rye was extremely well connected with leading figures in British and colonial society; philanthropically like-minded individuals, who opened many doors to her work. Her eagerness to tour the colonies was also a key to her influence. Between 1862 and 1886, when the FMCES was in existence, a total of 302 women were helped by the society. Most of the candidates went to Australia, followed by New Zealand and South Africa; only a handful went to Canada and the United States.[147]

By the 1880s new societies with an imperial hue eager to tap into a broader base were beginning to muscle in on the emigration field. From 1880 and after a series of societal mergers, the British Women's Emigration Association (BWEA), as it became known, dominated women's emigration for thirty-five years. This association and its offshoots—the South African Colonisation Society (1902) and the Colonial Intelligence League (1910)—was significant for several reasons. Firstly, it continued to follow and improve upon the fundamental principles of maintaining careful selection procedures, onboard chaperoning, and secure reception for female emigrants upon their arrival at a host of imperial destinations. Secondly, it made important contributions in the field of imperial education. Its journal, *The Imperial Colonist*, founded in 1902, was crucial in transmitting work produced by women for women. As well as promoting female emigration and celebrating the achievements of female imperialists, it was a highly valuable educational tool that informed and linked Britain with the wider British World.[148] Finally, perhaps the highest tribute it received and which put it head and shoulders above other sister organizations such as the Girls' Friendly Society (1874), the Primrose League (1883), and the Victoria League (1901), was official recognition from government. Its co-option by the arch-imperialists Joseph Chamberlain and Sir Alfred Milner in the British government's ill-fated reconstruction strategies in South Africa after 1902 were proof of the association's stature as one of the leading women's imperialist agencies.[149]

Similar strands of the same imperial philosophy were embedded in Victorian child migration strategies. Ever since the 1830s, middle class philanthropists, driven by their humanitarian impulses, had been worried about the growth of juvenile delinquency in Britain's sprawling urban centres and desired to salvage these wayward children and transform them into responsible citizens. Emigration to the open spaces and wholesome climates of the settlement colonies was central to this stratagem. As a result of growing criticism, the experiments of the 1830s were abandoned by 1840. However, the late 1860s witnessed a resurgence in these moral dynamics where those engaged in child philanthropy and emigration "acting with Victorian self-assurance . . . took sweeping actions which eventually became excesses."[150] Women, like the outspoken Rye, played a central role in promoting child emigration—or what Joy Parr has described as "philanthropic abduction." The crucial role played by Rye, Annie MacPherson, and her sister, Louisa Birt, among others, in promoting child migration, primarily to Canada, has been well documented.[151] What is essential is to situate these women in the wider context, national as well as imperial: "to regard them not as isolated figures, but as significant representatives of the growing number of women involved in public work of different kinds from the 1850s onwards."[152]

These schemes became highly politicized as supporters on both sides of the Atlantic engaged in heated debates with their critics about the pros and cons of child migration. Canadians, for instance, fearful that Britain was once again dumping its paupers, misfits, and delinquents on its shores, challenged the imperial authorities to provide evermore rigorous guidelines to the voluntary agencies which were doing the lion's share of the selection and screening in Britain. Imperial authorities, frustrated by a strident colonial nationalism, were equally critical of their counterparts overseas, who they charged were being overly selective when choosing child migrants, the future "bricks of Empire building."[153] The final number of children who were assisted overseas prior to the Great War is as yet unavailable. Canada, however, received the largest proportion: between 1868 and 1916 British charities and philanthropic groups helped 73,524. By 1928 this figure had reached 87,699.[154]

The fact remains that despite the increasing role played by philanthropic agencies in assisting emigration to imperial destinations, Whitehall remained remarkably uninterested in promoting or interfering with migration. When the CLEC was phased out in 1873, the administration of the passenger acts was transferred to the Board of Trade. The remaining functions of the Emigration Board were handed back to the Colonial Office. The onset of a severe economic depression in the mid-1870s, especially in the agricultural sector, led to increased agitation by industrial and agricultural trades unions for greater government direction, management, and above all, funding of the emigration process. Despite the growing hardship in many households throughout the land, London refused to override the dominant economic doctrine of the day—laissez faire. Central government's doggedness not to interfere in the migration process annoyed many philanthropists. In spite of the growing pressure from the National Association for Promoting State-directed Emigration and Colonization, founded in 1883, London's only concession to this lobby group was the establishment in 1886 of the Emigrants' Information Office. Although it did sterling work in publishing information handbooks and providing advice to would-be emigrants about conditions and opportunities overseas, it was a far cry from the National Association's demands for a state-aided empire migration strategy.[155]

Within Britain central government remained aloof right up to 1914, despite renewed calls by the Royal Colonial Institute in 1910 for government—in the name of imperial unity—to redirect British emigrants to destinations within rather than outside the empire. It was a different story at the parish and municipal level where local government, working with private charities and other philanthropic agencies, took the initiative to select and assist deserving candidates to migrate. For example, city councils in Bristol and Birmingham worked closely with Poor Law Guardians and used emigration as part of a larger strategy to help improve the plight of their deserving poor. The numbers involved were small but the fact remains that local government was willing to invest rate payers' funds in emigration initiatives. In the main, however, most British migrants were already making the decision to self-finance their relocation overseas, thus alleviating the government of any responsibility in the matter.

The Last Wave Before the Great War, 1880–1914

Only 28.2 percent of the emigrants leaving the British Isles between 1891 and 1900 went to destinations within the Empire; a drop of 1.1 percent from the previous decade. Between 1901 and 1910 the number reached a respectable 47.9 percent of the total, peaking at 65.1 percent between 1911 and 1913.[156] Bearing in mind the imprecise nature of migration statistics due to the vagaries of British officialdom's methods of calculation prior to 1912, the overall indicators are still impressive. In the 1880s, approximately 1,640,000 left the United Kingdom. For the decade 1900–09 an estimated 1,670,198 migrants left Britain. In 1913 alone, the astounding number of 389,394 British migrants headed overseas, with a massive 73 percent making for destinations within the British Empire and mainly to the "white" dominions.[157]

These global figures, however, belie changes to specific migrant flows and regional variations that impacted on particular colonies during this period. In 1880 the New Zealand government called for an immediate halt to free and assisted passage as it could not take in any more subsidized workers from overseas. The termination of state assistance was dramatic and was reflected in the total number of immigrants who landed in New Zealand in 1881, which fell sharply to 9,688. Even so, almost 150,000 immigrants arrived in New Zealand between 1881 and 1890, although almost as many left as stayed during the so-called 'Exodus' of the late 1880s and early

1890s. In 1888, for example, when the colony was in the strangling grip of economic depression, outflow exceeded intake.[158] Australia experienced similar economic hardships in the 1890s. Compounded by a banking crisis (1902–04) and some of the worst drought conditions at the turn of the twentieth century, these factors were a deterrence on migrant flows, which trickled in from Britain for years to come. For example, in 1889 the number of Britons entering Australia was just under 30,000; by 1893 they barely touched 7,900. In 1900 numbers had risen slowly to 10,000, but in the early years of the new century more people left Australia than entered.[159] This was a far cry from the hiatus of the 1850s.

Canada, too, had experienced these downward pressures in the latter decades of the nineteenth century. However, this trend was to change dramatically between 1896 and 1914. More than 3 million people migrated to Canada at this time; more than twice that registered in the preceding thirty years. Economic recovery was slow as reflected in the 1896 immigration statistics when only 17,000 immigrants of all nationalities arrived in the dominion that year. In 1900, fewer than 1,200 British migrants landed in Canada. Five years later the British contingent had rocketed to 65,000, surpassing the number of American arrivals. On the eve of war in 1914 overall numbers had risen to just over 400,000, of which 190,000 were from the United Kingdom. Even more illustrative, the senior dominion experienced six of the ten largest annual immigration levels ever recorded, over 200,000 each time between 1903 and 1913.[160] As for the mother country, well over one million British immigrants settled in Canada between 1900 and 1914, comprising the largest immigration flows of any ethnic group, at an annual average of 38 percent.

What was the key to Canada's overwhelming success in attracting more British migrants in the build-up to the Great War? If the nineteenth century had witnessed the fulfilment of America's manifest destiny, then the twentieth century belonged to Canada. This was certainly the vision of Sir Wilfrid Laurier, the Liberal prime minister between 1896 and 1911; and it was a message repeatedly echoed by government immigration pamphlets prior to 1914. The Laurier years had coincided with the beginning of one of the most spectacular periods of sustained global economic growth ever seen. Coupled with favourable domestic circumstances, this increasingly self-confident nation began to reap tremendous commercial advantages, which, in turn, accelerated its national development and allowed for the fulfilment of those promises echoed by the fathers of Confederation thirty years previously.[161]

Economic circumstances aside, one of the key factors behind the unprecedented flow of migrants to Canada prior to 1914 were the appointments of the energetic Clifford Sifton, as Minister of the Interior between 1896 and 1905, and his staunch political rival from Alberta, Frank Oliver, who succeeded Sifton as minister until 1911. Both men were committed to populating western Canada and settling "the last, best West" through a vigorous programme of almost unimpeded importation of British and European agriculturists. The reforms initiated by Sifton, and largely followed by Oliver, combined with aggressive marketing techniques, revolutionized Canadian immigration policy.

This impressive increase in immigration was accompanied by an equally spectacular shift in its ethnic composition. When Canada became a dominion in

1867, 60 percent of the population was of British descent, compared with 30 percent of French origin and roughly 7 percent of other European stock. Unsurprisingly, throughout the nineteenth century, the British Isles remained the primary source of Canada's immigrants: between 1867 and 1890, 60 percent of Canada's migrant intake originated from there. By 1911, despite the huge increases in the numbers emigrating from the United Kingdom, the British element of Canada's ethnic apportionment had dropped to 55 percent, with that of the other European constituents rising to approximately 9 percent.[162] Although British immigrants still topped the ethnic graph and accounted for 38 percent of the total intake by 1914, this downward trend began to alarm sections of Anglo-Canada's political and intellectual elites concerned about the threats racial dilution posed to the social fabric of the country.

The massive influx of immigrants into Canada whose origins were not Anglo-Saxon alarmed many Canadians who feared that, if left unchecked, it could lead to the balkanization of the young dominion.[163] Criticism of Ottawa's "open door" policy grew and xenophobic demands for a more exclusionist immigration policy were raised from a variety of quarters such as trades unions, eugenicists, and the Canadian medical profession. Indeed, prior to 1920, Canada's doctors were at the forefront of this growing discomfort over immigration, and championed stricter selection criteria based on ethnicity and race where the "widening of medical grounds for exclusion became their weapon."[164] Stirred by the growth of eugenics, and fears over racial degeneration, medical professionals—especially psychiatrists[165]—increasingly believed that the deluge of Slavic and Mediterranean peoples would eventually swamp Canada's Anglo-Saxon character. They also expressed concern about immigrants from Britain's slums, workhouses, and reformatories. The depiction of these immigrants as subversive led to demands for tighter medical controls and calls for the proper management of Canada's immigration policy, where deportation became an increasingly useful tool in preserving Canada's racial purity. New provisions introduced by the Immigration Act of 1902, interposed Canada's medical practitioners into frontline immigration duties where doctors contracted by the Department of Immigration and Colonisation controlled early deportation work.[166] Canadian immigration policy, which had prioritized the entry of immigrants on their economic utility, had, after 1905, shifted dramatically to one now founded upon ethnicity and race (ironically at a time when Britain was introducing similar entry restrictions on East European Jews through the 1905 Alien Act).

Within Britain itself at the turn of the twentieth century, empire migration became embroiled in the wider public debate about the state of British society. The military catastrophes suffered by British arms in the opening stages of the South African War (1899–1902) jolted an overconfident nation. "National efficiency" became a battle cry; tariff reform, compulsory military service, state-assisted emigration, eugenics and, more broadly, the concept of social imperialism, were all promoted as means of rebuilding Britain's resolve and national character.[167]

The dominions were also concerned with the condition of their own national fabrics during this period. The rigorous implementation of the "White" Australia policy after 1901, which effectively barred the vast majority of Asiatics from entering the dominion on a permanent basis, was paralleled by Canada's hardening nativistic attitudes towards recently arrived eastern European immigrants. To an increasing number of Canadians, these peasants clad in sheepskin coats were inassimilable and, moreover, untrustworthy. Similar racist views were echoed in South Africa. In response to intense anti-Indian agitation by the white settler minority in Natal during 1896–7, the colony pioneered restrictive immigration regulations in an attempt to solve the increasingly politicized "Indian" question. The restriction on non-white immigration into the colony by such means as language or dictation tests—known as the "Natal formula"—became the cornerstone of similar racially exclusionist legislation in the other dominions. Quotas, capitation taxes, and health and sanitation regulations rounded off what became a formidable arsenal in the dominions' war against racial adulteration.[168]

If restrictive immigration practices could be used by the dominions to safeguard their Anglo-Saxon heritage, state-assisted migration could also be used by the mother country in safeguarding its imperial interests. South Africa was a special case and must be examined in the light of the British government's attempt to foster white racial harmony and create a new rural order in South Africa after 1902. The architect of Britain's reconstruction policy was Sir Alfred Milner, British High Commissioner for South Africa and Governor of the Cape and Transvaal between 1897 and 1905. For Milner, economic recovery was the key to a new and vigorous *British* South Africa. His chief fear was Afrikaner nationalism, which he regarded as the most dangerous and destabilizing force in southern Africa. But to foster racial harmony, Afrikaners had to be encouraged to participate in the new industrial order and British immigrants had to be attracted and resettled in large numbers in the rural areas. The first duty of the reconstruction administration was therefore to settle and anglicize South Africa using British emigrants and capital. In order to offset Afrikaner political power, which was concentrated in the rural areas, Milner sought large numbers of loyal, English-speaking settlers to infiltrate the rural districts. The thousands of imperial troops awaiting demobilization provided an obvious source for if they could be induced to stay, despite their lack of agricultural experience, they would inculcate loyalty (and fear) among the rural Afrikaners, as well as establishing a firm foundation for additional government-sponsored settlement from Britain.[169]

Milner's policy, like its predecessors in the 1820s,[170] failed miserably. Of the 400,000 British and 30,000 imperial troops who had served in South Africa between 1899 and 1902, fewer than 2,000 participated in the government-sponsored resettlement programme. Most veterans showed little enthusiasm for the scheme, and those that did soon lost interest or grew disenchanted with an agonisingly slow and muddled bureaucracy. What is intriguing, however, is that South Africa did reflect the growing trend at the turn of the century that empire destinations were becoming increasingly popular with unassisted British migrants. Between 1901 and 1910, South Africa's share of the imperial total was 9.9 percent. Even though in percentage terms there was a drop of over three points during the brief census period of 1911–13, numbers remained buoyant until the outbreak of war.[171]

The onset of the Great War in August 1914 effectively halted the huge waves of outward migration which had been crashing on dominion shores. Post-war British migration would follow a different course at some levels, and although the numbers were remarkably buoyant—1,811,553 between 1918 and 1929—the patterns and flows took several new and noticeable twists, especially involving state-assisted migration, which became a highly contentious issue between the dominions and the British government during the interwar period.[172] The obvious counterfactual question remains: would these huge flood tides of humanity have continued to flow in the same directions and in the same volumes if war had not intervened? Would the dominions have continued to be the most popular destinations for British migrants or would the United States have reasserted itself as the foremost destination, as it had been throughout most of the nineteenth century? It is odd to think that child emigration continued up and until 1917 and was only halted for obvious humanitarian reasons when the Germans announced their campaign of unrestricted submarine warfare in February of that year.

One issue that migration historians have ignored as a fruitful field of endeavor, is the experience of thousands of British-born migrants who either came back to the United Kingdom to enlist in British regiments or enlisted in their respective dominion forces and served overseas. For instance, of the 34,500 volunteers who made up Canada's "first contingent," and which sailed to Britain in October 1914, 65 percent were British-born.[173] This predictably patriotic response to "King, Country, and Empire" was repeated throughout the Southern British World[174] as thousands more British migrants rallied to the Colours, temporarily arrived back "home," some forever remaining in foreign fields, never to return to either Blighty or their recently-adopted homes.

Conclusion

What threads can be drawn together about the histories of British migration between 1760 and 1914? One immediate observation is the sheer volume of outward migration: in the nineteenth century alone free British migrants accounted for 45 percent of the total number of European migrants heading overseas. Even more astounding are the figures for return migration. Dudley Baines has estimated that between one quarter and one third of all European migrants between 1815 and 1914 returned home. Returnee statistics for the United Kingdom are equally arresting. In England and Wales between 1870 and 1914 approximately 40 percent came back to the British Isles, while as many as a third of those of who left Scotland and Ireland at this time after years' sojourning in the United States, the neo-Britains and mini-Britains also returned home.[175] For the unfree or coerced non-Europeans—the enslaved, the indentured, or the convicted—their stories were much different. Most did not return to their places of origin. The same can be said about those who do not fit neatly into the "unfree" category, such as child emigrants of all kinds. Nonetheless, they made important contributions to the new societies they helped to establish and develop. The same can be said about imperial sojourners and returnee migrants. They too were important vehicles in transmitting back to Britain ideas, customs, and knowledge about a wider British World.

Migration, indeed, was the foundation upon which the colonies of white settlement and later the dominions were built. It was a key element within a larger imperial blueprint that reinforced the physical and psychological bonds of empire; people were the cultural adhesive that bound these neo-Britains and the mother country more closely together. It was not without its flash points, however. There were times when the dominions, for example, complained bitterly that London was dumping the dregs of British society on its slender financial shoulders; that it was trying to disaggregate its social responsibilities onto the newly-emerging nation-states within the empire. Emboldened by self-government and possessing a greater self-confidence in the management of their internal affairs, these neo-Britains did not flinch from taking controversial decisions about who they allowed through their borders, even if that meant causing friction within the imperial family. The debate over what constituted the settler or migrant of the "right type" would confound philanthropists, immigration officials and politicians in London and throughout the British World. And yet, when push came to shove as it did in August 1914, the response of Britons over the seas was phenomenal. In the end, whatever the intricate factors and intimate personal reasons as to why millions of people decided to leave (and return to) the British Isles between 1760 and 1914, it was a process of monumental proportions and dimensions, in which the people of the British Empire, or more appropriately, the British World, were constantly on the move.

Notes

1 Fitzpatrick, *Oceans of Consolation*, p. 25.
2 M. Harper, "British migration," p. 75.
3 Constantine, "Overseas settlement," pp. 16–35.
4 Bickers, *Settlers and Expatriates*, introduction.
5 The slavery literature and specifically the debate over figures, which range between nine and eleven million Africans, is vast. The key text which initiated much of the debate remains Curtin, *Atlantic Slave Trade*. Also see Eltis, *African Slavery*; Lovejoy, "Atlantic slave trade," pp. 473–501, for an excellent overview of the debate. As well, see Henige, "Measuring the immeasurable," pp. 295–313; and Eltis, "Volume and structure," table III, p. 45. Lovejoy calculates that between 1701 and 1800 the English carried the largest numbers of all the slaving nations—2,532,300 out of a total of 6,132,900 or 41 percent. Liberated African emigration has been analyzed by Asiegbu, *Politics of Liberation*.
6 The literature on indentured labour, although not as sizeable as that of slavery, is rich. See Tinker, *New System of Slavery*; Northrup, *Indentured Labor*; Carter, *Servants*; Saunders, *Indentured Labour*; Look Lai, *Caribbean Sugar*; P. Richardson, *Chinese Mine Labour*; Bhana and Brain, *Setting Down Roots*; Marks and Richardson, *International Labour Migration*; Emmer, *Colonialism and Migration*; Emmer and Mörner, *European Expansion*; Newbury, "Labour migration," pp. 234–56.
7 As borne out by the five-volume *OHBE*: D. Richardson, "Atlantic slave trade," II, pp. 440–64; P. D. Morgan, "Black experience in the British empire," *ibid*., pp. 465–86; Northrup, "Migration from Africa," III, pp. 88–100; Harper, "British migration," *ibid*., pp. 75–86; Constantine, "Migrants and settlers," IV, pp. 163–87. The African experience, which includes slavery and liberation, is explored in greater detail in one of the companion volumes edited by Morgan and Hawkins, *Black Experience and the Empire*.

8 Wrigley and Schofield, *Population History of England* demonstrates the complexities involved in the tabulation of this all-important data. For problems of sources on migration data see Whyte, *Migration and Society*, pp. 8–21.

9 Canny, *Europeans on the Move*; Emmer, *Colonialism and Migration*; Richards, *Britannia's Children*.

10 Akenson, *Half the World from Home*; id., *Small Differences*; id., *Irish Diaspora*; id., *Occasional Papers*; Fitzpatrick, "Emigration, 1801–70," pp. 562–609; id., "Emigration, 1871–1921," pp. 606–52.

11 Proudfoot, "Landscape, place and memory," p. 172.

12 Eltis, "Free and coerced transatlantic migrations," pp. 251–80; Horn and Morgan, "Settlers and slaves," pp. 19–44.

13 See Patterson, *Ulster-New Zealand Migration*; McCarthy, *Global Clan*; McCormack, "Networks among British immigrants," pp. 357–74. For insights into the development of information flows, networks and webs see Baines, "European emigration, 1815–1930," pp. 525–44; Lester, *Imperial Networks*; Laidlaw, *Colonial Connections*. For the web metaphor see Ballantyne, *Orientalism and Race*, pp. 1–17, and his "Empire, knowledge and culture," pp. 115–40.

14 Bailyn, *Voyagers to the West*, p. 244.

15 Walsh, "Introduction," to id. *Ireland Abroad*, pp. 9–10. The term career migrant is used by Tilly, "Transplanted networks," pp. 79–95. Lambert and Lester have gone further by using the term "imperial careering" in their edited collection *Colonial Lives*, pp. 1–31. For an earlier period which makes similar connections see MacKenzie, "Foreword," xiii–xxi. In the case of police as migrants and their contribution to colonial police forces see Fedorowich, "Problems of disbandment," pp. 88–110; Malcolm, "'What would people say if I became a policeman?'," pp. 95–107; Sinclair, *Colonial Policing*.

16 Kirk-Greene, *On Crown Service*; id., *Symbol of Authority*; Buettner, *Empire Families*, pp. 1–24.

17 Galenson, "Indentured servitude," p. 6; Wareing, "Migration to London," p. 358; Gemery, "Markets for migrants," p. 33.

18 Fogleman, "Slaves, convicts, and servants," p. 43.

19 Galenson, "Indentured servitude," p. 1; Fogleman, "Slaves, convicts, and servants," p. 43.

20 Fogleman, "Slaves, convicts, and servants," p. 56.

21 Ekirch, *Bound for America*, pp. 1–6 and 22–7; Fogleman, "Slaves, convicts, and servants," p. 58.

22 Fogleman, "New estimates," p. 691. Canny, "English migration," for a thought-provoking essay on sources, numbers and the historiographical debate so far. Also see Glass, *Numbering the People*.

23 Souden, "English indentured servants," pp. 19–33.

24 Canny, "English migration," pp. 49 and 58–9 is challenging Bailyn's figures on the total number of free emigrants which he sees as being inflated. Also see Fogleman, "New estimates," p. 698.

25 Canny, "English migration," p. 63; Horn, "British diaspora," pp. 35–6.

26 Whyte, *Migration and Society*, p. 125.

27 Games, "Migration," pp. 38, 32.

28 Cullen, "Irish diaspora," pp. 143–4. For the demographic and economic factors at work here see Cullen, "Economic development," pp. 159–95.

29 *Ibid.*; Jones, "Background to emigration," p. 4; Akenson, *Irish Diaspora*; Bielenberg, "Irish emigration to the British empire," pp. 215–16.

30 Morgan, "Unwelcome heritage," pp. 619–25; Jeffery, *An Irish Empire?*; Akenson, *If the Irish Ran the World*; Bielenberg, "Irish emigration," p. 216.

31 Miller, *Emigrants and Exiles*, pp. 137 and 149–50; Cullen, "Economic development," p. 161; Fitzgerald, "Aspects of Irish return migration," pp. 32–51; Jones, "Scotch-Irish in British America," pp. 284–313, esp. 287; Dickson, *Ulster Emigration*; Cullen, "Irish diaspora," p. 119; Jones, "Ulster emigration," p. 49.

32 Whyte, *Migration and Society*, p. 121.

33 MacKenzie, "Scotland and Empire," pp. 714–39.

34 Richards, "Atlantic empire," pp. 77–80; Landsman, "Scotland and the Americas," pp. 463–75; Hamilton, "Transatlantic ties," pp. 48–66; and his more in-depth study, *Scotland, the Caribbean and the Atlantic World*.

35 Bumsted, *People's Clearance*, pp. 9–13; Devine, "Paradox", pp. 1–15. Also see Smout, Landsman, and Devine, "Scottish emigration," pp. 76–112; Richards, *Highland Clearances*; Campbell, "Scotland," pp. 1–28; Gray, "Scottish migration," pp. 95–176.

36 Devine, "Landlordism," p. 87.

37 Devine, "Landlordism," p. 91; Richards, "Varieties of Scottish emigration," pp. 473–80.

38 Adams and Somerville, *Cargoes of Despair*, p. 142.

39 Fedorowich, *Unfit for Heroes*, pp. 5–6.

40 Bailyn, *Voyagers to the West*, p. 26. For the debate on the under- or over-estimation of numbers see Fogleman, "New estimates"; Smout, Landsman, and Devine, "Scottish emigration," pp. 76–112, esp. p. 97; Cullen, "Irish diaspora," pp. 113–49.

41 Fogleman, "Slaves, convicts, and servants," p. 49.

42 *Ibid.*, p. 46.

43 *Ibid.*, pp. 53–4, 59, 61, 65.

44 Gillen, "Botany Bay decision," pp. 740–66.

45 Bumsted, "Cultural landscape," pp. 363–92; Buckner, "Making British North America British," pp. 12–13; Adams and Somerville, *Cargoes of Despair*, p. 155; Murdoch, *British Emigration*, pp. 56–60.

46 Murdoch, *British Emigration*, p. 49.

47 Mackillop, *More Fruitful than the Soil*, pp. 41–76, 178–90.

48 *Ibid.*, p. 180.

49 *Ibid.*, pp. 181–90.

50 Jones, "Ulster emigration," pp. 49, 56, 58.

51 Jones, "Background to emigration," p. 9.

52 *Ibid.*, p. 10; MacDonagh, *Pattern of Government*, p. 64.

53 Murdoch, *British Emigration*, pp. 85–93.

54 Johnston, *British Emigration Policy*, p. 5.

55 Taylor, "Emigration," p. 61.

56 Buckner, "Whatever happened to the British empire?" p. 17; Bielenberg, "Irish emigration," p. 224; Thomas, *Migration and Economic Growth*, p. 57, table 7.

57 Elliott, *Irish Migrants*, p. 3; Bielenberg, "Irish emigration," pp. 218–20.

58 Taylor, "Emigration," pp. 61, 70.

59 Johnston, *British Emigration Policy*, pp. 1–56; Cowan, *British Emigration*; Edwards, *1820s Settlers*.

60 Cowan, *British Emigration*, p. 117.

61 Vance, "Politics of emigration," pp. 41–5.

62 *Ibid.*, p. 44.

63 *Ibid.*, pp. 41, 46–53. Gray has tabulated that there were eighty emigration societies in Scotland during the 1820s which helped over 2,000 emigrants, mostly weavers, to settle in Canada. "Course of Scottish emigration," p. 29.

64 Brynn, "Emigration theories," pp. 45–65; MacDonagh, *Emigration in the Victorian Age*, introduction; MacDonagh, *Pattern of Government*, pp. 22–3; Neal, "Irish steamship companies," pp. 28–61.

65 MacDonagh, "Emigration and the state," pp. 133–59. These ideas were explored in greater detail in his book, *Pattern of Government*. The corrective to some of this groundbreaking work has been provided by Dunkley, "Emigration and the state," pp. 353–80.

66 Erickson, "Emigration by British trade unions," pp. 248–73; Clements, "Trade unions and emigration," pp. 167–80; Horn, "Agricultural trade unionism," pp. 87–102; Malchow, "National lobby," pp. 92–116.

67 Jones, "Background to emigration," pp. 12, 54–5; Baines, *Migration in a Mature Economy*, p. 279; Devine, "Paradox," p. 11.

68 Jones, "Background to emigration," pp. 13–15; Gray, "Course of Scottish emigration," p. 21.

69 Jones, "Background to emigration," pp. 16–17.

70 Cowan, *British Emigration*, p. 229; MacDonald, *Canada*, pp. 265–311.

71 Baines, "European emigration, 1815–1930" p. 530; Jones, "Background to emigration", p. 16.

72 Cowan, *British Emigration*, p. 232.

73 Jones, "Background to emigration," pp. 18–19. For the debate on the problematical use, interpretation and 'hidden' meanings confronted by historians when analyzing emigrants' private letters see Erickson, *Invisible Immigrants*, pp. 1–21; Taylor, "Emigration", pp. 97–8; Miller, Boling, and Doyle, "Emigrants and exiles," pp. 97–125; Fitzpatrick, *Oceans of Consolation*, pp. 3–35; McCarthy, *Irish Migrants in New Zealand*, pp. 81–96 and other work by her cited in the bibliography. A must is Grant, *Representations of British Emigration*.

74 Cameron, Haines, and Maude, *English Immigrant Voices*, p. 47.

75 MacDonagh, *Pattern of Government*, pp. 27–9.

76 Taylor, "Emigration," p. 70.

77 Carrothers, *Emigration from the British Isles*, p. 205; Fitzpatrick, "Irish emigration," p. 128.

78 Payton, *Cornish Overseas*, p. 26; Burke, "The Cornish diaspora," pp. 57–75; Schwartz, "Cornish migration studies," pp. 136–65.

79 See Magee and Thompson, "Lines of credit," and their "Global and local," pp. 177–202.

80 Nalbach, "Software of empire," pp. 68–94.

81 Baehre, "Pauper emigration," p. 340.

82 Howells, "English pauper emigrant strategies," p. 181.

83 Howells, "Parish assisted emigration," p. 592.

84 Howells, "Emigration and the new poor law," p. 145. The Australian academics Richards and Haines have also been especially influential. Richards, "How did poor people emigrate", pp. 250–79; Haines, "Indigent misfits", pp. 223–47, and her more detailed study, *Emigration and the Labouring Poor*.

85 Howells, "Emigration and the new poor law," pp. 155–6. For this pessimistic view which dominated the pre-World War II literature and persisted into the early 1980s, see Madgwick, *Immigration*; MacDonald, *Canada*; Carrothers, *Emigration*; Johnson, *Emigration from the United Kingdom to North America*; Baehre, "Pauper emigration," pp. 339–67; Taylor, "Emigration," p. 59.

86 Howells, "Emigration and the new poor law," pp. 157–8. For the shortcomings of Madgwick's work see Shultz, "Immigration into eastern Australia," pp. 273–82. Apart

from Howells, this welcome corrective on the positive nature of assisted migration has been supported by the work of Haines. See her work cited above and "The new poor law," pp. 1–21.

87   Nicholas and Shergold, "Convicts as migrants," p. 47.

88   Harper, "British migration," p. 78; Shaw, *Convicts and the Colonies*, p. 162; McDonald and Shlomowitz, "Mortality on convict voyages," pp. 287, 291.

89   Robson, *Convict Settlers*, p. 4; Shaw, *Convicts and the Colonies*, pp. 148–9, 363–8; Richards, "Running home from Australia," p. 83.

90   Shaw, *Convicts and the Colonies*, pp. 147–8, 319–21; Nicholas and Shergold, "Transportation as global migration," p. 29.

91   *Ibid.*, pp. 149–53; Denoon and Mein-Smith, *History of Australia*, p. 161 for percentage breakdowns of convicts along ethnic lines; Oxley, *Convict Maids*; K. Reid, "Setting women to work," pp. 1–25; Nicholas and Shergold, "Convicts as migrants," p. 52 made this latter point which others like Oxley and Reid have taken on board.

92   Shaw, *Convicts and the Colonies*, pp. 166 and 183; Nicholas and Shergold, "Convicts as migrants," pp. 46–7; Denoon and Mein-Smith, *History of Australia*, p. 161.

93   McDowell, "Ireland in 1800," p. 658.

94   Madgwick, *Immigration into Eastern Australia*, p. 65.

95   Richards, "How did poor people emigrate?", pp. 253–5; Denoon and Mein-Smith, *Australia, New Zealand and the Pacific*, pp. 87–9, 159, 165–6.

96   For the all-important context to this see Burroughs, *Britain and Australia 1831–1855*; Macmillan, *Scotland and Australia 1788–1850*.

97   Richards, "How did poor people emigrate," pp. 258–9.

98   *Ibid.*, p. 259.

99   Hammerton, "Female immigration to Australia," pp. 539–66.

100 Bradlow, "Children's friend society," pp. 155–9; Hadley, "Natives in a strange land," p. 411; Jordan, "Stay and Starve," pp. 145–66.

101 Broeze, "Private enterprise," pp. 235–7; McDonald and Shlomowitz, "Passenger fares on sailing vessels," pp. 192–208.

102 McDonald and Richards, "Great emigration of 1841," p. 339. For the intricacies of the government and bounty systems see Madgwick, *Immigration*, pp. 130–68.

103 Broeze, "Private enterprise," p. 245; McDonald and Richards, "Great emigration of 1841," p. 338.

104 Broeze, "Private enterprise," p. 236.

105 *Ibid.*, pp. 242, 249. For recent work on the impact of British business and commercial networks see Pearson and Richardson, "Business networking," pp. 657–79.

106 Madgwick, *Immigration into Eastern Australia*, p. 112.

107 Richards, *Britannia's Children*, pp. 127, 138.

108 Newbury, "Labour migration," p. 241.

109 Donnachie, "Scots on the make," p. 143.

110 McDonald and Richards, "Great emigration of 1841," p. 346.

111 Mokyr and O'Gráda, "Prefamine Ireland," pp. 361–2, 366; Fitzpatrick, "Irish emigration," p. 131; Fitzpatrick, "Emigration, 1801–70," p. 565.

112 Fitzpatrick, "Over the foaming billows," p. 133.

113 Fitzpatrick, "Emigration, 1801–70," pp. 566–9. Also see O'Gráda, "Irish emigration statistics," pp. 143–9. Erickson's pioneering work has shown, however, that by the 1840s almost half of all Irish migrants were establishing new lives for themselves in the United States. See her *Leaving England*, p. 185.

114 R. Reid, "Irish convict families," pp. 69–96.

115 Haines, *Emigration and the Labouring Poor*, pp. 142–65.

116 McDonald and Richards, "Great emigration of 1841," p. 349.

117 Madgwick, *Immigration into Eastern Australia*, pp. 191–2; Swaisland, *Servants and Gentlewomen*, pp. 18–19; Hammerton, *Emigrant Gentlewomen*.

118 Gothard, "Pity the poor immigrant," p. 97; Archibald, "Exporting domesticity," pp. 228–47; C. Macdonald, *Good Character*.

119 Gothard, "Pity the poor immigrant," p. 104.

120 *Ibid.*, pp. 99, 105, 107.

121 *Ibid.*, pp. 114–16; P. Hamilton, "Poor female migration," p. 126.

122 Gothard, "Female migration to Tasmania," pp. 386–404.

123 Gothard, *Blue China*, pp. 211–12.

124 Belich, "Rise of the Anglo-world," p. 43.

125 Thomas, *Migration and Economic Growth*, p. 57, table 7.

126 Carrothers, *Emigration from the British Isles*, appendix 1, pp. 215, 305-6; Richards, *Britannia's Children*, p. 177; Sherrington, *Australia's Immigrants*, pp. 59–60; Thomas, *Migration and Economic Growth*, p. 57.

127 Sherrington, *Australia's Immigrants*, p. 61; O'Farrell, *The Irish in Australia*, p. 63; Denoon and Mein-Smith, *History of Australia*, p. 87.

128 Sherrington, *Australia's Immigrants*, p. 61.

129 *Ibid.*, p. 63.

130 Van Vugt, "Prosperity and industrial emigration," p. 339; Duncan, "Case studies," pp. 272–89.

131 Van Vugt, "Running from ruin," pp. 411–28; Erickson, *Leaving England*, pp. 34–59, 87–117.

132 Belich, *Making Peoples*, I, pp. 279–87, 316; Denoon and Mein-Smith, *History of Australia*, p. 166; Dalziel, "Emigration and kinship," pp. 112–28; Hudson, "English emigration to New Zealand," pp. 680–98.

133 Borrie, *Immigration to New Zealand*; Fedorowich, *Unfit for Heroes*, pp. 10–11; Belich, *Making Peoples*, I, p. 314.

134 Dalziel, *Julius Vogel*, pp. 104–9, 124–8.

135 Simpson, *The Immigrants*, pp. 169–87; Dalziel, *Origins of New Zealand Diplomacy*, pp. 25–90.

136 Belich, *Making Peoples*, I, p. 280.

137 Denoon and Mein-Smith, *History of Australia*, p. 88.

138 Gandar, "New Zealand net migration," pp. 163–4.

139 Denoon and Mein-Smith, *History of Australia*, p. 88.

140 Arnold, "Dynamics and quality," pp. 1–20.

141 Denoon and Mein-Smith, *History of Australia*, p. 87.

142 Belich, *Making Peoples*, I, p. 315.

143 Brooking, "Scots in New Zealand," p. 161.

144 Belich, *Making Peoples*, I, p. 315.

145 *Ibid.*, p. 318; Fitzpatrick, "Irish emigration," p. 133; Patterson, "Introduction" to *Ulster–New Zealand Migration*, p. 9; Phillips, "New Zealand's Ulster immigrants", p. 55.

146 Belich, *Making Peoples*, I, pp. 303 and 334.

147 Macdonald, *Good Character*, pp. 5–9, 28–30; Diamond, *Emigration and Empire*, pp. 93–196; Chaudhuri, "Victorian juvenile emigration," pp. 19–42; Swaisland, *Servants and Gentlewomen*, pp. 22–3.

148 Chilton, "New class of women," pp. 36–56.

149 Bush, *Imperial Power*, pp. 146–69.

150 Jordan, "Stay and starve," p. 161.

151 Wagner, *Children of the Empire*; Bean and Melville, *Lost Children*; Parr, *Labouring Children*.

152 Martin, "Pauper children," p. 26. Also see Bush, "The right sort of women," pp. 385–409.

153 Martin, "Pauper children," pp. 26, 48; Glynn, "Assisted emigration to Canada," pp. 209–38; Langfield, "Voluntarism, salvation, and rescue," pp. 86–114; Rooke and Schnell, "Imperial philanthropy," pp. 56–77.

154 Martin, "Pauper children," p. 48; Wagner, *Children of the Empire*, appendix 1, p. 259, which provides an excellent statistical breakdown of the various charities involved.

155 Malchow, *Population Pressures*; Plant, *Oversea Settlement*.

156 Thomas, *Migration and Economic Growth*, p. 57, table 7.

157 Constantine, "Overseas settlement," p. 19; Carrothers, *Emigration from the British Isles*, p. 242.

158 Gandar, "New Zealand net migration," p. 151; Simpson, *The Immigrants*, p. 187.

159 Sherrington, *Australia's Immigrants*, p. 87.

160 Kelley and Trebilcock, *Making of the Mosaic*, p. 111; Brown and Cook, *Canada 1896–1914*, p. 57; Thomas, *Migration and Economic Growth*, p. 56; Beaud and Prévost, "Immigration, eugenics and statistics," pp. 1–24.

161 Brown and Cook, *Canada 1896–1914*, p. 49.

162 Kelley and Trebilcock, *Making of the Mosaic*, p. 113.

163 Beaud and Prévost, "Immigration, eugenics and statistics," p. 4.

164 Godler, "Doctors and the new immigrants," p. 6.

165 Dowbiggin, "Immigration restriction," pp. 598–627.

166 Roberts, "Doctors and deports," pp. 17–36; Sears, "Immigration controls," pp. 91–112.

167 Searle, *National Efficiency*; Williams, "Politics of empire settlement," pp. 22–44; Constantine, "Empire migration and social reform," pp. 62–83.

168 Huttenback, *Racism and Empire*; Martens, "Natal and New South Wales," pp. 323–44.

169 Fedorowich, "British immigration to South Africa," pp. 222–46; Streak, *Milner's Immigration Policy*; Van Helten and Williams, "British women to the Transvaal," pp. 17–38.

170 Sturgis, "Anglicisation at the Cape of Good Hope," pp. 5–32; Bickford-Smith, "Revisiting anglicisation," pp. 82–95

171 Thomas, *Migration and Economic Growth*, p. 57, table 7.

172 Constantine, "Migrants and settlers," pp. 166–7; Fedorowich, *Unfit for Heroes*, pp. 191–9.

173 Bothwell, Drummond, and English, *Canada 1900–1945*, p. 142.

174 St J. Barclay, *The Empire is Marching*, p. 69.

175 Baines, *Migration in a Mature Economy*, pp. 28, 126; Harper, "Introduction" to *Emigrant Homecomings*, pp. 1–2.

Further Reading

The cornerstone for any quick reference work on British migration between 1760 and 1914 is the *OHBE*, volumes 2–4. The respective chapters by James Horn, Marjory Harper, and Stephen Constantine complete with their indicative bibliographies provide the foundation for more detailed study. Eric Richards's epic sweep *Britannia's Children* (2004) is a must: it not only complements the above scholarship, but his extensive bibliography is a veritable treasure trove for students interested in all facets of migration. Important surveys by Ian D. Whyte, *Migration and Society in Britain 1550–1830* (2000) and Alexander Murdoch, *British Emigration 1603–1914* (2004), provide important overviews as well. Contributions by economic historians such as Brinley Thomas, *Migration and Economic Growth* (1973) and Dudley Baines, *Migration in a Mature Economy* (1985) are invaluable when charting occupational trends, age cohorts, and overall patterns.

For the period 1500–1800, the pioneering collection of essays compiled by Nicholas Canny in *Europeans on the Move* (1994) is central to any analysis; as is the older but no less invaluable work of Bernard Bailyn and Barbara DeWolfe, *Voyagers to the West* (1986). For white indentured labour, David Galenson's *White Servitude in Colonial America* (1981) is a useful benchmark. So, too, for non-European peoples, is David Northrup's *Indentured Labor in the Age of Imperialism, 1834–1922* (1995); and the collection edited by P. C. Emmer, *Colonialism and Migration. Indentured Labour Before and After Slavery* (1986). The history of slavery is vast but David Eltis, *The Rise of African Slavery in the Americas* (2000) offers useful signposts. For convicts to Australia, see A. G. L. Shaw's *Convicts and the Colonies,* which has undergone numerous reprints since the 1960s and remains an important text. New analyses in the field have been provided by Stephen Nicholas's bicentenary collection *Convict Workers: Reinterpreting Australia's Past* (1988) which has taken the debate much further. For the all-important analysis of gender see Deborah Oxley's *Convict Maids* (1996).

Traditionally, studies of migration have been broken down according to ethnicity. Central to the discussion of Irish migration is the work by Donald Akenson and David Fitzpatrick, especially the latter's in the relevant volumes of *A New History of Ireland* (1989 and 1996). Kerby Miller's *Emigrants and Exiles* (1985) is also instructive. The Scots-Irish are discussed by R. J. Dickson in his timeless work *Ulster Emigration to Colonial America 1718–1775* (1966); but two more studies have been provided by Maldwyn Jones, in Bernard Bailyn and Philip D. Morgan, *Strangers within the Realm* (1991), and in E. R. R. Green's *Essays in Scotch-Irish History* (1969). For the Scots, two collections—edited by Tom Devine, *Scottish Emigration and Scottish Society* (1992) and R. A. Cage, *The Scots Abroad: Labour, Capital, Enterprise, 1750–1914* (1985)—are key. New and exciting work has been provided by Angela McCarthy for both communities in her edited work *A Global Clan. Scottish Migrant Networks and Identities since the Eighteenth Century* (2006) and *Irish Migrants in New Zealand, 1840–1937: "The Desired Haven"* (2005). Much more could be said about specific groups, communities, their destinations and host societies, but a quick glance at the bibliography will give the reader an idea of the sheer scale of scholarship. However, a new area of growth which must be flagged is return migration, and the work of Marjory Harper stands out in her recently published *Emigrant Homecomings. The Return Movement of Emigrants 1600–2000* (2005).

5

The Economics of Empire

A. R. Dilley[1]

In 1776, as the crisis in Britain's relations with her American colonies reached its climax, the first edition of Adam Smith's *Inquiry into the Nature and Causes of the Wealth of Nations* was published. Amongst other things, it considered the economics of European colonization, especially in North America. Smith did not doubt that benefits had arisen from this process, although these had not been expected when colonies were founded:

> The establishment of the European colonies in America and the West Indies arose from no necessity and although the utility which has arisen from them has been very great . . . [it] was not understood at their first establishment, and was not the motive either of that establishment or of the discoveries which gave occasion to it . . .[2]

Smith outlined how settlers, lightly taxed, could exploit the abundant land of these countries to achieve rapid rates of growth. Meanwhile, the new transatlantic trade had directly or indirectly increased the wealth of Europe, providing new products and a "vent" for surplus produce. He went on, however, to distinguish these "natural" and broadly beneficent developments from the consequences of the "mercantile" regulations of European colonial powers, including Britain. These either confined colonial imports and exports to the mother country, or channelled their trade through its ports. This, he argued, reduced the prices the colonies received for their produce while forcing them to pay more for imports, reducing their prosperity. Smith also doubted whether these artificially induced advantages ultimately benefited the mother country. They did not generate new business, he argued, but deflected attention from other channels. The regulations diverted merchants from shorter routes which, while perhaps being less profitable, handled a greater volume of goods at a faster rate, and thus generated more employment and placed more goods at the disposal of consumers. Despite lessening the wealth of the nation, Smith noted that the monopoly did raise the rate of profit among merchants. They, he believed, had been the "principal advisers" in the construction of the trading regulations and hence "we must not wonder . . . if, in the greater part of them, their interest has been more considered than either that of the colonies or that of the mother country."[3]

Smith was not the first to reflect upon the material effects of various forms of expansion, but his work is a useful starting point because it casts a long shadow over subsequent discussions.[4] Moreover, he offers a useful means of conceptualizing the economics of empire. In this chapter, following Smith, it is seen as the way in which various structures of empire interacted with processes of production, exchange, consumption, and accumulation in Britain and the colonies. Much of the most virulent discussion of these interactions has surrounded three broad questions which again emerge in Smith's work: How far do economic motives explain imperial expansion? What were the consequences of imperial rule for the economic development of the colonies? Did the colonising power itself benefit from the relationship? (A further question, that of the relationship between the dissolution of the empire and British economic decline, is discussed in Sarah Stockwell's chapter in this volume.) These questions have been at the heart of debate about empire and, during the twentieth century, were often a part of ongoing clashes between liberal and Marxist historians.[5] Since the end of the Cold War, attention has shifted towards non-economic and especially cultural issues (apart from an ongoing debate about "gentlemanly capitalism"). Ultimately, however, the interaction between inequalities of power and economic fortunes remains an indispensable component of the history of the empire. Interest looks likely to revive, not least under the stimulus of a growing preoccupation with "globalization" discussed at the end of this chapter.

In order to consider the issues outlined above, it will be useful to sketch the broad and shifting patterns of imperial trade and investment. We ought, perhaps, to note that migration (often forced) constituted a further important economic transfer, but is the subject of the previous chapter. The empire was never a "hermetically sealed unit" and intra-imperial transactions co-existed with other economic connections overseas (the changing imperial regulatory framework is discussed below).[6] During the eighteenth century, extra-European trade saw dramatic growth. Imports as a whole increased by 356.06 percent between 1700/1 and 1789/90, those to North America, the West Indies, Africa, and the East Indies by 658.33 percent; exports increased by 321.68 percent and 1156.71 percent respectively; and re-exports by 251.87 percent and 329.81 percent. By 1789/90 these regions accounted for 48.32 percent of imports, and received 52.88 percent of exports and 19.13 percent of re-exports.[7] Not all of this trade was conducted within the formal empire, especially after the loss of the Thirteen Colonies, but unfortunately statistics do not allow us to disaggregate the imperial component. The continued dynamism of the American market meant that, by the early nineteenth century, the importance of imperial trade declined.[8]

World trade expanded less dramatically in the first half of the nineteenth century, by approximately two and a half times; between 1850 and 1910 it increased tenfold. The empire held its own. By 1854–7 it provided 23.9 percent of British imports, and took 30.3 percent of all exports (by value), and in 1909–13 the totals were 24.9 percent and 35.4 percent. This relatively steady pattern masks important changes. The West Indian colonies declined to insignificance; their share of British exports fell from 45.2 percent in 1814–19 to 2.1 percent in 1909–13. The settlement empire became increasingly important, providing 32.2 percent of British empire imports and receiving 31.7 percent of British exports to the empire in 1854–7; by 1909–13 the figures were 50 percent and 54.6 percent respectively. India had risen to prominence by the mid-nineteenth century, and thereafter received about a third of British empire exports; her share of imports to Britain declined from 37.7 percent to 26.0 percent between 1854–7 and 1909–13.[9] Between the wars international trade lost much of the dynamism of the previous two centuries, and the 1930s saw dramatic reverses. Empire trade as a proportion of Britain's total increased, however, and by 1934 it provided 35.3 percent of British imports and received 43.9 percent of her exports. The settlement colonies (now dominions) reached new heights of importance, accounting for 61.09 percent and 53.01 percent of empire imports and exports respectively. India (16.34 percent and 22.29 percent) was eclipsed by the rest of the dependent empire (22.57 percent and 24.70 percent).[10] In the decade following World War II, empire trade accounted for just under half of all British trade, before beginning a dramatic decline in the late fifties.[11]

Flows of goods were accompanied by flows of investment. Before 1850 our knowledge of total volumes of capital export from Britain, and the empire's position, is sparse. Certainly a number of British companies operated overseas and raised capital in Britain, including such famous examples as the East India Company or the Hudson's Bay Company, as well as a host of lesser operations. It is likely that some money was also lent to colonial governments and, perhaps, some individual colonial enterprises.[12] After 1850 overseas investment increased dramatically and Britain placed a far greater volume of capital overseas than any other nation.[13] One recent estimate (echoing a long-established total) suggests that just under £4 billion was called up in overseas financial issues between 1865 and 1914. Of this, 37.71 percent was invested in the empire, of which 70 percent went to the white-settled empire, 19.29 percent to India, and 10.48 percent to the rest.[14] After the Great War both the volume of investment and the proportion placed overseas declined dramatically, the latter from an average of 38.9 percent in 1919–23 to 17.7 percent in 1934–8. With some official pressure, the empire received an increasing proportion of this, 66.4 percent in 1919–23 and 86.2 percent in 1934–7.[15] After World War II, which had seen the elimination of large volumes of British assets, capital export slowed to a trickle. Investment income, however, remained important to Britain's international position.[16] It is against this background that debates surrounding the economics of empire must be considered.

Economics and the Causes of the Expansion of Empire

The expansion of the British empire has proved both a striking feature and one of the great puzzles of modern British history. In 1883 J. R. Seeley warned of the temptation to attribute the process to a "fit of absence of mind."[17] Many late Victorian commentators, including Seeley, were inclined to see expansion as in part natural and in part the consequence of the interplay of the contingent and the unforeseen. Yet a long-established alternative tradition existed, explaining this expansion in economic terms. At the end of the eighteenth century Smith, as we have seen, believed that merchants were the architects of the mercantile system, while Edmund Burke suspected the East India Company's governor-general, Warren Hastings, of avarice in his expansion of the Company's Indian empire.[18] Many nineteenth-century radicals, such as Richard Cobden and John Bright, continued to oppose imperial advances as corrupt and economically unnecessary, although other "colonial reformers", such as Edward Gibbon Wakefield, thought colonies essential outlets for surplus capital, goods, and population.[19] Against this background came the work of three early twentieth-century writers often labelled "classical" theorists: J. A. Hobson, V. I. Lenin, and J. A. Schumpeter.[20] An important qualification must be made: each wrote upon "imperialism"—defined by them in various ways as an aggressive expansionism of which the construction of empire might be only one manifestation. This imperialism tended to be seen as a recent phenomenon—for Lenin beginning about 1900, for Hobson in 1870.[21] Although they often discussed something broader than the construction of formal empire, their works continue to influence debate and have drawn attention to the late nineteenth and early twentieth centuries.

J. A. Hobson, who stood squarely in the radical tradition, wrote extensively about imperialism between the mid-1890s and his death in 1940.[22] It is, however, the first part of his *Imperialism: A Study* (1902) which continues to exert a magnetic effect.[23] His approach was complex.[24] On the one hand, he suggested that, from 1870, the concentration of incomes in the hands of the upper classes led to excessive saving (oversaving). Imperial expansion opened investment outlets for this surplus capital.[25] On the other, he believed that the financiers who channelled these investments overseas were the "governor[s] of the imperial engine," manipulating politicians and other expansionist forces in society, not only in pursuit of new fields for investment, but also to make speculative profits on the stock market.[26] There is a tension between these two strands: was imperialism the result of a structural imbalance in the British economy, or of the manipulative power of a particular group?[27] Lenin drew upon Hobson, as well as a long line of other Marxist writers, in his *Imperialism: The Highest Stage of Capitalism* (1916).[28] He argued that, by 1900, capitalism had reached a new phase of development characterized by the rise of closely linked trusts and cartels in industry and finance. These sought to monopolize particular markets and industries, and required new outlets for goods and capital. This monopoly capitalism had developed, especially in Germany, after the world had been divided up during a previous phase of colonialism (about which he said little). World War I was an attempt by Germany—the main "have-not" power—to acquire territory to match its economic might.[29] J. A. Schumpeter, in his *Imperialism and Social Classes*, argued that, far from being the inevitable result of capitalism, imperialism (and Schumpeter, like Lenin, was mostly concerned with European foreign policy) was actually a perversion of its natural course arising from the survival of political elites (especially militaristic aristocracies) imbued with "atavistic" pre-capitalist values.[30]

These classical theories hold three distinct approaches to the relationship between imperial expansion and capitalism.[31] Hobson offers the idea that imperialism was not an inevitable result of capitalism, but rather of the particular form it took in Britain (and elsewhere in the world), chiefly serving the interests of certain classes (investors, financiers). Conversely, Lenin saw imperialism as an unalterable structural feature of a particular phase in the evolution of capitalism. Schumpeter suggested, with Hobson, that capitalism was not inherently imperialistic, but thought that it might become so under the influence of non-economic forces, as opposed to the economic interests of particular groups.[32] All agree upon two things: that the main explanation of imperialism (whatever its form) lay in the metropole, and that imperialism had taken a new form in the late nineteenth or early twentieth centuries.

These approaches inspired various others, and followers and critics increasingly transformed them into explanations for the expansion of formal empire. Moreover, despite the important distinctions noted, these theories, especially Hobson's and Lenin's, became a generalized "economic theory of imperialism."[33] From the early fifties, Ronald Robinson and Jack Gallagher's work sought to develop a comprehensive alternative to this "economic theory" of imperialism. They rejected its metropolitan focus and the idea that British expansion undertook a sharp change of pace in the 1870s. A mid-Victorian "imperialism of free trade," whose prime manifestation was "informal empire," had laid the foundations of subsequent formal expansion. This informal empire could be constructed either through belligerent acts by the British government to force potential trading partners to open their doors, or through the acquisition of power by elites dependent upon the British economic connection and willing to act as "collaborators" (an argument later developed and theorized by Robinson).[34] Formal annexation was a last resort for decision makers—characterized as a lofty and isolated "official mind"—only when they judged national interests to be threatened by events overseas.[35]

Robinson and Gallagher do not, however, deny the importance of economics. Interests overseas arose from the "many-sided expansion of British industrial society," while they defined imperialism as "a sufficient political function of [the] process of integrating new regions into the expanding economy."[36] Robinson and Gallagher's study of the "scramble" for Africa sought to show that Britain did not acquire colonies in Africa as outlets for surplus capital (as they believed Hobson and Lenin had alleged). Rather, Britain's main goal was to defend the routes to India via the Cape and Suez, both threatened by escalating crises in Southern Africa and Egypt. Yet they are also clear that much of the value placed upon India by the "official mind" lay in the high levels of British trade and investment in the subcontinent.[37]

By switching historiographical focus overseas, Robinson and Gallagher also highlighted the importance of so-called "sub-imperialist" groups based overseas who initiated imperial expansion for their own ends, often with reluctant official approval. These could include military officers, pro-consuls and other administrators, settlers, and missionaries. Among these, business interests could play a sub-imperialist role. During the late nineteenth-century partition of Africa, the South African mining magnate, Cecil Rhodes; the shipper, William Mackinnon; and the trader, George Goldie, were each instrumental in founding chartered companies to administer what became the Rhodesias, Kenya (British East Africa), and Nigeria.[38] It might be asked whether they were solely motivated by their material interests. Thus, there is a long and ongoing debate as to whether Rhodes was a capitalist masquerading as an imperialist or an imperialist masquerading as a capitalist.[39] Yet whether or not Rhodes and his counterparts always acted as businessmen, it was their businesses which delivered the wealth that placed them upon the imperial stage in the first place.

Robinson and Gallagher's work stimulated much new research. Their conceptual tools underpinned D. K. Fieldhouse's far larger study of the role of economic factors in specific instances of nineteenth-century European empire-building. Fieldhouse affirmed their conclusion that while economic interests (especially sub-imperial ones) were an important presence overseas, annexation ultimately occurred only when essentially non-economic political crises in the periphery forced decision-makers' hands.[40] Meanwhile, criticism of Robinson and Gallagher's work mounted. For example, D. C. M. Platt and W. M. Matthew questioned the applicability of the concept of "informal empire" in Latin America, the Middle East, and China. Platt also reasserted that British expansion shifted to a higher gear in the 1880s.[41] Experts on West Africa pointed out that "partition" there was begun by the French before the occupation of Egypt, and re-emphasized the role of economic interests in prompting advance.[42]

Much of this work was highly specialized, implicitly asserting that the expansion of the empire was a patchwork process produced by a chaotic maelstrom of impulses. Recently, however, P. J. Cain and A. G. Hopkins have developed a new model of British imperial advance, drawing upon elements of both Robinson and Gallagher and the "classical" theorists.[43] They seek to reintegrate the subject by re-emphasising the role of the evolving metropolitan economy in propelling formal and informal imperial expansion. In particular, they highlight the importance of the service sector—encompassing trade, finance, and a host of related services such as shipping and insurance.[44] The commanding heights of the service sector were concentrated in the City of London. According to Cain and Hopkins, its business leaders enjoyed close proximity to the aristocratic elements which dominated British policymaking, not only due to the inherent economic importance of their activities, but also because these could be conducted in accordance with aristocratic mores. Thus elites of the City and the government coalesced into a single "gentlemanly capitalist" class after the Glorious Revolution, dominated before 1850 by its landed elements, and thereafter by the service elite, especially financiers.[45]

Cain and Hopkins seek to demonstrate that the interests of these gentlemanly capitalists moulded the main goals of imperial policy.[46] Between 1688 and 1815, finance and trade enabled Britain to wage war on an increasingly global scale; a conjunction often labelled the "fiscal military state." Borrowing enabled Britain to mobilize military resources on an unprecedented scale, while trade provided tax revenues which helped to service this debt, and supplied strategic raw materials. British imperial expansion sought to defend and extend the aristocratic principles of the Glorious Revolution, and foster these crucial trading and financial activities.[47] Cain and Hopkins devote more attention to the ways in which a new form of gentlemanly capitalism resulted in formal and informal imperialism between 1850 and 1939. After 1850, as first agriculture and then industry declined, Britain's balance of payments came to rely on London-based services such as "invisible exports" (insurance, shipping, and the like) and investment income from abroad.[48] Many acts of formal expansion, and much policy within the dependent empire, turned upon their interests. India's status as the "jewel in the crown" rested upon her part in an increasingly complex web of international payments.[49] Britain invaded Egypt in 1882 to ensure that she paid her debts, rather than to secure Suez as Robinson and Gallagher argued.[50] Less emphasis is placed upon the partition of tropical Africa, which offered slim pickings for the City. Here, Britain selectively defended promising business interests whose leaders often allied themselves with the gentlemanly capitalist nexus to obtain support.[51]

Cain and Hopkins reiterate the importance of late nineteenth-century informal imperialism. In both the Middle and Far East, they argue that the goals of British policy were again determined by the interests of gentlemanly capitalists—pursued with considerable success through the collaboration of the British government and certain large businesses.[52] They particularly stress Britain's relations with "settler capitalist" countries, whether within or beyond the empire.[53] These loomed large as outlets for British investment in the late nineteenth century, and as trading partners. Following Robinson's theory of collaboration, Cain and Hopkins argue that, by the mid-nineteenth century, economic and political power in these societies resided with elites committed to export-led development. This required connections with Britain both for markets, and for capital to construct railways, port facilities, mines, and a host of other works to produce primary products. Reliance upon British capital meant that these countries had to play by "rules of the game" determined by London financiers to obtain capital on good terms. During debt crises the City's power reached its zenith as borrowers were forced to play by the rules to restore their credit. Thus Cain and Hopkins emphasize an unofficial imperialism controlled by gentlemanly capitalists in the City, with little role for the British government in relations with Argentina or, for that matter, Australia.[54]

Such a sweeping and bold account has, naturally, been met with skepticism. Critics have massed on two broad fronts: home and overseas. As far as the first goes, historians have questioned the distance between agriculture and services on the one hand and industry on the other, as well as the degree to which landowning, financial and mercantile elites formed a tight gentlemanly capitalist nexus.[55] For example, H. V. Bowen shows that the East India Company drew only limited amounts of capital from aristocrats and landowners.[56] Bowen and others also suggest that the British provinces, and overseas factors, played a more important role than Cain and Hopkins acknowledge.[57] J. R. Ward has argued that the East India Company's ability to finance Indian conquests between 1750 and 1850 depended upon the revenues of a triangular trade between India, China, and Britain facilitated (at times indirectly) by the products of Britain's industrializing north and the purchasing power of its workforce.[58] The unity of the City has also been challenged. Many have noted important divisions between and within commerce, finance, shipping, and the like. There were important conflicts of interest between merchants and shippers.[59] The financial sector absorbed large numbers of newcomers, and possessed distinctly ungentlemanly quarters, for example in the mining market.[60] However, divisions in personnel might mask unity of perceived interest, in other words a common conception of the "rules of the game." My own recent work suggests that the "City," or more accurately the crucial financial sector, did not "think" in any straightforward way, but rather reacted to events, displaying common views upon only some issues and then only occasionally. This leads to further questions about the pervasiveness of the City's informal imperialism, and the possibility that a coherent programme existed which could shape British government policy anything more than fitfully.[61] The connections between the two ends of the Strand through which such a programme might have been transmitted have also been queried. While institutional linkages existed between the Bank of England and the Treasury, no similar connections have been uncovered with the Foreign Office and Colonial Office.[62] Intermingling at official dinners and in smoke-filled rooms of London clubs may have fulfilled the same function, but how effectively remains to be established.

In a similar way some historians have challenged the details of Cain and Hopkins's account of British intervention overseas. Andrew Porter has reasserted the primacy of strategic motives in the annexation of Egypt.[63] For that other crucial African test case, the South African War, Ian Phimister has argued that the real enemy feared by the British was not so much a recalcitrant Afrikaner nationalism, but an independent United States of South Africa, dominated by the mining industry, profitable to British investors but firmly outside the empire. This suggests a division between the City's informal financial imperialism and the interests of policymakers.[64] More broadly, John Darwin argues that informal imperialism was not a deliberate choice of policy, but the maximum level of power Britain could realistically assert, varying with the level of penetration of a particular region by British interests (including business interests), and the constraints imposed by global forces, not least the competition of other imperial powers.[65]

Regardless of the criticisms, Cain and Hopkins' work has meant that, even with a growing interest in cultural approaches to the study of imperialism, there is a continuing debate about the economics of imperial expansion. This debate in turn presents new challenges. Firstly, as specialist criticism unintentionally reasserts traditional dividing lines, especially 1815, continued conscious efforts must be made to cross these boundaries. Secondly, given the questions which might be asked about the coherence of the thinking of British businessmen and politicians, there is a need to research their economic conceptions of the wider world.[66] A third and related line of enquiry, which Cain has recently explored, is how far racial stereotypes conditioned ideas about the economic probity of non-European peoples and in turn shaped British policy.[67] This may help to bridge the divide between those examining "culture" and those interested in economics and imperial policy.

Consequences Overseas

Whether constructed for economic reasons or not, by the early twentieth century the empire covered approximately a quarter of the globe. It encompassed a vast range of societies, which it ruled or influenced in very different ways and to different degrees. Understanding the economic effects of imperial rule is a daunting task; one which instantly raises a further question: how does economic development take place? This has generated a voluminous literature stretching back beyond the work of Adam Smith. Two broad approaches emerge, although there are variations within each: "diffusionist" or "modernization" theories on the one hand, and "dependency" or "world systems theories" on the other. The first sees economic development as the result of a linear process driven by increases in population, industrialization, and specialization, which in turn increase productivity and incomes.[68] It argues that these transformations are ultimately generated internally, but that trade can play an important role. For free traders, following the nineteenth-century British economist, David Ricardo, unrestrained international exchanges enable countries to specialize in those products that they are best placed to produce (in which they enjoy a "comparative advantage"). Some, such as Frederick List (a German critic of Ricardo), point out that some activities are more lucrative than others and advocate nurturing "infant" industries by temporarily protecting them from international competition. Both agree that economic advance is generated by internal change, facilitated by comprehensively or selectively engaging in trade.[69] Another variant, "staples thesis," developed particularly by Canadian economists and historians, suggests that an economy with a small population and a large natural resource endowment can best achieve internal development by exporting primary products.[70]

Marx ultimately shared a "diffusionist" approach to development, seeing a linear progression through different economic systems (feudal, mercantile, capitalist) as the motor of history, although predicting that the resultant capitalism would collapse under the weight of its own contradictions. However, radical and Marxist critics increasingly departed from Marx's views.[71] The experiences of Latin American economies in the first half of the twentieth century were particularly formative. As the value of their output fell during the Great Depression, reliance upon primary products seemed a path not towards accumulation but rather perpetual poverty.[72] Marxist-inspired radicals took up the cause, and formulated a new (un-Marxist) theory of development. A. G. Frank argued that the continent had become "underdeveloped" as a result of forceful and exploitative integration into the world economy.[73] Immanuel Wallerstein and Samir Amin, along with Frank himself, subsequently "globalized" this model, formulating "world systems theories." These argue that development in the world's economic "core" (effectively Europe and the US) depended upon the underdevelopment of the periphery (at times in alliance with a so-called "semi-periphery" of intermediate dependent countries).[74] Trade, along with international investment, becomes a means of unequal exchange, which expropriates the periphery's surplus to the core. A country's place in the world system, rather than its internal conditions of production, determines its level of development. Despite numerous pointed criticisms, the challenge has been sufficient to shake any easy assumption that trade and a conducive institutional mix are sufficient to promote development.[75]

The Latin American roots of dependency and world systems theories provide a warning against their uncritical application to the economics of empire. Formal empire may not be necessary to foster underdevelopment, only an exploitative economic connection. One analysis of African underdevelopment, which drew upon dependency theory, saw its origins in the slave trade rather than later colonization.[76] Trade often preceded the flag. While in Australia colonization may have virtually coincided with the advent of overseas commerce, many western Africans and Maoris were already engaged in international exchanges on the eve of annexation, while South Asia has been described as a "pivot" of the early modern global economy.[77] Matters are further complicated by the fact that many territories were acquired from other colonial powers. How, then, might we distinguish the impact of the (British) empire from the perks and pitfalls of an international connection? Smith provides one useful answer. For him the various restrictions imposed upon economic activities under the aegis of empire distinguished its effects. To broaden this a little, the impact of empire is here seen in the repercussions of the framework woven by the empire through pan-imperial regulation and the policies of specific colonial administrations.

The level of control imposed from the center over imperial trade shifted considerably during the empire's lifetime. From the mid-seventeenth century, a complex array of legislation, labeled the "mercantile system" by Smith, sought to channel colonial trade through Britain.[78] After some relaxations in the 1780s and 1820s, this system was dismantled between 1846 and 1860. Thereafter Britain operated a free trading empire, with the exception that, by 1914, the self-governing colonies had all taken measures to protect their industries and with concessions (known as preferences) for British goods.[79] Britain sought to return to this free-trading system after the First World War, an effort finally undermined by the Great Depression. The 1930s saw the revival of pan-imperial economic regulation, especially with the introduction of imperial preferences at the 1932 Ottawa conference. Metropolitan controls reached new heights during World War II.[80] The economic policies applied within particular colonies varied more widely: it was as much a patchwork as a pattern. Britain exerted differing degrees of control within different parts of the empire. After 1846, large parts of the settlement empire were granted "responsible government," gaining almost total internal control upon their economic policies.[81] Elsewhere in the empire, British officials could not necessarily impose their policies *carte blanche*; the need for political stability frequently shaped policy.[82]Administrators' actions were further moulded by their perceptions of local society, and were, at times, curtailed by a lack of funds and minimalist conceptions of the economic role of the state.[83]

Given this diversity, little was uniform in the economic impact of the empire overseas. Three questions will be considered in the remainder of this section, each representing potential ways in which the empire might have affected its territories; questions which have generated discussion among contemporaries and historians. Firstly, did the empire facilitate transfers of wealth to or from Britain? Secondly, did imperial rule facilitate unequal relations in trade or conditions of labour which might, in practice, amount to the same thing? Thirdly, did the empire create a context conducive to development in the colonies?

The Spanish, when they conquered the Inca and Aztec civilizations in Southern and Central America, received a flow of plunder that formed a plank of their power in the sixteenth and seventeenth centuries.[84] Was the British Empire an equally crude device to transfer wealth? Certainly there were times when this could be the case. One of the attractions for the East India Company of obtaining the *diwani* (the right to collect revenue in Bengal conceded by the Mughal emperor in 1765) was that it enabled the company to fund purchases (as well as debt repayments and military activities) in India with Indian revenues.[85] Many contemporaries, including Edmund

Burke in Britain, and Gholam Hossain-Khan Tabatabai in India, accused the British of draining the subcontinent of wealth.[86] Later nationalist writers argued that the "drain" had impoverished an economy that had functioned well before the British arrived.[87]

Many have pointed out that between 1870 and 1914 India's balance of payments surplus with the rest of the world was transformed into a deficit by its exchanges with Britain; one high estimate values this deficit at 4 percent of national income in 1882.[88] This deficit with Britain, and surplus elsewhere, certainly benefited Britain—enabling her to meet her own deficits with Europe and the United States, however, it also reflected India's position within a complex network of international trade settlements.[89] How far, then, were these transfers the result of British rule, as opposed to India's position in the international economy? Some so-called officially instituted "home charges" did transfer wealth to Britain, such as the payment of salaries and pensions of ex-Indian government officials resident in Britain. Their scale may not have been that great. A recent estimate values these home charges (including debt service) at 2 percent of the value of Indian exports around the turn of the twentieth century, and less than 1 percent in 1913.[90] Noting this, one mid-Victorian commentator considered that the main advantage of the Indian empire was "a perennial supply of old Indians spending Indian pensions at Bath and Cheltenham."[91]

There were similar "drains" elsewhere in the dependent empire. In colonial Africa, public spending was normally funded by taxing the colonized, and the revenues raised were also used to pay debts, pensions, and other charges in Britain.[92] There were, however, some subsidies in the other direction. A Treasury loan funded the construction of the Uganda Railway from Mombassa to Lake Victoria in East Africa. Direct aid could occasionally constitute a large proportion of colonial budgets. "Grants-in-aid" constituted 12–44 percent of Nigeria's revenues between 1900 and 1912; in 1901 such assistance provided 88 percent of the Gold Coast's funds. These transfers were not particularly great, costing each British taxpayer an estimated £0.02 per year between 1880 and 1914.[93] The Colonial Development Act of 1929 in practice did little to increase the flow from Britain. Little funding was provided and the legislation required that projects be formulated as much to create demand for British industry as to facilitate colonial development. Only after 1940 were larger sums devoted to empire development.[94] In the self-governing empire, there were even fewer subsidies either way, and payments from the colonies to Britain required the approval of increasingly democratic colonial assemblies. Overall, empire resulted in some "unrequited" payments both from and to colonies, which varied considerably and were rarely vast in scale.

If there was no significant or consistent "drain" of resources to or from Britain, was the empire a device to ensure that exchanges under its aegis were "exploitative"? Defining "exploitation" is difficult. Popular usage would see exploitation in low wages or prices given for products. Marxist theory suggests exploitation is inherent in a capitalist system, while dependency theory argues the same for international exchanges. All suggest exploitation is fundamentally an economic rather than a political process: it does not require imperial rule to operate. One alternate approach has been to see exploitation as intervention to secure transactions at better terms than those determined by the "free market."[95] This is not without its problems—free markets often prove elusive—but it allows us to distinguish the effect of empire from capitalism or an international connection.

To what extent did official actions facilitate exploitation in imperial commerce? Under free trade, British administrations did little to obtain colonial products at less than market prices. If there was exploitation it operated through unofficial channels. British trading houses in parts of India and West Africa often obtained semi-monopolies as purchasers of primary products and marketers of imports, using this position to maximize their profits, while shipping conferences were widely formed in the late nineteenth century to prop up freight rates.[96] Such measures were not confined to the empire; similar combinations sought to control Latin American shipping in the late nineteenth century.[97] They were only an effect of the empire inasmuch as imperial rule prevented any legislation being taken against "combinations" in the dependent empire. Anti-combination legislation was common in parts of the self-governing empire; after 1901 the Commonwealth of Australia passed such laws, although with mixed success.[98] Matters changed from the 1930s, when Britain abandoned free trade. The dominions tended to find their markets enhanced as metropolitan tariffs discriminated against the products of foreign rivals; one might say they enabled the dominions to exploit British consumers! On the other hand, many of the dependencies fared worse. Unless constrained by international treaties, many were forced to grant preferences to British manufactures with little gained in return. With a few exceptions—mainly those favourites of consumers, sugar, and tobacco— Britain did not impose tariffs upon tropical products and therefore could not make reciprocal concessions. The situation worsened after 1939 with the introduction of the compulsory bulk purchasing of much colonial produce. Although this was at times used to purchase output lacking a market due to wartime disruptions to shipping, it was increasingly used to lower prices.[99]

Much of the labour undertaken in the empire was, undoubtedly low paid, but how far was colonial labour "exploited"—in other words exacted at less than market price? Slaves in the West Indian sugar islands, and the Indian indentured labourers deployed throughout the empire after the abolition of slavery were both paid nothing or, through unfavorable contracts, given less than a "market rate."[100] Equally, western African (and later south Asian) societies were denied access to this labour. In the case of the former, few deny this had a negative—if highly regionalized—effect, although some question its overall significance.[101] Forced labour was also common in the early years of colonial rule in Africa. One officer in the Nyasaland Protectorate wrote to his mother that:

> One chief has to bring me 200 men to work for nothing and he brings me some every day, but he has to bring me a lot more yet. The hatred on his face when I tell him he has to bring more still or I'll make war on him is intense, but he's got to do it, or I'll burn all his villages and crops down.[102]

In Southern Rhodesia, controlled by Cecil Rhodes' British South Africa Company until 1923, a plethora of legislation sought to secure a plentiful supply of cheap labor for the colony's struggling gold-mining industry. Africans were forced into employment by taxation. The industry also formed the Rhodesian Native Labour Board which used a host of practices to obtain labor on cheap long-term contracts: a system nicknamed *Chibaro* (meaning slavery) by its victims. Its activities would have been futile without pass laws to prevent desertion and the colonial legal system to enforce unequal contracts.[103] Yet not all, or even most, labor undertaken in colonial Africa was forced. By the 1930s European enterprises in southern and central Africa were obtaining adequate supplies of labor. Partly population strains, often accentuated by restricted access to land (an indirect form of coercion), overtook direct coercion as a means of forcing down the price of labor. Moreover, wage labor had its own attractions, partly because earnings tended to be unevenly distributed across generations and genders. Often it provided the young men who most frequently undertook it access to a new source of resources and, potentially, social status.[104]

These dynamics of labor in early twentieth-century African colonies contrasted with those in the antipodes. The self-governing colonies there had already established a tradition of defending workers' rights and, even as the *Chibaro* system began to bite in Rhodesia, Australia was strengthening its labor laws. For instance, in 1908 the Australian federal government adopted the principle of "new protection," which stated that workers should share the fruits of gains from industrial protection, while the Australian High Court ruled that workers ought to be paid a wage high enough to support a wife and family. Bitter legal and political disputes surrounded these measures as employers and conservatives fought a rearguard action in the courts, delaying their full implementation.[105] In common with other settler colonies, legislation also ensured that non-white immigrants were excluded and unable to benefit from these measures.[106] Indigenous peoples also remained marginalized. Of course, as a self-governing colony Australia had virtual control over such matters. Its labor legislation, which proceeded further than British economic orthodoxy allowed, and the distribution of the benefits was not a feature of imperial control, but of its absence.[107] This is indicative of the varying trajectories of different parts of the empire at virtually the same time, and indeed of the contrasting nature of its components.

Did imperial rule promote development to the extent that, while some of the fruits may have unfairly accrued to Britain, there was, nonetheless, some advance for those under its aegis? One issue has been the degree to which British empire building created what A. G. Hopkins described in the West African case as an "open economy": one focusing upon a limited range of primary products for export with significant expatriate control. As we have seen, how one judges the merits of this depends upon the role assigned to trade in the development process. Moreover, since trade often preceded annexation, how far might open economies be the result of colonization? Hopkins' study of West Africa argues that its open economy had been developing at least since the transition to "legitimate commerce" following the abolition and suppression of the slave trade from 1807. While colonial rule may have removed certain "bottlenecks" in economic activity in matters such as transportation, it merely ushered in a new period in the area's long-standing engagement in the international economy.[108] Furthermore, the existence of this export trade may have shaped colonial expectations and policies. After partition, production in western

African colonies tended to be undertaken by Africans on a small scale, and large-scale production by expatriate interests (except in mining) tended to be discouraged by colonial officials in contrast to the situation elsewhere in the continent. The Nigerian administration would not permit the soap magnate William Lever to establish plantations and in the end he turned to the Belgian Congo. Partly Lever's overtures upset other established merchant interests, but administrators also saw that Africans were already producing for the world market (hence generating tax revenues), and feared that any widespread alienation of land of the kind that occurred elsewhere in British colonial Africa risked provoking African opposition with the potential to threaten the fragile colonial order.[109] Through the colonial period, western Africans proved particularly adaptive to the shifting demands and opportunities of the world economy. Farmers in southern Ghana, for example, migrated and developed new forms of social organization in order to produce cocoa.[110] Thus the distinctive form the "open economy" took in different regions of the empire might result from the interaction of pre-colonial economic activity and the "agency" and initiative of the colonized, as well as the assumptions of colonial rulers. It is unlikely that the latter painted upon a blank economic canvas.

Production for export remained largely concentrated upon a narrow range of primary products leaving many colonial economies vulnerable to shifts in the world price of a few products: something which was to prove catastrophic for many following decolonization. Yet concentration upon a few export "staples" also marked the development of many white settler colonies. Why, then, did the voluminous export trades developed in much of colonial Africa, not to mention the old West Indian sugar colonies, not produce the sustained economic development seen in Canada, Australia, and New Zealand? Why has Latin American dependency thesis rather than Canadian staples theory seemed more relevant in understanding their fortunes? Fieldhouse, contrasting the Ghanaian and Australian experiences, has recently suggested that the answer may lie in the failure of the export economy of the former to generate significant linkages with the wider economy.[111] Many of these linkages involve manufacturing goods to facilitate production (including sustaining labor), and processing and refining products.[112]

The policies of colonial rulers regarding industrialization have long been particularly controversial, nowhere more so than in India. At the advent of British rule, Indian artisans were leading producers of cotton goods. In the early nineteenth century this industry was, it has been argued, undermined by Lancashire cotton exports and by the disbanding of regional courts and armies reducing demand.[113] Later in the century, the British have been accused of implementing policies that prevented Indian industrialization, especially by denying protection to Indian industry before 1914. In 1895 the government of India moved to place a duty (for revenue purposes) upon cotton imports. Lobbying by Lancashire cotton interests led the secretary of state for India to insist a countervailing excise duty be placed upon Indian products to prevent any protection accruing to Indian cottons.[114] Free trade, combined with the fact that tenders for Indian railway contracts were offered in London, may have robbed the Indian economy of the full spur to industrialize that might have resulted from the vast sums invested in the 1870s and 1880s.[115] The self-governing empire, perhaps aided by protection, was able to gain more of these linkages. Canada had already seen significant industrialization, much associated with railway construction, urbanization, and the expansion of "staple" production before World War I, and other parts of the settlement empire were to follow suit between the wars, encouraged to some extent by tariff protection.[116]

Nonetheless, some industrial development occurred in India, especially in Bombay and Ahmedbad, from the 1850s. British attitudes to industrialization there began to shift after 1900. Lord Curzon came to believe that an Indian industrial complex would be an important strategic asset, providing the empire with an armoury east of Suez, and his government offered support to the Tatas development of an iron and steel industry, building a railway to the site and a guaranteed order of 20,000 tonnes of steel.[117] After the war, India received and used the right to protect industries, although it has been argued that the system, which considered each case for protection individually, did not permit a systematic protective policy.[118] By independence India possessed a significant industrial complex, although this still provided only a tiny proportion of employment. As for the rest of the dependent empire, by the end of the 1930s, the Colonial Office tacitly accepted the case for allowing industrialization, although any positive moves to this end were frustrated by the Board of Trade until World War II.[119]

Primary production and manufacturing both involve the direct or indirect exploitation of natural resources, and the effects of colonial rule upon the environment has become an expanding area of research.[120] Science and environmental management played an important role in ideas of a "civilising mission" which justified imperial rule. Such claims can be seen in policies as diverse as late eighteenth-century attempts to improve the lot of Caribbean slaves by transplanting breadfruit from Tahiti, irrigation schemes in India, or the conservation of forest lands.[121] The results of such interventions could be disastrous. The colonial state in Northern Rhodesia restricted access to firearms and sought to conserve wild animals (not least to preserve one favoured activity of colonial officials—hunting). For a time it also abolished the widespread *chitemene* system of "slash and burn" agriculture—highly productive but seen as wasteful by colonial officials—until revolt looked likely. Leroy Vail has argued that these measures led to the return of the bush and tsetse fly and reduced food supplies, making the environment far more hostile for humans.[122] Equally, in a recent study of Baringo in Kenya's Rift Valley, David Anderson has shown how colonial rulers' interventions to tackle problems caused by overstocking, overgrazing, and overcrowding only exacerbated ecological problems and, along with unpopular land policies, provoked resistance.[123] However, there is a danger in overestimating the power of the colonial state. J. McCracken has suggested that attempts at regulation in Nyasaland were only ever enforced fitfully, and hence could not be solely responsible for the spread of tsetse fly there in the early twentieth century.[124] Moreover, Tomlinson has recently observed that the most profound transformations of flora and fauna occurred in the temperate colonies of the Antipodes, and North America, rather than in Africa and Asia. Of course, similar developments in Latin America and the US should caution us against attributing these changes to imperial rule. The real challenge lies in Tomlinson's argument that the ecological barriers to transferring European technologies and plants imposed structural limitations upon the potential economic impact of empire.[125] Assessing this further perhaps awaits a full incorporation of environmental factors into theories of development.

Overall, the impact of imperial rule upon the wealth of the "nations" within the empire belies easy categorization. At times it could involve a drain of resources or exploitation, and at times colonial rulers may not have charted the best path to riches, but there was little consistency. Moreover, as the often-limited nature of the power of the colonial state becomes clear, it might be asked how far economic outcomes in different regions of the empire depended not only upon imperial policy but upon factors already present in colonial society. One thing perhaps is clear. There were few places where British imperial rule enabled a significant free transfer of resources to Britain in addition to those occurring through trade and interest payments. This in turn has led to a debate about the costs and benefits of the empire to Britain.

Consequences for Britain

As we have seen, Smith's *Wealth of Nations* argued that while trade and the development of at least the North American colonies benefited Britain, the "mercantile" system diminished these gains. Internationalism was economically beneficial, imperialism was detrimental. Smith was neither the first nor the last to consider the costs and benefits either of empire or of an international orientation. The implications of both for the British economy have been the subject of repeated controversy. Broadly, two questions have recurred. First, did gains from possessing an empire outweigh the costs? Second, did the possession of an empire distort the long-term evolution of the British economy?

Smith contributed to a pointed debate among his contemporaries concerning the benefits and costs of imperialism and internationalism.[126] As we have seen, trade with the extra-European world was particularly dynamic through the eighteenth century. Smith, as we also saw, recognized the value of this trade, but did not believe that it was enhanced by mercantile regulation. He, along with some others, expected that trade with the North American colonies would continue to flourish without imperial rule; a case vindicated as Anglo-American trade rapidly exceeded pre-1776 levels by the end of the 1780s.[127] With empire, it could be argued, came additional military expenditure through wars—most obviously the War of American Independence—and the maintenance of a large navy. To a great extent these might have been incurred anyway. Shipping would have needed defending and a large navy would also have remained necessary to defend mainland Britain, partly as the path of least strategic resistance, and partly due to a belief that the alternate—a large standing army—was inimical to British "liberty." The taxation of trade helped pay for these costs while even Smith noted that the Navigation Acts had aided defense by nurturing generations of seamen. Given this, P. K. O'Brien has argued that trade contributed fundamentally to British economic growth in the eighteenth century, facilitated to a great extent by imperial strategy.[128]

How far did this expanding trade, and its imperial component, lead to structural changes within the British economy, and especially stimulate industrialization? Eric Williams famously argued that the profits of the slave trade and slavery were important in providing the capital for the industrial revolution, while A. G. Frank thought it was funded by the "plunder" of Bengal.[129] Partly in response, there has been a tendency among many British economic historians to underplay the role of trade, and especially those trades associated with imperialism, and emphasize that of internal markets, natural resources, and sources of capital in instigating large-scale mechanization and manufacturing.[130] Recently, however, there has been a growing critique of analyses explaining the industrial revolution in purely endogenous terms.[131] Both O'Brien and J. M. Price have reasserted the importance of extra-European trade (and especially its imperial component) in generating the increased demand which stimulated the beginnings of industrialization during the eighteenth century.[132] Perhaps more contentiously, J. E. Inikori has argued that much of this increased demand came in an Atlantic trading system which derived much of its dynamism from the surplus of commodities produced by enslaved Africans, thus reiterating the link between African slavery (though not just in British colonies in the West Indies) and industrialization.[133]

Debates concerning the costs and benefits of empire, and its effect upon the evolution of the British economy in the eighteenth century, have counterparts in the late nineteenth and early twentieth centuries. Discussion of these latter periods has been stimulated by the dense coverage of the period in economic theories of imperialism and a concern to date and explain the origins of British economic "failure." Attempts to draw up "balance sheets" of late Victorian imperialism date back at least to Hobson.[134] The approach received a new impetus in the 1980s with the publication of a compendium of new data by Davis and Huttenback. They focus upon British overseas investment in the period 1865–1913, and seek to determine the profitability of the third which flowed to the empire. Previous studies based on stock market data had suggested that returns were higher in the empire than at home, but lower than in the foreign sector. Davis and Huttenback prefer calculating returns from the accounts of a sample of 482 firms. Between 1860 and 1884, they argued, empire investments did prove more profitable: returns were 5.8 percent at home, 5.8 percent overseas and 9.7 percent in the empire. Between 1885 and 1912, the position altered, these investments earning 5.5 percent, 5.3 percent, and 3.3 percent respectively. The empire, they concluded, did not yield higher profits after 1885; it was "a flame not worth the candle."[135] They then considered British expenditures in support of the empire, especially defense costs. Between 1860 and 1912 the average proportion of the UK budget spent on defense was 37 percent, compared to 3.3 percent in regions of responsible government, 32.5 percent in India (excluding the Princely States), and 2.8 percent in the rest of the dependent empire. Foreign developed countries spent 28.4 percent and foreign underdeveloped countries 28.7 percent.[136] Finally they analysed the distributions of these costs and benefits. Examinations of imperial stockholders found that "elites" ('financiers," "military," "gents and peers," and "misc. elites") based in the South East disproportionately invested in the empire, and, at least until 1909, tended to be taxed relatively lightly. This led them to conclude that returns from imperial investments did not match the outlay involved, but that two main groups gained: the British upper classes (who received those returns and shouldered fewer of the costs) concentrated in the South East, and the colonies of settlement (who were effectively subsidized by British defense expenditure).[137]

P. K. O'Brien has sought to incorporate trade into the analysis. By 1913, British agriculture produced only half of the non-tropical foodstuffs consumed in the United Kingdom, and (setting aside coal) 90 percent of the raw materials for British industry came from abroad. However, under free trade Britain paid prices determined in world markets for these products whether they came from the empire or not. All would have been available anyway.[138] It was only in the 1940s that devices such as bulk purchasing enabled Britain to purchase some products from tropical colonies below market prices.[139] O'Brien also suggests that without the distraction of defending the empire Britain might have been better prepared for the German challenge in the twentieth century while enjoying lower levels of taxation.[140]

The statistical basis for the case supplied by Davis and Huttenback can be questioned. Their data on rates of returns, for example, is based upon the accounts of 482 firms. While this may sound large, Davis and Huttenback do not indicate what proportion of total British investment they represent, or how typical they are of British investments. Their sample is entirely composed of firms registered in Britain. Yet according to their own figures, 54 percent of British investment in the empire was placed in government stocks.[141] Private companies registered overseas, including some important empire investments such as the Canadian Pacific Railway, or many South African gold mines, also borrowed heavily in Britain.[142] Davis and Huttenback, therefore, only sampled one type of British overseas investments, and this may not be representative of the performance of the whole, especially as British-owned companies operating overseas often seem to have been less successful than locally controlled rivals (which might also attract British capital).[143]

Davis and Huttenback's, and O'Brien's treatments of defense costs are also open to question. The figures may not compare like with like. Continental European states' use of conscripts reduced outlays and they frequently borrowed to defer defense expenditure. Neither, Paul Kennedy argues, was preferable to the British approach: conscription transferred labour out of productive sectors of the economy, while borrowing transferred present burdens—plus interest—to future generations.[144] Avner Offer wonders how far Britain's defense spending really did constitute a subsidy, especially to the self-governing colonies. Britain, so close to the cockpit of Europe was, perhaps, the most vulnerable of any part of the empire. Given this, Offer asks by how much would British military expenditure really have fallen if the empire had been abandoned? The Channel would have remained a logical line of defense, while Britain would still have had a vast international trade to protect. A large navy would have remained a necessity.[145]

Part of the difficulty, especially with Davis and Huttenback's work, is that they do not pursue the alternates which might have emerged without the empire. Michael Edelstein has made counter-factual estimates using two assumptions concerning the possible outcomes of the empire being independent. The weaker assumes similar international economic engagement among its components but suggests independence might still have led to higher protection (levels comparable to the very high *ad valorum* rates favoured by the US between 1870 and 1913) in both the self-governing and dependent empire, reducing trade with Britain. This, he calculates, would have led to the loss of 1.6 percent of British GNP in 1870, or 4.9 percent in 1913. On a stronger assumption, that without incorporation into the empire, he suggests the level of trade might have fallen still further—resulting in the loss of 4.3 percent of GNP in 1870, or 6.5 percent in 1913. Changes to investment income would, he claims, have been less profound as lower volumes of borrowing would have been counterbalanced by higher interest charges.[146]

These counterfactuals themselves are open to question. Considering the weaker assumption, O'Brien has pointed out that Edelstein fails to consider whether resources devoted to trade might have found more profitable employment elsewhere in the domestic economy, and whether protection overseas might not have been off-set by other opportunities—for example, in the provision of British capital goods. Turning to the stronger assumption, he also questions the extent to which patterns of trade might have altered. India's trade surpluses with the rest of the world enabled Britain to meet deficits in Europe and the United States, and the subcontinent might not have withdrawn from this trading pattern if outside the empire.[147] Paul Kennedy objected that without British rule providing a stable political and legal framework, Indian trade might have been seriously reduced. This was certainly an argument of nineteenth-century British imperialists, but by no means uncontentious ground given the dynamism of the pre-colonial Indian state formation and economic activity.[148] In other regions, as we have seen, open economies were built upon pre-colonial developments, again leading us to question how far trading patterns might have altered. However, the alternate to British rule in many areas might not have been independence, but domination by another European power. Would the British have lost out were another power to have administered their empire, or would they have benefited as "free-riders," letting someone else shoulder the costs?[149] More systematic consideration of British business in other empires might, however, help us to consider the repercussions.[150]

Curiously, debate on the costs and benefits has been confined in a number of ways. It overlooks their distribution, a central theme in Hobson's and Smith's critiques, revisited by Davis and Huttenback. One might, for instance, question the basis of their conclusion that imperial investment was the predilection of southern elites. How many of these were actually provincials using a London address?[151] Significant regional pockets of investment also existed, and certain classes of investors might have been particularly interested in certain types of imperial stocks.[152] Furthermore, attention has focused upon the period between c. 1870 and 1914, when a free-trading regime did little to distinguish relations with the empire from those with any other part of the world. More sustained attention is required to the partial resurrection of the "old colonial system" between the 1930s and 1950s.[153] Finally, the empire is often seen in relatively undifferentiated terms.[154] Between 1870 and 1914 the dominions (collectively) and India loomed largest as economic partners for Britain. Might it be possible to argue that while this economic core of the empire was worth the cost, much of the rest was extraneous?

The balance sheet debate has maintained a peaceful coexistence with a broader discussion about British economic "failure," especially the loss of the industrial lead she had acquired by the mid-nineteenth century. Late-Victorian Britain, it has been alleged, sacrificed its position to German and American competitors in the products of the "second industrial revolution": steel, chemicals, and electricals.[155] One frequent charge has been that the British capital market's international orientation meant that it failed to provide adequate investment for domestic industry.[156] Numerous factors have been offered as explanations, including investors' preferences for secure, fixed interest securities, or an anti-industrial "gentlemanly" culture.[157] Apologists for the City have pointed out that it could channel significant sums into industry at home and overseas. Barings, for example, raised £6 million for the Guinness Company in 1888, while in the decade prior to 1914, Canadian industrial financiers successfully tapped London.[158] Might, then, a lack of demand from domestic industrialists themselves explain the alleged bias? Alternatively, W. D. Rubinstein has argued that Britain's comparative advantage has always lain in the provision of services: any international bias was entirely rational even if detrimental to industry.[159]

This debate is more about the merits and pitfalls of internationalism rather than imperialism. Could the international orientation seen in the late nineteenth century be the legacy of an earlier phase of imperialism? O'Brien has argued that this orientation may indeed have its origins in the previous two centuries of mercantilism, and especially the determination of the British government to foster naval strength.[160] It is likely that naval construction might have generated advantages in trade and other overseas activities. How far though did the need to defend an empire, as opposed to basic geography, lead Britain to devote resources to nautical power? O'Brien begins his analysis in 1688, but the answer might well be sought far earlier. A preoccupation with maritime strength can be seen in the late middle ages and one might trace it back to the reign of Alfred![161]

A wide range of scholars have suggested that, in the late nineteenth century, the empire offered British exporters a "soft-market" which sustained mid-Victorian staple industries, blocking the adoption of more innovative business practices and newer products.[162] This alleged "softness" has recently been tested by Andrew Thompson and Gary Magee. They focus upon the self-governing colonies between 1870 and 1914, the fastest growing imperial markets, concluding that British exports did not receive an easy ride. Their growth reflected their rapid development and Britain's competitors' trade expanded more rapidly. British goods might enjoy some "sentimental preference," but this was not reflexive or unthinking. Circumstances overseas shaped demand. For example, by the 1890s Australians had developed a preference for continental style lager. British brewers such as Tennents, McEwan, and George Younger only retained their market by responding to the changing antipodean palate.[163] Might the dependent empire, where Britain possessed far more political control, have offered greater succour? In India it was certainly hard for foreign competitors to make inroads, although the proportion of imports coming from Britain declined from 85 percent in 1870 to 66 percent in 1913. There may have been a degree of official favouritism in the handling of government contracts (especially for railway construction between 1875 and 1885). This alone, Thompson argues, does not entirely account for the dominance of British firms, many being reliant upon the non-government sector. By 1900, exporters of British textile machinery only staved off stiff US competition by actively courting the market.[164] Overall, it seems, the late Victorian and Edwardian empire offered few easy rides for British industry.

The years prior to the Great War might also seem the wrong place to seek "softness." After all, the empire (with the exception of the dominions) remained committed to free trade, limiting the degree of overt discrimination possible. In 1931, Britain abandoned free trade in favor of protection and a measure of imperial preference. By the 1930s far more British exports were flowing into imperial channels. Fieldhouse has argued that while the imperial trading system constructed in the 1930s helped cushion British industry against the ravages of depression, it also removed pressures to improve products and levels of customer service.[165] Yet we might ask whether this thirty year period of neo-mercantilism was long enough to have a significant impact upon British industry, and how one assesses its impact on British industrial performance after 1945 as opposed to, for example, the militarization of the economy between 1939 and 1945.

The question still remains: was it worth it? Certainly, given that British trade, investment, and migration were never exclusively or even primarily confined within the empire, it is hard to find a flow of wealth from the empire decisive enough to make a considerable difference to British economic growth. Conversely, the outlays made to defend and sustain an empire do not seem to have been crushing. Yet perhaps more interesting issues emerge when we cease to consider the whole. Might certain parts of the empire have been crucial for certain groups at certain times? These need not have been "gentlemanly capitalists" or even elites. The balance sheet approach, arguably, tells us too little about the distribution of the economic costs and benefits of empire, regionally, by class, or by economic activity. Given the emphasis here upon the diversity of the empire, the attempt to generalize seems fraught with difficulties. A disaggregated analysis of the costs and benefits is, perhaps, much harder to achieve, not least because the basic unit of so much economic history remains the nation. Recent historiographical developments may help to overcome this.

Recent Developments: Globalization and the Economics of Empire

A new word has recently forced its attention upon historians: globalization. This has come partly through continuous usage in the media, and partly through increasing theorization in the social sciences. Globalization, like so many "metaconcepts," can be defined in a number of ways. Some approaches see it as the increasing integration of the world and its regions, others, as a growing consciousness of this integration.[166] In constructing their models, social scientists are increasingly drawing historical parallels. Part of the justification for the adoption of globalization as a research agenda, as outlined recently by A. G. Hopkins, comes from the dangers of the misuse of the past in debates among social scientists.[167] This is certainly a powerful enough case to maintain an interest in transnational economics and the economics of empire, as a crucial component of the history of empires and globalization. But are we generating significant *new* lines of enquiry?

There is a danger that any debate generated by the concept of "globalization" may simply result in the restatement of older positions in new language, or that its vagueness may mask important regional, temporal, and distributional disparities.[168] Yet "globalization" might open some enticing new avenues, or at least signpost less trodden routes rather more clearly. One merit, perhaps, is that the concept bridges the non-economic and the economic. It demands a total history encompassing economic, religious, political, social, and cultural developments, and an examination of their interrelationships. Particularly interesting is the relationship between economics, culture, and globalization. Research upon patterns of consumption which, after all, are the motor of so much economic activity, might prove a missing link in studies of imperial economics where, very often, the consumer is taken for granted. Tastes and preferences, combined with purchasing power, could have profound global and regional repercussions. Demand for sugar and tea propelled many early modern British trading and imperial ventures in both the Atlantic and Asia. Later, and more locally, production standards in late nineteenth-century New Zealand's dairy and meat industries were shaped to please the (rather asinine) tastes of British middle class consumers.[169] Consumption seems at least one place at which the study of culture and economics meet.

A second point, and one which has been a constant theme here, is the necessity of maintaining some conceptual division between the impact of empire and internationalization. Perhaps "globalization" provides us with a useful "metaconcept" to replace the sometimes confusing use of imperialism to denote acts of transnational cultural interaction, trade, investment, migration, and the like. Thus the way in which New Zealand's pastoral economy was shaped to British taste might easily be considered a feature of globalization and "market forces" without being in any way evidence of imperialism—a word we can reserve for direct and deliberate acts of, or attempts at, control.

This opens a third issue, the extent to which imperialism might shape such global interactions. Recently Magee and Thompson have examined the degree to which the empire wove a particularly dense and distinctive pattern of transnational networks, based upon a sense of community derived from shared values of Britishness. These may have facilitated international transactions by promoting information flows, and confidence between businessmen in Britain and overseas.[170] The empire may have spun particularly dense networks through, for example, the close ties between British and dominion newspapers; the dense web of social contacts forged by frequent circulation of individuals on ostensibly empire-related business; or pan-imperial trade organizations.[171] How far such networks, concentrated in the colonies of settlement, overlap with, or are distinct from, those connecting Britain and the dependent empire on the one hand, and neo-Europes beyond the empire, including the US and the Latin American Cone, will be particularly interesting to see.

Globalization, at least in popular usage, is synonymous with big business. There has been much work upon the evolution of British multinational companies, the various forms they have taken, and their relative success or failure.[172] Many able case studies have been made in regional or imperial contexts.[173] Just as there might be a distinctly imperial economic system in the "British World," can we find any patterns among "imperial businesses" in the non-European portions of the empire? Some current research suggests that business in the empire may indeed have possessed and transmitted an "imperial culture."[174] In addition, just as Andrew Thompson's chapter in this volume suggests that the empire could have subtle impacts upon the British state, might the same not have been true for the empire and culture of British business?[175]

Finally, many social scientists emphasize that globalization is eroding the power of nation-states.[176] We may question how far this is the case, but perhaps the de-privileging of the national can again open the way to a consideration of the differing regional, distributional, and sectoral impacts of imperialism, a theme repeatedly emphasized in this chapter. Of course, there is no need for a new concept to undertake any of these tasks (but then we do not need the concept of imperialism to analyze power in international relations, as Keith Hancock famously argued).[177] The real utility of a concept perhaps is not its absolute novelty but its ability to thrust new approaches to the fore.

Conclusion

The relationships between economics and empire explored in detail by Adam Smith over two hundred years ago remain a crucial strand in British imperial history. The economic questions he asked about the causes, and especially the consequences, of imperial expansion remain as pertinent as ever today. It looks likely that an emerging debate upon globalization may well revive interest and there is plenty of mileage in debates that, a few years ago, some considered passé.[178] For example, we still need to know more about the attitudes of many important economic groups in Britain to imperialism and empire. The attempt to consider the impact of imperialism overseas, and in Britain, while needing careful distinction from the impact of forces of trade, investment, migration, and the like unrelated to the empire, might still benefit from a full integration of recent work on environmental changes. Much writing in the mid-twentieth century considered the impact of the empire upon industry in both Britain and her various colonies. In a world where services are an increasingly important economic activity, perhaps the empire's ability to promote tertiary economic activity is worthy of equally comprehensive analysis.

And yet it is to be hoped that any renewed interest in questions of the economics of empire will not only follow Smithian lines. Should we continue to ask whether imperialism promoted or retarded the wealth of *nations*? One of the great opportunities provided by the recent focus upon globalization and transnationalism may be the opportunity to examine other angles. The impacts of empire upon consumption at home and overseas, the role of imperial culture in forging transnational networks and in the conduct of imperial business, and empire's effects upon the fortunes of different groups defined by race, gender, class, age, and location, can all too often fall through the cracks created by the questions posed by Smith. Perhaps this would no longer be economic history; it certainly would not involve econometrics and counterfactuals. But the impact of the material is not limited to the quantifiable, and the importance of the particular ought not to be masked by the general. This, it seems, is the real challenge posed to historians by the concept of globalization. The consideration of the economics of empire looks likely to return to scholarly attention. It is to be hoped that new approaches continue to emerge to complement the traditional debates about causes, costs, and benefits.

Notes

1 I would like to thank Jamie Counihan, Jill Campbell, Ian Phimister, and especially P. J. Marshall for their time and many helpful comments.
2 Smith, *Wealth of Nations*, IV, p. 138.
3 *Ibid.*, IV, pp. 156, 195.
4 Semmel, *Rise of Free Trade*; Cunningham Wood, *British Economists*, esp. pp. 7–8; Fieldhouse, *West and the Third World*, ch. 1.
5 See for example, Hancock, *Commonwealth Affairs*. For discussion, see Etherington, *Theories of Imperialism*, ch. 11.
6 Quoted from Tomlinson, "Periphery and the imperial economy," p. 62.
7 Due to changes in official statistical practices, figures for 1700/1 imports are for England and Wales, while for 1789/90 are for England and Scotland. 1700/1 export and re-export figures are for England, those for 1789/90 for Britain. Calculated from Price, "Imperial economy," tables 4.3, 4.4, p. 101.
8 Cain, "Metropolitan context," p. 32.
9 *Ibid.*, tables 2.2, 2.4, pp. 35, 44.
10 Calculated from Fieldhouse, "Metropolitan economics," Table 4.4, p. 102.
11 Fieldhouse, "Metropolitan economics," pp. 103–7.
12 Cain, "Metropolitan context," pp. 37–8.
13 For discussion, see Cain and Hopkins, *British Imperialism*, pp. 161–5; Foreman-Peck, *History of the World Economy*, fig.7.1, p. 121.
14 Calculated from Cain, "Metropolitan context," table 2.6, p. 48.
15 Cain and Hopkins, *British Imperialism*, tables 17.1, 18.7; pp. 415, 439.
16 Fieldhouse, "Metropolitan economics," p. 111.
17 Seeley, *Expansion*, p. 11.
18 Langford, "Burke, Edmund."
19 Semmel, *Rise of Free Trade*; Cunningham Wood, *British Economists*.
20 Although they too existed in the context of a vocal contemporary debate. See Etherington, *Theories of Imperialism*.
21 Earlier expansionisms are sometimes acknowledged. See *ibid.*, pp. 172–5.
22 Cain, *Hobson and Imperialism*.
23 *Ibid.*, ch. 8.
24 *Ibid.*, esp. pp. 5–14; Etherington, *Theories of Imperialism*, pp. 61–85.
25 Hobson, *Imperialism*, ch. 6.
26 *Ibid.*, pp. 51–61.
27 B. Porter, *Critics of Empire*, pp. 215–16.
28 Etherington, *Theories of Imperialism*, pp. 129–33.

29 Lenin, *Imperialism*; A. Brewer, *Marxist Theories*, pp. 116–23; Etherington, *Theories of Imperialism*, pp. 135–42.

30 Schumpeter, *Imperialism and Social Classes*; Etherington, *Theories of Imperialism*, pp.151–64.

31 Hobson and Lenin have frequently been conflated. See Stokes, "Mistaken identity"; Porter, *Critics of Empire*, p. 214.

32 Semmell, *Rise of Free Trade*, pp. 215–16, 222–6.

33 Etherington, *Theories of Imperialism*, chs 10–12, p. 235.

34 Robinson and Gallagher, "Imperialism of free trade"; Robinson, "Non-European foundations," esp. p. 124. See also Darwin, "Imperialism and the Victorians," p. 617.

35 Robinson, Gallagher, and Denny, *Africa and the Victorians*, pp. 19–24.

36 Robinson and Gallagher, "Imperialism of free trade," pp. 5–6.

37 Robinson, Gallagher, and Denny, *Africa and the Victorians*, esp. pp. 9–13.

38 See variously, Flint, *Sir George Goldie*; Galbraith, *Crown and Charter*; Rotberg, *The Founder*; Munro, *Maritime Enterprise and Empire*.

39 On the founding of Rhodesia, for example, see Flint, *Cecil Rhodes*; Phimister, "Rhodes, Rhodesia"; Butler, "Cecil Rhodes."

40 Fieldhouse, *Economics and Empire*, esp. pp. 459–77.

41 Platt, "Imperialism of free trade"; Platt, *Finance, Trade and Politics*; Platt, "Further objections"; W. M. Matthew, "Imperialism of free trade."

42 For summaries, see Louis, "Introduction," pp. 22–4, 27–32; Cain, *Economic Foundations*, pp. 51–7.

43 Cain and Hopkins, *British Imperialism*, pp. 31–4.

44 *Ibid.*, pp. 35–6. See also O'Brien, "Inseparable connections"; Brewer, *Sinews of Power*, and Andrew Thompson's contribution in this volume.

45 Cain and Hopkins, *British Imperialism*, esp. pp. 38–43.

46 *Ibid.*, pp.34–61, 645–55.

47 Cain and Hopkins, *British Imperialism*, pp. 63–98, 648–9.

48 *Ibid.*, pp. 648–9.

49 *Ibid.*, p. 278.

50 *Ibid.*, pp.312–17.

51 *Ibid.*, pp. 327–9.

52 *Ibid.*, pp. 340–79.

53 For this phrase, see Denoon, *Settler Capitalism*.

54 Cain and Hopkins, *British Imperialism*, chs 8–9.

55 Daunton, "Gentlemanly capitalism," pp. 134, 137, 140–1; Porter, "Gentlemanly capitalism," pp. 268–9.

56 Bowen, "Investment in the later eighteenth century"; Bowen, *Business of Empire*, p. 104.

57 Bowen, *Elites, Enterprise*, esp. pp. 16–21; Porter, "Gentlemanly capitalism," pp. 277–9; Munro, *Maritime Enterprise and Empire*, pp. 508–10.

58 Ward, "Industrial revolution and British imperialism."

59 Porter, "Which city, what empire?," p. 58.

60 Phimister, "Corners and company-mongering," pp. 38–9; *id.*, "Foreign devils"; Kynaston, *City of London*, pp. 333–4. See though, Cassis, *City Bankers*.

61 Dilley, "Gentlemanly capitalism."

62 Dumett, "Introduction" to *Gentlemanly Capitalism*, p. 10; Green, "Influence of the City," pp. 201–13; Green, "Gentlemanly capitalism," pp. 62–3.

63 Porter, "Gentlemanly capitalism."

64 Phimister, "Empire, imperialism and the partition," pp. 75–7.

65 Darwin, "Imperialism and the Victorians"; Darwin, "Globalism and imperialism."

66 Dilley, "Gentlemanly capitalism," esp. chs 3–4; Darwin, "Imperialism and the Victorians."

67 Cain, "Character and imperialism."

68 The classic is Rostow, *Stages of Economic Growth*.

69 Fieldhouse, *West and the Third World*, ch. 1.

70 For discussion, see Schedvin, "Staples and regions," p. 535; Neill, *Canadian Economic Thought*, ch. 8; W. A. Sinclair, *Process of Economic Development*, pp. 1–18.

71 Brewer, *Marxist Theories*, pp. 48–57, ch. 7.

72 Albert, *South America*, pp. 19–20; Abel and Lewis, "General introduction," pp. 2–18.

73 Frank, *Capitalism and Underdevelopment*, esp. pp. xv–xxii.

74 Wallerstein, *Modern World System*; Amin, *Accumulation on a World Scale*. For discussion, see Brewer, *Marxist Theories*, chs 8–9; Fieldhouse, *West and the Third World*, ch. 3.

75 For critiques, see Brewer, *Marxist Theories*, pp. 196–8; Brenner, "Capitalist underdevelopment"; Washbrook, "South Asia, the world system."

76 Rodney, *How Europe Underdeveloped Africa*.

77 Hopkins, *Economic History of West Africa*, ch. 4; Belich, *Making Peoples*, pp. 129–34, 148–55; K. R. Howe, *Where the Waves Fall*, p. 97; Bayly, *Rulers, Townsmen and Bazaars*. The quote is from Washbrook, "Problems and progress," p. 58.

78 Braddick, "Government, war, trade and settlement," pp. 293–305; Fieldhouse, "For richer, for poorer?," pp. 108–10; Semmel, *Rise of Free Trade*, pp. 28–9, 32–7, 138–57.

79 Cain, "Metropolitan context," pp. 38–41; Sullivan, "Revealing a preference."

80 Cain and Hopkins, *British Imperialism*, pp. 627–32; Krozewski, *Money and the End of Empire*.

81 Cain and Hopkins, *British Imperialism*, pp. 209–16.

82 Washbrook, "Law, state and agrarian society," esp. pp. 688–92.

83 Constantine, *British Colonial Development Policy*, ch. 2.

84 P. Kennedy, *Rise and Fall of Great Powers*, pp. 34–5, ch. 2.

85 Tomlinson, *Economy of Modern India*, p. 13.

86 Bayly, "Second British Empire," p. 56.

87 Tomlinson, *Economy of Modern India*, pp. 12–13.

88 Habib, "Studying a colonial economy," pp. 374–7. But see also Tomlinson, *Economy of Modern India*, pp. 13–14.

89 Saul, *Studies in British Overseas Trade*, esp. p. 62.

90 Tomlinson, *Economy of Modern India*, pp. 13–14.

91 Goldwin Smith, quoted in Symonds, *Oxford and Empire*, p. 81.

92 Wrigley, "Aspects of economic history," p. 118.

93 Davis and Huttenback, *Mammon*, p. 182.

94 Constantine, *British Colonial Development Policy*.

95 Landes, "Some thoughts," p. 14.

96 Ray, *Entrepreneurship and Industry*, pp. 27–8, 35–45; Hopkins, *Economic History of West Africa*, pp. 157–61, 200–3.

97 For example, see Greenhill, "Latin American trades."

98 Buckley and Wheelright, *No Paradise for Workers*, p. 16.

99 Fieldhouse, "For richer, for poorer," p. 112; *id.*, "Metropolitan economics," pp. 90–2; Ashton and Stockwell, "Introduction," pp. lxx–lxxi.

100 Marshall, "Diaspora of Africans and Asians," pp. 284–5.

101 Lovejoy, "Atlantic slave trade." See also Eltis, "Volume, age/sex ratios."

102 F. G. Poole to his mother, August 14, 1897, quoted Vail, "Political economy," p. 219.
103 Van Onselen, *Chibaro*, esp. pp. 80, 92–113.
104 *Ibid.*, pp. 118–19; Wrigley, "Aspects of economic history," pp. 125–7.
105 For overviews, see Buckley and Wheelwright, *No Paradise for Workers*, ch. 12; Norris, *Emergent Commonwealth*, ch. 6.
106 Offer, "Pacific rim societies."
107 Dilley, "Gentlemanly capitalism," pp. 139–40.
108 Hopkins, *Economic History of West Africa*.
109 Wrigley, "Aspects of economic history," pp. 85–7, 106; Phillips, *Enigma of Colonialism*.
110 Hill, *Migrant Cocoa-Farmers*.
111 Fieldhouse, *West and the Third World*, ch. 7.
112 Chandavarkar, "Industrialization in India," pp. 623–37.
113 Habib, "Studying a colonial economy," pp. 359–64; Ray, *Enterpreneurship and Industry*, pp. 6–7.
114 Tomlinson, *Political Economy of the Raj*, p. 15.
115 Ray, *Enterpreneursip and Industry*, pp. 66–9.
116 Schedvin, "Staples and regions," pp. 548–57.
117 Ray, *Enterpreneurship and Industry*, pp. 39–47.
118 Tomlinson, *Political Economy of the Raj*, pp. 61–3.
119 Butler, *Industrialisation and the British Colonial State*; Ashton and Stockwell, "Introduction," pp. lxiv–lxv.
120 For a recent collection, see Beinart and McGregor, *Social History and African Environments*.
121 Drayton, *Nature's Government*; Mackenzie, *Imperialism and the Natural World*.
122 Vail, "Political economy," pp. 228–9.
123 Anderson, *Eroding the Commons*.
124 McCracken, "Colonialism, capitalism and ecological crisis."
125 Tomlinson, "Periphery and the imperial economy," esp. pp. 55–6, 72–4. See also Crosby, *Ecological Imperialism*.
126 See Semmel, *Rise of Free Trade*, ch. 2.
127 Marshall, "Britain without America," pp. 584–5.
128 O'Brien, "Inseparable connections," pp. 67–76; Semmel, *Rise of Free Trade*, pp. 28–9.
129 Williams, *Capitalism and Slavery*, p. 105; Frank, *Dependent Accumulation and Underdevelopment*, pp. 72–3.
130 See, for example, McCloskey, "1780–1860: a survey," pp. 243–70.
131 O'Brien and Engerman, "Exports and the growth."
132 O'Brien, "Inseparable connections"; Price, "Imperial economy," pp. 98–9.
133 Inikori, *Africans and the Industrial Revolution*, esp. pp. 475–85.
134 Hobson, *Imperialism*, pp. 28–40. See also Cain, *Hobson and Imperialism*, pp. 106–14, 247–51.
135 Davis and Huttenback, *Mammon*, pp. 78–81, 107, 110.
136 *Ibid.*, pp. 160–5.
137 *Ibid.*, pp. 199, 306–14.
138 O'Brien, "Costs and benefits of British Imperialism," pp. 166–7.
139 Fieldhouse, "Metropolitan economics of Empire," pp. 90–2.
140 O'Brien, "Costs and benefits," pp. 198–9.
141 Davis and Huttenback, *Mammon*, table 2.1, pp. 40–1.
142 Innis, *Canadian Pacific Railway*, p. 276; Kubicek, *Economic Imperialism*.
143 Wilkins, "Free-standing company"; Paterson, *British Direct Investment*, pp. 103–13.

144 P. Kennedy, "Costs and benefits," pp.189–90.

145 Offer, "British Empire," pp. 216–19, 228–36.

146 Edelstein, "Costs and benefits," pp. 201–9.

147 O'Brien, "Costs and benefits," pp. 168–9.

148 Kennedy, "Costs and benefits," pp. 186–7; O'Brien, "Reply," pp. 192–3.

149 O'Brien intimates the latter, see O'Brien, "Reply," p. 193.

150 For example, see Katzellenburgen, "British businessmen."

151 Dilley, "Gentlemanly capitalism," pp. 38–9; Cain, *Hobson and Imperialism*, p. 245.

152 On Scottish investment, see Schmitz, "Scottish investment"; Bailey, "Australian company borrowing," esp. pp. 66–9.

153 See Sarah Stockwell's chapter in this volume.

154 Cain, *Hobson and Imperialism*, p. 248.

155 Dormois and Dintenfass, *British Industrial Decline*, ch. 1; J. F. Wilson, *British Business History*, ch. 4.

156 W. P. Kennedy, *Industrial Structure*, esp. pp. 144–3.

157 Wiener, *English Culture*.

158 Mitchie, *City of London*, pp. 2–9, 101–16; Marchildon, "Hands across the water"; Daunton, "Gentlemanly capitalism."

159 Rubinstein, *Capitalism, Culture and Decline*, esp. pp. 25–44.

160 O'Brien, "Imperialism and the rise."

161 P. Kennedy, *Rise and Fall*, pp. 13–35.

162 For references, see Magee and Thompson, "Soft touch," p. 689, n. 3.

163 *Ibid.*, pp. 692–4, 702–7.

164 Thompson, *Empire Strikes Back*, pp. 173–5.

165 Fieldhouse, "Metropolitan economics," pp. 101–12.

166 O'Rourke and Williamson, *Globalization and History*, pp. 8. The distinction is noted in Magee and Thompson, "Globalization from below," p. 1.

167 Hopkins, "Introduction," p. 9.

168 Porter, "Review"; Cooper, "Concept of globalisation."

169 Belich, *Paradise Reforged*, pp. 54–66.

170 Magee and Thompson, "Globalization from below."

171 Magee and Thompson, "Globalization from below"; Potter, *News and the British World*; Dilley, "Gentlemanly capitalism," ch. 5.

172 Chapman, *Merchant Enterprise*; Jones, *Merchants to Multinationals*; Wilkins, "Free-standing company"; Wilkins and Schröter (eds), *Free-Standing Company*.

173 Jones and Davenport-Hines, *British Business in Asia*; Platt, *Business Imperialism*; Hopkins, "Big business in Africa." Jones, *International Business*.

174 Current doctoral research by Valerie Johnson at King's College London.

175 See Thompson in this volume.

176 See, however, Hirst and Thompson, *Globalization in Question*.

177 Hancock, *Commonwealth Affairs*, p. 1.

178 Hopkins, "Utopian ideal," pp. 649–52.

Further Reading

Detailed and important overviews of the economics of empire in particular periods can be found in the five volumes in the *OHBE*. The work of Adam Smith is set in context by B. Semmel, *The Rise of Free Trade Imperialism*. The "classical" theories are discussed in N. Etherington, *Theories of Imperialism* and in A. Brewer, *Marxist*

Theories of Imperialism: A Critical Survey (which is also useful on "world systems theories").

The influence of Robinson and Gallagher continues to be felt. "The imperialism of free trade," (1953) in particular is worth revisiting. The subsequent debate is best followed in W. Roger Louis (ed.), *Imperialism: The Robinson and Gallagher Controversy* (1976). P. J. Cain and A. G. Hopkins, *British Imperialism, 1688–2000* ably synthesizes much specialist research upon economics and empire as well as offering a bold hypothesis. The ensuing discussions are best approached through two collections, R. E. Dummet (ed.), *Gentlemanly Capitalism and British Imperialism* (London, 1999), and S. Akita (ed.), *Gentlemanly Capitalism, Imperialism and Global History*. J. Darwin, "Imperialism and the Victorians" offers a stimulating critique of both Robinson and Gallagher's, and Cain and Hopkins' work.

The literature on empire, imperialism, and economic development overseas is voluminous. The various theories are reviewed, and "tested" in D. K. Fieldhouse, *The West and the Third World*. For an overview of colonial development policies, see M. Havinden and D. Meredith, *Colonialism and Development*. Much valuable work takes place in regional contexts. For settler societies, see D. Denoon, *Settler Capitalism*; C. B. Schedvin, "Staples and regions of *Pax Britannica*." For differing perspectives on British rule in India see I. Habib, "Studying a colonial economy— without perceiving the colonialism"; D. A. Washbrook, "Problems and progress: South Asian economic and social history, c. 1720–1860"; and B. R. Tomlinson, *The Economy of Modern India, 1860–1970*. J. F. Munro, *Britain in Tropical Africa* offers a useful review of the application of different theories of development. For general discussion of the environmental impacts and economics, see B. R. Tomlinson, "Empire of the dandelion."

Upon the economic impact of the empire upon eighteenth-century Britain, as well as chapters by O'Brien and Price in volume two of the *OHBE*, J. Inikori, *Africans and the Industrial Revolution* is controversial, but also offers a useful overview of the literature. L. E. Davis and R. A. Huttenback, *Mammon and the Pursuit of Empire* revived debate about the costs and benefits of late-Victorian imperialism and contains much useful data. Offer's chapter in volume 3 of the *OHBE* is a strongly argued rebuttal. P. K. O'Brien, "Imperialism and the rise and decline of the British economy, 1688–1989" attempts to bridge the two debates.

The best point of departure for globalization and imperial history are the contributions to A. G. Hopkins (ed.), *Globalization in World History*. See also the essays in Akita, *Gentlemanly Capitalism* and the "Afterword" in Cain and Hopkins, *British Imperialism*. For a skeptical voice, see F. Cooper, "What is the concept of globalization good for? An African perspective."

6

Religion in the British Empire

Elisabeth Elbourne

It is hard to separate out a clear domain occupied by "religion" in the British Empire. The subject spills over into the histories of an extraordinary range of groups. The topic touches on both the most intimate beliefs of individuals, even as it also relates to the political actions of very diverse communities of believers across the colonized world. The problem in some way mirrors that of imperial history itself: what might seem to be a coherent topic when viewed from the perspective of the imperial center breaks into a thousand fragments when it is necessary to encompass the multiplicity of views of the many communities that were subject to colonialism. British imperial history has, nonetheless, moved from a unifying focus on the imperial center to fragmentation into area studies and then perhaps back again to a more humbled effort to build a more complex global history.[1] The study of religion and imperialism similarly needs to focus on complexity and diversity, as well as acknowledging, at least for certain times and places, the sheer impossibility of adequately reconstructing the world views of many participants in the imperial enterprise.

The difficulty of defining the topic is related to the problem of defining "religion" itself. What counts as "religion" is partly determined by culture and prior assumptions, as David Chidester has convincingly argued in his history of the study of religion in the South African context.[2] Is it appropriate to see all ways in which a particular group tried to use non-material forces to influence the world as "religion"? How to think about African warriors chewing particular roots prepared in a certain way in order to deflect bullets, as part of a complex series of actions designed to improve performance in battle? Might root-chewing and the use of sacred specialists before warfare equally well be described as technology, for example? Is it appropriate to implicitly suggest that only the British had the possibility of *not* believing, since the British had "belief" whereas their colonized interlocutors had "worldviews," the different elements of which are less readily unpicked? The nub of the issue is, as Paul Landau and others suggest, that to separate out a sacred and a non-sacred realm is in itself a culturally determined move. Are beliefs "religion" if they do not involve the idea of a transcendent divinity?[3] Do ideas need to be systematically organized and widely shared in order to constitute religious belief? For much of the period under discussion, the British had a fairly clear idea of what religion was (an organized system of worship involving a transcendent deity) and generally thought that it was possible to disaggregate a religious and a non-religious sphere, at least analytically; many of their interlocutors wouldn't have thought of themselves as "having a religion."

Having said all that, I will nonetheless define religion as a set of beliefs shared by a number of members of a community about the non-material world and/ or about ways to influence the material world through appeal to non-material forces. This is a definition that tries to be as bland as possible, even though the material/non-material distinction is itself culturally shaped. Most importantly, "religious" ideas are scarcely fixed, even in cultures with religions based on sacred texts, but perhaps especially in oral cultures. Therefore it is not always helpful to think of unchanging "religions" confronting one another on the colonial stage, despite the obvious core of truth to this picture and its evident importance to adherents. This helps explain the particular ways in which religion shaped people's responses to colonialism, including very "material" responses, even as colonialism also in turn reshaped religious belief and contributed to a myriad of new ways of thinking about the sacred and about sacred power in a remarkable number of societies. In some cases the encounter with colonialism and with the self-conception of British Christianity pushed societies to define their own religious beliefs *as* systems, with exclusive boundaries, possibly in contrast to earlier, more open-ended ways of thinking about how the world worked.[4]

The diversity of the subject of the history of religion and empire is reflected in the multiplicity of pertinent scholarly fields.[5] Indeed, it is difficult to give a pointed summary of key trends because the historiographies of different regions are so varied even if regions were also knit together by imperial networks, global trends, and the movement of people and ideas. Key areas include the histories of particular regions; the history of imperialism; the history and anthropology, both of mission Christianity and of other forms of religion; and the history of colonial encounters. Clearly, the theme requires collaborative work on a global scale in addition to close local study, particularly given the linguistic challenges involved.

The first substantial written histories in English about religion and the British Empire were almost exclusively about British missionaries and mission societies, while nationalists in Africa and Asia often saw missionaries as powerful agents of imperialism. The legacy helped create a long-standing cleavage between different approaches to religion and colonialism, shaped by the geographical focus of historians and sharpened by the greater disciplinary influence of fields such anthropology and comparative religion on Africanists and Asianists. Since the 1980s, however, there has been an explosion of writing on missions and missionary Christianity from more diverse viewpoints (although the problem of the greater preponderance of archival evidence from a British missionary perspective persists). The post-colonial trend in imperial historiography, as well as a revived interest in identity formation, reawakened interest in missions as conveyors of knowledge and as agents of cultural imperialism.[6] From a more empiricist perspective, scholars such as Andrew Porter and Brian Stanley have helped to create a new field focusing explicitly on the relationship between missions and the British Empire, supported by the scholarly networks promoted by the Pew History of Christianity project.[7] Gender historians have fruitfully overhauled the field, reinserting female converts and missionaries and examining struggles over gender roles and sexuality in mission Christianity more broadly.[8] Meanwhile, debates that gathered force in the 1990s about the legacies of assimilation policies in general and residential schooling in particular lent an edge to discussion of religion and empire in former white settler colonies, notably Australia and Canada.[9] Regional specialists arguably pay more attention to religion in a variety of forms with the waning of materialist analyses. Certainly, Africanists have in recent years analyzed mission Christianity in exciting ways, building on a deep tradition of studying Christianity as an indigenous religion with its own dynamics.[10] The work of Jean and John Comaroff has been particularly influential, if controversial, among African historians, some of whom contest, among other things, its dialectical approach.[11]

A history of Christianity in colonial contexts nonetheless does not necessarily take imperialism as its main vector of analysis. The history of Christianity in general (rather than of missionaries in particular) reveals the importance of agents other than missionaries in the spread of Christianity and the complexity of the ways in which Christianity was spread and incorporated into indigenous societies, and changed in the process.[12] Indigenous converts were more important in interpreting and spreading Christianity than were European missionaries, for example, while Christianity was sometimes spread in forms not recognized by missionaries themselves as Christianity, as debate over the late nineteenth-century emergence of an African Initiated Church movement suggests.[13] This wider history clearly intersects with the history of religion and imperialism but is far from being defined by it, even if work such as that of the Comaroffs has in some ways re-opened a fundamental, long-standing debate about the relationship of Christianity and imperialism.[14] Beyond the history of Christianity, regional specialists grapple with the role of indigenous religions in shaping responses to colonialism.

The overall thrust of work in a variety of contexts is to demand a more cross-cultural analysis that considers the very different perspectives of participants in colonial encounters. This in turn raises the critical issue of translation, in its multiple senses, whether the literal translation between languages or the broader translation of concepts from one cultural setting to another.[15] This seems to me a particularly fruitful direction, as it compels the historian to look at diverse actors within a single frame, while prioritizing the issue of how these diverse actors actually communicated with one another, and how meaning might shift from one context to another. The difficult, and much-debated, issue of why colonized people converted to the religion of their conquerors looks somewhat different if one also factors in the ways in which the meanings of texts and beliefs change between contexts and languages, for example.[16]

Another critical issue is the interaction of different scales. Historians grapple with the relationships between religion, empire, globalization, and large-scale cultural and economic change. For example, from widely different and often antagonistic theoretical perspectives, many raise the issue of whether the high rates of adoption of Islam and Christianity in the colonized world were or were not a product of globalization and "modernity," however that vexed term is understood: the issue is one that the Victorians, with their progressivist assumptions, would have understood even if most would not have agreed with its premises.[17]

Not all of these pieces are always easy to place together, but they do add up to an overall argument for complication, and perhaps also for humility in the face of diversity. They also argue for the need to decentre the missionary, even if he (or she) should not be pushed completely to the margins. The remainder of this overview does not entirely live up that prescription: given the necessary brevity of the essay and the role of imperial Christianity as a connecting thread between regions, I focus more than I suggest is desirable on Christianity, the missionary movement and Christian imperial politics. I also explore the uses of religion in the creation of colonial group identities in the early modern period; the vernacularization of Christianity and its multiple uses by converts; cultural colonialism; and the mobilization of beliefs about the sacred in anti-colonial resistance, as one example of the diversity of religious responses to colonialism.

Christianity and the Colonial Self-Imagination in the Early Modern Period

When the first British entrepreneurs and settlers began in the seventeenth century to develop plantations, slaving forts, and small settlements in areas of the world as diverse as the Virginias, the Indian subcontinent, the west coast of Africa and the West Indies, they brought with them preconceptions that were shaped by Christianity, however inherently unlikely it is that all slavers, sailors, and settlers were fervently "religious." Despite the importance of Christian belief and indeed of sectarian conflict in many areas of established white settlement, the institutional structures of Christianity were, nonetheless, relatively weak throughout much of the early modern empire. Efforts to convert indigenous peoples, such as the New England missions of the fervent young Calvinist minister David Brainerd, were sporadic and mainly dependent on individual initiative, despite the rhetorical significance of the spread of Christianity to justifications for the plantation of new colonies.[18] Many people involved in empire were temporary migrants or lived mobile lives, such as merchants, fur traders, sailors, soldiers, whalers, or slave traders. Their mobile worlds did not coexist very easily with organized Christianity. Neither merchant ships nor the ships of the Royal Navy necessarily had chaplains on their payrolls in the eighteenth century, for example. Sailors generally only had access to organized religion if they were in a ship with a particularly religious captain, such as the evangelical John Newton who read prayers to the crew of his slave ship after a religious conversion in 1754. Soldiers were better served since individual army regiments often employed army chaplains, but this was neither centralized nor systematic until 1796.

Religion was nonetheless significant. The eighteenth century saw the slow growth of religious institutions in colonial contexts, aimed primarily at unruly British subjects. The Society for Promoting Christian Knowledge (SPCK) and the Society for the Propagation of the Gospel in Foreign Parts (SPG) were founded in 1699 and 1701 respectively by a group of high church Anglicans spearheaded by Thomas Bray, partly in response to the perception that British settlements overseas were inadequately provided with ministers, churches, and religious books. The preamble to the SPG charter complained about the inadequate provision of ministers and means for public worship overseas. Many

> do want the Administration of God's Word and Sacraments and seem to be abandoned to Atheism and Infidelity and also for Want of Learned and Orthodox Ministers to instruct Our . . . subjects in the Principles of true Religion, diverse Romish Priests and Jesuits are the more encouraged to pervert and draw over Our said Loving Subjects to Popish Superstition and Idolatry.[19]

New colonial bishoprics were formed after the American Revolution, as British administrators tried to create social and political order through a state church.[20]

Paradoxically, Christianity also created community identity and strengthened links of solidarity in new societies. However tenuous identity claims about being "British" or even "English" might have been in the early modern period, religion was a central source of group cohesion. Shared Protestantism was of course no guarantee of unity in the fractious theological climate of the early modern period. Even co-religionists were frequently divided among themselves on theological issues, as the multiple schisms and quarrels among the Puritan settlers of New England, including the foundation of Rhode Island by dissidents from the Massachusetts Bay colony, attests. Christianity did, however, help colonists in various settings to define themselves as different from others, such as slaves or hostile indigenous groups, while it also provided some underpinning of theological justification, where needed, for new settlements.

Whether indigenous groups could be or ought to be converted to Christianity was a more vexed question on which there were vigorous views but much less consensus either in Britain or on colonial frontiers than would be the case by the mid-nineteenth century. In contexts in which Christianity had political connotations, including cementing political and social allegiances, conversion might have political as well as theological weight, for example. Religion sealed allegiances. As James VI and I phrased it in his instructions to the Virginia Company, settlers ought to "well entreate" the Indians "whereby they may be the sooner drawne to the true knowledge of God, and the Obedience of us." When the young Powhaten woman Pocahontas was held hostage in the English fort at Jamestown for a year, the chaplain tried successfully to convert her to Christianity seemingly as part of a larger political move to create allies among the Powhaten; her conversion might be seen in the same light as her marriage to John Rolfe, by which the colony also hoped to cement alliances. The colony did not, however, send missionaries among the local people with whom they were frequently embroiled in violent conflict.[21] A number of the Six Nations Mohawk allies of Sir William Johnson in what is now upper New York State in the mid-eighteenth century similarly converted to Anglicanism, possibly in part as a means of fostering alliances; the war leader Joseph Brant (a key British ally during the American Revolution) became a Freemason as well for good measure.[22] Molly Brant, William's Johnson's sexual partner and Joseph Brant's sister, was a donor to the Anglican church in Kingston, Upper Canada, in the last years of her life, while Elizabeth Brant, Joseph's daughter, continued a family tradition of translating scriptures into Mohawk. Nonetheless, Christianity remained controversial among the Six Nations, as did the British alliance. This use of religion to seal allegiances worked in both directions: fur traders or Indian merchants might, for example, also move in the direction of indigenous religions in an effort to build new kin networks or business alliances.

In 1701 Parliament, under pressure from Dean Prideaux and Archbishop Tenison, revised the East India Company's charter to add a clause requiring EIC chaplains to learn local languages, "the better to enable them to instruct the Gentoos who should be the servants or slaves of the Company in the Protestant religion." Chaplains were not, however, expected to evangelize among the population more widely: again, shared Christianity was tied to allegiance and the common identity of the household. As late as 1793, it was still plausible for Lord Macartney to reassure the Chinese emperor that "the English never attempt to dispute the worship or tenets of others; they have no priests or chaplains with them, as have other European nations."[23]

In all this there was, of course, considerable variation between regions. In settlements with deep ethnic cleavages, Christianity was particularly important as a marker of group identity. In the West Indies, for example, Christianity was the defining religion of the masters. There was uncertainty about whether or not masters might be required in law to emancipate converted slaves. Many slave-owners thus resisted the efforts of Moravian missionaries to preach Christianity among slaves from the mid-eighteenth century onward. In the eighteenth century the Society for Propagation of the Gospel owned a slave plantation at Codrington in Barbados and concentrated on the spiritual needs of whites rather than on attempting to convert slaves. Tensions rose to a boiling point in the early 1800s when British Protestant missionary societies launched systematic conversion attempts that were tied to abolitionist activity. Christianity was more often spread by slaves and former slaves themselves in West Indian colonies in the seventeenth and eighteenth centuries, such as the formerly enslaved Moravian woman Rebecca Protten, who fostered an early eighteenth-century Christian community on the Danish island of St Thomas (later to become part of the British Empire) and later worked as a missionary in Africa.[24]

The distinction between Christian settlers and non-Christian slaves or indigenous peoples was one with legal bite. Early modern European law codes required that a person testifying in court take an oath in order for his or her testimony to have legal weight. Non-Christians were not able to swear on the bible to tell the truth, and thus were not able to testify in court. As late as the 1840s, this was a critical legal issue in the Australian colonies, where the incapacity of Aboriginal witnesses to give evidence in court made a mockery of the British insistence on equality under the law for white and black alike. Despite several appeals from governors on the spot, the Colonial Office did not grant the right to testify to Aboriginal witnesses until 1841.[25] Although many Christians supported the abolition of restrictions on Aboriginal testimony, including the 1823–5 New South Wales Attorney General Saxe Bannister and governor Sir George Gipps, the debate also pitted theists against secularists. In 1824 the NSW chief justice Forbes, a man who was not particularly religious, urged the home government to accept the verdict in a case in which the testimony of an Aboriginal witness to murder had been accepted despite putative legal problems:

Now was it not barbarous to exclude such testimony by a mere rule of Court, which was engendered in days of superstition, and framed by men who never heard of the consequences to which it would tend. Why is not competency confined to interest, and credibility left in all cases to the jury? Truth is a natural institute of mankind—it is founded in moral feeling—and providence has so guarded it, that perhaps it is next to impossible so to cover falsehood as to prevent its discovery, if sufficient care and means be used to expose it.[26]

The presumed Christianity of settler communities and the lack of Christianity of indigenous peoples, also laid the groundwork for legal distinctions in international law between peoples who were held to own land and those who occupied land but did not have inalienable property rights. Jurists and philosophers argued that civilization, including a high level of social and political organization, indicated inter alia by monotheism, enabled a people to develop land and thus to have a claim to it. Nomads without law or religion could not make the same property claims in land. Such arguments are present in seminal texts such as Locke's *Second Treatise*, even if Locke does not discuss religion. They also underlie the legal reasoning of Judge Burton in the 1836 Jack Congo Murrell case heard before the Supreme Court of New South Wales, in which Burton had to decide whether British courts had jurisdiction over crimes committed by Aboriginal people *inter se*, and thus by extension whether the British had a claim to rule in international law. Burton's reasoning turned around the civilization of Aborigines expressed in part by their religious practices. In a rough draft in his notebooks, Burton argued that the few and scattered Aboriginal inhabitants of New Holland "neither cultivated nor occupied in the sense of individual possession" the land and were not entitled to be considered "as so many Sovereign or Independent States." Because the practices of Aboriginal peoples were "only such as are consistent with a state of the grossest darkness & irrational superstition," their actions were not governed by "antient laws" but were "lewd practices entitled not to so much respect as the Brehon law of the Wild Irish."[27] Quite far into the nineteenth century, in sum, Christian monotheism was widely taken to be a marker of civility and of political development with implications for access to citizenship and, more broadly, to certain rights in international law.

Religion may have provided a means to help define membership in nascent colonial communities, but it also posed the dilemma to early modern colonial administrators of how to govern jurisdictions in which the religion of the majority was not a variant of Protestant Christianity. This was in some ways a continuation of the same problem: if religion created identity and helped mark group membership, then how was it possible to excite loyalty among groups that did not share the religious practices of the administrative elite? In several American colonies, Anglican administrators governed unhappy Protestant dissenters. In India, after the Battle of Plassey in 1757, at which the armies of the East Indian Company conquered the last independent Nawab of Bengal, Siraj-Ud-Daulah, the East India Company ruled over a majority Hindu population and a minority Muslim. The EIC depended on a network of largely Hindu intermediaries that it could ill afford to alienate. India's alien rulers, both the

EIC and subsequently the British state, experimented with various forms of legal pluralism, attempting to codify Muslim and Hindu law and custom; as was the case throughout colonial Africa, where a similar effort to identify and codify "traditional" law was a characteristic feature of indirect rule, the process changed the law codes, entrenched elites and removed much of the flexibility from earlier systems.[28] With less at stake economically, military officers expelled French Catholics from Nova Scotia in 1755, fearing for their loyalty as the region moved to war. In Quebec, however, with its larger population, the British were ultimately pushed towards policies that were relatively conciliatory towards the Catholic hierarchy after conquering New France during the Seven Years War: the objections of Protestant dissenters are enshrined in the Declaration of Independence.

In Ireland, divisions between Protestants and Catholics assumed some of the overtones of racial divisions between colonizers and colonized in different imperial contexts. Indeed, Burton's passing reference to the ancient Irish law, which coexisted for several hundred years with English common law, underscores the way that ideas about "wild Irish" and Scottish highlanders casually permeated discussions of civilization, civility, and law until quite far into the early nineteenth century. Around the same time, in 1828, John Philip of the London Missionary Society reminded readers of his crusading work *Researches in South Africa* that the civilization of the Scottish highlander was recent, and suggested that Africans too might be similarly transformed.[29] In both cases, but with particular political importance in Ireland, evangelicals saw Protestant Christianity as the agent of transformation. In Ireland, Protestants portrayed Catholics as uncivilized, in ways analogous to the portrayal of colonized peoples elsewhere who had not converted to Christianity. There is not space here to trace the history of the bitter and very complicated struggles between Protestants and Catholics in Ireland in the early modern period. It is significant, nonetheless, that this conflict was often framed in terms that recall colonial distinctions and called upon an assumed relationship between religion and civilization.[30]

The Missionary Movement

The late eighteenth century arguably saw a shift away from a dominant emphasis on Christianity as a marker of civility and potentially of difference and separation between groups, toward a greater stress on Christianity as a gateway to individual salvation that was potentially open to all, reflected, for example, in changes in Calvinist theology and in the growth of evangelicalism. Whether or not that is a fair generalization, an increasingly ambitious Christian reform movement that sought to convert and change the world gained influence in a number of spheres in Britain. In the watershed decade of the 1790s, three missionary societies were founded in Britain: the pioneering Baptist Missionary Society in 1792, the interdenominational London Missionary Society (LMS) in 1795, and the evangelical Anglican Church Missionary Society (CMS) in 1799. These three major societies were the precursors for an organized Protestant missionary movement that became a characteristic feature of modern British imperialism.

By the early nineteenth century, British missionaries often thought of themselves as spreading characteristically British virtues.[31] Nonetheless, British institutions had roots in the wider eighteenth-century world of evangelicalism, Calvinist revival and pietism across Protestant Europe and the Americas; the rhetoric of the early movement was determinedly international; and both the CMS and LMS employed a number of non-British missionaries.[32] An important early influence, for example, was the *Unitas Fratrum*, or Moravian church, which had branches in London and northern England. By the 1730s, the loosely linked refugees from religious warfare in Bohemia and Moravia who had eventually reconstituted themselves on the lands of Count Zinzendorff in 1727, had formed themselves into a missionary church whose young men drew lots in order to determine to which mission field God was directing them. Their publications, part of a burgeoning international evangelical print culture, influenced a young Norfolk shoemaker and occasional preacher, William Carey, to argue in 1792 for both the feasibility and urgent moral necessity of converting all non-Christians to Christianity to save them from damnation, as did the prior example of Catholic missions:

> Have not the popish missionaries surmounted all those difficulties which we have generally thought to be insuperable? Have not the missionaries of the *Unitas Fratrum*, or Moravian Brethren, encountered the scorching heat of Abyssinia, and the frozen climes of Greenland, and Labrador, their difficult languages, and savage manners?[33]

Carey went on to be a prime mover in the foundation of the Baptist Missionary Society, as well as a missionary and pioneering linguist in Bengal. The missionary movement was tightly linked to the capacity of Europeans to imagine and map the world as a whole.

Despite its international links, the missionary movement was also rooted in local conversionist evangelical culture, especially among the artisans, petty shopkeepers, and labourers who made up the bulk of the early missionary workforce. Although the key political movers in late eighteenth- and early nineteenth-century reform movements, such as Wilberforce, were almost necessarily middle and upper class, as were many members of the Boards of Directors of missionary societies, the energy behind the evangelical missionary movement in its earliest years came from below.[34]

The early missionary movement excited division, reflecting tensions between evangelicals and high church Anglicans, Methodists, and their critics, and the competing advocates of good order and of religious dissent in the charged atmosphere of the Napoleonic Wars and the aftermath of the French Revolution. Even the Church Missionary Society needed to fight against the many who viewed Anglican Evangelicals and Dissenters alike as dangerous, irrational and generally as the heirs of the disasters of the civil war and Cromwellian periods. If missionaries were not as widely supported in the opening years of the nineteenth century as they would be later, the frequently high Anglican administrators in the areas of the empire to which missionary societies despatched envoys tended to be even more wary. Central fears were that missionaries would stir up trouble, whether (in the case of the West Indies or the Cape Colony) by promoting the rights of unfree laborers, or, in situations in which the principal problem was how to win quiescence from the ruled, by provoking the anger of the targets of conversion. In the former case, the conversion of subaltern groups to Christianity breached the walls of religious division that had separated laborers from masters. In the latter, aggressive missionary attempts to change religion and culture might, it was feared, cause inhabitants to identify coerced cultural change with the British presence.

From the British perspective, a particularly vituperative debate took place in and about India. The Board of Directors of the East India Company was split about how many missionaries to admit and under what constraints, with the majority uneasy about excessive interference in indigenous customs and a minority, spearheaded by the Anglican Evangelical Charles Grant, determined to expand proselytizing and abolish certain Hindu customs. In 1806, Indian soldiers in the British army mutinied at Vellore. The revolt had deep roots and included an attempt to restore the sons of the Tippu Sultan, who were imprisoned at Fort St George in Vellore. The immediate trigger, however, was the British army's attempt to impose (backed up by extensive flogging) a new 1805 army dress code that forebade Hindus to wear religious marks on their foreheads and compelled Muslims to shave their beards, both of which orders violated religious practice. In the wake of Vellore, many in both Britain and India questioned the wisdom of interfering with Indian religions. In 1808, for example, Anglican clergyman Sydney Smith opined in the *Edinburgh Review* that it was not only futile but dangerous to attempt to convert Muslims and Hindus in India. Smith accused the evangelical members of the East India Company's Board of Directors of dangerous fanaticism:

> upon this subject they are quite insane and ungovernable; they would deliberately, piously and conscientiously expose our whole Eastern empire to destruction, for the sake of converting half a dozen Brahmins who, after stuffing themselves with rum and rice and borrowing money from the missionaries, would run away and cover the gospel and its possessors with every species of impious ridicule and abuse.

Not only were conversions largely unnecessary because "the Hindoos" were a "civilised and a moral people," but evangelical Christianity was "disgusting and dangerous enough at home." "Why are we to send out little detachments of maniacs to spread over the five regions of the world the most unjust and contemptible opinion of the gospel?"[35] While Smith's views were unusually vituperative and were certainly part of a domestic feud between evangelicals and high churchmen, they did express some real ambivalence about the missionary project that continued even amid the greater certainties of the later nineteenth century. In 1813, British evangelicals organized a petitioning campaign to persuade Parliament to make the renewal of the East India Company's license contingent on expanding the access of missionaries to Indian territory. A dramatic parliamentary debate turned around whether or not Hinduism required improvement, with different wings of the EIC taking contrasting positions. Those who supported Christianization and cultural transformation won.

Religious proponents of cultural transformation in South Asia were lent force by the liberal convictions of many Indian administrators in the high years of cultural assimilationism in the 1820s and 30s, as a new generation of administrators promoted English-language higher education for elites and the abolition of customs such as *sati*. Thomas Babington Macaulay exemplified the fusion of evangelical and liberal ideas in the self-confident atmosphere of the 1830s. Son of the evangelical abolitionist Zachary Macaulay and a Whig both as a member of parliament and as the archetypal "Whig historian," Macaulay became the first law member of the Governor General's Council in India in 1834. He argued passionately that a divided British administration ought to introduce English education at the secondary level rather than maintaining secondary-level education in Sanskrit or Arabic. As his *Minute on Indian Education* famously opined, since it was impossible with limited means to educate the "body of the people," administrators must instead "do our best to form a class who may be interpreters between us and the millions whom we govern; a class of persons, Indian in blood and color, but English in taste, in opinions, in morals, and in intellect."[36] In 1857, rebellion in the ranks of the British army of India was at least on some level facilitated by concern about the coerced violation of religious practice: in this case, famously, the British imposition of cartridges greased with pig and beef fat upon sepoys for whom to bite such greased cartridges in the course of loading a gun broke major taboos. The uprisings of 1857 caused a resurgence of doubt about the wisdom of cultural universalism, but it was no longer possible to reverse the missionary presence.

The overall trajectory of missions by the mid-nineteenth century was towards greater professionalization and closer cooperation with imperial officials, who in turn increasingly recognized the potential utility of working with missionaries. These tendencies were facilitated by the move of dissenters into the British mainstream, symbolized by the abolition of the Test and Corporation Acts in 1828; important also was the growing involvement of Anglicans of all theological stripes in missions, as the revitalization of the SPG in the 1830s and the 1859 formation of the Universities Mission to Central Africa indicate. Missionary societies provided vast networks of educational and medical facilities, ranging in scale from small bush schools to large urban hospitals. Many employees in fact developed professional administrative, teaching or medical careers that did not involve much direct proselytizing. The feminization of the movement by the late nineteenth century at first looks paradoxical but may not be: both married and single women arguably found professional outlets in missionary work that were less readily available at home, just as working class men had found similar possibilities in the 1790s and 1800s—none of which is to deny the profound religious motivation of many missionaries. In the late nineteenth century, the resurgence of faith-based missions brought a more evangelical approach back to missions. Notably, in 1862 Hudson Taylor founded the China Inland Mission that emphasized themes that would have been familiar to LMS directors in the 1790s, including evangelical work beyond imperial frontiers, itinerancy, and reliance on divine providence.

Christian Networks

One of the unintended consequences of the early missionary movement and of Christian humanitarian reform activity was the creation of powerful Christian information networks with implications both for the creation of "knowledge" and for political activity. Missionaries went to a number of parts of the world about which British information was relatively limited, often learned local languages, and sent back regular reports (frequently including diaries), which were then publicized through a remarkably active evangelical print culture. Missions were important to early modern science and to the development of anthropology as a result. The close relationship between the Royal Geographic Society and David Livingstone, LMS missionary and African explorer, is a noteworthy example.[37]

Missions also helped form popular conceptions of the non-Christian world. British Protestant missions adroitly exploited print culture, while telling stories, from personal conversion narratives to national histories, was a critical part of Protestant witness.[38] Periodical publications, pamphlets, biographies, and autobiographies streamed from the missionary world, not to mention board games, magic lantern shows, and a multitude of children's books, all designed to show the action of God in the world (while also fundraising). Concepts of civilization and savagery often informed such material, which helped build a popular conviction of the benefits of the British Empire.

Cumulatively, missionary societies often had more information at their disposal than did the Colonial Office, which relied heavily on the reports of high officials who usually stayed safely ensconsed in urban areas and stuck to English. Under certain circumstances, such as those of the Cape Colony in the 1830s, Christian activists were able to mobilize these information networks to their own ends and undermine local officials, as John Philip, superintendent of the LMS, was able to undercut the governor, Sir Benjamin D'Urban, and argue for the return of recently conquered land to the Xhosa. Public campaigns such as agitation against labor abuses in the Belgian Congo demonstrated the potential power of public lobbying, while the behind-the-scenes work of Sir Thomas Fowell Buxton, parliamentary leader of the campaign to abolish slavery and an advocate for indigenous rights, suggests the additional power of private networks. Nonetheless, such power remained strictly potential.

The movement for the abolition of first the slave trade and then of slavery itself in the late eighteenth and early nineteenth centuries provided a template for later campaigns. It is both an excellent example of a religious colonial lobby group and in some ways an exception, because abolitionists were arguing for a religious issue that had much wider backing on economic grounds. Abolitionism is surely reflective of larger intellectual and political changes such as the rise and entrenchment of liberalism and shifts in ways of thinking about man's relationship to God as an increasingly active agent: such shifts affected both British Christianity and economic theory simultaneously, so their mutual impact is difficult to disentangle.[39] At the same time, abolitionism was also made possible in part by international and local religious information networks.

In the late eighteenth century, abolition was primarily the cause of a cluster of relatively politically marginalized Quakers. Slave ship captain and eventual abolitionist John Newton later stated that as a young man he assumed that slavery was given of God and was not something it was possible to change. What changed crucially in the late eighteenth century was this belief: many Christians came to feel that on the contrary God was calling them to resist slavery. Quakers, dissenters, and Anglican evangelicals were in the forefront of a movement that gathered steam by the 1780s, marked by the creation in 1787 of the Society for the Abolition of the Slave Trade. Across the United Kingdom abolitionists adopted techniques that would later become familiar to missionary activists. Religious meetings dispersed information locally, while occasional large-scale national meetings helped create a sense of a reform movement that was united across denominations. In the meantime, adept exploitation of print culture and developing communication networks led to a steady stream of pamphlet literature. By the early 1830s, on the cusp of success in 1833, abolition was a widespread movement that enjoyed enormous popular support, despite much controversy, as it came to be seen as emblematic of British national virtue.[40]

A critical path to acceptance was the adoption of the abolitionist cause by well-placed Anglican evangelicals who gave the movement respectability and parliamentary prominence, albeit sometimes at the cost of heated disputes over the appropriate pace of abolition and the best tactics to adopt. Despite the iconic status of men such as William Wilberforce and Sir Thomas Fowell Buxton, successive parliamentary leaders of the abolitionist troops, they were clearly supported by large networks, both in the immediate sense of linked family and local religious networks and in the more obvious wider sense of armies of activists and volunteers. Abolitionism tended to run in families, such as the closely linked Cropper and Sturge families of Liverpool or the Buxton and Gurney families of Norfolk, whose members, including women, mutually supported one another in joint political endeavors. It seems symbolic that a great deal of Sir Thomas Fowell Buxton's correspondence, speech-writing and information-gathering was carried out by his daughter, Priscilla Buxton.[41] Priscilla was surely enabled to do this in part because evangelical Christianity of the period placed such emphasis on the centrality of the domestic sphere: here, public and private overlapped and dissolved into one another. Beyond the domestic support networks enjoyed by Buxton, anti-slavery activism engaged women across the western world.[42] Abolition captured the public imagination as a cause which was both political and exemplary of domestic virtue for its participants.

The optimism of the 1830s would be succeeded, however, by the greater pessimism and racism of the mid century, as predictions of the economic equivalence of slave and free labor proved too optimistic (at least under existing wage regimes in the West Indies) and as colonial lobby groups became increasingly vocal and successful on the British political stage. At the same time, the subsequent failures of the Aborigines protection movement, into which a number of key abolitionist activists, including the Gurney and Buxton families, moved after 1833, reflect the real limits to evangelical political agitation on issues that ran counter to a prevailing economic and political consensus. Buxton was influential in obtaining a parliamentary select committee that examined the status of "aborigines" in British settlements in 1835 and 1836. The committee reports, written primarily by Anna Gurney, made the case that the sin of settlers was destroying indigenous peoples across the empire; the solution was for indigenous peoples to have access to Christianity and to Western-style education and civilization in order to be able to protect themselves and to combat demoralization, while missionaries and administrators at the imperial center were to have paternalistic oversight of indigenous affairs.[43] Some imperial administrators made some efforts to put "protection" into practice, notably in the Australian colonies of New South Wales and Victoria. On the whole settler lobby groups overwhelmed what were usually half-hearted stabs at protection while indigenous groups themselves did not always welcome efforts at protection that infringed on their sovereignty, as the reception of George Robinson's tragic efforts to force indigenous people onto small parcels of reserved land in the Australian colonies suggests.[44] In the wake of this report, the Aborigines Protection Society was founded in 1837. It would, however, rapidly split into two factions, one of which was primarily interested in anthropology and the acquisition of knowledge about indigenous peoples: the convergence of missionary political networks and the networks of science is nicely illustrated in the fact that the Ethnological Society of London was an 1843 offshoot of a Christian imperial organization.

By the mid century mark, denominational struggles among the British themselves were less fervent but Christianity was, it seems to me, more explicitly woven into the fabric of the British Empire. Missionaries increasingly tended to adopt positions that were generally supportive of empire in general and of annexation in particular, often fuelled by the conviction that annexation would protect convert communities and, particularly in the high Victorian period, by ancillary belief in the mutually supportive benefits of Christianity, civilization, and commerce. Nonetheless, missionaries had ambiguous relationships with imperial authorities. They often opposed particular imperial actions and were uneasy about too close a relationship with secular administrators. Increasing ecumenicalism in the early twentieth century, expressed by the 1900 and 1910 World Missionary Conferences, provided an organizational counterweight to imperial structures, and missionaries themselves were sometimes targets of criticism by colonial officials.[45] "These missionaries are simply terrible," complained Sir Gerald Porter, the consul general in Zanzibar, to his wife in 1889:

> they have no common sense, they won't do what they're told, & go like mules in the opposite direction to what they are advised, & then when they get into a mess they expect to be pulled out of it by the Government.[46]

Nonetheless, even if the relationship between mission Christianity and imperialism was often uneasy, it was still close.

By the second half of the nineteenth century, as Brian Stanley argues, missionaries were no longer pioneers in unknown territory but often local political players, either with significant convert communities to nurture (in Bechuanaland or Fiji, for example) or largely unsuccessful (such as in China), in which case the temptation to co-operate with the state to improve the Christian position was sometimes irresistible.[47] Furthermore, the pressure of competing European powers in areas in which Britain had previously exercised informal economic control, helped push missionaries into seeing choices between British and other European annexation, rather than local independence. Among many examples, Wesleyan missionaries argued in the late 1860s and early 1870s that Fiji should become a Crown Colony; the CMS launched a passionate campaign for the annexation of Buganda; the LMS contended for the creation of British protectorates in southern Africa; John Smith Moffat and Charles Helm of the LMS helped broker the 1888 treaty and mineral concessions by which Lobengula, paramount chief of the Ndebele, surrendered territorial control over part of modern Zimbabwe to Cecil Rhodes' British South African Company, leading rapidly to war.[48] In China, missionaries benefited from, and indeed encouraged, treaty port provisions that compelled China to grant them access in the wake of deeply-resented wars in 1839–42 and 1856–60; they were taken by surprise by the virulent association between missionaries and imperialists for many, including the peasants who made up the backbone of the Boxer rebellion at the turn of the twentieth century and massacred thousands of missionaries and converts as part of their opposition to foreign imperialism.

Conversely, local uses of Christianity might also facilitate alliances between local Christians and the imperial state, however much this consequence was unintended or unwished for by converts. Paul Landau's work on the baNgwato in modern-day Botswana and the deployment of Christianity not only by Royal Family members but also by many commoners in the late nineteenth and early twentieth centuries reveals a world in which missionaries were relatively marginal, but Christianity was nonetheless enormously important to the rule of King Khama and his followers. The baNgwato did not wish for British interference in their lives. Nonetheless, the logic of Christianization and the alliances that Christianization required ultimately pushed the Bangwato into the British imperial ambit.[49]

Cultural Colonialism and the Vernacularization of Christianity

This final point raises two critical issues that in some ways overlap: the indigenization of Christianity and the broad topic of cultural colonialism. Christianity became not only a local but a majority religion in many parts of the colonized world, including British Africa, the Pacific, and much of indigenous North America. Cultural changes linked to mission Christianity accompanied that shift. Depending partly on differing views of the freedom of action of converts and of their aims, scholars might choose to emphasize the vernacularization of Christianity or, conversely, the "colonization" of culture and of the mind. Clearly, however, these were very broad processes, the study of which moves the historian of colonial Christianity beyond the agency of missionaries to the choices of the colonized.

There were many reasons that a community, or its leader, might express initial interest in receiving a missionary. In southern Africa these included the perceived capacity of missionaries through their networks to promote diplomatic alliances, and generally to act as both imperial and regional go-betweens.[50] Missionary networks also enabled access to technology and trade, including at times trade in arms. The Griqua received arms from the Cape Colony, for example, in exchange for their role as Christian intermediaries in a frontier zone. Groups such as the Khoekhoe of southern Africa, who were already incorporated in colonial structures, might be interested in missions for other reasons, including the potential freedom from coerced labour offered by the shelter of a mission station as well as, possibly, explanation for suffering.[51] Once established, missions frequently provided alternate sources of power for marginalized groups and in many cases particularly for marginalized women. An additional complication is that conversion clearly did not mean the abandonment of previous beliefs and practices to many converts. None of this explains, however, the real entrenchment of Christianity as an indigenous religion.

By the mid-nineteenth century, as Christianity became increasingly a religion of the colonized as well as of the colonizers, converts often struggled to gain control of Christianity on both the institutional and theological level. As early as the 1840s, black LMS congregations in the eastern Cape demanded "our church for ourselves," attempting to exercise the Congregationalist privilege of choosing their own ministers.[52] Lines of division were not always racial. Bishop Colenso of Natal caused a scandal in the Anglican church when he not only publicly doubted the literal truth of aspects of the Old Testament in response to questioning by Zulu interlocutors, including his translator John Ngidi, but argued that Anglican ritual should incoporate aspects of Zulu tradition.[53] Henry Venn, secretary of the CMS from 1841 to 1873, argued for the importance of an indigenous clergy and locally-run churches well before many of his own missionaries were able to accept indigenization. Samuel Crowther, bishop of Nigeria and the first black Anglican bishop, was promoted by Venn but undermined by local missionaries, for example.

Nonetheless, from the late nineteenth century onwards, many colonized people formed new churches that broke with older missionary denominations. Such breakaway churches were particularly common in Africa. In southern Africa, Ethiopianism challenged the so-called "mission churches" in the late nineteenth century, presenting a politicized interpretation of Christianity that drew on African beliefs, challenged racial subordination and enabled an all-black clergy in an environment of racism. In the Transvaal (now part of South Africa), for example, disillusioned black former Methodists and Anglicans clustered around breakaway Ethiopian leader Mangena Maake Mokone in the 1890s, moving in and out of alliances with the African-American denomination the African Methodist Episcopal Church. The complaints of Mokone, himself of royal lineage, against the Methodists included the persistence of racially segregated meetings, low wages for black clergy, and the poor advancement prospects for black clergy.[54]

African Initiated Churches (AICs) posed growing challenges to the mainstream mission churches throughout Africa, creating new loci of power. Whether the AICs should be seen as intrinsically anti-colonial is a much-debated question, but they did mark both the internalization and the transformation of Christianity within an African context.[55] AICs frequently offered healing and the defeat of witches and demons to congregants; whether or not to seek for healing was an anti-colonial gesture, it may perhaps be read as an effort to heal the psychic and material ills of unjust societies.

The vernacularization of Christianity ultimately freed communities and individuals to turn Christianity to diverse ends even if conversion also pulled converts more tightly into British-dominated worlds. These ends could and did include opposition to colonialism, from within the ambit of mission churches as well as without. John Chilembwe of colonial Nyasaland (now Malawi) was, for example, a Baptist preacher who ran industrial schools for the American National Baptist Convention in the southern Shire highlands explored by David Livingstone, and had briefly attended an African-American seminary in Virginia. In 1915 he led a brief and unsuccessful uprising against a brutal plantation owner named William Jervis Livingstone, a relative of David Livingstone, who abused his workers and had burned down Chilembwe's church. In calling his 200 followers to rise, before murdering Livingstone, Chilembwe urged them to "strike a blow and die, for our blood will surely mean something at last." He was killed as he fled to Mozambique, but despite his lack of short-term success he is now celebrated as a national hero in Malawi.[56]

What was the relationship of conversion to cultural change? In some ways this is a question about how far to take missionaries at their word. Christianity was frequently presented to potential converts as an agent of modernity. Christian agents were often in the forefront of introducing new technologies, such as literacy or bio-medicine, as well as associated ideological beliefs, such as a stress on particular gender roles or an equation between clothing, respectability, and civilization. The content of Christianity was not, however, necessarily "modern," whatever that vexed term is taken to mean. Furthermore, goods and technologies often already had a cultural weight that came from wider power relations in particular societies; the respectability denoted by hats, dresses, and corsets counted in the colonial Cape Colony more because labourers were cast as "unrespectable," than because missionaries said these things mattered.[57] It is not always easy, in sum, to determine the extent to which cultural change was a direct product of *missionary* activity in a context of broader processes of globalization and economic imperialism.

Missionary encounters did nonetheless clearly have a significant impact on many societies, if frequently in unpredictable ways. Take the example of language. Missionaries shaped many languages that they helped to transcribe almost always with the extensive assistance (or primary work) of local speakers, such as Zara Schmelen, the Nama wife of the German missionary who first transcribed Nama, or Biriban, the Akwabal man who enabled Lancelot Threlkeld to be the first person to transcribe an Australian Aboriginal language.[58] In some cases, missionary transcriptions of language, often by competing societies, contributed to ethnogenesis, as identities came to be defined by the creation of separate languages at different points in a dialect spectrum. The complicated processes of translation on which missions depended often inadvertently selected certain indigenous concepts as equivalencies of Christian concepts, sometimes with profound implications for these cultures' own understandings of themselves.[59] Missionaries were usually convinced (in common with many modernisers in colonized societies) that literacy was key to the development of both societies and individuals. Was this a form of cultural imperialism? Some scholars point to the cultural losses attendant on literacy; others such as Patrick Harries argue that in reality many people, such as Mozambiquan workers in South African mines, used texts and literacy in ways that were in continuity with their oral cultures and did not conform to the modernising precepts of either missionaries or Marxists.[60] In other words, the idea itself of modernization and what are often taken to be its characteristic features, such as literacy, need to be constantly challenged in order to escape from the self-understanding of British Christians themselves.

The impact of mission Christianity partly depended on the degree of power of indigenous groups. British Christians almost universally equated being sedentary with reaching a higher degree of civilization. Missionaries thus frequently urged vulnerable nomadic groups to settle down, and provided the institutional means for them to do so. As white settler states moved toward a greater degree of self-government, missionaries paradoxically often became increasingly arms of the colonial government in its dealings with indigenous groups. In both Australia and Canada, for example, Christian churches and former missionary societies were given extensive control over education. This came to include residential schools, which both colonial governments compelled indigenous children to attend, with often disastrous results that remain a subject before the courts.[61]

In other contexts in which indigenous groups wielded more power, missionaries did not establish the kind of total institutions that proved so problematic in Canada and Australia. Nonetheless, missionary schools, to take just one example, had an enormous influence on the daily lives of individuals. Christian agents also tried to remake the bodies of indigenous peoples. This was most directly expressed in the medical missions that became increasingly important in the late nineteenth centuries and that are one of the most important legacies of colonial Christianity. Missionaries ran the health systems of many developing countries up to, and in some cases past, independence. As was the case with schools, this does not mean either that they excited consent or that they were rejected outright. Scholars interested in the burgeoning field of the history of medicine and of science in colonial contexts have richly documented struggles between bio-medicine and indigenous ideas about the body and about healing, but they also show that individuals were often willing to access different methods at the same time, rather than seeing systemic conflict.[62]

Religion and Resistance

Colonized and colonising groups alike understood each other in terms of their own cosmologies well past first encounters. Many missionaries saw the hand of Satan in the challenges with which they were confronted, for example. There are some interesting parallels with the fact that people in many parts of Africa saw colonial officials and medical missionaries as evil and thus potentially as vampires or as witches. As the work of Luise White, Clifton Crais, and others suggests, colonialism was interpreted as a form of evil that needed to be expunged through techniques geared to that end, such as witchcraft eradication.[63] Both missionaries and their potential targets had well-developed ideas about evil and how to deal with it that only occasionally overlapped.

Colonized societies mobilised "religion" in a wide variety of ways to the ends of resistance, often partly in an attempt to encompass and overcome the sacred power of the invader. One such example, among many possibilities, is the prevalence of revitalization and prophetic movements.[64] This is difficult territory; close examination reveals deep differences between societies. Nonetheless, scholars do suggest that prophetic movements were, and are, common in many different parts of the world.

Typically, a prophet will cleanse the people of their evil in order to strengthen the community at a time of conflict, often through specific purification rituals. The cleansed community will then be stronger and better able to resist ills of a wide variety of kinds. Despite great variation, elements of this pattern were repeated in anti-colonial resistance movements in many different places.

In southern Africa in the mid-1850s the Xhosa were driven to desperation after crippling frontier wars and a pandemic of lung disease among cattle, the marker of wealth in Nguni societies. A young girl named Nongqawuse had a vision of the ancestors who told her that they would return on an appointed day, help drive the British into the sea, and usher in a new world of abundant cattle and wealth, if only the Xhosa would slaughter all their cattle and destroy their grain. Controversy over the prophecies split Xhosa society. In the end, nonetheless, enough people sacrificed that a great famine ensued. Many thousands of Xhosa people were driven to take refuge in the neighbouring Cape Colony where they were incorporated into the Cape economy, often as landless labourers.[65] The cattle killing movement, as it has come to be called, included religious innovation such as the belief in the resurrection and return in the flesh of the ancestors (possibly influenced by Christian beliefs in the resurrection of the dead, according to historian J. B. Peires). If Helen Bradford is correct, Nongqawuse may have been influenced by a desire to restore (or create) better gender norms, including the rejection of rape and incest at a time at which the decline in cattle made it difficult for young men to marry, as cattle were required for bridewealth.[66] At the same time, the idea of sacrifice and the cleansing of the community in order to eradicate the ill effects of witchcraft and sin and, among other things, strengthen society militarily were all elements of African practice with many parallels elsewhere. In other areas of colonial Africa, uprisings displayed a similar mix of innovation—sometimes incorporating elements of Christianity and characterized by the idea that prophets were receiving new revelations—and longstanding practices such as witchcraft eradication, the use of war magic, and the very deployment of prophets, spirit mediums, or other spiritual authorities. In 1906 rebels in the Zulu Bambatha rebellion against the poll tax and British colonial rule in Natal sacrificed white cattle and were doctored before going into battle. Among the Shona in modern Zimbabwe, *mhondoro* spirit mediums were possessed by the spirits of the ancestors who protected the land, conferred land ownership, and named chiefs; these mediums played key roles during both the 1896 combined uprising of the Shona and the Ndebele against British rule and the late twentieth-century war for independence against first the British and then the successor Rhodesian state.[67] As Terence Ranger argues, spirit mediums filled innovative as well as "traditional" roles: they helped villagers to exert some control over young guerrillas who were usually outsiders to the region, for example, and teach them appropriate behavioral norms. Some Christians either deployed Christianity to similar nationalist ends or were willing to move between religious forms, following mediums during the war.

In New Zealand, there were many Maori prophets who led movements against British incursions onto land in the nineteenth century.[68] Such movements included the Maori King Movement of 1858 to 1885, the Pai Marire (or Hauhau movement) of the 1860s, and the blood-soaked foundation of the Ringatu Church by the prophet

Te Kooti in the late 1860s and its rise against the colonial state. In each case and in many more a prophet was given revelations, often through visions and dreams, that enabled him or her to lead the community through actions designed to lead to revitalization and greater access to power. In North America, the ghost dance is only one example of many indigenous revitalization movements. When Pontiac led a loose coalition of Amerindian groups against the British Empire in 1763 in the wake of the Seven Years War, he was deeply influenced by the Delaware prophet Neolin, who had begun to receive visions in 1760–1. As Gregory Dowd recounts, as Pontiac laid out plans for an assault on Detroit, he told assembled warriors of the Ottawas, Hurons, and Potawatomis of the prophet's vision in which he had climbed to see the Master of Life, who had instructed him to lead his people to reject adultery, polygamy, fighting, and the medicine dance before battle, to moderate the use of alcohol and to abjure European goods. "As to those who come to trouble their lands,—drive them out, make war upon them. I do not love them at all."[69] Throughout the war, the warriors of the confederacy called upon sacred power to aid them through the black drink ceremony and other rituals.[70] Such innovative revivals of traditional means to mobilize power persisted in rebel movements in the north east well into the ninteenth century, and were often tied to a quest for unity among diverse groups, brought together by a shared revelation.[71] The prophet Tenskwatawa helped inspire the last push of indigenous groups to regain territory in the north east in the early nineteenth century, under the leadership of his brother Tecumseh. In a different setting, prophetic movements spread rapidly in the early nineteenth century Columbia Plateau in the far west, fuelled by a quest for healing as epidemic disease burned through the region.[72]

Literate cultures also, of course, deployed sacred power to anti-colonial ends. Islam, with a more tightly defined written text to which to appeal, was perhaps less open to syncretic influences in the creation of rituals designed to confer power, but its sacred texts nonetheless contained prophecies that could be applied to a variety of circumstances—as was and is, of course, the case with the Christian Bible. In Sudan in the late nineteenth century the Sufi leader Muhammed Ahmad claimed that he was the promised Mahdi, the prophesized redeemer who was to bring about a kingdom of justice before the day of the resurrection. He attracted a fervent following willing to attack the Anglo-Egyptian presence in the Sudan and establish a purified Islamic state. In 1884 the Mahdists besieged Khartoum, which the British general Charles Gordon refused to abandon before meeting a death that formed a centrepiece of the late Victorian imperial imagination. The Mahdists ruled Sudan until 1899, when British troops under Lord Kitchener brutally regained the territory. In the dominant British view of the day, the Mahdists were savage barbarians at whose hands Gordon died a saintly death.[73] There might nonetheless be some parallels between the beliefs of both Muhammed Ahmad and Charles Gordon in an interventionist god who acted through groups as well as through individuals and whose prophecies would be fulfilled. Surely there are also parallels between the sacrifice and purification of society carried out by the Xhosa in the mid-1850s and the drive of the Mahdis to re-establish just rule also in response to prophecy? Many Muslim rebels in India in 1857 were inspired by similar ideas about the need to return to a purified Islamic society in their pursuit of *jihad* against the British, as William Dalrymple has recently argued on the basis of newly uncovered records from the tragic siege of Delhi, seat of the last Mughal emperor, in 1857.[74]

These comparisons could be multiplied. China in the era of western dominance saw important millenarian movements such as the Taiping rebellion and the Boxer uprisings, for example. Is it arguable that cutting across diverse movements there was a concern to remake history, in light of prophecies about the past and the present? A re-imagined history summons worlds into being that are new and yet old: the purified Islamic state; the world of the ancestors, full of new cattle; the realm of the *mahdi*. Indeed, Christian missionaries in the 1790s and 1800s held many of the same types of beliefs, drawing on a venerable tradition of millenarian interpretation: the London Missionary Society originally wanted to convert the world in order to hasten the end time. James Read speculated in South Africa in 1807 that surely Napoleon was the antichrist. Christian millenarians among the Khoekhoe, the star converts of the LMS in South Africa, in 1850 rebelled and went into battle against the colonial state speaking of visions of white horses knee-deep in blood and the coming fulfilment of the prophecies of Isaiah.[75] It is difficult in looking at such movements to disentangle the "political" from the "religious." We are again up against the issue of how to define religion but also the difficult question of whether in such circumstances religious "belief" is a form of motivation in and of itself. What does seem clear is that anti-colonial resistance in many cases and across a wide range of religions cannot be understood without fuller attention to factors beyond the immediately material. This is not to claim primacy over economic and more obviously secular "political" motivations: it is to claim that in many cases the realms of the material and the non-material that historians might seek to disaggregate were simply not perceived as separate.

The importance of religion, including mission Christianity, is also evident in the perhaps more readily recoverable politics of nationalism and decolonization in the twentieth century. The fact that missions usually controlled higher educational institutions in colonies meant that many early nationalists, particularly in Africa, had Christian backgrounds. Late nineteenth- and early twentieth-century elite indigenous opposition to colonial policies often used Christian channels and deployed the trope of a righteous imperial center to critique local injustices. At the same time, mission Christianity characteristically shared a modernizing narrative with both Marxism and with organized nationalism, the main vector of opposition to colonial rule in the early twentieth century.[76] It was fairly easy for nationalists to build a nationalist narrative on Christian foundations, even if many thinkers of the post-war period from Frantz Fanon onward also urgently stressed the need to decolonize the mind, in part by escaping the assumptions of inferiority built into a Christian teleological vision.[77]

More broadly, religion might potentially hold together diverse communities confronted with the need for unity in the face of colonialism. In some contexts, Christianity could fill this role, as was the case among Yoruba Christians.[78] Elsewhere, revitalization movements might fill this function. Kenyan rebels sometimes moved between Christian and mau mau rituals, deploying both to promote unity. In many areas of the colonial world, nationalists naturally drew directly on indigenous religious traditions, which might also transform. Hindu nationalists in India created new visions of Hinduism, for example. Gandhi struggled to devise rituals and ideas to unite Hindus and Muslims, but he also deployed the notion of *dharma* to argue for individual right action in the face of injustice, while his followers used traditional chants and stories to mobilize the Hindu peasantry.

Consider South African examples. Early leaders of the South African National Congress (after 1912 the ANC), such as Sol Plaatje, John Dube, or Charlotte Maxeke had been mission educated. They appealed to the British imperial center but were also often influenced by interaction with African-American Christian networks. Plaatje supported the British cause in the South African War (1899–1902) although he was strongly disillusioned after the Act of Union and the unjust 1913 Native Lands Act. A later generation of activists, the ANC Youth League activists of the 1940s, including Nelson Mandela and Oliver Tambo, were similarly mission educated. They were, however, far less dependent on Christian imperial networks and influenced (to varying degrees) by Africanism. In this context Christianity might be reinvented as compatible with African traditions, as such advocates of African theology as John Mbiti and Gabriel Setiloane argued, but it was not a central ideology of resistance. By the 1960s, Black Consciousness advocates such as Steve Biko, Ramphela Mphale, and Barney Pityana also deployed Christianity but under the guise of Black Theology, which claimed that mission Christianity had perverted the true social justice message of Christianity. Christian paternalism was heavily criticized. In the meantime, apartheid was supported by the social exclusivity of white-only churches (as was true of segregation policies elsewhere in Africa) and by a theological superstructure. The way in which the anti-apartheid struggle was also a struggle over the meaning of Christianity is nicely illustrated by Alan Boezak's drive to persuade the World Council of Churches, of which he was moderator, to declare apartheid a heresy. South Africa is, of course, anomalous because of the development of apartheid, but it both illustrates dilemmas confronting colonized groups that were less powerful or less numerous in white settler colonies elsewhere, as well as some typical intellectual and organizational trends elsewhere in black Africa.

The history of religion in the British Empire can perhaps be divided into a history of institutions (both British and indigenous) that overlaps with, but certainly never completely coincides with, a different history that encompasses emotions, beliefs, and ideas. British missionaries thought they brought a readily well-defined "Christianity" to colonial places. That vision was constantly challenged in colonial contexts, however: converts may have accepted some precepts of Christianity but they certainly did not accept the meanings imputed by missionaries and still less did they necessarily accept the authority of missionaries themselves. Often converts reinterpreted Christianity or rewrote its theologies. Colonial environments thus often challenged the very boundaries and definitions both of Christianity and of indigenous religions. On the ground, struggles for sacred power, in Janet Hodgson's evocative phrase, overlapped with struggles for other forms of power. In the meantime, Christianity helped shape the self-image of the British as, indeed, Christian imperialists. Far more than window-dressing, religion shaped the outcomes of imperialism, just as imperialism in its turn rewrote the nature and uses of religion.

Notes

1 Fieldhouse, "Humpty-Dumpty"; D. Kennedy, "Imperial history."
2 Chidester, *Savage Systems*.
3 Landau, "Christian Conversion."
4 Comaroff and Comaroff, *Revelation and Revolution*, 1.
5 See also Porter, *Religion versus Empire?*, p. 7.
6 Thorne, *Congregational Missions*; Thomas, *Colonialism's Culture*; Hall, *Civilizing Subjects*.
7 A.N. Porter, *Religion versus Empire*; Stanley, *Bible and the Flag*; Stanley (ed.), *Christian Missions and the Enlightenment*; A. N. Porter (ed.), *British Protestant Missions*.
8 Among others, Hodgson, *Church of Women*; Semple, *Missionary Women*; Rutherdale, *Women and the White Man's God*; Grimshaw, "Missionary life"; Erlank, "Gendered reactions."
9 In an Australian context, Haebich, *Broken Circles*.
10 Some African examples, again in a vast field, might include Ranger, "Taking hold of the land"; Maxwell, *Christians and Chiefs*; Hawkins, *Writing and Colonialism;* Landau, *Realm of the Word;* Peel, *Religious Encounter*.
11 Peel, "Who hath despised"; Landau, "Hegemony and history."
12 Among a multiplicity of possible examples, Hastings, *Church in Africa*, and the essays in Maxwell and Lawrie (eds), *Christianity and the African Imagination*, including Lonsdale, "Kikuyu Christianities."
13 Etherington, "Introduction"; Brock, "New Christians as evangelists," p. 7, *passim*; Gray, *Black Christians*. Studies that make these broad arguments include Neylan, *Heavens are Changing*; Cox, *Imperial Fault Lines*; Elbourne, *Blood Ground*.
14 As David Maxwell points out: Maxwell, "Writing the history of African Christianity."
15 Landau, "Language"; Hofmeyr, *Portable Bunyan;* Saneh, *Translating the Message*; Bhabha, "Signs taken for wonders"; Maxwell, "Writing the history of African Christianity," p. 384.
16 Viswanathan, *Outside the Fold*. Robin Horton's seminal articles in the 1970s triggered a long-standing debate on the issue of conversion, modernity, and macrocosmic perspectives: Horton, "African conversion"; *id.*, "On the rationality of conversion."
17 Inter alia, Mudimbe, *Invention of Africa*; Hefner (ed.), *Conversion to Christianity*; Van der Veer (ed.), *Conversion to Modernities*; Brock (ed.), *Indigenous Peoples*.
18 Edwards, *Account of the Life*.
19 A. N. Porter, *Religion versus Empire*, pp. 17–18; Pascoe, *Two Hundred Years of the S.P.G.*, p. 932.
20 Porter, "Missionary enthusiasm."
21 Smith, *Generall History of Virginia, New England, and the Summer Isles*; Kupperman, *Indians and English*.
22 Stone, *Life of Joseph Brant*.
23 Stock, *History of the Church Missionary Society*.
24 Sensbach, *Rebecca's Revival*.
25 Shaw (ed.), *Gipps-Latrobe Correspondence*.
26 Francis Forbes to Wilmot Horton, August 14, 1824: Catton Papers, Australian Joint Copying Project, Reel M791; reproduced in Division of Law, Macquarie University, "Decisions of the Supreme Court, New South Wales," R v. Fitzpatrick and Colville, June 21, 1824, available at www.law.mq.edu.au.
27 Judge Burton, *Notebooks*: New South Wales State Archives.

28 Mamdani, *Citizen and Subject*; Dirks, "Little king to landlord."

29 Philip, *Researches in South Africa*.

30 Canny, *Making Ireland British*.

31 Thorne, *Congregational Missions*; Helly, *Livingstone's Legacy*.

32 Ward, *Protestant Evangelical Awakening*.

33 Carey, *Obligations of Christians*, p. 11.

34 For example, Hempton, *Religion of the People*.

35 S. Smith, "Indian missions."

36 Macaulay, *Minute on Indian Education*.

37 Sivasundaram, *Nature and the Godly Empire*.

38 Stevens, *Poor Indian*; Johnston, *Missionary Writing*.

39 Davis, *Inhuman Bondage*; Davis, *Problem of Slavery*.

40 Hall, *Civilizing Subjects*.

41 This is apparent from the correspondence of Sir Thomas Fowell Buxton: Rhodes House Library, Oxford, MSS Brit. Emp. s.444, papers of Sir Thomas Fowell Buxton.

42 Midgley, *Women Against Slavery*.

43 E. Elbourne, "The sin of the settler: The 1835–36 select committee on aborigines and debates over virtue and conquest in the early nineteenth-century British white settler empire," *Jl of Colonialism and Colonial History*, 4 (2003). *Report of the Select Committee on Aborigines (British Settlements)* (London, 1836–7).

44 Vivienne Rae-Ellis makes a strong case against Robinson (not accepted by all scholars) in her *Black Robinson*.

45 A. N. Porter, *Religion versus Empire*.

46 Rhodes House Library, Oxford, MSS Africa s.112, Gerald H. Portal to his wife, May 3, 1889, cited in Greenlee and Johnston, *Good Citizens*, p. 11.

47 Stanley, *Bible and the Flag*, p. 111.

48 *Ibid.*, pp. 112–16.

49 Landau, *Realm of the Word*.

50 Lester, *Imperial Networks*; Laidlaw, "Integrating metropolitan, colonial and imperial histories."

51 Ross, *Adam Kok's Griqua*.

52 Elbourne, *Blood Ground*.

53 Guy, *The Heretic*; Colenso, *Pentateuch*.

54 Campbell, *Songs of Zion*.

55 Comaroff, *Body of Power*; Sundkler, *Bantu Prophets*; id., *Zulu Zion*.

56 Rotberg, "John Chilembwe."

57 Ross, *Status and Respectability*.

58 Threlkeld, *Australian Grammar*.

59 Landau, "Language."

60 Harries, "Missionaries, marxists and magic"; Hofmeyr, "Jonah and the swallowing monster."

61 Chrisjohn, Young, and Maraun, *Circle Game*; Canadian government *Report* on status of Aboriginal peoples; Miller, *Shingwauk's Vision*.

62 Vaughan, *Curing Their Ills*; Arnold, *Science, Technology and Medicine*.

63 L. White, *Speaking with Vampires*; see also Crais, *Politics of Evil*.

64 Adas, *Prophets of Resistance*.

65 Peires, *The Dead Will Arise*.

66 Bradford, "Women, gender and colonialism."

67 Ranger, *Peasant Consciousness*, pp. 177–222, *passim*; Lan, *Guns and Rain*; Ranger, *Revolt in Southern Rhodesia*.
68 Binney, *Redemption Songs*; Elsemore, *Mana from Heaven*; Rosenfeld, *Island Broken in Two Halves*. See also Binney, Chaplin and Wallace (eds), *Mihaia*.
69 Anon (presum. Robert Navarre), "The journal of Pontiac's conspiracy" in Milo Milton Quaife (ed.), *The Seige of Detroit*, cited in Dowd, *War Under Heaven*, p. 104.
70 Dowd, *War Under Heaven*.
71 Dowd, *Spirited Resistance*.
72 Vibert, "Natives were strong."
73 Nicoll, *Mahdi of Sudan and the Death of General Gordon*.
74 Dalrymple, *Last Mughal*.
75 Read, *Kat River Settlement*.
76 Chatterjee, *Nation and its Fragments*.
77 Fanon, *Black Skin, White Masks*.
78 Peel, *Religious Encounter*.

Further Reading

A useful place to start for the student seeking to know more about missions and the British Empire is Norman Etherington's edited volume, *Missions and Empire*, one of the companion volumes of the *OHBE*. Etherington has assembled a number of experts to give overviews of key topics. The work of Andrew Porter, Brian Stanley, James Greenlee, and Charles Johnston, among others, explores the political dimensions of the missionary enterprise: see Porter, *Religion versus Empire?*; Stanley, *Bible and the Flag*; Greenlee and Johnston, *Good Citizens*. All of these works argue that relationships between missionaries and colonial administrations were complicated and multifaceted, with missionaries often functioning as critics, even if the overall thrust of missionary activity tended to be to support an imagined moral colonialism. There is a very complicated literature about missions, modernity, and cultural colonialism, which naturally overlaps with wider examinations of cultural colonialism. Jean and John Comaroff's *Of Revelation and Revolution* (two volumes of which have appeared so far) helped revivify the case for seeing missions as the cultural arm of imperialism. Different perspectives are provided by Paul Landau, *Realm of the Word*. Among historiographical discussions, see Landau, "Hegemony and history"; Peel, "For who hath despised?," and other works referred to in the 2003 forum on the work of the Comaroffs in the *American Historical Review*, including my own "Word made flesh." Nicholas Thomas is among the historians who include mission Christianity in wider discussions of cultural colonialism: Thomas, *Colonialism's Culture*. Significant studies of Christianity, missions, and colonialism in particular places include (among many possible examples) Neylan, *The Heavens are Changing* (on British Columbia); Jeffrey Cox, *Imperial Fault Lines* (on imperial India); Landau, *Realm of the Word*; Etherington, *Preachers, Peasants and Politics* (on south east Africa); Niel Gunson, *Messengers of Grace* (on the Pacific); Peel, *Religious Encounter and the Making of the Yoruba*. A growing body of literature also considers the domestic impact of the missionary movement. Thorne's *Congregational Missions and the Making of an Imperial Culture* raises the issue of how imperial missions and Christian humanitarianism shaped domestic cultures. So too do Catherine Hall's

Civilizing Subjects, David Turley's *The Culture of English Antislavery*, and, less directly, Lester's *Imperial Networks*. On gender and missions, see my note 8 above; note also the 1993 edited collection by Bowie, Kirkwood, and Ardener, *Women and Missions*.

Beyond mission Christianity, there is a dense history of Christianity in colonial contexts, in the first instance, and more broadly of the mobilization of a range of "religious" forms by indigenous peoples in colonial contexts. This literature includes examinations of the dynamics of conversion and its relationship to globalization and modernity, among other themes. Some key edited collections include Hefner (ed.), *Conversion to Christianity* and Van der Veer (ed.), *Conversion to Modernities*. The reader should explore the literatures of particular areas in more depth. A key study of Christianity in Africa that is only incidentally about religion and imperialism is Hastings, *The Church in Africa*. A visceral sense of the dynamics of cultural colonialism from the inside might be provided by Jamaica Kincaid, *A Small Place*. On revitalization and prophetic movements, see Michael Adas, *Prophets of Resistance*; Dowd, *A Spirited Resistance*; or Peires, *The Dead Will Arise*. To complicate the last picture the novel *Reds* by Zakes Mda is an interesting latter-day fictional account of the Xhosa cattle killing that gives a sense of the imaginative equation made by contemporary Xhosa people between Christianity and modernity on the one hand and tradition and cultural resistance on the other. Peter van der Veer's *Religion and Empire* shows how British Christianity and Indian Hinduism shaped one another during the colonial encounter as both Britain and India developed a sense of national identity. Isabel Hofmeyr's *The Portable Bunyan* is a rich example of the circulation of texts and beliefs across international networks, as well as of the mobilization of Christianity by Africans. These are only a few examples of a rich field that deserves to be explored in more depth through local examples as well as through comparative studies and through examination of the transnational networks of which the missionary movement was only the most vibrant example.

7

Empire and Ideology

Stephen Howe

Historians disagree widely and profoundly over how far imperial Britain may be said to have possessed or elaborated a distinctively imperialist ideology. They differ just as much on how important particular belief systems, ideologies or discourses[1] were in enabling, or indeed *causing*, imperial expansion, how great a role they played in the way the empire was ruled, how influential or widely held they were among Britain's own populations, what significance they had in British cultures, arts, and society, and what happened to such ideas as empire declined and fell.

This chapter seeks in the main to survey those disputes rather than to adjudicate them; though inevitably it reflects many of the author's own prejudices about the issues at stake. For reasons of space and manageability, the discussion which follows confines itself primarily to metropolitan British, and British-imperial, thought and action. It does not seek to embrace the "ideologies" of the colonized, developed in reaction to imperial rule, nor those cultivated among settler colonists—except briefly and insofar as they interacted especially closely with ideas put forward within Britain. It focuses mainly on the nineteenth and earlier twentieth centuries, discussing the ideologies associated with the "first British Empire" only in very abbreviated fashion and as background. Similarly, intellectual developments of the later twentieth century and beyond, the era of decolonization and its aftermath, cannot be explored here.

Very few concepts in the humanities and social sciences have been as contested or as multifarious in their meanings as has "ideology": in general, in relation to empires, and specifically in historical study of the British Empire. Since its coinage at the end of the eighteenth century, the term has oscillated, or been contested, between essentially pejorative uses where "ideology" denotes a particularly partisan, prescriptive, over-totalising, or simply invalid body of ideas, and more neutrally-intended ones which often employ it to mean sets of ideas with an especially important social-symbolic function.

These debates have, in all their complexity, tended to revolve around three types of question:

- Is ideology an inescapable component of all societies, all movements and organizations, or indeed of any argument or proposition anyone might ever put forward? Is there—or could there ever be in some future, better society (as some Marxist thinkers, among whom perhaps the most elaborate theories of ideology developed, especially argued or hoped)—anything outside ideology? Or is it the case, as another Marxist philosopher thought, that "all human societies secrete ideology as the very element and atmosphere indispensable to their historical respiration and life."[2]
- How formal and systematic does a body of thought have to be before it is aptly describable as an ideology?
- Is an ideology any more or less systematic body of thought, or should the term be reserved for "bad," false, and/or clearly instrumentally-intended bodies of ideas? For instance, should we distinguish sharply between "ideological" and "scientific" thought, as some theorists have done, or conversely see modern science as itself an ideology like others?

All these questions, as we shall see, have direct pertinence to British imperial history.

Increasingly often in the past couple of decades, writers on empire have replaced or supplemented reference to imperial or colonial *ideology* with allusion to *discourse*. Indeed a major body of recent work in the field is often referred to by such names as "colonial discourse theory." This term too requires brief explanation and contextualisation: not least because it so often seems to be used as a simple synonym for ideology.[3]

Originally, in linguistics, the term discourse simply meant a piece of language longer than a sentence. More generally and non-technically, the word was used to denote a formal treatment of a subject, in speech or writing; and in a broader sense to mean simply verbal communication or conversation. Contemporary academic uses derive above all from Michel Foucault, but seem frequently to slip towards corresponding to one (or more) of the three main earlier meanings. This vagueness is compounded by the numerous changes and uncertainties in Foucault's own use of the term, which reflect the protean nature of his thought. His core meaning, set out most fully and formally in *The Archaeology of Knowledge*, is simply sets of statements, arguments, classificatory schemas, and (sometimes) also *practices* which share a common set of rules and assumptions; or as Foucault puts it, a common "system of dispersion: discursive regularities."[4]

The use of the term discourse does not, as such, imply any judgment about whether its elements correspond to some reality outside it or not. What it does, in Foucault's normal usage, is declare this a non-issue: to say that it is pointless to concern ourselves about possible distinctions between the linguistic and the material or social, since the effectivity of discursive practices does not derive from their correspondences to truths about the real but from the systematic operation of the practices themselves. It requires a claim that language can never be *fully* referential, which is far from being a poststructuralist novelty but can be traced at least as far back as Saussure; but by no means a belief that there *is* no referent.[5] It is naturally possible to defuse the conceptual boobytraps here by adopting what one might call a "soft" version of historical discourse analysis (which is, in fact, what I think many historians are actually doing even when they loudly proclaim adherence to "hard" positions in theoretical debates). This "soft" position would be like that pronounced by Eleni Varikas: "The view that the common interests of a social group are constituted in the process of reflection and interpretation which give meaning to the common situations experienced daily by the actors, and that this meaning does not exist outside language"[6]—though the presumption is that the group and the daily situations *do* exist outside language.

All of these ideas are proclaimed and combined, often in uneasy association with Marxist and feminist arguments, in much contemporary colonial discourse theory. It is often proposed that there is a special relationship, a particular relevance, of these general claims to the colonial and postcolonial situation. However, not all such theorists accept all these arguments or interpret them similarly. Thus Edward W. Said, generally regarded as the "founder" of the approach, placed considerable and increasing (if not perhaps wholly consistent) distance between himself and Foucauldian notions of the relationship between power, knowledge and subjectivity.

Where there is a clear distinction, in imperial and colonial historical studies, between the concepts of ideology and of discourse, it is of the kind probably most lucidly summarized by Nicholas Thomas:

> colonialism is not best understood primarily as a political or economic relationship that is legitimized or justified through ideologies of racism or progress. Rather, colonialism has always, equally importantly and deeply, been a cultural process . . . Colonial cultures are not simply ideologies that mask, mystify, or rationalize forms of oppression that are external to them; they are also expressive and constitutive of colonial relationships in themselves.[7]

Others go further, asserting that colonialism was not only distinctively cultural, but specifically *textual*, as in the remarkable claim of Chris Tiffin and Alan Lawson: "Imperial relations may have been established initially by guns, guile and disease, but they were maintained in their interpellative phase largely by textuality . . . Colonialism (like its counterpart, racism), then, is an operation of discourse."[8] Chandra Mohanty, similarly, says that "The definition of colonization I invoke is a predominantly *discursive* one, focusing on a certain mode of appropriation and codification of 'scholarship' and 'knowledge.'"[9] Colonial discourse theory, following such protocols, has had a strong tendency to see colonial power everywhere, seeping into, controlling, transforming every tiny detail of colonized societies. Such a vision may be true to Foucault's programme and his theories of governmentality, but it is far more questionable how true it is to the colonial record itself. Colonized cultures were very often more resilient, and the colonial impact patchier, more superficial, less systematic, less effectual, than is assumed. The documents of colonial administration itself may sometimes envisage unchallenged dominance, utterly transformed social order, while the rhetoric and ritual of colonial government may often have created an image of total control and planned progression which the far more limited and improvisatory reality did not match.

Formal definitions of what is meant by colonial or imperial discourse have been rare even among those who routinely use the term. Homi Bhabha's programmatic statement provides what he calls, not a definition, but "the minimum conditions and specifications of such a discourse." These are framed, in Bhabha's typically elliptical style, as follows:

> It is an apparatus that turns on the recognition and disavowal of racial/cultural/historical differences. Its predominant strategic function is the creation of a space for a "subject peoples" [sic] through the production of knowledges in terms of which surveillance is exercised and a complex form of pleasure/unpleasure is incited. It seeks authorization for its strategies by the production of knowledges of colonizer and colonized which are stereotypical but antithetically evaluated. The objective of colonial discourse is to construe the colonized as a population of degenerate types on the basis of racial origin, in order to justify conquest and to establish systems of administration and instruction.[10]

Despite the obscurities and apparent paradoxes here—"recognition *and* disavowal" of difference, "pleasure/unpleasure"—the general thrust is fairly clear. Colonial discourse forms a symbolic system, a discourse in the strong Foucauldian sense. It always combines the production of knowledge with the wielding of power. It trades in archetypes and antitheses. It justifies itself with the very same moves by which it legitimises and indeed conceals repression. And it is singular, abstract and homogenous. Much recent historical writing on ideologies and discourses of empire has taken as its point of departure the questioning or dismantling of such abstraction and homogenisation.

We begin our main story at the point often seen as the High Noon of pro-imperial ideologies' hold in Britain, as of the empire itself: the end of the nineteenth century and beginning of the twentieth. This was not the period of the British Empire's greatest geographical extent. That came only after 1918, when large parts of the German and Turkish empires fell under British control via League of Nations mandates. It may not have been the peak of the empire's real power: already by 1900 Britain's industrial predominance was challenged by America and Germany, and many historians have written of British "relative decline" at the end of the Victorian era. It is, however, often seen as the period when empire was at its most important to Britain, when popular enthusiasm for imperialism was at its height, and when ideas about empire most thoroughly saturated domestic British culture. The main focus for this, as the new century dawned, was the South African War (at the time usually called the "Boer War") which had broken out the previous year. In that war, British forces had initially experienced utterly unexpected defeats; but by the spring of 1900 the tide had turned, and in May the end of the siege of Mafeking (actually quite an unimportant place and fight) was greeted with a remarkable outburst of national rejoicing.

Yet historians disagree widely over how important empire was to Britain, or to most British people, in this era, and over how to interpret its meanings and significance.[11] Perhaps the intense passions, fears and triumphs, which so much of Britain's public sphere expressed over South Africa in and around 1900 were an exceptional, unique episode, with neither deep roots nor long-term after-effects. The place of empire in British history has recently become a hot subject—and one with powerful contemporary implications. In the past few years more and more historians have turned to the subject; as literary and cultural critics, under Edward Said's influence, had done a little earlier.[12] Imperial themes and preoccupations have been uncovered not only in the obvious places like Rudyard Kipling's, Joseph Conrad's or John Buchan's fictions, but in almost the whole of modern British cultural production and performance. Moving ever wider, some historians then came to see all of British society, especially between the 1870s and the 1940s, as "permeated," "saturated," "steeped," or "suffused" (all these were key words in major 1990s texts on the subject) with imperialism. More, some claimed, the very ideas of Englishness and Britishness were formed by and utterly dependent on empire. Failure to recognize this, so some say, is at best myopic, at worst must be motivated by anxiety or disavowal towards Britan's descent from world power, by colonialist nostalgia or even, simply, by racism.

Both the influence of empire on British "domestic" history, and the significance of empire's legacies for Britain and Britishness today, have thus drawn ever more attention in recent years. Yet if the rapid expansion of work on such themes has shone light into previously neglected corners, and imparted a welcome new permeability to once rigid barriers between British and imperial history, there have been drawbacks too. Much of the resulting work has been notably speculative or polemical. In some hands, there has been an overcompensation for previous neglect, with incautious claims that absolutely all aspects of nineteenth- and twentieth-century British culture and society were products of imperialism. This new orthodoxy has already drawn vigorous counterattacks, perhaps most notably by Bernard Porter.[13]

Maybe, as critics like Porter suggest, claims about empire's significance for Britain are being pushed a little too far. Other historians have proposed powerful reasons for doubt about whether empire, even at its height of global power, was really so crucial to the lives and beliefs of the mass of Britain's people. They note what they see as the near-absence of empire from major nineteenth-century works of British literature, art, and music, its neglect in the schools and universities, and so on. Examining imperial themes in a broader British social and cultural context, Bernard Porter believes, better puts imperialism in its place: a relatively minor one. He uses an extended archaeological metaphor: there are thousands of imperial shards to be found when we excavate nineteenth- or early twentieth-century British society. Dug out and piled up at the side, they might look overwhelming. Studied *in situ*, however, you get a quite different impression. They're concentrated only in a few scattered spots.

The major repercussions of empire for Britain were, on this more skeptical view, almost all *indirect*. And the empire could have existed, and even expanded, with very little commitment towards or even awareness of it at home. More, such a lack of commitment and awareness may have been preferred by the empire's rulers. Not only did empire not require mass involvement among Britain's own populations, but such involvement might have been downright destabilising and was thus assiduously avoided—except, perhaps, for a relatively brief historical moment which peaked, indeed, around the end of the nineteenth century. Many things which are seen by recent writers as necessarily associated with Empire—the other shards that have been excavated and pieced together to form a supposed "imperial culture," like racism, patriotism, militarism, masculinism, adventure stories, the study of geography, and many more—could, and in the skeptical view did, exist quite independently of it. If many colonies were acquired almost costlessly, even reluctantly or absent-mindedly, and were ruled with few British personnel, little expenditure, often more bluff than substance, then on this count too one should not be surprised to find them remaining marginal to British society. Most broadly, something describable as "the national culture" could never have become profoundly imperialized, because there was no such thing. Class above all, but also religion, gender, region, language, and more meant that so disparate a population had almost no shared beliefs or ideals—about imperial matters, or anything much else. Scotland, Wales, and of course Ireland had very distinctive experiences and relations to empire.

Thus the sources of enthusiasm for empire, and the visions of empire which they mobilised, were more diverse and perhaps more restricted than is sometimes suggested. Campaigners for emigration and those for tariff reform employed entirely different rhetorics, appealed to different audiences, and subscribed not only to different philosophies but to utterly variant "map-images" of the empire itself. Pro-Imperial pressure groups like the Tariff Reform League, Navy League, and the Emigration Committee of the Royal Colonial Institute were each concerned with quite distinct aspects of Britain's global reach.[14] And it is sometimes hard to distinguish between specifically pro-Imperial sentiment and activity, and other facets of Britain's international relations or views about the country's place in the world. The Navy League, for instance, was evidently not only an "imperialist" body: even Little Englanders might support naval expansion, out of concern for the island's own security and fear of Germany. A whole complex of attitudes and policy preferences was in play. It is difficult, and may in some ways seem rather artificial, to separate out the distinctively imperialist elements—if one means by that, among other things, those which emphasized the formal, colonial Empire—from other strands like those concerned mainly with Britain's "informal empire" of trade and diplomacy, or indeed more diffuse currents of "jingo" patriotism or militarism. Yet much modern writing on the subject slides from talking about "patriotism," to "social imperialism," to "militarism" almost as if these were interchangeable expressions. These should properly be three quite distinct concepts, with the differences between them central to this enquiry.

How should we evaluate such starkly contending claims? Part of the problem of interpretation I am highlighting here lies in the sheer diversity, as well as size, of the empire—a diversity so great that some wonder whether it is even meaningful to speak at all of a singular "British Empire."[15] Serious attention to empire's impact on Britain itself has to start with recognition that imperialism and empire meant many different things in British political discourse to different people at different times. Some of the earliest British anticolonial critics recognized this, as did probably the most influential of them, J. A. Hobson.[16] And among these different meanings, some related specifically to particular parts of the empire, or particular kinds of British possession. It was more often than not the areas of considerable British settlement which were the main focus: the most important parts of the empire were seen as being Canada, Australia, and New Zealand; sometimes described as parts of a worldwide national family, a "Greater Britain." Indeed, the dominant languages of empire in the late-Victorian and Edwardian era clustered around the colonies (later dominions) of white settlement, and only encompassed the non-settlement possessions in Africa and Asia with difficulty. This has been neglected in much recent cultural history writing on colonialism, which has focused overwhelmingly on South Asia, and to a lesser extent Africa. Empire was understood and enthused about primarily in terms of a "Greater Britain" and a globalized Britishness (with the familiar ambivalence about whether the Irish were part of it) rather than a destiny to rule over non-European peoples. This is not to say that the ideas involved were not suffused with racialised belief; but relations with non-white subject groups were less central to them (or at least less *overtly* so) than is often thought. In some cases, as with Aboriginal Australians, it was indeed widely held that there was no need to think much about them, for they were inevitably doomed to rapid extinction anyway.

Differentiation of attitudes to empire by social class, and by region and nationality within the United Kingdom's multinational state, was obviously important. Thus, for instance, the groundbreaking work of P. J. Cain and A. G. Hopkins centers on their belief in the British Empire as creation and preserve of a socio-economic nexus they call "gentlemanly capitalism."[17] One aspect of this which Cain and Hopkins do not themselves much explore, but which has been taken up by other commentators, is to suggest that the image of the gentleman provided an important multinational bonding mechanism. Members of Scots, Welsh, and Irish elites could become gentlemen— *British* gentlemen—though this might be more difficult for the Irish if they claimed "indigenous" Catholic rather than "Ascendancy" Protestant ancestry. Later, one could add, members of the settler elites in the dominions could also come to be recognized as British gentlemen: again with varying degrees of difficulty, as wealthy, educated Canadians, for instance, seem to have been more readily accepted than otherwise equivalent Australians.[18] But (and this where the late-Victorian consolidation of certain ideas of race may have been most decisive to empire) that recognition was only ever extended to *any* non-white subjects of the empire in very tentative and precarious ways. A wealthy, and popular, figure like the cricketing Rajah Ranjitsinhji might, rather partially and provisionally, be so accepted, but such partial exceptions only underlined the general rule.

If some scholars believe active enthusiasts for empire were a smallish minority in British society, there is little doubt that active *opponents* were a yet smaller one, at least until decolonization was itself well advanced by the mid-twentieth century. There were always numerous critics of empire, to be sure, especially among Victorian radical liberals and later socialists, but few of these believed that British rule over or even conquest of overseas territories was always and in principle illegitimate. Calls for the immediate abandonment of all colonial possessions, or belief in some universal principle of self-determination even for "less advanced" peoples, remained rare at least until after World War I. Opposition to colonial rule or indeed expansion was most often either pragmatic or essentially parochial: because it was seen as economically irrational, because British (far more than "native") lives were put at risk, or because expansion overseas threatened the spirit of liberty at home. Many critics of what they called "aggressive imperialism" might contrast it with a more benign, progressive, "constructive" form, and see British colonial rule at its best as exemplifying that better kind. Such important enemies of *some* kinds of empire around 1900 as Hobson, E. D. Morel, or Roger Casement—and, for that matter, most of the pioneer British socialists and Labour leaders at the time—tended to adopt some variant on that mixture of attitudes. Even humanitarian concern for the victims of colonial conquest might appear disconcertingly selective: most strongly engaged when such victims were fellow whites (as with the Boer republics) or were mistreated by colonialists other than the British themselves (as in the Congo). Nonetheless, such internal critics of imperialism within Britain surely played a significant long-term role in pressing the empire's rulers towards doctrines of "trusteeship," of colonial development and welfare, and eventually of colonized peoples' self-government.

There is yet a further problem in analyzing the nature and the importance of British ideas about empire. This is that historians interested in political, economic and strategic studies of Britain's global power on the one hand; and cultural historians, literary and cultural studies scholars interested in the cultures and discourses of imperialism on the other, have tended to operate in separate spheres. There has indeed been an atmosphere of mutual inattention or even enmity (perhaps most sharply expressed in the over-polarized if not wholly artificial division between so-called "new" and "old" imperial historians). The post-1980s explosion of "new" cultural histories of empire and colonialism developed in significant part from literary studies, drew many of its theoretical and political influences from that quarter, and has continued to be marked by its origin. It has also diverged considerably from much earlier work on related issues in its basic assumptions about the nature of imperial power.

One side, broadly, sees the key to understanding imperial and colonial histories as lying in the relationship between knowledge and power, whereas the other views it as being that between *interest* (especially economic interest, in the most influential versions) and power. The focus on a knowledge–power relation tends (following Foucault, Said, and sometimes Bernard Cohn) to entail not only belief in the pivotal, powerful, and purposeful role of colonial discourses or ideologies, but on their ability to *create* much of that which they claimed to discover in colonized societies.[19] Some other historians have been highly sceptical about such claims, and have tended either to see "colonial knowledge" less as a source, tool, or form of power, more as essentially neutral "information" (with, often, an insistence that to be of value to rulers, it had to be largely accurate), or as something created by colonized as well as colonizers.[20] In some hands, such skepticism extends further, into denial that empire relied in any serious way on any system of thought or discourse such as a Saidian Orientalism. Ideologies of empire, on this view, were most often marginal in their influence, or were *ex post facto* rationalizations for acts of expansion typically driven by crisis on the "periphery," by mere opportunism, or by the availability of new means of control (especially in military and communications technology), rather than by any particular body of ideas. This kind of doubt is often further associated with a tendency to stress the weakness of colonial power in many situations, and hence the degree of autonomy, initiative, or agency often retained by the colonized. Such views have, however, almost inevitably been seen by hostile critics as amounting to a kind of exculpation of the colonial record.[21]

Some of these arguments were most influentially proposed from the 1950s onwards by Jack Gallagher and Ronald Robinson, in works which have had many followers ever since. They argued that Britain's preferred mode of expansion was always *informal*, the direct annexation of overseas territory being a last resort, and one undertaken not in response to pressure from public opinion or economic interests, but by a policy-making elite: the famous "official mind." This elite's actions, including the apparent shift to more extensive formal colonial acquisitions in the later nineteenth century, were not driven by any significant or elaborated imperialist ideology, but largely by force of circumstance. There is, one might note, no *necessary* connection between emphasis on informal rather than formal empire and downplaying of the role of ideology. It has proved possible (albeit perhaps rare) to believe in the importance or even semi-ubiquity of the latter in the context, for instance, of British ambitions and activities in Latin America.[22] However, in the main those who have followed Gallagher and Robinson in their stress on informal empire have ordinarily also done so in their disbelief in the power of ideology.

This relates to a further, equally contentious sphere of debate, on the significance of "collaboration" in shaping the nature of empire. Much writing on the British and other European empires, following Robinson and Gallagher and including that loosely identified by critics as a conservative "Cambridge School" of imperial historiography, sees British rule as depending heavily on the co-operation of major groups, especially elites, from among colonized populations. Collaborative bargains were not only inherent in the imperial relationship, but the nature of these bargains determined the character, and the longevity, of colonial rule. Again, ideas and ideology had little to do with it. Conversely, the social bases of anti-colonial nationalism lay in a web of particularistic relationships. Nationalist politics in India, for instance, was crucially formed by local patron-client networks, by the ways in which resources were fought over or bargained for, and thus by the very structures of the Raj, as the biggest controller of such resources. All this implies great scepticism about the claims of Congress either to represent a unified national will or to be driven by high principles of national liberation.[23] Yet the view just sketched is, in critics' eyes, in itself colonialist, according the colonized no meaningful role other than collaboration, no politics other than that structured by the imperial system itself. Historians associated with the Indian Subaltern Studies group have been especially persistent in their criticism of it.

Many of the key questions here—beyond those relating to the physical, in part measurable resources of colonial and imperial states—are about the extent to which systems of alien rule could achieve something aptly describable as hegemony. Many scholars have indeed seen colonial and imperial systems as exercizing this (though the term hegemony itself has been used in very varying and shifting ways).[24] On the other hand, there have been powerful arguments that colonial rulers, exercising dominance, failed utterly to achieve hegemony—the most famous and influential such case being made for India by Ranajit Guha.[25]

Insofar, though, as ideas or ideologies of empire were significant to the British around 1900, and insofar as we can generalize about these (bearing in mind the "warnings" about division and diversity noted above), what were these? Here we can only offer the broadest of outlines.

Empire depended, in the sphere of ideology, on ideas about difference, and usually on a belief in superiority. In earlier eras the form of such ideas had been predominantly religious. By about 1900, though these had not disappeared, the most powerful notions were cultural, civilizational, and—perhaps more than at any time before or since—racial. The superiority of Europeans (or more narrowly of the British, the English, or indeed "Aryan" or "Nordic" peoples) and thus their right to rule others, was established by their allegedly higher capacities, as manifested in all spheres from construction of systems of abstract thought or of political authority, through economic dynamism, to superior levels of artistic creativity or ethical behavior. Such superiority was seen by some as a result of contingent historical circumstances, so that in future and under proper tutelage, non-Europeans could match or emulate these achievements. This implied that the objective and justification of empire was to create such conditions: it was essentially an educational or civilizing enterprise. This belief, often expressed in a specifically Christian idiom, was certainly widely voiced in Britain around 1900.

Yet the turn of the century has often, surely rightly, been seen also as the apex of belief that differences in culture or technological achievement reflected biological ones. Such belief included a powerful strand of what is sometimes called "scientific (or pseudo-scientific) racism." Humanity was sharply divided into "racial" groups, arranged in a clear hierarchy of superiority and inferiority. European—sometimes specifically British or "Anglo-Saxon"—whites were at the top of this pyramid. Many Asian peoples occupied intermediate positions. Africans were lower still down the scale, often believed to be of innately inferior intelligence and creative, civilization-building or technological capacity. Indigenous peoples in much of the Americas and in the south Pacific, with few elaborate state forms or technological exploits to their name, and with some of them following customs like cannibalism or human sacrifice which colonialist ideology highlighted, exaggerated, or even maybe sometimes invented, were still more despised.

Such beliefs have a long ancestry, but became a major rationalization for empire, and (at least according to most, though not all, historians of the period) massively influenced all aspects of colonial policy, during the later nineteenth century. It is often pointed out that dominant ideas about race in Britain became markedly more illiberal in the mid-nineteenth century. There was a major shift between the 1830s and 1850s from humanitarian discourses to more racist and authoritarian ones.[26]

During this time, it was indeed believed in some influential circles that the existence of racial divisions and hierarchies was proved by science.[27] Historians again disagree, however, about how widely diffused these ideas were, either in general or in the specifically "Social Darwinist" form which they sometimes took in the early twentieth century. Daniel Pick, among others, has urged that the roots of such thinking were more domestic than imperial: "The 'aggression' of evolutionary discourse may have had as much to do with perceived 'terrors,' 'primitiveness' and fragmentation 'at home' as in the colonies."[28] Paul Crook, too, has argued forcefully and to some effect that social Darwinism played only a peripheral role in British imperial ideologies—there was no "Darwinised British imperial discourse."[29]

It was, on this view, neither the threat from the East, nor assertions of superiority over it, nor even (as in the standard interpretation of eugenicist arguments) the fear of "racial" degeneration through colonial miscegenation, which most pervasively dominated Social Darwinist and other later nineteenth-century evolutionary thought. Rather it was the fear of *internal* degeneration; an anxiety centered more on class than on race. Drives toward the formation of Social Darwinist, eugenicist and other evolutionist discourses came in substantial measure from pervasive late- Victorian British neuroses about national degeneration, centered on such images as "Outcast London" and the casually-labouring poor, prostitution, juvenile delinquency, and class-differential birth rates.[30] While they intersected with arguments about colonial expansion, emigration, and imperial defense, they were nothing like as persistently or pervasively focused on colonialism or race as most recent cultural theory assumes. Where these British debates became infused with concerns about external power relations, the focus was at least as much on intra-European rivalries and especially the perceived growing German threat as on colonial contexts. The "classic" texts of Social Darwinism did not concern themselves primarily with the imperial issue: thus for instance Benjamin Kidd's *Social Evolution* introduced the subject only in its concluding remarks, devoting to it a mere 23 pages (303–26) out of 350. And these passages are far from being a simple or straightforward celebration of imperial progress or racial hierarchy.[31] It may well be that racial ideas' place in imperialist ideologies was larger and more important, if more diffuse and less clearly articulated, in popular culture than in scholarship or (pseudo-) science. This is a possibility which we shall explore briefly below.

Closely linked to the role of racial beliefs in imperial ideology and practice is that of violence, repression, and atrocity. It is often argued that racist ideas ubiquitously underlay the seemingly standard assumption, to be found right across the history of Britain's colonial wars, that quite different rules applied when fighting "savages" than in warfare between European powers. Recent, intensely controversial works on the 1950s "Mau Mau" revolt have strongly emphasized such connections, and ensuing gross British brutality, at the very end of empire. [32]

It is indeed evident, even from staunchly patriotic and imperialist British accounts, that victory in colonial conflict was, time and again, accompanied by massacres of the defeated. James Grant's *British Battles on Land and Sea*—a massive four-volume work published in 1897, which fairly comprehensively lists, and lauds, every British colonial war up until that date—repeatedly notes such slaughters. In almost every case, the supposed racial characteristics of the enemy are invoked to explain imperial troops' savagery.[33] Arguments over the relationship between colonial rule and violence have also included stark claims that empire was inherently bound up with extreme, pervasive, structural, and even genocidal violence. Some historians suggest that most episodes of genocide and mass murder in world history have been associated with empire building: and in a particularly thought provoking and disturbing twist, Michael Mann has recently argued that "democratic" colonizers are the most likely to be genocidal.[34] Most of these claims, however, relate more to settler colonists' ideologies than to metropolitan British ones. There have also been intriguing suggestions that racial ideology massively shaped and distorted not only British behavior in imperial wars, but equally the interpretation of them. Thus James Belich's important analysis of the Maori wars uncovers systematic distortion in both contemporary and subsequent accounts of the conflicts—accounts which came almost exclusively, of course, from the European side.[35] Some of this distortion was of kinds found in most military contests: participants and their supportive chroniclers exaggerate both the numbers and the casualties of their opponents, seek to explain away defeats and reverses, embellish or invent atrocities by their foes and fall silent over irregularities on their own side's part. But the nature, extent and special features of both combatant and historiographical bias in this case exhibit a striking excess, Belich argues; one deriving from Victorian racial ideology.

Little, if any, less studied and less contentious than the role of "race" in imperial thinking has been the relationship between colonialism and gender.[36] The most powerfully persisting trope here has been identification and examination of a discourse by which imperialists supposedly identified themselves and their mission with masculine virtues, and the colonized with feminine weakness and dependency. There is an evident, powerful truth in this basic observation: but it has equally evidently been pushed much too far in some modern scholarship, in an essentialising fashion which ignores or drastically underrates the historical complexities of gendered discourses and practices in different colonial situations. Empire, it is often pointed out, was a man's world, not least in so often seeming like an open field for predatory male sexuality.[37] There were usually few European women in non-settler colonies, and the conquerors, rulers, administrators, theorists, publicists and artists of empire were overwhelmingly male. Ideas of a specifically "imperial masculinity," often associated with notions of adventure and of distinctive military virtues, were certainly very widespread.[38] So were related but perhaps significantly distinct ones of a pioneering male settler-colonial ethos.

Yet in British India, for instance, one might meaningfully speak of Bengalis as being feminized in colonial discourse; but India's so-called martial races—Sikhs, Baluchis, Pathans, and so on—were very clearly identified with sterotypes of masculinity. Indeed the whole martial race theory, later exported by the British from India to Africa, involved the masculinization of some subject populations just as clearly as it did the feminization of others. Moreover, as Mrinalini Sinha points out, much discussion of such issues tends to posit a specifically "modern" and "western" form of masculinity which was imposed on colonial contexts, failing to trace how this was itself inflected and altered by colonial relationships.[39] Likewise, "traditional" Indian or other ideas about gender roles among the colonized are often counterposed to the "modern/western/colonial" one, without registering either how these were also transformed by colonial impacts or how colonial ideologies themselves legitimated their stereotypes by reference to such local "traditions." The resources on which the British Raj drew to formulate martial races theory, images of an effeminate Bengali *bhadralok*, and so on, were taken at least as much from Indian as from European thought. Colonized men might be no less obsessed with masculinity, and with controlling "their" women's sexuality, than were their rulers.[40]

Students of British women as colonial writers, travellers or (in the few cases where such existed) power brokers have offered very diverse views on their ideological proclivities. The dominant tendency, however, remains the assertion that even western or colonialist feminism made its bid for women's equality only by, and through, assertions of intergender racial partnership in a colonial mission. Thus Moira

Ferguson finds only an implicit questioning and a far more decisive overt affirmation of colonial and racial hierarchies in the work of Mary Wollstonecroft and Jane Austen. Sara Mills, on the other hand, argues that women travellers in the East "were unable to adopt the imperial voice with the ease with which male writers did" and offered more nuanced, varied, less authoritative, or authoritarian images of native peoples than did male Orientalism. Billie Melman, too, finds women in the Middle East in the eighteenth and nineteenth centuries depicting (or constructing) a hugely varied set of "Orients," some involving sympathy with what they encountered abroad and criticism of their "own" patriarchal culture. Women's Orientalism, she also suggests, was often less monologically imperialist than that of men.[41] Judy Mabro's edited anthology, also dealing with western (mostly British) women travellers in the Middle East, does not seem to find their racist and elitist attitudes any more acceptable than those of men. Nor, in the end, does Felicity Nussbaum in her study of eighteenth-century men's and women's Orientalist writing. Despite various nuances and complications, she finds her female authors no less complicit in imperialism than the male. Sara Suleri believes that the marginality of European women to the colonial mission in India produced some questioning, but this was itself marginal to their collusion with imperialist oppression.[42] Julia Bush's study of aristocratic and "society" ladies in the early twentieth century finds them just as enthusiastic about empire building as their menfolk.[43] By the interwar years, by contrast, women interested in colonial affairs were far more likely to take a vigorous interest in reform, often with a specifically "maternalist" bias.[44] And Ann Laura Stoler, in a long series of particularly stimulating studies, sees in the sexual and other intimate encounters of multiple colonial situations a complex of ambiguities, anxieties and alterations which call into question not only many standard assumptions about colonial ideology but the very boundaries and definitions of "colonialism" itself.[45]

Still another aspect of debates over the historical salience and transformative force of British imperial ideology has recently been especially vigorous. This is over whether colonial rule should be viewed primarily in terms of modernization or of archaism. The notion of "colonial modernity" has been very widely invoked, especially among recent cultural historians of empire. The idea of colonialism as a modernizing, state-building, centralizing, developmentalist, and secularizing force has been deployed, too, by those urging a positive appraisal both of the British imperial record and of American "empire" today.[46] This clearly accords with much of the rhetoric and apparent self-image of empire builders themselves, and indeed with older notions of a distinctively liberal and commercial, rather than aristocratic or militaristic, British empire. Yet on the other hand, some British historians, like David Cannadine, stress instead the traditionalist and even archaizing features of British imperial ideology.[47] And many students of British India urge, in Maria Misra's words: "that, if anything, the British promoted the 'traditionalization' of India, halting many of the indigenous impulses toward modernization present in the late eighteenth century."[48] There is also a more structural problem with the "modernizing" picture. The notion of the colonial relationship coming from a rationalistic, homogenising drive by the expansionary power simply does not fit much of what we know about the British—or indeed any other colonialist—state in the nineteenth and earlier twentieth centuries. These were in many ways premodern, even precapitalist states; their ruling orders (and perhaps especially those fractions of the governing class most heavily involved in colonial expansion) largely aristocratic, only minimally subject to bourgeois rationality or fettered by popular democracy. Indeed there have been powerful arguments that one major social and ideological effect of empire within Britain was precisely to perpetuate such archaisms.[49] One does not have wholly to buy Joseph Schumpeter's view that imperialism was both utterly irrational and the product of feudal-military rather than capitalist elites, to recognize that the picture of a rationalistic capitalist imperialism painted by some historians—and the ideologically opposed but oddly congruent Fergusonian construct of an entirely "liberal empire"—is strikingly one-sided, if not entirely misleading.

Another big question which requires brief attention is that of *where* imperial ideologies were formulated and expressed. This has been pursued by historians and other scholars, with very divergent results, in cultural and especially literary production, in religious organizations, in scientific and medical discourses, and an ever-growing list of other fields.

Probably the largest body of modern writing on colonial ideology and discourse has persisted in the traditionally literary-critical vein of investigating texts from the English language literary canon and seeking to explore their depictions of empire—or, indeed, to demonstrate their complicity with British colonialism. As for the actual texts and authors investigated, the range involved has naturally grown over time. It remains, however, heavily focused on a fairly small number of mostly rather predictable figures. The biggest clusters of critical studies remain those around Kipling and Conrad.[50] Some other writers generally seen as of lesser literary merit but in whose work imperial themes play an especially large part, again mostly from the nineteenth and early twentieth centuries, have also attracted a large critical literature: prominent examples include, naturally enough, Rider Haggard.[51] Yet authors whose work had—apparently—an almost exclusively domestic focus have also been discussed extensively as completely bound up with empire, as has been the case with Thomas Hardy and Lewis Carroll.[52] There have indeed been attempts to argue that where nineteenth-century works of English literature do *not* refer to empire, this proves how crucial empire was to them—so crucial that their awareness of it had to be repressed. Suvendrini Perera, for instance, devotes an entire book to this implausible thesis, which amounts, as Bruce Robbins argues, to a kind of allegorical vulgar Freudianism in which empire becomes the universal unconscious of nineteenth-century culture, "a repressed but definitive truth that is always already obliged to return."[53] It might be added that the whole pseudo-Freudian emphasis in recent cultural theory on the fantasies, anxieties, and projections involved in empire "forgets" how much successful colonialism actually depended on real, accurate knowledge of the colonized.

As this suggests, the predominant focus has been on imperial ideas in the novel—and indeed it has sometimes been suggested that there is a particularly close and important relationship between this genre and the rise of empire.[54] There has perhaps been an excessive concentration on canonical, famous and literary texts, when we can surely learn more by looking at popular, mass market works. Other literary forms too, however, have been extensively investigated in this context: including drama, travel writing, children's literature, and newspapers.[55] Moving beyond literature, swelling bodies of work have investigated colonial and imperial themes in British cinema, photography, the visual arts, music, and more.[56] Each of these has been seen, by some commentators at least, as a crucial and influential vehicle for imperialist ideology.

The general tendency in recent scholarship on all these genres and milieux has been to stress their support for the "imperial mission" and their racist disparagement of colonized peoples. Here too, however, there have been voices raised in loud contradiction, as with John MacKenzie's polymathic gallop through Oriental themes and influences in British music, architecture, design, painting, sculpture, and the theatre, which insists that Orientalism in the arts included much which was innovative, and which displays genuine respect for the cultures from which it drew inspiration.[57] In somewhat parallel style, Robert Irwin joins the substantial chorus of those who assert that, contrary to the claims of critics like Edward Said, Orientalist scholarship was in the main very far from being monolithically racist or a handmaiden of colonialism.[58]

Institutions and practices which may be considered "cultural" in the broader, if not perhaps the more restricted sense have also been probed for their involvement with empire, and sometimes argued to have been key vectors of pro-imperial ideology. This has been done in relation to sport, in the linkages between imperial expansion and medical advance, including the racialization of various medical categories and techniques, in the advertising industry, youth organization, and many more.[59] Some social historians have identified as prime culprits in disseminating pro-imperial ideas those who founded, led and evangelized for the various semi-military youth organizations of late-nineteenth- and early twentieth-century Britain: Boy Scouts, Boys' Brigades, Church Lads' Brigades, and the rest. Perhaps the largest bodies of research and the most vigorous debates outside those in literary criticism, however, have centered on the place of empire in discourses of science and of religion.

Writing coming mainly from a cultural studies stable has frequently stressed—often in exaggerated ways—the "scientificity" of empire, its supposed powerful, distinctive, and even unique rationalizing, quantifying, organizing, knowledge-gathering thrust. Thus a very close association between empire and science has been suggested, and traced in numerous works, especially focused on British India.[60] If science has thus been seen as deeply complicit in imperial ideology, the story of religion is more complex. Whilst advocacy of empire was often conducted in religious terms, missionaries and other religious figures were also among the major critics of empire. Colonial mission activity, especially that of various nonconformist and evangelical groups, included significant involvement in anti-slavery agitation, in Caribbean anti-colonial protest, and later in opposition to white minority rule in Central and Southern Africa. The activities of colonial missionaries are indeed especially fertile territory for scholars keen to stress the ideological, cultural, and psychological aspects of colonialism. Missionaries did not usually have direct and powerful economic, or political-territorial, motivations for engaging in colonial projects. Their activities were more fully and purely directed towards cultural and psychological change than any other actors on colonial stages. And they were, on the whole, seeking explicitly to transform the consciousness of colonized subjects; whereas for governments and administrators (especially under Indirect Rule systems) such transformation was either peripheral and secondary, or even something deliberately to be avoided as a potentially destabilizing, unmanageable kind of interference. In many colonial situations, moreover, missionaries might be the only European residents from relatively poor backgrounds, the only ones with significant numbers of women in their ranks, the only ones living in intimate daily contact with colonized populations, and the only ones trying to provide education or health care to them. Yet they might also often be viewed as the most active and intrusive force of cultural imperialism, as is done by T. O. Beidelman, who sees Christian missions in East Africa as "the most naive and ethnocentric, and therefore the most thoroughgoing facet of colonial life . . . missionaries demonstrated a more radical and morally intense commitment to rule than political administrators or business men."[61]

Thus a huge range of cultural and social productions, institutions and forces may be identified as agents of imperial ideology—or indeed, more crudely, of propaganda. Whether, or in what ways, they were *successful* instruments of propaganda has proved far more difficult to establish. The messages presented in the multiple forms of pro-imperial entertainment and instruction, even were they univocal, were not merely passively accepted by audiences. Processes of reinterpretation—we might even call it deconstruction—would invariably take place, and these might well even be subversive of the intentions of the original producers. We know all too little of how such processes work.

And if we have far more questions than answers about the broad popular effects of such discourses, there are different but no less tricky problems of interpretation in relation to their impact on elites and policy makers. There were relatively few major, widely-read British "manifestos" for imperial expansion—perhaps the most famous arguable, albeit ambiguous, exception is Sir John Seeley's *The Expansion of England*—and even fewer of these were written by important political figures; though Charles Dilke's *Greater Britain* volumes could be read in this light, as perhaps could some works by Alfred Milner or Lord Cromer.[62]

There have, of course, been attempts by historians to argue that influential official minds not only accepted a grandiose conception of the imperial mission but consciously strove to implant that conception, by means of a variety of cultural apparatuses, in the British public. Such theories of "social imperialism" have probably been less influential among British historians than in Germany, and few British statesmen are as plausible candidates for the role of social-imperialist puppetmaster as is Bismarck. A number of names have, however, been canvassed: most obviously Joseph Chamberlain and Alfred Milner.[63] The problem with casting this pair as the villains of the piece is that whilst they played crucial roles in expanding British control over Southern Africa (Chamberlain as Colonial Secretary, Milner as High Commissioner), during the peak period of actual colonial expansion their broader ideas about Britain's world role were not endorsed by their colleagues, and after 1902 their empire policies were rejected both by their own party and by the electorate. Historians who cite the 1900 "Khaki election" as evidence of popular enthusiasm for such views tend to maintain a discreet silence about the 1906 Liberal landslide.

A more promising candidate might be Lord Salisbury, who was indeed at the helm of the state at a time when British colonial expansion was taking place with dramatic rapidity; and one can certainly find in Salisbury's scattered writings arguments that seem to suggest a belief in fostering imperial sentiment as a panacea for domestic ills.[64] Yet one can also find arguments of very different sorts: ones espousing colonialism on straightforward economic grounds, ones seeing the value of colonies as essentially strategic and defensive, and ones profoundly skeptical about whether colonies had *any* real value. Above all, one does *not* find arguments indicating that Salisbury believed the British voter or taxpayer to be an enthusiast for empire, let alone that such enthusiasm might be manipulated and capitalised upon by government. On the contrary, he felt that

> The misfortune—the root difficulty—we have in dealing with [colonial] questions . . . is that public opinion in its largest sense takes no note of them . . . The Members of the House of Commons are each like a ship without an anchor.[65]

Indeed one intriguing emphasis in recent writing on imperial mentalities has been to stress how much anxiety and insecurity these typically involved.[66] One need, surely, not press skepticism so far as to doubt that not only Salisbury or Chamberlain, but most British statesmen at least between the 1870s and the 1930s—perhaps across a much longer time period—had a sincere and profound belief in the greatness and goodness of the British Empire. Whether this amounted to their holding and seeking to spread a coherent or systematic imperial ideology is far harder to say. It may sometimes be more fruitful to pursue the influence of ideological predisposition as a force in imperial policy in more localized ways, as for instance Michael Cowen and Robert Shenton do in relation to Fabian and "neo-Hegelian" ideas among some British administrators in Africa.[67]

This brief sketch of aspects of British imperial ideas has proposed mostly "negative" conclusions, in the sense that it has emphasized how deeply divided students of these questions have been, perhaps especially in recent years, and how contradictory ideas about empire were, both at the time, and among recent historians of the phenomenon. This "negativity," however, should not be cause for depression, for the divisions, contradictions and complexities just indicate how richly fascinating the subject is, and how much work there still remains for historians to do.

Notes

1 These terms are explained in a broad sense at pp. 158–160 below.
2 Althusser, *For Marx*, p. 232.
3 Hunt and Purvis, "Discourse, ideology."
4 Foucault, *Archaeology*, p. 191.
5 See Cunningham, *Reading Gaol* for an extended, compelling argument that a great deal of contemporary theory is based on an egregious, systematic misreading of Saussure on this point.
6 Varikas, "Gender," p. 96.
7 Thomas, *Colonialism's Culture*, p. 2.
8 Lawson and Tiffin (eds), *De-Scribing Empire*, p. 3.

9   Mohanty, "Western eyes," p. 61.

10 Bhabha, *Location*, p. 70.

11 See also chapter by Catherine Hall.

12 See—amidst a rapidly swelling literature—Burton, "Rules of thumb,"; *id.*, "Who needs the nation?"; Ward (ed.), *British Culture*; Webster, "There'll always be an England"; Gilroy, *After Empire*; MacKenzie, *Propaganda and Empire*; Porter, *Absent-Minded Imperialists*; Thompson, *Imperial Britain*; *id.*, *Empire Strikes Back*.

13 Esp. Porter, *Absent-Minded Imperialists*.

14 See on these Thompson, "Language of imperialism'; *id.*, *Imperial Britain*.

15 See chapter by John Darwin.

16 Hobson, *Jingoism*; *id.*, *Imperialism*—and see Cain, *Hobson and Imperialism*.

17 Cain and Hopkins, *British Imperialism*.

18 Here, rapidly growing bodies of literature on ideas of "the British World" (e.g., Bridge and Fedorowich (eds), *British World*) and on the distinctive Scottish, Irish, Welsh, or indeed, say, Cornish, experiences of empire are making a crucial contribution. The latter cannot here, for reasons of space, be given even indicative citation.

19 Thus substantial literatures on "caste" in India and "tribe" in Africa see these as substantially colonial creations. Cohn's major relevant essays are collected in Cohn, *Anthropologist*; *id.*, *Colonialism*.

20 See, for example, Bayly, *Empire and Information*; and in this volume, the chapter by Tony Ballantyne.

21 For example, Dirks, *Castes of Mind*; *id.*, *Scandal of Empire*.

22 For example, Aguirre, *Informal Empire*.

23 See especially Gallagher, Johnson, and Seal (eds), *Locality*; Bayly, *Indian Society*; Washbrook, *Emergence*; and among Robinson's later essays, his 1986 "Excentric idea." An important recent reformulation of such arguments is in Newbury, *Patrons*.

24 See, for example, amidst a large literature, Engels and Marks (eds), *Contesting Colonial Hegemony*; Comaroff, *Body of Power*.

25 Guha, "Dominance."

26 For example, Hall, *Civilising Subjects*.

27 See, inter alia, Lorimer, *Colour*; *id.*, "Theoretical racism"; Goldberg, *Racist Culture*; Huttenback, *Racism and Empire*; McDougall, *Racial Myth*.

28 Pick, *Faces of Degeneration*, p. 38.

29 Crook, "Historical monkey business."

30 Respectively: Stedman Jones, *Outcast London*, Walkowitz, *Prostitution*, Soloway, *Birth Control*.

31 Kidd, *Social Evolution*; see also Crook, *Benjamin Kidd*.

32 D. Anderson, *Histories of the Hanged*; Elkins, *Britain's Gulag*: see also A. W. B. Simpson, *Human Rights*, which includes substantial discussion of abuses in late colonial wars.

33 Grant, *British Battles*; see also Lieven, "Butchering the brutes."

34 Mann, *Dark Side*.

35 Belich, *New Zealand Wars*.

36 Important surveys and overviews include Bryder, "Sex, race, and colonialism"; Burton (ed.), *Gender*; Chaudhuri and Strobel, *Western Women*; Levine (ed.), *Gender and Empire*; Lewis and Mills, *Feminist Postcolonial Theory*; Midgley (ed.), *Gender and Imperialism*. A growing sub-field, which cannot be adequately analyzed here, relates to the colonial dimensions of homosexuality and its representations. See for major statements, Aldrich, *Colonialism and Homosexuality*; Bleys, *Geography of Perversion*.

37 See, for instance, Hyam's pioneering but contentious *Empire and Sexuality*.

38 For example, Dawson, *Soldier Heroes*.
39 Sinha, *Colonial Masculinity*.
40 For example, Kelly, *Politics of Virtue*.
41 Ferguson, *Colonialism and Gender*; S. Mills, *Discourses of Difference*; Melman, *Women's Orients*.
42 Mabro (ed.), *Veiled Half-Truths*; Nussbaum, *Torrid Zones*; Suleri, *Rhetoric*.
43 Bush, *Edwardian Ladies*.
44 For example, Pederson, "National bodies"; *id.*, "Maternalist moment."
45 Stoler, *Carnal Knowledge*; *id.*,"Tense and tender ties"; *id.*, *Haunted by Empire*.
46 Most forcefully, if not stridently, N. Ferguson, *Empire*; *id.*, *Colossus*.
47 Cannadine, *Ornamentalism*.
48 Misra, "Lessons of empire," p. 133.
49 For example, Mayer, *Persistence*; Anderson, *English Questions*.
50 Amidst vast literatures on each: Husain, *Kipling and India*; Sullivan, *Narratives of Empire*; Wurgaft, *Imperial Imagination* (Kipling); Darras, *Conrad and the West*; Fincham and Hooper, *Postcolonial Eyes*; Firchow, *Envisioning Africa*; Parry, *Conrad and Imperialism* (Conrad). A very large, in part, separate polemical literature also developed in the wake of Chinua Achebe's famous denunciation of Conrad as a racist ("An Image of Africa"). Harrison, *Postcolonial Criticism* offers a thoughtful overview of some of these debates.
51 For example, Chrisman, *Rereading*; Etherington, *Rider Haggard*; Katz, *Haggard*.
52 Both given much space in Bivona, *Desire*.
53 Perera, *Reaches of Empire*; Robbins, "Colonial discourse," p. 213.
54 For example, Azim, *Colonial Rise* and, by far the most influential, Said, *Culture and Imperialism*.
55 For instance, Bratton *et al.* (eds), *Acts of Supremacy* on theatre; Grewal, *Home and Harem*; Pratt, *Imperial Eyes* on travel; Boyd, "Exemplars and ingrates'; Bristow, *Empire Boys*; Castle, *Britannia's Children*; Dunae, "Boys' Literature," on juvenile literature; Kaul, *Reporting the Raj* on the press.
56 Here, even more than in preceding sections, citation can only be the tip of the iceberg. On imperialism in photography: Bate, "Photography'; Ryan, *Picturing Empire*; in painting, Alloula, *Colonial Harem*; Tobin, *Picturing*; in architecture, Davies, *Splendours*; Metcalf, *Imperial Vision*; in music, Richards, *Imperialism and Music*; in cinema, Richards, *Visions of Yesterday*; *id.*, "Patriotism and profit"; in museums, Coombes, *Reinventing Africa*.
57 MacKenzie, *Orientalism*.
58 Irwin, *Lust of Knowing*.
59 Medicine: W. Anderson, "Medicine as colonial discourse"; Arnold (ed.), *Imperial Medicine*; McCulloch, *Colonial Psychiatry*; MacLeod and Leis (eds), *Disease*; Vaughan, *Curing Their Ills*; sport: Guha, *Corner*; McDevitt, *Best Man*; Mangan, *Cultural Bond*; *id.*, *Games Ethic*; advertising: Constantine, *Buy and Build*; Ramamurthy, *Black Markets*; *id.*, *Imperial Persuaders*; youth organizations: Blanch, "Organised youth; Rosenthal, *Character Factory*; Springhall, *Youth, Empire and Society* .
60 For example, Baber, *Science of Empire*; Kumar, *Science and the Raj*; Prakash, *Another Reason*.
61 Beidelman, *Colonial Evangelism*, p. 13. See also, for perhaps the most detailed and influential studies in this vein, Comaroff and Comaroff, *Revelation and Revolution*, and for an overview, Etherington, *Missions and Empire*.
62 Seeley, *Expansion*; Dilke, *Greater Britain*; *id.*, *Problems of Greater Britain*.
63 Perhaps first suggested in Semmel, *Imperialism*.
64 Salisbury was Prime Minister—with two short breaks—from 1885 to 1902.

65 Quoted in Gallagher and Robinson, *Africa and the Victorians*, p. 23.
66 For example, Cooper and Stoler, eds., *Tensions of Empire*.
67 See their important articles, "Fabian colonialism'; "Neo-Hegelian Idealism."

Further Reading

There is, to my knowledge, no satisfactory modern, general overview of this topic which embraces both a long timespan and the British Empire as a whole, though there are many important and illuminating works on particular parts of it.

The *OHBE* does not include chapters on "imperial ideology" as such, but naturally many of its authors cast light on varied aspects of the theme. Among the volumes of the project's continuing *Companion Series,* especially relevant are several contributions to Norman Etherington (ed.), *Missions and Empire* and Philippa Levine (ed.), *Gender and Empire.* The present author's forthcoming volume in that series, *Intellectual Consequences of Decolonisation* also intends to contribute to several relevant debates, and greatly expands on various arguments made very briefly in the chapter above. Specifically on British India, Thomas R. Metcalf, *Ideologies of the Raj* is succinct, readable, and erudite.

On "ideology" and related concepts in general, John B. Thompson, *Ideology and Modern Culture* is a lucid overview, accessible to those who are not specialists in political theory.

Edward W. Said's many writings on imperialism and "Orientalism," especially in literary culture—including *Culture and Imperialism*—have both had many imitators and prompted a vast body of hostile criticism, not least from imperial historians. Some of these works are listed in the bibliography.

For empire's place in British political thinking before the nineteenth century, perhaps the most important modern works are David Armitage, *The Ideological Origins of the British Empire* and—in comparative perspective—Anthony Pagden, *Lords of All the World.* P. J. Cain and A. G. Hopkins, *British Imperialism*, vol. 1, *Innovation and Expansion 1688–1914* and vol. 2, *Crisis and Deconstruction 1914– 1990*, though focused more on the economics than on the ideology of the British Empire, has had great impact on debate over the latter too.

On the much debated issue of how widespread, important and popular pro-imperial ideas were among Britain's populations, numerous writings by Antoinette Burton (some of them listed above) present a strong version of the case for their near-ubiquity. Bernard Porter, *The Absent-Minded Imperialists* offers a far more skeptical view; while Andrew S. Thompson, *Imperial Britain: The Empire in British Politics* and *The Empire Strikes Back?* proposes a more 'middle-ground' position. Catherine Hall, *Civilising Subjects* is among the most important of the more narrowly-focused works in this field.

On the complex interaction of ideologies, interests and local circumstances in particular colonial situations, especially important and influential recent works have included C. A. Bayly, *Empire and Information*, John and Jean Comaroff, *Of Revelation and Revolution*, and Ann Laura Stoler, *Carnal Knowledge and Imperial Power.*

8

Colonial Knowledge

Tony Ballantyne

One of the most significant shifts during the last two decades of research on the history of the British Empire has been the new centrality of "knowledge" as an analytical problematic. In the early 1980s, British imperial history was a marginal field within history as a discipline. During the 1970s and early 1980s, British "domestic" history had been revivified by the "new" social history, which had opened up new ways of writing about the past, especially the history of those social groups—such as children, women, the working class—who had enjoyed limited access to political power. These new approaches had relatively little impact on the study of empire, which remained preoccupied with testing and refining the theories of Ronald Robinson and John Gallagher. The work of Robinson and Gallagher in the 1950s and 1960s on imperial economics and the "official mind" of British imperialism had affected a paradigm shift in academic writing on empire. The agenda they set foregrounded questions of commerce, development, the emergence of proto-nationalism at the frontiers of empire, and the role of local crises in the periphery in driving imperial expansion.

Since the early 1980s, this established tradition of work on the empire has been challenged by a range of new approaches that have moved away from the domains of economics and high politics to focus on the question of culture. Scholars from a range of disciplinary backgrounds—literary studies, anthropology, gender studies, the history of education, geography, and art history—have fashioned a sprawling and disparate body of work that has radically reimagined empire, reading it not simply as a set of economic and political structures of dominance but as a cultural project. At the same time, a new generation of cultural historians have used an interdisciplinary body of theory to reread the archives of empire, focusing in particular on the centrality of cultural difference in structuring both colonial rule and the imperial imagination. This "new imperial history" has amounted to a profound shift in the way in which colonial domination and the dynamics of empire building have been imagined. Its cultural sensibility has greatly enlarged our sense of what colonialism was: it was not simply about extending informal political influence, establishing economic domination, or securing sovereignty, but it was a much broader set of asymmetrical relationships grounded in the desire of the colonizer to exert mastery over the colonized society, its natural and human resources, and its cultural forms.

Thus "colonial knowledge"—the form and content of the knowledge that was produced out of and enabled resource exploitation, commerce, conquest, and colonization—now stands at the center of work on the history of the British Empire. This essay examines the development of this analytical problematic and the ways in which it has transformed our understandings of the nature of colonial rule and its outcomes. While the other chapters in this collection address themes—such as religion, economics, and the state—that are long established in historical scholarship and have a ready legibility, given colonial knowledge's recent rise and prominence it requires careful explanation. This chapter charts the emergence of "colonial knowledge" as a subject of enquiry, highlights some of the fundamental points of contention and divergence within the historiography, traces the uneven purchase of "colonial knowledge" outside South Asia, and examines the connections between colonial knowledge and historical understandings of the nature of colonial states and construction of identity within the empire.

The Rise of Colonial Knowledge I: Orientalism and Colonial Knowledge

In 1978, the influential literary critic Edward Said published *Orientalism*, an elegant and powerful analysis of western representations of the "Orient" (the Islamic World, South and East Asia) and their role in both justifying European imperial dominance and in defining the nature of Europe itself. Said argued that Orientalism functioned as a system of knowledge production that produced a series of hierarchical oppositions between the "Occident" and the "Orient," oppositions that allowed the West to assert its superiority and control over "Oriental" societies.[1] While many of the themes of *Orientalism* had been anticipated by Raymond Schwab's study of the "Oriental Renaissance" in European thought and were addressed by post-war research on the role of ideology in shaping colonial administration and the colonial origins of anthropology, Said brought these concerns together in a new and provocative way.[2] Said's insistence on the power of representation and its complicity with European imperial enterprises has radically transformed understandings of translation, literary production, and the history of education in colonized societies. In foregrounding representation as a key aspect of imperialism, Said's work reoriented studies of empire towards cultural encounters, loosening the vice-like grip of Robinson and Gallagher (and their students) over the study of the imperial past. In the wake of Said, the production and dissemination of knowledge occupied an increasingly central position in shaping scholarly understandings of imperialism and was pivotal in enabling a growing recognition that colonialism was not simply a matter of military conquest, the extension of sovereignty, or economic dominance, but rather it was also a complex cultural project as well.

Although scholars were quick to the test the power of Said's thesis for many formerly colonized regions during the 1980s, it has been in the historiography of South Asia that *Orientalism* has proven most influential. By the end of the 1980s, the question of colonial knowledge had emerged as a central feature of the analytical terrain of South Asian studies. One of the earliest signs of this shift was an important 1986 article by the leading American South Asianist Ronald Inden, an essay that set out arguments he subsequently developed in his 1990 study *Imagining India*. Inden followed in the spirit of Said's text to launch a sustained critique of the Western tradition of Indology, the academic study of Indian texts, religion, and society. Inden argued that Indology had produced an understanding of South Asia that insisted "that the essence of Indian civilization is just the opposite of the West's." India's difference, Inden suggested, was defined by the two chief concerns of Indology: "caste" and "Hinduism." These categories, he contended, were chiefly the products of western concerns and served as potent markers of India's supposed backwardness.[3] At the same time, literary scholars were embracing the opportunities opened up by Said's work for a reassessment of colonial texts and the imperial history of literary studies as a discipline. The critic and theorist Gauri Viswanathan followed Said in seeking to locate colonialism's power as resting in the domain of culture. Her *Masks of Conquest* argued that literary studies and the very notion of literature itself were deployed by the colonial state in India as a powerful means of social control and as a bulwark to imperial power. From the 1830s, the study of English literature was seen by leading officials as a crucial force for reshaping the "character" of Indians and effectively functioned as an ideological instrument designed by an anxious colonial state to contain any inclination towards rebellion on the behalf of the colonized.[4]

Most importantly, however, Said's work provided an important set of intellectual tools for the newly formed Subaltern Studies collective whose work not only challenged established readings of South Asian history, but had a profound impact on humanities scholarship in general. This editorial collective emerged in response to the crisis that wracked the Indian state in the 1970s and set out to displace the elitist sensibilities of the historical models that developed under both British colonialism and India's bourgeois elite. While Antonio Gramsci's notion of the "subaltern" was central to the early volumes of *Subaltern Studies* produced by the collective, Said's use of Michel Foucault's work on power/knowledge and his own critique of European representations of the Orient were also increasingly important touchstones.[5] As Partha Chatterjee reflected:

> *Orientalism* was a book which talked of things I felt I had known all along but had never found the language to formulate with clarity. Like many great books, it seemed to say for the first time what one had always wanted to say.[6]

The influence of Said and Foucault on the Subaltern Studies project became marked from around the fifth volume (published in 1987), when some members of the collective began to frame their research into the history of the body and the power of representation in explicitly Saidian and Foucauldian terms.[7] This engagement with Foucault's work on knowledge regimes reflected the broader cultural turn within international humanities scholarship as well as a realization that asylums, prisons, and hospitals might be promising sites for recovering the colonial state's efforts to exercise the authority of western knowledge systems over its Indian subjects. But we must also recognize that the particular influence of Said's work in South Asia was a product of the particularity of the region's colonial history and the persistent question that scholars of Indian history have faced: how were a small group of Britons able to incorporate India into British trade networks and eventually colonize most of South Asia?

The Rise of Colonial Knowledge II: Power and Knowledge in South Asian Studies

Scholars from a range of disciplinary locations pursued this question in the 1980s and 1990s. One key figure here was the influential translator, literary critic, and theorist Gayatri Chakravorty Spivak. In a path-breaking 1985 essay, Spivak insisted that colonial archives were the product of the "commercial/territorial interest of the East India Company." In this essay, Spivak examined the nature of colonial knowledge through a critical reflection on her own archival search for the Rani of Sirmur, the wife of the ruler of a small hill-state in what is now Himachal Pradesh. As Spivak made clear, the Rani of Sirmur emerges in the colonial archives "only when she is needed in the space of imperial production." Spivak suggested that the Rani's occlusion from the archive meant that it was an impossible task to recover South Asian women's subjectivities from the colonial record.[8]

Spivak's conclusion that subaltern groups cannot speak has proved extremely controversial and has stimulated a large and discordant literature. Perhaps the most important gloss on Spivak's exploration of the gender and subalternity is Lata Mani's work on *sati* (widow burning). While Mani acknowledged the importance of Spivak's work, she warned against reading Spivak's argument as a set of "conclusions about colonial discourse in general," instead using it as a starting point for an extensive rereading of contemporary accounts of *sati*. Mani reconstructed the intense debates between evangelical missionaries, state functionaries, and indigenous male reformers over the scriptural basis of this contentious tradition. She contended that these exchanges generally erased female subjectivity, as women became the "grounds" for debate about the nature of custom and modernity. While Mani's analysis followed Spivak to the extent that she accepted the impossibility of any full recovery of female subjectivity, she also suggested that a nuanced reading of colonial texts was capable of unsettling the fundamental assumptions of male-produced eyewitness accounts. Mani traced acts of resistance to the coercive techniques that often enabled sati and highlighted the occasional accounts that disrupted official discourses by focusing on the physical and emotional pain inflicted upon women. Such narratives compromised and even ruptured key "fictions" about *sati*, especially the dominant representation of it as a "religiously inspired act of devotion to the deceased husband."[9] Equally importantly, Mani delineated the ways in which male indigenous elites were authorized as experts within the colonial system through debates on *sati*. Pandits and Brahman were subjected to "continual and instinctive questioning" by British authorities and out of their competing opinions and interpretations the British formulated a newly systematized vision of "tradition" as the bedrock of colonial policy. This "incitement to discourse" directed towards male "authorities" must be set in contradistinction to the muffling of female voices in colonial archives, revealing the fundamentally gendered dynamics that shaped British knowledge-construction and policy-making. This problematizing of the colonial archive by Spivak and Mani has been a key reference point for feminist historians of empire who have worked to document the history of colonized women as well as reconstruct the gendered dynamics of empire building.[10]

The question of the cultural consequences of colonial knowledge was not only posed by feminist scholars who were seeking to chart the ways in which colonial rule produced and codified new understandings of gender in the colonial realm. Another crucial vector of work was produced by anthropologists, especially those who were dedicated to historicizing the cultural forms that were fundamental to anthropological analysis. Foremost here was the work of Bernard Cohn, which opened up new perspectives on the place of knowledge in the political structures fashioned by the British in India. From the late 1950s, Cohn examined the institutional, textual, and cultural structures that shaped the colonial state's understanding of South Asian society. In pioneering essays on the colonial legal system, the census, and the development of western understandings of Indian society, Cohn analysed the contest between British and South Asian epistemic systems and the central role played by British understandings of Indian society in securing colonial dominance.[11]

He elaborated these arguments in his influential 1996 study *Colonialism and its Forms of Knowledge*. In this collection of essays, Cohn located the development of the colonial state in India within the broader dynamics of the construction of modern nation-states. Nation-states, Cohn argued, relied upon an innovative set of administrative processes that defined, codified, and controlled communities and their histories. These state practices, which relied upon the regularized production and ordering of knowledge, were profoundly different from the "theatre of power" that shaped pre-modern states and societies. Where the authority of the Mughal emperor was grounded in a "theatre of power" of ritual and spectacle, the colonial state's authority rested on its ability to collate and distill its knowledge of local terrains and cultures in maps, grammars, legal codes, and censuses. Through these processes Indian words, artifacts, and identities were wrenched out of their indigenous context and fashioned into new bodies of knowledge that served the needs of the British, but bore little relation to indigenous realities. The new forms of knowledge produced by the East India Company, such as grammars and dictionaries of South Asian languages that were vital to the everyday operation of colonial governance, allowed the British to assert their mastery of local cultural forms, enabling the invasion and conquest of India's "epistemological space." In *Colonialism and its Forms of Knowledge*, Cohn identified what he saw as the six key "investigative modalities" that were fundamental to the operation of colonial power: historiographic, observational/travel, survey, enumerative, museological, and surveillance.[12] Through an examination of these modalities in essays on the history of law, language, museums, and clothing Cohn opened up a vast cultural terrain for analysis and produced a compelling case for the centrality of culture as an analytical problem in the study of colonialism.

Nicholas Dirks has led the way in extending this perspective on colonialism as a cultural project. In his forward to *Colonialism and its Forms of Knowledge*, he argued:

It has not been sufficiently recognised that colonialism was itself a cultural project of control. Colonial knowledge both enabled conquest and was produced by it; in certain important ways, knowledge was what colonialism was all about. Cultural forms in societies newly classified as "traditional" were reconstructed and transformed by and through this knowledge, which created new categories and oppositions between colonizers and colonized, European and Asian, modern and traditional, West and East. Ruling India through the delineation and reconstitution of systematic grammars for vernacular languages, representing India through the mastery and display of archaeological memories and religious texts, Britain set in motion transformations every bit as powerful as the better-known consequences of military and economic imperialism.[13]

Much of Dirks's own work has focused on the production of archives, the collections of cartographic, linguistic, ethnographic, and historical knowledge fashioned by the colonial state and its functionaries. Dirks has made a strong case for regarding these not simply as repositories that record India's social structure and history, but as the very basis of British dominance in South Asia.[14]

The Rise of Colonial Knowledge III: Debating Colonial Knowledge and the Cultural Turn

It is true that within this new scholarship much less effort has been devoted to reconstructing the processes through which colonial knowledge actually produced dominance on the ground (or, for that matter, reshaped indigenous social realities), than to the deconstruction of colonial texts, there is also not doubt this emphasis on knowledge production has produced a radical reimagining of imperial power. This complex of work on colonial knowledge is united by both its deployment of Said's and Foucault's critical commentaries on the connections between power and knowledge and its general insistence that colonialism and its distinctive regimes of knowledge marked a profound rupture in South Asian history. Such attempts to radically reimagine the theory and practice of writing about the imperial past have proven contentious. Most importantly, practitioners of social history questioned the turn to culture and raised concerns about the ability of work on colonial knowledge to explain the structures of domination that have shaped life in South Asia. In critiquing Gyan Prakash's use of Said's work and the broader project of Subaltern studies, Rosalind O'Hanlon and David Washbrook not only highlighted theoretical tensions within the collective's work but also moved to reassert the primacy of older materialist understandings of class and the analytical power of "social history."[15] This argument needs to be read as part of the broader contest within the discipline of history over the "cultural turn." O'Hanlon and Washbrook were seeking to shore up the power of a language of criticism inherited from Marxist-inflected social history and in so doing they were challenging what they saw as the depoliticizing effects of work on "representation" and "identity." We must recognize that they staked out this position at a moment when British traditions of social history were being challenged and radically reworked by scholars who were interested in understanding class through language and symbol rather than relying on modes of analysis that focused on the intersections between economics and politics. More recently, Washbrook has revisited "colonial discourse theory," lamenting "the shift from 'social' to 'cultural' history," which has mean that "concepts of class and capital have gone missing."[16] For Washbrook, the cultural turn not only leaves deprivation and poverty unexplained, but it is both a product and a reflection of the westernization of South Asian intellectuals. Washbrook suggests that colonial discourse theory has allowed "Third World" elite émigrés in the west to remain privileged interpreters of their homelands: in effect, post-colonialism has become "a new mechanism of imperialism in an age of multicultural, globalized capitalism." More specifically, blind as he is to the strength of African, Australian, and Pacific post-colonial traditions that have enjoyed minimal support from the American academy, Washbrook suggests that post-colonialism marks the Americanization of the humanities: its concern with culture, ethnicity, and discourse mark its supposedly American nature.[17] The strength of the oppositions Washbrook drew between social history and cultural history, class and ethnicity, means "society" and "culture" are best read as part of an often heated transatlantic debate over the future of the humanities.

Critiques of the cultural turn in the study of empire have also been articulated by American South Asianists. In a "postmortem" for Subaltern Studies, Richard Eaton has made some important points about the uneven thematic and chronological interests of the Subaltern collective. Eaton's critique of the "postmodernism" of the collective, however, is primarily aimed to reassert the interpretative authority of history. Eaton denounced the shift towards knowledge and discourse as a move from "a positivist and empiricist orientation to one grounded more squarely in a literary criticism that draped itself in the banner of an amorphous, obscurantist phrasing: cultural studies." In his view, work on knowledge and discourse is closer to cultural studies than history, and cultural studies, for Eaton, is an "arm-chair" discipline, lacking the long-established methodological "traditions" of history. In this regard, Eaton sees the questioning of the colonial archive as particularly pernicious because it has enabled a marked transformation of the patterns of research and writing about the past:

> Indeed, the 1980s and 1990s saw a sharp drop from levels of earlier decades in the number of historians who applied for support or permission to conduct research out in the *mufassal*—that is, in district archives, local libraries, private collections, zamindari records, and so forth. Most ended up in London, and a few in national or state archives in India, studying colonial records that were then subjected to discourse analysis.[18]

But the study of colonial knowledge has not been simply the domain of anthropologists, literary scholars, and scholars based in women's studies programmes. Another arc of archivally-grounded research from within the British tradition of imperial history has explored the relationships between power and knowledge. Most important here is the work of C. A. Bayly. In contrast to the Foucauldian inflection of Cohn's work and the later volumes of *Subaltern Studies* and in Cohn's *Colonialism and its Forms of Knowledge*, Bayly's *Empire and Information* produced a reading of colonialism that wove together social and intellectual history. *Empire and Information*'s analytical framework drew on recent explorations in the sociology of knowledge. Particularly important here was Manuel Castells's exploration of the place of information technology in late twentieth-century social formations. Following Castells in his insistence that education, information technologies, and knowledge communities are central to any understanding of social change, Bayly framed this monograph as an exploration of the "information order" of colonial India. This interest in the structures that produced information and shaped Indian intellectual life meant that Bayly paid careful attention to the extent and meaning of indigenous literacy, local patterns of intelligence gathering, the power of long-established traditions of thought, the changing status of knowledge experts, and the impact of new technologies (especially the printing press). Bayly located the East India Company's rise to power in its engagement with these South Asian structures and traditions, placing particular emphasis on the Company's efforts to "turn" these to serve the interests of the colonial state (this is discussed further below). He also traced the encounters between western and Indian knowledge traditions, highlighting the long and extensive nature of these cross-cultural engagements.[19] Thus where Cohn suggested that colonial knowledge was foundational to British hegemony and marginalized indigenous traditions as it irrevocably transformed South Asian identities, Bayly argued that South Asian learned communities, religious leaders, and social reformers were able to mould and contest colonial knowledge, an argument that largely accords with the picture offered in Eugene Irschick's work on the colonial encounter in Tamil Nadu.[20] Bayly's work has provided an important stimulus for recent work that has mapped the contours of broader imperial "information order," including my own reading of imperial knowledge between 1760 and 1850, Alan Lester's examination of humanitarian knowledge networks, Zoë Laidlaw's study of the information revolution in colonial governance, and Simon Potter's monograph on the development of the imperial press system.[21]

The Rise of Colonial Knowledge IV: "Colonial Knowledge" outside Indian Historiography

It is very clear then that debates over "colonial knowledge" have fostered the development of new approaches to the colonial past, especially within the South Asian context. But it is important to recognize that the problematic of "colonial knowledge" does not enjoy quite the same purchase outside South Asia. This reflects both the variegated nature of colonialism itself and the very different intellectual trajectories and political conditions that have framed other colonial historiographies. The relatively late onset, for example, of large-scale European territorial rule in Africa has directed research toward a quite different set of concerns. Where South Asian historians have focused on the colonial state's project to describe, enumerate, and order cultural difference along the axes of caste and religion, such projects were not central to British imperial rule in Africa. As Frederick Cooper has observed, visions of colonial modernity based on this Indian model do not translate well to Africa where, for example, the British did not undertake a census that counted indigenous people in Kenya until 1948.[22] Africanists have seen the colonial state's project resting more firmly in its efforts to conquer and develop African environments. Most importantly, African historians have focused on the new medical understandings and technologies that enabled European powers to finally colonize and settle in tropical Africa.[23] A related avenue of research has focused on the ways in which the new social structures, political institutions, and economic patterns fostered by colonial regimes reshaped local ecologies and the material basis of everyday life in Africa.[24] This historiography on medicine and ecology has consistently returned to the connections between colonial regimes and the developmental strategies explored by post-colonial states, reflecting on the ongoing importance of intellectual and political debates over the impact of decolonization and the best path to development.[25] This question of state power has also been at the heart of the important reassessments of the place of the archive in the construction of white dominance in South Africa and on the powerful knowledge-producing apparatus constructed by the apartheid regime.[26]

In the former settler colonies of Canada, Australia, and New Zealand, significant bodies of historical research have addressed the role of knowledge production in enabling colonization, especially the role of exploration, cartography, and travel narratives in rendering indigenous landscapes legible and suitable for settlement by whites.[27] While some of this work addresses Foucault's knowledge/power problematic, this work also reflects the centrality of the land to the political economy of settler colonialism. Questions relating to land rights and resource control more broadly have stood at the heart of politics in Australia, Canada, and New Zealand over the past two decades and historians have played a prominent role in the legal processes initiated by the desire of indigenous communities to establish and assert their rights. Within this context, historians have devoted considerable effort to assessing the characteristics and evidentiary status of indigenous oral narratives.[28] And several historians have embraced the possibilities afforded by the careful use of various forms of oral testimony to experiment with new ways of narrating the colonial encounter as they strive towards a self-reflexive and decolonized form of historical practice. Most importantly, Judith Binney has juxtaposed Maori oral narratives with Pakeha (settler)-written texts to produce richly textured reassessments of the colonial encounter in New Zealand.[29] This kind of work reflects a fruitful interface between historical and anthropological approaches to colonialism, an interdisciplinary dialogue that has driven the key work of Nicholas Thomas on knowledge and empire in the Pacific.[30]

The other body of research that has contributed to the new prominence of colonial knowledge has been the study of science and empire. Until the 1980s, science enjoyed little prominence in imperial history. In the 1960s, George Basalla highlighted the importance of empires in spreading western science and over the next decade or so several historians of the former dominions traced the development of national scientific traditions from their colonial beginnings. Generally, however, science was seen as having limited significance for historical understanding of the British Empire.[31] This marginalization was challenged by important monographs published in the 1980s by Daniel Headrick and Michael Adas that demonstrated the importance of science and technology in enabling the new imperialism of the late nineteenth century as well as underscoring science's symbolic power as a marker of European dominance.[32] At the same time, Basalla's simple diffusionist model of western science was challenged by new work, especially Roy MacLeod's studies of both British and Australian science that affirmed the fundamental importance of science in the imperial project and produced a more complex model of the "architecture" of imperial science.[33]

A large and sophisticated historiography on colonial science developed from the early 1990s. In South Asia, for example, Partha Chatterjee edited a pioneering collection of essays that charted the consolidation of key discursive fields and disciplinary traditions in colonial Bengal.[34] Matthew Edney explored one key colonial discipline, cartography, in a history of the role of surveying in military campaigns, the assessment of taxation, and in the projection of "India" as a unified political unit.[35] A significant body of research has also explored the development of colonial science in the Pacific, paying particular attention to scientific networks and the role of imperial spaces opened up by imperial exploration in cementing the authority of fledgling disciplines such as botany and ethnography. Of particular importance here has been the work on the Pacific voyages of James Cook and the pivotal role of Joseph Banks, who was the naturalist on Cook's first voyage, in co-ordinating British imperial science in late eighteenth and early nineteenth centuries.[36] Medicine has also loomed large within the new work on colonial science and of particular importance here was David Arnold's *Colonizing the Body*, which examined the construction of a powerful system of scientific medicine that was deployed by the colonial state in India and, in a departure from Foucault's approach to biopower, emphasized the ability of South Asians to resist the authority attached to western medicine.[37] Megan Vaughan pursued a similar line of inquiry in Africa as she mapped the development of colonial medicine and highlighted the tensions between its claims to scientific neutrality and its profound embeddedness in imperial structures of domination. Her *Curing Their Ills* offered a careful reading of the full range of colonial medicine—ranging from psychiatry to the treatment of venereal diseases—and documented the pivotal role of medicine and doctors in the production of colonial understandings of African peoples.[38] But perhaps the strongest statement of the connection between science, medicine, and imperial authority was articulated by Sheldon Watts in his sweeping history of empires and epidemics, which identified medicine as fundamental to the exercise of British imperial power on the global stage.[39]

Much of the new work on colonial science has questioned the kind of image of an all-powerful western science produced by scholars like Watts. Richard Grove challenged prevailing stereotypes of science as an agent of the ruthlessness of early capitalist development, as he highlighted the crucial role of empires in shaping early forms of conservationist thought.[40] Other scholars have emphasized the ability of colonized peoples to engage with and contest western science. Bayly's *Empire and Information* records the engagement of South Asian elites with western forms of astronomy and geography and, in a similar vein, Michael Dodson has examined the ability of Hindu pandits to shape the diffusion of the new forms of knowledge that British missionaries and educational reformers presented to South Asians.[41] Beyond South Asia, Michael Bravo has explored the power of Inuit cartography and several contributions to the landmark *History of Cartography* series have highlighted the durability of non-western understandings of space under colonial rule.[42] Other scholars, especially Kavita Phillip and Gyan Prakash, have stressed the ways in which western science was translated and woven into indigenous epistemologies, to produce a kind of "mixed" or "alternative" modernity.[43] Science has thus become a central concern in imperial history, a new prominence that is perhaps best embodied in Richard Drayton's *Nature's Government*, which has charted the changing role of science in achieving the ends of "improvement" in the name of empire.[44]

When these disparate historiographies—on South Asia, on imperialism in Africa, the status of indigenous knowledge in former settler colonies and the history of colonial science and medicine—are viewed together, it is very clear that both local political issues and broad trends in humanities scholarship have rendered the archives of empire deeply problematic. Despite the divergent analytical languages and historiographical concerns within the historical literature on these former colonies, the weight of over two decades of research has demonstrated that the sources that historians conveniently use—from government records to photographs, manuscript collections to newspapers, from court archives to maps—are not simply transparent sources through which the colonial past can be accessed, but rather were themselves constitutive of the inequalities that were implicit within the imperial order. Archival repositories, libraries, and museums have been re-imagined as sites produced and saturated by power. Given that this is the nature of the archive of colonialism, how must it be read? What perspectives are foregrounded and what groups are privileged within colonial archives? More importantly, who is excluded, whose voices are silenced, what groups and individuals are reduced to fleeting traces and isolated textual fragments? These kinds of questions are increasingly shared by a range of different colonial historiographies.

Knowledge and Conquest

The precise relationships between knowledge and colonial power remain contested. Although a range of scholars have come to focus on the role of the colonial state in producing knowledge, it is important to highlight the substantial divergences between post-colonial anthropological readings of colonial knowledge and the work of scholars who are interested in the longer history of the production of knowledge by South Asian states and elites. Most of the studies produced by the Subaltern studies collective as well as the works by Cohn, Dirks, Spivak, and Mani share a common insistence on both the novelty and the great power enjoyed by the forms of knowledge sponsored by the colonial state. But this position is problematic. Not only has this anthropologically inflected work paid little attention to the processes through which the authority of this knowledge was secured, but it has largely disregarded the knowledge systems of early modern India and the complex ways in which the colonial state engaged with these forms of knowledge. In an important 1993 essay, the Sanskritist Sheldon Pollock offered a strong critique of the suggestion that colonialism "produced certain forms of domination *tout court*" and stressed the inattention paid to the power of precolonial social categories and forms of domination. He highlighted earlier periods in South Asian history (such as the eleventh and twelfth centuries CE) when powerful rulers sponsored the production of texts that offered prescriptive visions of the social order and carried substantial ideological weight. He also suggested that Mani's discussion of *sati* was grounded in a truncated vision of textual production, which neglected the importance of a "heirarchising textualisation" that had established the authority of certain elite forms of knowledge prior to the advent of British rule. Pollock argued that in the debates over *sati* indigenous discourses of power "intersected" with those of the colonial state and that such conjunctures contributed to the ability of the East India Company to establish its dominance in South Asia.[45]

The interfaces between Mughal and British state practices was also a crucial concern of Bayly's *Empire and Information*, which pieced together the East India Company's efforts to infiltrate, adapt, and finally turn South Asian knowledge traditions to serve British interests. Even though Nicholas Dirks has attacked Bayly's emphasis on the ability of Indians to shape and contest colonial knowledge, a growing corpus of work has began to explore the ways in which the texts, identities, and power structures that framed pre-colonial intellectual and political life continued to shape social and cultural change during British rule in the nineteenth century. Pollock himself has led a research team that has advanced our understanding of these transitions by mapping the flowering of Sanskritic knowledge between 1550 and 1750 CE and the complex processes that undercut its authority following the consolidation of British power at the turn of the nineteenth century.[46]

We need not only to explore the intersections between pre-colonial and colonial forms of knowledge, but also to recognize the limits of colonial knowledge. Even when colonial states exercised considerable power as they imposed new political boundaries, reoriented local economies, promoted new forms of knowledge, and constructed new regimes of surveillance and censorship, this control was never total. In *Empire and Information*, Bayly demonstrated the inability of the Company to develop reliable intelligence to guide their military operations at the fringe of its Indian empire. In conducting campaigns in Nepal (1814–16), Burma (1824–6), and on the northwestern frontier (1838–42), the Company's army had only scant and patchy information to guide their movements and enjoyed a shallow grasp of the armies and societies they were conducting campaigns against. These failures reflected the particularities of the indigenous "information orders" that developed beyond the plains of India as well as the Company's inability to find institutional or discursive points of engagement with these knowledge systems. Where some of the post-Saidian work has not always firmly established the connections between knowledge-production and the operation of colonial authority, Bayly's work stands as the richest and most nuanced assessment of the connections between knowledge and the colonial state's exercise of power.

Recent work on South Asian military history, particularly Randolf Cooper's study of the Company's campaigns against the Marathas and Douglas Peers' work on the intellectual culture of the Company army, has affirmed the importance of knowledge production in shaping both the military successes and failures of the Company.[47] In a similar vein, Michael Silvestri has reconstructed the efforts of the Indian police to cultivate networks of intelligence, the continuing dependence of the colonial state on its Indian subjects for information, and the very real limits of colonial policing.[48] Building on Bayly's notion of "information panics," D. K. Lahiri Choudhury has traced both the development of communication networks that were essential to the power of the colonial state and colonial official's anxieties over their inability to gain reliable information regarding local politics and anticolonial movements.[49]

The weaknesses of colonial knowledge were not only made manifest in the spectacular failures of the Company's campaigns on its northern borders or in the information panics triggered by the discovery of revolutionary anti-colonial movements. A small but suggestive body of research has begun to reveal the complex indigenous social spaces that remained beyond the purview of colonial knowledge. Bayly himself recorded the Company's struggles to access the valuable knowledge produced and circulated through women's talk in the seclusion of the zenana, the movement of eunuchs between the private and public worlds of South Asian courts, and the opinions and information that were laced together in the gossip of the bazaar. Other scholars have focused on the ways in which rumours both reflected the limits of colonial power and produced resistance against colonial rule. Martin Sökefeld has shown, for example, the power of rumour to call into question the Gilgit Agency in Yaghestan, in the western Himalaya. British authority in the region during World War I was challenged by rumors that queried Britain's position as a global power. To the consternation of the British, persistent rumours suggested Germany's Kaiser had converted to Islam and had joined forces with the Caliph of Turkey to launch a jihad against British rule. Sökefeld suggests that the "constant flow of multidirectional rumours" in Yaghestan was a key element in the shallow roots of colonial rule in the region.[50] Both Homi Bhabha and Ranajit Guha have seen rumour as central to the political confrontations of the colonial order and as embodiments of the anxieties that wracked a colonial state that was dominant but never quite hegemonic.[51]

Some of the most important work on rumour has come not from British India, but from the historiography of colonialism in Africa. Like Sökefeld's work on Yaghestan, George L. Simpson Jr has demonstrated how rumors revealed the shallowness of British authority in the East African Protectorate between 1915 and 1918. Simpson has traced the difficulties of British administrators in understanding the society that was under their control and highlighted the circulation of rumors that imagined a range of anti-colonial coalitions and uprisings. These rumors relating to the movement of various local leaders, clashes between different ethnic groups, and the development of rebellions against British authority caused considerable anxiety and revealed the very thin grasp that the British had of local politics.[52] Most importantly, Luise White has shown the value of using rumours to unpack the cultural contests inherent within the colonial order. She has reconstructed rumors that circulated from northern Zaire to central Tanganyika that identified Europeans—from mine supervisors to Catholic priests, labour recruiters to shopkeepers—as vampires. While many of these narratives dwelt on the otherness and threat posed by Europeans, White suggests that these rumours were not simply nativist responses to European intrusion, but rather they were innovative political narratives that wove together elements from the Bible, sermons, and missionary catechism. These narratives were fluid and mobile, they moved across time and space and were particularly important idioms through which both religious practices and labour relations could be contested.[53]

Knowledge and Subject Peoples

Just as the authority of colonial knowledge has been contested by historians, there has also been much debate over the ways in which colonial regimes defined and enumerated colonized communities. I have already noted that colonial states throughout the empire pursued a range of strategies for defining local societies and that the role of colonialism in reshaping indigenous identities has figured differently in a range of colonial historiographies. In light of this diversity, it is important to sketch some of these distinctive state strategies and these different literatures on the role played by colonial knowledge in the production of cultural difference.

In South Asia, the colonial state produced a massive body of historical and ethnographic knowledge that sought to map the operation of difference within South Asian society. Editions of South Asian texts, histories, ethnographic narratives, government reports, manuals for military officers, and popular travel narratives discussed the meaning of religion, caste, tribe, race, and region as factors that shaped the character, intellectual capacity, and customs of various colonized South Asian communities. From the beginning of the East India Company's effective rule in the 1760s, "religion" provided one of the key lenses for making sense of the historical development of India. As an analytical category, "religion" was an awkward but powerful imposition on Indian society. This European term had no close equivalents in Indian languages and, unlike Europeans, South Asians did not understand their cosmologies and devotional practices as constituting a clear and self-contained system that could be divorced from politics, economics, and social structure. For British officials and Orientalists, "religion" was a defining characteristic of Indian society and they believed that an opposition between Islam and Hinduism structured the pattern of Indian history. This reading of South Asian history provided evidence that seemingly reinforced the need to protect religious difference through the operation of the Company's administration. In 1772, the East India Company decided that its legal system would adhere as much as possible to the "antient usages and institutions" of South Asian communities. In effect, this meant that under the Company's rule Hindus and Muslims would be tried by the Company's legal codes which collated and standardized the customary law of each religion.

There is no doubt that as colonial rule progressed official pronouncements, governmental texts and popular British sentiment drew stark oppositions between Hinduism and Islam. Gyanendra Pandey's landmark *The Construction of Communalism in Colonial North India* argued that communalism was a "form of colonialist knowledge." The British understood "communalism" as the excessive religiosity that shaped life in India and which manifested itself in the violent conflict between religious communities. In the British imagination, "communalism" stood for the "puerile and the primitive" qualities of the colonized culture and marked India's primitiveness (and its need to be civilized through colonialism). Pandey argued that communalism was produced through the histories written by Orientalists and colonial officials, texts that identified religious conflict as the engine that drove Indian society and saw "communal riots" as symptomatic of the irrationality of Indian political life.[54]

Yet there is strong evidence that complicates this picture of colonialism, producing communal identity and conflict. In an important 1985 article, C. A. Bayly focused attention on communalism in the century before the 1860s (which conventionally was seen as marking the end point of Hindu-Muslim co-operation and the onset of a long period of increased communal conflict in the public sphere). Bayly reconstructed complex patterns of indigenous religious revitalization, the onset of communal conflicts that were fought over the socioeconomic and political standing of religious communities, and clashes that were focused more narrowly on the domain of religion itself. While Bayly underscored the persistence of syncretism and communal co-operation in rural areas and some urban centers (such as Delhi) into the nineteenth century, he highlighted the fierce battles waged between leaders from rival religious communities who sought to establish their sovereignty over sacred sites as well as the prominence of religious identity in the "land wars" waged by Hindus and Sikhs against elite Muslim landholders. He also recovered the role of mercenaries and demobilized soldiers, Muslim officers of the law (kazis, muftis, and kotwals), and broad shifts in the politico-economic balance of power between communities in triggering the religious conflict that became more common in urban centers in the second half of the eighteenth century and the first half of the nineteenth century.[55] This evidence demonstrated that religious categories like "Sikh," "Hindu" and "Muslim" had political meaning before the onset of British colonialism and suggested that the religious violence of the later nineteenth century exhibited some significant continuities with the cultural contests of the late Mughal period.

Katherine Prior's reassessment of official colonial understandings of religious conflict also challenged any easy equation between colonial knowledge and communalism. Prior showed that during the first half of the nineteenth century, colonial officials who presided over north Indian towns attempted to protect established patterns of religious display and preserve the balance of power between religious communities. This required the assemblage of local histories of religion that subsequently served as the intellectual basis for the practice of the colonial state in that locale. Prior suggested that these colonial histories were not all powerful constructions of the colonial imagination. Rather they were shaped by pre-colonial patterns of religious practice and contestation and they were also seized upon by groups who sought to use history to either shore up their dominance or to seek greater protection of their rights from the state.[56] From another angle, Cynthia Talbot's work on Andra Pradesh between the fourteenth and seventeenth centuries was an even stronger reminder of the importance of pre-colonial patterns of religious identification and conflict in shaping oppositions between Hinduism and Islam within South Asia. She demonstrated that on the Deccan frontier where the Kakatiya dynasty met the southward incursions of the Muslim Delhi Sultanate, the local propertied Hindu elite drew strong contrasts between themselves and the armies from the north by casting Muslims as demons and barbarians. These delineations of the otherness rested on a wide range of criteria, including language, clothing, marriage customs, military strategy, and ethnic origins, as well as religion. Her work reminds us that the categories "Hindu" and "Muslim" had long histories in South Asia prior to the East India Company's rise to power and that the definition of "Otherness" was also an important strategy for the construction of collective identity within South Asian cultures before the birth of European empires in Asia.[57]

Caste also assumed a central position in the colonial imagination and constituted the other key lens for colonial examinations of South Asian social structure. Here again the extent to which the colonial state produced Indian categories of identification has been disputed. The role of colonialism in shaping the caste system has recently overshadowed the work of an earlier generation of anthropologists and sociologists who focused on the process of "Sanskritisation," where low status groups modified their social standing by adopting the cosmology, ritual practices, and cultural customs of high caste groups and through this process reaffirmed the power of the caste ideologies that had initially defined them as being of low status.[58] In the late 1980s and 1990s, new work shifted the focus away from the social history of particular caste groups as it was contended that caste was essentially the product of British imaginations and the exigencies of colonial rule. In a powerful critique of established ways on imagining India, Nicholas Dirks argued in his *Castes of Mind* that caste was not the legacy of ancient texts nor was it a core element of Indian civilization, but rather should be understood as "a modern phenomenon . . . specifically, the product of the historical encounter between India and Western colonial rule." Under the British, "caste" became the key systematizing tool of colonial knowledge. In effect, "caste" provided an organizing principle for British understandings of Indian social structure and it operated as a powerful set of discourses that profoundly reshaped Indian society. Once it was embedded as the key governing principle in the colonial archive, caste became an important tool in anti-colonial nationalism and a constant point of reference for post-independence social policy. "In short, colonialism made caste what it is today."[59]

Susan Bayly has offered a very different reading of the history of caste. For her, caste is a longstanding and very real, if fluid, set of social practices within South Asian society, a complex of "ideals and practices that have been made and remade into varying codes of moral order over hundreds or even thousands of years." She argued that "traditional" caste society was a product of South Asia's pre-colonial cultural order. During the early modern period, particularly when centralized Mughal power was supplanted by various successor states, Brahmanical dominance was secured, but she suggests that even in the mid-eighteenth century Brahmanical notions of purity and ritual practice had an uneven reach across the region. These models, which were sponsored by scribal elites and warrior kings, were extended, but remained open to dispute. Such contestation remained a key feature of the cultural landscape of colonialism. Early orientalists and key functionaries within the colonial state did seize on caste as a key for unlocking the "mysteries" of Indian social forms, but it was colonialism's material transformations (especially deforestation, the spread of cash cropping, and urbanization) as well as competition between South Asian groups that were central in the extension and calcification of caste hierarchies during the nineteenth century. The colonial state's enumerative project was certainly novel in its scope, but she argued that the census and the state's ethnographic project owed a significant debt to long-standing efforts by South Asian rulers to classify their own subject populations. Thus, Susan Bayly did not deny the significance of colonial knowledge, but in contrast to Dirks she places much greater emphasis on the continuities between pre-colonial and colonial social orders. Rather than seeing colonialism as an abrupt rupture that produced a new sociology of knowledge that was capable of reconfiguring Indian society, she suggested that colonial rule sped up and intensified some key patterns of social change and argued that South Asians themselves were the central agents in redefining caste.[60]

Other recent work has called Dirks's reading of caste into question by highlighting both the profoundly localized nature of caste formations and significant regional variations in colonial knowledge relating to caste. John Rogers has traced the complex history of caste and colonialism in Sir Lanka. Rogers established that caste was an important feature of the indigenous social landscape in the eighteenth century and that early British accounts of the island did recognize the significance of caste. In the 1830s, however, caste was marginalized by the new weight attached to race in the state's ethnographic knowledge and subsequently the British attempted to excise caste from public life in the colony. But the invisibility of caste in colonial knowledge did not destroy the caste affiliations and caste practices which continued to shape both everyday life and elite politics. Thus colonial knowledge shaped state policy, but did not determine the patterns of local social relations and political activity.[61] Within India, Prachi Deshpande's work on Maharashtra has suggested that caste was a crucial element of the public sphere that developed under colonial rule. But she contends that it was debates and struggles conducted in Marathi over the intersections between caste and regional identity rather than an all-powerful colonial state that ultimately shaped the politics of caste in western India.[62] Further north in Punjab Brahmanical authority had shallow roots at best and the classical varna model of caste did not apply to the complex layering of identities found within a region that had been constantly remade by war, waves of migration, and long-distance trade networks. Within this region, broader colonial discourses that tried to map race and caste at an all-India level ran aground. Brian Caton has demonstrated that the analytical power of "caste" among the region's colonial administrators was disputed and as a category "caste" enjoyed less authority than the more flexible category of "tribe."[63] In a similar vein, my own work has shown how racial theories that sought to classify South Asian society into Aryan and Dravidian racial groupings and which suggested race and caste were analogous were unpopular with colonial administrators in Punjab who emphasized the "mixed" nature of the region's population.[64]

The massive body of ethnographic knowledge that mapped the operation of cultural difference within Indian society along multiple axes was not matched by any other colonial regime within the empire. In other colonial contexts, British dominance rested more firmly on large settler populations, military power, or the monopolization of the colony's productive capacity (whether this came in the form of valuable commodities, labour power, or the land itself). This has meant that historical work on the nature of imperial rule in other colonies has tended to place more weight on these other instruments of domination. Thus, for example, African historiographies have retained a strong concern with issues relating to economic development and the history of labor while work on settler colonies has tended to focus on patterns of land and resource alienation.

Nevertheless, over the past two decades historicizing the fundamental opposition between colonizer and colonized has been a prominent element in all colonial historiographies. In New Zealand historiography, for example, a central concern has been tracing the development of settler understandings of Maori culture and the gradual emergence of a Pakeha identity that defined the British and Irish colonists who settled in New Zealand against both their European peers and Maori. James Belich's *The New Zealand Wars*, which traced the influence of scientific racism in shaping British interpretations of Maori military resistance between 1845 and 1870, remains the most important study of the development of racial thought within the colony.[65] Much work on colonial Australia has focused on the ways in which European theories of property rights and sovereignty were used to define Australia as *terra nullius*, an empty land, and thereby denied the legal rights of indigenous communities.[66] Several other important works have highlighted the ways in which colonists justified their presence and power. Jeremy Beckett, for example, has argued that the "antiquity" of indigenous culture in Australia was widely recognized by European colonists, but this understanding did not encourage a wide belief in the rights that might accrue from a long occupation of the land. Rather in the hands of settler politicians and intellectuals, this antiquity meant that Aborigines stood as timeless primitives who were fundamentally different from civilized white settlers who were committed to "improvement."[67] More broadly still, Bob Reece and Bain Attwood have traced the ways in which the very category of "Aboriginal" was consolidated in colonial ethnography and government policy, as the diverse linguistic and social patchwork of indigenous groups were made legible through their reduction into a single overarching category that was defined against the values cherished by settler society.[68] Perhaps most importantly of all, a large historiography over the past two decades has traced the development of British understandings of Africans and the place of blackness in the imperial imagination (in Britain, the Caribbean, and Africa itself). This work is of particular importance because of the centrality of African slavery in the development of Britain's empire and the ways in which the oppositions between whiteness and blackness shaped British self identity, British understandings of other colonized peoples, and the political culture of the empire as a whole.[69]

Conclusion

Many of these attempts to historicize and deconstruct racial oppositions certainly have drawn some inspiration from the work of Edward Said, but they must be also be read as interventions in the heated public debates over race and colonialism that have been so prominent over the last three decades in Britain's former colonies and within Britain itself. Thanks in part to the work of activist-critics like Said, these political exchanges over the legacy of empire have increasingly turned on cultural questions and on understandings of history. Within such a context, work on "colonial knowledge" has not only offered new explanations of what colonialism was (a set of asymmetrical *cultural* relationships), but has also been driven by the search for forms of scholarly practice that break free from the discourses and intellectual practices that were institutionalized under imperial power. In this regard, the emergence of "colonial knowledge" as a key analytical problematic for recent work on empire reflects both the impact of the broad "cultural turn" within humanities scholarship as well as the more particular influence of post-colonialism's open commitment to writing *against* empire and its legacies. As we have seen, these approaches have stimulated heated debates as the importance of "culture" in the imperial project has been questioned by those who have either asserted the primacy of traditional "empirical" history over deconstructive readings of texts or by historians who remained committed to the materialist traditions of social history. There is no doubt that some work on colonial knowledge has failed to recover the connections between "culture" and other key analytical domains—such as politics, economics, and the "social"—but this variegated body of scholarship has greatly enlarged our understandings of the nature of the British Empire and its legacies. It has highlighted the value of a range of previously neglected sources—ranging from maps to doctors' notebooks, missionary magazines to grammars—while at the same time enabling a new tradition of self-reflexive scholarly practice, which interrogates the inherited concepts and language that continue to shape how we imagine the imperial past. Although the growing authority of this approach remains hotly contested, there is no doubt that the study of colonial knowledge has been absolutely central in revivifying work on empire and reconnecting the study of empire with the broader concerns of humanities scholarship. As a result, imperial history has moved from being an isolated area of speciality to a highly visible, if fractious, field of scholarship which speaks to a set of questions about power and knowledge that are central within a global public sphere energized by debates over religious conflict, globalization, and war.

At the moment there seems little likelihood of a rapprochement between these very different readings of the imperial past, but there is no doubt that the ensuing tension continues to stimulate new work on empire and invests the field with great energy.

Notes

1 Said, *Orientalism*.
2 Schwab, *La Renaissance orientale*; Asad (ed.), *Anthropology*; Guha, *Rule of Property*; Stokes, *English Utilitarians*.
3 Inden, "Orientalist Constructions," p. 402; *id.*, *Imagining India*.
4 Viswanathan, *Masks of Conquest*.
5 Guha, "Introduction," pp. ix–xxii; *id.*, "Historiography," pp. 1–8.
6 Chatterjee, "Their own words," p. 194.
7 Chaturvedi, "Introduction," p. xi; Sarkar, "Orientalism revisited," pp. 205–24.
8 Spivak, "Rani of Sirmur," pp. 263, 266, 270.
9 Mani, "Cultural theory," pp. 396, 403.
10 Burton, "Archive stories."
11 Cohn, "Indian status"; *id.*, "Law and change"; *id.*, "Indian society"; *id.*, "Social structure."
12 Cohn, *Forms of Knowledge*.
13 Dirks, "Foreword," p. ix.
14 Dirks, "Policing of tradition," pp.182–212; *id.*, *Hollow Crown*.

15 O'Hanlon and Washbrook, "After Orientalism," pp. 141–67.

16 Washbrook, "Colonial discourse theory," pp. 608–9.

17 *Ibid.*

18 Eaton, "(Re)imag(in)ing otherness," p. 60.

19 Bayly, *Empire and Information.*

20 Irschick, *Dialogue and History.*

21 Ballantyne, "Empire, knowledge and culture"; Laidlaw, *Colonial Connections*; Lester, *Imperial Networks*; Potter, *News and the British World.*

22 Cooper, *Colonialism in Question*, p. 143.

23 Curtin, "White Man's Grave"; Jennings, "Mysterious and intangible enemy."

24 Conte, "Colonial science and ecological change"; Vaughan, *Story of an African Famine*; Wolmer and Scoones, "'Civilized' agriculture."

25 Bonneuil, "Science and state building."

26 Hamilton *et al.* (eds), *Refiguring the Archive*; Pohlandt-McCormick, "In good hands."

27 Byrnes, *Boundary Markers*; Carter, *Road to Botany Bay*; *id.*, *Lie of the Land*; Clayton, *Islands of Truth*; Harris, *Resettlement of British Columbia*; Vibert, *Traders' Tales.*

28 Bell, "Cross cultural confusions"; Goodall, "Aboriginal history"; Perry, "Colonial archive on trial."

29 Binney, *Redemption Songs*; Bird Rose, *Hidden Histories*; Sissons, *Te Waimana.*

30 Thomas, *Colonialism's Culture*; *id.*, *Entangled Objects.*

31 Basalla, "Spread of Western science"; Hoare, *Reform in New Zealand Science*; Jarrell and Ball (eds), *Science, Technology, and Canadian History.*

32 Adas, *Machines as the Measure of Men*; Headrick, *Tools of Empire*; *id.*, *Tentacles of Progress.*

33 MacLeod, "Moving Metropolis"; *id.*, "Imperial to national science."

34 Chatterjee (ed.), *Texts of Power.*

35 Edney, *Mapping an Empire.*

36 Ballantyne (ed.), *European Exploration*; Sivasundaram, *Nature and the Godly Empire*; Gascoigne, *Science in the Service of Empire.*

37 Arnold, *Colonizing the Body.*

38 Vaughan, *Curing Their Ills.*

39 Watts, *Epidemics and History.*

40 Grove, *Green Imperialism*; *id.*, *Ecology, Climate and Empire.*

41 Bayly, *Empire and Information*, pp. 247–314; Dodson, "Re-presented for the Pandits"; *id.*, "Translating science."

42 Bravo, *Accuracy of Ethnoscience*; Woodward and Lewis (eds), *History of Cartography.*

43 Philip, *Civilizing Natures*; Prakash, *Another Reason.*

44 Drayton, *Nature's Government.*

45 Pollock, "Deep Orientalism?," pp. 97, 99–101.

46 Pollock, "Working papers"; *id.*, "Death of Sanskrit."

47 Cooper, *Anglo-Maratha Campaigns*; Peers, "Colonial knowledge."

48 Silvestri, "Dressing up."

49 Choudhury, "Sinews of panic."

50 Sökefeld, "Rumours and politics," p. 338.

51 Bhabha, "Calm violence," p. 332.

52 G. L. Simpson, "British perspectives."

53 White, "Vampire priests"; *id.*, "Telling more."

54 Pandey, *Construction of Communalism*, pp. 6, 24.

55 Bayly, "Communalism."

56 Prior, "Making history."
57 Talbot, "Inscribing the other."
58 Srinivas, *Caste in Modern India*.
59 Dirks, *Castes of Mind*, pp. 5–6.
60 S. Bayly, *Caste, Society and Politics*.
61 Rogers, "Early British rule."
62 Deshpande, "Caste as Maratha."
63 Caton, "Social categories."
64 Ballantyne, *Orientalism and Race*, pp. 52–4.
65 Belich, *New Zealand Wars*.
66 Reynolds, *Law of the Land*.
67 Beckett, "Past in the present," p. 205.
68 Reece, "Inventing aborigines"; Attwood, "Introduction."
69 Hall, *Civilising Subjects*; M. Wood, *Blind Memory*.

Further Reading

The key entrance point into the literature on colonial knowledge is Edward Said's *Orientalism*. Ronald Inden's *Imagining India* and Gauri Viswanathan's *Masks of Conquests* are two important attempts within the South Asian context to build on Said's work on the construction of "Otherness." Said's influence and the contentious nature of the Subaltern Studies project are nicely summed up in the anthology *Mapping Subaltern Studies*, edited by Vinayak Chaturvedi. Bernard Cohn's *Colonialism and its Forms of Knowledge* is a very influential study of knowledge in British India and has been a pivotal work in showing the value of cultural approaches to the history of the empire. Working in the space opened by Cohn, Nicholas Dirks's *Castes of Mind* is a powerfully argued reading of caste in colonial India. The culturally-inflected work of Cohn and Dirks can be fruitfully contrasted with the abiding concern with the intersections between social, intellectual, and political history that characterize C. A. Bayly's *Empire and Information* and Susan Bayly's *Caste, Society and Politics*. Zoë Laidlaw's *Colonial Connections* is an important extension of C. A. Bayly's work on the place of information in imperial governance. Matthew Edney's *Mapping an Empire* charts the role of cartography in colonial governance in India and it can be usefully read against Giselle Byrnes's study of surveying in New Zealand, *Boundary Markers*. Readers interested in the history of science and empire should start with Richard Drayton's *Nature's Government*, Richard Grove's *Green Imperialism* and Gyan Prakash's *Another Reason*. My own *Orientalism and Race* is a useful starting point for discussions of the connections between colonial knowledge and racial difference, while Antoinette Burton's essay "Archive Stories" is an indispensable introduction to debates over gender and the colonial archive. Finally, the leading Africanist Frederick Cooper offers a set of thoughtful reflections on knowledge and colonialism in his *Colonialism in Question*.

9

Culture and Identity in Imperial Britain

Catherine Hall

Empire was part of everyday life for Britons between the late eighteenth century and the end of World War II, when decolonization began.[1] The shift from an empire of commerce and the seas, the form of empire that dominated in the seventeenth and much of the eighteenth century, to a territorial empire of conquest and settlement meant that the effects of this growing imperial world were ever more apparent in Britain as crossings between metropole and colonies increased.[2] As early as 1820 Britain ruled a quarter of the world's population and the Victorian period saw the zenith of her power. By the end of the nineteenth century Britain retained world dominance, but was locked in competition with the US, Germany, and Japan. In the period after World War I and during the interwar years British dominion continued to increase, despite anti-colonial nationalisms and the imminent disintegration, in the wake of World War II, of the great European empires. Britain was constructed as the metropole, the center of this empire, the place from which power flowed. To describe Britain as imperial draws attention not just to British economic, political, and military power and its exercise over others, but also to the ways in which British culture was permeated with things and ideas associated with empire.

There has been a lively debate amongst historians as to the significance of empire in British culture. This debate has long antecedents, one of the most influential of which was Eric Williams's classic text *Capitalism and Slavery*. In 1944 the young Oxford-educated Trinidadian historian, later to become Prime Minister, challenged the orthodoxy that Britain's abolition of the slave trade and slavery was a grand humanitarian gesture. He was developing a thesis first articulated by C. L. R. James, the renowned Trinidadian critic. Williams argued that profits from slavery were critical to the industrial revolution and that merchants and manufacturers saw that free labor was more productive than the labor of the enslaved.[3] The linkage that he suggested between abolition and the development of capitalism has been explored in a variety of ways by historians and seen as central to the empowerment of the nineteenth-century middle class.[4] Since the publication of Edward Said's seminal text, *Orientalism*, in 1978, these debates have taken a new turn for it became the iconic text which linked culture with colonialism. Many historians were deeply critical of Said for his lack of historical depth; others have been profoundly influenced by the arguments that he made about the ways in which "European culture was able to manage—and even produce—the Orient politically, sociologically, militarily, ideologically, scientifically and imaginatively during the post-Enlightenment period."[5] The new questions about imperialism and culture surfaced at a time when it had become clear that while the era of the great European empires was over, the effects of those empires lived on. In the newly independent countries it was evident that gaining political independence had not resulted in the decolonization of people's minds. In the old metropolitan centers the arrival of large numbers of erstwhile imperial citizens brought questions of race to the top of the political agenda in new ways. Colonial culture, it was clear, had lasting legacies and scholars from many disciplines began to reflect on this. A vigorous debate has ensued among historians; large numbers of books and articles have been published, university courses established and research projects pursued. Some are convinced that British metropolitan culture was shaped by the imperial experience. John MacKenzie, whose edited series for Manchester University Press has been in the forefront of publishing work in this area, has recently concluded: "Empire constituted a vital aspect of national identity and race-consciousness, even if complicated by regional, rural, urban, and class contexts."[6] Others are much more skeptical. Bernard Porter claims that empire was irrelevant to most Britons most of the time: in his assessment it was only in the late nineteenth century that imperial sentiment really affected large numbers.[7]

Questions of theory and method are critical here. Porter puts great emphasis on the test of empirical evidence. A historical subject must explicitly state, for example, that he or she has been influenced in a particular way by empire. This narrow empiricism makes no attempt to understand the world of assumptions in which decisions are made, or how, when those assumptions change, things which were taken for granted in one period have to be stated explicitly in another. No study of the political ethos, or of the intellectual framework within which political or cultural debate takes place can work effectively with such a limited and restrictive notion of historical evidence. The most elementary understanding of how background assumptions operate suggests that they are largely unconscious, and form the consensual understandings—the common sense of the period—which is never explicitly stated. Of course, using this material depends on the quality of interpretation and the care with which interpretative readings are related to material circumstances and institutional frameworks. But to refuse the work of any of this interpretative evidence is to fall into the darkness of empiricism.

This chapter draws on the recent scholarship that makes use of discursive analysis and argues that Britons encountered the empire in myriad ways. It was nothing special, just ordinary, part of the world in which they lived.[8] A substantial number of Britons spent some years, or all of their lives, on one imperial site or another. There were innumerable opportunities across the empire for men seeking their fortune—as settlers, soldiers or sailors, convicts or indentured servants, fur traders or farmers, merchants or planters, medical men or missionaries, teachers or clerks, or colonial officials. The possibilities for women—as wives, teachers, and missionaries—increased greatly from the mid-nineteenth century.[9] The experiences of these varied colonists were shaped by the places they went to, the times at which they went, and the kind of colonial project on which they were engaged, whether it was rescuing "the heathen," mapping new territories, or serving in the British army or navy. Their experiences were also shaped by who they were—men or women, with capital or without, English, Irish, Scottish, or Welsh. Their families and friends heard about their lives through letters or listened to the tales of those who returned from their adventures. They might have been tobacco growers or indentured laborers in the North American colonies, sugar planters or book-keepers in the West Indies, soldiers or camp followers in the East India Company army in Bengal, farmers on the Cape, slave traders on the west coast of Africa, missionaries or teachers in New Zealand, clerks on the rubber plantations of Malaya. Each brought their stories home. Their listeners told those stories to others, spreading the word about the imperial world. At the same time peoples of the empire came to Britain. African sailors, Indian servants, enslaved men and women from the Caribbean, students, colonial politicians, Aboriginal cricketers all passed through, along with many other sojourners in the "mother country."[10] Some, especially sailors and dockers, settled in Britain—establishing mixed communities in the ports of London, Cardiff, Bristol, Liverpool, and Glasgow. Most Britons had seen people of color by the mid-nineteenth century, whether servants, the illegitimate children of white West Indians, or Anglo-Indians sent home to be schooled, lascars working in the docks, freed Africans on the missionary and anti-slavery lecture circuits, Indian ayahs tending the children of their masters and mistresses, or even princely Indians staying in aristocratic country houses.

Britons were also entirely familiar with the fruits of empire—tobacco from North America, sugar from the West Indies, tea from India—all enjoyed by the majority of the population. For the rich there were Kashmiri shawls. There was opium from the East, cocoa and coffee from the West Indies, wheat from Canada, exotic plants for the gardens of the middle classes burgeoning across the country from the early nineteenth century. Then there were the raw materials, from cotton and wool to oil and rubber, flowing in from the empire and feeding manufacturing and processing industries.[11] And a significant number of Britons had some kind of direct economic connection to empire—through trade, commerce, or investments.

But knowledge of empire was not confined to direct encounter with its peoples, places, and products, for ideas *about* Empire played a significant part in the imaginative life of Britons. They read of colonial wars in their newspapers and periodicals, sang missionary hymns in their churches and chapels, funded missionary activities across the globe.[12] Some heard talks about the inevitability of the disappearance of aboriginal peoples, or the new theories of racial difference, at their mechanics' institutes or literary and philosophical societies. Large numbers supported the campaign for the abolition of the slave trade in the late eighteenth century, or the anti-slavery movement in the 1820s and 1830s.[13] At the time of the "Indian Mutiny" in 1857 the country was galvanized by stories in the press of horrible violence while the events following the rebellion at Morant Bay in Jamaica in 1865 split the British public between those who supported the actions of Governor Eyre and those who were his critics.[14] The Liberal party under Gladstone was not explicitly in favor of imperial expansion, yet Liberals assumed that empire was a part of their universe. By the late nineteenth century, however, Disraeli's turn to empire and the growth of popular Toryism was one factor in the rising tide of imperial sentiment, fuelled by European rivalries over Africa.[15] Music-hall songs, postcards, the popular press, advertisments, youth movements, magazines, and fiction all played on this enthusiasm and articulated a nationalist and patriotic message.[16] Yet in the South African War opinion was sharply divided with passionate support both for the British and for the Boers.[17] There was never one view of empire in Britain—rather a cacophony of voices, debating the rights and wrongs of what kind of empire there should be and how it should be ruled. Few, however, questioned the existence of empire itself or imagined a Britain without it.

Empire was visible in innumerable ways. Major international events such as the Great Exhibition of 1851 or the 1924 Wembley British Empire Exhibition (visited by over 27 million people—over half the population) provided opportunities to admire the rich products of empire and reflect on the benefits of Britain's "civilizing mission."[18] At a more modest level the shows that traveled the country exhibiting in towns and cities sometimes included representations of the lives of native peoples, replete with their "primitive" paraphernalia. Dioramas dramatizing great imperial events such as the "Indian Mutiny" of 1857 drew large crowds. Theatres provided dramatic renditions of imperial dilemmas; visual artists, from Hogarth to Frith, represented racial and ethnic difference; public sculpture celebrated the achievements of empire; and museums organized their collections through the categories of the "primitive" and the "civilized."[19]

The culture of Britain, in other words, was permeated with empire. The definition of culture here is not a set of *things*—paintings, novels, exhibitions, music-hall songs, or newspapers—rather it is about a set of *practices*. Culture is associated primarily with the production and exchange of meanings—how we make sense of the world. It is not simply about ideas in the head, for it is also about how those ideas organize and regulate social and institutional worlds. Meanings are constructed in languages, and languages work through representation. They use signs and symbols to stand for or represent ideas and feelings in ways that allow others to decode or interpret them. Meaning is constructed through language, and language is therefore crucial to culture. Foucault's understanding of the relation between language and discourse has greatly influenced the ways in which we understand the workings of culture. For Foucault discourses are tied not only to languages but to practices, institutions, and power: discourses include institutional practices and technologies of power. Stuart Hall puts it this way:

> The discursive approach . . . examines not only how language and representation produce meaning, but how the knowledge which a particular discourse produces connects with power, regulates conduct, makes up or constructs identities and subjectivities, and defines the way certain things are represented, thought about, practised and studied. The emphasis in the *discursive* approach is always on the historical specificity of a particular form or "regime of representation": not on "language" as a general concern, but on specific *languages* or meanings, and how they are deployed at particular times, in particular places. It points us towards greater historical specificity—the way representational practices operate in concrete historical situations, in actual practices.[20]

Historians and critics concerned with understanding the place of empire in metropolitan culture have made discursive analysis central, attending carefully to the context, the particular moment, and the specific ways in which, for example, different peoples are represented.

Discourses play a part in the construction of identities. The conception of identity that is in play here is one that is not essential or fixed. A girl is not born English, or feminine, or working class. Rather, those identities are brought into being through discursive or symbolic work that demarcates the self from the other. A little girl identifies with the sameness of her mother's body, with feminine talk and play, and sees the differences between herself and her brother. She identifies with the mother, knows that she is not the same as her brother. Identity is formed by "the outside": by the interconnections between the positive presence taken into the self and the negative and excluded dimensions distinguished as the other. Gender is one of the earliest differences to be recognized, along with ethnicity and class. Being feminine or masculine, English or Irish or British, meant being some things and not others. This distinction between self and other, between included and excluded, is not neutral, for it carries with it a desire to mark boundaries of social and political authority, who has power and of what kinds. But what is seen as outside an identity, different, other to it, is in fact constitutive of it. The "fullness" of identity depends on what it lacks. The Bengali's "effeminacy," for example, in nineteenth century metropolitan discourse was counterposed to the Englishman's "manliness": effeminacy signaled an incapacity for independence and for self-government associated with the subaltern position in the world. Male identification with what was labeled feminine was repressed and split off, projected as a negative element, onto the other—the imagined Bengali. Likewise, the Bengali's "passivity" was contrasted with the Englishman's capacity for conquest. Thus, identities were always constructed in a process of mutual constitution—the making of self through the making and marking off of others.[21]

In imperial Britain this making of self and other, this process of mutual constitution, was profoundly influenced by colonial relations. From the sixteenth century colonial encounters had produced understandings of the differences between one people and another. Ideas of race were used to explain these differences. By the eighteenth century British men and women understood themselves in relation to multiple others of the nation, the empire, and beyond.[22] They interpreted their experiences through regimes of representation, "grammars of difference" which placed peoples hierarchically, some being seen as having greater capacities and more rights than others.[23] Africans or Indians were not the same as Britons. In the wake of the loss of the American colonies Britain's success in the Napoleonic Wars marked a new confidence in empire and Britons' right to rule. There was a period of conservatism and absolutism across the empire with military governors, for example, ruling colonies as if they were accountable only to themselves.[24]

By the 1830s this was giving way to an era of reform marked by changes in colonial rule and new ideas of difference. Definitions of difference were critical to empire building for this was legitimated on the grounds that Britons were suited to conquest and settlement, and would bring the benefits of their superior civilization to others. Colonized peoples were classified, their habits recorded and judged, their distinctive characteristics, as they were defined, seen as the basis on which to make decisions about appropriate forms of government. Scales of comparison were constructed and race (understood in terms of climate, culture, or biology) was seen as a critical marker of difference: Anglo-Saxons were the most civilized people in the world, others must serve them and in time some would learn to live like them. Such differences, between Anglo-Saxon and Celt, African and Indian, Maori and Australian Aboriginal, never could be fixed for they were neither natural nor self-evident and indeed they were constantly contested. But across the British Empire there was a never-ending process of attempting to fix the binaries between colonizer and colonized, establishing the "natural" inequalities that legitimated colonial rule. At the same time the distinctions within the colonizers—men or women, rich or poor, English or Irish—were also marked. These grammars of difference informed the practices of government and citizenship both in the metropole and across the empire. In theory all British subjects were equal: in practice few had the right to political citizenship.[25] The Irish were not the same as the English, it was widely believed, and must be ruled differently.[26] In the 1830s the Colonial Office believed that freed Africans in the West Indies would one day be capable of self-government. By 1865 this day looked very far away.[27] But it was not just the practices of government and citizenship that were at issue. Grammars of difference cut across public and private worlds shaping practices of everyday life, in the family, in the workplace, and in the most intimate domains of sexual life. Colonial sexualities were pathologised—from the figure of the "Venus Hottentot" to the "effete Bengali" or the oversexed African man of the European imagination—and fantasies of exotic otherness shaped metropolitan sexualities.[28]

Grammars of difference operated across metropole and colony and were multidimensional. Differences of class, of race, of ethnicity, of gender and sexuality were all in play in the process of identity construction. At particular times, during the "Indian Mutiny" of 1857, or the debates provoked by the events at Morant Bay in Jamaica in 1865, or the Fenian "outrages" on the mainland in 1866/7, questions of empire and its relation to the metropole may have been pre-eminent. At other times, during the Napoleonic wars, the Crimean war, or the Great War for example, enmities with France or Germany were more significant in defining Britons' sense of themselves. At times of European war continental antagonisms might come to the fore as France, or Germany, or Russia were constructed as the antithesis of Englishness or Britishness. At times of acute class tension, as in the 1830s and 1840s, the 1880s, or the 1920s and 1930s, issues of class belonging might seem the determining factor in shaping a sense of self. Between the 1760s and the 1940s religious affiliation played an important part in placing men and women in the social world. Hostility to the Irish in Britain was endemic throughout this period, informed both by anti-Catholicism and a sense of racial otherness, while anti-Jewish sentiment erupted in the context of the arrival and settlement of large numbers of East European refugees, labeled as "aliens," in the late nineteenth century. Meanwhile, in the intimate encounters of everyday life differences of gender may often have seemed to be the most significant in shaping a person's experience, but gender was always inflected by class and race, just as race was always gendered and classed. But empire never went away—it was always there—simply one of the factors shaping British identities, articulating for men and women who they were, what their place was in the world, and how they might relate to others.

Historians and critics have explored the place of empire in metropolitan culture and identity through a wide variety of sources and with different methods. A large body of scholarship now exists, much of it informed by post-colonial analysis, focused on visual culture, on exhibitions, on poetry, on travel writing, on the press, theatre and music-hall, on the political culture of anti-slavery, and on the popular imperialism of the late nineteenth century. Each and every one of these could provide a vehicle through which to investigate the specificities of how the colonial connection was imagined and lived and how it informed Britons' sense of themselves. Different sources reveal different discourses and open up the multiple voices speaking on questions of empire. Parliamentary reports yield official discourse, the missionary press abolitionist discourse, business papers commercial discourses; each can say different things. Many historians have chosen to focus on one specific genre—advertisements, or boys' adventure stories, or the music-hall—as a way into the imperial aspects of British culture. Here the focus is on the cultural form that is being analyzed, asking questions such as how were the nation and empire being represented, or how were colonized peoples imagined? Such studies cannot tell us how audiences received these materials, what particular viewers thought about them, or to what extent readers were affected by what they read. One way of exploring how empire impacted on people's lives is through the study of individuals, both men and women who traveled the empire and those who stayed at home. Letters and diaries that record personal feelings and reactions are particularly valuable in telling us about what people thought and felt. Sources of this kind are sadly more available for certain kinds of individuals—those with a public presence. It is harder to find out about the reactions of working class Britons to empire than that of the middle and upper classes. Yet unusual cases do exist, such as that of the soldier and policeman John Pearman whose diary reveals something of his thinking about his service in India, or Hannah Cullwick, a domestic servant for most of her life, who enacted the part of an enslaved woman for her middle class lover.[29] Micro studies across generations of particular families who lived and worked across Britain and the empire can also be very revealing.[30] Another way in is to study specific historical moments, as, for example, a very contested event or an election that focused on imperial questions, and see what people said and how people voted at that time.[31] Detailed local studies of communities can also be rewarding, revealing how attitudes to empire shifted over particular historical periods. In Birmingham, for example, there was very substantial support for anti-slavery activities in the 1830s but by the time of Morant Bay in Jamaica in 1865 there was very limited enthusiasm for the Jamaican rebels.[32]

Those historians who have been influenced by post-colonial thinking see the particular task of post-colonial analysis, whatever sources are being examined, as to reveal the ways in which colonial power was central to Britain's place in the world and to British identities.[33] Empire was taken for granted and that which is taken for granted can be almost unseen. There was much that was discomforting about empire, that people wanted not to know about, or think about, or indeed to forget.

The scale of conquest and dispossession, the numbers of deaths, the reliance upon violence to maintain colonial possessions, the realities of poverty, of ill health and of famine—these were the aspects of empire that most Britons preferred to ignore—whilst enjoying the cheap goods and labour and comforting themselves with stories of British justice, of the introduction of roads and railways, and of the "civilizing mission." Post-colonial analysis aims to reveal the subjects that have been hidden, the agendas that are obscured when stories are told one way rather than another. It aims to open up silences, reveal gaps and absences, explore what gets left out when a history is related this way rather than that.

"The most difficult thing to get hold of," Raymond Williams has argued, "in studying any past period, is [the] felt sense of the quality of life at a particular place and time: a sense of the ways in which the particular activities combined into a way of thinking and living."[34] Williams named this "way of thinking and living," the "structure of feeling" of any particular historical moment. It is the *imperial* "structure of feeling," the ways in which ideas about empire were lived and felt, the discursive practices and regimes of representation that distinguished between colonizers and colonized, and offered particular forms of identification to audiences, that we will now explore. Our example comes from the 1840s, but it could come from any moment between the late eighteenth century and 1945. In giving "reign to the space of imagination and fantasy," as Cora Kaplan has written, literature can give us access to ways of thinking and feeling about nation, empire, and identity.[35] How did Britons "live the empire" at that time, how did it shape what they thought and felt about themselves and others? The remainder of this essay will focus on reading British culture through one novel, for fiction undoubtedly provided one of the most popular ways of imaginatively "living the empire."[36]

In January 1847, *Vanity Fair*, William Thackeray's panoramic comic and satirical novel about the lives and fortunes of "a set of people living without God in the world . . . greedy pompous mean self-satisfied for the most part and at ease about their superior virtue" as he himself described it, began to appear in monthly installments.[37] The title drew on Bunyan's celebrated account in *The Pilgrim's Progress* (a work said to be the most widely read in Britain after the Bible), of Vanity Fair as the place where anything and anybody could be bought and sold, a world dominated by the market. The novel did well, was a critical success, and has been read, dramatized and filmed ever since. It is still widely read, available in a number of paperback editions, studied in schools and colleges, and enjoyed by a wide range of audiences. It is immensely readable and very funny. Initially subtitled *Pen and Pencil Sketches of English Society* and with its great centerpiece the battle of Waterloo, it presents a picture of a complex early nineteenth-century social world, ranging from London to Bath, Brighton and Hampshire, and crossing the channel to Brussels, Ostend, and Paris. With a large cast of characters including financiers, merchants, the military, "Society," and the lesser aristocracy, not to speak of the domestics who serviced them all, there were, in Thackeray's words:

scenes of all sorts: some dreadful combats, some grand and lofty horse-riding, some scenes of high life, and some of very middling indeed: some love-making for the sentimental, and some light comic business; the whole accompanied by appropriate scenery and brilliantly illuminated with the Author's own candles.[38]

Not surprisingly in this dramatization of English life there were plenty of signs of empire. It was simply there, far from the heart of the action but part of the world in which people lived, informing them of who they were.

Thackeray, like many British people, had close associations with the empire.

Born in Calcutta in 1811, he was the son of the Secretary of the Board of Revenue in the East India Company. His mother also came from a Company family. His father, in common with many other Company officials in the late eighteenth century, had had an illegitimate daughter with an Indian mistress before his marriage. The child was recognized in his will and Thackeray was later to feel a considerable sense of guilt about this half-sister, a guilt which may have contributed to the deep ambivalence so present in his fiction about children of mixed heredity. At five, after an early childhood cared for by a loving mother and innumerable domestics, he was sent to England to school, accompanied by a native servant. He never returned but the India connections on both sides of his family, and that of his wife-to-be, were very present. After school at Charterhouse and his undergraduate days in Cambridge, Thackeray embarked on the life of a young man of fortune. His inheritance from his father, however, was lost in the collapse of a number of Indian banks in 1833. Writing became a way of making a living: from the regular magazine articles and travel narratives to the novels that secured his public reputation. After his father's death his mother remarried, to her first love, Henry Carmichael-Smyth, an ensign of the Bengal Engineers, a man initially deemed unsuitable by her family. They returned to England and Thackeray spent his summers with them. Carmichael-Smyth's brother was appointed Governor of British Guiana in 1833, ensuring that Thackeray had close connections with both the East and West Indies.[39]

Thackeray was also fascinated by history. *Vanity Fair* was a novel that was set in the past, but was about the present. *The History of Henry Esmond*, which he published in 1852, was his spectacularly successful historical novel, set at the time of the Glorious Revolution and its aftermath. The writing of *Esmond* gave him, in Thackeray's words, "as much trouble" as the *History of England* (the first two volumes of which were published to great acclaim in 1849) had given Macaulay.[40] It was commonly said to be the best historical novel of the nineteenth century. One of Thackeray's lifelong, but frustrated, ambitions was to write a history of Queen Anne's reign and in his lectures on "The Four Georges" he rivaled the success of Dickens as a public performer. His attention to detail and to specificity, to the nuance of time and place, to the material conditions of life and the commodities that were consumed, whether in the past or the present, make his texts particularly appropriate vehicles through which to investigate the specificities of colonial connection. In his recording of the everyday he prefigured Trollope, who regarded him as a great master.

From the opening pages of *Vanity Fair* traces of empire are present, part of the great theatrical scene. At the heart of the narrative are two young women—Becky Sharp, the spirited and self-seeking orphan who has to secure her own fortune through the marriage market, and the meek and docile Amelia Sedley, whose rich stockbroker father loses his money. In this anti-heroic novel their adventures with the odious George Osborne, the generous and loyal "Dobbin," the kindly but stupid Rawdon Crawley and his relatives, and the wicked Lord Steyne provide the backbone of the action. "Wives, husbands, children, masters, servants, lives, blood, bodies," as Bunyan had put it, all were for sale in this godless society.[41] In Thackeray's novel almost every man and woman is out for themselves and masterminding this drama was the narrator, the skeptical observer, inviting his readers to enjoy the spectacle of greed and hypocrisy, with the sacred cows of Victorian morality—the family, marriage, religious belief, and social hierarchy—at the center of the gaze.

Empire provides some of the wallpaper and color for this grand scene: from the commodities, the guava jelly, the muslin and Kashmir shawls, the chutneys and chilies, to the regiments which have fought in the West Indies, India, and Canada, the missionary meetings concerning Timbuctoo and Quashimaboo, to the frightful colony of Coventry Island with its newspapers, the *Swamp Town Gazette* and the *Swamp Town Sentinel*. Then there are the people: the black and Indian servants, the "mahogany" West Indian heiress, the greedy Anglo-Indian and the vulgar Irishwoman. On the very first page we are introduced to Sambo, "the black servant," "bandy legged" and "grinning," who stands for the African presence in Britain. Sambo is part of the scenery, not a real person. Sambo has been named by his masters. He is a sign of the prosperity of the Sedley family, the new rich demonstrating their status by their employment of an African. He has no past or future, he flits through the novel, surfacing in the Sedley household from time to time, as footman, as butler, as comically in love with the cook and locked in rivalry with the coachman over her favors. For Thackeray, Trollope argued, "it was essential that the representations made by him should be, to his own thinking, lifelike."[42] But Sambo did not need to be lifelike, for he was simply an African, identified by the color of his skin, "black Sambo." Sambo is a fantasy African, not living and breathing so that readers could identify with him, feel his pleasures and his pains. He is a shadow, a black shadow, haunting the imperial imagination, a trace of colonial power.

Thackeray was drawing on one discourse of "the African" current in the 1840s. Abolitionist sentiment was waning in Britain as doubts increased as to the "success" of emancipation in the West Indies and the possibilities of "civilizing" Africans, making them into black Britons. His pencil sketch of Sambo had nothing in common with the dignified emancipated negro of the anti-slavery imagination, a person to be taken seriously in his own right. Rather he drew on a tradition of satirical writing and visual representations of the limited capacities of "the African"—a tradition informed by pro-slavery thinkers.

There had been a black population in Britain from the Elizabethan period, when the slave trade became established, but it had grown as the triangular trade developed. Newspaper advertisements from as early as the seventeenth century demonstrate that sales of enslaved people were taking place in Britain, particularly in the port towns. Families whose money had come from the West Indies returned home with their "property" in people, and indeed sometimes had their portraits painted with an enslaved man or woman as a "possession," akin to their houses, dogs, and land.

Free Africans were also a presence, many of them working as sailors, dockers, or servants. By the mid-1760s Granville Sharp, who was to take up the case of James Somerset and challenge the legality of slavery inside Britain, estimated that there were approximately 20,000 black servants in London.[43] The end of the American War of Independence saw a significant number of black loyalists, who had fought for the British in return for their freedom, escaping re-enslavement by fleeing to the United Kingdom. Some Africans managed to do relatively well economically and establish themselves in trade but the visibility of a poor black community in London by the 1780s drew much adverse comment. At a time when anti-slavery sentiment was gathering force in Britain, fuelled by an evangelical revival across Protestant denominations, a scheme was hatched to establish a community for freed Africans in Sierra Leone. This ill-fated plan was initially strongly supported by Olaudah Equiano, who was to become the best-known African in Britain.

Not all Africans were destined to survive in the historical records only as Sambo, Caesar, or John—names imposed upon them by their masters. Equiano had been given a series of names by his owners, despite his protestations, and he used one of them—Gustavus Vassa, for much of his life in Britain. In 1789, however, he published his autobiography, *The Interesting Narrative of Olaudah Equiano or Gustavus Vassa the African*, under his own birthname. Born into a prosperous family in what is now Eastern Nigeria, he was seized, aged ten, into slavery and passed from one master to another before suffering the horrors of the "Middle Passage" to the West Indies. Bought by a naval lieutenant, he spent some years serving with him in the Seven Years War and was then sold on to a Quaker merchant who lived in Philadelphia. Having already learned to speak English, read, write, and do arithmetic he proved useful to his master and was able to buy his freedom at the age of twenty-one. He spent much of the rest of his life in England and was one of the Africans in Britain actively concerned with the abolition of the slave trade and slavery. Equiano's autobiography, a bestseller in its time, provided a powerful refutation of the pro-slavery belief, maintained in numerous pamphlets and travel accounts, that Africans were mentally inferior to white people and born to be their subjects. The first-person account it gave of the kidnapping and enslavement of a child, the "Middle Passage" and the dehumanizing daily routines and brutalities of slavery fundamentally challenged the claims of the plantocracy and the West India interest that enslaved Africans enjoyed better lives than those of British workers.

The "war of representation" between pro-slavery and anti-slavery forces continued apace between the 1780s and the 1830s. Both sides published pamphlets and speeches, organized public meetings and petitions, and lobbied members of both Houses of Parliament. By the 1820s it was abundantly clear that the ending of the slave trade in 1807 had not resulted in slavery dying away, as many had hoped. A new popular movement emerged in Britain, supported across classes and regions and by large numbers of women as well as men, insisting on immediate emancipation. At the same time resistance to slavery in the Caribbean was escalating, culminating in 1831 with a major rebellion in Jamaica. This convinced even the West India interest in Britain that emancipation was inevitable and that the most important consideration was what concessions could be won from the British Parliament. Colonial slavery was abolished in the British Empire in 1833 but full freedom was not finally established until August 1, 1838. The 1830s marked the highpoint of anti-slavery and humanitarian concern across the country, when large numbers of white men and women strongly identified with the idea of "the poor negro," victimized by brutal white West Indians. In this anti-slavery discourse Africans, if properly tutored, could become "like us," Christian, industrious, and domesticated. Similarly, indigenous peoples, who had been abandoned to their fate at the hands of cruel settlers in Australia, New Zealand, Canada, and the Cape, were constructed in humanitarian discourse as in need of rescue and protection. They should be made anew in a British idiom.[44] By the 1840s, however, sympathy for freed Africans and native peoples was receding in the face of the constant lamentations of the planters over the economic plight of their properties, and the refusal of native peoples, particularly in New Zealand and the Cape, to accept colonial rule. A harsher racial rhetoric of the fundamental differences between races, now seen as "natural," became more salient.

This was the place from which Thackeray was writing in 1847. He had probably absorbed from his evangelical mother the view that slavery was immoral, but he was never actively identified with the anti-slavery movement and had no formal political alignments. He worked imaginatively with the metaphor of slavery in his writing, but it was the ties that bind white men and women in relations of inequality and that reduced white people to objects that preoccupied him, not colonial slavery. Having visited the Ottoman Empire in 1845 it was "Oriental slavery" that fascinated him—Becky Sharpe's enslavement of men, Lord Steyne as the sultan with his harem.[45] It was white people whose dehumanization he was concerned with, not the ways in which those same white people dehumanized their colonial subjects.

It was, therefore, not men like Equiano that Thackeray chose to represent, but Sambo, a cipher deprived of personhood. Miss Swartz, the second person of color in the novel, "the rich woolly- haired mulatto from St.Kitts" (p. 6), was granted a slightly more elaborate pencil sketch and a function in the plot. Miss Swartz was one of the boarders at Miss Pinkerton's academy (where Amelia and Becky were educated), paying double for the privilege of being allowed to mix with the daughters of the English middle classes. In Amelia's mind she was good natured, despite her hysterical "yoops" (p. 8), but in every other account she was reduced to a rather grotesque object, only acceptable because her money was sufficient to offset the color of her skin. Amelia and George had been designated for each other by their respective fathers since childhood. Once Mr Sedley's stockbroking business had gone under, however, Mr Osborne no longer wanted his son allied to a bankrupt. Miss Rhoda Swartz was "reported to have I don't know how many plantations in the West Indies, a deal of money in the funds, and three stars to her name in the East India stockholders' list. She had a mansion in Surrey, and a house in Portland Place" (p. 183) and her money quite made up, in Mr Osborne's eyes, for the unfortunate accident of her birth. He instructed his son to marry her, for love may be "felt for any young lady endowed with such qualities as Miss Swartz possessed" (p. 186). Her hundred thousand pounds would ensure her plenty of attention and "vast respect" in the Osborne household. But George had been educated as a gentleman and while his father had worked his way up in trade, his son was of a different generation. As he reported to Amelia:

My sisters say she has diamonds as big as pigeon's eggs . . . how they must set off her complexion! A perfect illumination it must be when her jewels are on her neck. Her jet-black hair is as curly as Sambo's. I dare say when she went to court; and with a plume of feathers in her topknot she would look a perfect Belle Sauvage. . . Diamonds and mahogany, my dear! Think what an advantageous contrast—and the white feathers in her hair—I mean in her wool. She had earrings like chandeliers: you might have lighted 'em up, by Jove. . . (pp. 183–4)

Furthermore, "her father was a German Jew—a slave-owner they say—connected with the Cannibal islands in some way or other" (p. 184). Here poor Rhoda's sins were magnified: her father was German, a Jew, and a slaver, linked with the barbarisms of Africa, in particular cannibalism. And on top of all that her mother was black. This was not a woman that George could accept. Compared with the kind, gentle, sweet, docile, and ladylike Amelia in her simple white muslin, she was vulgarity personified, and racialized. Bedecked in her "favourite amber-coloured satin, with turquoise bracelets, countless rings, flowers, feathers, and all sorts of tags and gimcracks," she was "about as elegantly decorated as a she chimney-sweep on Mayday." Her bejeweled hands sprawled in her amber satin lap and "her big eyes rolled about" (p. 190). When ordered by his father to marry her, George responded:

Marry that mulatto woman? . . . I don't like the color, sir. Ask the black that sweeps opposite Fleet market, sir. *I'm* not going to marry a Hottentot Venus. (p. 194)

While Thackeray was deeply critical of aspects of the marriage market his representation of Miss Swartz, drawing as it did on the discourse of miscegenation, the assumption that it was "unnatural" for white to mix with black, was itself dehumanized. Miss Swartz, like Sambo, was a white fantasy.

Thackeray's lack of sympathy for anti-slavery sentiment was further exercised in his portrait of Pitt Crawley, the canting and hypocritical humanitarian. But this was a living and breathing man. The oldest son of Becky's first employer, Sir Pitt Crawley (a dirty, degenerate and mean-spirited baronet), he is "a very polite and proper gentleman," yet condemned as effeminate for his lack of manly attributes (p. 74). After time in the diplomatic service, he turned country gentleman, "wrote a pamphlet on Malt," for he liked to be in the public eye, and "took a strong part in the Negro Emancipation question." He "became a friend of Mr. Wilberforce's," engaged in a celebrated correspondence on "the Ashantee Mission," always attended the evangelical meetings in London in May and did all that he could to improve religious instruction in his neighborhood. He subjected the household at Queen's Crawley to regular prayers and supported an independent meeting house to the disgust of his uncle, the local Rector. He tried unsuccessfully to persuade his father to give up his parliamentary seat to him, "for the good of the nation and the Christian world." Yet his desire to support the abolitionist cause was not sufficient to make him want to unseat Mr Quadroon, who paid fifteen hundred pounds a year for the second family seat owned by the Crawleys. And Mr Quadroon, a West Indian whose name meant that he was of mixed descent, was pro-slavery (p. 75). Money was more important than principles, and anti-slavery sentiment easily discarded when self-interest was at stake.

Pitt Crawley's marriage into an evangelical family only magnified these tendencies. His mother-in-law was "a tall and awful missionary of the truth," who "rode about the country in her barouche" launching "packets of tracts among the cottagers and tenants." She was on the female committee of the "Warmingpan fund for the Feejee Islanders," while his sister-in-law was a "mature spinster," "whose love for the blacks occupied almost all her thoughts" and who eventually married a missionary at the Cape (p. 309). Here Thackeray was giving imaginative shape to the frequent criticism of anti-slavery and missionary and evangelical enthusiasts that their interest in far-distant lands and heathens abroad stemmed from a failure of sympathy with those closer to home. Like Dickens' famous portrait of Mrs Jellaby in *Bleak House*, whose preoccupation with Africa was at the expense of her own horribly neglected children.

India in the 1840s figured differently in the British imagination from the West Indies. Writing about India and its ancient culture, its horrid superstitions, abounded—from novels, travel books, and histories, to treatises and pamphlets. Public debate on aspects of Indian government or culture surfaced at intervals, often associated with the renewal of the Charter for the East India Company. Thackeray's childhood experience of Bengal, combined with the wealth of continuing family connections, meant that Anglo-Indians were part of his world and Jos Sedley, one of his most memorable comic creations, is a rich expression of this. Before she has even met him, he is the subject of Becky Sharp's fantasized future as she imagines herself mounted on an elephant and "dressed in an infinity of shawls, turbans and diamond necklaces" paying a visit to the Grand Mogul (p. 19). Jos, Amelia's older brother, is fat, greedy, narcissistic, vain, indolent, and self-deluding. He works for the Bengal Division of the East India Company, as collector of Boggley Wollah, a "fine, lonely, marshy, jungly district, famous for snipe-shooting, and where not infrequently you may flush a tiger." No other Europeans live there so Jos sits in lonely splendour, waited upon by native servants and eating and drinking to his heart's content. The resulting liver complaint means a period of respite in Britain—and Becky's first unsuccessful attempt to ensnare him. Meeting later in Brussels, when Becky is married to Rawdon Crawley, she mercilessly plays upon his fears relieving him of a great deal of money and eventually, at the end of the novel, it is suggested that she has poisoned him, gaining a life insurance in the process. Jos is indeed one of Becky's victims, enslaved to her charms. After Waterloo, a time at which Jos distinguishes himself by his cowardice, he returns to Bengal for ten years before once again coming home. Having been promoted in the Company service he is now a rich man and settles in a comfortable Anglo-Indian district of London, joins the Oriental Club and mixes with his Company friends. Dressed in his astonishing waistcoats, his satins and velvets, smoking his hookah, he tells his tales of hunting prowess and military adventure, "Waterloo Sedley" as he likes to be called, was the very picture of an Anglo-Indian returnee.

Thackeray must have known many such Anglo-Indians. By the 1840s a significant change had taken place in the form of colonial rule in India. In the eighteenth century the country had been ruled in an Indian or "Orientalist" idiom, with efforts made to co-operate with existing structures of power and social organization, to respect the ancient languages and culture, to adapt rather than attempt to transform. The reforming spirit of the 1820s and 1830s, influenced by both evangelicalism and utilitarianism, brought major changes and it was increasingly seen as Britain's responsibility to intervene in Indian society and make manners and morals anew. By the 1830s the idea of India as a site of "thick darkness," which would be brought into civilization by British rule, had circulated widely.[46] From the late 1790s a new evangelical discourse of heathenism and depravity began to compete with orientalist accounts: it was Britain's duty to take the Christian religion to the "lamentably degenerate and base . . . people of Hindostan."[47] In the debates over *sati*, the ritual burning of the Hindu widow on the funeral pyre of her husband, the figure of the oppressed Hindu woman became a potent symbol for the legitimacy of British colonial rule. Hindu women had to be protected from the barbarisms and cruelties of Hindu men.[48] Utilitarians were just as enthusiastic as evangelicals in their schemes for Indian improvement. James Mill's *History of India,* published in 1818 to significant acclaim, defined a liberal reforming programme that would free India from its own culture and superstitions. These issues were not, however, the ones that interested Thackeray. There is no trace in *Vanity Fair* of these debates. His India was one dominated by the Company and by the military, there were no descriptions of the landscapes or the peoples, it was in effect a white world and one as seen from the metropole, intimately interlocked with a British social world.

Thackeray was witty at the expense of the Anglo-Indian world. He caricatured their habits and preoccupations, their obsession with their own small world, their levels of corruption, as in "the great Calcutta house of Fogle, Fake and Cracksman" which "failed for a million, and plunged half the Indian public into misery and ruin" (p. 569). He satirized the ways in which colonizers carry with them their "pride, pills, prejudices, Harvey sauces, cayenne peppers . . . making a little Britain" wherever they settled down (p. 612). But once again his critique of the greed and hypocrisy of British society never disturbed his assumptions of native inferiority—the otherness of colonized peoples. Jos is accompanied on his return by his native servant, Loll Jewab, who carries a ready supply of mangoes, chutneys, and curry powders. Loll Jewab is a mute, degraded and effeminized figure: a "shuddering native," his brown face "livid with cold and of the colour of a turkey's gizzard," wrapped in a shawl, "moaning in a strange and piteous way, and showing his yellow eyeballs and white teeth" (p. 561). His life is a misery on account of his master's tyranny. Jos's arrogance of manner and assumptions of superiority are belied by his total dependence on his servants. Yet while Thackeray is sympathetic to life below stairs in relation to European servants, his tolerance ends with a dark skin. Loll Jewab is mistaken for the Devil by the maidservants at the inn, made fun of by the boys of the neighbourhood on account of his "dusky countenance," and once he has taught the art of curry making to a newly employed white servant he is packed off back to Calcutta (p. 546).

While Company servants do not get a good press from Thackeray, the military escapes unscathed. Dobbin's regiment served in the West Indies in the period before Waterloo, and in India immediately afterwards, where they were actively involved with the Burmese wars. What is not explored is the colonizing work with which they were engaged. This is one of the erasures in Thackeray's history, for his representation of the regiment is a kindly one, focused on the social world of the officers and their gallant service, whether at Waterloo or in the colonies. One wonders what the *History of the Punjaub*, which Dobbin was writing at the end of the novel, would have had to say about the peoples that they conquered. The life of the regiment was ordered by Mrs Major, Peggy O'Dowd for while "O'Dowd goes in command of the regiment," Peggy "goes in command of O'Dowd" (p. 245). Thackeray's loquacious and warm-hearted Irishwoman is his most generous sketch of one who is both colonizer and colonized. For the Irish, colonized by the British, were both inside and outside the United Kingdom. The regiment does the work of empire, whether in the West Indies, India, or, if they had been posted there, Ireland. For Ireland, as their Irish-born hero Wellington put it, could never be ruled in the same way as England. It required a strong military presence.

Thackeray had spent six months in Ireland in 1842 and published an account, his *Irish Sketch Book*, of his travels. He was troubled by the poverty and want, and disgusted by the "loathsome" figures of the beggars, so evident especially in the south and west, but hopeful that the country was improving. The growth of a middle class, he was convinced, would ensure progress, reducing the power "both of the Protestant aristocracy and the Catholic peasantry."[49] He frequently noted the presence of dragoons, but made no observations on the ways in which law and order were enforced in Ireland. And while very aware of the ways in which the "sister island" was blamed for all ills by those who saw themselves as "hereditary bondsmen," he was much more inclined to blame the Irish themselves, their indolence and partiality for dirt, for the problems they faced. Between this journey and the writing of *Vanity Fair* came the Great Famine, but nothing of this is evident in Thackeray's account of Mrs O'Dowd. The discourse on which he draws here is that of the Irish as Britons, contributing to the power of the empire. Both Irish and Scots were disproportionately represented in the British army and navy, where there was always a demand for their services. Major O'Dowd has served in every quarter of the globe and is a brave commander, though a man of few words. She is as brave as any man, as much at home in Madras or in Brussels, in a cantonment or under a tent, a stout, jolly lady, who rides at the head of the regiment on an elephant, "kind in act and thought, impetuous in temper, eager to command" (p. 408). She mothers the young men, cares for the wounded, tyrannizes her husband, and is a dragon to all the ladies of the regiment. She is a passionate patriot, proud of her pedigree, convinced that everything Irish is best. With her exaggerated Irish dialect she is ever voluble and vulgar, but honest and kind at heart.

Thackeray's comic and satirical panorama of the social world, conducted by his narrator who provided a commentary on the doings of these self-interested and self-deluded characters, did not invite simple identifications from his readers. Here there was no glorious hero or heroine, no David Copperfield or Jane Eyre, developing through the novel into mature people with better understandings of themselves and others. There is no stable point of identification, no full belonging anywhere. Indeed, Thackeray represents the instability of the non-essential self. In his galaxy of flawed characters the most engaging is the wicked Becky Sharpe who "performs" identities in a remarkably modern manner. Becky is not born, she is made and re-made, and her identity is always in process as she responds to the new situations in which she finds herself. By the end of the novel, in a desperate bid for respectability, she attends missionary meetings and supports worthy causes as vigorously as any of the evangelical enthusiasts she has previously despised. This Becky had little resemblance to the Society lady who neglected her husband and son and risked her reputation by mixing too freely with a dubious aristocrat. Could white women readers have identified totally with Becky, wanted to be her, modeled themselves on her, dreamed of her at night? Rather, their identifications would have been divided between some aspects of Becky, some of Amelia, but nothing of Miss Swartz, the excluded and negative dimensions of the self. Similarly with the men—there was no hero, but there were aspects of Rawdon and of Dobbin that were admirable, inviting identification, while Sambo and Loll Jewab could be easily discarded. It is through this process of identification—recognising self in other, abjecting negative dimensions, fantasizing ways of being—that identities are made and re-made, that men and women fashion themselves as gendered and raced beings, as British women and men.

Vanity Fair is not an imperialist novel, in the sense that it actively promulgates imperial expansion with a self-consciously colonial setting. Thackeray eschewed politics. Yet his writing was informed through and through by the politics and presence of empire. His novel is one in which empire, and the grammars of difference associated with it, are simply part of everyday social experience positioning characters in the racial hierarchies through which power was lived and regulated. This was the rich world into which readers were invited. We cannot know precisely what generations of readers have taken from the book. But we can know what Thackeray could take for granted without making explicit. And we are at liberty to infer that this is part of the long process that made the British imagination imperial. This is how British identities were constituted through empire.

Notes

1 Thanks to Stuart Hall, Gail Lewis, and Jokhim Meikle.
2 There was a well-established imperial culture in Britain by the eighteenth century, but traffic between metropole and colonies increased exponentially in the nineteenth century.
3 Williams, *Capitalism and Slavery*.
4 Davis, *Problem of Slavery*; Turley, *Culture of English Antislavery*; Drescher, *Capitalism and Antislavery*. For a helpful short discussion of the class implications, see Epstein, "Taking class notes."
5 Said, *Orientalism*, p. 3; for a critique by a historian see MacKenzie, *Orientalism*.
6 MacKenzie, "Empire and metropolitan cultures." For another recent assessment, see Thompson, *Empire Strikes Back?*.
7 Porter, *Absent-Minded Imperialists*. For a different account, see Thompson, *Empire Strikes Back?*.

8   Hall and Rose (eds), *At Home with the Empire,* Introduction.
9   Levine (ed.), *Gender and Empire.*
10 Fryer, *Staying Power;* Shyllon, *Black People in Britain;* Burton, *At the Heart of the Empire;* Visram, *Asians in Britain.*
11 de Groot, "Metropolitan desires."
12 Thorne, *Congregational Missions.*
13 Oldfield, *Popular Politics;* Midgley, *Women Against Slavery.*
14 Bolt, *Victorian Attitudes to Race;* Dawson, *Soldier Heroes;* Hall, *Civilising Subjects.*
15 Eldridge, *Disraeli;* Porter, *Critics of Empire;* Taylor, "Imperium et libertas"; Thompson, *Imperial Britain.*
16 MacKenzie, *Propaganda and Empire; id., Imperialism and Popular Culture.*
17 Krebs, *Writing of Empire.*
18 Auerbach, *The Great Exhibition;* Coombes, *Reinventing Africa.*
19 Dabydeen, *Hogarth's Blacks;* Cherry, *Beyond the Frame;* Bennett, *Birth of the Museum.*
20 S. Hall, *Representation,* p. 7.
21 Sinha, *Colonial Masculinity;* Hall, *Civilising Subjects.*
22 K. Wilson, *Island Race;* Wilson (ed.), *New Imperial History.*
23 Cooper and Stoler (eds), *Tensions of Empire.*
24 Bayly, *Imperial Meridian.*
25 Hall, McClelland, and Rendall, *Defining the Victorian Nation;* McClelland and Rose, "Citizenship and empire."
26 Kinealy, "At home with the empire."
27 Holt, *Problem of Freedom.*
28 Levine, "Sexuality and empire."
29 Steedman, *Radical Soldier's Tale;* Davidoff, "Class and gender."
30 Caine, *Bombay to Bloomsbury.*
31 Semmel, *Governor Eyre Controversy;* Price, *Imperial War;* Schneer, *London 1900.*
32 Hall, *Civilising Subjects.*
33 Said, *Culture and Imperialism;* Hall, "Thinking the postcolonial, thinking the empire"; Loomba, *Colonialism/Postcolonialism.*
34 Williams, *Long Revolution,* p. 47.
35 Kaplan, "Imagining empire: history, fantasy and literature."
36 Brantlinger, *Rule of Darkness.*
37 Cited in Pollard (ed.), *Thackeray,* pp. 33–4.
38 Thackeray, *Vanity Fair,* p. xxii.
39 Thackeray by Shillingsburg, *Oxford Dictionary of National Biography;* D. Thomas, *Thackeray and Slavery.*
40 Sutherland, introduction to Thackeray, *Henry Esmond,* p. 8.
41 Bunyan, *Pilgrim's Progress.*
42 Trollope, *Thackeray,* p. 94.
43 Gerzina, *Black England,* p. 5.
44 Hall, *Civilising Subjects;* Lester, *Imperial Networks.*
45 Thomas, *Thackeray and Slavery.*
46 Macaulay, *Speeches,* p. 117.
47 C. Grant, *Observations on the State of Society among the Asiatic Subjects of Great Britain, particularly with Respect to Morals and on the Means of Improving it. Written chiefly in Year 1792* (privately printed, 1797), pp. 71–4.
48 Mani, *Contentious Traditions.*
49 Thackeray, *Irish Sketch Book,* pp. 42–3, 365.

Further Reading

This is a very flourishing field and it is impossible to do more than make a few suggestions from the rich historiography—but see the bibliography. One of the first studies to explore the significance of empire to the making of British identities was Antoinette Burton's *Burdens of History*. This focuses on the ways in which British feminism was profoundly influenced by ideas of empire, a theme that has subsequently been taken up most notably by Clare Midgley in her book *Women Against Slavery* and a number of articles. Lata Mani's *Contentious Traditions* includes much material on British missionaries. For the impact of gender, class, and empire on political culture see Catherine Hall, Keith McClelland and Jane Rendall's *Defining the Victorian Nation*. There are two book-length studies of the mutual constitution of colonizer and colonized in the British Empire: Mrinalini Sinha, *Colonial Masculinity* and Catherine Hall, *Civilising Subjects*. The first deals with England and Bengal in the late nineteenth century, the second with England and Jamaica between the 1830s and the 1860s. Susan Thorne's *Congregational Missions and the Making of an Imperial Culture in Nineteenth Century England* explores the significance of mission work to British culture. A groundbreaking recent study that looks at sexuality and prostitution across metropole and colony is Philippa Levine's *Prostitution, Race and Politics*. A new collection edited by Catherine Hall and Sonya Rose, *At Home with the Empire* has articles on key issues by many of the foremost writers in this field.

10

Imperial Identities Abroad

Stuart Ward[1]

Historians have long debated the question of whether the British Empire had any "fatal impact" on the history, culture and identity of the British Isles. While some have maintained that the empire provided the crucial common project that helped to weld the English, Scottish, Welsh, and (some) Irish into a credible community of Britons,[2] others have remarked upon the extraordinarily limited impact of empire in Britain, and its failure to leave any lasting imprint on the dominant patterns of national self-definition.[3] Those seeking to establish a tangible link between empire and identity-formation are invariably faced with an exacting burden of proof, and the problem of weighing imperial factors against other, more domestic determinants of metropolitan Britishness.

The situation is entirely different, however, when it comes to assessing the cultural underpinnings of imperial identities abroad. Here, the material and ideological agencies of empire are readily assumed as the obvious starting point for understanding the origins and evolution of new world identities. For the millions of settlers, merchants, missionaries, convicts, and military personnel who participated in the expansion of empire, the task of establishing viable new communities invariably required a heightened sense of collective self-awareness. Ideas and assumptions about community and belonging that may only have been latent at home were thrown into sharper relief by the sheer, incomprehensible distance from the mother country, and the strange and often threatening encounter with indigenous peoples. Adapting European systems of land use, social organization, economic exchange and religious belief to new, often harsh and hostile environments, with only limited resources, inevitably brought new departures from established "British" ways. At the same time, the task of applying British concepts of law and liberty to these circumstances often involved a determination to preserve and uphold the political and cultural markers of Britishness. It was the interplay between familiar ideas and institutions from home and the unfamiliar exigencies of colonial experience that produced the dynamics of imperial identity-formation.

It is only in recent years that historians have begun to re-examine settler identity-formation as part of a singular, integrated historical experience. The generation that produced the *Cambridge History of the British Empire* in the 1930s readily assumed that the histories of British settler colonies (restyled as "dominions" from 1907) could be comprehended within the same frame. The experience of post-war reconstruction and decolonization, however, brought centrifugal tendencies in the historiography, and a new emphasis on identity-formation as a central plank in the story of national autonomy. Russel Ward's *The Australian Legend* (1958) was emblematic of this shift in emphasis, raising the question of the origins of a distinctive "Australian character." Similarly, J. M. S. Careless's influential essay on "Limited identities in Canada" (1969) encouraged a trend away from viewing Canadian identities in their wider, imperial setting. These insular tendencies developed to the point where, by the 1990s, A. G. Hopkins could confidently pronounce that Australian and Canadian history were "scarcely studied elsewhere."[4] What is even more remarkable is that it took so long for anyone to notice. Only J. G. A. Pocock, in a lecture in Christchurch in 1973, had seen cause for concern in these devolutionary tendencies. His famous "plea for a new subject," in which British history would be reconceived as the sum of its many, globally integrated parts, was taken up enthusiastically by scholars in the British Isles, but made almost no impression on the study of British identities "abroad." Pocock's underlying lament for the passing of the imperial world was completely out of tune with a new generation of historians who seemed more intent on extricating their past from its imperial antecedents. It would be left to a later, post-1980s generation of historians, taking their cue from a renewed interest in the study of "Britishness" in the United Kingdom, to reconceptualize Pocock's plea in the form of new, reintegrated histories of the identities and culture of "the British World."[5]

Identity is a notoriously slippery field of study because it is so subjective and multifaceted. No group identity is ever truly stable or coherent, and even the most homogenous communities are prone to fragmentation due to the countless distinctions of age, class, gender, occupation, religion, political persuasion, and so on. Yet few would dispute that all social groupings share certain assumptions about their distinctive characteristics, without which they would be unable to function as communities. In some cases, this will amount to little more than tacit agreement on the outer definitions of the realm within which internal disputes can legitimately be fought. Yet this pegging out of the broad categories of inclusion and exclusion is a powerful agent of social change, particularly when it comes to traumatic experiences like war, revolution and—for our purposes—empire-building. Historians now routinely point to the "contested" and "unstable" nature of imperial identities, but it is equally important to consider what held these communities together, and how they managed to wield so powerful a collective influence on subject peoples. As Philip D. Morgan cautions:

> Not everything is indeterminate and permeable, not everything is contested, not everything is fragile. Multiple and hybrid these identities may have been, but their integrity, their totality, their continuities with a past, their ability to maintain boundaries should not be underestimated. The British, for all their diffuseness, were, after all, rather unified linguistically and culturally.[6]

It is the evolving trajectories of the broader outlines and prevailing assumptions about imperial Britishness that are pursued in this chapter, rather than (for reasons of space as much as anything else) the infinite sources of internal division, dissent, and dispute. In particular, it is worth considering the contextual factors that influenced the changing tenets and texture of imperial Britishness over time, and from one settler context to the next. Above all, the chapter will focus on the tensions and contradictions between metropolitan and colonial conceptions of Britishness that were such a key factor in the composition of settler identities, and which ultimately proved crucial to the break-up of an imagined community of "Greater Britain."

An Empire of Rights

The American Revolution represented the first of many flashpoints between rival conceptions of imperial Britishness. The Declaration of Independence is commonly remembered in popular mythology as the moment when the inhabitants of a diffuse and widely dispersed array of colonies found their collective voice as a distinctive American people. Yet research in recent decades has lent increasing support to the idea that the colonists "always strove to be Britons" and achieved their independence "without ever declaring their common character or distinctive identity." According to this view, the causes of the revolution were entirely political, legal, and administrative, and involved no "deeper disconnection between the antagonists."[7] This, of course, is not to say that American society was not radically different from metropolitan Britain. Indeed it has been suggested that it was precisely the gap between the relatively simple agricultural societies in the American colonies and the increasingly refined and cultivated old world that made settlers anxious to secure "metropolitan recognition" of their attachments to Britain.[8] To the extent that notions of identity fueled the revolutionary passions, this was more a case of unrequited Britishness—of American colonists taking umbrage at the refusal of the imperial metropole to treat them as equals.

One striking feature of the taxation crises that sparked the conflict is the way that both sides drew on notions of a transatlantic community of Britishness to promote their cause. On the one hand, the revolutionary slogan "no taxation without representation" implied that American colonists were entitled to the same rights and liberties as their fellow Britons on the other side of the Atlantic. As one anonymous colonist wrote despairingly in the *Boston Journal* in 1765: "Are not the people of *America*, BRITISH Subjects? Are they not *Englishmen*?"[9] On the other hand, metropolitan supporters of the Stamp Act found it equally useful to frame their arguments in terms of a common subjecthood. Writing in 1765, Soame Jenyns noted that one in twenty Englishmen were not directly represented in Parliament, and saw no reason why the same inconvenience should not be borne by the American colonists: "Are they not alike British subjects? are they not Englishmen? or are they only Englishmen when they sollicit for protection, but not Englishmen when taxes are required to enable this country to protect them?"[10] Few, if any, of the colonial protagonists staked their claims on a distinctive cultural identity as "Americans."

The concept was more commonplace in Britain than the Thirteen Colonies at the time, and it was only in the later stages of the conflict that it was increasingly used by the colonists themselves as a way of implying that they had been "deprived of their Britishness."[11] In this respect, it is possible to interpret the American response to the taxation crises of the 1760s and 1770s as "a fundamental schism between metropolitan and provincial definitions of patriotism."[12] As P. J. Marshall concludes, although Britons on both sides of the Atlantic shared a sense that the empire "constituted one nation in terms of language and liberty," by the 1770s "there were significant differences across the Atlantic as to what British Protestantism and British liberty implied."[13]

T. H. Breen takes this line of reasoning further, arguing that the fundamental political and civic ideals of the American Revolution were not, in themselves, sufficient to forge a sense of trust between widely dispersed colonists, and sustain them through years of war and deprivation. Rather, he suggests that the resort to rights rhetoric was a strategy deployed by "a people who had not yet invented a nation and, therefore, who had not yet constructed a common history."[14] For Breen, it was not a self-confident American patriotism but the fundamental disorientation wrought by "changing perceptions of identity within the British Empire" that provided the emotional fuse that fired the revolution.[15] The experiences of Benjamin Franklin are a prime (albeit extreme) example of the motivating power of colonial resentment at the shoddy treatment meted out by their erstwhile fellow Britons. During the latter stages of his conversion from British imperialist to American patriot, Franklin could scarcely disguise his disbelief that Americans were regarded in London as "the lowest of Mankind and almost of a different Species from the English of Britain."[16] Other prominent patriots like Thomas Jefferson and John Adams are also said to have held out as long as possible for some kind of reconciliation. In a working draft of the Declaration of Independence, Jefferson gave voice, not to robust, self-assured patriotism, but feelings of rejection at the hands of his indifferent countrymen: "These facts," he avowed,

> have given the last stab to agonizing affection, and manly spirit bids us to renounce for ever these unfeeling brethren. We must endeavour to forget our former love for them ... We might have been a free and great people together.[17]

To borrow J. G. A. Pocock's verdict on the identity of the American revolutionaries: "They ceased being 'British' when they could not be 'British' as they understood the term."[18]

The American Revolution was not only deeply implicated in notions of transatlantic Britishness, it was also instrumental in redrawing the boundaries of empire in the post-revolutionary era. The need to find a new homeland for the American Loyalists who had fought alongside the British provided the initial rationale for the colonization of Australia—several years before anyone thought about a dumping ground for felons. The American Revolution had an even greater impact in India, where Lord Cornwallis was despatched in 1786 as the first Governor-General directly answerable to Westminster. His mission was inevitably framed by the imperative of making good the losses he personally had sustained as a commander of British forces in the War of Independence. Meanwhile in Ireland, the revolutionary climate of the 1780s had a formative influence on nationalist and loyalist identities alike, with the 1798 rebellion of the "United Irishmen" providing the key stimulus to the Union of 1801 (again, remarkably, with Cornwallis presiding). Loyalism was also the predominant response of white planters in the British West Indies, for whom the social, cultural and material ties with Britain "restrained the development of a nationalistic creole consciousness."[19] In short, there was scarcely a corner of the British imperial world where the American Revolution failed to resonate in white British subjectivities. Above all, the tens of thousands of Loyalist refugees who poured into the northern provinces of the Maritimes, Quebec, and Ontario bear witness to the fact that the American Revolution represented, not the termination of pan-British imperial identities, but their radical realignment and reinvigoration.

Canadian Loyalism was an amalgam of personal allegiance to the King, a desire to preserve the political and cultural ties with Britain, and an abiding faith in the British constitution. It was a version of Britishness that was bolstered by the proximity of "others" in the form of the French settler community of Quebec (whom it was hoped might ultimately be absorbed into the British community) and the American presence to the South (whom it was feared might ultimately absorb the Canadian Loyalists, whether by invasion, annexation, or the insidious movements of population). By the time of the War of 1812, this unique set of circumstances had provided the makings of a fully fledged Loyalist myth. As the York *Observer* proclaimed in the aftermath of the war:

> Rather than submit to a successful rebellion they forsook the land of their forefathers— their homes,—their families,—in many instances, their friends, and all they hitherto held dear upon earth; and plunged unhesitatingly into the depths of difficulties of a boundless forest, there to teach their children, amidst every species of privation those lessons of patriotism and faithfulness, they had so nobly illustrated in action.[20]

The Loyalist myth, as it evolved in nineteenth-century English-Canadian discourse, has often been understood in terms of a *failure* of identity-formation. Paquet and Wallot, for example, have argued that the Loyalists' attachment to "an explicitly British program of action" meant that "the process of identity-formation was somewhat slowed down"—that it was somehow "retarded" compared to their French counterparts.[21] What this view overlooks is the extent to which Canadian Loyalism was as much a unique adaptation of Britishness as American republicanism. In seeking to establish "a counter-revolutionary society on the borders of revolutionary one," English Canadians were, from the outset, at a considerable remove from their metropolitan counterparts.[22] The sense of vulnerability in the face of a perceived American threat gave the imperial ideal an edge and urgency that it could never have acquired in Britain.

It was not merely the external threat of American continental dominance that shaped a peculiarly Canadian species of Britishness, but also—paradoxically—the American origins of English Canada itself. Writing in the early 1960s, W. L. Morton pointed out that one of the "most obvious" things about the Loyalist refugees that was often overlooked was "that they were Americans, unreconstructed Americans."[23] Historians have increasingly emphasized the cultural and political inheritance that the (otherwise disinherited) Loyalists brought with them from the American colonies, which manifested itself in a variety of ways. Specifically, it is now well established that the Loyalists were not merely "exponents of a metropolitan philosophy of provincial subordination," but rather saw themselves as conservative defenders of liberty.[24] They saw themselves, not as founding a bastion of metropolitan British conservatism, but as recreating the pre-revolutionary American homes they had lost.[25] For this reason, Loyalist leaders in Upper Canada did not always see eye to eye with the British officials who administered the province.[26] While English Canadians would continue to describe themselves for generations in terms uncompromisingly loyal and British, it was a Britishness that was largely home spun, and tailored to a peculiarly American set of aspirations, rights, and liberties.

This tendency to shape the outlines of imperial identity in accordance with local requirements often brought frontier communities into conflict with metropolitan opinion—not least over the treatment of indigenous peoples. The humanitarian and abolitionist sentiments that took root in Britain in the early nineteenth century were difficult to reconcile with the acquisitive and aggressive project of settler colonialism, particularly on the turbulent frontiers of the Cape Colony and New South Wales. Alan Lester has shown how settlers reshaped their social identities according to their common material interests and collective insecurity. In the Eastern Cape, the violent struggle with the Xhosa of 1834–5 "prompted most of the settlers to close ranks and to forge an unprecedentedly clear and embattled political identity."[27] This sense of embattlement arose, however, not merely from the violent "outrages" of the enemy, but also a perceived threat from within—namely the metropolitan humanitarians who sympathized with the Xhosa's cause. What particularly offended humanitarian sensibilities was the tendency among settlers to resort to exterminatory rhetoric (and practices) as the solution to the conflict of interest with indigenous peoples, and to justify these within an imperial ethic of progress. Settlers, for their part, deeply resented humanitarian condemnations of their behavior, and remained anxious about the prospect of metropolitan betrayal of their interests. As one prominent Eastern Cape settler protested: "England, instead of protecting us, accuses us, who were born and bred in her bosom, and have the like feelings as the rest of her sons, of cruelty and oppression."[28] The expectation that England ought properly to "protect us" was itself the product of assumptions rooted in an imagined community of imperial Britishness. Settler communities were vitally dependent on the metropole, not only for their commercial viability but also their cultural self-definition. This inevitably invested the relationship with a unique set of tensions and anxieties.

In 1836, humanitarian pressure groups at the height of their influence in Britain were instrumental in setting up the parliamentary Select Committee on Aborigines, and later the Aborigines Protection Society, which consolidated the rift between settler communities and metropolitan humanitarians. In New South Wales, the need to defend settler colonial practices from liberal critique also had the subtle effect of marking settlers off from their fellow countrymen in Britain. The *Sydney Morning*

Herald complained in March 1838 that the Colonial Office had become overrun with "those kind-hearted 'Liberals' who bestow so much of their pity on devastating and murdering savages, that they have none to spare for the white people." Conversely, humanitarians depicted settlers as having strayed from the fundamental principles of Protestant liberalism—a species of "aberrant Briton" in Lester's phrase. Seen in this context, settler anxieties about the internal threat of indigenous violence tended not to endear the colonists to a wider imperial identity, but quite the opposite. Or more precisely, the recurring disputes between settlers and humanitarians often resembled "struggles over the nature of Britishness itself"—and how far indigenous people could be included in the empire of rights.[29]

In reality, the humanitarian-settler divide did not run strictly along metropolitan-provincial lines. Humanitarian opposition to settler practices in the Eastern Cape stemmed as much from influences in Cape Town, and New South Wales had its share of dissenters on the ethics of aboriginal dispossession. Yet perceptions were more important than realities, and the depiction of humanitarianism as a species of maternal infidelity invested it with a special emotive power. Moreover, the metropolitan-provincial framing of the problem provided humanitarians with additional leverage in pressing the Colonial Office to take direct responsibility for indigenous affairs. If settlers could be depicted as inherently lacking the moral fibre to behave justly towards "the natives," who else was to protect their property and livelihood?

This line of argument was instrumental in promoting the annexation of New Zealand to the empire in 1840. The influx of settlers from Australia, humanitarians claimed, had left the Maori at the mercy of settler rapaciousness, unchecked by the sobering influence of British sovereignty. As the British Resident, James Busby argued, if Britain failed to acquire New Zealand, it would abandon the country to "the evil ascendancy of its own unprincipled subjects."[30] The precise reasons for annexation were complex, but humanitarian concerns were prominent both in the appointment of a British Resident in 1831, and the decision to proceed with annexation at the end of the decade.[31] In the event, metropolitan authority proved to be no protection against settler excesses, and thus the emergence of a New Zealand settler identity was to be equally marked by the experience of frontier conflict.

But the timing of these developments is significant—the New Zealand wars came later, into the 1850s and 1860s when the humanitarian and abolitionist movements were in rapid decline. Thus whereas the Cape settlers had grappled with metropolitan condemnation of their violent dealings with the Xhosa, the New Zealanders were confronted with exaggerated expectations of swift and total victory. James Belich has shown how the assumption of indigenous racial inferiority determined how the New Zealand wars were fought and, ultimately, remembered. The unexpected military prowess of the Maori (with innovations such as "Pa" fortifications, trench-style defensive systems and effective use of European weaponry) produced a string of military victories over their would-be conquerors that brought jeers from the London press. *The Times*, for example, encapsulated metropolitan incredulity in 1860: "Can it be that the very insignificance coupled with the boastful insolence of the enemy unsteadies our men and puzzles our commanders?"[32] The settlers, for their part, were inclined to ascribe these setbacks to the poor quality of the British regulars who had been despatched to assist in the suppression of Maori "insolence." Thus the *New Zealander* was "driven to a very painful contrast between our commanders who imperil New Zealand, and those who saved our Indian Empire two years ago."[33] Maori resistance was an affront to contemporary perceptions of Britishness, and therefore needed to be explained away as short-lived, imitative (rather than innovative), and fundamentally aberrant. The expectation of British martial superiority also meant that the ultimate victory over the Maori could not easily be incorporated into a heroic-foundational myth of settler identity. Although the wars offered ample raw material for a commemorative tradition, subsequent New Zealand accounts were dominated by "a suppressive reflex: a tendency to play down, obscure or forget the unacceptable."[34]

An Empire of Race

In the space of only three decades, the humanitarian, paternalist assumptions that had influenced the decision to colonize New Zealand had given way to ideas about the inevitability of Maori defeat at the hands of racially superior settlers. This same pattern can be traced in the fate of the Treaty of Waitangi—conceived in 1840 as an instrument to curtail the excesses of the newcomers, by 1877 it had been declared a "simple nullity" by New Zealand Chief Justice James Prendergast, having been signed "between a civilised nation and a group of savages."[35] This trend was by no means unique to New Zealand, but represented a much wider embrace of racial ideas across the settler-colonial world, including the United States. Catherine Hall has argued that, in the imperial metropolis itself, "the period from the mid-1840s to the mid-1860s saw a marked shift in the discursive terrain . . . and an increasing turn to the language of race to explain and justify the inequalities and persistent differences between peoples."[36] This was partly a response to the widely publicized horrors of colonial rebellion from Lucknow to Morant Bay. But the deeper causes lay in two closely related developments: first, the emergence, mid-century, of scientific racism in influential works by polygenist and evolutionist theorists, and second, the romantic embrace of nationalism as a powerful new source of civic identification. Nationalism was, itself, a response to complex processes of modernization and industrialization, in which new technologies, production techniques, capital investments, and urbanization eroded older patterns of community and allegiance and forged new, more interdependent societies. "The search was on," to quote Benedict Anderson, "for a new way of linking fraternity, power and time meaningfully together."[37] For the young Birmingham intellectual and preacher George Dawson, profoundly affected by the events of 1848, the future trend seemed clear: "This principle of races is about to regulate the new division of Europe, and the square large-headed man does ever rule the world."[38]

These ideas increasingly influenced metropolitan understandings of the nature of British imperial expansion. Charles Dilke's travels in the 1860s brought to mind an expansive vision of the British nation—a "Greater Britain" where "in essentials, the race was always one."[39] A decade later John Seeley argued that "our Empire . . .

does not consist of a congeries of nations held together by force, but in the main one nation, as much as if it were no Empire but an ordinary state." The idea of race lay implicit in Seeley's thinking, and he thus saw no place for India in his conception of "Greater Britain." The Indian population, he argued, was completely unlike "those tens of millions of Englishmen who live outside of the British Islands. The latter are of our own blood, and are therefore united to us by the strongest tie."[40] Seeley's lectures would have a profound influence on a later generation of imperial administrators, not least Alfred Milner, who would famously declare in his posthumously published "Credo": "I am an Imperialist and not a Little Englander because I am a British Race Patriot."[41]

There were, however, limits to the appeal of race nationalism in mid-Victorian Britain, as Peter Mandler has argued. What he terms the "civilisational perspective" of an earlier generation of English intellectuals proved remarkably adaptive and resilient, promoting the alternate view that race nationalism—so prevalent in Europe post-1848—was "an atavism from which England had providentially escaped."[42] But this was emphatically not the case in the settler colonies, where ideas about racial destiny and national vigor were taken up with a far more immediate sense of urgency and significance. In southern Africa, for example, the discovery of diamonds and later gold brought profound demographic changes and problems of rapid urbanization, which fuelled a growing trend towards racial segregation. In the aftermath of the Zulu Wars, the *Cape Times* editorialized on the struggle for "supremacy of race," while other English journals like *Lantern* resorted to scientific racism as a means of promoting ethnic pride.[43] Meanwhile in Oxford, a young Cecil Rhodes recorded his personal reflections on race nationalism in his 1877 "Confessions of Faith":

> I contend that we are the finest race in the world and that the more of the world we inhabit the better it is for the human race . . . every acre added to our territory means in the future birth to some more of the English race who otherwise would not be brought into existence.

By the early 1890s, there were frequent calls for the "dirty white half-bred orientalism" of Cape Town's architecture to be replaced by "that splendid audacity of national egotism that has been acknowledged to be one of the secrets of our mastery in British colonization"—a wish that was soon granted with the erection of an unmistakably Victorian Town Hall, and other municipal buildings.[44]

In Australia, race nationalism became an inherently defensive doctrine as the revolution in transport and communications brought potential dangers in the region closer to shore. In the aftermath of the defeat of France by Prussia in 1870, the *Sydney Morning Herald* proclaimed the arrival of a new "epoch in which the war of the races has clearly begun," with immediate repercussions for the Australian colonies: "The course of events is tending to destroy the security which Australians hitherto found in isolation . . . Space and distance have lost their old meaning."[45] These anxieties about a coming race war were initially fuelled by the threat of rival European colonial ambitions in the Pacific, particularly the French in the New Hebrides and the Germans in New Guinea. By the 1890s, however, they were increasingly framed in terms of fears of an "awakening Asia." In 1893, Charles Henry Pearson was one of the first to raise the alarm in predicting that the Chinese "will sooner or later overflow their borders and spread over new territory, and submerge weaker races." Australia's proximity to these dangers seemed self-evident. "We will wake," he warned, "to find ourselves elbowed and hustled, and perhaps even thrust aside."[46] In this setting, it became commonplace to seek comfort in imperial and racial self-imagery. By the turn of the century Australia's "great national ideal," wrote the union leader W. G. Spence, was "purity of race and the preservation of Greater Britain for the Anglo-Saxon stock."[47] It was an ideal that became embodied in the "White Australia" immigration policy—a measure that was unambiguously geared towards preserving the "British character" of Australian society.

By contrast, the language of race nationalism was tempered to some extent in Canada by the needs of national unity, particularly among Canadian politicians who had to take account of the French minority. But this did not stop prominent English Canadian editors, intellectuals and community leaders from drawing on ideas of blood, breed, and kinship. The poet Wilfred Campbell, for example, made little allowance for Quebec sensibilities in his 1914 anthology, *Sagas of Vaster Britain: Poems of the Race, the Empire and the Divinity of Man.*[48] Conservative politicians, too, drew on the language of Britishness to portray the Liberals as weak on the problem of securing the nation against American encroachment. The 1891 election, for example, was fought almost entirely on the Liberals' proposals for tariff reciprocity with the United States, which prompted John A. Macdonald's celebrated retort: "A British subject I was born, and a British subject I will die." Patricia K. Wood argues that MacDonald's British subjecthood had distinct ethnic undertones that privileged the status of English Canadians and served the additional purpose of branding Americans as aliens.[49] In this fraught view of Canada's southern border, talk of independence from Britain was tantamount to a renunciation of Canada itself. Future prime minister R. B. Bennett declared on the eve of World War I:

> An independent Canada means this, that we Canadians are afraid of responsibility and the obligation of power, afraid to accept the responsibilities of our race and breed; afraid to think that we are Britons, afraid to face the future in the eye.[50]

Whereas the original generation of Canadian Loyalists had stressed "love for the King and our happy constitution" as the primary markers of their Britishness,[51] a century later they were widely commemorated as "the very cream . . . of the British race in America"—the "purest blood" of the old colonies.[52]

The South African War tapped into these racial sensibilities throughout the settler empire. The outbreak of hostilities was greeted with exhilaration in Australia and New Zealand, and in neither case did opposition to the conflict reach the level of intensity of that in Britain. As one newspaper reported in rural Australia:

> The vigour with which . . . an Englishman can and does criticise the Government policy in South Africa would be a source of infinite discomfort if not positive danger to him in New South Wales . . . We are more imperial than the British, more ready to bristle up against any daring critic than Birmingham.[53]

Australia's pre-eminent balladist, A. B. Patterson, captured settler understandings of the conflict in *With French to Kimberley* (1900):

> His column was five thousand strong—all mounted men—and guns:
> There met, beneath the world-wide flag, the world-wide Empire's sons;
> They came to prove to all the earth that kinship conquers space,
> And those who fight the British Isles must fight the British race!

Seen from a colonial perspective, securing the fringes of empire could more easily be portrayed as a legitimate and worthy cause, calling on the combined strength of a unified race. The mere fact that the empire seemed to be responding as one people offered reassurance to the thinly dispersed communities of Australia and New Zealand, regardless of the merits of the dispute. One New Zealand Member of Parliament frankly conceded: "I do not know what the quarrel is, but I believe our case to be just."[54] The situation was somewhat different in Canada, where Francophone sensibilities were generally opposed to sending troops to imperial wars. Premier Wilfred Laurier was initially reluctant to commit himself, claiming that the South African conflict posed no danger to Canada. But he was soon compelled by a surge of English-Canadian race nationalism to despatch an official contingent. This provoked an immediate reaction in Quebec, with government backbencher Henri Bourassa resigning his seat in protest. Although Bourassa's name was to become synonymous with Francophone nationalism, in his resignation letter he stressed the betrayal of British principles: "The principle at stake is the prize axiom of British liberalism: No Taxation Without Representation. And the tax in blood constitutes the heaviest form of public contributions."[55] He later complained in the House of Commons that "we are not yet imbued with the real British spirit of self-government."[56]

Bourassa's protest illustrates that the language and rhetoric of Britishness was not the exclusive preserve of Anglo-Saxon race nationalism. Donal Lowry has argued that "ethnic outsiders could and frequently did" feel a "profound sense of loyalty to the Crown and Empire." Laurier himself proclaimed the benefits of the British flag "which floats over our heads without a single British soldier in the country to defend it, its sole defence resting in the gratitude which we owe it to our freedom."[57] Similarly, a minority of Cape Afrikaners maintained a somewhat strained loyalty to the empire during the South African War. Ethnic and racial accommodation could even extend to the indigenous peoples of southern Africa. As Andrew Thompson points out, "Blacks and Coloureds developed their own strains of Loyalist ideology, which saw the Crown as a source of protection against the machinations of labour- and land-hungry settler politicians."[58] This mirrored developments in Australia, where from as early as 1846 Aboriginal peoples developed the habit of petitioning Queen Victoria to redress settler abuses of British sovereignty, often adopting the language and sentiments of loyal subjects.[59] And in an entirely different context, the history of the Indian National Congress reveals the stories of any number of educated nationalist leaders who started their careers as moderates and British Loyalists of one kind or another.

While Thompson is right to stress the "fluidity and hybridity" of imperial identities, and to caution against "the temptation to equate loyalism with 'Anglo-Saxon Imperialism,'" this should not come at the cost of obscuring the pervasive appeal of ethnic identification in the white-settler empire. Imperial Britishness was sufficiently elastic to allow certain ethnic outsiders to lay claim to a British identity, but these groups were rarely accepted fully (or even partially in most instances) by the "core" Anglo-Saxon constituency. For all Bourassa's talk about "British" principles, he was widely regarded as a traitor and a scoundrel among English Canadians. Similarly, the Cape Afrikaner Loyalists rightly protested that their loyalty went unacknowledged and unrewarded. Alfred Milner was deeply suspicious of Afrikaner Loyalism—a view which Rudyard Kipling apparently shared.[60] And in Australia, while Aborigines were classed as British subjects for the purposes of legitimating British sovereignty, no Aborigine was ever taken seriously as a "fellow Briton," no matter how loudly they may have professed loyalty to the Queen.

Racialized conceptions of Britishness were even more rigid and absolute in settings where the British population was clearly in the minority. For British settler communities in Chinese Treaty ports such as Shanghai, race was the "defining constant" in their dealings with outsiders and their self-perception as a coherent group. This produced its own peculiar culture of rites and taboos vis-à-vis the local Chinese, not least in the realm of sexual conduct. As Robert Bickers argues, although these rules were often more honoured in the breach, the perpetrators "knew that what they were doing was rule breaking: they knew that there were rules and they knew what they were." More to the point, these rules applied equally to Indians recruited to China as merchants, police, and nightwatchmen, despite being nominally afforded "British" protection.[61] Similar customs proliferated in Kenya and Rhodesia, where the social distance between Africans and British settlers was rigidly maintained as a means of alleviating their constant physical proximity. Dane Kennedy has shown how the veneer of settler self-confidence disguised deeper anxieties about African "savagery." This produced a distinctive variant of settler Britishness, in which the highly ritualized observance of racial boundaries was not only a means of harnessing cheap labor, but also a form of "emotional gratification." Indeed, some of these customs were positively inimical to labour efficiency, such as the extraordinary settler aversion to conversing with Africans in English (most preferring to use pidgin variants of Swahili, Matabele, or Mashona even with their own servants, despite the constant misunderstandings that inevitably ensued). These habits were predicated on an absolute demarcation of the boundaries of imperial identities, and a settler insistence "that a basic biological gap separated themselves from Africans."[62]

Similarly in India, ethnic outsiders were kept at arm's length regardless of their "loyal" credentials, as Mrinalini Sinha's study of Britishness and "clubbability" in colonial society amply illustrates. She quotes one vernacular Bengali newspaper from 1883: "a native may adopt English customs, wear the English dress, change his paternal name, and move in English society with his wife, yet nothing can lead the Englishman to think that a native is his equal." While colonial clubs were ostensibly run along metropolitan lines, their colonial setting invested them with a distinctive function of "fashioning a white British self."[63] To the extent that the boundaries of imperial Britishness in India were blurred, this related more to relations between Raj society and mixed-race "Anglo-Indians." It was more common, for example, for ethnic whites to suffer exclusion on socioeconomic or mixed-racial grounds, than for ethnic outsiders to be granted equality of status.[64] In short, "non-ethnic" strains of loyalism rarely resonated mutually, and this placed clear limitations on the more fluid, hybrid versions of Britishness that prevailed in the Victorian and Edwardian empire.

A further complication arises from the fact that the empire was not monolithic in its appeal, even to the most ardent race nationalists. This same era also saw the emergence of more localized attachments to regional identities, and early indications of what was termed "colonial nationalism." Marcus Clarke predicted in *The Future Australian Race* (1877) that the "best bone and sinew of Cornwall, the best muscle of Yorkshire, the keenest brains of Cockneydom," would combine with the balmy Australian climate and healthier diet to produce "the making of a great nation."[65] In Canada, it was the beneficial effects of the northern winter that was said to produce a more virile and virtuous character. Medical authorities claimed that the climate would produce a "*Canadian* people . . . a taller, straighter, leaner people—hair darker and drier and coarser; muscles more tendinous and prominent and less cushioned."[66] These ideas carried clear masculinist overtones—it was rarely the frontier woman who was celebrated as a new colonial breed. On the contrary, as Marilyn Lake has argued, the "politics of respectability" rendered problematic the notion that colonial women might deviate from the received standards of metropolitan domesticity. But largely because of these gendered assumptions, the frontier became the object of a masculine fantasy—a place where colonial men might liberate themselves from the domestic drudgery of the old world.[67]

Ideas about the vast colonial landscape as the cradle of new nationhood found expression in the popular verse and prose of the Sydney *Bulletin*, the *plein air* landscapes of the "Heidelberg" school in Victoria, and later in the work of the "Group of Seven" painters in Canada, with their emphasis on the "pristine and replenishing air which sweeps out of that great hinterland."[68] Similarly in New Zealand, it was claimed that the country's "insular position must assist in the development of a national type." Here again it was the environment and local scenery that brought the promise of a national culture "fired with the beauty and bloom of the native bush and . . . the cluck of weka and kiwi and the harsher note of the kakariki and kaka."[69] In the reconstruction era in South Africa, nativist themes were prominent in the journal *The State*, and framed the essential South-Africanness of Sir Percy Fitzpatrick's highly popular 1907 novel *Jock of the Bushveld*, with its "cast of rugged characters."[70] It was with these expressions of local pride and provincial self-assertion in mind that the influential author and journalist, Richard Jebb, following an extended sojourn in the settler colonies at the turn of the century, famously declared that "new nations are bursting the colonial chrysalis."[71]

For a later generation of historians, this era came to represent the key to unlocking the dynamic of identity-formation in the British settler-colonies. An early phase of imperial false consciousness, it was widely claimed, gradually gave way to a new, more authentically "national" self-awareness. According to this model, separation from the imperial metropole was the inevitable outcome of a relationship where Britain was the "mother country" and the colony was "the child who reaches maturity, flexes its muscles and engages in several other pleasing metaphors."[72] As such, imperial patriotism and colonial nationalism were interpreted as inherently conflicting identities within settler societies, perhaps even indicative of rival social groupings, with the former bound by natural law to give way to the latter. Carl Berger sought to correct this tendency in the early 1970s in his depiction of Canadian imperialism as "one variety of Canadian nationalism—a type of awareness of nationality which rested upon a certain understanding of history, the national character, and the national mission." Berger's model challenged the received wisdom that imperial patriotism "did not grow out of the Canadian soil," but it left open the possibility that Canadian imperialism was inherently at odds with other "varieties of Canadian nationalism" that sought separation from the parent state.[73]

It was on this point that Berger, in turn, was challenged by Douglas Cole, who questioned whether "colonial nationalism" deserved the label of "nationalism" at all. He drew a distinction between "nationalism" on the one hand—embodying an ethnic, linguistic, and cultural community—and a more localized "patriotism" on the other, which expressed affection for a homeland and its inhabitants, but which stopped short of an exclusive, self-sufficient folk myth. He argued that, for Australians and Canadians (and by extension, New Zealanders and the various British settler communities in Africa) it was the worldwide community of the British race—or "Britannic nationalism" as he termed it—that possessed all of "the most potent elements for nationhood—language, origin, cultural heritage, common loyalty, the inspiration of past achievement, a foreign menace" and so on.[74] What had often been mistaken for "colonial nationalism," he claimed, was really an expression of pride of place and community of interest. Or as he put in the case of English Canadians, "there is a recognition of a distinction of interest between the Canadian state and the United Kingdom, and a feeling that colonial status is humiliating, but not a feeling that Canadians constitute a new ethnic group."[75] His fundamental point was that colonial and imperial identities could not be conceived as rival expressions of nationalism because the former remained "vitally dependent" on the latter for its primary categories of inclusion and exclusion.[76] As such, it made no sense to understand the demise of "Greater Britain" in the twentieth century in terms of the full flowering of self-sufficient colonial national identities.

Cole's nomenclature raises difficulties, because contemporaries did not distinguish rigidly between "nationalism" and "patriotism" in the same way. On the contrary, these terms were used interchangeably, and blurred easily with other concepts such as "race," "loyalty," and "empire." But there is something to be said for treating local patriotic sentiments as part of a continuum with the wider ethnic and cultural identification with the British world. The founding father of Australian Federation, Henry Parkes, for example, appealed to the "crimson thread of kinship" as the common bond uniting all Australians. For Parkes, the sole criteria of who was (and was not) entitled to a stake in the new nation was the ethnic and cultural ties to the old world. Or as Prime Minister of the new Commonwealth of Australia, Alfred Deakin, put it a decade later: "The same ties of blood, sympathy, history and tradition which make us one Commonwealth here, make the British of to-day one people everywhere."[77] In Canada, the 1884 Centennial of the Settlement of Upper Canada brought forth a torrent of rhetoric extolling the virtues of the founders of the Canadian nation, while at the same time honouring their commitment to remaining British. The Chancellor of Trinity College, Toronto and member of the Canadian Senate, G. A. Allan, intoned:

> I yield to no one in my love for my native country. The very soil of Canada is dear to me. I love her lakes and forests, her mighty rivers, her broad and fertile fields. I am proud of the past history of my country . . . the fitness our people have displayed for free and constitutional government, and that observance of law and order which is the noblest characteristic of the Anglo-Saxon race. But all this is entirely consistent with a deep and abiding love and attachment to the Motherland, whose glorious traditions we inherit, and which are the common property of every subject of the empire.[78]

Allan emphasized the physical features of soil, climate, and geography when speaking of his affection for Canada, but resorted to the language of loyalty, liberty and Britishness in conveying a sense of the people. The same can be said of Sir Percy Fitzpatrick, who identified fiercely with South Africa as "home" while adhering to a Milnerite conception of imperial community.[79]

This is not to say that these self-styled colonial Britons were unable to distinguish themselves as a social grouping from their metropolitan (or for that matter fellow settler-colonial) counterparts. It is simply that they did so in ways that were compatible with the idea of an overarching ethnic and cultural unity. New Zealand accounts of the South African War, for example, were quick to emphasize the outstanding physical and martial attributes of the New Zealand Mounted Rifles vis-à-vis the British regulars, or their temperance and moral bearing compared to the undisciplined Australians.[80] But none of this suggested an independent destiny for an exclusive New Zealand "volk." In Australia, the same tendencies were mirrored in the writings of C. E. W. Bean—chief promoter of the "ANZAC legend" and tireless chronicler of Australian national distinctiveness. In his 1910 travelogue, *On the Wool Track*, he lauded the Australian bushman's "extraordinary versatility, the capacity to do anything," but went on to explain that this special quality "obviously exists pre-eminently in the British race. But it does not come out till the race gets to places like Australia, where it has to."[81] Bean's love for Australia was an extension of his race nationalism—his idealized Australian warrior was a tribute to the fact that "Australia is as purely British as the people of Great Britain—perhaps more so."[82]

The converse of this was that British migrants to the dominions were often reminded that they were somehow a lesser breed. One Montreal resident wrote in a letter to *The Times* that "Canada is a land for a superior and conquering type, the picked, strong, diamond edged kind of man . . . Any Britisher who thinks of going out there should be able to measure up."[83] In Canada, concerns about the fitness and moral fibre of urban-bred, working class Britons led to calls for a greater proportion of rural migrants, or even restriction of migration altogether. But as Janice Cavell argues, this was not so much a case of burgeoning Canadian nationalism, as a closing of ranks against "a serious threat to Britishness as Canadians understood it."[84] This ambivalence toward new British migrants was encapsulated in the New Zealand custom of disparaging recent arrivals as "homies." The term simultaneously branded the newcomers as outsiders, while at the same time acknowledging that they were anything but "foreigners."[85]

An Empire of Irreconcilable Interests

Even Richard Jebb reached the conclusion that what he termed "colonial nationalism" posed no inherent threat to imperial cohesion, so long as the settler communities of Australia, Canada, New Zealand, and South Africa were never presented with a stark choice between imperial federation and separatism. He saw no inconsistency in championing the "separate national aspirations" of the dominions while at the same time celebrating the "Soul of the Empire"—on the contrary he insisted that the former was a precondition of the latter. He observed that the nature of "Colonial loyalty" had undergone subtle changes, and was increasingly embraced "in proportion as it subserves the interests and ideals of separate nationalism."[86] Or in other words, the British "soul" incorporated a wide variety of interpretations of the meaning and utility of imperial Britishness. In order for the overarching sense of unity to flourish, it was necessary that the policies, practices, and institutions of empire should be sufficiently flexible as to support a variety of often conflicting interests. Herein lies a more plausible explanation for the unraveling of imperial identities in the twentieth century.

Jebb's fundamental problem had been a recurring feature of imperial relations for generations. During the Crimean War, for example, the Australian Republican John Dunmore Lang expressed his grave doubts "whether Britain now would be able in times of war to defend all her numerous colonies."[87] An expectation that "British interests" would coincide happily with the community of race and culture frequently fell foul of the realities of a highly dispersed empire. John A. MacDonald may be best remembered for his determination to preserve Canada's Britishness in the face of the threat of American domination, but he also worked tirelessly to secure Canadian autonomy from the interference of Westminster. The same goes for the Cape colonists, who in the immediate aftermath of the South African War staunchly resisted Alfred Milner's plans to suspend the Cape constitution—a move widely resented as a "raid upon the liberties of this country."[88] As Neville Meaney has observed in an Australian context, experience had shown "that there was no natural coincidence of interests, or at the least that such a coincidence could not be relied upon."[89]

For Meaney, it was the tensions and contradictions between an imperial "community of culture," and the more narrow delineation of a colonial "community of interest" that provided the key co-ordinates of settler identity formation.[90] It was because of these tensions that the "imperial federation" movement failed to make significant inroads in any of the settler colonies. The idea of forming an imperial parliament as the embodiment of the aspirations of the British race around the globe first emerged in the 1880s and remained alive until World War I. Although an Imperial Federation

League was formed, with branches in virtually all of the settler colonies, the idea was never more than an abstraction. The mere suggestion that colonial interests might be legislated from London invited nagging doubts about the capacity of metropolitan leaders to identify fully with the multifarious interests of the British world.

World War I had the effect of affirming the instinctive "community of culture," while at the same time aggravating rival conceptions of the "community of interest." While there was little significant opposition in Australia, New Zealand, or English-speaking Canada and South Africa to the idea that the dominions were duty bound to rally to the cause, considerable disagreement emerged over how the dominions might influence the conduct of the war effort. Lloyd George's Imperial War Cabinet was an ad hoc expedient which brought little satisfaction, with Billy Hughes—ever anxious about Australia's exposed position in the Pacific—demanding a more formal, better structured mechanism for imperial co-operation. At the other extreme, sections of Canadian opinion feared that any kind of Canadian participation in a common imperial policy would tend to undermine Canadian sovereignty.[91] R. F. Holland suggests that the failure to solve the problem of minimal dominion input in operational matters served to "differentiate 'British' identities," and "made Dominion policy-makers all the more determined to protect the confined realm over which they presided."[92] This was clearly in evidence at the 1917 Imperial Conference in London, where dominion leaders called for "full recognition of the Dominions as autonomous nations of an Imperial Commonwealth," and the right "to an adequate voice in foreign policy."

These pressures carried over into the imperial conferences of the 1920s, culminating in the Balfour Declaration of 1926 (which defined the dominions as "autonomous communities within the British Empire, equal in status, and in no way subordinate one to another in any aspect of their domestic or external affairs") and the Statute of Westminster of 1931, which set the seal on the devolution of legislative authority from Westminster. The dominions were now formally "independent" but only in the Irish Free State and South Africa could this be said to have been the product of a self-sufficient, unifying national myth. In neither case, however, was nationalist separatism rooted in a break-away British settler community striving for maturity from the parent state. Rather, it was the ready availability of an alternate, non-British ethnic community that provided the main impetus for change. In the case of South Africa, World War I had witnessed the emergence of a more strident Afrikaner nationalism under the influence of J. B. M. Herzog, who saw the British as foreigners and oppressors. It was Herzog who gave South Africa its own flag in 1927, amidst bitter opposition from the British minority, and who took every opportunity to promote South Africa's independence vis-à-vis the empire, not least on the question of wartime neutrality. In Ireland the situation was more complex, and cannot easily be comprehended within a settler-colonial nationalist framework. What is significant, however, is that Republicans drew on a rhetoric and symbolism that underlined their ethnic difference from "the Saxon foe" (in the words of the Republican "anthem," *The Soldier's Song*). The revival of the Irish language as a political symbol was a crucial plank in this strategy, as was the use of symbols like the harp and the tricolor. Yet the civil war that occasioned the birth of the Irish Free State rendered the national myth-making process shaky and ambivalent. Both the pro- and anti-Treaty factions claimed the mantle of nation-builders, and thus held rival stakes in the history and symbolism of Irish nationalism. The 1920s were thus marked by a series of heated disputes in which "Republicans quarrelled with Free Staters over the right to use Sinn Féin's symbols, while ex-unionists . . . lamented the replacement of their symbols by those of Sinn Féin."[93] As a result, the position of the Free State within the empire in the interwar years was highly ambivalent, and cannot easily be characterized as a robust new nation shaking off the burden of imperialism.

Apart from these two exceptions, the spirit of separatist nationalism trailed significantly behind the legal and constitutional process of carving out separate nation-states. This was particularly so where anti-British separatist feeling was at its strongest, as in South Africa where the English-speaking community rallied aggressively around the British flag—quite literally so in the bloody riots of the late 1920s.[94] More consensual were the New Zealand Centennial celebrations a decade later, where enthusiasm for the British connection was as commonplace as expressions of national pride (indeed the two invariably went together). The Minister responsible for the event noted that it would be too much to expect "a separate national culture" to have developed in less than a hundred years.[95] Interwar Canada, too, showed every sign of an enduring commitment to Empire and Britishness, with intensely loyal organizations like the Orange Lodge and the IODE (International Order Daughters of the Empire) continuing to thrive. The Canadian historian, W. L. Morton, recalled his interwar childhood in Manitoba in terms that encapsulated the distinctive meaning of Britishness in a settler-colonial context:

> British we were, but English in the sense of southern English we never were. On the contrary every English-Canadian in my childhood milieu disliked an English Lord, an Oxford accent, and English style . . . our Britishness, then, was not Englishness, but a local brew which we called Canadian.[96]

Throughout these years, Canadian Liberals and Conservatives continued to debate the meaning and importance of the imperial connection, with prominent figures like John Ewart, O. D. Skelton, and John W. Dafoe warning of the danger the empire posed to Canadian autonomy. Yet even the most trenchant critics of empire could stress the "moral unity" of the British people and "an instinctive sense of a common destiny."[97] As Simon Potter concludes, these disagreements were not so much about the fate of "Britishness" in English Canada per se, but "a more basic difference of opinion over how far Canadian and British interests were compatible."[98]

In some respects, the interwar years were characterized by a determination to make good the logic of the Balfour Declaration—to nurture and preserve a Greater British community of culture while recognizing that separate statehood placed clear limitations on the imperial community of interest. This logic could function effectively so long as there were sufficient grounds to believe that the divergence of interest could be managed and resolved within an overarching scheme of common objectives and aspirations. And in the interwar years there was much to go on in this respect—empire co-operation and interdependence in migration policies, capital investments, security policies, and trade and tariff regulations were often remarkably harmonious, as evidenced by the imperial preference arrangements that emerged from the 1932 Ottawa Conference. And any doubts about the capacity of the British World to respond as a single entity to an external crisis were (temporarily) dispelled by the onset of World War II.

It was only into the post-war era, with the collapse of British imperial power and a profound reorientation of British priorities towards Europe, that the myth of Greater Britain unravelled completely—a process that Jim Davidson has termed "De-dominionisation."[99] It is a phenomenon that is not yet fully understood, and only recently have the muddied waters of a generation of nationalist-inspired historiography begun to clear. The impetus came from many sources—at times from the dominions themselves (Canada's move towards separate citizenship in the 1940s, or South Africa's withdrawal from the Commonwealth in 1961) while at other times it was the British government that set the pace (Harold Macmillan's "Wind of Change" policies in Africa, and the general downgrading of the Commonwealth that was implicit in his bid for EEC membership in 1961). In each instance, what became clear was that the imperative of imperial unity could no longer restrain the centrifugal tendencies in an empire of irreconcilable interests. Macmillan slowly came to an awareness of this, recording in his diary in September 1962 amid the clamour of Commonwealth complaint over his EEC aspirations: "It is ironical to hear countries which have abused us for years now beseeching us not to abandon them. The thought that UK might declare herself independent seems so novel as to be quite alarming."[100] Symbolically, Macmillan had taken the initiative the previous year to reclaim the term "British" (for diplomatic purposes) exclusively for "UK" usage.[101]

Among the erstwhile "Dominions," the loosening of ties to Britain was welcomed in some quarters as a unique opportunity to forge a "new nationalism."[102] But it is equally clear that the break-up of the British world was wholly unwelcome to millions of self-styled "Britishers," and caused considerable anxiety and disorientation. In Canada, for example, the move to establish a separate Canadian nationality in the 1940s sparked a long-running and heated debate about the importance of being British. Even something as innocuous as the appointment of the first Canadian-born Governor-General (Vincent Massey in 1952) brought howls of protest, with the *Calgary Herald* describing it as "a drab and melancholy milestone in Canadian history" imposed on the people by a "stealthy, furtive, weak-willed and knavish" government in Ottawa.[103] These sentiments were voiced across a range of issues, from the diminishing official use of the term "dominion," to the St Laurent government's opposition to Britain's actions at Suez in 1956. The culmination was the flag debate of 1964, when Opposition Leader John Diefenbaker fought a rearguard action against the Pearson government's Maple Leaf design, insisting that the new flag must preserve a place for the Union Jack. For a large section of English Canadian opinion, the packing away of the symbols and sentiments of Britishness implied the spiritual redundancy of Canada itself.

A similar pattern emerged in Australia and New Zealand, although the context and causation was somewhat different. Issues of economic and defense co-operation had a special capacity to arouse concern because of the ongoing importance of the British defense guarantee and Commonwealth trade preferences. Thus, when the Wilson government announced its decision to withdraw all British service personnel from "East of Suez," the significance was immediately apparent. Newspapers in Melbourne and Sydney reacted to the news with headlines that were almost apocalyptic in tone. "Waken to our peril" was the verdict of the *Melbourne Herald*, while in Sydney the *Daily Mirror* wrote of a "Far East Death Warrant."[104] The *Auckland Star* was more sentimental:

> The enthusiasm for Kipling, the nostalgia for the "sun-shine an' the palm trees an' the tinkly temple bells" has dwindled. Oddly enough, the Kipling spirit seems to be kept alive more by non-Britons than the British themselves. Who was most shocked by Mr Wilson's announcement this week? . . . If anyone received a traumatic shock it was in this part of the world, not in Britain.[105]

New Zealanders were more ill at ease over the successive attempts by British governments to join the European Economic Community. What was at stake was more than the livelihood of the New Zealand pastoral industry (as critical as this was). As J. G. A. Pocock explains:

> We were to learn that you [Britain] cared as little for our past as for our future. What you did, of course, was irrevocably and unilaterally to disrupt a concept of Britishness which we had supposed that we share with you . . . In effect, you threw your identity, as well as ours, into a condition of contingency.[106]

In South Africa, the situation was markedly different in the light of the triumph of Afrikaner nationalism at the 1948 election. Here, as Thompson remarks, the "British" community increasingly looked like "a cultural minority struggling to find a home in an 'Afrikanerized' South Africa."[107] The Republican referendum of 1960, and the subsequent withdrawal of South Africa from the Commonwealth the following year, were shocking and traumatic events, but they came at a time when South African "Britishness" had long since lost its credibility. The opposite was the case, however, for the white Rhodesian community of the Central African Federation. Here, Macmillan's "Wind of Change" speech of January 1960 brought unwelcome repercussions and bitter recriminations. The Federation required the support of the British government to resist secessionist pressures from African nationalists in Northern Rhodesia and Nyasaland, and Rhodesian leaders frequently resorted to the language of loyalism as a means of securing it. By the 1960s, however, appeals to the integrity of the race were of dubious legitimacy. Race had become a liability for the "British" Rhodesians, particularly in their ambition to secure an independent constitution under white minority rule. The British government's unwillingness to meet these demands culminated in the Unilateral Declaration of Independence of Ian Smith's Rhodesian Front Government in November 1965. Modelling their text on the American Declaration of Independence of 1776, the Rhodesian rebels deliberately drew a parallel between their own plight and the feelings of unrequited loyalty of Jefferson, Franklin and the generation of "thwarted Britons" of the 1770s. But in a new twist, Smith issued a further statement:

If Sir Winston Churchill were alive today, I believe he would probably emigrate to Rhodesia—because I believe that all those admirable qualities and characteristics of the British that we believed in, loved and preached to our children, no longer exist in Britain.[108]

If the Americans rebels in 1776 had "ceased being 'British' when they could not be 'British' as they understood the term,"[109] then for Smith and his followers, it was the United Kingdom that had "ceased being British" when it failed to live up to the Rhodesian version of the "Greater British" ideal.

At a time when Enoch Powell was eagerly promoting the resurgence of Englishness, it is an open question whether Britain did indeed "cease to be British" at Empire's end. But it is beyond dispute that the self-styled "British" communities around the globe had been transformed by the complex processes of imperial decline. By the end of the 1960s, the rhetoric, rituals, and civic culture of Greater Britain had gone the way of the American colonies two hundred years earlier—up to a point. The Americans had framed their British identities primarily (but not exclusively) in terms of a discourse of rights and freedoms, which could be successfully repackaged and promoted as the core ingredient of a new, self-sufficient American national myth. But for the later generation of neo-Britains whose imperial identities had been filtered through the prism of race nationalism (again, not exclusively), there was no ready-made, alternate ethnic myth to help reconstitute their idea of nationhood. Having never struggled for their independence, these English-speaking communities were forced to rely on ambiguous emblems of place (maple leaves, beavers, kiwis, and boxing kangaroos) and tenuous generalizations about a distinctive "way of life" as the hallmarks of their nationhood. It is no coincidence that "multiculturalism" was formally adopted as a civic ideal by Canadian and Australian governments in the immediate wake of imperial decline. The celebration of a uniquely harmonious, multi-ethnic social composition was a creative and ingenious way of dealing with the post-imperial ethnic void.[110] In the meantime, the annual national holidays of Canada, Australia, and New Zealand since the 1960s have been characterized by an almost ritualized questioning of the national identity (as in: "do we have one?").[111] While this may be part of a more general postmodern condition in a world where nationalism has run its course as the primary means of harnessing individual and group loyalties to the state, it nonetheless bears the imprint of a peculiar imperial legacy in these former "dominions." In the very nature of its demise and its ambivalent afterlife, "Britishness became a reality abroad in ways it never did at home."[112]

Notes

1   Many thanks to Carl Pedersen and Simon Potter for reading and commenting on an earlier draft.
2   See Colley, *Britons*; Samuel, *Patriotism*.
3   Porter, *Absent-Minded Imperialists*, pp. 165, 253.
4   Hopkins, "Back to the future," p. 216.
5   The literature is steadily growing, but a useful starting point is Bridge and Fedorowich (eds), *British World*.

6 P. D. Morgan, "Encounters," p. 49.

7 Zuckerman, "Identity in British America," p. 115.

8 Greene, "American Revolution."

9 Quoted Breen, "Ideology and Nationalism," p. 29.

10 S. Jenyns, *Objection to the Taxation of our American Colonies by the legislature of Great Britain, briefly Consider'd* (London, 1765), p. 8.

11 See Marshall, "Nation defined by empire," p. 220; also Breen, "Ideology and nationalism," pp. 30–1.

12 Gould, *Persistence of Empire*, p. 133.

13 Marshall, "Nation defined by empire," pp. 216, 220.

14 Breen, "Ideology and nationalism," p. 37.

15 *Ibid.*, p. 39.

16 G. S. Wood, *Americanization of Benjamin Franklin*, p. 150.

17 Breen, "Ideology and nationalism," p. 34. See also Conway, "Fellow-nationals."

18 Pocock, *Discovery of Islands*, p. 182.

19 O'Shaughnessy, *Empire Divided*, p. 4.

20 Quoted Mills, *Idea of Loyalty*, pp. 16–17.

21 Paquet and Wallot, "Nouvelle France," pp. 111, 101.

22 S. F. Wise, quoted Errington and Rawlyk, "Creating a British-American Political Community," p. 188.

23 Morton, *Canadian Identity*, p. 23.

24 Calhoon *et al.* (eds), *Loyalists and Community*, p. 2.

25 See Errington and Rawlyk, "Creating a British-American political community," pp. 188–9.

26 Mills, *Idea of Loyalty*, p. 17.

27 Lester, *Imperial Networks*, p. 63.

28 John Mitford Bowker, quoted Lester, *Imperial Networks*, p. 66.

29 See Lester, "British settler discourse," pp. 25, 33, 39.

30 Quoted Belich, *Making Peoples*, p. 187.

31 Moon, *Path to the Treaty of Waitangi*, pp. 55–6, ch. 3.

32 Quoted Belich, *New Zealand Wars*, p. 315.

33 1860, quoted Belich, *New Zealand Wars*, p. 314.

34 Belich, *New Zealand Wars*, p. 318.

35 See G. Morris, "James Prendergast."

36 Hall, *Civilising Subjects*, p. 338.

37 B. Anderson, *Imagined Communities*, p. 36.

38 Dawson, "On the present state of Europe," 1849 lecture quoted Hall, *Civilising Subjects*, p. 365.

39 Dilke, *Greater Britain*, pp. vii–viii.

40 Seeley, *Expansion*, pp. 11, 301–2.

41 *The Times*, July 25, 1925.

42 Mandler, "Mid-Victorian thought," p. 230.

43 Bickford-Smith, *Ethnic Pride and Racial Prejudice*, p. 78.

44 *Ibid.*, pp. 134–5.

45 Quoted Meaney (ed.), *Under New Heavens*, p. 398. Meaney demonstrates that in Australia, too, a prior emphasis on settler rights and constitutional principles gave way to a more racialized conception of Britishness from roughly mid-century.

46 Pearson, *National Life and Character*, pp. 41, 90.

47 Quoted Cole, "Crimson thread," pp. 515–16.

48 Published in Toronto.
49 Wood, "Defining 'Canadian'."
50 Quoted Francis, *National Dreams*, p. 63.
51 Upper Canadian Anglican clergyman John Strachan, quoted Mills, *Idea of Loyalty*, p. 27.
52 Quoted Berger, *Sense of Power*, p. 99.
53 *Evening Penny Post* (Goulburn), Feb. 22, Mar. 16, 1900.
54 Crawford and McGibbon (eds), *One Flag*, pp. 3, 9.
55 Quoted Monet, "Canada," p. 166.
56 *Ibid.*, p. 171.
57 Lowry, "Empire loyalism," pp. 99, 104.
58 Thompson, "Languages of Loyalism," p. 635.
59 See McKenna, *This Country*, pp. 65–8.
60 Kipling paid a visit to Milner at the Cape and, according to the latter, "saw through that utter imposture, the simple-minded Boer patriot, dear to the imagination of British radicals." See Tamarkin, "Cape Afrikaners," pp. 126–7.
61 Bickers, *Britain in China*, pp. 71–2.
62 D. Kennedy, *Islands of White*, pp. 155, 164.
63 Sinha, "Clubbability," pp. 514–15, 504.
64 Buettner, *Empire Families*, ch. 2; Sinha, "Clubbability," p. 501, 505.
65 Clark, *Future Australian Race*, pp. 14–16.
66 Quoted Berger, *Sense of Power*, p. 129.
67 Lake, "Politics of Respectability."
68 Lawren Harris, quoted Berger, *Sense of Power*, p. 133.
69 H. A. Talbot Tubbs and C. Stuart Ross, quoted K. Sinclair, *Destiny Apart*, p. 49.
70 Dubow, "Colonial Nationalism," pp. 72–3.
71 Quoted Eddy and Schreuder (eds), *Rise of Colonial Nationalism*, p. 1.
72 As critiqued by McQueen, *New Britannia*, p. 21. Philip Buckner has commented on these tendencies in Canadian historiography in "Whatever happened to the British Empire." See also Neville Meaney's critique of the "thwarted nationalism" thesis in Australia in "Britishness and Australian identity."
73 Berger, *Sense of Power*, pp. 8, 9.
74 Cole, "Problem of 'nationalism'," p. 178.
75 *Ibid.*, p. 166.
76 Cole, "Crimson thread," p. 523.
77 *Ibid.*, p. 522.
78 United Empire Loyalist Centennial Committee, *Centennial of the Settlement*, p. 61.
79 Dubow, "Colonial nationalism," pp. 73–4.
80 Crawford, "Impact of the war," pp. 206–10.
81 Bean, *On the Wool Track*, pp. 146–7.
82 *Ibid.*, p. 139.
83 Cavell, "Imperial race," p. 362.
84 *Ibid.*, p. 350.
85 Sinclair, *Destiny Apart*, pp. 104–6.
86 Jebb, *Colonial Nationalism*, pp. vii, 1–2, 327.
87 *Sydney Morning Herald*, May 23, 1854.
88 Cape Opposition Leader John X. Merriman, quoted Dubow, "Colonial nationalism," p. 56.
89 Meaney, "Britishness and Australian identity," p. 85.

90 This distinction was originally developed in Meaney's *Search for Security*, pp. 3–7.

91 See Potter, "Richard Jebb," pp. 16–18.

92 Holland, "British Empire and the Great War," pp. 129–30.

93 Morris, *Our Own Devices*, p. 219.

94 Saker, *South African Flag Controversy*.

95 Quoted Renwick (ed.), *Creating a National Spirit*, p. 15.

96 Quoted Buckner, "Long Goodbye," p. 191.

97 Dafoe quoted Cole, "Problem of 'nationalism'," p. 175.

98 Potter, "Richard Jebb," p. 26.

99 See Davidson, "De-dominionisation of Australia"; *id.*, "De-dominionisation revisited."

100 Sept. 12, 1962: Macmillan, *At the End of the Day*, p. 132.

101 It had previously been reserved for the UK and the dominions collectively, but by the 1960s this had fallen into disuse. See Ward, "End of empire," pp. 251–2.

102 The term "new nationalism" was used independently in Canada, Australia, and New Zealand in the 1960s. See Ward, "New nationalism."

103 *Calgary Herald*, Jan. 26, 1952.

104 *Melbourne Herald* and *Daily Mirror*, July 19, 1967, quoted Kristensen, "Still a British country," p. 46.

105 "Not Quite Cricket," *Auckland Star*, Jan. 20, 1968.

106 Pocock, "Contingency, identity, sovereignty," p. 297.

107 Thompson, "Languages of Loyalism," p. 646.

108 Quoted Webster, "There'll always be an England," p. 581.

109 Pocock, cited n. 18 above.

110 Some English South Africans and Rhodesians chose to throw in their lot with Afrikaner race-nationalism. White New Zealanders increasingly adopted the Maori term "Pakeha" to distinguish themselves as a cultural and quasi-ethnic grouping, in a rare inversion of centuries of colonizing practice.

111 As manifested in the countless feature articles and opinion pieces in the pages of the *Globe and Mail*, the *Australian*, and the *New Zealand Herald* (among many others) each year on Jul. 1, Jan. 26, and Feb. 6, respectively.

112 Morgan, "Encounters," p. 45.

Further Reading

Imperial culture and settler identity occupies a vast body of scholarship with any number of potential points of entry. Following the trajectory of the themes sketched out here, one obvious starting point is Linda Colley's *Britons: Forging the Nation*, in which she includes empire alongside religion and war as one of the primary determinants of eighteenth-century British identities.

For the American colonies see Jack. P. Greene's essay on "Empire and identity," in P. J. Marshall (ed.), *OHBE, Vol. 2*. On the ideological underpinnings of the American Revolution, it is useful to contrast Bernard Bailyn's *The Ideological Origins of the American Revolution* with T. H. Breen's more recent *The Marketplace of Revolution*. For an interesting British perspective on the parting of the ways between British and American identities see Stephen Conway, "From fellow-nationals to foreigners."

The varieties of post-revolutionary loyalism can be traced for Canada in Norman Knowles, *Inventing the Loyalists* and for the British West Indies in Andrew Jackson O'Shaughnessy, *An Empire Divided*.

Settler identities and the encounter with indigenous peoples are usefully surveyed, albeit with an American emphasis, in M. Daunton and R. Halpern (eds), *Empire and Others*. On the Cape Colony see Alan Lester, *Imperial Networks* and for New Zealand James Belich, *The New Zealand Wars and the Victorian Interpretation of Racial Conflict*. The Australian experience of frontier conflict has been documented in a series of books by Henry Reynolds and a host of others, but see, for example, Henry Reynolds, *Frontier*.

On humanitarianism and the emergence of mid-Victorian race nationalism, the debate in metropolitan Britain can be easily accessed by comparing Catherine Hall, *Civilising Subjects* with Peter Mandler, *The English National Character*. For the settler colonies there is no single, all-encompassing work, but for South Africa see Clifton C. Crais, *White Supremacy and Black Resistance in Pre-industrial South Africa*; and for Kenya and Rhodesia, Dane Kennedy, *Islands of White*. Empire and race nationalism in Australia has been examined in a series of essays by Neville Meaney, the most recent of which is "In History's page: Identity and myth" in Deryck M. Schreuder and Stuart Ward (eds), *Australia's Empire* (Oxford, forthcoming).

The problem of "colonial nationalism" continues to draw debate. Critics notwithstanding, a useful place to begin is Douglas Cole's "The problem of 'nationalism' and 'imperialism' in British settlement colonies." Neville Meaney's thesis on the role of the "community of interest" in forging separate settler nationalities is best summarized in Neville Meaney, "Britishness and Australian identity: The problem of nationalism in Australian history and historiography."

Attempts to integrate the historical experiences across the many British settler communities is beginning to emerge within the new "British World" historiography. Three recent examples are Carl Bridge and Kent Fedorowich (eds), *The British World: Diaspora, Culture and Identity* (2003); Philip Buckner and Doug Francis (eds), *Rediscovering the British World* (2005); and Kate Darian-Smith, Patricia Grimshaw and Stuart Macintyre (eds), *Britishness Abroad: Transnational Movements and Imperial Cultures* (2007).

11

Agency, Narrative, and Resistance

Jon E. Wilson

Since at least the early 1990s, the concept of agency has been central to the historical study of colonial societies. But the term "agency" is a perplexing one. An agent is a person that does something, a person or thing that "produces an effect," as the *Oxford English Dictionary* puts it. Sometimes, it refers to someone who acts on behalf of another, the agent of a business for example. But in another sense, the sense that historians and other scholars of colonial societies have used the word recently, agency is the free capacity people have to do things for themselves. The concept of agency describes how people have the power to act in a self-directed way, to put their own aims and objectives into practice, rather than being the victims of someone else's designs. If a laborer picks cotton for fear of violence or starvation she does not exert her own agency in doing so. But if she consciously goes against the wishes of her master, and deliberately ploughs the field badly or runs away, it is much easier to show that she was acting on her own behalf, and so exercising agency.

"Agency" is not a clearly definable concept with a single meaning, more a cluster of notions that share resemblances and similarities. Rather than trying to define it, this chapter will show how the concept has been used in different circumstances by scholars, and what the implications of these uses are. In many of its uses, the concept of "agency" has two elements. First of all, there is a cognitive component: "agency" refers to the way people think about what they do. The term describes a subject's ability to think for themselves and tell stories about their own actions which are not given to them by other people. Instead, those stories are developed from within "their own" culture that places them at the center of their own worlds. Secondly though, the idea of agency denotes action itself. Historians and others using the term assume that "agency" occurs when stories about action are put into practice, when talking stops and the subject has real causal power to change the world they live within a little.

For more than a decade now the attempt to discover the "agency" of non-European subjects of colonialism has been an important—perhaps the most important—theme in the historical study of colonial societies. Whether they have been successful or not, scholars have sought to identify both the narrative voice and active causal power of people who they perceive as marginalized or downtrodden. They have attempted to make the "subaltern"—the subordinated—the "sovereign subject of history, to listen to their voices, [and] take their experience and thoughts . . . seriously."[1] In doing so, historians and others aim to show that "colonized subjects [we]re not passively produced by hegemonic projects but are active agents whose choices and discourses are of fundamental importance in the formation of their societies," as Carol Breckenridge and Peter van der Veer put it in an important volume published in 1993.[2] Even the most marginalized people had some capacity to tell their own stories and act for "themselves," often employing what the political scientist James C. Scott called *Weapons of the Weak* against power and authority.[3]

The word "agency" has only entered scholarly vocabulary quite recently. It has been a particular latecomer in the academic discipline of history, emerging earlier in fields less concerned with the explanation of historical change over time, such as anthropology and political science. Despite the seemingly novel themes and intellectual influences that its use signals, this chapter argues that a concern with what is now called "agency" is not new. It has underpinned the history of anti-colonial scholarship since the middle of the twentieth century at least. But in spite of its long history, the quest to identify and recover "agency" has always been a precarious enterprise. This chapter argues that the concept does not denote a coherent methodological approach or field of study. All it does is describe scholars' insistence that non-European peoples are "fully human," and have the same capacities as Europeans or Americans, in particular the ability to tell their own autonomous stories and to influence events for themselves. While looking for agency, scholars bundle together a number of different and contradictory approaches to the study of colonial history, in particular mixing consciousness and causal power in ways that are incoherent and do not help the historical understanding of colonized societies. Laudable, indeed sometimes entirely necessary from an ethical or political point of view, the historical limits of such an approach need to be recognized. Recognizing those limits might allow the historian to recognize that the idea of a single common "humanity" has a politically charged history itself. Together with the fashionable notion that all human beings should be able to "make their own history," and act out their own political and cultural lives "for themselves," it is a concept that entails its own forms of exclusion as well as inclusion, of disempowerment as well as empowerment, each of which have important effects.[4]

Without explicitly describing their enterprise as the search for "agency," progressive scholars of Europe, North America, as well as the non-European world have written "history from below" for a long while. In doing so, they attempted to recover the voice and action of the poor and marginalized in the process. E. P. Thompson's *Making of the English Working Class* is a classic example of the genre, with its attempt to "rescue the poor stockinger, the Luddite cropper, the 'obsolete' hand-loom weaver . . . from the enormous condescension of posterity" as Thompson put it.[5] Similarly, Marxist accounts of class struggle between peasants or workers and colonial elites, or interpretations by European or American scholars of the attempt by Africans or Asians to exercise their own autonomous cultural identity against imperial institutions were concerned with the way colonial subjects asserted their active ability to do things for themselves against forces outside their own control like capitalist economic structures and colonial forces of cultural domination. The concern with free, self-directed activity was a theme in many liberal imperialist narratives—one was written by E. P. Thompson's father—in which colonial institutions were said to gradually unleash the ability of non-European peoples for self-rule.[6]

But the line of "influence" responsible for the development of "history from below" does not flow neatly from West to East.[7] From the late nineteenth century, politicians and commentators who lived within or were writing about colonized societies tried to identify the conditions that allowed the self-directed capacity of non-European subjects of imperial rule to think and act for themselves, to narrate their own stories, and influence the world. Non-elite "agency" has been a concern in academic and non-academic thought about the world outside Europe for as long—if not longer—as Europe. In India, for example, nationalist writers such as Rabindranath Tagore celebrated the history of folk, popular culture in ways that have intriguing parallels with later attempts to write history from below.[8] From the early years of the twentieth-century, third world nationalist historians told stories about the clash between non-European people's desire to run their own lives and the forces of imperial domination. In India and elsewhere, these arguments existed alongside non-European attempts to write a form of history—in some senses a history from below—that challenged the colonial regime's exclusive claim to liberate the "agency" of its subjects.[9]

Scholars have rarely shared a consensual sense of what it actually means to exert "agency" for very long. Nonetheless, these various debates did have a common, if rather vague concern: to recognize the "fully human" characteristics of peoples whose common humanity had been doubted by imperial officials and Eurocentric historians exclusively concerned with the actions of a small band of white men. Being human, from this point of view, is to act in a self-motivated fashion, to possess one's own distinctive way of life or culture, and act according to one's own will rather than being manipulated or objectified by others. Nationalist, post-nationalist, feminist, colonial, and post-colonial scholars engage in the humanist project of attempting to demonstrate that social groups that were previously forgotten or marginalized possessed a degree of autonomy and independence in being able to play an important role in a "history of their own."

To today's generation of scholars and students, used to working in institutions that have at least a token presence of African or Asian historians, it might seem obvious that every population group has "its own history." But as late as 1963, Oxford's Regius Professor of History suggested that Africans were a people without historical significance, whose societies did not possess their own historical consciousness, and never substantially changed as a result of their action. "Perhaps in the future," Hugh Trevor-Roper said,

> there will be some African history to teach. But at present there is none: there is only the history of the Europeans in Africa. The rest is darkness . . . and darkness is not a subject of history.[10]

Trevor-Roper wrote as country after country achieved its independence from European imperial rule, when stories about African agency were commonplace and the leaders of newly independent African nations "electrified university audiences" in Britain. "European colonialism was a living denial of the ability of Africans to organize their own sovereignties, and African studies emerged," alongside independent African nation-states "in part as a sort of recantation," as John Lonsdale puts it.[11] "Asianist" and "Africanist," as well as Caribbean and Australasian scholarship was written, which vehemently opposed racist sentiments of the kind articulated by Trevor-Roper, to show that history was something which "happens among all people at all times."[12]

In these various European and non-European settings, what it meant for someone to act in a fully human way, and to think and act freely for themselves was defined by historians in different ways. In the period of "decolonization" from the 1940s to the 1960s, historians tended to concern themselves with the collective, institutional conditions of non-European agency: with the ways in which non-European peoples narrated and asserted their "freedom" by struggling to create independent nation-states or post-capitalist societies. In order to underpin these stories, historians demonstrated the existence of sophisticated and dynamic polities, cultures, and economies. "History"—the thing that everyone was supposed to possess—was written, which emphasized the importance of the collective stories that "cultures" and "nations" told about themselves, and which allowed them to act in a purposive fashion to assert their own destiny.

These concerns were inflected in the scholarship on different regions in different ways. Early Indian nationalist historians and politicians celebrated the continuities and connections of history on an all-India scale, for example. Jawarhalal Nehru's *Discovery of India*, written in the 1940s, linked a common Indian (for which read largely Hindu and sometimes Buddhist) national culture he believed could be traced back to ancient times with the post-colonial nationalist state's project of modernization.[13] The connection between storytelling and action, between narratives that were supposed to depict millennia-long lines of continuous "Indian" cultural activity in the past and the agency of the "nation" in the present is illustrated well by Nehru's appropriation of the ancient Mauryan emperor Asoka's figure of four lions on four pillars as the symbol of the Indian state. The history-making agency of the independent Indian state to make laws and govern a population in the twentieth century was based on the attempt to project a history of "India's" political and cultural activity that stretched long into the past.[14]

Pre-colonial histories of this kind informed the way non-European peoples' engagement with and resistance to the imperial presence during the eighteenth, nineteenth and twentieth centuries was understood. This kind of analysis occurred in India from at least the 1870s, in the writing of the Bengali intellectual Bankimchandra Chattopadhyaya, for example.[15] In 1907, in a book that was banned before it was printed, the Maratha Hindu nationalist V. D. Savarkar saw the anti-colonial Indian rebellion of 1857 as a "war of independence" that was part of a long campaign to preserve the autonomy of Hindu culture against foreign encroachment.[16]

Between India and Pakistan's independence in 1947 and the 1970s, those who contemplated the modern history of South Asia turned away from seeing culture as a determining force. Instead, they tended to emphasize the impact of colonial educational institutions, the role of economic forces, or the charismatic leadership of particular nationalist heroes, in determining the shape of resistance.[17] Influenced by debates about Russia's revolutions, Marxist and Marxist-influenced scholars argued about the role of the so-called "rich peasant" as a leader of insurgency.[18] It was pre-colonial India's Asiatic, feudal, or quasi-feudal social structure whose role was emphasized in studies of resistance, together with the ideas and personality of men such as M. K. Gandhi, Jawaharlal Nehru and Subhas Chandra Bose. Each, nonetheless, took for granted the idea that a coherent form of national life existed, whether it was defined by its socioeconomic conditions or willingness to be mobilized by a narrow nationalist elite. But as scholarship in Britain and India became more economistic, from the 1960s anthropologically-minded scholars in the USA gave a renewed emphasis to the role of pre-colonial cultural continuities in determining the shape of Indian practice. Here historians of the Indian subcontinent often explicitly drew from models created to understand the African past.[19]

In the history of the Caribbean, Marxist forms of class analysis were combined with an account of the power of enlightenment political rhetoric to explain mass resistance to colonialism and slavery. C. L. R. James' *Black Jacobins* is a good example of such an approach.[20] Only more recently have Caribbean historians begun to perceive cultural continuities between black African and Caribbean culture. In contrast, the history of modern Africa emphasized the role of such pre-colonial continuities from the 1960s. A group of "nationalist" scholars in Dar es Salaam in the 1960s with some connections to Julius Nyerere's newly independent Tanzanian regime were interested in unearthing the pre-colonial African cultural roots of modern East African national identity.[21] Like their earlier peers in the Indian subcontinent, they believed "history" involved the possession of forms of cultural organization and identity that occurred on a large—at least national—scale. Those genuinely "indigenous" forms of organization were said to influence the shape of both African resistance and British colonial rule.

For example, in an important series of arguments made during the late 1960s, Terence Ranger showed how pre-colonial forms of political and cultural organization influenced the first phase of resistance to British rule, and went on to inform later nationalist campaigns for independence. Ranger's point was that supposedly "traditional" forms of tribal and pan-tribal identity were often capable of being mobilized by later insurgents and nationalist politicians, not least because they could unite diverse groups of people on a large scale. Zimbabwe's Ndebele and Shona people were able to unite in opposition to the British in 1896 because they shared common memories of pre-colonial political centralization, as well as common traditions of charismatic, revolutionary leadership. Like other historians writing at the same time, Ranger's point was that these people possessed the attributes which elsewhere were seen as responsible for causing the events of "history." Their history could be understood as one which involved classes and revolutions, government and states, wealth and poverty, for example, attributes which, incidentally, many leaders of many independent African states denied they possessed.[22] A little more than a decade later John Iliffe made a similar intellectual move when he argued that pre-colonial Africa knew poverty in a similar way as modern Europe, a point that the romanticized view of Africa's past espoused by some of the continent's rulers denied.[23]

As John Lonsdale noted, indigenous pressures also affected "the establishment and character of colonial rule." Large-scale indigenous forces in the form of the "cycle of African state-building and decay, forces which occurred independently of outside European influences," powerfully influenced when, where, and how Europeans were able to occupy African territory, for example.[24] Following arguments made by Ronald Robinson and John Gallagher, historians such as Lonsdale and Ranger argued that the character of African resistance to European imperialism played a significant role in shaping the nature of colonial rule, influencing the heavy deployment of violent imperial troops in some places, and the development of forms of "indirect rule" elsewhere.[25] But where "Africanist" scholars differed from "imperial historians", such as Robinson and Gallagher, was in their emphasis on the sophisticated nature of African political organization and resistance. The latter were primarily concerned to chart the processes that shaped the development of the British Empire; the former engaged instead in the ethical project of demonstrating that non-European peoples possessed forms of organization and "agency."

The various narratives described in this chapter so far were about the destiny of nations and states. In different ways, each attempted to recover and celebrate the common human attributes of non-European peoples by plotting them onto large-scale forms of political, cultural, and economic organization or identity: Hindu culture, Indian potentialities for capitalist development, Ndebele and Shona political traditions, for example. But, since the early 1980s, the equation made between agency and the nation has been widely criticized. Narratives about the destiny of national political communities have been broken down into smaller stories that are supposed to better reflect the genuine diversity of non-European human experience.

Here, first of all, historians examined "subaltern" resistance by peasants and workers who did not share the values or culture of the elites who led nationalist campaigns. The work of India's *Subaltern Studies* collective challenged what they saw as the elitist bias of dominant strands of imperial and nationalist historiography. With the work of this group in the early 1980s culture returned as an important category in South Asian scholarship. But this literature emphasizes the autonomy of the fragmentary life-worlds of the poor rather than the homogeneity of "national" cultural life. Ranajit Guha and his colleagues suggested that India's poor possessed their own native forms of insurgent culture that could not be subsumed into a single, supposedly "nationalist," way of life. It was that culture, not purely economic forces or a desire for national liberation, which drove peasant rebellion in colonial India.[26]

Secondly, historians based in Britain and the United States showed how "agency" was something exercised in a more small-scale fashion in everyday life and the intimate sphere of domestic life, as well as large institutions. The growing importance of feminist history from the late 1970s encouraged this localizing, disaggregating tendency. Feminist scholars showed how many stories about the emancipation of nations or classes silenced the voices and hid the perspective of women from view. Scholars have more recently become interested in examining complex interactive situations where "resistance" seems to involve complicity, and collaboration implies resistance, where action is halting and fragmentary, and voices multivocal.

While in the 1970s and 1980s historians celebrated the actions of nationalist leaders and peasant rebels, recently historians have tried to recover the agency of once unfashionable figures who played a less heroic role. The middle-ranking "native" official, the Sikh soldier fighting for the British during World War I, the South African convert to Christianity, the working class Ulster Unionist, and the Kikuyu loyalist during Mau Mau have all become figures of historical interest who had complex projects and desires of their own. In the last few years, the titanic clash between empire and emerging national cultures has been replaced by a more diffuse emphasis on the complexity of human responses to colonial institutions.[27]

Where it concerns the history of the most marginalized or downtrodden, the recent analysis of non-European activity has become less self-confident and more complex. Scholars of non-European history have been troubled about whether it is possible to ever truly understand and "recover" the historical role that non-European subjects, especially marginalized groups such as the poor and women, played in engaging with and resisting European colonial rule. They have asked whether the "subaltern can speak," or at least whether their voice can be heard, a question I'll consider in more detail later on. From some points of view, the very act of writing history itself is seen as a way of subordinating the complexity of non-European life into an overly straightforward set of stories that subjugates or annihilates the "quiet voice" of the marginalized.[28]

Nonetheless, these more complex recent arguments about "agency" are no less concerned with the humanist project of identifying "a history of their own" for previously marginal social groups. Despite their hesitancy and sophistication, at the root of all these vexed debates lies the ethical injunction to recognize the common humanity of all colonized peoples, an injunction which has been central to anti-colonial politics and scholarship since at least World War II. Nowadays, it is just that they recognize that the task is far more fraught and complex than scholars a generation ago thought.

In their various forms, these various attempts to "recover" the agency of the marginal and downtrodden can be connected to the twentieth-century humanist project of recognizing all human beings, whether European or not, as bearers of universal capacities and rights. Such arguments were explicitly made when a critique of the supposedly "dehumanising" effects of colonialism emerged in the middle of the twentieth century. During and after World War II, they gathered pace alongside decolonization, the emergence of newly independent, Caribbean, African and Asian states into the "family of nations," and the construction of global bodies such as the United Nations, UNESCO and the Ford Foundation. These new bureaucracies spoke a new global language that emphasized the common capacities, attributes, and rights of "humanity."

The need to recognize every human being's free capacity to formulate and act out their wishes for themselves is taken for granted as a basic task for every student or scholar of the colonized world. But it is a far less straightforward process than it might at first appear, especially for the historian. This is not merely because the colonial archive lies in the way of the historian's recognition of the subaltern's humanity or capacity to act freely for themselves. There are more deep-rooted philosophical problems. To begin with, no one can agree what it means to be either human or free. As the German philosopher Martin Heidegger suggested, "if one understands humanism in general as a concern that man become free for his humanity and find its worth in it, then humanisms differ according to one's conception of the 'freedom' and 'nature' of man."[29] Heidegger's point was that every proclamation in defense of one conception of human capacities or another involved an abstract, metaphysical definition of the supposedly objective characteristics of humanity. People are human in ways that no single definition can define nor single story narrate. The stories people do tell are often connected to the kinds of institutions they inhabit or support, whether the post-colonial nation-state or the liberal, global academic institution. Whilst offering their own recuperative histories of non-European consciousness, agency, and humanity, scholars have constrained human "being" with their own, particular sense of what it means to exercise human agency, excluding others' ways of being from their account. Each particular definition has its own particular lines of exclusion, and involves the articulation of its own forms of power. The different definitions of human "agency" that scholars have formulated over the last generation and more have been important in helping to explain how people acted in the past, and understand the process of historical change over centuries. But they have failed in their primary purpose. They have not been able to recognize the "fully human" character of the subjects they have analyzed.

The rest of the chapter will explore three moments in scholarship on resistance, agency, and the colonial encounter to develop this argument. The first moment concerns the history of the nationalist campaign against British rule in India during the late nineteenth and early twentieth century, and occurred in the late 1970s. The second, in the late 1980s, concerns the attempt by literary critics to think about the way in which scholars might—or might not—be able to listen to the genuine voice of the most marginalized. The third from the early 1990s has to do with the role of narrative and storytelling in the relationship between missionaries and Christian converts in colonial South Africa.

After examining each of these moments in the history of colonial studies, the chapter concludes by offering a series of suggestions about the way historians might approach the history of non-European engagement with and resistance to colonial rule. The concern here will not be to consider when or how Africans or Asians exercised autonomous "agency" and when they did not. Instead, the chapter will end with a discussion of the one category that is crucial to the way historians discuss the agency of non-Europeans, the idea of the "native." As we shall see, the ethical imperative to recover and celebrate "native agency" involves a set of assumptions about the relationship between culture, power, and place which have a recent history, and which are deeply problematic. These assumptions prevent scholars from asking more important historical questions about the way understandings of political action, and the operation of different forms of power, have changed across the world over the past two or three hundred years.

II

In 1979, the Oxford historian Tapan Raychaudhuri published a vociferous attack on the study of Indian nationalism by a group of historians, most of whom were British and most at one time or another from Cambridge, known to their critics as "the Cambridge school."[30] The group had developed "a critique of Indian nationalism and the nationalist interpretation of history."[31] That critique exposed the stories which nationalist politicians and historians made about their ability to speak on behalf of a single, homogenous nation as a series of hollow claims. Instead, scholars such as Christopher Baker, D. A. Washbrook, and Anil Seal showed how the roots of "national" politics were forged in highly differentiated "local arenas of power," often also dependent on long-standing indigenous social and economic practices which focused on particular towns and regions. The group argued that nationalist politicians often used all-India political arenas to preserve and augment their local authority and economic power. As David Washbrook noted, "[e]ven as the Congress stood proclaiming victory for a national ideal [in 1947], the ambiguities of trying to construct provincial politics on district-level institutions stood out clearly."[32]

Raychaudhuri argued that this approach denied the "humanity" of Indian political actors. It imputed base motives to men (and they were almost all men) who he believed had performed noble deeds in pursuit of national aspirations. Quoting a sentence from an article by Conor Cruise O'Brien, Raychaudhuri argued that the Cambridge School had reduced Indian nationalism to "animal politics." The Cambridge group was unable to recognize the "hopes, passions, and heartbreak of millions," subsuming them instead within "endless narratives of factional squabbles." Instead, in the Cambridge approach, Indian politicians as well as British officers seemed to be directed by "mechanical" socioeconomic forces. Raychaudhuri believed the Cambridge School had dehumanized Indian politicians, reducing dignified human beings to "creature[s] in pursuit of rationally calculated clearly defined specific material ends in the short term." The "humanistic discipline" of history had been reduced to a dessicated social science in which human passion and commitment were subjugated under the determining force of abstract social structures.[33]

For Raychaudhuri, recognizing the humanity of Indians involved recognizing their free capacity to act on the basis of their own, dignified aspirations, not to be a pawn in someone else's game. Yet Raychaudhuri was fairly categorical about precisely what it actually meant to freely formulate dignified aspirations—any old set of desires and intentions would not do. The only "human" aspiration worth narrating was the desire for national liberation, the aim of constructing an independent nation free from British rule. The ethical function of history was to recognize Indians' ability to exercise "agency" in one very particular respect: to fight for, and later live within, the bureaucratic structures of the independent, post-colonial nation-state.

The argument Raychaudhuri made about what is and what is not good history was based on a very particular set of claims about what it meant to be "human." Those claims are contestable. But they can only be judged on ethical and not historical grounds. As we noted, from his point of view, being "human" involves the realizable desire to belong to the institutions of an independent, modern, secular, sovereign, and (for historians on the left) socialist nation-state. Raychaudhuri's nationalist history perceives human beings as entities whose teleological destiny lies in the realization of their participation in a nation-state. There is no room within this definition of humanity for those who do not share such aspirations; or for others whose "freedom" was itself limited by the nation-state. As historians writing since Raychaudhuri have emphasized, nationalist narratives often justify homogenizing and sometimes oppressive post-colonial institutions by flattening out and annihilating "minority" cultures, and ignoring the role of women. Other analysts might see other attributes, for example the fight against patriarchy or the struggle between social classes to eke out a livelihood, as more fundamental to what it means to be a human being.

Historians looking to recover the human agency of non-European peoples face a series of judgments about the particular kind of agency they wish to narrate. Those judgments involve a consideration of the essential attributes and capacities that make up a "human being," and how they might best be realized. Judgments such as these pose ethical questions that cannot be answered with the tools of historical analysis. The historical academy is no more equipped to judge than any other institution. Indeed, if Alasdair Macintyre is right to suggest that the modern-day humanities and social sciences don't offer any coherent form of moral enquiry at all, the academy is probably the place least likely to allow one to work out an answer.[34]

Here we can make a second point. Raychaudhuri draws a sharp opposition between his own attempt to celebrate the aspiration of national liberation—the great deeds of nationalist heroes—on the one hand, and what he sees as the Cambridge School's sense of Indian victimhood. His problem with Seal, Washbrook *et al.* is that they emphasized the forces which Indian politicians had no control over, and their inability or (worse) unwillingness to overcome them. Certainly, the early work of the so-called "Cambridge School" can be accused of economism, cynicism and a reluctance to take the history of ideas, aspirations, and the cognitive component of human life seriously. Raychaudhuri is right to criticize some of the works he reviews for an overly rigid rational-actor model of human conduct. But amidst such criticism, one must also recognize that the "Cambridge School" touched on an important truth: that historical actors are not always driven by grand aspirations; that grand aspirations sometimes fail; that a sense of victimhood, frustration, and the inability to escape one's immediate circumstances are important and frequent aspects of the human condition. Such feelings (and we are in the realm of feelings here) don't necessarily lead to a sense of power, agency or commitment to the cause of liberation, although they do sometimes. They don't always result in the narration of stories which scholars who want to ethically recognize the dignity of the marginalized and oppressed feel comfortable retelling. But such complex and heterogeneous responses should, however, be taken account of by the historian of non-European encounters with European colonial rule.

III

In 1988, the literary critic Gayatri Chakravorty Spivak published an article that posed the question, "Can the Subaltern Speak?." Spivak's text was published a few years after a number of scholars—historians, anthropologists, and literary critics—had begun to criticize the kind of nationalist approach to anti-colonial resistance articulated by historians such as Raychaudhuri. Instead, in India and elsewhere, historians had attempted to recover the authentic voice of the "subaltern", which had been hidden or suppressed by elitist—nationalist and imperialist—approaches. Spivak asked whether such a project was possible. Could scholars ever retrieve the authentic voice of the marginalized, especially of marginalized women? Her answer was no. The subaltern could not speak for herself.

This wasn't merely because it was technically difficult to find evidence of the voice of marginalized people in places such as colonial India. Because the archive largely consists of documents written by elite and middle class men, that is often the case. As Premesh Lalu puts it, "[t]o claim that subaltern consciousness, voice or agency can be retrieved through colonial texts is to ignore the organisation and representation of colonized subjects as a subordinate proposition within primary discourses."[35] Certainly not oblivious to the difficulty of using colonial archives for evidence of marginalized voices, Spivak was nonetheless making a more sophisticated point. Even where records of her speech remained, her "voice" was always subsumed by more powerful subjects who gave her voice authority and, in a sense, controlled what "she" said.[36]

Spivak discusses the case of *sati*, the practice of women burning to death on the funeral pyres of their husbands in early colonial India. The figure of the *sati*—the woman—herself was spoken for and argued about in a series of debates between those trying to abolish and others wishing to preserve the practice in the 1810s and 1820s. British officials and Indian reformers trying to abolish *sati* said they were acting in the woman's best interests, arguing that they alone knew what she would do if she had free will; supporters of the practice disputed these claims, arguing that the *sati* burnt voluntarily. As Spivak put it, "[w]hat the British see as poor victimised women going to the slaughter [wa]s fact an ideological battleground."[37] The *sati* was a cause célèbre, a subject of controversy. But she had become this after being objectified by others, rather than being able to find a place for her own thoughts to be taken seriously on her own terms.[38]

Following Spivak's argument, one can see how attempts by scholars to recover the voice of the subaltern, whether E. P. Thompson's "stockinger," Eugene Genovese's slave, or Spivak's Indian woman, inevitably treat it as a sign of something else in such a way that it loses authentic content of its own. However well intentioned they are, historians and others cannot help projecting their own interests and fantasies, making the subaltern appear as a stereotyped figure within their own discourse. By invoking the power of the western academy to speak for the "voiceless" of the "third world," historians in fact seem simply to confirm global inequalities of power, proving once again that it is only when their voice is mediated and subsumed by the voice of powerful institutions such as colonial reformers, western missionary organizations,

NGOs, or universities that the "third world" poor have any "agency" at all. The academic project of "recovering agency" is in danger of perpetuating precisely the kind of colonial inequalities of power it sets out to critique. After all, those European men who criticized and abolished *sati* in India in the early nineteenth century did not set out to dehumanise or silence Indian women. Instead they claimed to speak on behalf of the "humanity" of the "victims" of *sati*, to speak for them and so give them agency for the first time. Like progressive scholars listening to so-called "native voices" today, they alone claimed to be able to listen to the long-suppressed speech of the subaltern. In the process, though, they merely project their own thoughts onto the "native voice," a concept we will return to in the last section of this chapter.

Instead of indulging in the fantasy that the authentic subjectivity of the subaltern can be restored, Spivak argues that the critic needs instead to trace the way the figure of the subaltern—the "native," for example—is both produced and then silenced by others' speech and writing. Critics should analyze who did speak, how their words were authorized, and what those articulate voices silenced; to identify the "location and reinscription of subject-positions which are instrumental in forms of control and insurgency," as Robert Young puts it.[39] Here, one cannot presume that either colonialism or capitalism are all-powerful monoliths that always act the same way to oppress and marginalize. The critical scholar pays attention to the complex and highly differentiated forms of power that create the field on which the subjects of colonialism speak and act in an uneven fashion.

Alongside Edward Said's *Orientalism* and Homi K. Bhabha's *Location of Culture*, Spivak's 1988 essay forms an essential component of the canon of post-colonial studies, a field that emerged from within literary criticism not history.[40] Despite the literary context to her work, the emphasis in Spivak's writing on the need to trace the complex history of the institutions that allocate subject-positions, and which give some people and not others "voice," forces her into archival research and leads to the use of historical techniques, and a form of analysis that is useful for historians. What Spivak reminds us is that attempts to "recover agency" necessarily reduce the heterogeneity of non-European responses to European colonial institutions to a simplistic story about the voice of a single, monolithic subject—a story which is told by those with the power to make their words heard, even if it is only the fairly limited power which those of us who write from within academic institutions have.

IV

In particular, I'd like to suggest that Spivak's argument offers a useful corrective to an increasingly common concern within colonial studies: an emphasis on the stories and narratives of non-European subjects of colonial regimes. Above all, in the last decade or so "agency" has been associated with the way non-European subjects tell stories about themselves. As we shall see, scholars have paid greater attention to their ability to speak and tell stories than their power to act.

This narratalogical literature assumes that the capacity people have to tell stories is closely connected to their power in the world. Humans are regarded as beings who dwell in narrative, who "make themselves up" by telling stories about the connection between the choices they made in the past, and their "identity" or "subjectivity" (in other words who they are) in the present. From this point of view, it is the ability to tell coherent stories about one's self that gives human beings coherence, which allows them to act in a rational and concerted way, and which therefore enables them to "wield" power or agency over the world they inhabit. "[N]arrative is an expression of power." It empowers those who tell stories, whether nationalists who narrate the glorious deeds of the states and empires they belong to, peasants who detail the events of a subaltern rebellion or, one might add, early twenty-first century consumers explaining the consistent forms of identity which underpin their shopping choices. As the historical anthropologist J. D. Y. Peel puts it, "narrative empowers through enhancing the capacity for action."[41]

Like many other scholars working on the history of colonial societies in the last few years, Peel has attempted to identify traces of authentic indigenous narratives from records of the colonial encounter, and to criticize other scholars who "den[y] indigenous narrative." The scene of his particular inquiries has been the interaction between Christian missionaries and the Yoruba population in what is now southwestern Nigeria. Peel argues that the arrival of Christianity to the Yoruba, a process that occurred alongside the emergence of colonial rule, did not simply annihilate indigenous culture. The local population were "active participants" in the construction of a specifically Yoruba form of Christianity. But their engagement with missionaries also led to the creation of a distinctively Yoruba identity for the first time. A previously diverse population began to see themselves as they were seen by European outsiders, as a relatively homogenous population governed by a common identity and culture even if it was an identity and culture missionaries were trying to annihilate. Far from simply having an identity imposed on them by others though, Peel argues that the Yoruba possessed agency in so far as they told their own stories about themselves.

Peel's argument here depends on his attempt to trace an authentically "Yoruba" element in the stories which African converts to Christianity such as Samuel Ajayi Crowther—the first African Bishop of the Anglican Church—told about themselves and their society. Instead of simply arguing that the character of Yoruba Christianity was entirely determined by the shape of pre-missionary Yoruba culture, Peel emphasizes the active powers of men such as Crowther to recast old stories to fit new ways of life. In particular, European missionaries and African converts both encouraged Yoruba to "buy into a new version of how Yoruba history might go, to invite them to rescript their history in terms of a unidirectional narrative of social progress" about the emergence of Christianity, civilization and commerce in West Africa.[42] This was possible because existing storytelling traditions allowed a new, Christian ending to be grafted onto old, Yoruba forms of narrative. The result was a very complex set of individual stories in which there was considerable "interplay or even merging of the Christian narrative brought by the missionaries and the ongoing histories of the Yoruba communities." Those narratives, nonetheless, gave their tellers a sense of their own agency. Not only that, they give them the practical ability to act powerfully upon the world which people who were not able to tell coherent stories—dislocated slaves dragged from place to place, for example—did not have.

This is, no doubt, a sophisticated account of the colonial encounter, offering a complex interpretation of the relationship between Europeans and Africans, and the consolidation of "native" Yoruba identity in the process. It provides an important interpretation of the role of both Yoruba resistance and agency in the process of colonization and conversion. The problem, however, is that Peel's search for signs of "indigenous narrative" forces him toward an overly simplistic account of "European" and "Yoruba" culture in a way which cannot avoid producing an overly stereotyped account of the "native" voice. If the tendency to assert power by telling stories about oneself belongs to all human beings, how does one identify which narrative is constructed by Europeans, and which is an instance of "African initiative?" I'm not sure it is possible for the historian to tell. It is impossible to assess what is specifically Yoruba, rather than Igbo, or Tswana, or Zulu, or even British or German about "Yoruba" culture without producing an overly static and simplistic account of Yoruba culture. The attempt to recover authentic native stories ends up flattening out the complex range of positions people occupied, and the arguments they articulated into an overly simplistic account of the "native" voice. As I'll suggest in a moment, the very idea of the "native" is something with a problematic history.

The history of Asia and especially Africa has increasingly come to be dominated by this concern to show how colonized as well as colonising peoples "made themselves up" by telling stories about themselves—a process which is seen as evidence of native "initiative" or agency. From this point of view, Christianity in Africa was appropriated into authentically "African" narratives, for example.[43] Intended to counter a supposed overemphasis on the power of colonial institutions to "invent" features of the African or Asian social landscape such as caste, tribe, identity, or even nationality, this emphasis often ends up being highly elitist. As John L. and Jean Comaroff point out, it privileges the men and (more rarely) women who had access to means of communication such as print. Discussion of the African nature of African Christianity concentrates on elite figures such as Samuel Ajayi Crowther or Samuel Johnson. Ironically, it is those who were closest to European missionaries who are seen as the most authentically "African." A similar emphasis on narrative and indigenous forms of history-writing in South Asian history—albeit one which often leads to very different arguments—has accompanied a turn away from the "masses" toward the scholarly concentration on elite writing from the Indian subcontinent. The problem here is not that the work of elites is being studied; it is that too often they are taken as representing an authentically indigenous agency or a genuinely "native" culture in an overly simplistic fashion. First of all, it often assumes there is a single "native" voice. Secondly, it presupposes the existence of a Manichean opposition between native and colonial, African/Asian, and European points of view.

As the Comaroffs suggest, attempts to delineate non-European agency in this way neglect the extent to which many (but certainly not all) aspects of the lives of both colonial "subjects" and their European "masters" were produced in a far more complex dialectical process. In a variety of arena across the colonized world "a process of reciprocal determination" occurred in which new, European and non-European, ways of life were forged, the lives of Europeans and Africans and Asians were intertwined in ways that had a dramatic, transformative effect on each other.

Christianity and reformist Hinduism or Islam, new forms of ethnic and national identity, novel configurations of tribe and caste, commodity production, and peasant agriculture were attributes of modern life in Africa and Asia that one group of historians or another have attributed to the colonial encounter. These were not colonial "inventions," straightforwardly imposed by a monolithic power. Instead, they came into being in a complex process of encounter and response, working themselves out in an often fraught and anxious process of colonial interaction. As historians rapidly remind themselves (but are seemingly as quick to forget), colonialism had an effect on the colonizer as well as the colonized, even if new forms of colonizing subjectivity were not always straightforwardly transported back home.[44] As the Comaroffs suggest, colonialism represented "a bewilderingly tangled field of cross-cutting social and cultural ties" between Europeans and their subjects.[45] Upon such a complex field, identifying the isolated narrative voice or causal agency of one group of subjects or another is very difficult. It becomes impossible—and meaningless—to ask whether African Christianity was more a product of "African" than "European" agency, or if an institution such as Hindu caste owed more to Indian agency than European institutions, for example.

The complex process of colonial entanglement which scholars such as the Comaroffs describe forces one to ask a new set of questions. One begins to wonder why the multivalent process of encounter and interaction between Europeans and non-Europeans is so frequently described by both contemporary historical actors and historians as a Manichean clash between native and European ways of life? The partially non-European origins of European rule is undoubted; the role of non-European actions in the making of colonial institutions is a matter of little controversy.

So why has this "tangled" force-field of cross-cutting action and resistance so often been narrated as an "engagement between two 'sides'," a straightforward struggle for native agency against an intrusive, alien power?

V

To answer this question one needs, in part, to explain the emergence of the idea of the "native" itself. The attempt to recover "indigenous agency" relies on a form of nativism. It involves the assumption that non-European peoples' native cultures or ways of life endured with enough coherence from long enough ago to be recognizably "indigenous," and are not merely the product of short-term, contingent events. From this point of view, asserting one's "agency" is to articulate oneself in the idiom or culture of one's native land, not in the language or cultural idiom of the foreigner. The idea of the native in this sense is connected to the notion that cultures are attached to particular territorial localities. It depends on the opposition between the "native" whose existence is rooted in a particular locality and the vagrant, alien, outsider, or stranger whose way of life is created somewhere else. For the last few decades at least, the link between culture, native place, and agency has been crucial to the different ways scholars have tried to ethically recognize the humanity of the non-European subjects they study.

Since at least the late middle ages the English word "native" has been used as both an adjective and a noun to describe where someone was born. Jonathan Swift's *Gulliver's Travels*, first published in 1736, speaks of Gulliver's "native country" on a number of occasions. Early modern Britons often described someone as "native of" a particular place, denoting their birthplace, even if they did not live there. But the use of the word to describe something more than one's birthplace, to refer instead to their residence in a place they belong to in a more deep-rooted cultural sense began only in the early nineteenth century. This new notion emerged alongside a British empire based not on European settlement, but on the colonial administration of non-European societies by a white governing class who dreamt of their return "home": what some refer to as "the Second British Empire." At this point in time, "the native" or "natives" became (an) exclusively non-European figure(s). "Native" only described Europeans in an ironic sense. In South Asia at least, it emerged as a way for Europeans to speak about Indians, and Indians to speak about themselves at roughly the same time.

As Arjun Appadurai suggests, this notion of "the native" implies physical immobility: "[t]he natives are immobilised by their belonging to a place . . . Natives are those who are somehow confined to places by their connection to what the place permits," as opposed to the colonialists, missionaries, and observers who arrive from another place.[46] Appadurai suggests that the American or European anthropologist's use of the idea of the "native" incarcerates them, imprisoning them within overly rigid notions of culture and thought that are linked to a particular confined place. Amongst anthropologists and, more belatedly, historians, the use of the word "native" as a noun has been seen as having imperialist political overtones since at least the 1930s, and has fallen out of use. But the concept of a people immobilized—incarcerated, perhaps—by their culture to a particular place has remained with us with terms such as "indigenous people" and "first nations." The implication remains that global citizens of European place can travel the world, while Asians, Africans and "native" Americans are only truly themselves if fixed to their native place.

More, perhaps, than Appadurai recognizes, this process of incarceration provided the strange basis for resistance and "agency" by the "native themselves." From the mid-nineteenth century until at least the 1970s, many non-European campaigns against colonial rule consisted of an attempt to expel a purportedly malign, alien presence from "native" space. Early forms of constitutional critique of British rule in India, such as those articulated by Rammohun Roy in the 1820s, challenged British "interference" with "native" Bengali ways of life even while it supported some British institutions and encouraged some British migration. The far more dramatic insurrection of 1857–8 in north India was mobilized with a call against the British introduction of practices from outside that would pollute the South Asian body politic. The Mau Mau insurrection in the 1950s opposed native Kikuyu cultural practices to the intrusive force of European settlers, and colonial forms of rule to the Kenyan highlands. Each of these very different instances of resistance occurred as stories were told about the opposition between supposedly coherent forms of "native" cultural practice and identity rooted in a particular physical place—Bengal, Hindustan, Kenya—on the one hand, and the intrusive force of British rule on the other.[47] These forms of nativism existed alongside other global ways of engaging with and criticizing European domination. But paradoxically, these notions of "native" autonomy depended on global interconnection and the operation of forces which operated on a worldwide scale. They relied on the flow of ideas and institutional practices that occurred within the colonial encounter, but also on connections between insurgents and rebels on a continental or global scale. They might encompass the colonial, missionary, and elite institutions, such as the law court, that tried to map the identity and culture of a mobile population onto a restricted "native" territory. But they also incorporated the vernacular, sometimes transnational press. Rammohun Roy's conception of being a native Bengali depended on an implicit and explicit comparison between Bengal and the other "social institutions" of both British and north Indian society. These contrasts in turn relied upon colonial legal institutions and both Bengali and British newspaper technology.[48] Mau Mau rebels had fought for the British in Southeast Asia during World War II and some historians would say they developed a sense of "their own" culture in the process. Considering the subjects of French imperialism, one might note that Ho Chi Minh lived in Brooklyn, Pol Pot in Paris. It shouldn't surprise us that some of the most fervent "native" cultural nationalists were as widely travelled as the imperial officers they opposed.

The invocation of this idea of "native" territory as the dwelling place of one particular type of person involves a reduction—or confinement—of complex and heterogeneous histories of global interaction and colonial encounter to a straightforward opposition between two pre-constituted entities, the native and the alien. There is an intrinsic contradiction in the idea of the "native voice" here. Historians looking for "indigenous voices," or who emphasize the ability of "natives" to tell stories about themselves need to pay attention to the external, sometimes global forces which acted from outside to make the native "self" what it was. Yet they find it difficult to do so precisely because those forces came from outside that self's "native" place. If, after all, a particular story showed signs that it was partially produced by forces from outside, how could it be the voice of the "native" to begin with? If one ends up, as many historians do, of ethically privileging the native voice one cannot understand the global operation of power within which it emerged.

The idea of "native agency" also makes it difficult to explore aspects of non-European "initiative" that are silent and cannot be narrated with reference to a culture that adheres to a native place. It makes it difficult to tell stories about migration, for example. The colonial idea of the intransigent "native" emerged to an eighteenth- and early nineteenth-century world in which movement and the flow of both people and goods were centrally important. The pre-colonial populations of South Asia and Africa probably moved in search of employment, land and trade far more than they do now. Sometimes, long-distance migration occurred in ways that allowed individuals to consciously retain many of the cultural practices they started out with. In multinational, multicultural merchant cities such as Alexandria, Calcutta, Mombasa, Salonica, or Shanghai, immigrants settled among "their own" people. Arabs, Armenians, Gujuratis, Jews, and many other ethnic and religious groups created self-policing local communities around institutions and local courts.[49] In these situations, individuals were able to tell coherent stories "of their own" about cultural continuities which stretched into the distant past and gave them a sense of who they were. But more often, outside these early modern multicultural cities, cultures did not so straightforwardly move with people.

In some contexts, the Atlantic slave trade being the most obvious, mobility was coerced. It involved a deliberate uprooting and definite sense of cultural loss, what Orlando Patterson calls social death.[50] However hard historians have recently tried, it is impossible to see the movement of people in the Atlantic slave trade as a process in which African culture was simply transplanted from one place to another. The culture of slaves of African descent in the Americas had as much—perhaps far more—to do with the institutions of slavery in America as of African culture.[51] It is as important to try to understand enslavement as a process of loss and alienation, as it is to chart the ways in which they made themselves "at home" by continuing to articulate cultural continuities which extended back into the African past. Indeed, the two might be seen as closely intertwined. Slave narratives which presented Africa as the (literally) native, origin point for the slave's life, such as the Carolina-born Olaudah Equiano's fictional account of his early years in Benin, were to construct stories of a putative "home" in the face of such alienating anxiety.[52] Equiano's story was also an effort to find a voice in a world where claiming to be the authentic representative of a respectable "native" place, especially one that could be placed within a Biblical lineage, was an important way of acquiring public credibility. What is fascinating is the way Equiano's own text—just like the work of historians who see his writing as the genuine expression of African culture—effaces the role of his mobility, and global travel and connection rather than the culture of his birthplace, that made him who he was. Equiano's "agency"—his actions, and the voice he possessed to tell stories about them—were produced by mobile forces he had no control over, forces that did not dwell for long in any "native" place. Making Equiano into an informant about native African culture reduces important aspects of his story.

The same is true where mobility was less traumatic, and more of a conscious choice. Elites and poor alike were highly mobile in eighteenth-century India, for example. It is impossible to tell the story of their movement, or explain the role of mobility in the making of both pre-colonial "Indian" or colonial states, or social formations if one is looking for signs of "indigenous" (i.e., immobile) subjectivity or agency. Someone who moved from one place to another was as likely to jettison elements of their "native" culture as to transport them to a new place. In doing so they would tell stories which neglected the importance of mobility and migration, and which instead rooted them in their new place. In the eighteenth century the Burdwan Raj seemed to be Bengal's most characteristically "Bengali" landed estate, supporting Bengali-language scholarship, being central to many canonical Bengali texts and, in the early nineteenth century, defending the particularities of Bengali culture and law. The Burdwan *raja* extolled their "ancient" connection to western Bengal. Yet the family that ruled the Burdwan raj came from a peripatetic north Indian Mughal bureaucratic class, about which historians know very little other than that they migrated from Punjab in the 1690s. To survive and prosper as landholders in Bengal they needed to abandon traces of this past, and rapidly narrativise themselves as members of Bengal's regional ruling class.[53]

Thousands, perhaps millions, of less prominent or prosperous Indians made similar journeys in the seventeenth and eighteenth centuries, moving to less densely populated areas where they thought they could improve their livelihood. Sometimes people moved in groups that allowed them to retain a sense of continuous collective identity. More often they did not.[54] Migration on a massive scale accompanied instances of rural "rebellion" that are seen by subaltern historians as the violent articulation of "local" (i.e., immobile) cultures. The most common response to threatening economic conditions was "exit" not "voice" or insurrection. Our understanding of subaltern consciousness relies on colonial records, and comes from those who stayed in place to make itself heard in front of the colonial state. Celebrating the native subaltern voice ignores the "initiative" of those who are silently mobile.[55]

But peasant movement was an important factor in shaping the character of both India's pre-colonial politics and the British colonial state. It was a force that was voiceless, but nonetheless had important effects. Indian rulers responded to the danger of rural mobility by combining "enticement" and "chastisement," offering better conditions than other local rulers while displaying their power to protect and punish at key moments. In Bengal and much of South India at least, most seem to have assumed that, however hard one tried, a large number of cultivators would simply move on each year, and constructed their administrative apparatus accordingly. The British responded very differently. They regarded mass migration as a sign of the pathological character of Indian society, seeing it as either the noble yeoman-cultivator's legitimate response to the typical and tyrannical "oppression" of local elites, or evidence of the barbarous peasant's treachery and disaffection. The conscious or unconsciously formulated solution in each case was to try to immobilize India's mobile population, fixing them with a system of revenue and law which incentivized "rich peasants" who occupied the same soil for generations, but penalized those who moved from place to place. The "peasantization" of India's mobile rural population is seen by most historians as one of the most important dynamics occurring in the subcontinent's nineteenth century. It occurred as the colonial regime developed new forms of rule and forged new relationships with Indian elites in response to a highly mobile population it found almost impossible to govern to begin with.[56]

In one sense, then, British imperialism developed its categories and techniques of governance in response to the active, mobile powers of the population being governed. Mobile peasants were participants in processes that produced the practices of colonial governmentality and also, for many, new forms of impoverishment. What could, perhaps, be simplistically called "native agency" had a constitutive role in the making of both colonial state and indigenous society. But these instances of non-European activity have been marginalized in stories told by both the colonial regime and its nationalist opponents about the relationship between "natives" and their foreign rulers. In order to collect revenue more effectively, colonial institutions fixed Indians in their villages, and assumed that the "real" India was rural and static, not mobile.[57] In their attempt to show that colonialism was a force that existed outside the authentic Indian nation, nationalists used a similar perspective to celebrate the "agency" of a supposedly static, immobile society. Figures such as Mohandas K. Gandhi and Rabindranath Tagore conjured a fantastical image of India as a self-governing community of people who were happily incarcerated in their villages, bound together by the continuous transmission of local culture and tradition from generation to generation not by their movement from place to place. Nationalism was interested in the way Indians could shake off colonialism's external oppressive force by articulating and modernizing those traditions "for themselves." In the process it ignored and marginalized the silent, mobile, and often literally unplaceable forces that made its existence possible in the first place. In the late eighteenth century, the cultivator who moved from place to place was able to negotiate with different landholders and possessed a considerable degree of power as a result. By the 1930s mobile peasants had become "landless labourers," marginal figures driven to the edge of subsistence by peasants with fixed rights to occupy the soil, silent in a political world that only listened to the supposedly authentic voice of the "sons of the soil."[58]

With its attempt to connect consciousness and agency to native place, colonialist, nationalist, and subaltern approaches to peasant consciousness have privileged the latter. Historians—especially historians interested in identifying and recovering "native" agency—assume that Asia, America, Australasia, and Africa are populated by "indigenous people" whose activity consists in their expression of authentic cultural idioms tied to their "native" place. Such a perspective makes migration and mobility seem an inauthentic and unnatural form of economic and cultural expression—as something that people only do when they are pushed to the brink, and which causes unnatural levels of alienation and anxiety. Of course that isn't the case. Mobility is as natural or as normal a phenomenon as staying in one place. Many of the societies we inhabit, in Asia as well as America, were constituted by recent migration. Immobility and stasis are as liable to induce social or psychic crises of one sort or another as movement. But the assumptions explored in this chapter about the relationship between culture, narrative, place, and action in the non-European world make it hard to tell celebratory stories about the triumph of "indigenous" agency or "native" culture without fixing those subjects to one place.

The fixing of people in place is one way in which the present-day search for "agency" acts to exclude, marginalize and silence its subjects. It offers a good example of the limits of this particular approach to the study of non-European societies. But instead of wholly abandoning the emphasis on "agency," this chapter has argued that its limits and contradictions need to be recognized. The search for "agency" is part of the anti-racist ethical or political project of recognizing the common humanity of non-European peoples. But like all forms of historical scholarship, it involves the use of technique that limits the particular political or ethical uses to which they might be put. Like all instances of historical enquiry it tells a story about what it means to be human in a particular place and time that marginalizes and excludes other ways of being human.

With its emphasis on the vocal, active power of individuals bound to a "culture" which belongs to a particular place, perhaps the literature that this chapter has examined tends to operate with rather a narrow notion of what it means to be a human being. Not everyone tells stories about their action all the time; sometimes they talk about their passivity, talking about the way things have been done to them rather than done by them. Sometimes they are even silent. Everyone feels active and empowered some of the time. But feeling powerless, perhaps even victimized, is an important part of what it means to be human as well. Instead of imagining they can change the world by recovering the active narrative powers of the most marginalized, historians should try to understand the complex, contradictory, and often incoherent ways in which people in the past have responded to the worlds of human and non-human action they have inhabited.

Notes

1 Chakrabarty, *Provincialising Europe*, p. 102.
2 Breckenridge and van der Veer (eds), *Orientalism*, pp. 4–5.
3 Scott, *Conscripts of Modernity*.
4 The argument here is indebted to the work of Talal Asad: see his *Genealogies of Religion* and *Formations of the Secular*.
5 E. P. Thompson, *Making of the English Working Class*. Another classic in the genre is Hobsbawm and Rudé, *Captain Swing*.
6 Thompson and Garratt, *Rise and Fulfilment*.
7 For the relationship between Edward Thompson and Tagore see Thompson, *Alien Homage*; Dasgupta (ed.), *A Difficult Friendship*.
8 On this element in Tagore's work see Openshaw, "Radicalism"; Thompson, *Alien Homage*.
9 For various accounts of this challenge in the Indian subcontinent, see O'Hanlon, *Caste, Conflict, and Ideology*; Raychaudhuri, *Europe Reconsidered*; Chatterjee, *Nation and its Fragments*; Kaviraj, *Unhappy Consciousness*.
10 Trevor-Roper, "Rise of Christian Europe."
11 Lonsdale, "How to study Africa"; Lonsdale, "Emergence of African Nations," p. 139.
12 For an earlier "Caribbeanist" attempt to do the same, see James, *Black Jacobins*. For the Africanist literature, see Denoon and Kuper, "Nationalist historians"; Ranger, *Emerging Themes of African History*. For the idea of "people without history" see Wolf, *Europe and the People without History*; Miller, "History and Africa."
13 Nehru, *Discovery of India*.
14 For a discussion of some of these issues, see Chakrabarty, "Postcoloniality."
15 Kaviraj, *Unhappy Consciousness*.
16 Savarkar, *Indian War of Independence*.
17 For some of these approaches, see Kopf, *British Orientalism*; Sarkar, *Modern India*; Chandra, *India's Struggle for Independence*; id., *Rise and Growth of Economic Nationalism*.
18 Low, *Congress and the Raj*; Ray, *Social Conflict*; Charlesworth, *Peasants and Imperial Rule*.
19 Rudolph and Rudolph, *Modernity of Tradition*; Cohn, *India*; Cohn, *Anthropologist*.
20 James, *Black Jacobins*. See Scott, *Conscripts of Modernity* for a nuanced account of James's argument.
21 Ranger, "Connexions."
22 For example, Lonsdale, "States and social processes"; Iliffe, *African Poor*.
23 Ranger, *Revolt in Southern Rhodesia*; id., "Connexions"; Iliffe, "Maji Maji rebellion."
24 Lonsdale, "Emergence of African nations," p. 14. For the development of African historiography since the 1960s, and also an insightful discussion of the idea of resistance, see Cooper, "Conflict and connection."
25 Robinson and Gallagher with Denny, *Africa and the Victorians*; Robinson, "Non-European foundations."

26 Culture is particularly foregrounded in Chakrabarty, *Rethinking Working-Class History*. Also Guha and Spivak (eds), *Subaltern Studies*; Guha (ed.), *Subaltern Studies Reader*; Chakrabarty, *Habitations of Modernity*; Ludden, *Reading Subaltern Studies*. For two critical perspectives see O'Hanlon, "Recovering the subject"; Haynes and Prakash, *Contesting Power*.

27 For some of these perspectives, see Ballantyne and Burton (eds), *Bodies in Contact* and Ballantyne, *Between Colonialism*; S. Howe, *Ireland and Empire*; Branch, "Mau Mau rebellion"; Elizabeth Elbourne's chapter in this volume.

28 Jameson, *Political Unconscious*; Bhabha, *Nation and Narration*; Guha, "Small voice of history."

29 Heidegger, "Letter on Humanism," p. 225.

30 Raychaudhuri, "Indian nationalism."

31 Bayly, "Judith Brown," p. 267.

32 Washbrook, "Country politics," p. 539. Other examples of the genre are Seal, *Emergence of Indian Nationalism*; Baker and Washbrook, *South India*; Bayly, *Local Roots of Indian Politics*.

33 Raychaudhuri, "Indian nationalism," p. 750.

34 MacIntyre, *After Virtue*; *id.*, *Three Rival Versions*.

35 Lalu, "Grammar of domination," Spivak, "Can the subaltern speak?"; *id.*, *Critique of Postcolonial Reason*.

36 Spivak, "Can the subaltern speak," revised as chapter 3 of Spivak, *Critique of Postcolonial Reason*.

37 Spivak, *Critique of Postcolonial Reason*, p. 163. For an important criticism of Spivak's argument, which suggests instead that the critic can recover "a conception of the native as historical subject and agent," see Parry, "Problems in current theories."

38 For widely differing accounts of the European discussion of *sati* see Mani, *Contested Traditions*; Major, *Pious Flames*.

39 R. Young, *White Mythologies*, p. 160.

40 Said, *Orientalism*; Bhabha, *Location of Culture*.

41 Peel, "For who hath despised," pp. 606, 593. See Ricoeur, *Time and Narrative*; Carr, *Time, Narrative, and History* for the philosophical underpinnings of this approach.

42 Peel, "For who hath despised," p. 602.

43 For a discussion of these approaches in African history see Spear, "Neo-traditionalism"; Lonsdale, "Agency in tight corners."

44 See Catherine Hall's chapter in this volume.

45 Comaroff and Comaroff, *Revelation and Revolution*, 2.

46 Appadurai, "Putting hierarchy in its place," p. 37; for a discussion of the relationship between supposedly autonomous culture and place, see also Gupta and Ferguson, "Beyond 'culture'."

47 See the last chapter of J. E. Wilson, *Domination of Strangers*; Bayly, *Empire and Information*; Anderson, *Histories of the Hanged*.

48 For a discussion of Rammohun's cosmopolitanism see Bayly, "Rammohan Roy."

49 Mazower, *Salonica*.

50 Patterson, *Slavery and Social Death*.

51 For a pioneering account of slave culture see Genovese, *Roll, Jordan, Roll*.

52 Carretta, *Equiano, the African*.

53 Calkins, "Regionally oriented ruling group"; McLane, *Land and Local Kingship*; J. E. Wilson, *Domination of Strangers*.

54 See the discussion of "tribal breakouts" in Bayly, *Indian Society*.

55 Hirschman, *Exit, Voice, and Loyalty*; J. E. Wilson, "A thousand countries to go to."
56 Bayly, *Indian Society*; Washbrook, "Land and labour"; *id.*, "Eighteenth-century issues."
57 Inden, *Imagining India*.
58 See, for example, Bose, *Agrarian Bengal*; Chatterjee, "Colonial state and peasant resistance."

Further Reading

The life cycle of an analytical concept such as "agency" is perhaps somewhere between ten and twenty years in the humanities and social sciences—just long enough for a scholar to publish a book or two based on a particular approach and then begin to revise their views. The word "agency" became a central concern in the history of colonized societies during the early 1990s. It is only now that critical appraisals and review essays that treat "agency" as a general concept which dominates a field are being published.

Scholarship from the early 1990s foregrounded the role of culture rather than economics and state formation, and included C. Breckenridge and P. van der Veer (eds), *Orientalism and the Postcolonial Predicament* and John Illife, *Africans: The History of a Continent*. Around this time, a number of scholars revised earlier arguments about the monodirectional power of European institutions in making non-European culture. Key revisions were Edward Said's *Culture and Imperialism* (1993), which partially criticizes the argument of *Orientalism* (1978); and Terence Ranger's "The invention of tradition revisited" in T. Ranger and O. Vaughan (eds), *Legitimacy and the State in Twentieth-century Africa*, which gives agency a greater role than his essay in the volume edited with Eric Hobsbawm, *The Invention of Tradition*. Studies of colonial discourse began to show how imperial regimes denied and undermined indigenous agency, offering their own theories of agency instead—for example, R. Inden's *Imagining India*. By contrast, others suggested that the relative weakness of colonial institutions allowed room for "indigenous" cultural assertion, as in Bruce Berman and John Lonsdale's *Unhappy Valley*, or C. A. Bayly's *Indian Society and the Making of the British Empire* and *Empire and Information*. William Pinch, "Same difference in India and Europe" considers the relationship between these two strands in South Asian history.

Since the 1990s, the work of historians has been fertilized by social sciences concerned to consider the idea of agency in a more theoretical—and often more rigorous—fashion. Appraisals of the concept in various different disciplines include L. M. Ahearn, "Language and Agency"; J. L. Dornan, "Agency and Archaeology: Past, Present, and Future Directions" and M. Emirbayer and A. Mische, "What is agency?".

The concept has, of course, been central within different philosophical traditions. In the essays collected in his *Human Agency and Language* Charles Taylor tries to produce a positive definition of the relationship between agency, language, and human subjectivity, which suggests that language is a form of social action, and inaugurates the linguistic and narratological turn mentioned in this chapter. Taylor's arguments are taken in an important direction by Saba Mahmood in *The Politics of Piety. The Islamic Revival and the Feminist Subject*, which argues that agency can be exercised in an embodied, not merely intellectual form. Also important in trying to define agency in philosophical terms are the works of P. Bourdieau, *Outline of a Theory of Practice* and A. Giddens, *New Rules of Sociological Method*. By contrast the anthropologist Talal Asad unravels some of the contradictions and ambivalences implicit in using the concept in the introductory chapter of *Genealogies of Religion* and his more recent *Formations of the Secular*, an approach which has influenced this chapter.

12

Ends of Empire

Sarah Stockwell[1]

At midnight on June 30, 1997, Britain transferred Hong Kong back to China. This most recent episode in British decolonization came approximately a half-century after British withdrawal from India in 1947, often seen as initiating the end of empire. By 1967 over twenty British territories had achieved independence. So rapid and widespread was the dissolution of empire in the first post-war decades that today only sixteen British dependencies remain (all, save Gibraltar and the British Antarctic Territory, small island territories).

Scholarly analysis of these developments is of relatively recent origin, but unlike some of the other areas of imperial history discussed in this book this blossoming of scholarship has been driven by the gradual opening of relevant archival deposits rather than major methodological shifts.[2] The resulting literature has often been "traditional" in appearance; high politics takes center stage, with historians essentially concerned with why and how the empire was lost. Historians have concentrated on "interesting" or "important" territories whose transitions could be easily traced in British archives; only recently have some smaller or apparently marginal decolonizations received much scholarly attention. Moreover, in the rush to write the history of decolonization, the (admittedly "minor") British dependencies that remain have largely been excluded from accounts of post-1945 empire (including the Falkland Islands erupting from obscurity in 1982, but otherwise neglected; and the smaller island dependencies).[3] Perhaps because of the abundance of source material, the potential for comparative European study has yet to be fully realized; British historians, with one or two notable exceptions,[4] focus largely on the British experience.

Nearly two decades ago a leading scholar decried the intellectual weakness of writing about decolonization in "chronological slabs."[5] Some years and many publications on, the picture looks in many ways dispiritingly similar. That this should be so is in part a consequence of the tremendous output of the *British Documents on the End of Empire* project, which, continuing a tradition that began with the twelve volumes of documentary material relating to the *Transfer of Power* in India edited by Nicholas Mansergh, has made accessible great swathes of archival material from the

British National Archives in general (series A) and country (series B) volumes.[6] The project has made a huge contribution to our understanding of British imperial policy and decolonization, but it has arguably also allowed scholarship to continue within broadly familiar parameters without appearing stale, thanks to the novel insights drawn from its pages. The pattern of archival concessions has continued to shape the literature, with growing attention being paid to the 1960s and the 1970s, although the passage of time has in turn inevitably nuanced understanding of the 1940s and 1950s.[7]

If this all looks worthy but dull (especially since the steam has gone out of major ideological disputes associated with Marxist or early nationalist accounts), in recent years the field has also undergone something of a metamorphosis: the end of empire now looks much more exciting. Themes are beginning to receive the attention they deserve. The continued vigor of regional studies is contributing ever more sophisticated analyses of colonial politics, societies and economies. Recent endeavors to put empire back into British history, coupled with post-colonialism's interest in locating the "post-colonial" among colonizers as well as colonized, has resulted in new attention to the metropolitan consequences of decolonization, chipping away at the received wisdom that the end of empire had little significant impact on Britain.

Perhaps most strikingly, British decolonization has in the early twenty-first century provoked more jagged controversy,[8] both academic and public. The BBC series *Empire Warriors* (2004) disseminated new and more disturbing images of British decolonization, in stark contrast to the nostalgic manner in which, for example, at the time of the Hong Kong handover in 1997 the British press had briefly contemplated Britain's imperial past and its legacy (the *Daily Telegraph* was moved to publish a commemorative empire history of "a story we all should know" with "much to cherish and to celebrate").[9] In Kenya late colonial politics has become the subject of charged contemporary political debate.[10]

The variety in subject and analysis of recent historical writing has generated images of British decolonization that seem hard to reconcile. For George Boyce, the "relative ease with which England got rid of its empire" (though "there were hard and difficult decisions to make: lives were lost, [and] military and police repression were used from time to time"), meant that "the thing was done with remarkably few scars, or so it was perceived." This reflected an "English tradition of resolving political issues in a way that enabled the old order to give way to the new, and that combined the benefit of practical thinking with the language of constitutional development." Frank Heinlein similarly judges that Britain did "all told . . . rather well." For David Anderson, on the other hand, "British justice in 1950s Kenya was a blunt, brutal and unsophisticated instrument of oppression."[11]

The contrasting characterizations we now possess reflect in part historians' different methodologies, sources, and sympathies. It is generally accepted that late British colonialism could flex its military muscles, as Suez demonstrated. Yet as British records became accessible under the thirty-year release rule, much first-generation scholarship focused on the 1930s and 1940s, when there seemed sufficient evidence of reform and accommodation to suggest a British "way" in decolonization contrasting with that of other European powers, and which some even contended laid the foundations for the development of African nationalism. This may partly have been so: there are no direct parallels in British decolonization to Algeria, IndoChina, or Mozambique. But perhaps Britain's late colonial wars have been *perceived* as different to those of the French or the Portuguese partly because they did not have the same contemporary domestic political impact, and because in the case of the latter, at least by the time Portugal engaged in conflict over Angola and Mozambique, this had become less acceptable to a largely post-imperial and increasingly liberal Britain.

Encouraged by the linguistic turn we can now adopt a more critical eye when reading the official record, bringing into sharper focus both the prejudice and more benevolent paternalism (if still embedded in a sense of racial difference and British superiority) that informed the workings of the "official mind" perhaps disguised by an aura of objectivity imparted by neat papers filed by Whitehall bureaucrats. As the focus of historical research expands to encompass individuals and subjects previously neglected, we also have more evidence of the ways in which empire news was spun,[12] arguably with consequences not just for contemporary perceptions of British decolonization, but also for how historians have written about the British experience. As one writer commenting on the transfer of power in India reflects, contemporary newsreels "perhaps more than any other mass medium, have defined the way in which we see the first major decolonization of the twentieth century."[13]

However, that British decolonization produces such different characterizations also reflects the fact that the history of the British Empire encompasses genuinely very different experiences, reflecting in part the geographically and constitutionally diffuse nature of British imperial interests. The British Empire in 1945 included some 700 million people spread across the world. The historian of Nigeria may have a very different picture of British decolonization to, say, the historian of India or the historian of Fiji. It is a commonplace, but important nonetheless, that there was not one British empire but several: an empire of the "white" dominions (the "old" Commonwealth); the informal empire of the Middle East (a region perhaps more crucial to late colonial British interests than some tropical and island dependencies); and, most pertinent to this chapter, the very different dependent empires of Asia, Africa, the Mediterranean, and Caribbean. Contemporaries probably shared this view. The empire was not centrally managed: until at least the late 1930s British policy was "reactive," and, although World War II invigorated imperial administration, this occurred at a point when shifting local and international opinion made direct rule from London increasingly inappropriate.

This mixed bag of territories was run by individuals of varying abilities and moral sensibility. Many were well intentioned (if immersed in the cultural mores of their time), but some were downright nasty. It had always been so, but we can speculate as to whether the end of empire exposed these human idiosyncrasies more deeply: from those who grappled conscientiously with their duties to "dependent" peoples to those who, confronted with new forms and levels of resistance, fell back upon repression and violence. Many faced multiple and sometimes conflicting responsibilities, reflecting the peculiar position of colonial administrators and officials, caught between colony and metropole, majorities and minorities, white "kith and kin" and black African nationalists. If Britain's record in decolonization looks increasingly sullied, it remains very difficult to reach global judgments.

This chapter considers some of these "ends" of empire and some of the ambiguities and conflicts within the history of the end of the British Empire. It first examines their unraveling: briefly, that of the dominions and informal empire, and, in much greater depth that of the dependent empire, reflecting its more developed historiography. It then reviews thinking on the causation of end of empire. A third and final section considers Britain's "empires" of finance, and as well as of missionary activity: empires which are only now beginning to be studied in the end-of-empire period, and whose own "decolonizations" could proceed at a different pace, as well as the impact of decolonization on Britain itself.

I

Britain's post-1945 relations with Canada, South Africa, Australia and New Zealand have rarely been accorded significant historical attention.[14] Yet these "white dominions" were a key component of British imperial identity. Defined in 1926 as "autonomous Communities within the British Empire, equal in status . . . and freely associated as members of the British Commonwealth of Nations,"[15] the dominions still remained part of the British imperial system, bound by a web of cultural, defense, and economic ties reinforced by the continuation of preferential trading agreements within the empire, first introduced in 1932. For British statesmen and officials they occupied a central place in British cultural, economic and diplomatic worlds through the 1940s and the 1950s, as myriad official and informal networks illustrate. The formation of a Defence Advisory Committee on Commonwealth Minerals in 1951, chaired initially by an Australian, provides one small example;[16] successive governments' concern with the Commonwealth connection in their deliberations over the European project a more substantial one.[17]

Dating the point at which the dominions ceased to be "British" is notoriously difficult. This is not only because nationalist sentiments developed in different dominions at different times (associated especially with the late nineteenth century and World War I)[18] but also because of the problems of singling out a decisive moment when "local" national identities eclipsed the British. Certainly, however, the Commonwealth bond was increasingly fractured by declining complementarity in economics, defense, and politics and by increased concern with the United States both in Britain and the dominions. It was also undermined by Britain's first European application in 1961.[19] But as the periodic debates over Australian republicanism illustrate, this story has yet to reach its full conclusion.

Establishing a single chronology of decolonization for the dependent empire can be equally problematic. In part this is because of the deep historical roots of both British decline and anti-colonial nationalism. The Indian National Congress formed in 1885; elsewhere subject populations had long manifested resistance in a variety of ways. The hegemonic cultural discourse of colonialism was challenged by movements like pan-Africanism, as often located at the imperial metropole or in the Americas as in the colonies. Imperial historiography once sought to distinguish between early modes of opposition and later "nationalism"—the former what Ronald Robinson and Jack Gallagher described as "romantic reactionary struggles against the facts," contrasting with later "defter nationalisms" employing Western political idioms. Others, however, such as Terence Ranger, focusing especially on central and southern Africa, emphasized the complex interplay between "primary" and "secondary" resistance and the continuities in resistance over time, thus anticipating post-colonialism's project of tracing lines of resistance with less concern for immediate historical context.[20]

Commentators, like contemporaries, recognize too that transfers of power did not necessarily end imperial influence. Marxists argued that formal rule gave way to "neo-colonialism" where independence could not alter economies forged under colonialism.[21] Post-colonial theory also sees the independence achieved as far from complete. But where neo-colonialism posits essentially passive colonized subjects, post-colonialism stresses their agency, and places its fulfillment among colonizers as well as colonized as occurring after the transfers of power, or even as yet to come.[22]

We return to these themes later. But a less ambitious narrative organized in the traditional way around transfers of power concentrated in the twenty years after 1945 still risks telescoping diverse events into a single "end of empire." Even here there is no one story of decolonization. This is especially true for the 1940s, which saw the first great wave of British decolonization: the independence of India and the creation of Pakistan in 1947, and in 1948 withdrawal from the former League of Nations-mandated territory of Palestine and independence for Burma and Ceylon (Sri Lanka). The date of independence in each case reflected distinct constitutional and political histories.

India had a long history of organized nationalist opposition. By the late 1930s British India had already achieved provincial self-government. The decision by the majority Hindu nationalist organization, the Indian National Congress, to launch a campaign of civil disobedience in protest at Britain's failure to consult before taking India into war, served with the unanticipated arrival of the Japanese enemy on India's borders to persuade the British government in 1942 to offer future self-government in return for wartime co-operation. The offer was rejected and Congress embarked upon its "Quit India" movement. The post-war Labour government nonetheless felt effectively committed to early withdrawal. Communal conflict between the country's majority Hindu population and the minority Muslims (now under Jinnah's leadership demanding a separate state) scuppered hopes that power would be transferred to a united India and, amid fears that the country had become ungovernable, led Mountbatten to expedite retreat.[23]

In Palestine, unable to reconcile competing Arab and Jewish ambitions (the latter now given added moral force by Jewish wartime suffering and political weight by American interest) and the target of escalating Zionist terrorism, the British referred the issue to the United Nations. However, they rejected UN plans for partition, fearing that this would alienate opinion throughout the crucial oil-producing and strategically important Arab world. The British resigned from the mandate and evacuated personnel, one of the few occasions when the manner of their departure lacked even the pretense of forethought.[24]

While the writing was on the wall for British colonialism in south Asia and Palestine, elsewhere a renewed sense of imperial purpose was evident. This developed before the war in response to labor protest and colonial unrest—most serious in the sugar-producing British West Indies between 1935 and 1938—and a series of critiques of Britain's colonial record from quite different quarters. Wartime administrative reorganization and colonial mobilisation supplied added impetus. This refurbishment of colonial policy is illustrated by empire-wide initiatives concerning labor, housing, and education, and expanded development provision under the Colonial Development and Welfare Act (1940), successive revisions of which so increased the sums available that between 1946 and 1970 nearly £344 million was expended.[25] These measures lent at least surface legitimacy to British claims regarding its colonial role and underpinned other more political wartime initiatives: in 1942 the old rhetoric of "trusteeship" was revised in favour of a new language of "partnership" with the colonies, and in 1943 the secretary of state for the colonies, Oliver Stanley, declared British policy to be to "guide Colonial peoples along the road to self-government within the framework of the British empire."[26]

In south-east Asia, where the Japanese occupation created both an opportunity and a need to plan for the future, Britain proposed a new Malayan Union conjoining various territories with the Federated Malay States, and abandoning collaboration with the Malay sultans in favor of direct rule and the creation of a common citizenship among the region's Malay, Chinese, and Indian communities. The (long-term) goal was democratic self-government. The union was swiftly abandoned in the face of Malay protests (they feared political usurpation by non-Malays) and sovereignty was restored to the sultans; nevertheless the Federation established in 1948 represented London's attempt to preserve the essentials of the modernizing policy.[27] In post-war Africa too, the British retreated from systems of "indirect rule" through local native chiefs and advisors in favour of elected representative local government with the objective, elaborated at a 1947 conference of Britain's African governors, of promoting eventual self-government.

Too much should not be made of these initiatives: variously conceived, they sought inter alia to bolster British authority locally and in the eyes of the international community (especially Britain's wartime anti-colonial ally, America). There remained distinct limits to the British government's willingness to diverge from the classic model of imperial-colonial economic relations, while country-case studies reveal Britain had only mixed success in realizing welfare initiatives.[28] The same is true of "reform" of local government. Richard Rathbone's pioneering study suggests that in the 1950s Gold Coast chronically underfunded local government was a "dreadful mess."[29] Yet conceived with no expectation of imminent political change, the bureaucratic activity of the early to mid-1940s (as seen, the focus of much early scholarship) still reflects a reinvigoration in aspects of British imperial policy.[30]

This renewed sense of purpose could manifest itself in other ways. The Labour foreign secretary Ernest Bevin initially believed the empire to hold the key to a reassertion of a British world role, as he briefly sought to ally Britain with other European colonial powers in Africa as a "third force" to match the USA and USSR.[31] In the context of financial difficulties, however, as important was that an abortive attempt to restore sterling convertibility in 1947 was followed by a retreat into the "sterling area" (formed by the wartime introduction of currency and trade controls among the loose association of countries basing their currency on sterling). Britain maintained controls on colonial spending in the dollar area and on sterling convertibility, thereby intensifying imperial economic integration.[32] Britain's plight increased the value of Malaya and Africa, whose dollar-earning exports helped finance Britain's (and the independent Commonwealth's) dollar-area import requirements, which outvalued their exports to America.[33] Simultaneously Britain sought to increase production of colonial substitutes for imports from beyond the sterling area. These policies stymied some existing development and welfare initiatives, ushering in a period of greater imperial exploitation overseen by an army of new British personnel memorably characterized as a "second colonial occupation," although they may not everywhere have been as ruthlessly applied as a reading of general imperial policy suggests.[34]

This mixed and in many ways contradictory picture continued into the 1950s, which saw perhaps the most striking juxtapositions of accommodation and reform with violence and conflict. The latter reflected problems associated with those colonies with "plural" (mixed race) societies and especially those with entrenched settler communities.

It would be misleading to characterize the transfers of power in Britain's west African colonies as "straightforward" or peaceful. Each produced its own particular challenges and conflicts: rioting in the Gold Coast (Ghana) in 1948; and here and in Nigeria the development of disputes between regionally-based political parties. Yet in general terms, and in contrast to the settler colonies of east and central Africa, west African territories illustrate that strain of British decolonization characterized by negotiation and accommodation: end of empire mapped out in constitutional discussions in colonial capitals and in meetings at Lancaster House in London. The Gold Coast riots in that "model colony" initiated a sequence of events that within three years resulted in the first elected Assembly in British Africa, and three years later in full internal self-government, comprehensively outpacing the leisurely reform timetable envisaged as recently as 1947. A domino effect ensued, especially in nearby Nigeria, which achieved independence in 1960.[35]

In West Africa policymakers chose to protect British interests through negotiation and concession. Elsewhere the 1950s support quite different characterizations of British decolonization. The Conservative governments of Churchill and Eden sustained a counter-insurgency campaign in Malaya, where in 1948 a state of emergency had been declared. A new High Commissioner and Commander-in-Chief, Sir Gerald Templer, from 1952 developed new approaches to the communist revolt, which helped turn the tide in Britain's favor by 1954.[36] Thereafter Malaya, like the Gold Coast and Nigeria, was steered swiftly towards independence. The declaration of further states of emergency saw new military campaigns in Cyprus (1955–9), and Kenya (1952–60). The outstanding example of this willingness to use force in defense of British interests came in 1956 when Eden authorised British collusion with France and Israel to attack Egypt after President Nasser nationalized the Suez Canal. International isolation and the threat to the pound forced the government into humiliating retreat, followed by the ailing Eden's resignation and his replacement by Harold Macmillan.

Different again was the decision in 1953 to create a federation of three central African territories, the white self-governing Southern Rhodesia, and Nyasaland and Northern Rhodesia, with a view to establishing a dominion that might progress towards independence under white rule. Justified on economic grounds, this flew in the face of African opposition. Yet although the inauguration of the Central African Federation (CAF) looks bold in a period when elsewhere in Africa the British were increasingly on the defensive, a recent interpretation presents it as a concession to nationalism, although here the "nationalists were white."[37]

These contrasting developments are reflected in historians' varied characterizations of the decade before Suez. David Goldsworthy argues that the Churchill and Eden administrations sought to "contain change"; W. D. McIntyre identifies instead the "ambiguous fifties"; while Martin Lynn and others see Britain not only attempting to "hold the line against imperial retreat, but [contemplating] . . . a determined attempt at imperial reassertion." As L. J. Butler argues, "even on the eve of the withdrawal from Africa, British officials . . . display[ed] an almost astonishing confidence in their own ability to shape the long-term development of the colonial territories."[38]

Developments in the late 1950s and the early 1960s, in contrast, constituted a more straightforward process of imperial retreat. Famously declaring that a "wind of change" was blowing through Africa, from late 1959 Macmillan initiated the second great phase of British decolonization. Government officials now openly spoke of the end of empire and, with the various emergencies now ended, accommodation and negotiation became the order of the day.[39] Between 1960 and 1964 (when Labour returned to power) ambitions to transfer power to multiracial governments in east Africa and to the settler-led CAF were abandoned as colonies were steered towards independence: Nigeria and Cyprus in 1960; Sierra Leone and Tanganyika (Tanzania) in 1961; Uganda, Jamaica, and Trinidad in 1962 (the former's decision to secede bringing to an end a Caribbean federation established in 1958);[40] Kenya in 1963, the year the CAF was dissolved in response to Northern Rhodesia and Nyasaland's progress towards independence under black majority rule, and Sabah and Sarawak were integrated into a Malaysian Federation; Nyasaland (Malawi), Northern Rhodesia (Zambia) and Malta in 1964. Soon after came independence for the former High Commission southern African territories and smaller Caribbean dependencies; later Fijian independence in 1970 and the transfer of Hong Kong to China in 1997.

Official reports commissioned in the later 1950s reveal the background to this imperial retreat. As late as 1957 one concluded that the "costs" and "benefits" of colonial rule were evenly matched: evidence that, although Suez exposed Britain's financial weakness and inability to act without American support, while damaging its relations with the United States and Commonwealth,[41] it did not immediately provoke disavowal of empire. By spring 1959, however, the ground was shifting. Members of an Africa Committee of officials were by now torn: if "Western governments appear to be reluctant to concede independence to their dependent territories" this might "alienate African opinion and turn it towards the Soviet Union." Yet premature withdrawal might leave "large areas of Africa ripe for Communist exploitation." Events tipped the scales in favor of early retreat on March 3, 1959, as Ronald Hyam and W. R. Louis characterized it "the fateful day which signalled the moral end of the British empire in Africa." Eleven Mau Mau detainees died in the Hola Camp in Kenya. Elsewhere twenty Africans were killed protesting at the arrest of Dr Hastings Banda, leader of the Nyasaland African Congress;[42] in the subsequent Devlin enquiry the colonial administration was likened to a "police state." The newly appointed colonial secretary Iain Macleod would later recall that these events constituted "the decisive moment when it became clear to me that we could no longer continue with the old methods of government in Africa, and that meant inexorably a move towards African independence."[43]

If the core of the colonial empire had gone by 1964, it took a crisis following sterling devaluation in 1967 for Britain to abandon a defense role east of Suez.[44] Successive post-war governments had debated the future of defense commitments in the Middle East and beyond. In 1952 foreign secretary Eden had noted that the "more gradually and inconspicuously we can transfer the real burdens from our own to American shoulders, the less damage we shall do to our position and influence in the world";[45] a 1957 Defense White Paper had envisaged reliance on a nuclear strategy with a concomitant reduction in conventional forces. But policymakers had clung stubbornly to an "informal" empire, as much for prestige as for access to resources or military facilities.[46] It is widely argued that Britain following Suez finally passed its mantle in the Middle East to the United States,[47] although, as Simon Smith has emphasized, until its eventual withdrawal in the early 1970s Britain retained paramountcy in the Gulf and in particular in the important oil-rich state of Kuwait.[48]

II

Much scholarly ink has been spent debating the causes of death of the British Empire. Post-war politicians situated it within a historical framework encompassing the progressive British devolution of authority to white self-governing colonies from the late 1830s, a self-serving whiggish interpretation presenting the wholesale dissolution of empire after 1945 as the culmination rather than the wreck of British ambitions.

One does not have to dig deep for evidence belying Macmillan's contention that the British had "not lost the will, or even the power to rule. But they did not conceive of themselves as having the right to govern in perpetuity."[49] One could cite the abandonment of Conservative plans for multiracial government in Africa and the preservation of the CAF, or the retreat from territories once deemed essential to Britain's interests at dates inconceivable only a few years before. Instead most scholars see Britain responding to variously the rise of the two superpowers and the Cold War,[50] anti-colonial nationalism,[51] weakening British appetite for empire in the era of the welfare state,[52] and, related to this, the declining value of empire,[53] or more broadly to the interplay between these shifting domestic, colonial, and international circumstances.[54]

Most of these developments had earlier antecedents. Following World War I Britain, now holding more territory than ever, had struggled to manage crises in Egypt, Ireland, and India, while the interwar depression had corroded Britain's colonial authority. Jack Gallagher argued that in these already difficult circumstances World War II revived empire as far-flung possessions mobilized in support of an "imperial" war.[55] But more enduring was its longer-term impact through economic and political dislocation. Throughout the colonial empire, whether in south-east Asia (overrun by the Japanese in 1941–2), India, the West Indies (exposed to unprecedented American influence), or Africa (where some colonies found themselves at war with Vichy neighbours or compelled to up production of essential supplies by whatever means including conscription), the war contributed at varying times and complex ways to emergent political movements.[56] The same was true of the intrusive colonialism of the immediate post-war era, for example in Malaya where the British sought to reassert control of the forest frontier.[57]

On the domestic front, with debts of around £3,500 million (much owed to the colonies), British gold and currency reserves spent, and industry no longer geared to consumer and export production, post-war Britain faced a massive imbalance in the value of exports and imports. In 1945 Britain went cap in hand to the United States for a loan, the terms of which required a disastrous attempt to restore sterling convertibility in summer 1947. As we have seen, the effects of the financial crisis temporarily increased the perceived importance of the African and south-east Asian colonies. But the mid-1950s fall in the market value of primary commodities rendered the colonies less useful economically—especially after the independence of the more valuable territories of Malaya and the Gold Coast. As Britain moved towards economic liberalization, culminating in the restoration of sterling convertibility in 1958, historians such as Gerold Krozewski and Allister Hinds have argued that the perceived irrelevance of formal empire explains the subsequent rapid decolonization; A. G. Hopkins contends that Macmillan believed that "he could remodel the empire without damaging Britain's economic interests." In contrast, W. R. Louis and Ronald Hyam found little evidence that financial considerations were crucial determinants in the transfers of power.[58] But it is important to acknowledge that British economic decline comparative to the United States undermined its ability to fully commit to the continued development of colonies as they approached independence while fulfilling its defense commitments and ambitions for an independent nuclear deterrent, both determinants of "superpower status" in the transition to a "post-imperial" world.

In comparison to economic problems, the impact of domestic politics appears less important, particularly in the 1940s and early 1950s, where David Goldsworthy identifies a cross-party consensus on colonial questions.[59] However, there were differences of principle and allegiance between Labour and the Conservatives, as Labour's flirtation with nationalizing British firms overseas and the pro-settler Conservative commitment to achieving "multiracial" governments and the CAF indicate.[60] These differences sharpened in the later 1950s. Labour, its approach to empire radicalized by continued evidence of colonial nationalism, pressurized the Conservatives in ways which Kenneth Morgan claims contributed both impetus and content to Macmillan's "wind of change" policy after 1960.[61]

In an international context the United States could be an uncomfortable ally, ideologically opposed to colonialism and its vision of a multilateral free-trade system frustrated by British imperial preference and sterling area arrangements. Yet Britain successfully weathered American anti-colonialism during the war,[62] and the onset of the Cold War complicated American attitudes. On occasion America could now be seen as coming "to the rescue" of the British empire.[63] In British Guiana the United States, fearful that independence might hand power to the nationalist Cheddi Jagan, whom they saw as a potential Castro, even pressed Macmillan to intervene politically as it was "not possible for us to put up with an independent British Guiana under Jagan."[64] Anglo-American differences still surfaced in the United Nations, however, its membership swelled with former colonies: Britain often found itself the target of criticism.[65] More generally the Cold War changed political calculations. By the late 1950s an overriding concern was the need to manage transfers of power in the manner least likely to facilitate the spread of communism. Meanwhile Belgian and French decolonization left Britain more isolated in its colonial activity, especially in Africa, where developments in Algeria and the former Belgian Congo further discredited colonialism.[66] The post-war international order had become less accommodating to the imperial project.

We have already seen that these shifting domestic and international contexts interacted in complex and diverse ways with emergent nationalist movements. One significant strain of scholarship nonetheless credits Britain with having made the running at least in the case of African decolonization. Ronald Robinson argued that by 1947 "the door to independence had already been unlocked for African nationalists . . . It had been unlocked, not in response to, but in anticipation of nationalist pressure, by British economic need and moral utopianism." John Flint further suggests that "the emergence of nationalist political parties seeking mass support was the result of the decision to decolonize and a creation of imperial policy."[67] Yet as records open up for the later 1950s and the 1960s, it emerges that even where colonies followed a largely peaceful transition to independence London was pushed by reports of nationalist politics and the fear that local politics would spiral out of British control, often penned by British governors, like Arden-Clarke in the Gold Coast or Sir Glyn Jones in Nyasaland.[68]

In the late colonial period resistance in all its guises, from labor protest to religious revivalism, accompanied and sometimes collaborated with new political organizations campaigning for independent nationhood. Against backgrounds of both social and economic dislocation and war, such organizations won support and produced a cast of nationalist heroes commemorated in statuary, street names, autobiographies, and celebratory nationalist histories across the ex-colonial world. An ongoing and vigorous tradition of regional studies has permitted more academic assessments of the role and purchase of national identities in engendering resistance in communities fragmented by religion, ethnicity, geography, and income, as Jon Wilson discusses in the case of India elsewhere in this volume. Most recently, post-colonial and gender studies have made possible even fuller understandings of the complexity of late-colonial politics, exposing the significant contributions of gender, class, generational, and ideological disputes. For example, in Kenya, where political exclusion, labor laws, and, above all, alienation of Kikuyu land to European settlers had by the 1930s provoked African opposition, a crisis of gender relations and anxieties about moral decline within Kikuyu society and inter-village disputes contributed significantly to the emergence of Mau Mau.[69] In the Gold Coast generational, regional, and economic differences propelled the rise of an Ashanti-based National Liberation Movement that in the last years of British rule campaigned unsuccessfully for a federal constitution to protect Ashanti interests against the southern-based Convention People's Party of "commoners" and "verandah boys" led by the charismatic Kwame Nkrumah.[70]

III

If the *dynamics* and causation of the end of empire have inevitably attracted most attention from historians, the *management* of "decolonization" as a process has now become a prominent theme[71], although the two cannot entirely be separated. Historians see similarities in the origins of the various European decolonizations; British handling of the process, however, is often portrayed as distinctive. For some, the means by which Britain negotiated decolonization reflects a "liberal" turn in policy-making manifest in the reforms of the 1930s and 1940s and later accommodation and negotiation. Many note that Britain sought sometimes to anticipate nationalist pressure, debating whether it was better to move "fast" or "slow," and for some this served to "unlock" the door for African nationalism. As already noted, George Boyce, for example, argues that when forced to accept the inevitability of change the British were at least pre-equipped with a "whole vocabulary that implied adjustment, accommodation, gradualism," acquired in major colonial losses in the eighteenth century and consistent with a Burkean political tradition—and in which the ideal of Commonwealth was important.[72]

If the British rhetoric of accommodation and Commonwealth certainly illuminates how Britain handled the retreat from empire, it also risks casting British management of nationalism in an overly benevolent light, glossing over sometimes devastating legacies of turmoil and violence. In India, while finessing the details of the independence ceremony, the British deliberately left the details of the partition line concealed in Mountbatten's safe until after their authority expired on Independence Day.[73] Many thousands had already died in communal violence; but an estimated half million more were killed during partition. In other places British authorities intervened to sometimes brutal effect to shape political outcomes. In Kenya, David Anderson identifies a strategy to "cultivate an African opposition, by arming vigilantes, styled as Home Guards, to protect villagers from attack and to assist the police and military in operations against the Mau Mau fighters." The war against Mau Mau, he argues, was waged in such a way that it might strip rebels and their sympathizers "of every possible human right, while at the same time maintaining the appearance of accountability, transparency, and justice"; a conclusion most starkly demonstrated by the extensive use of state execution that resulted in the trial of around 3,000 Kikuyu on capital charges, of whom some 1,090 were hung between 1952 and 1960.[74] Anderson believes that the use of state execution on this scale is unparalleled in the history of British imperialism, but, if not to the same degree, there is evidence of British abuse in other places during decolonization.[75] In comparison to these extremes the Cyprus emergency was less brutal; even so Robert Holland's account of the "dangerous" game played by the then foreign secretary, Harold Macmillan, in deliberately attempting to draw Turkey into the Cyprus problem to bring greater international leverage to bear on Greece during negotiations in 1955, hardly reflects well on the future premier and illustrates what Holland elsewhere describes as a cynicism at the heart of British policy-making: a concern with British prestige and appearances as opposed to what was genuinely right or wrong.[76] More generally Frank Furedi suggests that the declaration of states of emergency by encouraging ethnic tensions bought Britain valuable "breathing space" during which the colonial authorities could disable radical nationalism and foster moderate alternates.[77] Declaring a "state of emergency" permitted the assumption of extraordinary powers (including a mandatory death sentence for "terrorist" crimes) but technically fell short of "war," thus sparing British actions scrutiny under the Geneva convention. It also maintained the illusion of continued civil rule—and thus probably influenced not only contemporary perceptions of British decolonization but also arguably historians distinguishing Britain's "emergencies" from the colonial wars of other European powers. Cyprus, with its majority Greek Orthodox and minority Muslim population, illustrates that the experience of British force was not confined to non-Christian and non-white populations. But generally speaking, Enoch Powell was right to warn that Britain risked applying one standard to the white man and one to the black; strikingly, if unsurprisingly, British governments, while sorely vexed by the activities of the recalcitrant and finally rebellious white settlers in Rhodesia, were still unwilling to pit British forces against the federal forces of white "kith and kin."[78]

Ironically it was "weaker" nationalisms that could prove most challenging, as British governments sought to extricate themselves from regions which looked likely to be a long-term drain on the imperial exchequer or where competing nationalisms threatened or had caused civil war, yet where once resolved to go, Britain wanted to identify plausible "national" leaders to whom to devolve power. Another irony was that it was white "kith and kin" who could be most resistant to strategies for decolonization. For example, it was hard to reconcile white South African prejudices with British hopes to transform the Commonwealth into a larger, multiracial vehicle for "post-imperial" British influence through the admission of black African states. British ministers also feared the influence of the apartheid state among white settlers in neighbouring southern Rhodesia, as well as its potential to complicate what had become the overwhelming priority of shoring up western influence among the newly emerging independent black African states. For the 1960s Conservative governments, notwithstanding the variety of connections white settlers had with the party,[79] the biggest headache associated with decolonization lay in reconciling the settlers' ambitions with black African nationalism in Kenya, but especially in central Africa.

Analysis of different aspects of policy-making and regions thus reveals that British management of the difficult business of decolonization could vary markedly. But most historians would agree that while the "means" varied, they were generally directed to an "end" which aimed at salvaging from unhappy circumstances as much prestige and influence for Britain as possible. Ronald Robinson and W. R. Louis dub this the "imperialism of decolonization." This formulation adapted to the political and strategic priorities of the 1950s and 1960s the classic but economically focused thesis of "the imperialism of free trade" in which, forty years before, Robinson and Jack Gallagher had described British governments' pursuit of their interests by "informal" means if possible, formal where not.[80] A. J. Stockwell has described this as maintaining "an imperial role as opposed to imperial rule," even though, in Louis and Robinson's words, British imperial power underpinned by American wealth and power had became "substantially an Anglo-American revival."[81] Where Britain had already replaced "rule" with "role," the retreat from informal empire, John Kent points out, "translated directly into a loss of global prestige and influence"; a reflection that helps to account for the considerable domestic concern at the staged British withdrawal of troops from the Suez canal zone that preceded the Suez crisis.[82] As these interpretations illustrate, and contrary to Macmillan's self-serving explanation of British decolonization, even at the end of empire, British officials and statesmen had not necessarily become less "imperial"; this reflects wider society's attitudes to empire, a theme explored in the next section.

IV

Decolonization was always about more than a transfer of sovereignty. Central to its study must be its impact on Britons whose lives took them overseas, sometimes in collaboration with the imperial or colonial state, and sometimes in locations which were never formally part of the British Empire but where they constituted a cultural and economic force which can rightly be described as "imperial." With a few notable exceptions,[83] only recently have historians considered the "ends" of this aspect of empire and other dimensions of the impact of decolonization on British culture, economy, and society. It is to these matters we now turn.

On the eve of decolonization, colonies and the Commonwealth housed and employed hundreds of thousands of Britons. Indeed between 1946 and 1963 an average of 127,524 left British shores each year for either temporary or permanent residence overseas. Of these, around 82 percent of seaborne British emigrants succumbed to the powerful appeal of the empire-Commonwealth, no doubt encouraged by continued commitment on the part of the British state and the governments of Australia, New Zealand, and Canada to help finance re-settlement.[84] Colonies had less attraction than the dominions: nonetheless by 1958 there were 287,300 Britons living in the "settler" colonies of central Africa and 67,700 in Kenya in 1960.[85]

Among those leaving Britain's shores were men—and, in increasing if still limited numbers, women—taking up temporary employment in the colonies. Ironically, the late colonial era saw significant expansion in their numbers. Between 1947 and 1954 the total number of expatriates employed in the colonial service rose from 11,000 to 18,000. Numbers peaked in 1954, but as late as 1960 new recruits were still being appointed to the East African colonies on permanent and pensionable terms. Indeed the empire-Commonwealth continued to provide openings for British graduates, especially in the scientific and technical branches where staff were needed to oversee the post-war development drive. That between 1947 and 1956 somewhere between a quarter and a half of all new British geology graduates found employment on the colonial geological surveys provides one illustration of how professional opportunities could remain extensively integrated with empire. In the 1950s in Africa there was also a significant growth in the numbers of both Protestant and Catholic missionaries (of all nationalities, including British) in the field, which combined with their expansion into new areas has led to the decade being described as "the last great missionary era in Africa's history."[86]

These examples further illustrate the divergent trajectories of British decolonization and remind us that the imperial history of the 1950s cannot simply be read via the trope of "end of empire." As Oglu Kalu observes, writing on Nigerian missions, different timetables of "decolonization" applied to different aspects of colonial activity.[87] For many missionaries, businessmen, and others this was unquestionably an era of change, but in varying degrees it was also one of "business as usual," reflecting the indeterminate nature of British imperial policy. Investigating these communities' experiences of decolonization is not simply an matter of aligning the literature on the post-1945 period with that of earlier phases of British imperialism. The end-of-empire era offers the opportunity to reconsider familiar themes in imperial historiography in a context quite different from that of earlier periods. Some such themes are those of the relations between settlers, missionaries, or businessmen and the imperial and colonial state. For example, studies of British business during decolonization reveal its often fraught dealings with officialdom. These could be further complicated by the unfamiliar challenges of the late colonial era, and the picture that emerges is consequently far from that posited in "neo-colonialist" interpretations of business-imperial state collusion.[88] My own study of British firms in the Gold Coast argues that differences between government and business intensified following the 1948 riots. These underscored the intense local unpopularity of business and led the Labour government to try and divorce African popular perceptions of British colonialism and British commerce.[89] For some missions, identification with the state at this transitional time undermined their local standing, and, as Caroline Howell shows in her study of the Church Missionary Society in Uganda, did not always bring commensurate influence. In Kenya and Central Africa, where decolonization was accompanied by violent conflict or bitter controversy, the potential impact on state-missionary relations was all the greater, as John Stuart demonstrates in the case of Scottish missionaries in Central Africa in the 1950s, who, however ambivalent in their response to political developments, found themselves at odds with both the Nyasaland colonial government and the Federation authorities by the end of the decade.[90]

It would be a shame, however, to investigate these communities only in relation to the imperial or colonial state (or indeed chiefly to deploy wider-ranging research to investigate their input into imperial policy-making) rather than as subjects of interest in their own right, not least as a window on to how elements of British society viewed empire and its demise and of how these may have helped shape metropolitan culture generally. The success or otherwise with which British interests adapted to the changing environment, perhaps by forging new linkages overseas, also constitutes a crucial part of the history of Britain's transition towards a "post-imperial" state; and one to which as an emerging literature on female missionaries in the later twentieth century shows, there was also a gendered dimension.[91]

The response of British settlers in east and central Africa is most readily retrievable by the historian and best known—and hence will receive only passing attention here–encompassing as it did vigorous engagement with political issues, including the formation of political parties representative of different sections of the settler communities. In Central Africa, settlers led by Roy Welensky lobbied for federation and, as influence in London ebbed away in the early 1960s, to oppose the introduction of African majority rule in Northern Rhodesia. Settler action in this region culminated in a unilateral declaration of independence by the white government of (Southern) Rhodesia in 1965, catapulting the country into prolonged civil war.

Among the British business community, recent research on India, Malaya and Africa reveals contrasting experiences and a plurality of attitudes towards the end of empire. The drive to accelerate economic development of the colonial empire through private enterprise and the post-war commodity boom provided new business opportunities, but companies remained anxious about the consequences of political instability (including, in some colonies, war) and, as local politicians gained access to power, programmes of economic nationalism.[92] Confronted with these circumstances, businessmen sometimes proved—as Robert Tignor has argued in relation to Kenya, Egypt, and Nigeria—willing "to intervene at critical moments" in the decolonization process.[93] Sometimes this extended to financial and other involvement in colonial politics as a way of buying influence with successor regimes or on occasion to shape political outcomes.[94] Businesses demonstrated varying attitudes towards constitutional change, and their contrasting responses do not lend themselves to easy analysis on lines of sector, scale or location. There is, however, evidence that some business interventions—and not just those of multinational corporations—were negotiated through networks that included commodity groups which crisscrossed the empire: so in 1955 members of an association of British businesses in West Africa sought advice of a similar organization in India, Pakistan and Burma to see if this would "help in dealing with the changing constitutional situation in West Africa."[95]

Recent writing on missions suggests it is equally hard to generalize here. Like some in the business community, missions could be slow to comprehend the changes afoot, and as Andrew Porter has shown, their responses reflected variations in belief and theology, and divergent attitudes even within one location towards nationalism and British imperial policy.[96] India was a case apart (here independence raised especially acute and difficult issues for Christians since politics and religion were closely interwoven).[97] But for African missions too, what could be times of opportunity also witnessed the transformation of familiar features of the colonial and ecclesiastical landscapes, including the continued growth in "independent" Christian churches, most famously as a result of the "East African Revival." After decades in which little advance had been made towards an indigenous Anglican episcopate, the first twentieth-century African diocesan bishop was appointed in 1951. African ministry in general expanded, and local churches were established with their own juridical autonomy (autonomous Anglican provinces no longer subordinate to Canterbury were created in West Africa in 1951, in Central Africa in 1955, and in East Africa in 1960–1).[98]

This discussion can be at best only suggestive of the ways in which different communities experienced and responded to late colonial developments, and of the ways in which Britons beyond those employed by the imperial and colonial state were a dynamic element in decolonization. Much remains to be investigated.

However, a more critical issue might be the outcome of constitutional change for these communities and for Britain itself. Decolonization inevitably involved a winnowing away of the administrative apparatus through which the British state had managed imperial affairs. The India Office closed in 1947, and the Colonial Office and the Commonwealth Relations Office, brought under the leadership of one minister in 1962, were amalgamated in 1966. Some of the Colonial Office's brief had in 1961 been hived off to a new Department of Technical Co-operation (later the Ministry of Overseas Development), while an increasing proportion of British aid was targeted at Latin America, where it seemed likely to achieve most for British interests overall.[99] As this last example illustrates, decolonization changed more than administrative structures. Departmental management can nonetheless be a barometer of shifting attitudes within the heart of the British establishment: as the functions of areas of Whitehall shrank, the Foreign Office (later the Foreign and Commonwealth Office), which had taken on some ex-Indian civil servicemen, expressed reluctance to employ ex-colonial service personnel, partly fearing that they might be a liability as representatives of a "post-imperial" Britain in former colonies.[100]

The Commonwealth also saw changes. There was a shift towards "multilateralism" after 1965, a new Secretariat assuming the managerial role previously undertaken by the Commonwealth Relations Office and Cabinet Office, and in the early 1970s biennial peripatetic Heads of Government Meetings replaced prime ministerial gatherings in Downing Street. From the later 1960s the separation became more than institutional, with the former mother country frequently isolated in Commonwealth discussions, including those concerning South Africa.[101]

The economic consequences of decolonization defy easy quantification. Although the intense interest in imperial economic integration of the late 1940s had waned by the mid-1950s, the resources and opportunities of the empire-Commonwealth were still valued, in particular the financial structures of the Sterling Area.[102] The economies of Britain and areas of the empire-Commonwealth became progressively less complementary, but in 1960 the Commonwealth still took 40 percent of British exports and supplied one third of all imports.[103] Where access to former colonial markets and resources became more difficult, the consequences were mitigated by the availability of alternate sources for some primary commodities, the development of synthetic substitutes, and the availability of other trading partners.

In weighing such evidence, historians are in any case divided over the extent to which the empire lost from the late 1940s was of genuine value to Britain. Some have concluded that empire had ceased to matter economically. Others focusing on the burdens it imposed on British resources, the allegedly financially destabilizing effects of the debts represented by colonial sterling balances, and the obstacle it presented to participation in the European project, argue that empire was contributing to economic decline.[104]

Although, as in any period, it is thus difficult to produce a "costs-benefits" analysis of empire, specific impacts can be identified that resulted not just from the transfers of power but from other aspects of the end of empire. For example, the adoption of nationalist policies by local politicians often produced environments less receptive to British businesses which also now found themselves competing for trade with foreign companies. One aspect of economic nationalism with potentially far-reaching consequences was the establishment of central banking systems and locally-issued and managed currencies which could affect a country's financial stability and thus both British concerns operating there and future participation in all aspects of the sterling area.[105] The progressive dismantling of the financial structures of empire removed some of the advantages previously enjoyed by British interests.

Some of these economic issues relate to the yet more elusive question of the social impact of decolonization. An important theme here is post-war immigration to Britain from the West Indies, south Asia, and anglophone Africa, and the related question of British race relations in the later twentieth century.[106] While the great increase in numbers arriving from the New Commonwealth after the war—fulfilling in many cases a need for labor in key transport, construction, and other industries— was not strictly a consequence of decolonization, Stephen Constantine argues that it helps explain the abandonment of the principle of free entry for all empire subjects into Britain, previously reaffirmed in the 1948 British Nationality Act. Legislation in 1962, 1968, and 1971 restricted the free movement of Commonwealth citizens until the position of those seeking entry to Britain was little different to that of other immigrants. Constantine further shows that there was a concurrent decline in demographic complementarity between Britain and the Old Commonwealth.[107]

All aspects of the end of empire, from constitutional change to colonial war, were also of personal consequence to British men and women in the colonies, attenuating careers and threatening lifestyles. In India appointments had been increasingly Indianised for some time, but elsewhere, where scant attention had been paid to local higher education, change before 1945 was limited. In consequence the late colonial period saw a sharp acceleration in policies of localization, prompting vigorous action by serving British administrators on pensions and future career security.[108] Aware of their importance for future administrative and political stability, the British government instituted arrangements designed to encourage British officials to stay on even once the direction and speed of constitutional change became apparent.[109] As successive transfers of power gradually closed off opportunities for redeployment elsewhere in the empire, however, many in the colonial service found their overseas careers brought to a premature end: by late 1970 the Overseas Resettlement Bureau, established to assist former colonial service personnel in finding new posts, had placed its 10,000th client.[110] Some had entered into colonial employment with their eyes wide open: Bruce Nightingale, recruited in 1957 to the colonial service in Northern Nigeria, later claimed to have had what can be read as a sophisticated understanding of contemporary trends. Conscious of the direction policy was going—a relative had advised him to opt for Tanganyika "as being likely to last longer"—he nevertheless embarked on a career in the service partly because hearing an official "attempting to explain the apparent failures of British policy in Kenya and Cyprus" had encouraged him "to see what was happening on the ground."[111] Others "stayed on"—often with NGOs or in advisory capacity to independent governments—contributing in still under-explored ways to Britain's overseas and development activities "after" empire.[112] We know as yet too little of the institutional consequences of these contracting professional career opportunities, but there are hints of the kind of changes which may have been at work: the careers master at Marlborough, the school which between the 1920s and the 1950s had provided 50 percent more recruits to the Colonial Administrative Service than any other English public school, was by the early 1950s advocating a career in business rather than in overseas government service to the boys.[113]

For some the foreshortening of careers must have exacerbated what Elizabeth Buettner's research on earlier "Anglo-Indians" homecomings found was often a difficult adjustment, perhaps more difficult for women than men. The contrast between life overseas with access to cheap domestic labour and British patterns of domesticity and lifestyle must have been even more marked in the late colonial period than in the interwar years, especially given the shrinking opportunities to relocate to other corners of the empire where an expatriate lifestyle could be reproduced.[114] Buettner argues that those Anglo-Indians who settled back in Britain, keen to promote a positive reading of Britain's imperial past in publications and other media, helped inculcate a "nostalgic" take on the British Raj within late twentieth-century metropolitan culture.[115] Research of my own indicates that some—perhaps unfairly—may have been regarded by those who had remained in Britain as a curious hangover from a bygone age.

These last examples bear upon the broad question of how British society as a whole viewed empire and its decline. It has been only very recently, partly encouraged by post-colonialism's desire to look for a post-colonial moment in the society of the colonizer as well as the colonized, that there has been much attempt to redress what has been deemed a "stunning lack of curiosity about the impact of decolonization within the metropolitan formation."[116] The cultural and social impact of imperialism on Britain has been one of the most contested areas of imperial historiography and it is consequently no surprise that as historians extend their gaze to incorporate the post-1945 era that there should be sharp differences of interpretation.[117] As Stephen Howe has recently advised, in our rush to explore this aspect of Britain's past, some writers risk taking "as their starting point what they should be trying to find out: that imperial rule must necessarily have been fundamental to Britishness."[118] Perhaps we should be wary of privileging the imperial dimension in Britain's recent past over other maybe more significant traditions (one might argue that in post-1945 Britain a more prominent discourse drew on the recent experience of World War II). Yet one cannot question the impact of research in this field, which to date has demonstrated that there *was* a greater imprint of empire on a variety of aspects of British cultural (as well as political) life after 1945 than once suspected. Challenging the view of public indifference to empire after 1945, it has provided ample evidence of the "persistence" of "imperialism" in British culture,[119] and of the various ways in which this culture of empire was subtly changing in the late 1940s and 1950s reflecting the new rhetoric of development, partnership, and Commonwealth.[120]

Having accepted that empire still mattered to people, raises in turn the question of when, if at all, its decline was registered in the wider public consciousness. With overall trends disguised by the divergent nature of decolonization, the continuing force of British imperialism in some areas into the 1950s and the refashioning of empire as Commonwealth, the prevailing view is that it was not before the Suez crisis that society at large woke up to the demise of British imperialism,[121] although others identify a considerably greater lag between decolonization and its domestic impact.[122] Making a slightly different point, Andrew Thompson concludes that despite the enduring appeal of an imperial political economy, it was from 1959 that "an increasing number of people became disengaged from the empire in the sense that they seemed less likely to support or hold an opinion about it."[123]

As historians turn to investigating the domestic impact of the loss of empire—as opposed to the broader question of the legacies of empire in general—some have raised tantalizing suggestions about the further ways in which the loss of empire had a major transformative effect on British politics or society.[124] Thus in recent years historians have argued that the declining power of white "kith and kin" in east and central Africa is reflected in domestic British racial discourse.[125] They have also considered the emasculation of white British masculinity that resulted from the "demise of narratives of white male adventure and power in vast territory";[126] collective amnesia in a nation not quite able to square up to its change in role;[127] and the erosion of hierarchy and the decline of deference.[128] There is interest in the ways the concerns of political literature and debate since 1980 have reflected the delayed impact of end of empire; including, as Andrew Thompson recounts elsewhere in this volume, discussion of regional devolution within the United Kingdom.[129]

As this chapter has sought to show, the history of the end of the British Empire can lend itself to very different characterizations, reflecting in part the historiographical development of this area of study, but also the ambivalent nature of British imperial policy notably in the 1940s and 1950s. It may be that the piecemeal way in which the British Empire was dismantled has also contributed to the relative neglect of the consequences of the decolonization process in Britain. As historians increasingly turn to this aspect of decolonization and undertake further comparative and thematic studies of this aspect of the history of the British Empire, not only will the history of the end of empire benefit, but also our understanding of the dynamics of the most recent period of British history. It is an exciting prospect.

Notes

1 I am grateful to Arthur Burns, Andrew Porter, John Stuart, Andrew Thompson, and Jon Wilson for comments on a draft of this chapter.
2 Near-contemporaneous works included Strachey, *End of Empire* and Lee, *Colonial Development*. Only after 1980 did a significant literature develop: the best general account from the period being Darwin, *Britain and Decolonisation*.
3 With only very limited exceptions: see, for example, Drower, *Britain's Dependent Territories*.
4 For example, Holland, *European Decolonisation*.
5 Holland, "Decolonization craze," p. 107.

6 For an alternate regional perspective see the published volumes of primary sources on the movement for independence in India published in the *Towards Freedom* series, for example, Gupta (ed.), *Towards Freedom*.

7 For example, Lynn (ed.), *British Empire in the 1950s.*

8 The controversy centered on Anderson, *Histories of the Hanged* and Elkins, *Britain's Gulag.*

9 See, for example, *Independent*, May 27, 1997, p. 14; June 3, 1997, pp. 14–15; *Daily Telegraph, The British Empire, 1497–1997: 500 Years that Shaped the World* (London, 1997), p. 2.

10 For these see Ogot, "Mau Mau and Nationhood."

11 Boyce, *Decolonisation*, pp. 267, 270; Heinlein, *British Government Policy*, p. 309; Anderson, *Histories of the Hanged*, p. 7.

12 Carruthers, *Winning Hearts and Minds*; Lewis and Murphy, "Old pals' protection society."

13 Woods, "Business as usual?"

14 This is changing: see Ward, *Australia*; Buckner (ed.), *Canada*; F. MacKenzie, *Redefining the Bonds.*

15 See chapter by John Darwin.

16 NA, CO 537/7056, minutes, Aug. 22, 1951.

17 May, "Commonwealth or Europe?."

18 See, for example, Eddy and Schreuder (eds), *Rise of Colonial Nationalism.*

19 See chapter by Stuart Ward; also Rooth, "Economic tension and conflict."

20 Gallagher and Robinson, "Partition of Africa," p. 640; Ranger, "Connexions," parts I and II.

21 See, e.g, Wasserman, *Politics of Decolonization*; Leys, *Underdevelopment.*

22 Young, *Post-Colonialism*, p. 45.

23 See Brown, *Modern India*; Jalal, *Sole Spokesman*; Sarkar, *Modern India*; Moore, *Escape from Empire.*

24 See Cohen, *Palestine*; Ovendale, *Palestine Mandate*; Louis, *British Empire in the Middle East.*

25 See Ashton and Stockwell (eds), *Imperial Policy*, pt. 1, introduction; Lee and Petter, *Colonial Office*; Cooper, *Decolonization and African Society*, pt. 1; Havinden and Meredith, *Colonialism and Development*, p. 258.

26 *H of C debs.*, vol. 380, col. 2015, June 24, 1942 (speech by Macmillan); and vol. 391, col. 48, July 13, 1943 (Stanley).

27 Smith, *British Relations*; A. J. Stockwell (ed.), *Malaya*, pt. 1, intro.

28 Butler, *Industrialisation and the British Colonial State*; Lewis, *Empire State-Building.*

29 Rathbone "Things fall apart," pp. 122–43. See also Pearce, *Turning Point*, pp. 198–9; Flint, "Planned decolonisation."

30 On the 1946–7 reform of administration, Pearce, *Turning Point*; Cell, "On the eve of decolonisation," pp. 235–57; Pearce, "Colonial Office in 1947," pp. 211–15; Flint, "Planned decolonisation'; Robinson, "Andrew Cohen."

31 Kent, "Bevin's imperialism."

32 See Schenk, *Britain and the Sterling Area.*

33 Krozewski, "Sterling."

34 Low and Lonsdale, "Introduction," pp. 1–63; on last point see Stockwell, *Business of Decolonization*, ch. 7.

35 See Rathbone (ed.), *Ghana*; Lynn (ed.), *Nigeria.*

36 Stubbs, *Hearts and Minds.*

37 Murphy, "Government by blackmail," p. 54; see also Murphy (ed.), *Central Africa.*

38 Goldsworthy, "Keeping change"; McIntyre, *British Decolonization*, ch. 3; Lynn (ed.), *British Empire in the 1950s*, intro., pp. 7, 10–11; Butler, *Britain and Empire*, p. 193.

39 Hyam and Louis (eds), *Conservative Governments*, intro, pp. xxxviii–xli, xlv.

40 Ashton and Killingray (eds), *West Indies*.

41 See especially Louis and Owen (eds), *Suez 1956*; Louis and Robinson, "Imperialism of decolonization," esp. p. 481, Adamthwaite, "Suez revisited," p. 225.

42 NA, FO 371/137972, no. 24, June 1959, report, "Africa: the next ten years"; Hyam and Louis (eds), *Conservative Governments*, intro., pp. xxvii, xlv; Ashton, "Keeping change within bounds," pp. 32–52, esp. 42–6.

43 Shepherd, *Iain Macleod,* pp. 159–61.

44 Ashton and Louis (eds), *East of Suez*; Dockrill, *Britain's Retreat*.

45 NA, CAB 129/53 C(52) 202: "British Overseas Obligations," Cabinet Memo by Eden, June 18, 1952; see Ovendale, *Transfer of Power*.

46 Brasted, Bridge, and Kent, "Cold War," pp. 20–1; see also Kent (ed.), *Egypt*, pt. 1, intro. p. xli.

47 Kyle, *Suez*; Lucas, *Divided We Stand*; McNamara, *Balance of Power*.

48 Smith, "Power transferred," pp. 1–23; see also Smith, *Britain's Revival and Fall in the Gulf*; id., *Kuwait*.

49 For example, Macmillan, *Pointing the Way*, pp. 116–17.

50 Discussed in Louis, *Imperialism at Bay*; Louis, "American Anti-Colonialism."

51 For example, Low, *Eclipse of Empire*, esp. ch. 1; Furedi, *Colonial Wars*.

52 Holland, *European Decolonisation*.

53 See, for example, in case of India: Tomlinson, *Political Economy of the Raj*.

54 Darwin, *Britain and Decolonisation*.

55 Gallagher, *Decline*; see also Jackson, *British Empire*.

56 See, for example, Thorne, *Issue of War*, esp. ch. 5; Killingray and Rathbone, *Africa and the Second World War,* esp. Lonsdale, "Depression and the Second World War"; Kent, *Internationalization of Colonialism*.

57 See Harper, *End of Empire*, ch. 3.

58 Krozewski, *Money and the End of Empire*; Hinds, *Britain's Sterling Colonial Policy*; Hyam and Louis (eds), *Conservative Governments*, intro., pp. xxv–xxvi; Hopkins, "Macmillan's audit of empire," esp. p. 252.

59 Goldsworthy, *Colonial Issues*; but see Owen, "Decolonisation and post-war consensus."

60 On Labour: Stockwell, *Business of Decolonization*, ch. 3; Murphy, *Party Politics and Decolonisation*.

61 K. Morgan, "Imperialists at bay." On the left generally, see S. Howe, *Anti-Colonialism*.

62 Louis, *Imperialism at Bay*; Wolton, *Lord Hailey*.

63 Louis and Robinson, "Imperialism of decolonization."

64 Cited Ashton, "Anglo-American revival," p. 177.

65 Louis, "Public enemy number one."

66 Ovendale, "Macmillan."

67 Robinson, "Andrew Cohen," p. 65; Flint, "Planned decolonisation," p. 390.

68 See, for example, the various documents reproduced in the relevant *BDEE* volumes. Rooney, *Arden-Clarke*; Baker, *Glyn Jones*.

69 Peterson, "Writing in revolution"; Lonsdale, "Moral economy."

70 Allman, *Quills of the Porcupine*.

71 With, for example, literature on policing and handling of colonial emergencies: see Anderson and Killingray, *Policing and Decolonization;* Holland (ed.), *Emergencies and Disorder*.

72 Boyce, *Decolonisation*, p. 269.

73 Owen, "Transfer of power."

74 Anderson, *Histories of the Hanged*, pp. 4, 7–8.

75 Smith, "Communal conflict and insurrection in Palestine," p. 77.

76 Holland, *Revolt in Cyprus* pp. 58–9; *id.*, "British experience."

77 Furedi, "Creating a breathing space"; *id.*, *Mau Mau War*, pp. 214, 216, 218–19.

78 Murphy, "Intricate and distasteful subject." For Powell, see *H of C debs*, vol. 610, cols 232–7, July 27, 1959.

79 Murphy, *Party Politics and Decolonisation.*

80 Robinson and Gallagher, "Imperialism of free trade."

81 Louis and Robinson, "Imperialism of decolonization," p. 469; Stockwell, *Ending the British Empire*, p. 24.

82 Kent, *Egypt*, pt. 1, intro., p. xxxvii.

83 In addition to the literature on British politics and decolonization discussed above, see, for example, Kahler, *Decolonization.*

84 Calculated from Constantine, "Migrants and settlers," table 7.2, p. 165, see also pp. 167–8, 175.

85 Kahler, *Decolonization*, table vi, p. 317.

86 Kirk-Greene, *On Crown Service*, tables 3.2–3, pp. 50–3, 73; Symonds, *Oxford and Empire*; S. E. Stockwell, "African prospects," p. 93; Hastings, *African Christianity*, p. 108.

87 Kalu, "Passive revolution," pp. 250–77.

88 See esp. N. White, "Business and politics," pp. 544–64.

89 S. E. Stockwell, *Business of Decolonization*, esp. ch. 3.

90 Howell, "Church and state," esp. p. 210; Stuart, "Scottish missionaries," esp. p. 426.

91 See inter alia (on missionaries) Hastings, *African Christianity*, ch. 4; on business, N. White, *British Business*; and on missions and gender, Gaitskell, "Independent Africa."

92 A useful survey in N. White, "Decolonization in the 1950s," pp. 100–21.

93 Tignor, *Capitalism and Nationalism*, p. 11.

94 S. E. Stockwell, *Business of Decolonization*, chs 5–6.

95 *Ibid.*, p. 130.

96 Porter, "British experience"; *id.*, "Universities mission"; Stuart, "Scottish missionaries," p. 413.

97 See Brown, "Who is an Indian?"

98 Hastings, *African Christianity*, pp. 46, 48, 51–3, 96, 112.

99 Hyam and Louis (eds), *Conservative Governments*, intro, pp. xxxiii, lxvi.

100 NA, CO 1017/659, no. 4, Selwyn Lloyd to I. Macleod, July 21, 1960.

101 McIntyre, "Commonwealth legacy," esp. pp. 693, 699.

102 Tomlinson, "Decline of the empire"; S. E. Stockwell, "African prospects"; *id.*, "Fiscal context"; Hyam and Louis (eds), *Conservative Governments*, p. lxii, doc. 304.

103 Darwin, *End of the British Empire*, p. 50.

104 See review of literature in Tomlinson, "Decline of the empire"; Feinstein, "End of empire."

105 On which see Uche, "Bank of England"; Schenk, "Origins of a central bank"; S. E. Stockwell, "Sterling Tradition."

106 See Paul, *Whitewashing Britain.*

107 Constantine, "Migrants and settlers," pp. 184–5.

108 Rathbone, "Transfer of power."

109 See Kirk-Greene, *On Crown Service*, ch. 4.

110 NA, LAB 8/2908, minutes of the 12th meeting of the Advisory Council of the OSRB, July 2, 1970.

111 Nightingale, *Seven Rivers to Cross*, pp. 32–3, 36.

112 On second careers see Kirk-Greene, "Decolonization"; *id.*, *Britain's Imperial Administrators*, ch. 9, esp. pp. 267–73. This section also draws on ongoing research of my own.

113 Kirk-Greene, *Britain's Imperial Administrators*, p. 137, citing work by Nile Gardiner; NA, CO 1017/2?43, H. Wylie, housemaster, to J. W. Calvert, parent and chairman of the Rubber Trade Association, UK, Feb. 5, 1953, enclosed with Calvert to H. Poynton, Feb. 10, 1952.

114 Buettner, *Empire Families*, ch. 5; Procida, *Married to the Empire*, p. 217.

115 Buettner, *Empire Families*, pp. 254–69.

116 Schwarz, "The only whiteman in there."

117 Contrast the contributions to Ward (ed.), *British Culture* and Hall, "Post-colonial," p. 246, with Porter, *Absent-Minded Imperialists*, p. 282.

118 S. Howe, "Internal decolonization," p. 218.

119 See Mackenzie, "Persistence of empire."

120 See, for example, chapters by Peter Hansen, Alex May, and Kathryn Castle in Ward (ed.), *British Culture*.

121 See Mackenzie, "Persistence of empire"; Ward, "Introduction" in *id.*(ed.), *British Culture*.

122 S. Howe, "When if ever did empire end?"

123 Thompson, *Empire Strikes Back?*, p. 216.

124 Hall, "Post-colonial," p. 246.

125 *Ibid.*, p. 219.

126 Webster, *Imagining Home*, p. xiv.

127 Gilroy, *After Empire*, cited Howe, "Internal decolonization," p. 220.

128 Ward, "No nation could be broker."

129 Howe, "Internal decolonization"; for a critique of the connection between devolution and decolonization, see Devine, "Break-up of Britain."

Further Reading

There are now any number of general histories of British decolonization. The best of the recent crop are L. J. Butler's *Britain and Empire: Adjusting to a Post-Imperial World* and F. Heinlein's *British Government Policy and Decolonization, 1945–63: Scrutinising the Official Mind*; R. Hyam's *Britain's Declining Empire: The Road to Decolonization, 1918–1968* is likely to become a standard text. Of those works published earlier, J. Darwin's *Britain and Decolonisation: The Retreat from Empire in the Post-War World* has stood the test of time, and J. Gallagher's elegant *The Decline, Revival and Fall of the British Empire* remains a stimulating read.

In addition to these general works, there is now a considerable periodical literature on aspects of the end of empire process (of which W. R. Louis and R. Robinson's "The imperialism of decolonization" is perhaps the most important), and an equally voluminous collection of monographs and books exploring different aspects of the end of empire process, often through reference to local or regional case studies. It is difficult to single out individual texts from among this extensive literature, but perhaps among the most influential are those that address issues or themes that bear most closely on the broader lines of imperial policy-making, such as P. Murphy, *Party Politics and Decolonization: The Conservative Party and British Colonial Policy in Tropical Africa, 1951–1964*, D. Goldsworthy, *Colonial Issues in British Politics, 1945–1961*, G. Krozewski, *Money and the End of Empire. British International Economic Policy and the Colonies, 1947–1958*, and W. R. Louis's various writings, including *Imperialism at Bay, 1941–1945: The United States and the Decolonization of the British Empire*.

For a comparative approach, see, R. Holland's *European Decolonization 1918–1981: An Introductory Survey* and F. Cooper, *Decolonization and African Society: The Labor Question in French and British Africa*. More often, however, comparative treatment has been undertaken via edited collections of essays, including R. Holland (ed.), *Emergencies and Disorder in the European Empires after 1945*, and K. Fedorowich and M. Thomas (eds), *International Diplomacy and Colonial Retreat*. There are also edited collections discussing particular themes, for example, S. Ward (ed.), *British Culture and the End of Empire* and B. Stanley (ed.), *Missions, Nationalism, and the End of Empire*.

Those interested in reading beyond the secondary literature are richly served by N. Mansergh (ed.), *Constitutional Relations between Britain and India: the Transfer of Power, 1942–1947*, 12 vols (London, 1970–83) and H. Tinker (ed.), *Constitutional Relations between Britain and Burma: the Struggle for Independence 1944–1948*, 2 vols (London, 1983–4), as well as by the general volumes in the *BDEEP* project general volumes (series A) covering the period from 1925 to 1970 and country volumes (series B), comprising, at the time of going to press, fifteen sets of multipart volumes. As well as reproducing official records, the introductions to the series A *BDEEP* volumes offer comprehensive overviews of imperial policy-making, while the country volumes are in many cases the most authoritative guides to developments leading to the transfers of power in individual territories.

The literature on colonial politics and nationalism is too large to survey here, suffice to say that there are an enormous number of stimulating and sophisticated country and local studies, although inevitably some countries, such as India and Malaya, have attracted more scholars than others. D. Anderson's *Histories of the Hanged* merits particular mention, however, for its impact on recent historiography of British decolonization generally.

Consolidated Bibliography

Abel, C. and Lewis, C. M., "General introduction," in *id.* (eds), *Latin America, Economic Imperialism and the State*.

Abel, C. and Lewis, C. M. (eds), *Latin America, Economic Imperialism and the State: The Political Economy of the External Connection from Independence to the Present* (London, 1985).

Achebe, C., "An image of Africa," *Research on African Literatures*, 9 (1978).

Adams, I. and Somerville, M., *Cargoes of Despair and Hope: Scottish Emigration to North America, 1603–1803* (Edinburgh, 1993).

Adams, R. J. Q., *Bonar Law* (London, 1999).

Adamthwaite, A., "Suez revisited," *International Affairs*, 64 (1988), repr. in J. W. Young (ed.), *The Foreign Policy of Churchill's Peacetime Administration, 1951–1955* (London, 1988).

Adas, M., *Prophets of Resistance: Millenarian Protest Movements Against the European Colonial Order* (Chapel Hill, 1979).

Adas, M., *Machines as the Measure of Men: Science, Technology, and Ideologies of Western Dominance* (Ithaca, NY, 1989).

Aguirre, R., *Informal Empire: Mexico and Central America in Victorian Culture* (Minnesota, 2005).

Ahearn, L. M., "Language and Agency," *Annual Review of Anthropology*, 30 (2001).

Aikman, L. S. Wells, *The Journal of a Voyage from Charlestown to London* (New York, 1968).

Akenson, D. H., *Half the World from Home: Perspectives on the Irish in New Zealand, 1860–1950* (Wellington, 1990).

Akenson, D. H., *Occasional Papers on the Irish in South Africa* (Grahamstown, 1991).

Akenson, D. H., *Small Differences: Irish Catholics and Irish Protestants, 1815–1922, an International Perspective* (Kingston and Montreal, 1991).

Akenson, D. H., *The Irish Diaspora: A Primer* (Toronto and Belfast, 1993).

Akenson, D. H., *If the Irish Ran the World: Montserrat, 1630–1730* (Liverpool, 1997).

Akita, S. (ed.), *Gentlemanly Capitalism, Imperialism and Global History* (London, 2002).

Albert, B., *South America and the World Economy from Independence to 1930* (London, 1983).

Aldrich, R., *Colonialism and Homosexuality* (London, 2003).

Allman, J. M., *The Quills of the Porcupine: Asante Nationalism in an Emergent Ghana* (Madison, 1993).

Alloula, M., *The Colonial Harem* (Manchester, 1986).

Almon, J. (ed.), *A Collection of Papers Relative to the Dispute between Great Britain and America, 1764–1775* (New York, 1971).

Althusser, L., *For Marx* (London, 1965).

Amin, S., *Accumulation on a World Scale* (New York, 1974).

Amin, S. and Chakrabarty, D. (eds), *Subaltern Studies IX. Writings on South Asian History and Society* (Delhi, 1996).

Anderson, B., *Imagined Communities* (London, 1991).

Anderson, D., *Eroding the Commons. The Politics of Ecology in Baringo, Kenya, 1890–1963* (Oxford, 2002).

Anderson, D., *Histories of the Hanged: Britain's Dirty War in Kenya and the End of the Empire* (London, 2005).

Anderson, D. and Grove, R. (eds), *Conservation in Africa: People, Policies and Practice* (Cambridge, 1987).

Anderson, D. and Killingray, D. (eds), *Policing and Decolonisation: Politics, Nationalism and the Police, 1917–1965* (Manchester, 1992).

Anderson, P., *English Questions* (London, 1992).

Anderson, W., "Medicine as colonial discourse," *Critical Inquiry*, 18 (1992).

Appadurai, A. "Putting hierarchy in its place," *Cultural Anthropology*, 3 (1988).

Archibald, D. C., "Angel in the bush: exporting domesticity through female emigration" in Kranidis (ed.), *Imperial Objects*.

Armitage, D., *The Ideological Origins of the British Empire* (Cambridge, 2000).

Armitage, D., "The Declaration of Independence and international law," *William and Mary Quarterly*, 3rd ser., 59 (2002).

Armitage, D. and Braddick, M. (eds), *The British Atlantic World, 1500–1800* (Basingstoke, 2002).

Arnold, D., *Colonizing the Body: State Medicine and Epidemic Disease in Nineteenth-Century India* (Berkeley, CA, 1993).

Arnold, D., *Science, Technology and Medicine in Colonial India* (Cambridge 2000).

Arnold, D. (ed.), *Imperial Medicine and Indigenous Societies* (Manchester, 1988).

Arnold, R., "The dynamics and quality of trans-Tasman migration, 1885–1910," *Australian Economic History Rev.*, 26 (1986).

Asad, T., *Genealogies of Religion: Discipline and Reasons of Power in Christianity and Islam* (Baltimore, 1993).

Asad, T., *Formations of the Secular: Christianity, Islam, Modernity, Cultural Memory in the Present* (Stanford, CA, 2003).

Asad, T. (ed.), *Anthropology and the Colonial Encounter* (London, 1973).

Ashton, N., *Eisenhower, Macmillan, and the Problem of Nasser: Anglo-American Relations and Arab Nationalism, 1955–1959* (Basingstoke, 1996).

Ashton, N., "Anglo-American revival and empire during the Macmillan years, 1957–63," in Lynn (ed.), *British Empire in the 1950s*.

Ashton, S. R., "Keeping change within bounds: A Whitehall reassessment," in Lynn (ed.), *British Empire in the 1950s*.

Ashton, S. R. and Killingray, D. (eds), *The West Indies* (BDEEP, Series B, London, 1999).

Ashton, S. R. and Louis, W. R. (eds), *East of Suez and the Commonwealth, 1964–1971* (BDEEP, Series A, 3 pts, London, 2004).

Ashton, S. R. and Stockwell, S. E., "Introduction," to id. (eds), *Imperial Policy and Colonial Practice*.

Ashton, S. R. and Stockwell, S. E. (eds), *Imperial Policy and Colonial Practice 1925–1945* (BDEEP, Series A, 2 pts, London, 1996).

Asiegbu, J. U. J., *Slavery and the Politics of Liberation 1787–1861* (London, 1969).

Atieno Odhiambo, E. S. and Lonsdale, J. (eds), *Mau Mau and Nationhood: Arms, authority and narration* (Nairobi, 2003).

Attwood, B., "Introduction," in Attwood and Arnold (eds), *Power, Knowledge and Aborigines*.

Attwood, B. and Arnold, J. (eds), *Power, Knowledge and Aborigines*, (Clayton, OH, 1992).

Auerbach, J. A., *The Great Exhibition of 1851: A Nation on Display* (London, 1999).

Austen, R. A., *African Economic History* (London, 1987).

Avery, D., *"Dangerous Foreigners." European Immigrant Workers and Labour Radicalism in Canada, 1896–1932* (Toronto, repr. 1983).

Azim, F., *The Colonial Rise of the Novel* (London, 1993).

Baber, Z., *The Science of Empire: Scientific Knowledge, Civilization, and Colonial Rule in India* (Albany, NY, 1996).

Baehre, R., "Pauper emigration to Upper Canada in the 1830s," *Histoire sociale – Social History*, 14 (1981).

Bailey, J. D., "Australian company borrowing, 1870–1893: A study in British overseas investment" (Oxford Univ. D.Phil. thesis, 1957).

Bailyn, B., *The New England Merchants in the Seventeenth Century* (Cambridge, MA, 1955, new edn 1979).

Bailyn, B., *The Ideological Origins of the American Revolution* (Cambridge, MA, 1967).

Bailyn, B. with DeWolfe, B., *Voyagers to the West: A Passage in the Peopling of America on the Eve of the Revolution* (New York, 1986).

Bailyn, B. and Morgan, P. D. (eds), *Strangers within the Realm. Cultural Margins of the First British Empire* (Chapel Hill, 1991).

Baines, D., *Migration in a Mature Economy* (Cambridge, 1985).

Baines, D., "European emigration, 1815–1930: looking at the emigration decision again," *Economic History Rev.*, 47 (1994).

Baker, C., *Sir Glyn Jones. A Proconsul in Africa* (London, 2000).

Baker, C. J. and Washbrook, D. A., *South India: Political Institutions and Political Change, 1880–1940* (Delhi, 1975).

Ballantyne, T., "Empire, knowledge and culture: from proto-globalization to modern globalization," in Hopkins (ed.), *Globalization in World History* (London, 2002).

Ballantyne, T., *Orientalism and Race: Aryanism in the British Empire* (Basingstoke, 2002).

Ballantyne, T., *Between Colonialism and Diaspora: Sikh Cultural Formations in an Imperial World* (Durham, NC, 2006).

Ballantyne, T. (ed.), *Science, Empire and the European Exploration of the Pacific* (Aldershot, 2004).

Ballantyne, T. and Burton, A. M., *Bodies in Contact: Rethinking Colonial Encounters in World History* (Durham, NC, 2005).

Basalla, G., "The spread of Western science," *Science*, 156 (1967).

Bate, D., "Photography and the colonial vision," *Third Text*, 22 (1993).

Baugh, D. A., "Maritime strength and Atlantic commerce: The uses of 'a Grand Marine Empire'," in Stone (ed.), *Imperial State at War*.

Bayly, C. A., *The Local Roots of Indian Politics: Allahabad, 1880–1920* (Oxford, 1975).

Bayly, C. A., *Rulers, Townsmen and Bazaars: North Indian Society in the Age of British Expansion, 1770–1870* (Cambridge, 1983).

Bayly, C. A., "The pre-history of 'Communalism?' Religious conflict in India 1700–1860," *Modern Asian Studies*, 19 (1985).

Bayly, C. A., "Judith Brown, The Origins of An Asian Democracy," *English Historical Rev.*, 103 (1988).

Bayly, C. A., *Imperial Meridian. The British Empire and the World, 1780–1830* (London, 1989).

Bayly, C. A., *Indian Society and the Making of the British Empire* (Cambridge, 1988).

Bayly, C. A., *Empire and Information. Intelligence Gathering and Social Communication in India, 1780–1870* (Cambridge, 1996).

Bayly, C. A. "The second British Empire," in Winks (ed.), *OHBE*, 5.

Bayly, C. A., "Rammohan Roy and the emergence of constitutional liberalism in India, 1800–1830," *Modern Intellectual History*, 4 (2007).

Bayly, C. A. and Prior, K., "Cornwallis, Charles, first Marquess Cornwallis (1738–1805)" in Matthew and Harrison (eds), *Oxford Dictionary of National Biography*.

Bayly, S., *Caste, Society and Politics in India from the Eighteenth Century to the Modern Age* (Cambridge, 1999).

Bean, C. E. W., *On the Wool Track* (New York, 1910).

Bean, P., and Melville, J., *Lost Children of the Empire* (London, 1989).

Beaud, J. -P. and Prévost, J. -G., "Immigration, eugenics and statistics: measuring racial origins in Canada (1921-1941)," *Canadian Ethnic Studies*, 28 (1996).

Beckett, J. R., "The past in the present; the present in the past: Constructing a national aboriginality," in Beckett (ed.), *Past and Present*.

Beckett, J. R. (ed.), *Past and Present: the Construction of Aboriginality* (Canberra, 1988).

Beidelman, T. O., *Colonial Evangelism: A Socio-Historical Study of an East African Mission at the Grassroots* (Bloomington, IN, 1982).

Beinart, W. and McGregor, J. (eds), *Social History and African Environments* (Oxford, 2003).

Belich, J., *The New Zealand Wars and the Victorian Interpretation of Racial Conflict* (Auckland, 1986).

Belich, J., *Making Peoples: A History of New Zealanders from Polynesian Settlement to the End of the Nineteenth Century* (Auckland, 1996).

Belich, J., *Paradise Reforged: A History of New Zealanders from the 1880s to the Year 2000* (Auckland, 2001).

Belich, J., "The rise of the Anglo-world: settlement in North America and Australasia, 1784-1918," in Buckner and Francis (eds), *Rediscovering the British World*.

Bell, D., "Cross cultural confusions: Indigenous traditions, legal confrontations and ethnographic uncertainties," *Australian Cultural History*, 18 (1999).

Bennett, T., *The Birth of the Museum: History, Theory, Politics* (London, 1995).

Berger, C., *The Sense of Power: Studies in the Idea of Canadian Imperialism, 1867–1914* (Toronto, 1970).

Berman B. and Lonsdale, J., *Unhappy Valley: Conflict in Africa and Kenya*, 2 vols (London, 1992).

Bhabha, H. K., *Nation and Narration* (London, 1990).

Bhabha, H. K., *The Location of Culture* (London, 1994).

Bhabha, H. K., "Signs taken for wonders: Questions of ambivalence and authority under a tree outside Delhi, May 1817," in Bhabha, *Location of Culture*.

Bhabha, H. K., "In a spirit of calm violence," in Prakash (ed.), *After Colonialism*.

Bhana, S. and Brain, J. B., *Setting Down Roots. Indian Migrants in South Africa 1860–1914* (Johannesburg, 1990).

Bickers, R., *Britain in China* (Manchester, 1999).

Bickers, R. (ed.), *Settlers and Expatriates: Britons over the Seas* (Oxford, forthcoming 2008).

Bickford-Smith, V., *Ethnic Pride and Racial Prejudice in Victorian Cape Town* (Cambridge, 1995).

Bickford-Smith, V., "Revisiting anglicisation in the nineteenth-century Cape Colony," in Bridge and Fedorowich (eds), *British World*.

Bielenberg, A., "Irish emigration to the British empire, 1700–1914," in *id.* (ed.), *Irish Diaspora*.

Bielenberg, A. (ed.), *The Irish Diaspora* (Harlow, 2000).

Binney, J., *Redemption Songs: A Life of Te Kooti Arikirangi Te Turuki* (Auckland, 1995).

Bird Rose, D., *Hidden Histories: Black Stories from Victoria River Downs, Humbert River and Wave Hill Stations* (Canberra, 1991).

Birmingham, D. and Martin, P. M. (eds), *History of Central Africa*, 2 vols (London, 1983).

Bivona, D., *Desire and Contradiction: Imperial Visions and Domestic Debates in Victorian Literature* (Manchester, 1990).

Blackburn, R., *The Making of New World Slavery: From the Baroque to the Modern, 1492–1800* (London, 1997)

Blackstone, W., *Commentaries on the Laws of England* (ed. Stanley N. Katz), 4 vols (Chicago, 1979).

Blanch, M., "Imperialism, nationalism and organized youth," in Clarke *et al.* (eds), *Working-Class Culture*.

Bleys, R. C., *The Geography of Perversion: Male-to-Male Sexual Behavior Outside the West and the Ethnographic Imagination 1750–1918* (London, 1996).

Bolt, C., *Victorian Attitudes to Race* (London, 1971).

Bonneuil, C., "Science and state building in late colonial and postcolonial Africa, 1930–1970," *Osiris*, 15 (2000).

Borrie, W. D., *Immigration to New Zealand, 1854–1938* (Canberra, 1991).

Bose, S., *Agrarian Bengal: Economy, Social Structure and Politics, 1919–1947* (Cambridge, 1986).

Bothwell, R., Drummond, I., and English. J., *Canada: 1900–1945* (Toronto, 1992).

Bourdieu, P., *Outline of a Theory of Practice* (Cambridge, 1972).

Bowen, H. V., "Investment in the later eighteenth century: East India stockholding 1756–1792," *Economic History Rev.*, 2nd ser., 42 (1989).

Bowen, H. V., *Revenue and Reform: The Indian Problem in British Politics, 1757–1773* (Cambridge, 1991).

Bowen, H. V., *Elites, Enterprise and the Making of the British Overseas Empire, 1688–1775* (London, 1996).

Bowen, H. V., *The Business of Empire: The East India Company and Imperial Britain, 1756–1833* (Cambridge, 2006).

Boyce, G., *Decolonization and the British Empire, 1775–1997* (Basingstoke, 1999).

Boyd, K., "Exemplars and ingrates: Imperialism and the Boys' Story Paper, 1880–1930," *Historical Research*, 67 (1994).

Braddick, M. J., "Government, war, trade and settlement" in Canny (ed.), *OHBE*, 1.

Bradford, H., "Women, gender and colonialism: Rethinking the history of the British Cape Colony and its frontier zones, c. 1806–70," *JAH*, 37 (1996).

Bradlow, E., "The children's friend society at the Cape of Good Hope," *Victorian Studies*, 27 (1984).

Branch, D., "Loyalism during the Mau Mau rebellion in Kenya, 1952–60" (D.Phil, Univ. of Oxford, 2005).

Brantlinger, P., *Rule of Darkness. British Literature and Imperialism 1830–1914* (Ithaca, 1988).

Brasted, H., Bridge, C., and Kent, J., "Cold War, informal empire, and the transfer of power: Some paradoxes in British decolonization resolved?" in M. Dockrill (ed.), *Europe Within the Global System, 1938–1960* (Bochum, 1995).

Bratton, J. S., *et al* (eds), *Acts of Supremacy: The British Empire and the Stage, 1790–1930* (Manchester, 1991).

Bravo, M. T., *The Accuracy of Ethnoscience: A Study of Inuit Cartography and Cross-Cultural Commensurability* (Manchester, 1996).

Breckenridge, C. A. and van der Veer, P. (eds), *Orientalism and the Postcolonial Predicament: Perspectives on South Asia* (Philadelphia, 1993).

Breen, T. H., "Ideology and nationalism on the eve of the American Revolution: Revisions *once more* in need of revising," *Jl of American History*, 84 (1997).

Breen, T. H., *The Marketplace of Revolution: How Consumer Politics Shaped American Independence* (New York, 2004).

Brenner, R., "The origins of capitalist underdevelopment: a critique of neo-Smithian Marxism," *New Left Rev.*, 104 (1977).

Brewer, A., *Marxist Theories of Imperialism: A Critical Survey*, 2nd edn (London, 1990).

Brewer, J., *The Sinews of Power: War, Money and the English State, 1688–1783* (London, 1989, 1st edn).

Bridge, C. and Fedorowich, K. (eds), *The British World: Diaspora, Culture and Identity* (London, 2003).

Bristow, J., *Empire Boys: Adventures in a Man's World* (London, 1991).

Brock, P., "New Christians as evangelists," in Etherington (ed.), *Missions and Empire*.

Brock, P. (ed.), *Indigenous Peoples, Christianity and Religious Change, Jl. of Religious History*, 27 (2003).

Brocklehurst, H. and Phillips, R. (eds), *History, Nationhood and the Question of Britain* (London, 2004).

Brockliss, L., "The professions and national identity" in Brockliss and Eastwood (eds), *Union of Multiple Identities*.

Brockliss, L. and Eastwood, D. (eds), *A Union of Multiple Identities: the British Isles, c.1750–c.1850* (Manchester, 1997).

Broeze, F. J. A., "Private enterprise and the peopling of Australasia, 1831–50," *Economic History Rev.*, 35 (1982).

Brooking, T., "'Tam McCanny and Kitty Clydeside' – the Scots in New Zealand," in Cage (ed.), *Scots Abroad*.

Brown, C. L., *Moral Capital: Foundations of British Abolitionism* (Chapel Hill, 2006).

Brown, J. M., *Modern India: The Origins of an Asian Democracy*, 2nd edn (Oxford, 1994).

Brown, J. M., "Who is an Indian? Dilemmas of national identity at the end of the British Raj in India," in Stanley (ed.), *Missions*.

Brown, J. H. and Louis, W. R. (eds), *OHBE*, 4, *The Twentieth Century* (Oxford, 1999).

Brown, R. C. and Cook, R., *Canada, 1896–1914: A Nation Transformed* (Toronto, 1974).

Bryder, L., "Sex, race, and colonialism: an historiographical review," *International History Rev.*, 20 (1998).

Brynn, E., "The emigration theories of Robert Wilmot Horton 1820–1841," *Canadian Jl of History*, 4 (1969).

Buckley K. and Wheelwright, T., *No Paradise for Workers: Capitalism and the Common People in Australia* (Melbourne, 1988).

Buckner, P., *The Transition to Responsible Government: British Policy in British North America 1815–1850* (Westport, CN, 1985).

Buckner, P., "Whatever happened to the British Empire," *Jl of the Canadian Historical Association*, 3 (1993).

Buckner, P., "Making British North America British, 1815–1860," in Eldridge (ed.), *Kith and Kin*.

Buckner, P., "The long goodbye: English Canadians and the British world," in Buckner and Francis (eds), *Rediscovering the British World*.

Buckner, P. (ed.), *Canada and the End of Empire* (Vancouver, 2005).

Buckner, P. and Francis, D. (eds), *Rediscovering the British World* (Calgary, 2005).

Buettner, E., *Empire Families: Britons and Late Imperial India* (Oxford, 2005).

Bumsted, J. M., *The People's Clearance. Highland Emigration to British North America* (Edinburgh, 1982).

Bumsted, J. M., "The cultural landscape of early Canada," in Bailyn and Morgan (eds), *Strangers within the Realm*.

Bunyan, J., *The Pilgrim's Progress* (London, 1904).

Burke, G., "The Cornish diaspora of the nineteenth century" in Marks and Richardson (eds), *International Labour Migration*.

Burroughs, P. B., *Britain and Australia 1831–1855* (Oxford, 1967).

Burton, A., "Rules of thumb: British history and 'imperial culture' in nineteenth- and twentieth-century Britain," *Women's History Rev.*, 3 (1994).

Burton, A., *At the Heart of the Empire: Indians and the Colonial Encounter in Late Victorian Britain* (Berkeley, CA, 1994).

Burton, A., *Burdens of History. British Feminists, Indian Women, and Imperial Culture, 1865–1915* (Chapel Hill, 1994).

Burton, A., "Who needs the nation? Interrogating 'British' history," *Jl of Historical Sociology*, 10 (1997).

Burton, A. (ed.), *Gender, Sexuality, and Colonial Modernities* (London, 1999).

Burton, A., "Archive Stories: Gender in the Making of Imperial and Colonial Histories," in Levine (ed.), *Gender and Empire*.

Burton, A. (ed.), *Archive Stories: Facts, Fictions, and the Writing of History* (Durham, NC, 2005).

Bush, J., "'The right sort of women': female emigrators and emigration to the British Empire, 1890–1910", *Women's History Rev.*, 3 (1994).

Bush, J., *Edwardian Ladies and Imperial Power* (London, 2000).

Butler, J., "Cecil Rhodes," *International Jl of African Historical Studies*, 10 (1977).

Butler, L. J., *Industrialisation and the British Colonial State: West Africa, 1939–1951* (London, 1997).

Butler, L. J., *Britain and Empire. Adjusting to a Post-Imperial World* (London, 2002).

Byrnes, G., *Boundary Markers: Land Surveying and the Colonization of New Zealand* (Wellington, 2001).

Cage, R. A. (ed.), *The Scots Abroad: Labour, Capital, Enterprise, 1750–1914* (London, 1985).

Cain, P. J., *Economic Foundations of British Overseas Expansion: 1815–1914* (London, 1980).

Cain, P. J., "Economics and empire: The metropolitan context," in Porter (ed.), *OHBE*, 3.

Cain, P. J., "The economic philosophy of constructive imperialism" in Navari (ed.), *British Politics and the Spirit of the Age*.

Cain, P. J., *Hobson and Imperialism. Radicalism, New Liberalism and Finance, 1887–1938* (Oxford, 2002).

Cain, P. J., "Character and imperialism: the British financial administration of Egypt, 1878–1914," *JICH*, 34 (2006).

Cain, P. J. and Hopkins, A. G., *British Imperialism*, 2 vols (London, 1993).

Cain, P. J. and Hopkins, A. G., *British Imperialism 1688–2000* (2nd edn, Harlow, 2002).

Caine, B., *Bombay to Bloomsbury: A Biography of the Strachey Family* (Oxford, 2005).

Calhoon, R. M. *et al.* (eds), *Loyalists and Community in North America* (Westport, CN, 1994).

Calkins, P., "The formation of a regionally oriented ruling group in Bengal, 1700–1740," *Jl of Asian Studies*, 29 (1970).

Callahan, R., *The East India Company and Army Reform, 1783–1798* (Cambridge, 1972).

Calloway, C. G., *The American Revolution in Indian Country: Crisis and Diversity in Native Americans Communities* (Cambridge, 1995).

Cameron, W., Haines, S., and Maude, M. M., *English Immigrant Voices: Labourers' Letters from Upper Canada in the 1830s* (Kingston and Montreal, 2000).

Campbell, R. H., "Scotland," in Cage (ed.), *Scots Abroad*.

Campbell, J. T., *Songs of Zion: The African Methodist Episcopal Church in the United States and South Africa* (New York and Oxford, 1995).

Cannadine, D., "The empire strikes back," *Past and Present*, 147 (1995).

Cannadine, D., *Ornamentalism: How the British Saw Their Empire* (London, 2001).

Canny, N., *Making Ireland British, 1580–1650* (Oxford, 2001).

Canny, N., "English migration into and across the Atlantic during the seventeenth and eighteenth centuries," in *id.* (ed.), *Europeans on the Move.*

Canny, N. (ed.), *Europeans on the Move. Studies on European Migration, 1500–1800* (Oxford, 1994).

Canny, N. (ed.), *OHBE*, 1, *The Origins of Empire* (Oxford, 1999).

Cardell, D., Cumming, C., Griffiths, P., and Jones, B., "Welsh identity on the Victorian goldfields in the nineteenth century," in Cardell and Cumming (eds), *World Turned Upside Down.*

Cardell, D. and Cumming, C. (eds), *A World Turned Upside Down: Cultural Change on Victoria's Goldfields 1851–2001* (Canberra, 2001).

Carey, W., *An Enquiry into the Obligations of Christians, to use Means for the Conversion of the Heathens* (Leicester, 1792).

Carr, D., *Time, Narrative, and History: Studies in Phenomenology and Existential Philosophy* (Bloomington, 1986).

Carretta, V., *Equiano, the African: Biography of a Self-made Man* (Athens, GA, 2005).

Carrothers, W. A., *Emigration from the British Isles* (London, 2nd edn, 1965).

Carruthers, S. L., *Winning Hearts and Minds: British Governments, the Media, and Colonial Counter-Insurgency 1944–1960* (Leicester, 1995).

Carter, M., *Servants, Sirdars and Settlers. Indians in Mauritius, 1834–1874* (Delhi, 1995).

Carter, P., *The Road to Botany Bay: An Essay in Spatial History* (London, 1987).

Carter, P., *The Lie of the Land* (London, 1996).

Cartwright, F. D. (ed.), *The Life and Correspondence of Major Cartwright* (London, 1826).

Cassis, Y., *City Bankers: 1890–1914* (Cambridge, 1994).

Cassis, Y. (ed.), *Finance and Financiers in European History, 1880–1960* (Cambridge, 1992).

Castle, K., "Imperial legacies, new frontiers, children's popular literature and the demise of empire," in Ward (ed.), *British Culture.*

Castle, K., *Britannia's Children: Reading Colonialism through Children's Books and Magazines* (Manchester, 1996).

Caton, B. P., "Social categories and colonization in Panjab, 1849–1920," *Indian Economic and Social History Rev.*, 41 (2004).

Cavell, J., "The imperial race and the immigration sieve: The Canadian debate on assisted British migration and empire settlement, 1900–30," *JICH*, 34 (2006).

Cecil, J. (ed.), *The Works of the Rev. John Newton*, new ed., 2 vols (Philadelphia, 1839).

Cell, J., "On the eve of decolonization: the Colonial Office's plans for the transfer of power in Africa, 1947," *JICH*, 8 (1980).

Chakrabarty, D., *Rethinking Working-class History: Bengal, 1890–1940* (Princeton, 1989).

Chakrabarty, D., "Postcoloniality and the artifice of history: Who speaks for 'Indian' Pasts?," *Representations*, 38 (1992).

Chakrabarty, D., *Provincialising Europe: Postcolonial Thought and Historical Difference* (Princeton, 2000).

Chakrabarty, D., *Habitations of Modernity: Essays in the Wake of Subaltern Studies* (Chicago, 2002).

Chambers, I. and Curti, L. (eds), *The Post-Colonial Question: Common Skies, Divided Horizons* (London, 1996).

Chandavarkar, R., "Industrialization in India before 1947: Conventional approaches and alternate perspectives," *Modern Asian Studies*, 19 (1985).

Chandra, B., *The Rise and Growth of Economic Nationalism in India: Economic Policies of Indian National Leadership, 1880–1905* (New Delhi, 1966).

Chandra, B., *India's Struggle for Independence 1857–1947* (New Delhi, 1989).

Chapman, S. D., *Merchant Enterprise in Britain* (Cambridge, 1992).

Charlesworth, N., *Peasants and Imperial Rule: Agriculture and Agrarian Society in the Bombay Presidency, 1850–1935* (Cambridge, 1985).

Chatterjee, P., "The colonial state and peasant resistance in Bengal 1920–1947," *Past and Present*, 110 (1986).

Chatterjee, P., "Their own words: An essay for Edward Said," in Sprinker (ed.), *Edward Said*.

Chatterjee, P., *The Nation and its Fragments: Colonial and Postcolonial Histories* (Princeton, 1993).

Chatterjee, P. (ed.), *Texts of Power: Emerging Disciplines in Colonial Bengal* (Minneapolis, 1995).

Chaturvedi, V., "Introduction," in Chaturvedi (ed.), *Mapping Subaltern Studies*.

Chaturvedi, V. (ed.), *Mapping Subaltern Studies and the Postcolonial* (London, 2000).

Chaudhuri, N., "'Who will help the girls?': Maria Rye and Victorian juvenile emigration to Canada, 1869–1895," in Kranidis (ed.), *Imperial Objects*.

Chaudhuri, N. and Strobel, M. (eds), *Western Women and Imperialism: Complicity and Resistance* (Bloomington, IN, 1992).

Cherry, D., *Beyond the Frame. Feminism and Visual Culture, Britain 1850–1900* (London, 2000).

Chidester, D., *Savage Systems: Colonialism and Comparative Religion in Southern Africa* (Charlottesville, 1996).

Chilton, L., "A new class of women for the colonies: *The Imperial Colonist* and the construction of empire," in Bridge and Fedorowich (eds), *British World*.

Choudhury, D. K. L., "Sinews of panic and the nerves of Empire: The imagined state's entanglement with information panic, India c.1880–1912," *Modern Asian Studies*, 38 (2004).

Chrisjohn, R., Young, S., and Maraun, M., *The Circle Game: Shadows and Substance in the Indian Residential School Experience in Canada*, 2nd edn (Penctiton, 2006)

Chrisman, L., *Rereading the Imperial Romance: British Imperialism and South African Resistance in Haggard, Schreiner, and Plaatje* (Oxford, 2000).

Clark, M., *The Future Australian Race* (Melbourne, 1877).

Clarke, J. *et al.* (eds), *Working-Class Culture: Studies in History and Theory* (London, 1979).

Clarke, P., and Trebilcock, C. (eds), *Understanding Decline: Perceptions and Realities of Britain's Economic Performance. Essays in Honour of Barry Supple* (Cambridge, 1997).

Clavin, P., "The World Economic Conference of 1933: the failure of British internationalism," *Jl of European Economic History*, 20 (1991).

Clayton, D. W., *Islands of Truth: The Imperial Fashioning of Vancouver Island* (Vancouver, 2000).

Clements, R. V., "Trade unions and emigration, 1840–80," *Population Studies*, 9 (1955).

Clive, J., and Bailyn, B., "England's cultural provinces: Scotland and America," *William and Mary Quarterly*, 3rd ser., 11 (1954).

Cobden, R., *England, Ireland and America* (Edinburgh, 1836).

Codell, J. F. (ed.), *Imperial Co-Histories. National Identities and the British and Colonial Press* (London, 2003).

Cohen, M., *Palestine: Retreat from the Mandate 1936–1945* (London, 1978).

Cohn, B. S., "Some notes on law and change in North India," *Economic Development and Cultural Change*, 8 (1959).

Cohn, B. S., "From Indian status to British contract," *Jl of Economic History*, 21 (1961).

Cohn, B. S., *India: The Social Anthropology of a Civilization* (Englewood Cliffs, NJ, 1971).

Cohn, B. S., "Notes on the history of the study of Indian society and culture," in Singer and Cohn (eds), *Structure and Change in Indian Society*.

Cohn, B. S., "The Census, Social Structure, and Objectification in South Asia," in Cohn, *An Anthropologist Among the Historians*.

Cohn, B. S., *An Anthropologist Among the Historians and Other Essays* (Delhi, 1987).

Cohn, B. S., *Colonialism and its Forms of Knowledge: The British in India* (Princeton, 1996).

Cole, D., "'The crimson thread of kinship': Ethnic ideas in Australia, 1870–1914," *Historical Studies*, 56 (1971).

Cole, D., "The problem of 'nationalism' and 'imperialism' in British settlement colonies," *Jl of British Studies*, 10 (1971).

Coleman, D. (ed.), *Maiden Voyages and Infant Colonies: Two Women's Travel Narratives of the 1790s* (London, 1999).

Colenso, J. W., *The Pentateuch and the Book of Joshua Critically Examined* (London, 1862).

Colley, L., "Britishness and otherness: an argument," *Jl of British Studies*, 31 (1992).

Colley, L., *Britons. Forging the Nation, 1707–1837* (London and New Haven, 1992).

Collini, S., *Public Moralists. Political Thought and Intellectual Life in Britain, 1850–1930* (Oxford, 1991).

Collini, S. *et al.* (eds), *History, Religion and Culture: Intellectual History 1750–1950* (Cambridge, 2000).

Colls, R., *Identity of England* (Oxford, 2002).

Comaroff, J., *Body of Power, Spirit of Resistance: The Culture and History of a South African People* (Chicago, 1985).

Comaroff, J. and Comaroff, J., *Of Revelation and Revolution.* 2 vols. (Chicago, 1991–1997).

Compton, J. M., "Open competition and the Indian civil service, 1854–76," *English Historical Rev.*, 83 (1968).

Connolly, S. J. (ed.), *Kingdoms United? Great Britain and Ireland. Integration and Diversity since 1500* (Dublin, 1999).

Constantine, S., *The Making of British Colonial Development Policy, 1914–40* (Manchester, 1984).

Constantine, S., *Buy and Build: The Advertising Posters of the Empire Marketing Board* (London, 1986).

Constantine, S., "Migrants and settlers," in Brown and Louis (eds), *OHBE*, 4.

Constantine, S., "Empire migration and social reform 1880–1950," in Pooley and Whyte (eds), *Migrants, Emigrants and Immigrants.*

Constantine, S., "British emigration to the Empire-Commonwealth since 1880: from overseas settlement to diaspora?" in Bridge and Fedorowich (eds), *British World.*

Conte, C. A., "Colonial science and ecological change: Tanzania's Mlalo Basin, 1888–1946," *Environmental History*, 44 (1999).

Conway, S., *The British Isles and the War of American Independence* (Oxford, 2000).

Conway, S., "From fellow-nationals to foreigners: British perceptions of the Americans, circa 1739–1783," *William and Mary Quarterly*, 59 (2002).

Coombes, A. E., *Reinventing Africa: Museums, Material Culture and Popular Imagination* (London and New Haven, 1994).

Cooper, F., "Conflict and connection: Rethinking colonial African history," *American Historical Rev.*, 99 (1994).

Cooper, F., *Decolonization and African Society: The Labor Question in French and British Africa* (Cambridge, 1996).

Cooper, F., "What is the concept of globalization good for? An African perspective," *African Affairs*, 100 (2001).

Cooper, F., *Colonialism in Question: Theory, Knowledge, History* (Berkeley, CA, 2005).

Cooper, F. and Stoler, A. L., "Between metropole and colony: rethinking a research agenda," in Cooper and Stoler (eds), *Tensions of Empire.*

Cooper, F. and Stoler, A. L. (eds)., *Tensions of Empire: Colonial Cultures in a Bourgeois World* (Berkeley, 1997).

Cooper, R. G. S., *The Anglo-Maratha Campaigns and the Contest for India: The Struggle for Control of the South Asian Military Economy* (Cambridge, 2004).

Corrigan, P., and Sayer, D., *The Great Arch. English State Formation as Cultural Revolution* (Oxford, 1985).

Cowan, H. I., *British Emigration to British North America: The First Hundred Years* (Toronto, revd edn, 1961).

Cowen, M. P. and Shenton, R. W., "The origin and course of Fabian colonialism in Africa," *Jl of Historical Sociology*, 4 (1991).

Cowen, M. P. and Shenton, R. W., "British Neo-Hegelian Idealism and official colonial practice in Africa: The Oluwa land case of 1921," *JICH*, 22 (1994).

Cox, J., *Imperial Fault Lines: Christianity and Colonial Power in India, 1818–1940* (Stanford, 2002).

Crais, C., *White Supremacy and Black Resistance in Pre-industrial South Africa* (Cambridge, 1992).

Crais, C., *The Politics of Evil: Magic, State Power and the Political Imagination in South Africa* (Cambridge, 2002).

Craton, M., *Sinews of Empire: A Short History of British Slavery* (Garden City, NY, 1974).

Crawford, J., "The impact of the war on New Zealand military forces and society," in Crawford and McGibbon (eds), *One Flag, One Queen, One Tongue*.

Crawford, J. and McGibbon, I. (eds), *One Flag, One Queen, One Tongue: New Zealand, the British Empire and the South African War, 1899–1902* (Auckland, 2003).

Crook, D. P., *Benjamin Kidd: Portrait of a Social Darwinist* (Cambridge, 1984).

Crook, D. P., "Historical monkey business: The myth of a Darwinized British imperial discourse," *History*, 84 (1999).

Crosby, A. W., *Ecological Imperialism: The Biological Expansion of Europe, 900–1900* (Cambridge, 1986).

Cullen, L. M., "The Irish diaspora of the seventeenth and eighteenth centuries," in Canny (ed.), *Europeans on the Move*.

Cullen, L. M., "Economic development, 1750–1800," in Moody and Vaughan (eds), *New History of Ireland*, 4.

Cunningham Wood, J., *British Economists and the Empire* (London, 1983).

Cunningham, V., *In the Reading Gaol: Postmodernity, Texts, and History* (Oxford, 1994).

Curran, J. and Porter, V. (eds), *British Cinema History* (London, 1983).

Curtin, P. D., *The Atlantic Slave Trade: A Census* (Madison, 1969).

Curtin, P. D., "The end of the 'White Man's Grave'? Nineteenth-century mortality in West Africa," *Jl of Interdisciplinary History*, 21 (1990).

Cuthbertson, G., Grundlingh, A., and Suttie, M.-L. (eds), *Writing a Wider War. Gender, Race and Identity in the South African War, 1899–1902* (Athens, 2002).

Dabydeen, D., *Hogarth's Blacks: Images of Blacks in Eighteenth Century English Art* (Manchester, 1987).

Dalrymple, W., *The Last Mughal: The Fall of a Dynasty, Delhi, 1857* (London, 2006).

Dalziel, R., *Origins of New Zealand Diplomacy: The Agent-General in London 1870–1905* (Wellington, 1975).

Dalziel, R., *Julius Vogel: Business Politician* (Auckland, 1986).

Dalziel, R., "Emigration and kinship: migrants to New Plymouth 1840–1843," *New Zealand Jl of History*, 25 (1991).

Darian-Smith, K., Grimshaw, P., and Macintyre, S. (eds), *Britishness Abroad: Transnational Movements and Imperial Cultures* (Melbourne, 2007).

Darras, J., *Joseph Conrad and the West: Signs of Empire* (New York, 1982).

Darwin, J. G., *Britain and Decolonization: The Retreat from Empire in the Post-War World* (London, 1988).

Darwin, J., "Durham in the East: India and the idea of responsible government, 1858–1939," *Jl of Canadian Studies*, 25 (1990).

Darwin, J. G., *The End of the British Empire. The Historical Debate* (Oxford, 1991).

Darwin, J., "Imperialism and the Victorians: The dynamics of territorial expansion," *English Historical Rev.*, 112 (1997).

Darwin, J., "Globalism and imperialism: The global context of British power, 1830–1960" in Akita (ed.), *Gentlemanly Capitalism*.

Darwin, J., "The descent of empire: Post-colonial views of Britain's imperial history," (annual lecture to Institute of Colonial and Postcolonial Studies, University of Leeds, May 4, 2006).

Dasgupta, U. (ed.), *A Difficult Friendship: Letters of Edward Thompson and Rabindranath Tagore, 1913–1940* (Delhi, 2003).

Daunton, M., "'Gentlemanly capitalism' and British industry 1820–1914," *Past and Present*, 122 (1989).

Daunton, M., *Trusting Leviathan. The Politics of Taxation in Britain, 1799–1914* (Cambridge, 2001).

Daunton, M. and Halpern, R. (eds), *Empire and Others: British Encounters with Indigenous Peoples, 1600–1850*, (London and Philadelphia, 1999).

Davidoff, L., "Class and gender in Victorian England" in Newton, Ryan and Walkowitz (eds), *Sex and Class in Women's History*.

Davidson, J., "The de-dominionisation of Australia," *Meanjin*, 38 (1979).

Davidson, J., "De-dominionisation revisited," *Australian Jl of Politics and History*, 51 (2005).

Davies, P., *Splendours of the Raj: British Architecture in India 1660–1947* (London, 1985).

Davies, R. R., *The First English Empire: Power and Identities in the British Isles 1193–1343* (Oxford, 2000).

Davis, D. B., *The Problem of Slavery in the Age of Revolution, 1770–1823* (Ithaca, NY, 1975).

Davis, D. B., *Inhuman Bondage* (Oxford, 2006).

Davis, J., *A History of Britain, 1885–1939* (Basingstoke, 1999).

Davis, L.E. and Huttenback, R. A., *Mammon and the Pursuit of Empire: The Political Economy of British Imperialism, 1860–1912* (Cambridge, 1988).

Dawson, G., *Soldier Heroes: British Adventure, Empire and the Imagining of Masculinities* (London, 1994).

de Groot, J., "Metropolitan desires and colonial connections: Reflections on consumption and empire," in Hall and Rose (eds), *At Home with the Empire*.

Denoon, D., *Settler Capitalism: The Dynamics of Dependent Development in the Southern Hemisphere* (Oxford, 1983).

Denoon, D. and Kuper, A., "Nationalist historians in search of a nation: The 'new historiography' in Dar es Salaam," *African Affairs*, 69 (1970).

Denoon, D. and Mein-Smith, P. (with Wyndham, M.), *A History of Australia, New Zealand and the Pacific* (Oxford, 2000).

Deshpande, P., "Caste as Maratha: Social categories, colonial policy and identity in early twentieth-century Maharashtra," *Indian Economic and Social History Rev.*, 41 (2004).

Devine, T. M., "Introduction: the paradox of Scottish emigration," in *id.* (ed.), *Scottish Emigration and Scottish Society*.

Devine, T. M., "Landlordism and highland emigration," in *id.* (ed.), *Scottish Emigration and Scottish Society*.

Devine, T. M. (ed.), *Scottish Emigration and Scottish Society* (Edinburgh, 1992).

Devine, T. M., *Scotland's Empire, 1600–1815* (London, 2004).

Devine, T. M., "The break-up of Britain? Scotland and the end of empire," *Transactions of the Royal Historical Society*, 16 (2006).

Dewey, C., "The education of a ruling caste: the Indian civil service in the era of competitive examination," *English Historical Rev.*, 88 (1973).

Dewey, C., *Anglo-Indian Attitudes: The Mind of the Indian Civil Service* (London, 1993).

Diamond, M., *Emigration and Empire: The Life of Maria S. Rye* (New York, 1999).

Dickson, R. J., *Ulster Emigration to Colonial America 1718–1775* (London, 1966).

Dilke, C., *Greater Britain* (London, 1868).

Dilke, C., *Problems of Greater Britain*, 2 vols. (London, 1890).

Dilley, A. R., "Gentlemanly capitalism and the Dominions: London finance, Australia and Canada, 1900–1914" (Oxford Univ. D.Phil. thesis, 2006).

Dirks, N. B., "Foreword" to Cohn, *Colonialism and its Forms of Knowledge*.

Dirks, N. B., *The Hollow Crown: The Ethnohistory of an Indian Kingdom* (New York, 1987).

Dirks, N. B., "From little king to landlord: Colonial discourse and colonial rule," in *id.* (ed.), *Colonialism and Culture*.

Dirks, N. B. (ed.), *Colonialism and Culture* (Ann Arbor, 1992).

Dirks, N. B., "The policing of tradition: Colonialism and anthropology in Southern India," *Comparative Studies in Society and History*, 39 (1997).

Dirks, N. B., *Castes of Mind: Colonialism and the Making of Modern India* (Princeton and Oxford, 2001).

Dirks, N. B., *The Scandal of Empire: India and the Creation of Imperial Britain* (Cambridge, MA, 2006).

Dockrill, M. (ed.), *Europe Within the Global System, 1938–1960* (Bochum, 1995).

Dockrill, S., *Britain's Retreat from East of Suez: The Choice Between Europe and the World* (Basingstoke, 2002).

Dodson, M. S., "Re-presented for the Pandits: James Ballantyne, "useful knowledge," and Sanskrit scholarship in Benares College during the mid-nineteenth century," *Modern Asian Studies*, 36 (2002).

Dodson, M. S., "Translating science, translating empire: the power of language in colonial north India," *Comparative Studies in Society and History*, 47 (2005).

Donnachie, I., "The Making of 'Scots on the make': Scottish settlement and enterprise in Australia, 1830-1900," in Devine (ed.), *Scottish Emigration and Scottish Society*.

Dormois, J. P., and Dintenfass, M., *British Industrial Decline* (London, 1998).

Dornan, J. L., "Agency and Archaeology: Past, present, and future directions," *Jl of Archaeological Method and Theory*, 9 (2002).

Dowbiggin, I., "'Keeping this country sane': C. K. Clarke, immigration restriction, and Canadian psychiatry, 1890–1925," *Canadian Historical Rev.*, 76 (1995).

Dowd, G. E., *A Spirited Resistance: The North American Indian Struggle for Unity, 1745–1815* (Baltimore, 1992).

Dowd, G. E., *War Under Heaven: Pontiac, the Indian Nations and the British Empire* (Baltimore and London, 2002).

Drayton, R., *Nature's Government: Science, Imperial Britain, and the "Improvement" of the World* (New Haven, 2000).

Drescher, S., *Capitalism and Anti-Slavery: British Mobilization in Comparative Perspective* (London, 1986).

Drower, G., *Britain's Dependent Territories. A Fistful of Islands* (Aldershot, 1992).

Dubow, S., "Colonial nationalism, the Milner kindergarten and the rise of 'South Africanism,' 1902–10," *History Workshop Jl*, 43 (1997).

Dubow, S., "Imagining the new South Africa in the era of reconstruction" in D. Omissi and A. Thompson (eds), *The Impact of the South African War* (Basingstoke, 2002).

Dummett, R. E. (ed.), *Gentlemanly Capitalism and British Imperialism* (London, 1999).

Dunae, P., "Boys' literature and the idea of empire," *Victorian Studies*, 24 (1980).

Duncan, R., "Case studies in emigration: Cornwall, Gloucestershire and New South Wales, 1877–1886," *Economic History Rev.*, 16 (1963).

Dunkley, P., "Emigration and the state, 1803–1842: the nineteenth-century revolution in government reconsidered," *Historical Jl*, 23 (1980).

Eastwood, D., "'Recasting our lot': Peel, the nation and the politics of interest," in Brockliss and Eastwood (eds), *A Union of Multiple Identities*.

Eastwood, D., Brockliss, L., and John, M., "From dynastic union to unitary state: the European experience," in Brockliss and Eastwood (eds), *A Union of Multiple Identities*.

Eaton, R. M., "(Re)imag(in)ing otherness: A postmortem for the postmodern in India," *Jl of World History*, 11 (2000).

Eddy, J. and Schreuder, D. (eds), *The Rise of Colonial Nationalism: Australia, New Zealand and South Africa First Assert Their Identities, 1880–1914* (London and Sydney, 1988).

Edelstein, M., "Imperialism: Costs and benefits" in Floud and McCloskey (eds), *Economic History of Britain since 1700*.

Edelstein, M., *Overseas Investment in the Age of High Imperialism: The United Kingdom, 1850–1914* (London, 1982).

Edney, M. H., *Mapping an Empire: The Geographical Construction of British India, 1765–1843* (Chicago, 1997).

Edwards, I. E., *The 1820 Settlers in South Africa* (London, 1934).

Edwards, J., *An Account of the Life of the Rev. David Brainerd* (Boston, 1749).

Ekirch, A. R., *Bound for America. The Transportation of British Convicts to the Colonies 1718–1775* (Oxford, 1987).

Elbourne, E., *Blood Ground: Colonialism, Missions and the Contest for Christianity in Britain and the Eastern Cape, 1799–1853* (Montreal and Kingston, 2002).

Elbourne, E., "The sin of the settler: The 1835–36 select committee on aborigines and debates over virtue and conquest in the early nineteenth-century British white settler empire," *Jl of Colonialism and Colonial History*, 4 (2003).

Eldridge, C. C., *Disraeli and the Rise of a New Imperialism* (Cardiff, 1996).

Eldridge, C. C. (ed.), *Kith and Kin: Canada, Britain and the United States from the Revolution to the Cold War* (Cardiff, 1997).

Elkins, C., *Britain's Gulag: The Brutal End of Empire in Kenya* (London, 2005).

Elliot, B. S., *Irish Migrants in the Canadas* (Kingston and Montreal, 1988).

Ellis, J., "Reconciling the Celt: British national identity, empire, and the 1911 investiture of the Prince of Wales," *Jl of British Studies*, 37 (1998).

Eltis, D., "Free and coerced transatlantic migrations: some comparisons," *American Historical Rev.*, 88 (1983).

Eltis, D., "The volume, age/sex ratios and African impact of the Slave Trade: Some refinements of Paul Lovejoy's review of the literature," *Jl of African History*, 31 (1990).

Eltis, D., *The Rise of African Slavery in the Americas* (Cambridge, 2000).

Eltis, D., "The volume and structure of the transatlantic slave trade: a reassessment," *William and Mary Quarterly*, 3rd ser., 58, 1 (2001).

Emirbayer, M. and Mische, A., "What is agency?," *American Jl of Sociology*, 103 (1998).

Emmer, P. C. (ed.), *Colonialism and Migration. Indentured Labour Before and After Slavery* (Dordrecht, 1986).

Emmer, P. C. and Mörner, M. (eds), *European Expansion and Migration* (Oxford, 1992).

Empire Warriors, BBC DVD, dd22924.

Engels, D. and Marks, S. (eds), *Contesting Colonial Hegemony: State and Society in Africa and India* (London, 1994).

Epstein, J., "Taking class notes on empire" in Hall and Rose (eds), *At Home with the Empire*.

Equiano, O., *The Interesting Narrative: And Other Writings*. (ed. and intro. V. Carretta), (Harmondsworth, 1995).

Equiano, O., *The Interesting Narrative of the Life of Olaudah Equiano* (ed. R. J. Allison), (Boston, 1995).

Erickson, C., "The encouragement of emigration by British trade unions, 1850-1900," *Population Studies*, 3 (1949).

Erickson, C., *Invisible Immigrants: The Adaptation of English and Scottish Immigrants in Nineteenth-Century America* (London and Ithaca, 1990).

Erickson, C., *Leaving England* (London and Ithaca, 1994).

Erlank, N., "Gendered reactions to social dislocation and missionary activity in Xhosaland, 1830–1847," *African Studies*, 59 (2000).

Errington, J. and Rawlyk, G. A., "Creating a British-American political community in Upper Canada," in Calhoon *et al.* (eds), *Loyalists and Community in North America*.

Etherington, N., *Rider Haggard* (Boston, 1984).

Etherington, N., *Theories of Imperialism: War, Conquest, and Capital* (London, 1984).

Etherington, N., "Introduction," in Etherington (ed.), *Missions and Empire*.

Etherington, N. (ed.), *Missions and Empire* (OHBE companion series, Oxford, 2005).

Evans, P. B., Rueschemeyer D., and Skocpol, T. (eds), *Bringing the State Back In* (Cambridge, 1985).

Fairbank, J. K., *Trade and Diplomacy on the China Coast* (Stanford, 1953).

Falconbridge, A. M., *Two Voyages to Sierra Leone (1794)*, in Coleman (ed.), *Maiden Voyages and Infant Colonies*.

Falls, C., *The Birth of Ulster* (London, 1996).

Fanon, F., *Black Skin, White Masks* (London, 1952).

Fedorowich, K., "Anglicisation and the politicisation of British immigration to South Africa, 1899–1929," *JICH*, 19 (1991).

Fedorowich, K., *Unfit for Heroes. Reconstruction and Soldier Settlement in the Empire between the Wars* (Manchester, 1995).

Fedorowich, K., "The problems of disbandment: the Royal Irish Constabulary and imperial migration, 1919-1929," *Irish Historical Studies*, 30 (1996).

Fedorowich, K. and Thomas, M. (eds), *International Diplomacy and Colonial Retreat*, special issue of *JICH*, 28 (2000).

Feinstein, C., "The end of empire and the golden age," in Clarke and Trebilcock (eds), *Understanding Decline*.

Ferguson, M., *Colonialism and Gender Relations from Mary Wollstonecraft to Jamaica Kincaid: East Caribbean Connections* (New York, 1993).

Ferguson, N., *Empire: How Britain Made the Modern World* (London, 2003).

Ferguson, N., *Colossus: The Rise and Fall of the American Empire* (London, 2004).

Fieldhouse, D. K., *Economics and Empire* (London, 1973).

Fieldhouse, D. K., "Can Humpty-Dumpty be put together again? Imperial history in the 1980s," *JICH*, 12 (1984).

Fieldhouse, D. K., "For richer, for poorer?," in Marshall (ed.), *Cambridge Illustrated History of the British Empire*.

Fieldhouse, D. K. "The metropolitan economics of empire," in Brown and Louis (eds), *OHBE*, 4.

Fieldhouse, D. K., *The West and the Third World* (Oxford, 1999).

Fincham, G. and Hooper, M. (eds), *Under Postcolonial Eyes: Joseph Conrad after Empire* (Cape Town, 1995).

Firchow, P. E., *Envisioning Africa: Racism and Colonialism in Conrad's Heart of Darkness* (Lexington, 2000).

Fitzgerald, P., "'Come back Paddy Reilly': Aspects of Irish return migration 1600–1850," in Harper (ed.), *Emigrant Homecomings*.

Fitzpatrick, D., "Irish emigration in the later nineteenth century," *Irish Historical Studies*, 22 (1980-1).

Fitzpatrick, D., *Oceans of Consolation. Personal Accounts of Irish Migration to Australia* (Ithaca and London, 1994).

Fitzpatrick, D., "Emigration, 1801–70" in Vaughan (ed.), *A New History of Ireland*, 5.

Fitzpatrick, D., "Emigration, 1871–1921" in Vaughan (ed.), *A New History of Ireland*, 6/II.

Fitzpatrick, D., "'Over the foaming billows': The organisation of Irish emigration to Australia" in Richards (ed.), *Poor Australian Immigrants*.

Flint, J. E., *Sir George Goldie and the Making of Nigeria* (London, 1960).

Flint, J. E., *Cecil Rhodes* (London, 1976).

Flint, J. E., "Planned decolonization and its failure in British Africa," *African Affairs*, 82 (1983).

Floud, R. and McCloskey, D. (eds), *The Economic History of Britain since 1700*, 2nd edn, 2 vols (Cambridge, 1994).

Fogleman, A. S., "Migrations to the thirteen British North American colonies, 1700-1775: new estimates," *Jl of Interdisciplinary History*, 22 (1992).

Fogleman, A. S., "From slaves, convicts, and servants to free passengers: The transformation of immigration in the era of the American revolution," *Jl of American History*, 85 (1998).

Foreman-Peck, J., *A History of the World Economy: International Economic Relations Since 1850*, 2nd edn (Hemel Hempstead, 1995).

Foucault, M., *The Archaeology of Knowledge* (London, 1972: orig. pub. 1969).

Francis, D., *National Dreams: Myth, Memory and Canadian History* (Vancouver, 1997).

Frank, A. G., *Capitalism and Underdevelopment in Latin America* (London, 1969).

Frank, A. G., *Dependent Accumulation and Underdevelopment* (London, 1978).

Freedman, L., Hayes, P., and O'Neill, R. (eds), *War, Strategy, and International Politics* (Oxford, 1992).

Friedberg, A. L., *The Weary Titan. Britain and the Experience of Relative Decline, 1895–1905* (Princeton, 1988).

Fryer, P., *Staying Power. The History of Black People in Britain* (London, 1994).

Fuller, A. J. and Béné, V., *The Everyday State and Society in Modern India* (London, 2001).

Furedi, F., *The Mau Mau War in Perspective* (London, 1989).

Furedi, F., "Creating a breathing space: The political management of colonial emergencies," *JICH*, 21 (1993), reprinted in Holland (ed.), *Emergencies and Disorder*.

Furedi, F., *Colonial Wars and the Politics of Third World Nationalism* (London, 1994).

Gaitskell, D., "Apartheid, mission and independent Africa: from Pretoria to Kampala with Hannah Stanton," in Stanley (ed.), *Missions*.

Galbraith, J. S., *Crown and Charter: The Early Years of the British South Africa Company* (London, 1974).

Galenson, D. W., *White Servitude in Colonial America: An Economic Analysis* (Cambridge, 1981).

Galenson, D. W., "The rise and fall of indentured servitude in the Americas: an economic analysis," *Jl of Economic History*, 44 (1984)

Gallagher, J., *Decline, Revival and Fall of the British Empire. The Ford Lectures and Other Essays* (ed. A. Seal), (Cambridge, 1982).

Gallagher, J., Johnson, G., and Seal, A. (eds), *Locality, Province and Nation: Essays on Indian Politics* (Cambridge, 1977).

Gallagher, J. and Robinson, R., "The imperialism of free trade," *Economic History Review*, 6 (1953).

Gallagher, J., and Robinson, R., "The partition of Africa," in Hinsley (ed.), *New Cambridge Modern History*, 11.

Gallo, K., *Great Britain and Argentina. From Invasion to Recognition, 1806–26* (Basingstoke, 2001).

Gambles, A., *Protection and Politics. Conservative Economic Discourse, 1815–52* (Oxford, 1999).

Games, A., "Migration," in Armitage and Braddick (eds), *British Atlantic World*.

Gandar, J. M., "New Zealand net migration in the latter part of the nineteenth century," *Australian Economic History Rev.*, 19 (1979).

Gascoigne, J., *Science in the Service of Empire: Joseph Banks, the British State and the Uses of Science in the Age of Revolution* (Cambridge, 1998).

Gemery, H. A., "Markets for migrants: English indentured servitude and emigration in the seventeenth and eighteenth centuries," in Emmer (ed.), *Colonialism and Migration*.

Genovese, E. D., *Roll, Jordan, Roll: The World the Slaves Made* (New York, 1974).

Gerzina, G., *Black England. Life before Emancipation* (London, 1995).

Ghosh, D., "Household crimes and domestic order: Keeping the peace in colonial Calcutta, c. 1770–c. 1840," *Modern Asian Studies*, 38 (2004).

Giddens, A., *New Rules of Sociological Method* (London, 1976).

Gillen, M., "The Botany Bay decision, 1786: Convicts, not empire," *English Historical Rev.*, 97 (1982).

Gilmour, I., *Riot, Risings, and Revolution: Governance and Violence in Eighteenth-Century England* (London, 1993).

Gilroy, P., *The Black Atlantic: Modernity and Double Consciousness* (Cambridge, MA, 1993).

Gilroy, P., *After Empire: Melancholia or Convivial Culture* (London, 2004).

Glass, D. V., *Numbering the People: The Eighteenth-Century Population Controversy and the Development of Census and Vital Statistics in Britain* (Farnborough, 1973).

Glass, D. V. and Taylor, P. A. M., *Population and Emigration* (Dublin, 1976).

Glynn, D., "'Exporting outcast London': assisted emigration to Canada, 1886–1914," *Histoire sociale—Social History*, 15 (1982).

Godler, Z., "Doctors and the new immigrants," *Canadian Ethnic Studies*, 9 (1977).

Goldberg, D. T., *Racist Culture: Philosophy and the Politics of Meaning* (Oxford, 1993).

Goldsworthy, D., *Colonial Issues in British Politics, 1945–1961* (Oxford, 1971).

Goldsworthy, D., "Keeping change within bounds: Aspects of colonial policy during the Eden and Churchill governments, 1951–1957," *JICH*, 17 (1990).

Goodall, H., "Aboriginal history and the politics of information control" in White and Russell (eds), *Memories and Dreams*.

Gothard, J., "'Radically unsound and mischievous': female migration to Tasmania, 1856–1863," *Australian Historical Studies*, 23 (1989).

Gothard, J., *Blue China. Single Female Migration to Colonial Australia* (Melbourne, 2001).

Gothard, J., "'Pity the poor immigrant': assisted single female migration to colonial Australia," in Richards (ed.), *Poor Australian Immigrants*.

Gould, E. H., "American independence and Britain's counter-revolution," *Past and Present*, 154 (1997).

Gould. E. H., "A virtual nation: Greater Britain and the imperial legacy of the American Revolution," *American Historical Rev.*, 104 (1999).

Gould, E. H., *The Persistence of Empire: British Political Culture in the Age of the American Revolution* (Chapel Hill, 2000).

Gould. E. H., "Zones of law, zones of violence: The legal geography of the British Atlantic, circa 1772," *William and Mary Quarterly*, 3rd ser., 60 (2003).

Gould, E. H., and Onuf, P. S., eds., *Empire and Nation: The American Revolution in the Atlantic World* (Baltimore, 2005).

Gould, J. D., "European inter-continental emigration: the role of 'diffusion' and 'feedback,'" *Jl of European Economic History*, 9 (1980).

Grant, A. and Stringer, K. J. (eds), *Uniting the Kingdom? The Making of British History* (London, 1995).

Grant, J., *British Battles on Land and Sea*, 4 vols (London, 1897).

Grant, R. D., *Representations of British Emigration, Colonisation and Settlement: Imagining Empire, 1800–1860* (Basingstoke, 2005).

Gray, M., "Scottish migration: the social impact of agrarian change in the rural lowlands, 1775–1875," *Perspectives in American History*, 7 (1973).

Gray, M., "The course of Scottish emigration, 1750–1914: enduring influences and changing circumstances" in Devine (ed.), *Scottish Emigration and Scottish Society*.

Gray, R., *Black Christians and White Missionaries* (New Haven, 1990).

Green, E. H. H., *The Crisis of Conservatism. The Politics, Economics and Ideology of the British Conservative Party, 1880–1914* (London, 1995).

Green, E. H. H., "Gentlemanly capitalism and British economic policy, 1880–1914," in Dummett (ed.), *Gentlemanly Capitalism and British Imperialism*.

Green, E. H. H., "The influence of the City over British economic policy, c. 1880–1960," in Cassis (ed.), *Finance and Financiers*.

Green, E. R. R. (ed.), *Essays in Scotch-Irish History* (London, 1969).

Green, S. J. D. and Whiting. R. C. (eds), *The Boundaries of the State in Modern Britain* (Cambridge, 1996).

Greenberg, M., *British Trade and the Opening of China 1800–1842* (Cambridge, 1951).

Greenblatt, S., *Marvelous Possessions: The Wonder of the New World* (Chicago, 1991).

Greene, D. J. (ed.), *Political Writings*, vol. 10, *The Yale Edition of the Works of Samuel Johnson* (New Haven, 1977).

Greene, J. P., "Negotiated authorities: The problem of governance in the extended polities of the early modern Atlantic World," in *id. Negotiated Authorities*.

Greene, J. P., *Negotiated Authorities: Essays in Colonial Political and Constitutional History* (Charlottesville, VA, 1994).

Greene, J. P., "The American Revolution," *American Historical Rev.*, 105 (2000).

Greene, J. P. (ed.), *Colonies to Nation, 1763–1789: A Documentary History of the American Revolution* (New York, 1975).

Greenhill, R., "Merchants and the Latin American trades: An introduction," in Platt (ed.), *Business Imperialism 1840–1930*.

Greenlee, J. S. and Johnston, C. M., *Good Citizens: British Missionaries and Imperial States, 1870–1918* (Montreal and Kingston, 1999).

Grewal, I., *Home and Harem: Nation, Gender, Empire and the Cultures of Travel* (London, 1996).

Grimshaw, P., "Faith, missionary life and the family" in Levine (ed.), *Gender and Empire*.

Grove, R. H., *Green Imperialism: Colonial Expansion, Tropical Island Edens, and the Origins of Environmentalism, 1600–1860* (Cambridge, 1995).

Grove, R. H., *Ecology, Climate and Empire: Colonialism and Global Environmental History, 1400–1940* (Cambridge, 1997).

Guha, R., *A Rule of Property for Bengal: an Essay on the Idea of Permanent Settlement* (Paris, 1963).

Guha, R., "On some aspects of the historiography of colonial India," *Subaltern Studies I* (Delhi, 1982).

Guha, R., "Dominance without hegemony and its history," in Guha (ed.), *Subaltern Studies VI*.

Guha, R., "Introduction," in Guha (ed.), *Subaltern Studies Reader*.

Guha, R., "The small voice of history" in Amin and Chakrabarty (eds), *Subaltern Studies IX. Writings on South Asian History and Society* (Delhi, 1996).

Guha, R., *A Corner of a Foreign Field: The Indian History of a British Sport* (London, 2002).

Guha, R. (ed.), *Subaltern Studies VI* (Delhi, 1989).

Guha, R. (ed.), *A Subaltern Studies Reader, 1986–1995* (Minneapolis, 1997).

Guha, R. and Spivak, G. C. (eds), *Selected Subaltern Studies* (New York, 1988).

Gupta, A. and Ferguson, J., "Beyond 'culture': Space, identity, and the politics of difference," *Cultural Anthropology*, 7 (1992).

Gupta, P. S. (ed.), *Towards Freedom: Documents on the Movement for Independence in India, 1943–1944* (Delhi, 1997).

Guy, J., *The Heretic* (Athens, OH, 1985).

Habib, I., "Studying a colonial economy—Without perceiving the colonialism," *Modern Asian Studies*, 19 (1985).

Hadley, E., "Natives in a strange land: the philanthropic discourse of juvenile emigration in mid-nineteenth century England," *Victorian Studies*, 33 (1990).

Haebich, A., *Broken Circles: Fragmenting Indigenous Families 1800–2000* (Fremantle, 2000).

Haines, R., "Indigent misfits or shrewd operators? Government-assisted emigrants from the United Kingdom to Australia, 1831–1860', *Population Studies*, 48 (1994).

Haines, R., *Emigration and the Labouring Poor: Australian recruitment in Britain and Ireland, 1831–1860* (Basingstoke, 1997).

Haines, R., "'The idle and the drunken won't do there': Poverty, the new poor law and nineteenth-century government-assisted emigration to Australia from the United Kingdom," *Australian Historical Studies*, 28 (1997).

Hall, C., "The nation within and without" in Hall, McClelland and Rendall, *Defining the Victorian Nation*.

Hall, C., "Introduction: thinking the postcolonial, thinking the empire," in *id.*, *Cultures of Empire. A Reader*.

Hall, C., *Civilising Subjects: Metropole and Colony in the English Imagination, 1830–1867* (Cambridge, 2002).

Hall, C., "Roundtable on Catherine Hall's *Civilizing Subjects*: Response," *Jl of British Studies*, 42 (2003).

Hall, C. (ed.), *Cultures of Empire: A Reader. Colonizers in Britain and the Empire in the Nineteenth and Twentieth Centuries* (Manchester, 2000).

Hall, C., McClelland, K., and Rendall, J. (eds), *Defining the Victorian Nation. Class, Race, Gender and the British Reform Act of 1867* (Cambridge, 2000).

Hall, C. and Rose, S. (eds), *At Home with the Empire. Metropolitan Culture and the Imperial World* (Cambridge, 2006).

Hall, D. D., *Worlds of Wonder, Days of Judgment: Popular Religious Belief in Early New England* (New York, 1989).

Hall, H. L., *The Colonial Office. A History* (London, 1937).

Hall, S., "When was the 'post-colonial'? Thinking at the limit," in Chambers and Curti (eds), *The Post-Colonial Question*.

Hall, S. (ed.), *Representation: Cultural Representations and Signifying Practices* (London, 1997).

Hamilton, C. *et al.* (eds), *Refiguring the Archive* (Cape Town, 2002).

Hamilton, D. J., *Scotland, the Caribbean and the Atlantic World, 1750–1820* (Manchester, 2005).

Hamilton, D. J., "Transatlantic ties: Scottish migration networks in the Caribbean, 1750–1800" in McCarthy (ed.), *A Global Clan*.

Hamilton, P., "The 'servant class': poor female migration to Australia in the nineteenth century" in Richards (ed.), *Poor Australian Immigrants*.

Hammerton, A. J., "'Without natural protectors': female immigration to Australia, 1832–36', *Historical Studies*, 16 (1975).

Hammerton, A. J., *Emigrant Gentlewomen. Genteel Poverty and Female Emigration 1830–1914* (London, 1979).

Hancock, W. K., *Survey of British Commonwealth Affairs: Problems of Economic Policy, 1918–1939*, 2 vols (London, 1942).

Hansen, P. H., "Coronation Everest: The empire and Commonwealth in the 'second Elizabethan Age'" in Ward (ed.), *British Culture*.

Harling, P. and Mandler, P., "From 'fiscal-military' state to laissez-faire state, 1760–1850," *Jl of British Studies*, 32 (1993).

Harlow, V. T., *The Founding of the Second British Empire 1763–1793*, 2 vols. (London, 1952, 1964).

Harper, M., "British migration and the peopling of the empire," in Porter (ed.), *OHBE*, 3.

Harper, M. (ed.), *Emigrant Homecomings. The Return Movement of Emigrants 1600-2000* (Manchester, 2005).

Harper, T., *The End of Empire and the Making of Malaya* (Cambridge, 1999).

Harries, P., "Missionaries, marxists and magic: Power and the politics of literacy in South-East Africa," *Jl of South African Studies*, 27 (2001).

Harris, C., *The Resettlement of British Columbia: Essays on Colonialism and Geographic Change* (Vancouver, 1997).

Harrison, B. H., *The Transformation of British Politics 1860–1995* (Oxford, 1996).

Harrison, N., *Postcolonial Criticism* (Cambridge, 2003).

Hastings, A., *A History of African Christianity 1950–1975* (Cambridge, 1979).

Hastings, A., *The Church in Africa, 1450–1950* (Oxford, 1996).

Havinden, M. and Meredith, D., *Colonialism and Development: Britain and its Tropical Colonies, 1850–1960* (London, 1993).

Hawkins, S., *Writing and Colonialism in Northern Ghana: The Encounter between the LoDagaa and the "World on Paper"* (Toronto, 2002).

Haynes, D. E. and Prakash, G., *Contesting Power: Resistance and Everyday Social Relations in South Asia* (Delhi, 1991).

Headrick, D. R., *The Tools of Empire: Technology and European Imperialism in the Nineteenth Century* (Oxford, 1981).

Headrick, D. R., *The Tentacles of Progress: Technology Transfer in the Age of Imperialism, 1850–1940* (Oxford, 1988).

Heathcote, T. A., *The Indian Army. The Garrison of British Imperial India 1822–1922* (Newton Abbot, 1974).

Hefner, R. W. (ed.), *Conversion to Christianity: Historical and Anthropological Perspectives* (Berkeley, CA, 1993).

Heidegger, M., "Letter on Humanism" in *Basic Writings: Martin Heidegger* (ed. D. Krell), (London, 1993).

Heinlein, F., *British Government Policy and Decolonization, 1945–1963. Scrutinising the Official Mind* (London, 2002).

Helly, D. O., *Livingstone's Legacy: Horace Waller and Victorian Mythmaking* (Athens, OH, 1987).

Hempton, D., *Religion of the People: Methodism and Popular Religion, c. 1750–1900* (London, 1996).

Henige, D., "Measuring the immeasurable: the Atlantic slave trade, West African population and the Pyrrhonian critic," *Jl of African History*, 27 (1986).

Henretta, J., *"Salutary Neglect": Colonial Administration under the Duke of Newcastle* (Princeton, 1972).

Hevia, J., *English Lessons: The Pedagogy of Imperialism in Nineteenth-Century China* (Durham, NC, 2003).

Hill, P., *The Migrant Cocoa-Farmers of Southern Ghana* (Cambridge, 1963).

Hinds, A., *Britain's Sterling Colonial Policy and Decolonization, 1939–1958* (Westport, CT, 2001).

Hinsley, F. H. (ed.), *New Cambridge Modern History*, 11 (1962).

Hirschman, A. O., *Exit, Voice, and Loyalty: Responses to Decline in Firms, Organizations, and States* (Cambridge, MA, 1970).

Hirst, P. and Thompson, G., *Globalization in Question: The International Economy and the Possibilities of Governance*, 2nd edn (London, 1999).

Hoare, M. E., *Reform in New Zealand Science, 1880–1926* (Melbourne, 1976).

Hobsbawm, E., *The Invention of Tradition* (Cambridge, 1993).

Hobsbawm, E. J. and Rudé, G., *Captain Swing* (London, 1969).

Hobson, J. A., *The Psychology of Jingoism* (London, 1901).

Hobson, J. A., *Imperialism: A Study*, 3rd edn (1938, repr. Michigan, 1965; first pub. 1902).

Hodgson, D., *The Church of Women: Gendered Encounters between Maasai and Missionaries* (Bloomington, IN, 2005).

Hofmeyr, I., "Jonah and the swallowing monster: orality and literacy on a Berlin mission station in the Transvaal," *Jl of Southern African Studies*, 17 (1991).

Hofmeyr, I., *The Portable Bunyan: A Transnational History of the Pilgrim's Progress* (Princeton, 2003).

Holland, R. F., *Britain and the Commonwealth Alliance 1919–1939* (London, 1981).

Holland, R. F., *European Decolonization, 1945–1961: An Introductory Survey* (London, 1985).

Holland, R. F., "The decolonization craze," *Itinerario*, 12 (1989).

Holland, R. F., "The British experience of decolonization," *Itinerario*, 20 (1996).

Holland, R. F., *Britain and the Revolt in Cyprus, 1954–1959* (Oxford, 1998).

Holland, R. F., "The British Empire and the Great War," in Louis and Brown (eds), *OHBE*, 4.

Holland, R. F. (ed.), *Emergencies and Disorder in the European Empires after 1945* (special issue of *JICH*, 21, 1993).

Holt, T. W., *The Problem of Freedom. Race, Labor and Politics in Jamaica and Britain, 1832–1938* (Baltimore, 1992).

Hopkins, A. G., *An Economic History of West Africa* (London, 1973).

Hopkins, A. G., "Big business in Africa," *Jl of African History*, 27 (1987).

Hopkins, A.G., "The Future of the Imperial Past" (inaugural lecture, Cambridge, 1997).

Hopkins, A. G., "Back to the future: From national history to imperial history," *Past and Present*, 164 (1999).

Hopkins, A. G., "Macmillan's audit of empire, 1957," in Clarke and Trebilcock (eds), *Understanding Decline*.

Hopkins, A. G., "Introduction: Globalization—An agenda for historians," in *id.* (ed.), *Globalization in World History*.

Hopkins, A. G., "Development and the utopian ideal" in Winks (ed.), *OHBE*, 5.

Hopkins, A. G. (ed.), *Globalization in World History* (London, 2002).

Hoppen, K. T., *The Mid-Victorian Generation, 1846–1886* (Oxford, 1998).

Horn, J., "British diaspora: emigration from Britain, 1680–1815" in Marshall (ed.), *OHBE*, 2.

Horn, J. and Morgan, P. D., "Settlers and slaves: European migrations to early modern British America" in Mancke and Shammas (eds), *Creation of the British Atlantic World*.

Horn, P., "Agricultural trade unionism and emigration, 1872–1881," *Historical Jl*, 15 (1972).

Horton, R., "African conversion," *Africa*, 41 (1971).

Horton, R., "On the rationality of conversion," pt 1, *Africa*, 45 (1975).

Howe, A., "From Pax Britannica to Pax Americana: Free trade, empire, and globalization, 1846–1948," *Bulletin of Asia-Pacific Studies* (2003).

Howe, A., *Free Trade and Liberal England, 1846–1946* (Oxford, 1997).

Howe, K. R., *Where the Waves Fall: A New South Sea Islands History from First Settlement to Colonial Rule* (London, 1984).

Howe, S., *Anti-Colonialism in British Politics: The Left and the End of Empire* (Oxford, 1993).

Howe, S., *Ireland and Empire: Colonial Legacies in Irish History and Culture* (Oxford, 2000).

Howe, S., "Internal decolonization? British politics since Thatcher as post-colonial trauma," *Twentieth Century British History*, 14 (2003).

Howe, S., "When—if ever—did empire end? Recent studies of imperialism and decolonization," *Jl of Contemporary History*, 40 (2005).

Howe, S., "When if ever did empire end? Internal decolonization in British culture since the 1950s," in Lynn (ed.), *British Empire in the 1950s*.

Howell, C., "Church and state in crisis: The deposition of the Kabaka of Buganda 1953–1955," in Stanley (ed.), *Missions*.

Howells, G., "'For I was tired of England Sir': English pauper emigrant strategies, 1834-60," *Social History*, 23 (1998).

Howells, G., "Emigration and the new poor law: the Norfolk emigration fever of 1836," *Rural History*, 11 (2000).

Howells, G., "'On account of the disreputable characters': parish assisted emigration from rural England, 1834–1860," *History*, 88 (2003).

Hudson, P., "English emigration to New Zealand, 1839–1850: Information diffusion and marketing a new world," *Economic History Rev.*, 54 (2001).

Hume, D. *Essays: Moral, Political, and Literary* (ed. E. F. Miller), (Indianapolis, 1985).

Husain, S. S., *Kipling and India* (Dacca, 1964).

Huttenback, R. A., *Racism and Empire: White Settlers and Colored Immigrants in the British Self-Governing Colonies 1830–1910* (Ithaca, NY, 1976).

Hyam, R., "British imperial expansion in the late eighteenth century," *Historical Jl*, 10 (1967).

Hyam, R., *Empire and Sexuality* (Manchester, 1990).

Hyam, R., *Britain's Declining Empire: The Road to Decolonization, 1918–1968* (Cambridge, 2006).

Hyam R. and Louis, W. R. (eds), *The Conservative Governments and the End of Empire 1957–1964* (*BDEEP*, Series A, 2 parts, London, 2000).

Ignatieff, M., *Blood and Belonging. Journeys into the New Nationalism* (London, 1993).

Iliffe, J., "The organization of the Maji Maji rebellion," *Jl of African History*, 8 (1967).

Iliffe, J., *The African Poor: A History* (Cambridge, 1987).

Illife, J., *Africans: The History of a Continent* (Cambridge, 1995).

Inden, R., "Orientalist constructions of India," *Modern Asian Studies*, 20 (1986).

Inden, R., *Imagining India* (Oxford, 1990).

Inikori, J. E., *Africans and the Industrial Revolution* (Cambridge, 2002).

Innis, H. A., *A History of the Canadian Pacific Railway* (Toronto, 1923).

Irschick, E. F., *Dialogue and History: Constructing South India, 1795–1895* (Berkeley, CA, 1994).

Irwin, R., *For Lust of Knowing: The Orientalists and Their Enemies* (London, 2006).

Jackson, A., "Irish Unionists and the empire," in Jeffery (ed.), *An Irish Empire?*

Jackson, A., *The British Empire and the Second World War* (London, 2006).

Jalal, A., *The Sole Spokesman: Jinnah, the Muslim League and the Demand for Pakistan* (Cambridge, 1985).

James, C. L. R., *The Black Jacobins: Toussaint L'Ouverture and the San Domingo revolution* (New York, 1938).

Jameson, F., *The Political Unconscious: Narrative as a Socially Symbolic Act* (London, 1981).

Jarrell, R. A. and Ball, N. R. (eds), *Science, Technology, and Canadian History: Les Sciences, la Technologie et L'Histoire Canadienne* (Waterloo, 1980).

Jebb, R., *Studies in Colonial Nationalism* (London, 1905).

Jeffery, K. (ed.), *An Irish Empire? Aspects of Ireland and the British Empire* (Manchester, 1996).

Jennings, M., "'This mysterious and intangible enemy': Health and disease amongst the early UMCA Missionaries, 1860–1918," *Social History of Medicine*, 15 (2002).

Johnson, S. C., *Emigration from the United Kingdom to North America, 1763–1912* (London, 1913).

Johnston, A., *Missionary Writing and Empire 1800–1860* (Cambridge, 2003).

Johnston, H. J. M., *British Emigration Policy 1815–1830. "Shovelling out Paupers"* (Oxford, 1972).

Jones, C. A., *International Business in the Nineteenth Century: The Rise and Fall of a Cosmopolitan Bourgeoisie* (New York, 1987).

Jones, G., *Merchants to Multinationals: British Trading Companies in the Nineteenth and Twentieth Centuries* (Oxford, 2000).

Jones, G. and Davenport-Hines, R. P. T., *British Business in Asia since 1860* (Cambridge, 1989).

Jones, H. and Kandiah, M. D. (eds), *The Myth of Consensus. New Views of British History, 1945–64* (London, 1996).

Jones, M., "The background to emigration from Great Britain in the nineteenth century," *Perspectives in American History*, 7 (1973).

Jones, M. A., "The Scotch-Irish in British America," in Bailyn and Morgan (eds), *Strangers within the Realm*.

Jones, M. A., "Ulster emigration, 1783–1815" in Green (ed.), *Essays in Scotch-Irish History*.

Jordan, T. E. "'Stay and starve, or go and prosper!' Juvenile emigration from Great Britain in the nineteenth century," *Social Science History*, 9 (1985).

Kahler, M., *Decolonization in Britain and France. The Domestic Consequences of International Relations* (Princeton, 1984).

Kalu, O., "Passive revolution and its saboteurs: African Christian literature in the era of decolonization, 1955–1975" in Stanley (ed.), *Missions*.

Kaplan, C., "Imagining empire: history, fantasy, literature" in Hall and Rose (eds), *At Home with the Empire*.

Katz, W., *Rider Haggard and the Fiction of Empire* (Cambridge, 1987).

Katzellenburgen, S. E., "British businessmen and German Africa 1885–1919," in Radcliffe (ed.), *Great Britain and her World*.

Kaul, C., *Reporting the Raj: The British Press and India, c. 1880–1922* (Manchester, 2003).

Kaul, C. (ed.), *Media and the British Empire* (Basingstoke, 2006).

Kaviraj, S., *The Unhappy Consciousness: Bankimchandra Chattopadhyay and the formation of Nationalist Discourse in India* (Delhi, 1995).

Kelley, N. and Trebilcock, M., *The Making of the Mosaic: A History of Canadian Immigration Policy* (Toronto, 1998).

Kelly, J. D., *A Politics of Virtue: Hinduism, Sexuality, and Countercolonial Discourse in Fiji* (Chicago, 1991).

Kendle, J., *Federal Britain. A History* (London, 1997).

Kennedy, D., *Islands of White: Settler Society and Culture in Kenya and Southern Rhodesia* (Durham, 1987).

Kennedy, D., "Imperial history and post-colonial theory," *JICH*, 24 (1996).

Kennedy, P., *The Rise and Fall of British Naval Mastery* (London, 1976).

Kennedy, P., "The costs and benefits of British imperialism, 1846–1914," *Past and Present*, 125 (1989).

Kennedy, P., *The Rise and Fall of Great Powers: Economic Change and Military Conflict from 1500 to 2000* (London, 1989).

Kennedy, W. P., *Industrial Structure, Capital Markets and the Origins of British Economic Decline* (Cambridge, 1987).

Kent, J., *The Internationalization of Colonialism. Britain, France, and West Africa, 1939–1956* (Oxford, 1992).

Kent, J., "Bevin's imperialism and the idea of Euro-Africa 1945–1949," in Dockrill and Young (eds), *British Foreign Policy*.

Kent, J. (ed.), *Egypt and the Defence of the Middle East, 1945–1956* (*BDEEP*, series B, 3 parts, London, 1998).

Kidd, B., *Social Evolution* (London, 1894).

Killingray, D. and Rathbone, R., *Africa and the Second World War* (London, 1986).

Kinealy, C., "At Home with the empire: The example of Ireland," in Hall and Rose (eds), *At Home with the Empire*.

King, R. D. and Kilson, R. W. (eds), *The Statecraft of British Imperialism. Essays in Honour of Wm. Roger Louis* (special issue of *JICH*, 27, 1999).

Kirk-Greene, A. H. M., *On Crown Service. A History of HM Colonial and Overseas Civil Services, 1837–1997* (London, 1999).

Kirk-Greene, A. H. M., *Britain's Imperial Administrators, 1858–1966* (Basingstoke, 2000).

Kirk-Greene, A. H. M., "Decolonization: the ultimate diaspora," *Contemporary British History*, 36 (2001).

Kirk-Greene, A. H. M., *Symbol of Authority. The British District Officer in Africa* (London, 2006).

Knowles, N., *Inventing the Loyalists: The Ontario Loyalist Tradition and the Creation of Usable Pasts* (Toronto, 1997).

Kopf, D., *British Orientalism and the Bengal Renaissance: The Dynamics of Indian Modernization 1773–1835* (Berkeley, CA, 1969).

Kranidis, R. S. (ed.), *Imperial Objects. Victorian Women's Emigration and the Unauthorized Imperial Experience* (New York, 1998).

Krebs, P., *Gender, Race and the Writing of Empire: Public Discourse and the Boer War* (Cambridge, 1999).

Kristensen, J., "In essence still a British country: Britain's withdrawal from East of Suez," *Australian Jl of Politics and History*, 51 (2005).

Krozewski, G., "Sterling, the 'minor' territories, and the end of formal empire, 1939–1958," *Economic History Rev.*, 46 (1993).

Krozewski, G., *Money and the End of Empire. British International Economic Policy and the Colonies, 1947–1958* (Basingstoke, 2001).

Kubicek, R. V., *The Administration of Imperialism: Joseph Chamberlain at the Colonial Office* (Durham, NC, 1969).

Kubicek, R. V., *Economic Imperialism in Theory and in Practice: the case of South African Gold Mining Finance, 1886–1914* (Durham, NC, 1979).

Kumar, D., *Science and the Raj 1857–1905* (Delhi, 1995).

Kupperman, K., *Indians and English: Facing Off in Early America* (Cornell, 2000).

Kyle, K., *Suez: Britain's End of Empire in the Middle East* (London, 2003).

Kynaston, D., *The City of London: Golden Years, 1890–1914* (London, 1994).

Laidlaw, Z., "'Aunt Anna's report': the Buxton women and the Aborigines Select Committee, 1835–37," *JICH*, 32 (2004).

Laidlaw, Z., "Integrating metropolitan, colonial and imperial histories—the Aborigines Select Commitee of 1835–37," in Mar and Evans (eds), *Writing Colonial Histories*.

Laidlaw, Z., *Colonial Connections, 1815–1840: Patronage, the Information Revolution and Colonial Government* (Manchester, 2005).

Lake, M., "The politics of respectability: Identifying the masculinist context," *Historical Studies*, 22 (1986).

Lalu, P., "The grammar of domination and the subjection of agency: Colonial texts and modes of evidence," *History and Theory*, 39 (2000).

Lambert, D. and Lester, A. (eds), *Colonial Lives Across the British Empire* (Cambridge, 2006).

Lambert, S. (ed.), *House of Commons Sessional Papers of the Eighteenth Century*, 147 vols (Wilmington, Del., 1975).

Lan, D., *Guns and Rain: Guerillas and Spirit Mediums in Zimbabwe* (London, 1985).

Landau, N. (ed.), *Law, Crime, and English Society, 1660–1830* (Cambridge, 2002).

Landau, P., *The Realm of the Word: Language, Gender and Christianity in a Southern African Kingdom* (Portsmouth, 1995).

Landau, P., "'Religion' and Christian conversion in African history: A new model," *Jl of Religious History*, 23 (1999).

Landau, P., "Hegemony and history in Jean and John Comaroff's *Of Revelation and Revolution*," *Africa*, 70 (2000).

Landau, P., "Language" in Etherington (ed.), *Missions and Empire*.

Landes, D. S., "Some thoughts on the nature of economic imperialism," *Jl of Economic History*, 21 (1961).

Landsman, N. C., "Nation, migration, and the province in the first British empire: Scotland and the Americas, 1600–1800," *American Historical Rev.*, 104 (1999).

Langfield, M., "Voluntarism, salvation, and rescue: British juvenile migration to Australia and Canada, 1890–1939," *JICH*, 32 (2004).

Langford, P., "Burke, Edmund (1728/30–1797)," in *Oxford Dictionary of National Biography* (Oxford, 2004). Available at www.oxforddnb.com/view/article/4019 (accessed Apr. 26, 2007).

Lawrence, J., "The politics of place and the politics of nation," *Twentieth Century British History*, 11 (2000).

Lee, J. M., *Colonial Development and Good Government. A Study in the Ideas Expressed by the British Official. Classes in Planning Decolonization, 1935–64* (Oxford, 1967).

Lee, J. M. and Petter, M., *The Colonial Office, War, and Development Policy: the Organization and Planning of a Metropolitan Initiative, 1939–1945* (London, 1982).

Lenin, V. I., *Imperialism: The Highest Stage of Capitalism* (1917) in *id.*, *Selected Works*, 1.

Lenin, V. I., *Selected Works*, 2 vols (Moscow, 1950).

Lester, A., *Imperial Networks. Creating Identities in Nineteenth-Century South Africa and Britain* (London, 2001).

Lester, A., "British settler discourse and the circuits of empire," *History Workshop Jl*, 4 (2002).

Levine, P., *Prostitution, Race and Politics: Policing Venereal Disease in the British Empire* (London, 2003).

Levine, P., "Sexuality and empire," in Hall and Rose (eds), *At Home with the Empire*.

Levine, P. (ed.), *Gender and Empire* (OHBE companion series, Oxford, 2004).

Lewis, J., *Empire State-Building: War and Welfare in Kenya, 1923–1952* (Ohio, 2000).

Lewis, J. and Murphy, P., "'The old pal's protection society.' The Colonial Office and the British press on the eve of decolonization" in Kaul (ed.), *Media and the British Empire*.

Lewis, R. and Mills, S. (eds), *Feminist Postcolonial Theory: A Reader* (Edinburgh, 2003).

Leys, C., *Underdevelopment in Kenya: The Political Economy of NeoColonialism 1964–1971* (London, 1975).

Lieven, M., "'Butchering the brutes all over the place': Total war and massacre in Zululand, 1879," *History*, 84 (1999).

Long, E., *The History of Jamaica. Or, General Survey of the Antient and Modern State of That Island*, 3 vols (London, 1774).

Lonsdale, J., "The emergence of African nations: A historiographical analysis," *African Affairs*, 67 (1968).

Lonsdale, J., "States and social processes in Africa: A historiographical survey," *African Studies Rev.*, 24 (1981).

Lonsdale, J., "The depression and the Second World War in the transformation of Kenya" in Killingray and Rathbone (eds), *Africa and the Second World War*.

Lonsdale, J., "Moral economy" in Berman and Lonsdale, *Unhappy Valley*.

Lonsdale, J., "Agency in tight corners: Narrative and initiative in African history," *Jl of African Cultural Studies*, 13 (2000).

Lonsdale, J., "How to study Africa: From victimhood to agency," *openDemocracy* (2005).

Lonsdale, J., "Kikuyu Christianities: A history of intimate diversity," in Maxwell and Lawrie (ed.), *Christianity and the African Imagination*.

Look Lai, W., *Indentured Labor, Caribbean Sugar. Chinese and Indian Migrants to the British West Indies, 1838–1918* (Baltimore, 1993).

Loomba, A., *Colonialism/Postcolonialism*, 2nd ed. (London, 2005).

Lorimer, D., *Color, Class and the Victorians* (Leicester, 1978).

Lorimer, D., "Theoretical racism in late-Victorian anthropology 1870–1900," *Victorian Studies*, 31 (1988).

Loughlin, J., *Ulster Unionism and British National Identity since 1885* (London, 1995).

Loughlin, J., "Imagining 'Ulster': The north of Ireland and British national identity, 1880–1921," in Connolly (ed.), *Kingdoms United?*

Louis, W. R., "Introduction" to id. (ed.), *Imperialism*.

Louis, W. R., *Imperialism at Bay, 1941–1945. The United States and the Decolonization of the British Empire* (Oxford, 1977).

Louis, W. R., *The British Empire in the Middle East, 1945–1951* (Oxford, 1984).

Louis, W. R., "American anti-colonialism and the dissolution of the British empire," *International Affairs*, 61 (1985), repr. Louis and Bull (eds), *Special Relationship*.

Louis, W. R., "Public enemy number one: the British Empire in the dock at the United Nations, 1957–1971," in Lynn (ed.), *British Empire in the 1950s*.

Louis, W. R. (ed.), *Imperialism. The Robinson and Gallagher Controversy* (New York and London, 1976).

Louis, W. R. and Brown, J. (eds), *OHBE*, 4, *The Twentieth Century* (Oxford, 2000).

Louis, W. R. and Bull, H. (eds), *The Special Relationship* (London, 1986).

Louis, W. R. and Owen, R. (eds), *Suez 1956. The Crisis and its Consequences* (Oxford, 1989).

Louis, W. R. and Robinson, R., "The imperialism of decolonization," *Jl of Imperial and Commonwealth History*, 22, 3 (1994).

Lovejoy, P. E., "The volume of the Atlantic slave trade: A synthesis," *Jl of African History*, 23 (1982).

Lovejoy, P. E., "The impact of the Atlantic Slave Trade on Africa: A review of the literature," *Jl of African History*, 30 (1989).

Low, D. A., *Congress and the Raj: Facets of the Indian struggle, 1917–47* (London, 1977).

Low, D. A., *Eclipse of Empire: Commonwealth and Decolonization* (Cambridge, 1990).

Low, D. A. and Lonsdale, J. M., "Introduction: Towards the new order, 1945–1963," in Low and Smith (eds), *History of East Africa*, 3.

Low, D. A. and Smith, A. (eds), *History of East Africa*, 3 (Oxford, 1976).

Lowry, D., "The crown, empire loyalism and the assimilation of non-British white subjects in the British world: An argument against 'ethnic determinsm,'" in Bridge and Fedorowich (eds), *British World*.

Lowry, D. (ed.), *The South African War Reappraised* (Manchester, 2000).

Lucas, W., Scott, *Divided We Stand: Britain, the United States, and the Suez Crisis* (London, 1991).

Ludden, D., *Reading Subaltern Studies: Critical History, Contested Meaning and the Globalization of South Asia* (London, 2002).

Lynn, M. (ed.), *Nigeria 1943–1960* (BDEEP, Series B, 2 parts, London, 2001).

Lynn, M. (ed.), *The British Empire in the 1950s. Retreat or Revival?* (London, 2005).

Mabro, J. (ed.), *Veiled Half-Truths: Western Travellers' Perceptions of Middle Eastern Women* (London, 1991).

Macaulay, T. B., *Minute on Indian Education* (1835), in *Selected Writings*, ed. John Clive and Thomas Pinney (Chicago, 1972).

Macaulay, T. B., *Speeches on Politics and Literature* (London, 1909).

McCarthy, A., *Irish Migrants in New Zealand, 1840–1937: "The Desired Haven"* (Woodbridge, 2005).

McCarthy, A. (ed.), *A Global Clan. Scottish Migrant Networks and Identities since the Eighteenth Century* (London, 2006).

McCloskey, D., "1780–1860: a survey," in Floud and McCloskey (ed.), *Economic History of Britain since 1700*.

McCormack, A. R., "Networks among British immigrants and accommodation to Canadian society—Winnipeg, 1900–1914," *Histoire sociale—Social History*, 17 (1984).

McCracken, D., *The Irish Pro-Boers, 1877–1902* (Johannesburg, 1989).

McCracken, D., *MacBride's Brigade: Irish Commandos in the Anglo-Boer War* (Dublin, 1999).

McCracken, J., "Colonialism, capitalism and ecological crisis in Malawi: A reassessment," in Anderson and Grove (eds), *Conservation in Africa*.

McCulloch J., *Colonial Psychiatry and the "African Mind"* (Cambridge, 1995).

McDevitt, P. F., *"May the Best Man Win": Sport, Masculinity and Nationalism in Great Britain and the Empire, 1880–1935* (New York, 2004).

MacDonagh, O., "Emigration and the state, 1833–55: An essay in administrative history," *Transactions of the Royal Historical Society*, 5th ser., 5 (1955).

MacDonagh, O., *A Pattern of Government Growth 1800–60* (London, 1961)

MacDonagh, O., *Emigration in the Victorian Age* (Farnborough, 1973).

Macdonald, C., *A Woman of Good Character* (Wellington, 1990).

McDonald, J. and Richards, E., "The great emigration of 1841: Recruitment for New South Wales in British emigration fields," *Population Studies*, 51 (1997).

McDonald, J. and Shlomowitz, R., "Mortality on convict voyages to Australia, 1788-1868," *Social Science History*, 13 (1989).

McDonald, J. and Shlomowitz, R., "Mortality on immigrant voyages to Australia in the nineteenth century," *Explorations in Economic History*, 27 (1990).

McDonald, J. and Shlomowitz, R., "Passenger fares on sailing vessels to Australia in the nineteenth century," *Explorations in Economic History*, 28 (1991).

MacDonald, N., *Canada, 1763–1841: Immigration and Settlement* (London, 1939).

McDougall, H. A., *Racial Myth in English History: Trojans, Teutons, and Anglo-Saxons* (Hanover, NJ, 2004).

McDowell, R. B., "Ireland in 1800," in Moody and Vaughan (eds), *New History of Ireland*, 4.

MacIntyre, A., *After Virtue: a Study in Moral Theory* (London, 1981).

MacIntyre, A., *Three Rival Versions of Moral Enquiry* (London, 1990).

McIntyre, W. D., *British Decolonization, 1946–1997. When, How, and Why did the British Empire Fall?* (London, 1998).

McIntyre, W. D., "Commonwealth legacy," in Brown and Louis (eds), *OHBE*, 4, *The Twentieth Century* (Oxford, 1998).

Mackay, D. L., "Direction and purpose in British imperial policy, 1783–1801," *Historical Jl*, 17 (1974).

McKenna, M., *This Country: A Reconciled Republic?* (Sydney, 2004).

MacKenzie, F., *Redefining the Bonds of Commonwealth, 1938–48: The Politics of Preference* (London, 2002).

MacKenzie, J. M., *Propaganda and Empire: the manipulation of British public opinion 1880–1960* (Manchester, 1984).

MacKenzie, J. M., "Essay and reflection: on Scotland and Empire," *International History Rev.*, 15 (1993).

MacKenzie, J. M., *Orientalism: History, Theory and the Arts* (Manchester, 1995).

MacKenzie, J. M., "Empire and national identities: The case of Scotland," *Transactions of the Royal Historical Society*, 6th ser., 8 (1998).

MacKenzie, J. M., "Empire and metropolitan cultures," in Porter (ed.), *OHBE*, 3.

MacKenzie, J. M., The persistence of empire in metropolitan culture," in Ward (ed.), *Culture*.

MacKenzie, J. M., "Foreword," in A. Mackillop and S. Murdoch (eds), *Military Governors and Imperial Frontiers c.1600–1800* (Leiden/Boston, 2003).

MacKenzie, J. M. (ed.), *Imperialism and Popular Culture* (Manchester, 1985).

MacKenzie, J. M. (ed.), *Imperialism and the Natural World* (Manchester, 1990).

Mackillop, A., *"More Fruitful than the Soil." Army, Empire and the Scottish Highlands, 1715–1815* (Edinburgh, 2000).

Mackillop, A. and Murdoch, S. (eds), *Military Governers and Imperial Frontiers c. 1600–1800* (Leiden/Boston, 2003).

McLane, J. R., *Land and Local Kingship in Eighteenth-Century Bengal* (Cambridge, 1993).

McClelland, K. and Rose, S., "Citizenship and empire, 1867–1928," in Hall and Rose (eds), *At Home with the Empire*.

MacLeod, R., "On visiting the 'Moving Metropolis': Reflections on the architecture of imperial science," *Historical Records of Australian Science*, 5 (1982).

MacLeod, R., "From imperial to national science," in MacLeod (ed.), *Commonwealth of Science*.

MacLeod, R. (ed.), *The Commonwealth of Science: ANZAAS and the Scientific Enterprise in Australasia, 1888–1988* (Melbourne, 1988).

MacLeod, R. and Leis, M. (eds), *Disease, Medicine and Empire* (London, 1988).

McMahon, C., *Republicans and Imperialists: Anglo-Irish Relations in the 1930s* (London, 1984).

Macmillan, D. S., "Scottish enterprise and influences in Canada, 1620–1900" in Cage (ed.), *Scots Abroad*.

Macmillan, D. S., *Scotland and Australia 1788–1850* (Oxford, 1967).

Macmillan, H., *Memoirs*, vol.6, *At the End of the Day* (London, 1973).

Macmillan, H., *Memoirs*, vol. 5, *Pointing the Way, 1959–1961* (London, 1972).

McNamara, R., *Britain, Nasser, and the Balance of Power in the Middle East, 1952–1967: From the Egyptian Revolution to the Six Day War* (London, 2003).

McQueen, H., *A New Britannia: An Argument Concerning the Social Origins of Australian Radicalism and Nationalism* (Ringwood, Vic., 1970).

Madden, A. F. "1066, 1776 and all that: The relevance of English medieval experience of 'Empire' to later imperial constitutional issues," in J. E. Flint and G. Williams (eds), *Perspectives of Empire: Essays Presented to Gerald S. Graham* (London, 1973).

Madden, A. F. with Fieldhouse, D. K. (eds), *Select Documents on the Constitutional History of the British Empire and Commonwealth*, 8 vols. (Westport, CT, New York, and London, 1985–2000): 1, *"The Empire of the Bretaignes," 1175–1688: The Foundations of a Colonial System of Government; 2, The Classical Period of the First British Empire, 1689–1783: The Foundations of a Colonial System of Government; 3, Imperial Reconstruction, 1763–1840: The Evolution of Alternative Systems of Colonial Government; 4, Settler Self-Government, 1840–1900: The Development of Representative and Responsible Government; 5, The Dependent Empire and Ireland, 1840–1900: Advance and Retreat in Representative Self-Government; 6 (with John Darwin), The Dominions and India since 1900; 7 (with John Darwin), The Dependent Empire: Colonies, Protectorates, and Mandates, 1900–1948; 8, The End of Empire.*

Madgwick, R. B., *Immigration into Eastern Australia, 1788–1851* (London, 1937).

Magee, G. B. and Thompson, A. S, "'A soft touch?' British industry, empire markets and the self-governing Dominions, 1870–1914," *Economic History Rev.*, 2nd series, 56 (2003).

Magee, G. B. and Thompson, A. S., "'Lines of credit, debts of obligation': migrant remittances to Britain, c. 1875–1913," *Economic History Rev.*, 59 (2006).

Magee, G. B. and Thompson, A. S., "The global and local: explaining migrant remittance flows in the English-speaking world, 1880–1914," *Jl of Economic History*, 66 (2006).

Magee, G. B. and Thompson, A. S., *"Globalization from below": A cultural economy of the British Empire, 1860–1914* (forthcoming).

Mahmood, S., *The Politics of Piety. The Islamic Revival and the Feminist Subject* (Princeton, 2004).

Maitland, F. W., *The Constitutional History of England* (ed. H. A. L. Fisher), (Cambridge, 1963).

Major, A., *Pious Flames: European Encounters with Sati* (New Delhi, 2006).

Malchow, H. L., "Trade unions and emigration in late Victorian England: a national lobby for state aid," *Jl of British Studies*, 15 (1975–6).

Malchow, H. L., *Population Pressures: Emigration and Government in Late Nineteenth Century Britain* (Palo Alto, 1979).

Malcolm, E., "'What would people say if I became a policeman?': The Irish policeman abroad," in Walsh (ed.), *Ireland Abroad*.

Mamdani, M., *Citizen and Subject: Contemporary Africa and the Legacy of Late Colonialism* (Princeton, 1996).

Mancke, E. and Shammas, C. (eds), *The Creation of the British Atlantic World* (Baltimore, 2006).

Mandler, P., "'Race' and 'nation' in mid-Victorian thought," in Collini *et al.* (eds), *History, Religion and Culture*.

Mandler, P., *The English National Character* (New Haven, 2006).

Mangan, J. A., *The Games Ethic and Imperialism: Aspects of the Diffusion of an Ideal* (Harmondsworth, 1986).

Mangan, J. A., *The Cultural Bond: Sport, Empire, Society* (London, 1992).

Mani, L., *Contentious Traditions: The Debate on Sati in Colonial India* (Berkeley, CA, 1998).

Mani, L., "Cultural theory, colonial texts: Reading eyewitness accounts of widow burning," in Nelson and Grossberg (eds), *Marxism and the Interpretation of Culture*.

Mann, M., *The Dark Side of Democracy: Explaining Ethnic Cleansing* (Cambridge, 2004).

Manning, H. T., *British Colonial Government after the American Revolution 1782–1820* (New Haven, CT, 1933).

Mansergh, N., *The Commonwealth Experience* (London, 1969).

Mar, T. B. and Evans, J. (eds), *Writing Colonial Histories: Comparative Perspectives* (Melbourne, 2002).

Marchildon, G. P., "The hands across the water: Canadian industrial financiers in the City of London, 1905–20," *Business History*, 34 (1992).

Marks, S. and Richardson, P. (eds), *International Labour Migration. Historical Perspectives* (London, 1984).

Marquand, D., "How united is the modern United Kingdom?," in Grant and Stringer (eds), *Uniting the Kingdom?*.

Marquand, D., "The twilight of the British state? Henry Dubb versus sceptred awe," in Green and Whiting (eds), *Boundaries of the State*.

Marshall, P. J., "Empire and authority in the later eighteenth century," *JICH*, 15 (1987).

Marshall, P. J., "The whites of British India, 1780–1830: A failed colonial society?," *International History Rev.*, 12 (1990).

Marshall, P. J., "'Cornwallis triumphant': War in India and the British public in the late eighteenth century," in Freedman, Hayes, and O'Neill (eds), *War, Strategy, and International Politics*.

Marshall, P. J., "A nation defined by empire, 1755–1776," in Grant and Stringer (eds), *Uniting the Kingdom?*.

Marshall, P. J., "Imperial Britain," *JICH*, 23 (1995).

Marshall, P. J., "The diaspora of Africans and Asians," in *id.* (ed.), *Cambridge Illustrated History of the British Empire*.

Marshall, P. J., "Imperial Britain," in *id.*, *Cambridge Illustrated History of the British Empire*.

Marshall, P. J., "The British state overseas, 1750–1850," in Moore and Van Nierop (eds), *Colonial Empires Compared*.

Marshall, P. J., *The Making and Unmaking of Empires: Britain, India, and America c. 1750–1783* (Oxford, 2005).

Marshall, P. J., "Britain without America—A second empire?," in Marshall (ed.), *OHBE*, 2.

Marshall, P. J., "The first British Empire," in Winks (ed.), *OHBE*, 5.

Marshall, P. J. (ed.), *OHBE*, 2, *The Eighteenth Century* (Oxford, 1999).

Marshall, P. J. (ed.), *The Cambridge Illustrated History of the British Empire* (Cambridge, 1996).

Martens, J., "A transnational history of immigration testriction: Natal and New South Wales, 1896-97," *JICH*, 34 (2006).

Martin, M., "'A future not of riches but of comfort': The emigration of pauper children from Bristol to Canada, 1870–1915," *Immigrants and Minorities*, 19 (2000).

Matthew, H. C. G., *Gladstone, 1875–98* (Oxford, 1995).

Matthew, H. C. G. and Harrison, B. H. (eds), *The Oxford Dictionary of National Biography* (Oxford, 2004).

Matthew, W. M., "The imperialism of free trade in Peru, 1820–70," *Economic History Rev.*, 2nd series, 21 (1968).

Maxwell, D., *Christians and Chiefs in Zimbabwe: A Social history of the Hwesa People c. 1870s–1990s* (Edinburgh, 1999).

Maxwell, D., "Writing the history of African Christianity: Reflections of an editor," *Jl of Religion in Africa*, 36 (2006).

Maxwell, D. and Lawrie, I. (eds), *Christianity and the African Imagination: Essays in Honour of Adrian Hastings* (Leiden, 2002).

May, A., "Commonwealth or Europe? Macmillan's dilemma, 1961–63," in May (ed.), *Britain, the Commonwealth and Europe*.

May, A., "Empire loyalists and 'Commonwealth men': The Round Table and the end of empire," in Ward (ed.), *British Culture*.

May, A. (ed.), *Britain, the Commonwealth and Europe: the Commonwealth and Britain's Applications to Join the European Community* (Basingstoke, 2001).

Mayer, A. J., *The Persistence of the Old Regime: Europe to the Great War* (London, 1981).

Mazower, M., *Salonica, City of Ghosts: Christians, Muslims and Jews 1430–1950* (London, 2004).

Meaney, N., *The Search for Security in the Pacific* (Sydney, 1976).

Meaney, N., "Britishness and Australian identity: The problem of nationalism in Australian history and historiography," *Australian Historical Studies*, 32 (2001).

Meaney, N. (ed.), *Under New Heavens: Cultural Transmission and the Making of Australia* (Melbourne, 1989).

Melman, B., *Women's Orients: English Women in the Middle East, 1718–1918* (London, 1992).

Metcalf, T. R., *An Imperial Vision: Indian Architecture and Britain's Raj* (Berkeley, CA, 1989).

Metcalf, T. R., *Ideologies of the Raj* (Cambridge, 1994).

Midgley, C., *Women Against Slavery: The British Campaigns, 1780–1870* (London, 1992).

Midgley, C. (ed.), *Gender and Imperialism* (Manchester, 1998).

Miller, J. C., "History and Africa/Africa and History," *American Historical Rev.*, 104 (1999).

Miller, J. R., *Shingwauk's Vision: A History of Canadian Residential Schools* (Toronto, 1996).

Miller, K. A., *Emigrants and Exiles: Ireland and the Irish Exodus to North America* (Oxford, 1985).

Miller, K. A. with Boling, B., and Doyle, D. N., "Emigrants and exiles: Irish cultures and Irish emigration to North America, 1790–1922," *Irish Historical Studies*, 22 (1980–1).

Mills, D., *The Idea of Loyalty in Upper Canada, 1784–1850* (Kingston and Montreal, 1988).

Mills, S., *Discourses of Difference: An Analysis of Women's Travel Writing and Colonialism* (London, 1991).

Minchinton, W. E. (ed.), *Politics and the Port of Bristol in the Eighteenth Century: The Petitions of the Society of Merchant Venturers, 1698–1803* (Bristol, 1963).

Misra, M., "Lessons of empire: Britain and India," *SAIS Review*, 23 (2003).

Mitchie, R. C., "Dunn, Fischer and Co in the City of London, 1906–14," *Business History*, 30 (1988).

Mitchie, R. C., *The City of London: Continuity and Change 1850–1990* (London, 1992).

Mohanty, C., "Under western eyes: Feminist scholarship and colonial discourses," *Feminist Rev.*, 30 (1988).

Mokyr, J. and O'Gráda, C., "Emigration and poverty in prefamine Ireland," *Explorations in Economic History*, 19 (1982).

Mommsen, W. J. and Osterhammel, J. (eds), *Imperialism and After: Continuities and Discontinuities* (London, 1986).

Monet, J., "Canada," in Eddy and Schreuder (eds), *Rise of Colonial Nationalism*.

Moody, T. W. and Vaughan, W. E. (eds), *A New History of Ireland, 4, Eighteenth Century Ireland 1691–1800* (Oxford, 1986).

Moon, P., *The Path to the Treaty of Waitangi* (Auckland, 2002).

Moore, B. and Van Nierop, H. (eds), *Colonial Empires Compared. Britain and the Netherlands, 1750–1850* (Aldershot, 2003).

Moore, R. I., *Escape from Empire: the Attlee Government and the Indian Problem* (Oxford, 1983).

Moran, G., *Sending Out Ireland's Poor: Assisted Emigration to North America in the Nineteenth Century* (Dublin, 2004).

Morgan, H., "An unwelcome heritage: Ireland's role in British empire-building," *History of European Ideas*, 19 (1994).

Morgan, K., "Imperialists at bay: the British Labour party and decolonization," *JICH*, 27 (1999), repr. in King and Kilson (eds), *Statecraft of British Imperialism*.

Morgan, P. D., "The Black experience in the British empire, 1680–1810," in Marshall (ed.), *OHBE*, 2.

Morgan, P. D., "Encounters between British and 'indigenous' peoples, c. 1500–1800," in Daunton and Halpern (eds), *Empire and Others: British Encounters with Indigenous Peoples, 1600–1850*.

Morgan, P. D. and Hawkins, S. (eds), *Black Experience and the British Empire* (OHBE Companion series, Oxford, 2004).

Morley, J., *The Life of William Ewart Gladstone*, 3 vols (London, 1903).

Morris, E., *Our Own Devices: National Symbols and Political Conflict in Twentieth-Century Ireland* (Dublin, 2005).

Morris, G., "James Prendergast and the Treaty of Waitangi: Judicial attitudes to the Treaty during the latter half of the nineteenth century," *VUW Law Review*, 35 (2005).

Morris-Jones, W. H. and Fischer, G. (eds), *Decolonization and After: the British and French Experience* (London, 1980).

Morton, W. L., *The Canadian Identity* (Toronto, 2nd ed., 1972).

Mudimbe, V. Y., *The Invention of Africa* (Bloomington, 1988).

Munro, J. F., *Britain in Tropical Africa* (London, 1984).

Munro, J. F., *Maritime Enterprise and Empire: Sir William Mackinnon and his Business Network, 1823–93* (Woodbridge, 2003).

Murdoch, A., *British Emigration 1603–1914* (Basingstoke, 2004).

Murphy, P., *Party Politics and Decolonization: the Conservative Party and British Colonial Policy in Tropical Africa, 1951–1964* (Oxford, 1995).

Murphy, P., "'Government by blackmail': The origins of the Central African Federation reconsidered," in Lynn (ed.), *British Empire in the 1950s*.

Murphy, P., "'An intricate and distasteful subject': British planning for the use of force against the European settlers of Central Africa, 1952–1965," *English Historical Rev.*, 71 (2006).

Murphy, P. (ed.), *Central Africa, 1945–1965* (*BDEEP*, Series B, 2 parts, London, 2005).

Nalbach, A., "'The software of empire': Telegraphic news agencies and imperial publicity, 1865–1914," in Codell (ed.), *Imperial Co-Histories*.

Navari, C. (ed.), *British Politics and the Spirit of the Age* (Keele, 1996).

Neal, F., "Liverpool, the Irish steamship companies and the famine Irish," *Immigrants and Minorities*, 5 (1986).

Nehru, J., *The Discovery of India* (London, 1946).

Neill, R., *A History of Canadian Economic Thought* (London, 1991).

Nelson, C. and Grossberg, L. (eds), *Marxism and the Interpretation of Culture* (Urbana, IL, 1988).

Newbury, C., "Labour migration in the imperial phase: an essay in interpretation," *JICH*, 3 (1975).

Newbury, C., *Patrons, Clients, and Empire: Chieftaincy and Over-rule in Asia, Africa, and the Pacific* (Oxford, 2003).

Newton, J. L., Ryan, M. P., and Walkowitz, J. R. (eds), *Sex and Class in Women's History* (London, 1983).

Neylan, S., *The Heavens are Changing: Nineteenth-Century Protestant Missions and Tsimshian Christianity* (Montreal and Kingston, 2002).

Nicholas, S. (ed.), *Convict Workers: Reinterpreting Australia's Past* (Cambridge, 1988).

Nicholas, S. and Shergold, P. R., "Convicts as migrants," in Nicholas (ed.), *Convict Workers*.

Nicholas, S. and Shergold, P. R., "Transportation as global migration," in Nicholas (ed.), *Convict Workers*.

Nightingale, B., *Seven Rivers to Cross. A Mostly British Council Life* (London, 1996).

Norris, R., *The Emergent Commonwealth: Australian Federation: Expectations and Fulfilment 1889–1910* (Melbourne, 1975).

Northrup, D., *Indentured Labor in the Age of Imperialism, 1834–1922* (Cambridge, 1995).

Northrup, D., "Migration from Africa, Asia, and the South Pacific," in Porter (ed.), *OHBE*, 3.

Nussbaum, F. A., *Torrid Zones: Maternity, Sexuality and Empire in Eighteenth-Century English Narratives* (Baltimore and London, 1995).

O'Brien, P. K., "The costs and benefits of British imperialism, 1846–1914," *Past and Present*, 120 (1988).

O'Brien, P. K., "Reply," *Past and Present*, 125 (1989).

O'Brien, P. K., "Imperialism and the rise and decline of the British economy, 1688–1989," *New Left Rev.*, 238 (1999).

O'Brien, P. K., "Inseparable connections: Trade, economy, state, and empire," in Marshall (ed.), *OHBE*, 2.

O'Brien, P. K. and Engerman, S. L., "Exports and the growth of the British Economy from the Glorious Revolution to the Peace of Amiens," in Solow (ed.), *Slavery and the Rise of the Atlantic System*.

O'Farrell, P., *The Irish in Australia* (Sydney, 1986, rev. 3rd edn 2001).

O'Gráda, C., "A note on nineteenth-century Irish emigration statistics," *Population Studies*, 29 (1975).

O'Hanlon, R., *Caste, Conflict, and Ideology: Mahatma Jotirao Phule and Low Caste Protest in Nineteenth-Century Western India* (Cambridge, 1985).

O'Hanlon, R., "Recovering the subject: Subaltern studies and histories of resistance in colonial South Asia," *Modern Asian Studies*, 22 (1988).

O'Hanlon, R. and Washbrook, D., "After Orientalism: Culture, criticism, and politics in the Third World," *Comparative Studies in Society and History*, 34 (1992).

O'Rourke, K. H. and Williamson, J. G., *Globalization and History: The Evolution of a Nineteenth-Century Atlantic Economy* (Massachusetts, 1999).

O'Shaughnessy, A. J., *An Empire Divided: The American Revolution and the British Caribbean* (Philadelphia, 2000).

Offer, A., "Pacific rim societies: Asian labour and white nationalism," in Eddy and Schreuder (eds), *Rise of Colonial Nationalism*.

Offer, A., "The British Empire, 1870–1914: A waste of money?," *Economic History Rev.*, 46 (1993).

Ogot, B, "Mau Mau and Nationhood," in Atieno Odhiambo and Lonsdale (eds), *Mau Mau and Nationhood*.

Oldfield, J., *Popular Politics and British Anti-Slavery. The Mobilisation of Public Opinion Against the Slave Trade, 1787–1807* (London, 1998).

Onuf, P. S. and Onuf, N. G., *Federal Union, Modern World: The Law of Nations in an Age of Revolutions, 1776–1814* (Madison, 1993).

Openshaw, J., "The radicalism of Tagore and the Bauls of Bengal," *South Asia Research*, 17 (1997).

Ovendale, R., *Britain, the United States, and the End of the Palestine Mandate, 1942–1948* (London, 1989).

Ovendale, R., "Macmillan and the wind of change in Africa, 1957–1960," *Historical Jl*, 38 (1995).

Ovendale, R., *Britain, the United States, and the Transfer of Power in the Middle East 1945–1962* (London, 1996).

Owen, N., "'More than a transfer of power': Independence day celebrations in India, 15 August 1947," *Contemporary Record*, 6 (1992).

Owen, N., "Decolonization and post-war consensus," in Jones and Kandiah (eds), *Myth of Consensus*.

Owen, R., *Lord Cromer: Victorian Imperialist, Edwardian Proconsul* (Oxford, 2004).

Owen, R. and Sutcliffe, B. (eds), *Studies in the Theory of Imperialism* (London, 1972).

Oxley, D., *Convict Maids. The Forced Migration of Women to Australia* (Cambridge, 1996).

Pagden, A., *Lords of All the World: Ideologies of Empire in Spain, Britain and France c.1500–c.1800* (New Haven, 1995).

Pagden, A., "The struggle for legitimacy and the image of empire in the Atlantic, to c. 1700," in Canny (ed.), *OHBE*, 1.

Pagden, A. and Canny, N. (eds), *Colonial Identity in the Atlantic World* (Princeton, 1987).

Page, B., *Prelude to Partition: the Indian Muslims and the Pattern of Imperial Control* (Delhi, 1982).

Paley, R., "After *Somerset*: Mansfield, slavery and the law in England, 1772–1830," in Landau (ed.), *Law, Crime, and English Society*.

Paley, W., *The Principles of Moral and Political Philosophy* (1785), in *The Works of William Paley* (Philadelphia, 1857).

Pandey, G., *The Construction of Communalism in Colonial North India* (Delhi, 1990).

Paquet, G. and Wallot, J.-P., "Nouvelle France/Québec/Canada: A world of limited identities," in Pagden and Canny (eds), *Colonial Identity in the Atlantic World*.

Parr, J., *Labouring Children. British Immigrant Apprentices to Canada, 1869–1924* (Toronto, 2nd edn, 1994).

Parry, B., *Conrad and Imperialism: Ideological Boundaries and Visionary Frontiers* (London, 1983).

Parry, B., "Problems in current theories of colonial discourse," *Oxford Literary Rev.*, 9 (1987).

Pascoe, C. F., *Two Hundred Years of the S.P.G.: An Historical Account of the Society for the Propagation of the Gospel in Foreign Parts 1701–1950* (London, 1951).

Paterson, D. G., *British Direct Investment in Canada 1890–1914* (Toronto, 1976).

Patterson, B. (ed.), *Ulster-New Zealand Migration and Cultural Transfers* (Dublin, 2006).

Patterson, O., *Slavery and Social Death: A Comparative Study* (Cambridge, 1982).

Paul, K., *Whitewashing Britain. Race and Citizenship in the Postwar Era* (Ithaca, 1997).

Pawlisch, H., *Sir John Davies and the Conquest of Ireland* (Cambridge, 1985).

Payton, P., *The Cornish Overseas* (Fowey, 2nd edn, 2005).

Payton, P. (ed.), *Cornish Studies*, 10 (Exeter, 2002).

Pearce, R. D., "The Colonial Office in 1947 and the transfer of power in Africa: An Addendum to John Cell," *JICH*, 10 (1982).

Pearce, R. D., *The Turning Point in Africa: British Colonial Policy, 1938–1948* (London, 1982).

Pearson, C. H., *National Life and Character: A Forecast* (London, 1894).

Pearson, R. and Richardson, D., "Business networking in the industrial revolution," *Economic History Rev*, 54 (2001).

Pederson, S., "National bodies, unspeakable acts: The sexual politics of colonial policy-making," *Jl of Modern History*, 63 (1991).

Pederson, S., "The maternalist moment in British colonial policy: The controversy over 'child slavery' in Hong Kong, 1917–1941," *Past and Present*, 171 (2001).

Peel, J. D. Y., "'For who hath despised the day of small things?' Missionary narratives and historical anthropology," *Society for Comparative Study of Society and History*, 37 (1995).

Peel, J. D. Y., *Religious Encounter and the Making of the Yoruba* (Bloomington, 2001).

Peers, D. M., *Between Mars and Mammon. Colonial Armies and the Garrison State in India, 1819–35* (London, 1995).

Peers, D. M., "Colonial Knowledge and the Military in India, 1780–1860," *JICH*, 33 (2005).

Peires, J. B., *The Dead Will Arise: Nongqawuse and the Great Xhosa Cattle-Killing Movement of 1856–7* (Bloomington, 1989).

Perera, S., *Reaches of Empire: The English Novel from Edgeworth to Dickens* (New York, 1991).

Perkin, H., *The Rise of Professional Society: England since 1880* (London, 1989).

Perry, A., "The colonial archive on trial: Possession, dispossession and history in *Delgamuukw v. British Columbia*," in Burton (ed.), *Archive Stories*.

Peterson, D., "Writing in revolution. Independent schooling and Mau Mau in Nyeri," in Atieno Odhiambo and Lonsdale (eds), *Mau Mau and Nationhood*.

Peterson, M. D. (ed.), *Thomas Jefferson, Writings*, vol. 15, *The Library of America* (New York, 1984).

Petter, M. and Lee, J. M., *The Colonial Office, War and Development Policy: the Organization and Planning of a Metropolitan Initiative, 1939–1945* (London, 1982).

Philip, J., *Researches in South Africa* (London, 1828).

Philip, K., *Civilizing Natures: Race, Resources, and Modernity in Colonial South India* (New Brunswick, NJ, 2004).

Phillips, A., *Enigma of Colonialism. British Policy in West Africa* (London, 1989).

Phillips, J., "Who were New Zealand's Ulster immigrants?", in Patterson (ed.), *Ulster-New Zealand Migration*.

Phimister, I. R., "Rhodes, Rhodesia, and the Rand," *Jl of African Studies*, 1 (1974).

Phimister, I. R., "Corners and company-mongering: Nigerian Tin and the City of London," *JICH*, 28 (2000).

Phimister, I. R., "Empire, imperialism and the partition of Africa," in Akita (ed.), *Gentlemanly Capitalism*.

Phimister, I. R., "Foreign devils, finance, and informal empire: Britain and China, c. 1900–1912," *Modern Asian Studies*, 40 (2006).

Pick, D., *Faces of Degeneration: A European Disorder, c. 1848–c. 1918* (Cambridge, 1989).

Pimlott, B., *Harold Wilson* (London, 1992).

Pinch, W., "Same difference in India and Europe," *History and Theory*, 38 (1999).

Plant, G. F., *Oversea Settlement* (London, 1951).

Platt, D. C. M., *Finance, Trade and Politics 1815–1914* (Oxford, 1968).

Platt, D. C. M., "The imperialism of free trade: Some reservations," *Economic History Rev.*, 2nd ser., 21 (1968).

Platt, D. C. M., "Further objections to an 'Imperialism of free trade,' 1830–60," *Economic History Rev.*, 2nd ser., 26 (1973).

Platt, D. C. M. (ed.), *Business Imperialism 1840–1930: An Inquiry Based on the British Experience in Latin America* (Oxford, 1977).

Pocock, J. G. A., "British history: A plea for a new subject," *New Zealand Jl of History*, 8 (1974).

Pocock, J. G. A., "British history: A plea for a new subject," *Jl of Modern History*, 47 (1975).

Pocock, J. G. A., "The limits and divisions of British history: In search of the unknown subject," *American Historical Rev.*, 87 (1982).

Pocock, J. G. A., "History and sovereignty: The historiographical response to the Europeanization in two British cultures," *Jl of British Studies*, 31 (1992).

Pocock, J. G. A., "Conclusion: Contingency, identity, sovereignty," in Grant and Stringer (eds), *Uniting the Kingdom*.

Pocock, J. G. A., "Empire, state, and confederation: The War of American Independence as a crisis in multiple monarchy," in Robertson (ed.), *Union for Empire*.

Pocock, J. G. A., *The Discovery of Islands: Essays in British History* (Cambridge, 2005).

Pocock, J. G. A., "Law, sovereignty and history in a divided culture: The case of New Zealand and the Treaty of Waitangi," in *id.*, *Discovery of Islands*.

Pohlandt-McCormick, H., "In good hands: Researching the 1976 Soweto Uprising in the State Archives of South Africa," in Burton (ed.), *Archive Stories*.

Pollard, A. (ed.), *Thackeray: Vanity Fair* (London, 1978).

Pollock, S., "The death of Sanskrit," *Comparative Studies in History and Society*, 43 (2001).

Pollock, S., "Introduction: Working papers on Sanskrit knowledge systems on the eve of colonialism," *Jl of Indian Philosophy*, 30 (2002).

Pollock, S., "Deep orientalism? Notes on Sanskrit and power beyond the Raj," in Breckenridge and van der Veer (eds), *Orientalism and the Postcolonial Predicament*.

Pooley, C. G. and Whyte, I. D. (eds), *Migrants, Emigrants and Immigrants: A Social History of Migration* (London, 1991).

Porter, A. N., "Which city, what empire? Shipping, government, and the limits of co-operation. 1870–1914," in Turrell and Van Helten (eds), *City and Empire*.

Porter, A. N., "'Gentlemanly capitalism' and Empire: The British experience since 1750," *JICH*, 18 (1990).

Porter, A. N., "War, colonialism and the British experience: The redefinition of Christian missionary policy, 1938–1952," *Kirkliche Zeitgeschichte*, 5 (1992).

Porter, A. N., "Religion, missionary enthusiasm and empire," in Porter (ed.), *OHBE*, 5.

Porter, A. N., "Church history, history of Christianity, religious history: Some reflections on British missionary enterprise since the late eighteenth century," *Church History*, 71 (2002).

Porter, A. N., "The Universities Mission to Central Africa: Anglo-Catholicism and the twentieth century colonial encounter," in Stanley (ed.), *Missions*.

Porter, A. N., Online review of Niall Fergusson's *Empire: How Britain Made the Modern World*. Available at www.history.ac.uk/reviews/paper/porterA.html (accessed December 2006).

Porter, A. N., *Religion versus Empire. British Protestant Missionaries and Overseas Expansion, 1700–1914* (Manchester, 2004).

Porter, A. N. (ed.), *OHBE, 3, The Nineteenth Century* (Oxford, 1999)

Porter, A. N. (ed.), *The Imperial Horizons of British Protestant Missions 1880–1914* (Cambridge, 2003).

Porter, B., *Critics of Empire: British Radical Attitudes to Colonialism in Africa 1659–1914* (London, 1968).

Porter, B., *The Absent-Minded Imperialists. Empire, Society and Culture in Britain* (Oxford, 2004).

Potter, S., "Richard Jebb, John S. Ewart, and the Round Table, 1898–1926," *English Historical Rev.*, 122 (2007).

Potter, S. J., *News and the British World: the Emergence of an Imperial Press System, 1876–1922* (Oxford, 2003).

Prakash, G., *Another Reason: Science and the Imagination of Modern India* (Princeton, 1999).

Prakash, G. (ed.), *After Colonialism: Imperial Histories and Postcolonial Displacements* (Princeton, 1995).

Pratt, M. L., *Imperial Eyes: Travel Writing and Transculturation* (London, 1992).

Price, J. M., "The imperial economy," in Marshall (ed.), *OHBE, 2*.

Price, R., *An Imperial War and the British Working Class: Working-Class Attitudes to the Boer War 1899–1902* (London, 1972).

Price, R., "One big thing: Britain, its empire, and their imperial culture," *Jl of British Studies*, 45 (2006).

Prior, K., "Making history: the state's intervention in urban religious disputes in the North-Western Provinces in the early nineteenth century," *Modern Asian Studies*, 27 (1993).

Procida, M. A., *Married to the Empire. Gender, Politics and Imperialism in India, 1883–1947* (Manchester, 2002).

Proudfoot, L., "Landscape, place and memory: towards a geography of Irish identities in colonial Australia," in Walsh (ed.), *Ireland Abroad*.

Purvis, T. and Hunt, A., "Discourse, ideology, discourse, ideology, discourse, ideology . . .," *British Jl of Sociology*, 44 (1993).

Quaife, M. M. (ed.), *The Seige of Detroit in 1763: The Journal of Pontiac's Conspiracy and John Rutherford's Narrative of a Captivity* (Chicago, 1958).

Radcliffe, B. M. (ed.), *Great Britain and Her World* (Manchester, 1975).

Rae-Ellis, V., *Black Robinson: Protector of Aborigines* (Melbourne, 1996).

Ramamurthy, A., *Black Markets: Images of Black People in Advertising and Packaging in Britain, 1880–1990* (Manchester, 1990).

Ramamurthy, A., *Imperial Persuaders: Images of Africa and Asia in British Advertising* (Manchester, 2003).

Ranger, T. O., *Revolt in Southern Rhodesia, 1896–7: A Study in African Resistance* (London, 1967).

Ranger, T. O., "Connexions between 'primary resistance' movements and modern mass nationalism in east and central Africa," parts I and II, *Jl of African History*, 9 (1968).

Ranger, T. O., *Peasant Consciousness and Guerilla War in Zimbabwe: A Comparative Study* (London, 1985).

Ranger, T. O., "Taking hold of the land: Holy places and pilgrimages in twentieth-century Zimbabwe," *Past and Present*, 117 (1987).

Ranger, T. O., "The invention of tradition revisited: the case of colonial Africa," in Ranger and Vaughan (eds), *Legitimacy and the State in Twentieth-Century Africa.*

Ranger, T. O. (ed.), *Emerging Themes of African History: Proceedings of the International Congress of African Historians held at University College, Dar es Salaam, October 1965* (London, 1969).

Ranger, T. and Vaughan O. (eds), *Legitimacy and the State in Twentieth-Century Africa* (London, 1993).

Rankin, H. F., *The Golden Age of Piracy* (Williamsburg, VA, 1969).

Rathbone, R., "The colonial service and the transfer of power in Ghana," in Smith (ed.), *Administering Empire.*

Rathbone R., "Things fall apart: The erosion of local government, local justice and civil rights in Ghana, 1955–1960," in Lynn (ed.), *British Empire in the 1950s.*

Rathbone, R. (ed.), *Ghana, 1941–1957* (BDEEP, series B, 2 parts, London, 1992).

Ray, R. K., *Social Conflict and Political Unrest in Bengal, 1875–1927* (Delhi, 1984).

Ray, R. K., *Entrepreneurship and Industry in India, 1800–1947* (Delhi, 1992).

Raychaudhuri, T., "Indian nationalism as animal politics," *Historical Jl*, 22 (1979).

Raychaudhuri, T., *Europe Reconsidered: Perceptions of the West in Nineteenth-Century Bengal* (Delhi, 1988).

Read, J., jnr, *The Kat River Settlement* (Cape Town, 1852).

Reece, R. H. W., "Inventing aborigines," *Aboriginal History*, 11 (1987).

Reid, K., "Setting women to work: the assignment system and female convict labour in Van Diemen's land, 1820–1839," *Australian Historical Studies*, 34 (2003).

Reid, R., "'That famine is pressing each day more heavily upon them': The emigration of Irish convict families to NSW 1848–1852," in Richards (ed.), *Poor Australian Immigrants.*

Renwick, W. (ed.), *Creating a National Spirit: Celebrating New Zealand's Centennial* (Wellington, 2004).

Reynolds, H., *Frontier* (Sydney, 1987).

Reynolds, H., *The Law of the Land* (Ringwood, 1987).

Richards, E., *A History of the Highland Clearances* (London, 1982).

Richards, E., "Varieties of Scottish emigration in the nineteenth century," *Australian Historical Studies*, 21 (1985).

Richards, E., "Australia and the Scottish connection, 1788–1914," in Cage (ed.), *Scots Abroad.*

Richards, E., "Scotland and the uses of the Atlantic empire," in Bailyn and Morgan (eds), *Strangers within the Realm.*

Richards, E., "How did poor people emigrate from the British Isles to Australia in the nineteenth century?," *Jl of British Studies*, 32 (1993).

Richards, E., *Britannia's Children. Emigration from England, Scotland, Wales and Ireland since 1600* (London, 2004).

Richards, E., "Running home from Australia: intercontinental mobility and migrant expectations in the nineteenth century," in Harper (ed.), *Emigrant Homecomings.*

Richards, E. (ed.), *Poor Australian Immigrants in the Nineteenth Century. Visible Immigrants: Two* (Canberra, 1991).

Richards, J., *Visions of Yesterday* (London, 1973).

Richards, J., "Patriotism and profit: British imperial cinema in the 1930s," in Curran and Porter (eds), *British Cinema History.*

Richards, J., *Imperialism and Music: Britain 1876–1953* (Manchester, 2001).

Richardson, D., "The British empire and the Atlantic slave trade, 1660–1807," in Marshall (ed.), *OHBE*, 2.

Richardson, P., *Chinese Mine Labour in the Transvaal* (London, 1982).

Rickard, J., "The anti-sweating movement in Britain and Victoria: The politics of empire and social reform," *Historical Studies* (1978–9).

Ricoeur, P., *Time and Narrative* (Chicago, 1984).

Robb, P. (ed.), *Dalit Movements and the Meanings of Labour in India* (Delhi, 1993).

Robbins, B., "Colonial discourse: A paradigm and its discontents," *Victorian Studies*, 35 (1992).

Robbins, K., *Nineteenth Century Britain: Integration and Diversity* (Oxford, 1995).

Roberts, A. D. (ed.), *Cambridge History of Africa*, 7 (Cambridge, 1986).

Roberts, B., "Doctors and deports: the role of the medical profession in Canadian deportation, 1900–1920," *Canadian Ethnic Studies*, 18 (1986).

Roberts, R. A. (ed.), *Calendar of Home Office Papers of the Reign of George III, 1773–1775* (London, 1899).

Robertson, J. (ed.), *A Union for Empire: Political Thought and the British Union of 1707* (Cambridge and New York, 1995).

Robertson, R., *Globalization: Social Theory and Global Culture* (London, 1992).

Robinson, R. E., "Non-European foundations of European imperialism: sketch for a theory of collaboration," in Owen and Sutcliff (eds), *Studies in the Theory of Imperialism*.

Robinson, R. E., "The excentric idea of imperialism, with or without empire" in Mommsen and Osterhammel (eds), *Imperialism and After*.

Robinson, R., "Andrew Cohen and the transfer of power in tropical Africa, 1940–1951" in Morris-Jones and Fischer (eds), *Decolonization and After*.

Robinson, R. E., and Gallagher, J. A., "The imperialism of free trade," *Economic History Rev.*, 2nd ser., 6 (1953).

Robinson, R. E. and Gallagher, J. A., with Denny, A., *Africa and the Victorians: The Official Mind of Imperialism* (London, 1961).

Robson, L. L., *The Convict Settlers of Australia* (Melbourne, 1973).

Rodger, N. A. M., *The Command of the Ocean: A Naval History of Britain 1649–1815* (London, 2004).

Rodney, W., *How Europe Underdeveloped Africa*, revd edn (Washington DC, 1981).

Rogers, J. D., "Early British rule and social classification in Lanka," *Modern Asian Studies*, 38 (2004).

Rooke, P. T. and Schnell, R. L., "Imperial philanthropy and colonial responses: British juvenile emigration to Canada, 1896–1930," *The Historian*, 46 (1983).

Rooney, D., *Sir Charles Arden-Clarke* (London, 1982).

Rooth, T., "Economic tension and conflict in the Commonwealth 1945–51," *Twentieth-Century British History*, 13 (2002).

Rose, J. H., "Frederick the Great and England, 1756–1763 (continued)," *English Historical Rev.*, 29 (1914).

Rose, S., *Which People's War? National Identity and Citizenship in Wartime Britain, 1939–1945* (Oxford, 2003).

Rosenthal, M., *The Character Factory: Baden-Powell's Boy Scouts and the Imperatives of Empire* (New York, 1986).

Ross, R., *Adam Kok's Griqua: A Study in the Development of Stratification in South Africa* (Cambridge, 1976)

Ross, R., *Status and Respectability in the Cape Colony, 1750–1850: A Tragedy of Manners* (Cambridge, 1999).

Rostow, W. W., *The Stages of Economic Growth: A Non-Communist Manifesto* (Cambridge, 1960).

Rotberg, I., *The Founder: Cecil Rhodes and the Pursuit of Power* (Oxford, 1988).

Rotberg, R., "John Chilembwe: Brief life of an anticolonial rebel, 1871?-1915," *Harvard Magazine*, 107 (2005).

Rubinstein, W. D., *Capitalism, Culture and Decline, 1750–1990* (London, 1993).

Rudolph, L. I. and Rudolph, S. H., *The Modernity of Tradition: Political Development in India* (Chicago, 1967).

Rushdie, S., "The new empire within Britain," in *id. Imaginary Homelands. Essays and Criticism*.

Rushdie, S., *Imaginary Homelands. Essays and Criticisms, 1981–1991* (London, 1991).

Rutherdale, M., *Women and the White Man's God: Gender and Race in the Canadian Mission Field* (Vancouver, 2002).

Ryan, J. R., *Picturing Empire: Photography and the Visualization of the British Empire* (London, 1997).

Said, E. W., *Orientalism* (Harmondsworth and New York, 1978).

Said, E. W., *Culture and Imperialism* (London, 1993).

Saker, H., *The South African Flag Controversy, 1925–28* (Cape Town, 1980).

Samuel, R., *Patriotism: The Making and Unmaking of British National Identity* (London, 1989).

Saneh, L., *Translating the Message: The Missionary Impact on Culture* (Maryknoll, NY, 1989).

Sarkar, S., *Modern India 1885–1947* (Delhi, 1983; Basingstoke, 1989).

Sarkar, S., "Orientalism revisited: Saidian frameworks in the writing of modern Indian history," *Oxford Literary Rev.*, 16 (1994).

Saul, S. B., *Studies in British Overseas Trade, 1870–1914* (Liverpool, 1960).

Saunders, K. (ed.), *Indentured Labour in the British Empire, 1834–1920* (London, 1984).

Savarkar, V. D., *The Indian War of Independence (National Rising of 1857)* (Bombay, 1946).

Schedvin, C. B., "Staples and regions of *Pax Britannica*," *Economic History Rev.*, 2nd ser., 43 (1990).

Schenk, C., "The origins of a central bank in Malaya and the transition to independence, 1954–1959," *JICH*, 21 (1993).

Schenk, C., *Britain and the Sterling Area from Devaluation to Convertibility in the 1950s* (London, 1994).

Schmitz, C., "Nature and dimensions of Scottish investment, 1860–1914," *Business History*, 39 (1997).

Schneer, J., *London 1900: The Imperial Metropolis* (London, 1999).

Schoen, B., "The fragile fabric of Union: The Cotton South, federal politics, and the Atlantic world, 1783–1861" (PhD diss., University of Virginia, 2004).

Schumpeter, J. A., *Imperialism and Social Classes* (New York, 1951, 1st pubd 1919).

Schwab, R., *La Renaissance orientale: La découverte du Sanscrit—Le siècle des écritures déchiffrées* (Paris, 1950).

Schwartz, S. P., "Cornish migration studies: An epistemological and paradigmatic critique" in Payton (ed.), *Cornish Studies*, 10.

Schwarz, B., "The only whiteman in there; the de-racialisation of England 1956–1968," *Race and Class*, 38 (1996).

Scott, D., *Conscripts of Modernity: The Tragedy of Colonial Enlightenment* (Durham, 2004).

Scribner, R. L. (ed.), *Revolutionary Virginia: The Road to Independence*, 7 vols (Charlottesville, VA, 1973).

Seal, A., *The Emergence of Indian Nationalism: Competition and Collaboration in the Later Nineteenth Century* (Cambridge, 1968).

Seal, A., "Imperialism and nationalism in India," in Gallagher, Johnson and Seal (eds), *Locality, Province and Nation*.

Searle, G. R., *The Quest for National Efficiency* (Oxford, 1971).

Searle, G. R., *Entrepreneurial Politics in Mid-Victorian Britain* (Oxford, 1993).

Sears, A., "Immigration controls as social policy: the case of Canadian medical inspection 1900-1920," *Studies in Political Economy*, 33 (1990).

Seeley, J. R., *The Expansion of England* (ed. and intro. J. Gross), (Chicago, 1971).

Sellar, W. C. and Yeatman, R. J., *1066 and all That: A memorable history of England* (New York, 1931, first pub. 1930).

Semmel, B., *Imperialism and Social Reform: British Social-Imperial Thought 1895–1914* (London, 1960).

Semmel, B., *The Governor Eyre Controversy* (London, 1962).

Semmel, B., *The Rise of Free Trade Imperialism. Classical Political Economy, the Empire of Free trade and Imperialism, 1750–1850* (Cambridge, 1970).

Semple, R., *Missionary Women: Gender, Professionalism and the Victorian Idea of Christian Mission* (Rochester, NY, 2003).

Sensbach, J. F., *Rebecca's Revival: Creating Black Christianity in the Atlantic World* (Cambridge, MA, 2005).

Shaw, A. G. L., *Convicts and the Colonies* (Dublin, 5th edn, 1998).

Shaw, A. G. L. (ed.), *Gipps-Latrobe Corresondence* (Melbourne, 1989).

Shepherd, R., *Iain Macleod* (London, 1994).

Sherrington, G., *Australia's Immigrants 1788–1988* (Sydney, 2nd edn, 1990).

Shillingsburg, P., "Thackeray, William Makepeace," in Matthew and Harrison (eds), *Oxford Dictionary of National Biography* (Oxford, 2004).

Shultz, R. J., "Immigration into eastern Australia, 1788–1851," *Historical Studies*, 14 (1970).

Shyllon, F., *Black People in Britain 1555–1833* (Oxford, 1977).

Silver, A. W., *Manchester Men and India Cotton, 1847–1872* (Manchester, 1966).

Silvestri, M., "The thrill of 'simply dressing up': The Indian police, disguise, and intelligence work in colonial India," *Jl of Colonialism and Colonial History*, 2 (2001).

Simmons, R. C. and Thomas, P. D. G. (eds), *Proceedings and Debates of the British Parliaments Respecting North America, 1754–1783*, 5 vols (Millwood, NY, 1982).

Simpson, A. W. B., *Human Rights and the End of Empire: Britain and the Genesis of the European Convention* (Oxford, 2001).

Simpson, G. L., "British perspectives on Aulihan Somali unrest in the East Africa Protectorate, 1915–18," *Northeast African Studies*, 6 (1999).

Simpson, T., *The Immigrants: The Great Migration from Britain to New Zealand, 1830-1890* (Auckland, 1997).

Sinclair, G., *At the End of the Line. Colonial Police Forces and the Imperial Endgame, 1948–1980* (Manchester, 2006).

Sinclair, K., *A Destiny Apart: New Zealand's Search for National Identity* (Wellington, 1986).

Sinclair, W. A., *The Process of Economic Development in Australia* (Melbourne, 1976).

Singer, M. and Cohn, B. S. (eds), *Structure and Change in Indian Society* (Chicago, 1968).

Sinha, M., *Colonial Masculinity: The "Manly Englishman" and the "Effeminate Bengali" in the Late Nineteenth Century* (Manchester, 1995).

Sinha, M., "Britishness, clubbability, and the colonial public sphere: The genealogy of an imperial institution in colonial India," *Jl of British Studies*, 40 (2001).

Sissons, J., *Te Waimana: The Spring of Mana: Tuhoe History and the Colonial Encounter* (Dunedin, 1991).

Sivasundaram, S., *Nature and the Godly Empire: Science and Evangelical Mission in the Pacific, 1795–1850* (Cambridge, 2005).

Skocpol, T., "Bringing the state back in: Strategies of analysis in current research," in Evans, Rueschemeyer and Skocpol (eds), *Bringing the State Back In*.

Smith, A., *The Wealth of Nations: Books IV–V* (ed A. Skinner), (London, 1999, first pubd 1776).

Smith, C., "Communal conflict and insurrection in Palestine," in Anderson and Killingray (eds), *Policing and Decolonisation*.

Smith, J., *The Generall History of Virginia, New England, and the Summer Isles* (London, 1624).

Smith, J. (ed.), *Administering Empire. The British Colonial Service in Retrospect* (London, 1999).

Smith, S., "Indian missions," *Edinburgh Review* (1808).

Smith, S., *British Relations with the Malay Rulers from Decentralisation to Malayan Independence 1930–1957* (Oxford, 1995).

Smith, S., *Kuwait, 1950–1965: Britain, the al-Sabah, and Oil* (Oxford, 1999).

Smith, S., *Britain's Revival and Fall in the Gulf: Kuwait, Qatar and the Trucial States, 1950–1971* (London, 2004).

Smith, S., "Power transferred? Britain, the United States, and the Gulf, 1956–1971," *Contemporary British History*, 21 (2007).

Smollett, T., *The Expedition of Humphry Clinker* (ed. A. Ross), (London, 1985).

Smout, T. C., Landsman, N. C., and Devine, T. M., "Scottish emigration in the seventeenth and eighteenth centuries," in Canny (ed.), *Europeans on the Move*.

Sökefeld, M., "Rumours and politics on the Northern Frontier: The British, Pakhtun Wali and Yaghestan," *Modern Asian Studies*, 36 (2002).

Solow, B. L. (ed.), *Slavery and the Rise of the Atlantic System* (Cambridge, 1991).

Soloway, R. A., *Birth Control and the Population Question, 1877–1930* (North Carolina, 1982).

Souden, D., "English indentured servants and the transatlantic colonial economy," in Marks and Richardson (eds), *International Labour Migration*.

Spear, T., "Neo-traditionalism and the limits of invention in British Colonial Africa," *Jl of African History*, 44 (2003).

Spivak, G. C., "Can the subaltern speak?," in Nelson and Grossberg (eds), *Marxism and the Interpretation of Culture*.

Spivak, G. C., "The Rani of Sirmur: An essay in reading the archives," *History and Theory*, 24 (1985).

Spivak, G. C., *The Post-Colonial Critic: Interviews, Strategies, Dialogues* (ed. Sarah Hasrasym), (London, 1990).

Spivak, G. C., *A Critique of Postcolonial Reason: Toward a History of the Vanishing Present* (Cambridge, MA, 1999).

Springhall, J., *Youth, Empire and Society* (London, 1977).

Sprinker, M. (ed.), *Edward Said: A Critical Reader* (Oxford, 1992).

Srinivas, M. N., *Caste in Modern India: And Other Essays* (Bombay, 1962).

Stanley, B., *The Bible and the Flag* (Trowbridge, 1990).

Stanley, B. (ed.), *Christian Missions and the Enlightenment* (Richmond, 2001).

Stanley, B. (ed.), *Missions, Nationalism and the End of Empire* (Cambridge, 2003).

Stedman Jones, G., *Outcast London: A Study in the Relationship Between Classes in Victorian Society* (London, 1971).

Steedman, C., *The Radical Soldier's Tale: John Pearman 1819–1908* (London, 1988).

Steele, I. K., *The English Atlantic 1675–1740: An Exploration of Communication and Community* (New York, 1986).

Steele, I. K., *Betrayals: Fort William Henry and the Massacre* (New York, 1990).

Stevens, L., *The Poor Indian: British Missionaries, Native Americans and Colonial Sensibility* (Philadelphia, 2004).

Stock, E., *The History of the Church Missionary Society: Its environments, its men and its work* (4 vols, London, 1899–1916).

Stockwell, A. J., *Ending the British Empire: What did they think they were doing?* (Inaugural Lecture Series, Royal Holloway, 1999).

Stockwell, A. J. (ed.), *Malaya 1942–1957* (BDEEP, series B, 3 parts, London, 1995).

Stockwell, A. J., and Burroughs, P. (eds), *Managing the Business of Empire. Essays in Honour of David Fieldhouse* (London, 1998).

Stockwell, S. E., "'Instilling the "sterling tradition': decolonization and the creation of a central bank in Ghana," *JICH*, 28 (1998).

Stockwell, S. E., *The Business of Decolonization: British Business Strategies in the Gold Coast* (Oxford, 2000).

Stockwell, S. E., "Trade, empire, and the fiscal context of imperial buiness during decolonization," *Economic History Rev.*, 57 (2004).

Stockwell, S. E., "African prospects. Mining the empire for Britain in the 1950s" in Lynn (ed.), *British Empire in the 1950s*.

Stokes, E., *The English Utilitarians and India* (Oxford, 1959).

Stokes, E., "Late nineteenth century colonial expansion and the attack on the theory of economic imperialism: A case of mistaken identity?," *Economic History Rev.*, 2nd ser., 27 (1969).

Stoler, A. L., "Tense and tender ties: The politics of comparison in North American history and (post)colonial studies," *Jl of American History*, 88 (2001).

Stoler, A. L., *Carnal Knowledge and Imperial Power: Race and the Intimate in Colonial Rule* (Berkeley, CA, 2002).

Stoler, A. L. (ed.), *Haunted by Empire: Geographies of Intimacy in North American History*, (Chapel Hill, 2006).

Stone, L. (ed.), *An Imperial State at War: Britain from 1689 to 1815* (London, 1994).

Stone, W., *Life of Joseph Brant—Thayendanegea, Including the Border Wars of the American Revolution* (New York, 1838).

Strachey, E. J., *The End of Empire* (London, 1959).

Streak, M., *Lord Milner's Immigration Policy for the Transvaal, 1897–1905* (Johannesburg, 1970).

St. J. Barclay, G., *The Empire is Marching* (London, 1976).

Stuart, J., "Scottish missionaries and the end of empire. The case of Nyasaland," *Historical Research*, 76 (2003).

Stubbs, R., *Hearts and Minds in Guerilla Warfare: The Malayan Emergency, 1948–1960* (Singapore, 1989).

Sturgis, J., "Anglicisation at the Cape of Good Hope in the early nineteenth century," *JICH*, 11 (1982).

Suleri, S., *The Rhetoric of English India* (Chicago, 1992).

Sullivan, E., "Revealing a preference: Imperial preference and the Australian tariff, 1901–1914," *JICH*, 29 (2001).

Sullivan, Z. T., *Narratives of Empire: The Fictions of Rudyard Kipling* (Cambridge, 1993).

Sundkler, B., *Bantu Prophets in South Africa* (Oxford, 1961)

Sundkler, B., *Zulu Zion and Some Swazi Zionists* (Oxford, 1976).

Swaisland, C., *Servants and Gentlewomen to the Golden Land* (Oxford, 1993).

Symonds, R., *Oxford and Empire: The Last Lost Cause* (Basingstoke, 1986).

Talbot, C., "Inscribing the other, inscribing the self: Hindu-Muslim identities in pre-colonial India," *Comparative Studies in Society and History*, 37 (1995).

Tamarkin, M., "The Cape Afrikaners and the British Empire from the Jameson Raid to the South African War" in Lowry (ed.), *South African War Reappraised*.

Taylor, C., *Human Agency and Language* (Cambridge, 1995).

Taylor, M., "Imperium et libertas? Rethinking the radical critique of Imperialism during the nineteenth century," *JICH*, 19 (1991).

Taylor, M., "The 1848 revolutions and the British empire," *Past and Present*, 166 (2000).

Taylor, P. A. M., "Emigration," in Glass and Taylor (eds), *Population and Emigration*.

Taylor, W. S., and Pringle, J. H. (eds), *Correspondence of William Pitt, Earl of Chatham*, 4 vols (London, 1838–40).

Thackeray, W. M., *The History of Henry Esmond* (Harmondsworth, 1985).

Thackeray, W. M., *The Irish Sketch Book*, first pub. 1842 in *The Oxford Thackeray*, 17 vols, 5 (London, n.d.).

Thackeray, W. M., *Vanity Fair. A Novel without a Hero*, first pub. 1848 (Ware, 2001).

The Elgin-Grey Papers II (ed. A. G. Doughty) (Ottawa, 1937).

Thomas, B., *Migration and Economic Growth: A Study of Great Britain and the Atlantic Economy*, (Cambridge, 2nd edn, 1973).

Thomas, D. A., *Thackeray and Slavery* (Athens, OH, 1993).

Thomas, H., *The Slave Trade: The Story of the Atlantic Slave Trade, 1440–1870* (New York, 1997).

Thomas, N., *Entangled Objects: Exchange, Material Culture, and Colonialism in the Pacific* (Cambridge, MA, 1991).

Thomas, N., *Colonialism's Culture: Anthropology, Travel and Government* (Oxford, 1994).

Thompson, A. S., "The language of imperialism and the meanings of Empire," *Jl of British Studies*, 36 (1997).

Thompson, A. S., *Imperial Britain: The Empire in British Politics c. 1880–1932* (London, 2000).

Thompson, A. S., "Imperial propaganda during the South African War," in Cuthbertson, Grundlingh, and Suttie (eds), *Writing a Wider War*.

Thompson, A. S., "The languages of Loyalism in Southern Africa, c. 1870–1939," *English Historical Rev.*, 118 (2003).

Thompson, A. S., "Gallagher, John Andrew (1919–80)" in Matthew and Harrison (eds), *Oxford Dictionary of National Biography*.

Thompson, A. S., "Robinson, Ronald Edward (1920–1999)," in Matthew and Harrison (eds), *Oxford Dictionary of National Biography*.

Thompson, A. S., with Begum, R., "Asian 'Britishness': A study of first generation Asian migrants in Greater Manchester," *Asylum and Migration Working Paper Series*, 4.

Thompson, A. S., *The Empire Strikes Back? The Impact of Imperialism on Britain from the Mid-Nineteenth Century* (Harlow, 2005).

Thompson, E. P., *The Making of the English Working Class* (London, 1963).

Thompson, E. P., *"Alien Homage": Edward Thompson and Rabindranath Tagore* (Delhi, 1998).

Thompson, E. J. and Garratt, G. T., *Rise and Fulfilment of British Rule in India* (London, 1934).

Thompson, J. B., *Ideology and Modern Culture* (Cambridge, 1990).

Thompson, R. C., *Australian Imperialism in the Pacific* (Melbourne, 1980).

Thorne, C., *The Issue of War. States, Societies, and the Far Eastern Conflict of 1941–1945* (London, 1985).

Thorne, S., *Congregational Missions and the Making of an Imperial Culture in Nineteenth-Century England* (Stanford, CA, 1999).

Threlkeld, L. E., *An Australian Grammar, comprehending the Principles and Natural Rules of the Language, as spoken by the Aborigines, in the vicinity of Hunter's river, Lake Macquarie, New South Wales* (Sydney, 1834).

Tiffin, C. and Lawson, A., "Introduction," to id. (eds): *De-scribing Empire: Post-colonialism and Textuality* (London, 1994).

Tignor, R., *Capitalism and Nationalism at the End of Empire: State and Business in Decolonising Egypt, Nigeria and Kenya, 1945–1963* (Princeton, 1998).

Tilly, C., "Transplanted networks," in Yans-McLaughlin (ed.), *Immigration Reconsidered*.

Tinker, H., *A New System of Slavery. The Export of Indian Labour Overseas, 1830-1920* (Oxford, 1974).

Tobin, B. F., *Picturing Imperial Power: Colonial Subjects in Eighteenth-Century British Painting* (Durham, NC, 1999).

Tomlinson, B. R., *The Indian National Congress and the Raj 1929–1942* (London, 1976)

Tomlinson, B. R., *The Political Economy of the Raj, 1914–1947: the Economics of Decolonization in India* (London, 1979).

Tomlinson, B. R., *The Economy of Modern India, 1860–1970* (Cambridge, 1993).

Tomlinson, B. R., "Empire of the dandelion: Ecological imperialism and economic expansion, 1860–1914," *JICH*, 26 (1998).

Tomlinson, B. R., "Economics and empire: The periphery and the imperial economy," in Porter (ed.), *OHBE*, 3.

Tomlinson, J., "The decline of the empire and the economic 'decline' of Britain," *Twentieth Century British History*, 14 (2003).

Trevor-Roper, H., "The rise of Christian Europe," *The Listener*, Nov. 28, 1963.

Trollope, A., *Thackeray*, first pub. 1879 (London, 1997).

Tsokhas, K., *Markets, Money and Empire: The Political Economy of the Australian Wool Industry* (Carlton, Victoria, 1990).

Turley, D., *The Culture of English Antislavery, 1780–1860* (London, 1991).

Turrell, R. V. and Van Helten, J. J. (eds), *The City and Empire*, 2 vols (London, 1984).

Uche, C. U., "Bank of England versus the IBRD: Did the Nigerian colony deserve a central bank?," *Explorations in Economic History*, 34 (1997).

United Empire Loyalist Centennial Committee, *The Centennial of the Settlement of Upper Canada by the United Empire Loyalists, 1784–1884* (ed. G. A. Billias), (Boston, 1972).

Vail, L., "The political economy of East-Central Africa," in Birmingham and Martin (eds), *History of Central Africa*, 2.

Vance, M. E., "The politics of emigration: Scotland and assisted emigration to Upper Canada, 1815–26," in Devine (ed.), *Scottish Emigration*.

Van der Veer, P. (ed.), *Conversion to Modernities: The Globalization of Christianity* (New York, 1996).

Van Helten, J. J. and Williams, K., "'The crying need of South Africa': The emigration of single British women to the Transvaal, 1901–1910', *Jl of Southern African Studies*, 10 (1983).

Van Onselen, C., *Chibaro: African Mine Labour in Southern Rhodesia, 1900–1933* (London, 1975).

Van Vugt, W. E. "Prosperity and industrial emigration from Britain during the early 1850s," *Jl of Social History*, 22 (1988–9).

Van Vugt, W. E. "Running from ruin?: The emigration of British farmers to the USA in the wake of the repeal of the Corn Laws," *Economic History Rev*, 41 (1988).

Varikas, E., "Gender, experience and subjectivity: The Tilly-Scott disagreement," *New Left Rev.*, 211 (1995).

Vaughan, M., *The Story of an African Famine: Gender and Famine in Twentieth-Century Malawi* (Cambridge, 1987).

Vaughan, M., *Curing Their Ills: Colonial Power and African Illness* (Cambridge, 1991).

Vaughan, W. E. (ed.), *A New History of Ireland*, 5, *Ireland Under the Union*, part 1 1801–70 (Oxford, 1989).

Vaughan, W. E. (ed.), *A New History of Ireland*, 6, *Ireland Under the Union*, part II 1870–1922 (Oxford, 1996).

Vibert, E., "'The natives were strong to live': Reinterpreting early-nineteenth century prophetic movements in the Columbia plateau," *Ethnohistory*, 42 (1995).

Vibert, E., *Traders' Tales: Narratives of Cultural Encounters in the Columbia Plateau, 1807–1846* (Norman, 1997).

Visram, R., *Asians in Britain. 400 Years of History* (London, 2002).

Viswanathan, G., *Masks of Conquest: Literary Study and British Rule in India* (New York, 1989).

Viswanathan, G., *Outside the Fold: Conversion, Modernity and Belief* (Princeton, 1998).

Wagner, G., *Children of the Empire* (London, 1982).

Walkowitz, J., *Prostitution and Victorian Society* (Cambridge, 1980).

Wallace, A. F. C., *The Long, Bitter Trail: Andrew Jackson and the Indians* (New York, 1993).

Wallerstein, I., *The Modern World System*, 3 vols (London, 1974–89).

Walsh, O. (ed.), *Ireland Abroad: Politics and professions in the nineteenth century* (Dublin, 2002).

Walton, J. K., "Britishness" in Wrigley (ed.), *Companion to Early Twentieth Century Britain*.

Ward, J. M., *Colonial Self-Government: The British Experience 1759–1856* (London, 1976).

Ward, J. R., "The Industrial Revolution and British imperialism, 1750–1850," *Economic History Rev.*, 2nd ser., 47 (1994).

Ward, S., "'No nation could be broker': the satire boom and the demise of Britain's world role," in *id.* (ed.), *British Culture*.

Ward, S., *Australia and the British Embrace* (Melbourne, 2001).

Ward, S., "The end of empire and the fate of Britishness," in Brocklehurst and Phillips (eds), *History, Nationhood and the Question of Britain*.

Ward, S., "The 'new nationalism' in Australia, Canada and New Zealand: Civic culture in the wake of the British world," in Darian-Smith, Grimshaw, and Macintyre (eds), *Britishness Abroad*.

Ward, S. (ed.), *British Culture and the End of Empire* (Manchester, 2001).

Ward, W. R., *The Protestant Evangelical Awakening* (Cambridge, 1992).

Wareing, J., "Migration to London and transatlantic emigration of indentured servants, 1683–1775," *Jl of Historical Geography*, 7 (1981).

Washbrook, D. A., "Country politics: Madras, 1880 to 1930," *Modern Asian Studies*, 7 (1973).

Washbrook D. A., *The Emergence of Provincial Politics: Madras Presidency, 1870–1920* (Cambridge, 1976).

Washbrook, D. A., "Law, state and agrarian society in Colonial India," *Modern Asian Studies*, 15 (1981).

Washbrook, D. A., "Problems and progress: South Asian economic and social history, c. 1720–1860," *Modern Asian Studies*, 22 (1988).

Washbrook, D. A., "South Asia, the world system, and world capitalism," *Jl of Asian Studies*, 49 (1990).

Washbrook, D. A., "Land and labour in late eighteenth-century South India: the golden age of the pariah?," in Robb (ed.), *Dalit Movements*.

Washbrook, D. A., "India 1818–1860: Two faces of colonialism," in Porter (ed.), *OHBE*, 3.

Washbrook, D. A., "Eighteenth-century issues in South Asia," *Jl of the Economic and Social History of the Orient*, 44 (2001).

Washbrook, D. A., "Colonial discourse theory and the historiography of the British Empire," in Winks (ed.), *OHBE*, 5.

Wasserman, G., *The Politics of Decolonization: Kenya, Europe and the Land Issue, 1960–1965* (Cambridge, 1976).

Watts, S., *Epidemics and History: Disease, Power and Imperialism* (New Haven, 1997).

Webster, W., *Imagining Home: Gender, "Race" and National Identity, 1945–64* (London, 1998).

Webster, W., "'There'll always be an England': Representations of colonial wars and immigration, 1948–68," *Jl of British Studies*, 40 (2001).

Webster, W., *Englishness and Empire, 1939–45* (Oxford, 2005).

White, L., "Vampire priests of Central Africa: African debates about labor and religion in colonial Northern Zambia," *Comparative Studies in Society and History*, 35 (1993).

White, L., *Speaking with Vampires: Rumor and History in Colonial Africa* (Berkeley, CA, 2000).

White, L., "Telling more: Lies, secrets, and history," *History and Theory*, 39 (2000).

White, N., "The business and politics of decolonization: The British experience in the twentieth century," *Economic History Rev.*, 53 (2000).

White, N., *British Business in Post-Colonial Malaysia, 1957–1970: "Neo-Colonialism" or "Disengagement"?* (London, 2004).

White, N., "Decolonization in the 1950s: The version according to British Business," in Lynn (ed.), *British Empire in the 1950s*.

White, R., *The Middle Ground: Indians, Empires, and Republics in the Great Lakes Region, 1650–1815* (Cambridge, 1991).

White, R. and Russell, P. (eds), *Memories and Dreams: Reflections on Twentieth Century Australia* (Sydney, 1997).

Whyte, I. D., *Migration and Society in Britain 1550–1830* (Basingstoke, 2000).

Wickwire, F. and Wickwire, M., *Cornwallis: The Imperial Years* (Chapel Hill, 1980).

Wiener, M. J., *English Culture and the Decline of the Industrial Spirit, 1850–1980* (Cambridge, 1981).

Wight, M., *The Development of the Legislative Council 1606–1945* (London, 1946).

Wight, M., *British Colonial Constitutions 1947* (Oxford, 1952).

Wilkins M., "The free-standing company 1870–1914: An important type of British foreign direct investment," *Economic History Rev.*, 2nd ser., 49 (1988).

Wilkins M. and Schröter, H. (eds), *The Free-Standing Company in the World Economy* (Oxford, 1998).

Williams, E., *Capitalism and Slavery* (London, 1944).

Williams, K., "'A way out of our troubles': The politics of empire settlement, 1900–22," in Constantine (ed.), *Emigrants and Empire*.

Williams, G. A., *The Welsh in Their History* (London, 1982).

Williams, R., *The Long Revolution* (London, 1961).

Williams, R. A., *The American Indian in Western Legal Thought: The Discourses of Conquest* (Oxford, 1990).

Wilson, J. E., "'A thousand countries to go to': Peasants and rulers in late eighteenth-century Bengal," *Past and Present*, 189 (2005).

Wilson, J. E., *The Domination of Strangers. Modern Politics in Colonial India, c. 1780–1830* (Basingstoke, 2008).

Wilson, J. F., *British Business History 1720–1994* (Manchester, 1995).

Wilson, K., *The Sense of the People: Politics, Culture, and Imperialism in England, 1715–1785* (Cambridge, 1995).

Wilson, K., *The Island Race. Englishness, Empire and Gender in the Eighteenth Century* (London, 2003).

Wilson, K. (ed.), *A New Imperial History: Culture, Identity and Modernity in Britain and the Empire, 1660–1840* (Cambridge, 2004).

Winks, R. W. (ed.), *OHBE*, 5, *Historiography* (Oxford, 1999).

Winn, P., "Britain's informal empire in Uruguay in the nineteenth century," *Past and Present*, 73 (1976).

Wolf, E. R., *Europe and the People without History* (Berkeley, CA, 1982).

Wolmer, W. and Scoones, I., "The science of 'civilized' agriculture: The mixed farming discourse in Zimbabwe," *African Affairs*, 99 (2000).

Wolton, S., *Lord Hailey, the Colonial Office and the Politics of Race and Empire in the Second World War* (Basingstoke, 2000).

Wood, G. S., *The Americanization of Benjamin Franklin* (New York, 2004).

Wood, M., *Blind Memory: Visual Representations of Slavery in England and America, 1780–1865* (New York, 2000).

Wood, P. K., "Defining 'Canadian': Anti-Americanism and identity in Sir John A. Macdonald's nationalism," *Jl of Canadian Studies*, 36 (2001).

Woods, P., "Business as usual? British newsreel coverage of Indian independence and partition, 1947–8," in Kaul (ed.), *Media and the British Empire*.

Woodward, D. and Lewis, G. M. (eds), *The History of Cartography: Volume 2, Book 3: Cartography in the Traditional African, American, Arctic, Australian, and Pacific Societies* (Chicago, 1998).

Wrigley, C. (ed.), *A Companion to Early Twentieth Century Britain* (Oxford, 2003).

Wrigley, C. C., "Aspects of economic history," in Roberts (ed.), *Cambridge History of Africa*, 7.

Wrigley, E. A. and Schofield, R. S., *The Population History of England 1541–1871: A Reconstruction* (London, 1981).

Wurgaft, L. D., *The Imperial Imagination: Magic and Myth in Kipling's India* (Middletown, CN, 1983).

Yakota, K. A., "Post-Colonial America: Transatlantic networks of exchange in the early national period," (Ph.D., Univ. of California, Los Angeles, 2002).

Yans-McLaughlin, V. (ed.), *Immigration Reconsidered: History, Sociology, and Politics* (Oxford, 1990).

Young, A., *Political Essays Concerning the Present State of the British Empire* (London, 1772).

Young, J. W. (ed.), *The Foreign Policy of Churchill's Peacetime Administration, 1951–1955* (1988).

Young, R., *White Mythologies: Writing History and the West* (London, 1990).

Young, R., *Post-Colonialism. An Historical Introduction* (Oxford, 2001).

Yudelman, D., *The Emergence of Modern South Africa. State, Capital, and the Incorporation of Organized Labour on the South African Gold Fields, 1902–1939* (Westport, CT, 1983).

Zuckerman, M., "Identity in British America: Unease in Eden," in Pagden and Canny (eds), *Colonial Identity in the Atlantic World*.

Index

Aborigines 136–7, 147, 163, 194, 204, 229–30
Aborigines Protection Society 144, 224
  Parliamentary Select Committee on (1835–6) 143, 234
Act of Union (1707) 66–7
Adams, John 222
Adams, R. J. Q. 49
Adas, Michael 185
Aden 2, 44
Afghanistan 2, 56
Africa 22–3, 25, 29, 33, 47, 102–3, 105, 107, 112, 115, 145, 189, 204, 211, 230, 271–284, 286, 288; see also country entries
  historiography of 184–7, 193, 248–52, 257–65
  Partition of 106–7
  "Scramble for" 105
African Initiated Church movement 133, 146
African Methodist Episcopal Church 146
African National Congress 152
Africans, in Britain 208–9
Afrikaaners (Boers) 16, 51, 91, 108, 229–30, 235
"agency" 245–68
Ahmedbad 115
Akenson 65
Alabama 32
Algeria 271, 279
Allan, G. A. 233
America, central 110
America, Latin (South America) 14–15, 43, 106, 109–10, 112, 114–15, 122, 165
America, North 43, 101–2, 145; see also American colonies, Canada, and the United States

American Civil War (1861–65) 83
American colonies, British (the thirteen colonies) xiv, 4–5, 21–33, 65, 67–8, 101, 137–9, 201
  loyalists 24, 68, 222–4
  native Americans 21, 25–6, 28–32, 135–6
  taxation of 4, 24–5, 221–2
  trade with 25, 102, 116
American Congress 26
American National Baptist Convention 147
American revolution ("crisis" and revolutionary war) xiv, 4–5, 21–33, 64, 67–8, 116, 203, 209, 220–1
Amin, Samir 109
Anderson, Benedict 226
Anderson, David 115, 270, 280
Anglican Church and Anglicanism 42, 134–5, 138–9, 146, 284
  colonial bishoprics 135, 284
Angola 271
anthropology 144, 178, 181
  and history 132
Appadurai, Arjun 260
Apthorp, East 23
Arden-Clarke, Sir Charles 279
Argentina 2, 14, 63, 107
army, British 19n26, 40, 47, 52, 92, 116, 200, 214
  and soldier settlement schemes 84, 91
  and South African War 91
  and World War I 92
Arnold, David 186
Arrowsmith, John 7
Ashanti 210, 280
Asia 33, 115, 271; see also India, south Asia, and south-east Asia
Attwood, Bain 194

Auckland 84
Austen, Jane 169
Australia 2, 7, 16, 18, 32, 44, 49–50, 63,
   68, 71, 74–89, 91, 107, 120, 133, 162–3,
   272, 282, 185, 194, 210, 220, 222, 228–
   30, 232; *see also* Aborigines, colonies of
   white settlement, dominions, and colony/
   state entries
   Britishness, decline in 237–9
   economic development of 114
   emigration to and colonization of 49, 63,
      75–89, 109
   federation of 232
   gold rushes 71, 82–3, 85
   historiography of 220
   labour legislation in 112–13
   racial discrimination and "white"
      Australia policy 91, 113, 227–8, 233
   religion in 148
   and World War I 233–5

Bailyn, Bernard 64
Baines, Dudley 92
Baldwin, Stanley 46
Balfour declaration (1926) 16, 235–6, 272
Baluchis 168
Baker, Christopher 253
Banda, Hastings 277
baNgwato 145
Bank of England 108
Banks, Joseph 186
Baptist Missionary Society 138
Barbados 24, 136
Barings 120
Basaka, George 185–6
Bayly, Christopher 183–4, 186, 188–9, 191
Bayly, Susan 192–3
Bean, C. E. W. 233
Bechuanaland (Botswana) 144–5
Beckett, Jeremy 194
Beidelman, T. O. 172
Belfast 77
Belgian Congo 164, 279
Belich, James 85, 167, 194, 225
Bengal 5–6, 22, 27, 110, 117, 137, 186,
   210, 212, 260, 262, 264
Bengalis 168, 203–4
Benin 262
Bennett, R. B. 228
Berger, Carl 232
Bermuda 30
Bevin, Ernest 274
Bhaba, Homi 160, 256, 189
Bickers, Robert 63, 230
Biko, Steve 152
Binney, Judith 185
Birmingham 88, 205

Birt, Louisa 87
Bismarck 172
Blackstone, William 23
Bland, Richard 24
Board of Trade 87, 115
Boezak, Alan 152
Bombay 115
Bonar Law, Andrew 49
Bose, Subhas Chandra 249
Botany Bay 68, 75; *see also* New South
   Wales
Botswana *see* Bechuanaland
Bourassa, Henri 229
Bowen, H. V. 107
Boxer rebellion 145, 151
Boyce, George 270, 280
Boys' Brigades 171
Boy Scouts 171
Brainerd, David 134
Brant, Joseph 135
Brant, Molly 135
Bravo, Michael 186
Bray, Thomas 134
Breckenbridge, Carol 246
Breen, T. H. 222
Bright, John 44, 104
Bristol 88, 201
Britain
   aristocracy 46
   citizenship 53, 55–7
   civil service 46–7, 69
   economy 54, 102–8, 116–21, 123, 275,
      277–8, 285–6
   immigration 40, 49, 55–7, 286
   industrialization 44, 46
   multiculturalism 40, 56–7
   "official mind" 41, 105, 165
   parliament 11, 25, 31–2, 40, 41, 52–3,
      55, 209, 276
   politics *see* political parties
   state xiv, 33, 39–61, 286
      "fiscal military" 4, 39, 42–3, 106
      "laissez-faire" 43
   union 39, 50–51, 219
      break-up of 52, 288
British American Land Company 73
British Antarctica 269
British Broadcasting Corporation 56
British Committee of the Indian National
   Congress 54
British Documents on the End of Empire
   project 269–70
British East Africa Company 105
British empire 162–3; *see also* culture,
   economics, ideology, religion, and class
   end of (decolonisation) xiv, 18, 52, 56,
      220, 269–93

and engineering 51, 53
expansion 4–8, 15, 39, 41–4, 51–2,
    101–8, 172–3
"first" xiv, 4, 7, 8, 19n8
impact 39–57, 160–4, 170–2, 199–
    217, 219, 287–8; see also culture,
    economics of empire, and legacies of
    empire
legacies of in Britain 55–7, 270, 286–8
and monarchy 40, 42, 52
and professionalization 46–8, 282–3
"second" xiv, 19n8, 42
"third" 43–4
violence 167–8, 280–1
British Empire Exhibition, Wembley 202
British Guiana (Guyana) 207, 279
British Ladies Female Emigrants'
    Society 81–2
British Medical Association 48
British Nationality Act (1948) 55, 60n90,
    286
British North America see Canada
British South Africa Company 105, 112,
    145
British Trade Boards Act (1909) 49–50
British Women's Emigration Society 86–7
British World xi, 39, 64, 75, 92–3, 123,
    174n18, 220
"Britishness" 50–1, 56–7, 64, 161, 287; see
    also culture of empire
Buchan, John 161
Buettner, Elizabeth 287
Buganda 145
Bumsted 66
Bunyan, John 206, 208
Burke, Edmund 26–7, 31, 104, 110–11
Burma 2, 44, 273, 284, 188
Burnard, Trevor 32
Busby, James 225
Bush, Julia 169
Butler, L. J. 276
Buxton, Priscilla 143
Buxton, Thomas Fowell 142–3

Cain, Peter 41, 106–8, 163
Calvinism 138–9
Cambridge History of the British Empire 220
"Cambridge School" (south Asian
    history) 165, 253–4
Cambridgeshire 74
Campbell, Wilfred 228
Canada (British North America) 2, 7, 9,
    13, 16, 18, 32, 49–50, 53, 63, 67–8,
    70, 73–5, 77, 80, 83, 86–7, 89–90, 92,
    133, 162–3, 208, 220, 223–4, 228–30,
    234, 236–7, 272, 282; see also province
    entries

Britishness, decline in 237–9
economic development 114–15
emigration to 49, 63–75, 86–92, 282
historiography of 185, 220
immigration policy and race, in the
    twentieth century 89–91, 228
immigration Act (1902) 90
nationalism 232–3
religion 148
and World War I 235
Canada, Lower 5, 8–9, 73
Canada, Upper 8–9, 69–71, 73, 224, 233
Canada Acts
    1840 53
    1867 53
Canada Company 73
Canadians, French 5, 67–8
Canadian Pacific Railway 118
Cannadine, David 169
Canny, Nicholas 65
Cardiff 201
Careless, J. M. 220
Carmichael-Smyth, Henry 207
Carroll, Lewis 170
Cape 7, 10, 71, 91, 105, 145–7, 149, 201,
    210, 224–5, 229–30, 234, 241n60
Cape Town 227
Carey, William 139
Cartwright, John 28
Casement, Roger 164
Castro, Fidel 279
Caton, Brian 193
Cavell, Janice 23–33
Central Africa 113, 275, 282–5, 288; see
    also country entries
Central African Federation 18, 276, 278,
    283–4
Ceylon (Sri Lanka) 7, 13, 17, 193, 273
Chamberlain, Joseph 52, 87, 172
Chartered companies 4, 41, 105–6; see also
    company entries
Chatham, Earl of 31
Chatterjee, Partha 186
Chattopadhyaya, Bankimchandra 248
Chibaro 113
Chidester, David 131
Chilembwe, John 146–7
China 2, 7, 14–15, 17, 43, 106–7, 144–5,
    151, 269, 276; see also Boxer rebellion,
    Opium Wars, and Shanghai, Taiping
    rebellion
    British in 230
China Inland Mission 141
Chisholm, Caroline 81
Choudhury, D. K. L. 189
Church Lads' Brigades 171
Church Missionary Society 138–9, 144–6,
    283

Churchill, Winston 275–6
City of London 17–18, 41, 44, 45, 106–8, 117–21
Clarke, Marcus 231
Clive, Robert 5
Cobden, Richard 14, 44, 104
cocoa 114, 201
coffee 201
Cohn, Bernard 164, 181, 183–4, 187
Cold War 102, 277, 279
Cole, Douglas 232
Colenso, Bishop J. W. 146
"collaboration," theories of 107
Colonial conference (1907) 2
colonial development 18, 52, 108–16, 274, 285
Colonial Development Acts
   1929 52, 111
   1940 111, 274
colonial discourse xi, 158–60, 170–1, 178–83
Colonial Intelligence League (est. 1910) 86
colonial knowledge 53, 164, 177–97
Colonial Land and Emigration Commission 74, 79, 82, 87
Colonial Office 10, 13, 41, 48, 52, 55, 72, 79, 87, 108, 115, 136, 142, 225, 205, 285
Colonial Service 47–8, 64, 282–3, 285–7
colonial state 47–8, 112–13, 115, 179–82, 184–5, 187, 190–2
colonies of white settlement 2, 5, 8–10, 16, 39, 45, 52, 103, 111, 148; see also dominions and country entries
   emigration to and settlement in 63–100
   identities in 219–43
   gendered identities 231
Colquhoun, Patrick 70
Comaroff, Jean and John 133, 258–9
Commission for Racial Equality 56
Commonwealth, the 17–18, 55, 237, 272, 275–6, 280–3, 285–7
Commonwealth Immigrants Act (1962) 60n92
Commonwealth Relations Office 285
Conrad, Joseph 161, 170
Conservative Party, Britain ("Tories") 202, 276–8, 281
Constantine, Stephen 286
"constructive imperialism" 45, 52, 164
Convention People's Party (Gold Coast) 280
convicts see transportation
Cook, James 186
Cooper, Frederick 184
Cooper, Randolph 188
Cork 77
Corn Laws, repeal of (1846) 43–4, 77

Cornwall 74, 83, 174n18
Cornwallis, Lord 43, 58n19, 222
cotton 32, 73, 114, 201
Cowen, Michael 173
Crais, Clifton 148
Crimea War 204, 234
Cromer, Lord (Evelyn Baring) 15, 172
Crook, Paul 166
"crown colony" government 8, 13–14
Crowther, Samuel (Bishop) 146, 257–8
Cullen, L. M. 65
Cullwick, Hannah 205
culture and empire xiii, 56–7, 108, 123–4, 177–97, 195, 199–217; see also race
   British imperial culture 160–3, 199–217, 287–8
   British women and 200–1
   class and 204, 210–11
   and colonialism 159
   fiction and 170–1, 179, 206
   gender and 204, 211, 213
   imperial economic culture 108, 123–4
   "militarism" and 162, 168
   missionaries and 145–8, 200, 212
   museums and 202
   music halls and 202
   patriotism and 162
   travel literature and 205
Cyprus 275–6, 280–1, 286

Dafoe, John W. 236
Dalrymple, Sir John 25, 27
Dalrymple, William 151
Darwin, John 108
Daunton, Martin 33
Davidson, Jim 237
Davies, Sir John 3
Davis, L. E. 117–19
Dawson, George 226
Deakin, Alfred 232
Delhi 5
Derbyshire 83
Deshpande, Prachi 193
Devine, Tom 66, 72
Dickens, Charles 212
Dickinson, John 25
Diefenbaker, John 237
Dilke, Charles 172, 226
Dirks, Nicholas 181–2, 187–8, 192–3
D'Urban, Benjamin 142
defense, British costs of 117–21
Disraeli, Benjamin 202
Dodson, Michael 186
dominions 2, 15–16, 18, 63, 92–3, 112, 119, 219–43, 233–9, 272, 282; see also colonies of white settlement and country

entries
"dominion" status, of 2
nationalism in 232–9
Douglas, Thomas (5th Earl of Selkirk) 70
Douglass, William 28
Dowd, Gregory 150
Drayton, Richard 187
Dube, John 152
Dublin 76–7
Dundas, Henry 69–70, 72
Durham, Lord (and Durham Report) 8
Dutch empire 7

East Africa 111, 172, 249, 275, 282, 288;
   see also country entries
East African railway 111
"East African Revival" 284
East Anglia 75
East India Company 5, 8, 10, 23, 26–7,
   31–2, 42–3, 47, 103–4, 107, 136–8, 140,
   152, 180–1, 184, 190, 201, 207, 212–13
   Board of Control 6, 10
   Charter Act (1813) 43, 140
East Indies 102, 207
Eaton, Richard 183
economics of empire xii, 101–29; see
   also colonial development, free trade,
   "gentlemanly capitalism," imperial
   preference, mercantilism, tariffs, and
   taxation
   and British industrialisation 11, 107,
      109, 112, 118
   business and empire 105–8, 283–4, 286
   and colonial industrialisation 109,
      114–15
   economic impact of in Britain (costs and
      benefits of) 54, 116–21, 123, 285–6
   economic impact overseas 102, 108–16
   investment in empire 103–4, 117–18
   trade 7, 8, 14–15, 41, 42, 44–5, 47, 51,
      53, 70, 101–3, 105–6, 110, 112, 114,
      201, 285–6
   "underdevelopment" 108–16
Edelstein, Michael 118–19
Eden, (Robert) Anthony 275–7
Edney, Michael 186
Elgin, Lord 10
Eltis, David 64
Emigrants' Information Office 88
England (and British Isles) 3, 21–2
English emigration 65, 71, 76, 78, 80, 85
Egypt 2, 15, 17, 48, 63, 105–8, 277, 284;
   see also Suez
Elliot, T. F. 79
Equiano, Olaudah 29, 209–10, 262
Ethiopianism 146
Ethnological Society of London 144

Europe 22–3, 45, 49, 51, 64, 101, 104,
   109, 118–19, 139
European Economic Community 50, 237–8,
   272
Ewart, John 236
exploration 51, 53, 186
Eyre, Edward John (Governor) 201

Falconbridge, Anna Maria 28–9
Falkland Islands 44, 80, 269
Family Colonisation Loan Society 81
Fanon, Franz 151
Far East 107
Featherston, Sir Issac 84
Female Middle Class Emigration Society 86
Ferguson, Moira 169
Fieldhouse, D. K. 106, 114, 121
Fiji 144, 271, 276
Fitzpatrick, David 80
FitzPatrick, Sir Percy 231, 233
Flint, John 279
Foreign and Commonwealth Office 285
Foreign Office 41, 108, 285
forestry 115
Foucault, Michel 158–60, 164, 179, 182,
   185, 202
Fox, Charles James 26, 27
France 5, 7, 18, 22, 28, 42, 106, 204, 275,
   279
Franklin, Benjamin 222, 238
French imperialism 227, 261, 279
Frank, A. G. 109, 117
Franklin, Benjamin 25
free trade 6–7, 17, 33, 43–5, 105, 112
   and "Manchester School" 44
"free trade imperialism" (empire of free
   trade) xiv, 6–7, 39–42, 105–6, 165; see
   also informal empire
Furedi, Frank 281

Gallagher, Jack 1, 40–1, 44, 105–7, 165,
   177–8, 250, 273, 278
Gambia 44
Games, Alison 65
Gandhi, Mohandas K. 152, 249, 263–4
George III 26, 63
Georgia 32
gender xii–iii
   colonial women and 149, 180–1, 255–6,
      279
   European women and empire 143–4,
      200–1
   and imperialism 168–9, 180–1, 203–4,
      255–6
   masculinity and imperialism 168, 203,
      288
   and religion 133

"gentlemanly capitalism" xiv, 39, 41–2, 106–8, 163
Germany 104, 120, 160, 162, 167, 199, 227
Gibraltar 269
Girls' Friendly Society 87
Gladstone, William Ewart 45, 53, 201
Glasgow 72–3, 201
Glasgow Committee on Emigration 73
globalization xi, 121–3, 133
Gold Coast (Ghana) 44, 111, 114, 274–5, 278–80, 283
Goldie, Sir George 105
Goldsworthy, David 276, 278
Gordon, (General) Charles 150
Gramsci, Antonio 179
Grant, Charles 140
Grant, James 167
Great Exhibition (1851) 202
Greece 281
Grey, Sir George 76
Griqua 145
Grove, Richard 186
Guha, Ranajit 165, 189, 250
Guiness Company 120
Gulf 2, 277
Gurney, Anna 143

Haggard, Rider 170
Haileybury College 47
Halifax (Canada) 68
Hall, Catherine xii, 56, 226
Hall, Stuart 202
Halpern, Rick 33
Hamilton, Lord Archibald 72
Hancock, Keith 123
Hardy, Thomas 170
Harries, Patrick 147
Harper, Marjory 77
Hastings, Warren 27, 104
Headrick, Daniel 185
Heidegger, Martin 252
Heinlein, Frank 270
Helm, Charles 145
Herbert, Sydney 82
Herzog, J. B. M. 235
Hinduism see India
Hinds, Allister 278
Ho Chi Minh 261
Hobson, J. A. 53, 104–5, 117, 119, 162
Holland, Robert 235, 280–1
Hong Kong 8, 15, 44, 63, 269–70, 276
Hopkins, Anthony 41, 106–8, 113, 121, 220, 278
Hopkinson, Henry 55
Horton, Sir Robert Wilmot 72, 78
Howe, Stephen 287

Howell, Caroline 283
Howells, Gary 75
Hudson's Bay Company 103
Hughes, Billy 235
humanitarianism 8, 31–2, 41, 143–4, 164, 166, 199, 201, 224–6; see also anti-slavery and abolitionism, Aborigines Protection Society
Hume, David 23
Huttenback, R. A. 117–19
Hyam, Ronald 276, 278

ideology and empire 157–76
identities xiii
   in Britain 199–215
   in white settlement colonies 219–39
Iliffe, John 249
Imperial Colonist 86
Imperial federation 15, 48–9, 234–5, 53
Imperial Federation League 234–5
Imperial preference 42, 45–6, 58n37, 110, 112, 236
Imperial War Cabinet 235
Imperial War Conference (1917) 16
Imperialism
   critics of 45, 51, 53, 104–5, 109, 162–5
   economic theories of 109, 104–5, 109, 112
   and the environment 115–16
   and resistance 248–54, 262–4
   and underdevelopment 109
Inden, Ronald 179
indentured labour 63–5, 67–8, 112
India xiv, 2, 5–6, 8, 10–13, 15–18, 23, 25, 32, 41, 43–4, 47–8, 63, 103, 105, 107, 112, 114–15, 137, 134, 140–1, 165, 169, 186, 204, 207–8, 222, 226–7, 248–9, 253–6, 269, 271, 273, 277–8, 280, 284, 286–7, 289n6; see also south Asia
   caste 12, 47, 179, 192–3, 259
   communalism 190–1, 273
   Council of 11
   economy of 114–15
   emigration from 40, 55–6
   Hinduism in 137–8, 140, 152, 248, 179, 190–1, 213, 259
   historiography of 248
   'home charges' 12, 111
   Indian army 2, 10, 12, 19n26, 43, 47, 140–1, 188
   Indians, Anglo- 212–13, 287
   industrialisation in 114–15
   Islam in 190
   land reform 93
   law 43, 190
   missionaries in 6, 180

Mughal empire 5, 26–7, 110, 151, 181, 191–2, 262
  "permanent settlement" (1793) 43
  police 43
  princely states 2, 11, 58n40, 117
  railways 114–15
  Rebellion ("Mutiny") (1857–8) 11, 141, 150–1, 201–2, 204
  Simon Commission (1928–30) 9
  taxation in 43, 110
  trade 102–3, 119, 120–1
  transition to independence 17–18, 253–4, 269, 271–3
India Acts
  (1919) 17
  (1935) 17
India Office 41, 48, 285
Indian Civil Service 6, 11–12, 47, 51, 64, 111, 140–1
Indian Medical Service 51
Indian National Congress (INC) 12–13, 54, 165, 229–30, 253
Indians, in Britain 201
"indirect rule" 17, 172, 274
IndoChina 271
Indology 179
industrialisation see economics of empire
"informal empire" 1–3, 8, 14–15, 41, 105–7, 165, 271, 277, 282
Inikori, J. E. 117
Innes, William 31
International Order Daughters of the Empire 236
Iran 17
Iraq 17, 56
Ireland 2–3, 50, 138, 162, 223, 277
  Home Rule 51, 53
  migration 51
  republicanism 235–6
  Union (1802) 223
Irish 50–1, 163, 174n18, 204, 214, 219
  migration 51, 65–6, 68, 71–2, 74–8, 80, 82–3, 97 n. 113
    Catholic 65–6, 67, 69, 70, 80–1, 85–6
    Protestant 65–6, 69–71, 80–81, 85–6
Irish Famine 70–2, 77, 80–1, 214
Irish Free State (Southern Ireland) 2, 16, 235
Irschick, Eugene 184
Irwin, Robert 171
Islam 56, 133, 150, 137–8, 140, 152
Israel 275

Jaggan, Cheddi 279
Jamaica 22, 24, 32, 66, 201, 204–5, 276;

  see also Morant Bay
  Rebellion in (1831) 209
James, C. L. R. 199, 249
Japan 199, 273–4
Jebb, Richard 231, 234
Jefferson, Thomas 33, 222, 238
Jenyns, Soame 221
Jinnah, Mohammed Ali 273
Johnson, Samuel 25, 30, 258
Johnson, William 135
Jones, Sir Glyn 279
Jones, Maldwyn 73

Kalu, Oglu 283
Kaplan, Cora 206
Kennedy, Dane 230
Kennedy, Paul 118–19
Kenya (British East Africa) 105, 115, 230, 251, 260–1, 270, 275–7, 279–83; see also Mau Mau
Kent 75
Kent, John 282
Kidd, Benjamin 167
Kikuyu 251, 260
Kipling, Rudyard 161, 170
Kitchener, Lord 150
Khoekhoe 145, 151
Krozewski, Gerold 278
Kuwait 277

labour 112–13
  in Africa 113–14
  in Australia 113
  forced 112–13
  legislation 49, 112–13
Labour Party (Britain) 276, 278, 283
Laidlaw, Zoe 184
Lake, Marilyn 231
Lalu, Premesh 255
Lanarkshire 72
Lancashire 11
Landau, Paul 131, 145
Lander, Richard 7
Lang, John Dunmore 234
Laurier, Sir Wilfrid 89, 229
law 22–8, 32, 136–8
Lawson, Alan 159
League of Nations 17, 273
  Mandates 160, 273
Lenin, V. I. 104–5
Lester, Alan 184, 224–5
Lever, William 114
Liberal Party (Britain) 201–2
List, Frederick 109
Liverpool 71, 201
Liverpool, Lord 13, 71

Liverpool Strike (1775) 28
Livingstone, David 142, 147
Lloyd-George, David 235
Lobengula 145
Locke, John 30, 137
London 67, 69, 70, 201; see also City of
    London
London Economic Conference (1933) 46
London Missionary Society 138–9, 141–2,
    145–6, 151
Long, Edward 24, 32
Lonsdale, John 248, 250
Louis, W. R. 276, 281–2
Lowry, Donal 229
Lucknow 226
Lynn, M. 276

Mabro, Judy 169
Macaulay, Thomas Babington 141, 207
McCracken, John 115
MacDonagh, O. 74
MacDonald, John A. 228, 234
Macintyre, Alasdair 254
McIntrye, W. D. 276
MacKenzie, John 50, 171, 200
Mackinnon, William 105
Macleod, Iain 277
MacLeod, Roy 186
Macmillan, Harold 237–8, 275–6, 278–9,
    281
MacPherson, Annie 87
Madras 6
Mafeking, relief of 160
Magee, Gary 120–2
Maitland, F. W. 32
Malacca 44
Malaya 17, 18, 58n40, 201, 274–5, 278,
    284
    Union of 274
    Federation 274
Malaysia 276
Malta 276
Mandela, Nelson 152
Mandler, Peter 227
Mani, Lata 180–1, 187–8
Mann, Michael 167
Mansergh, Nicholas 269–70
Mansfield, Lord 24
Maori 32, 84–5, 109, 149–50, 185, 194,
    201, 210, 225–6
    Prophet movements 149–50
Maori Wars 167, 225–6
Marathas 188, 193
Marquand, David 48
Maritime Provinces 223; see also New
    Brunswick, Nova Scotia, Prince Edward

Island
Marshall, P. J. 22, 222
Marx, Karl 109
Marxist historiography 246, 249, 270, 273
Marxist theories of imperialism 102, 104–5,
    109, 111–12, 158–9
Maryland 64
Massachusetts Bay 135
Massachusetts Company 4
Massey, Vincent 237
Matthew, W. M. 106
Mau Mau 151, 167, 251, 260–1, 277,
    279–80
Mauritius 7
Maxeke, Charlotte 152
Mbiti, John 152
Meaney, Neville 234
medicine and imperialism 48, 51, 53, 148,
    171, 186–7
Mediterranean 271
Melman, Billie 169
mercantilism 6, 101, 110, 116
Middle East 18, 106–7, 169, 271, 277; see
    also country entries and Suez
Middlesex 76
migration xiii, 18, 42, 49–50, 54, 63–100,
    102, 162, 262–4, 236, 282; see also
    English, Irish, Scots and Welsh emigration
    assisted migration 71–2, 75, 78–9, 82,
        87–8
    child migration 76, 78, 82, 86–7, 92
    return migration 92
    unfree or forced migration 64–5, 67–8,
        75–7, 92
    women and 76–8, 81–2, 86–7
migrant remittances 54, 74–5
military and empire 64, 67–8
Mill, James 213
Mills, Sara 169
Milner, Sir Alfred 87, 91, 172, 227, 230,
    234, 241n60
mining 107–8, 113–14
Misra, Maria 169
missions and missionaries xiv, 6–7, 33, 41,
    53, 57n1, 64, 132–52, 172, 201, 257–9,
    283–4
    and African nationalism 151–2, 283–4
    Catholic missions 138, 283
    and the colonial and imperial state 139–
        42
    and conversion 135–6, 138–9, 146–7,
        257–9
    and cultural imperialism 258–9
    and education 147–8, 151–2
    and evangelicalism 138–40, 143, 211–12
    female missionaries 141, 283

and independent churches 146, 284
and medicine 148
Methodist 139, 144, 146
and millenarianism 151
and "modernity" 147
and non-European women 146
Protestant 33, 135–42, 283
translation 147
Mississippi 32
Moffat, John Smith 145
Mohawk 135
Mokone, Mangena Maake 146
Montserrat 66
Morant Bay, rebellion (1865) 201, 204–5, 226
Moravians 136, 139
Morel, E. D. 164
Morgan, Kenneth 278
Morgan, P. D. 220
Morley, John 13
Morton, W. L. 223, 236
Mountbatten, Louis (First Earl of Burma) 273, 280
Mozambique 147, 271
Mphale, Ramphela 152

Napoleonic Wars (1803–15) 7, 42–3, 67, 70, 203–4
Nasser, Gamal Abdel 275
Natal 10, 44, 51, 91, 146
National Association for Promoting State-directed Emigration and Colonization (est. 1883) 88
National Liberation Movement (Gold Coast) 280
nationalism, anti-colonial 272–3, 277, 279–81
"native," the idea of 259–65
Navy, the British Royal 45, 116, 118–21, 134, 200, 214
"Blue Water" theory 45
Navy League 162
Navigation Acts 4–5, 25, 42–3, 101, 110, 116
the Ndebele 145, 249–50
Nehru, Jawarhalal 248–9
"neo-colonialism," 273
Nepal 2, 188
New Brunswick 49, 67–8, 73; see also Maritime Provinces
New Brunswick and Novia Scotia Land Company 73
New England 32, 133, 135
"new" imperial history xii, 164, 177
New South Wales 77, 79, 80–2, 136–7, 144, 224–5; see also Botany Bay, Port Philip Bay, Van Diemen's Land

New York 68, 135
New Zealand 2, 7, 10, 16, 18, 44, 49–50, 149, 162, 185, 194, 201, 225–6, 273, 282; see also colonies of white settlement, dominions, Maori, and Waitangi
economic development of 114, 122
emigration to 49, 63, 78–80, 82–6, 88–9, 223–4, 282
gold strikes 85
identity in 228–9, 231–3, 236–9
and World War I 235
New Zealand Company 79, 84
Newfoundland 2
Newton, John 30–1, 134, 142
Ngidi, John 146
Nigeria 17, 105, 111, 114, 146, 258–9, 271, 271, 275–6, 283–4, 286
Nightingale, Bruce 286
Nile 7
Nkrumah, Kwame 280
Nongqawuse 149
North Borneo 44
Northern Rhodesia (Zambia) 238
Norton, Fletcher 24
Nova Scotia 9, 67–8, 73, 138; see also Maritime Provinces
Nussbaum, Felicity 169
Nyasaland (Malawi) 18, 112, 115, 146–7, 238, 276–7, 279, 283
Nyasaland African Congress 277
Nyerere, Julius 249

O'Brien, Conor Cruise 253
O'Brien, Patrick K. 117–20
O'Hanlon, Rosalind 182
Offer, Avner 117
Oliver, Frank 89
Ontario 68, 223
opium 201
"Opium Wars" (1839–42, 1856–60) 7, 45, 145
Orange Lodge 236
orientalism 169, 171, 178, 199–200, 255–6
Otago 82, 85
Ottawa 71, 110
Ottawa conference (1932) 46, 237
Ottoman Empire 2, 7, 16, 160, 189
Oxford History of the British Empire xiii

Pacific Islands 63, 83, 166, 185–6
Paine, Thomas 25
Pakistan 248, 273, 284
Palestine 273–4
Paley, William 32
palm oil 114, 201
Pandey, Gyanendra 190

Papineau, Louis 9
Paquet, G. 223
Parkes, Henry 232
Parr, Joy 87
Passenger Acts 69–70, 72
Pathans 168
Patterson, A. B. 229
Patterson, Orlando 262
Pearman, John 205
Pearson, Charles Henry 228
Peel, J. D. Y. 257–8
Peel, Sir Robert 44, 76
Peers, Douglas 188
Peires, J. B. 149
Pennsylvania 25, 68
Perera, Suvendrini 170
Peterloo (1819) 72
Philip, John 138, 142
Phillips, Trevor 56
Phimister, Ian 108
Pick, Daniel 166
Pimlott, Ben 49
piracy 27–8
Pityana, Barney 152
Phillip, Kavita 187
Plaatje, Sol 152
Plassey, Battle of (1757) 5, 137
Platt, D. C. M. 106
Pocahontas 135
Pocock, J. G. A. 50, 220, 222, 238
Poor Law Amendment Act (1834) 75
Poor Law Relief 81
Pontiac's War (1763–74) 150
Pol Pot 261
policing 188–9, 290n71
Pollock, Sheldon 187–8
Port Philip Bay 75; see also New South
    Wales and Victoria
Porter, Andrew 108, 132, 284
Porter, Bernard 161, 200
Porteus, Beilby 26
post-colonialism (and post-colonial
    studies) xii–iii, 183, 194, 205–6, 256,
    270, 273
Potter, Simon 184, 236
Powell, Enoch 239, 281
Powhaten 135
Prakash, Gyan 182, 187
Prendergast, James 226
Price, J. M. 117
Primrose League (est. 1883) 87
Prince Edward Island 68, 70; see also
    Maritime Provinces
Prior, Katherine 191
prophet movements 148–9
Protten, Rebecca 136
Punjab 193, 262

Quakers 142
Quebec xiv, 5, 13, 67–8, 138, 223, 238

race and racism xii–iii, 13–14, 32, 146,
    193–4, 226, 281–2
  in Britain and in British imperialism 42,
    55–7, 161, 163, 166–9, 171, 194,
    203–15, 281–2, 286, 288
  in the dominions 227–30, 233, 238–9
    in Australia 90–1
    in Canada 89–91
    in South Africa 91
railways 11, 107
Ramsay, Allan 31
Randolph, John 24
Ranger, Terence 149, 249–50, 273
Ranjitsinhji, Rajah 163
Rathbone, Richard 274
Raychaudhuri, Tapan 253–5
Red River Colony (Manitoba) 70
Reece, Bob 194
religion xiv, 41, 56, 57n1, 131–56, 190–1;
    see also Anglicanism, Hinduism, Islam,
    missionaries, and prophet movements
  and anti-slavery 142–3
  and resistance 148–52
Renfrewshire 72
resistance 245–65 esp. 247–54, 272–3,
    279–80; see also nationalism
  and religion 148–52
  in American colonies 21–33
"responsible government" 9–10
Revolutionary Wars (1793–1802) 42–3
Rhode Island 135
Rhodes, Cecil 105–6, 112, 145, 227
Rhodesia, Northern (Zambia) 18, 105, 115,
    238, 275–6, 284; see also Central African
    Federation
Rhodesia, southern (Zimbabwe) 18, 51,
    105, 112–13, 145, 149, 230, 238, 249,
    276, 281, 284; see also Central African
    Federation
  labour legislation in 112–13
  mining industry 112–13, 145
  taxation 113
  UDI 238–9
Ricardo, David 109
Richards, Eric 78
Robbins, Bruce 170
Robinson, George 145
Robinson, Ronald 1, 40–1, 44, 105–6, 107,
    165, 177–8, 250, 273, 279, 281–2
Rogers, John 193
Rolfe, John 135
Roy, Rammohun 260–1
Royal Colonial Institute 88, 162
Royal Colonial Society 54

Royal Geographical Society 7, 142
rubber 201
Rubinstein, W. D. 120
Rushdie, Salman 55
Russia 46, 204
Rye, Maria 86

Sabah 276
Said, Edward 159, 161, 164, 170–1, 178–9,
    182, 194, 199–200, 256
St Kitts 66
Salisbury, Lord 173
Sarawak 276
sati 141, 189, 188, 213, 255–6
Savarkar, V. D. 248
Schumpeter, J. A. 104–5, 170
Schwab, Raymond 178
science, technology and empire 45, 48, 51,
    115, 144, 166–7, 185, 187
Scotland 49–51, 53, 56, 66, 138, 212
    emigration from 65–6, 68–9, 71–2, 77,
        80, 82, 85, 95n63
    and empire 49–51, 162–3, 174n18, 214,
        283
    Highlands 22, 66, 67–9, 82
    Highland (People's) Clearance 66–7
    Islands 66–7
    Lowlands 67, 72, 85
Scott, James C. 246
Seal, Anil 253–4
Seeley, Sir John xii, 48, 103–4, 172, 226–7
Setiloane, Gabriel 152
Seven Years War (1756–63) 4, 5, 30, 43, 66,
    138, 150
Shanghai 230
Shenton, Robert 173
Shona 149, 249–50
shipping 45, 51, 72–4, 78, 106–7, 112
Sierra Leone 29, 209, 276
Sifton, Clifford 89
Sikhs 158, 251
Silvestri, Michael 188
Simcoe, John G. 69
Simpson, George L. 189
Sind 44
Sinha, Mrinalini 168, 230
Singapore 44
Sinn Fein 236
Siraj-Ud-Daulah 5, 137
Sirmur, Rani of 180
Six Nations (Mohawk) 135
Skelton, O. D. 236
slavery and the slave trade 4, 5, 21, 29, 45,
    63, 67, 93n5, 112–13, 115, 117, 194,
    199, 208–12, 250, 262
    anti-slavery and abolitionism 8, 29, 41,

45, 63, 112–13, 136, 142–3, 171,
    199, 201, 205, 208–10
    British women and 143
    Somerset case (1772) 29
Smith, Adam 3, 6, 101–2, 109–10, 116,
    119, 123–4
Smith, Iain 239
Smith, Simon 277
Smith, Sydney 140
Smollett, Tobias 28
Smuts, Jan 16
"Social Darwinism" 46, 166–7
"social imperialism" 104–5, 172
Society for the Abolition of the Slave
    Trade 143
Society for Promoting Christian
    Knowledge 134
Society for the Propagation of the Gospel in
    Foreign Parts 134–5, 141
Somerset, James 29, 35n58
South Africa 2, 16, 18, 32, 50, 105, 108,
    131, 145, 160, 164, 172, 201, 210, 231,
    234–6, 272; *see also* Afrikaaners, colonies
    of white settlement, and dominions
    apartheid in 18, 152, 185
        anti-apartheid movement 152, 171
    Asians in 91
    black Africans 229
    emigration to 49, 63, 74, 80, 91
    mining in 118, 227
    race 91, 227, 238
    withdrawal from Commonwealth 237–8
    and World War I 235
South African Colonisation Society 86
South African "kindergarten" 54
South African National Congress 152
South African War (1899–1902, the "Second
    Boer War") 45, 51, 90–1, 108, 152, 160,
    172, 202, 228–9, 233–4
South Asia 110, 112; *see also* India,
    Pakistan, and East India Company
    historiography of 178–84, 186–7,
        190–4, 247–56, 259–65
South Australia 82
South Australian Company 79
South Carolina 32
Southeast Asia 278; *see also* country entries
southern Africa 113
Spanish empire 7, 22, 110
Spence, W. G. 228
Spivak, Gayatri Chakravorty 180–1, 187,
    255–6
sport and empire 50
Stair, Earl of 27
Stanley, Brian 132, 144
Stanley, Oliver 274
Statute of Westminster (1931) 16, 235

Stephen, Sir James 13
sterling 277
sterling bloc 17
Sterling Area 275, 278, 285
Stockwell, A. J. 282
Stoler, Anna Laura 169
Stuart, John 283
"sub-imperialism" 105–6
Subaltern Studies collective 165, 179–80,
    182–3, 187, 250, 255–6
Sudan 150
    Mahdists 150
Suez, east of 277
Suez Canal 15, 83, 105, 107
Suez crisis (1956) 270, 237, 275–7, 288
sugar 112, 114, 122, 201
Suleri, Sara 169
Swan River Colony 76
Swift, Jonathon 260

Tabatabai, Gholam Hossain-Khan 111
Tagore, Rabindranath 247, 264
Tahiti 115
Taiping rebellion (China) 151
Tambo, Oliver 152
Tanzania (Tanganyika) 189, 249, 276, 286
tariffs
    protective, in the colonies 114–15
tariff reform 46; see also imperial
    preference
Tariff Reform League 162
Tasmania 75, 82
taxation (British) 42–3, 45–6, 54, 106,
    116–18
taxation, colonial 113–14; see also
    American colonies and country entries
Taylor, Hudson 141
tea 122, 201
telegraph 74–5
Templer, Sir Gerald 275
Thackeray, William 206–15
Thomas, Nicholas 159, 185
Thompson, Andrew 120–2, 229–30, 238,
    288
Thompson, E. P. 246–7, 255
Tiffin, Chris 159
Tignor, Robert 284
timber 73
Titmouse, Simeon 74
Tippu Sultan 140
tobacco 112, 201
Tobago 66
Tomlinson, B. R. 115
tradition 180
Transfer of Power in India (Mansergh, N.)
    volumes 279

transnationalism 122–3
transportation (of convicts) 65, 75–7, 79
    gender and 76–8
Transportation Act (1717) 65
Transvaal 51, 146
Treasury 52, 108, 111
Trevor-Roper, Hugh 247–8
tribalism 193, 259,
Trinidad 7, 13, 275
"trusteeship" 41, 274
Turkey see Ottoman Empire

Uganda 111, 276, 283; see also Buganda
Ulster 51
Ulster Unionists 56, 251
United Empire Loyalists 68
United Nations 251, 273, 279
UNESCO 251
United States 18, 46, 49, 64–5, 68, 71, 80,
    83, 86, 92, 109, 115, 122, 160, 199,
    226, 272, 274–9, 282
Universities Mission to Central Africa 141
USSR 274–6; see also Russia
Utilitarianism 11, 140–1, 213

Vail, Leroy 115
Van der Veer, Peter 246
Van Diemen's Land see Tasmania
Van Vugt, William 83
Vanity Fair 206–15
Varikas, Eleni 159
Vattel, Emer de 23, 26, 31
Vaughan, Megan 186
Venn, Henry 146
Verelst, Harry 27
Victoria 50, 71, 82, 85, 144; see also Port
    Philip Bay and New South Wales
Victoria, Queen 229–30
Victoria League 87
Virginia 24, 64, 66, 133
Virginia Company 4, 135
Viswanathan, Gauri 179
Vogel, Sir Julius 84

Waitangi, Treaty of (1840) 32
Wales (and the Welsh) 50–1, 53, 56, 162–3,
    174n18, 219
    Welsh emigration 71, 80, 83, 85
Wakefield, Edward Gibbon 78, 84, 104
Wallerstein, Immanuel 109
Walsh, Oonagh 64
Ward, J. R. 107
Ward, Russel 220
Washbrook, David 182–3, 253–4
Watts, Sheldon 186

Welensky, Roy 284
Wellesley, Earl of 43
Wells, Louisa 26
West, Richard 24
West Africa 7, 26, 29, 106, 109, 112–3,
    275; *see also* country entries
West Indies, British (the Carribean) 4–5, 8,
    13, 23–4, 32, 40, 52, 64–6, 101–3, 114–
    15, 117, 134, 136, 139, 143, 171, 194,
    201, 207–10, 212, 223, 249, 251, 272,
    274, 277–8, 286; *see also* country entries
    culture of 249
    historiography of 249
    immigration to Britain from 55–6
    planters 53, 59n74
    trade with 102–3
Western Australia 76
White, Luise 148, 189
Wilberforce, William 139, 142, 211
Wilkes, John 24
William II 47
Williams, Eric 117, 199
Williams, Raymond 206
Wilson, Harold 49, 237–8
witchcraft 148

Wollstonecraft, Mary 169
Wood, Patricia 228
World Council of Churches 152
World Missionary Conference (1900,
    1910) 144
World War I 15–17, 87–8, 91, 93, 103–4,
    110, 115, 118, 121, 199, 204, 228,
    234–5, 251
World War II 18, 40, 55, 56, 103, 110, 199,
    212, 237, 251, 271, 273–4, 278, 287

Xhosa 142, 149, 224–5
    and the Cattle Killing Movement 149

Yoruba 151, 257–8
Young, Arthur 31
Young, Robert 256

Zaire 189
Zanzibar 144
Zimbabwe *see* Rhodesia
Zionism 273
Zulu 146, 149
Zulu Wars 227

Lightning Source UK Ltd.
Milton Keynes UK
UKOW07f2155120216

268263UK00003B/5/P